THE DEMOCRACY CLOCK

THE DEMOCRACY CLOCK

A CONTEMPORANEOUS PUBLIC RECORD OF
GOVERNANCE ACTIONS, JANUARY 2025-
JANUARY 2026

JIM VINCENT

VINCENT PRESS

Copyright © 2026 Jim Vincent

All rights reserved.

No part of this book may be reproduced, stored in a retrieval system, or transmitted in any form or by any means—electronic, mechanical, photocopying, recording, or otherwise—without prior written permission of the publisher or author, except for brief quotations used in reviews, scholarship, journalism, or news reporting.

This work is a non-fiction record and analysis of publicly documented events. It is based on information available in the public record at the time of publication and reflects developments as they occurred within that period.

The events documented herein are drawn from publicly available sources, including government records, court filings, legislative actions, executive orders, and contemporaneous reporting. Inclusion of any event does not imply endorsement of any individual, institution, or viewpoint.

Every effort has been made to ensure accuracy at the time of publication. Given the evolving nature of public records, corrections, clarifications, or supplemental volumes may be published separately.

The author asserts the moral right to be identified as the author of this work.

First edition.

ISBN: 978-1-7642233-0-0 (Paperback)

ISBN: 978-1-7642233-1-7 (Hardback)

Published by Vincent Press: https://thedemocracyclock.com

Printed and distributed by IngramSpark and BookVault.

Available through Amazon, Barnes & Noble, and international distributors.

For those who refused to stay quiet.

"The ideal subject of totalitarian rule is not the convinced Nazi or the convinced Communist, but people for whom the distinction between fact and fiction no longer exists."

— HANNAH ARENDT

CONTENTS

Preface   xi
Introduction   xiii

    Source Basis and Verification   1
    Part I   3
1. The Problem of Measuring Democracy   5
2. Why Government — and Why Democracy   9
3. Promises as Constitutional Design   15
4. The Six Democratic Imperatives   21
5. The Six Civic Deliverables   25
6. The Moral Floor   31
7. Diagnostics of a Failing Republic   37
8. Time as Democratic Evidence   49
9. Interlude: From Inheritance to Measurement   55
    Part II   59
10. Reading Democratic Time: A Note on Method   61
11. Week 1: Emergencies as Operating System   65
12. Week 2: Law and Memory as Weapons   77
13. Week 3: Systems as Spoils   89
14. Week 4: DOGE as Parallel Statecraft   101
15. Week 5: The State as Personal Instrument   113
16. Week 6: Bureaucracy as Patronage Engine   125
17. Week 7: Tools as Habit, Not Exception   137
18. Week 8: Citizenship and Service as Leverage   151
19. Week 9: Emergency Powers as Routine Governance   163
20. Week 10: Voter Rolls as Leverage   175
21. Week 11: Chaos as Methodical Governance   185
22. Week 12: Emergency Powers as Routine Governance   197
23. Week 13: Loyalty as Daily Governance   209
24. Week 14: Universities and Borders as Levers   219
25. Week 15: Emergency Rule as Routine Governance   231
26. Week 16: Stratified Rights as Routine Governance   243
27. Week 17: Citizenship as Leverage   255
28. Week 18: Inequality as Operating System   267
29. Week 19: Institutions as Instruments of Loyalty   279

30.	Week 20: Surveillance as Everyday Governance	291
31.	Week 21: Emergency Powers as Routine Governance	303
32.	Week 22: Citizenship as Sorting Mechanism	315
33.	Week 23: Secrecy as War-Making Method	325
34.	Week 24: Hardwiring Inequality as Governance	337
35.	Week 25: Immunity as Architecture of Power	351
36.	Week 26: Data and Force as Governance	363
37.	Week 27: Databases and Detention as Governance	373
38.	Week 28: Confinement as Governance	383
39.	Week 29: Law, Maps, and Memory as Control	393
40.	Week 30: Emergency as Method in Washington	405
41.	Week 31: Emergency as Governing Method	417
42.	Week 32: Emergencies as Everyday Rule	429
43.	Week 33: Authoritarian Powers as Policy	439
44.	Week 34: Military Governance as Routine	451
45.	Week 35: Security as Presidential Clay	465
46.	Week 36: Law, Hunger, and Silence as Leverage	477
47.	Week 37: Shutdown as Quiet Purge	487
48.	Week 38: Shutdown as Weaponry	497
49.	Week 39: Shutdown as Weaponized Governance	509
50.	Week 40: Ballroom as Blueprint	521
51.	Week 41: Shutdown and Ballrooms as Rule	533
52.	Week 42: Hunger and Pardons as Power	541
53.	Week 43: Memory and Law as Weapons	553
54.	Week 44: Belonging Redrawn by Force	565
55.	Week 45: Law as Sorting Mechanism	579
56.	Week 46: Impunity as Operating System	589
57.	Week 47: Citizenship and Power for Sale	601
58.	Week 48: Memory as Instrument	613
59.	Week 49: Files as Instruments of Power	627
60.	Week 50: Consolidation as Governance	635
61.	Week 51: War, Oil, and Enforcement as Rule	645
62.	Week 52: Occupation as Governance	657
	Epilogue	669
	About the Author	671
	Also by Jim Vincent	673

PREFACE

This book began as a weekly act of attention. Each entry was written in real time, connected to recent events, and published with the understanding that the work would continue. Week after week, the record steadily grew, without a fixed ending. That open-ended approach was intentional. Democracies evolve, and any attempt to draw conclusions too early risks distortion. The Democracy Clock was designed to shift forward or backward as circumstances changed, not to provide a final judgment. Its purpose was to monitor democratic health as it developed, without presuming where it might end. However, there comes a point when an ongoing record must be finalized—not because the story is complete, but because the moment it captures has gained historical significance. The first year of a presidential term is not just a prelude; it's when governing strategies are set, institutional limits are tested, and the costs of resistance or compliance become clearer. By the end of that year, patterns are no longer hypothetical—they can be measured. Choosing to turn this record into a book was a deliberate decision. It transforms a flow of events into a reference, enabling the year to be understood as a whole rather than just a series of impressions.

That stability matters. Democratic erosion is often debated not only in terms of content but also in how it is remembered. Events are minimized, reframed, or denied once their immediate urgency passes. A fixed record resists this tendency. It preserves not just what happened, but how each development affected the state of democratic governance at the time. This volume does not claim finality. It does not suggest that the forces it documents will inevitably prevail, nor that they are irreversible. It asserts something narrower and more defensible: that the first year of this term caused measurable changes to democratic structures, limits, and resilience, and that these changes can only be understood clearly when they are held steady long enough to be observed.

Readers who followed the project week by week will recognize familiar ground here, but will also find something different. When read continuously, the record reveals cumulative effects that are harder to notice when viewed in isolation. What felt like isolated events becomes part of a pattern, and what seemed minor gains weight. First-time readers are encouraged to approach this work not as commentary but as documentation. The judgments presented are not reactions to headlines; they are the result of a consistent effort to assess democratic health against fixed standards, week after week, regardless of whether the findings are reassuring or unsettling.

For archivists and historians, this book serves as a source document: a contemporaneous account of how democratic erosion was tracked as it unfolded, before outcomes were clear. It is intentionally limited, time-stamped, and methodologically transparent. Future interpretations may vary, but the record will endure. Converting a living process into a book always involves compromises. It sacrifices immediacy for coherence and flexibility for longevity. In this case, that compromise was justified. Time kept moving while this record was being created, and it will continue after this volume ends. But for one year, democratic time has been measured, recorded, and fixed. This is what this book is.

INTRODUCTION

Democratic collapse rarely announces itself. It does not come with a single proclamation or a clear break between before and after. More often, it unfolds gradually: a rule bent here, a safeguard bypassed there, a precedent ignored, a silence allowed to stand. Each step seems manageable on its own, but together, they transform what a system is and what it can no longer be.

This book exists because such change is difficult to see as it happens. Democracies are rarely undone by dramatic reversals; instead, they weaken through repetition, normalization, and fatigue. What feels tolerable in one week can become decisive over time. By the moment the consequences are clear, the path that led there is often blurred, contested, or forgotten. The Democracy Clock was created to cut through that confusion. It is neither a metaphor nor a prediction but a measuring tool. Its purpose is to track democratic erosion as it occurs—increment by increment—using time as the measure. Not outrage. Not ideology. Just time. Time matters because democratic damage accumulates over time. A captured institution is harder to restore than one under pressure. A precedent once set becomes easier to reuse. Norms that survive one violation may not withstand multiple violations. What seems reversible early on can become entrenched later. The key question is not only what happened but how each development impacts the difficulty of restoring democratic governance afterward.

This book measures that difficulty. The following record covers the first year of Donald Trump's second term. It does so weekly because weeks are how power is exercised: through executive actions, court decisions, legislative maneuvers, administrative changes, and acts of omission that go unchallenged. Each week is treated as a unit of democratic time, evaluated in relation to what came before and what it leaves behind. The Clock itself functions as a cumulative ledger. It advances when democratic constraints weaken, and retreats when credible resistance or repair occurs.

These movements are not symbolic; they are based on consistent assessments of how specific developments affect the structure, resilience, and reversibility of democratic governance. The result is a continuous measurement of democratic health over time, not a final verdict. What this book does not do is claim that any single action "ended" democracy. That framing is tempting but wrong. Democracies fail not because one moment is decisive, but because many moments go by without measurement. The Clock exists to highlight those moments. It is also not a comprehensive record of everything that happened. It does not catalog personalities. It is not an expression of partisan outrage nor a forecast of election results. Many volumes will explain what occurred during this period. Few will measure the impact of those events on democracy itself. That is the gap this work aims to fill. Supporting documentation is maintained separately. This volume focuses on measurement and cumulative effects rather than a detailed chronology.

Measurement depends on standards. The Democracy Clock functions based on a fixed set of democratic principles—limits on power, institutional independence, equal access to participation, the rule of law, and the conditions essential for peaceful self-governance. These standards are not created for this project; they are derived from constitutional design, comparative democratic practices, and historical lessons. What's unique here isn't the principles themselves but the insistence on applying them consistently, week after week, without softening the narrative.

Consistency is crucial because cherry-picking alerts makes it hard to tell real issues from noise. A system that only reacts to major abuses will overlook quieter forms of corruption. Changes in administration, procedural shifts, and strategic delays don't usually make headlines but can cause long-term harm. By viewing each week as part of an ongoing record, the Clock reveals those subtler changes.

Readers should understand how to interpret what follows.

Each chapter covers a single week. It begins by placing that week within the larger timeline of democratic health—showing the Clock reading at the start of the week and how it ended. Then, it details events that significantly impacted democratic structures and limits, explaining what happened and why it matters. The focus is always on impact: how a specific action shifted the balance of power, affected institutional independence, or made reversal harder.

Some weeks cause only slight shifts in the Clock. Others cause larger changes. A lack of significant movement in a given week should not be seen as reassurance. Stagnation can be as revealing as movement, especially when pressures build up without clear breaking points. Similarly, resistance moments are noted if they are credible and meaningful, not just rhetorical.

This is a careful record, not a perfectly balanced one. Balance suggests symmetry between forces that are often unequal. Measurement promotes fidelity to evidence and method. When democratic erosion speeds up, the Clock moves accordingly; when constraints are maintained or restored, it shows that too. The direction of change is a result of the process, not a premise.

Readers seeking catharsis won't find it here. The tone is intentionally calm. This isn't because the events are harmless; rather, it's because panic clouds judgment. Alarm without a foundation drains attention and clouds judgment. The goal is to make the pattern clear enough so that urgency is rooted in understanding, not fear.

This also means resisting the urge to frame every week as unprecedented. Some developments are new; many are not. Part of democratic erosion involves reusing old tactics under new conditions or reactivating dormant authorities once thought constrained. By providing historical and institutional context, the record distinguishes between escalation and repetition, innovation and recycling. That distinction matters for anyone concerned with repair.

The first year of a presidential term is especially consequential. Early actions shape institutional expectations. Personnel choices become part of administrative reality. Courts define the boundaries they are willing to defend—or abandon. Congress shows whether it will serve as a coequal branch or an auxiliary one. By the second year, many key trajectories are already set.

That's why this volume ends where it does. It does not claim to be final. It offers a baseline.

Future volumes may extend the record. If they do, the Clock will not reset. Democratic time does not reset. What is lost remains lost unless actively restored, and restoration leaves traces. That's why the Clock accumulates rather than averages. It remembers.

Readers might disagree with some judgments. That's expected. What matters is that judgments are clear, consistent, and based on publicly observable events. Disagreement is healthier than forgetfulness. The Clock serves not as an oracle but as a disciplined framework to see what might otherwise be dismissed as isolated or temporary.

Most importantly, this book is an act of civic memory. Democracies don't survive without records of how they were tested. When institutions fail, it's often because the path to failure wasn't clearly marked. The Democracy Clock traces that path as it unfolds, week by week, while opportunities to respond still exist.

Time is not yet over. But it's no longer abstract, and it's no longer invisible.

SOURCE BASIS
AND VERIFICATION

Events discussed in this book are based on contemporary public records and reports from the period covered. These include official government documents, court filings and rulings, agency announcements, legislative records, executive actions, and verified reports of institutional activity from reputable news organizations and watchdog groups. All events included can be verified at the time they entered the public record through primary documents, corroborated reporting, or institutional records. No event is included solely on guesses, assumptions, or unverified claims. When facts changed, conflicted, or were clarified over time, the analysis reflects what could be confirmed during the relevant period.

Unlike the related *Democracy Clock Event Log*, this book does not aim to provide a complete chronological record of every action taken. Instead, it summarizes verified events within a structured analytical framework that shows how power was exercised, limited, redirected, or consolidated over time. Events are selected and discussed based on their significance to democratic institutions and their overall impact on the system's health. Individual source citations are not included in-line. This is a deliberate choice, reflecting the book's purpose as a narrative and analytical record rather than a comprehensive documentary archive.

The full evidentiary record is maintained separately in the *Democracy Clock Event Log*, which preserves complete chronological context. Readers seeking original documents or contemporaneous reports should consult public records and coverage from the relevant period. The interpretations, judgments, and clock-movement assessments presented here are the author's analytical conclusions drawn from that verified record. The distinction between evidence and analysis is intentional and foundational to this project.

PART I
THE FRAMEWORK

CHAPTER 1
THE PROBLEM OF MEASURING DEMOCRACY

Modern democracies are often thought to be self-sustaining. They are expected to withstand shocks, correct mistakes, and survive periods of poor leadership or political conflict through the normal functioning of institutions and norms. However, history suggests otherwise. Democratic systems can weaken, distort, and collapse—not usually suddenly, but through gradual decline. Republican Rome decayed into empire. Athenian democracy faded into oligarchy. More recently, democratic governments in Hungary, Russia, Venezuela, and elsewhere have eroded from within as restrictions on power were steadily loosened or ignored.

The United States is no exception. Over the past few decades, trust in government has decreased, institutional norms have weakened, and the separation of powers has become less effective. Courts have become more politicized. Executive authority has grown. Alliances that once supported American influence have frayed. Elections still happen, but trust in their legitimacy has diminished. Each of these issues is often seen as separate, a partisan issue, or a temporary problem. Together, they point to a democratic system under ongoing pressure.

Historians and political theorists have studied these patterns in detail. What remains difficult is to track democratic decline as it happens. Right now, very different claims are made about the state of American democracy. One side says it remains strong and resilient; the other warns that it is damaged and nearing failure. Approval ratings, polls, and media stories are used as evidence by both sides. None of these measures is definitive. All can be influenced by the very forces they aim to evaluate. This leads to disagreements without resolution and concerns without clear answers.

This book starts with that problem. If democracy is weakening, how can we tell? How much damage has been done, where has it happened, and how reversible is it? Without a way to assess democratic health, decline remains a matter of interpretation until it becomes an irreversible fact. Observation alone isn't enough. What's needed is a framework that can see democratic change as it happens—across institutions, rights, governance, and moral obligations.

To meet this need, this book develops a measurement system for democracy itself. Measurement without clear definitions is just noise; definitions without guiding principles are arbitrary. So, the analysis begins with fundamental questions: why government exists, why democracy was chosen as a form of self-rule, what it promises, what it requires, and what it must deliver to maintain legitimacy. From these basics, the book defines a comprehensive set of democratic indicators and combines them into a single, overall measure: the Democracy Clock. Noon indicates a fully functioning democracy. Midnight shows the absence of democratic governance. Movement along the clock reflects accumulated structural and moral changes over time. The clock doesn't predict collapse or assign blame; it records change.

Part II tracks this measure weekly throughout Donald Trump's second term, viewing it as a continuous case study of democratic stress and response. Each week highlights actions that either moved American democracy toward recovery or further deterioration. A companion volume provides a complete record of the underlying governmental actions. Together, they create an ongoing public record of democratic loss and renewal.

The goal of this book is to make democratic conditions visible. It captures change as it happens, tracks its progress, and preserves the evidence behind those measurements. Without such a record, democratic failure is only recognized in retrospect, when fixing it becomes much harder—if not impossible.

CHAPTER 2
WHY GOVERNMENT — AND WHY DEMOCRACY

The United States did not expect to confront a fundamental question in the third century of its existence: why does a nation need a government at all? For much of its history, that question seemed settled. Government was assumed to be permanent, its institutions resilient, its constitutional design sufficient to absorb shocks and correct excesses. Recent events have forced that assumption into doubt. Not because they created America's vulnerabilities, but because they made visible what the country had long taken for granted—that institutions would always hold, leaders would always respect limits, and democratic self-correction could be relied upon indefinitely. Those assumptions are no longer secure. When assumptions fail, inquiry must return to first principles.

Government is not an American invention. It is not even a political invention. It is a human one. From the smallest family to the largest empire, every group of people develops rules, roles, expectations, and consequences. There has never been a society without governance. Even in conditions often romanticized as "unstructured," power flows, decisions are made, conflicts are resolved, and someone determines what happens next. Government is the form human cooperation inevitably takes. Life without it is unstable, fragile, and often short.

The underlying insight is simple: government is inevitable because human beings cannot live together without structure. The moment two people form a partnership, they negotiate roles. The moment a family forms, it creates rules. A village generates customs. A market generates norms. A clan produces leadership. A nation produces law. Government is not the opposite of freedom; it is the condition that allows freedom to exist at all. The alternative is not liberty, but exposure—to violence, to scarcity, and to the unchecked power of the strong.

This inevitability has nothing to do with virtue. People do not create governments because they are noble, but because conflict is unavoidable and must be managed. A system that resolves disputes prevents feuds. A system that distributes resources prevents collapse. A system that enforces rules prevents chaos. The question has never been whether a society will have a government. The question is what kind of government it will have, and for whose benefit. Authority always exists. Legitimacy does not.

From the beginning, the central problem of government has not been whether authority will arise, but how—and whether—it will be justified. Authority is the capacity to command. Legitimacy is the right to do so. A government is legitimate when people accept its authority not because they fear punishment, but because they recognize themselves in its decisions and see its power exercised on their behalf. History offers countless examples of governments with authority but without legitimacy—regimes that commanded obedience but not consent. Such systems endure by force until force fails. When legitimacy collapses, government does not disappear; it becomes extractive rather than protective, coercive rather than representative.

For most of human history, power has been allocated by methods unrelated to legitimacy: strength, lineage, age, gender, wealth, priesthood, conquest, or corruption. Monarchs claimed divine right. Emperors claimed destiny. Oligarchies claimed superiority. Councils claimed wisdom. Technocrats claimed expertise. Each of these systems faced the same limitation. They could rule, but they could not justify their rule to those they governed. Authority rested on tradition or violence, not on consent.

Nor were these systems stable. Hereditary monarchies decayed as unfit heirs inherited power. Warrior states fractured when dominant leaders died. Priest-kings lost control when prophecy failed. Aristocracies ossified. Technocracies detached themselves from the public. Coup regimes splintered. Even admired ancient models proved fragile. Greek city-states were exclusive and volatile. The Roman Republic drifted toward oligarchy and then empire. None produced a durable model of justified, self-correcting governance.

It is in this context that democracy becomes extraordinary. Democracy is the only form of government designed to ground authority in the governed. It is the only system structured to distribute power broadly enough to prevent permanent domination. It is the only form that requires leaders to justify their actions rather than merely enforce them. Its premise is simple but radical: those affected by political decisions have the right to shape them. This idea is neither natural nor inevitable. It is a choice—and a rare one.

Democracy's moral claim is that all human beings possess equal political dignity. Its practical claim is that shared and constrained power produces stability. Its central advantage is that it contains mechanisms for peaceful correction. Elections allow leaders to be replaced without violence. Legislatures provide channels for grievance without revolt. Courts restrain abuse without coups. A free press exposes wrongdoing without insurrection. Democracy is the only system explicitly designed to detect its own failures and respond without destroying itself.

Authoritarian systems cannot do this. They can centralize authority, but they cannot correct their own errors. They suppress dissent, distort information, and eliminate feedback. They mistake obedience for strength and silence for stability. Their failures, when they come, are often sudden because no one can safely warn of danger. The defining weakness of authoritarianism is not brutality, but blindness. It cannot see itself clearly enough to endure.

If democracy represents a radical departure from human political history, American democracy represents an even more radical experiment. What emerged in Philadelphia in 1776—and again with greater precision in 1787—was not a copy of Athens, Rome, or Westminster. It was not a refinement of monarchy or an imitation of ancient republics. It was a system with no working prototype: representative government with separated powers, written constraints, independent courts, and lawful succession. Nothing like it existed at the time.

The architects of this system were not seeking to replicate history. They were trying to avoid it. Greece was unstable. Rome was corruptible. France was convulsing. England was hereditary and hierarchical. The American design studied these failures not to emulate them, but to prevent their repetition. It aimed to create a government strong enough to govern, yet restrained enough to be governed. The result was an experiment—audacious and unfinished.

Its authors understood that the experiment could fail. They said so plainly. Madison warned that power would concentrate. Jefferson warned that self-government required civic virtue. Washington warned of faction. Hamilton warned of demagogues. American democracy was not handed down as a finished achievement. It was constructed—unevenly and imperfectly, and in ways that excluded millions—but built with the intention of demonstrating that ordinary people could govern themselves through justified institutions.

That intention mattered as much as the structure. It produced a republic grounded not only in law, but in the belief that legitimacy flows from the people rather than birth, conquest, or force. It created a system in which authority could be questioned without treason, conflict resolved without violence, and succession achieved without bloodshed. These ideas were astonishing in a world dominated by kings and empires. They remain rare today.

The United States expanded its democracy unevenly, denying rights to Indigenous nations, enslaved people, women, immigrants, and the poor. Yet over time, the circle of legitimacy widened. That expansion was not automatic; it was fought for. Democracy grows only when people demand it. It erodes when they stop defending its principles.

The modern era has tested these commitments. Inequality, disinformation, polarization, and institutional neglect have weakened public confidence. Many Americans now experience government as distant or captured, democracy as procedural rather than substantive, and institutions as protective of themselves before the public. These perceptions, rooted in real failures, create openings for leaders who reject democratic restraint and promise simpler, more forceful rule.

This is the situation American democracy faces today: a system designed to constrain power confronting pressures that treat restraint as an inconvenience rather than a core purpose. Government will persist; it always does. The question is what kind of government it becomes—and whom it serves. When institutions are repurposed to concentrate power rather than justify it, democracy does not collapse. It converts.

A democracy rarely disappears overnight. It erodes as practices once considered intolerable become routine. Each breach becomes precedent. Each precedent becomes expectation. Over time, the extraordinary becomes ordinary, and a society loses sight of what legitimacy once required. Decline accelerates not through crisis, but through normalization; not through drama, but through habit.

To measure this erosion, we must first understand what is being eroded. Government is inevitable; democracy is not. Government structures collective life; democracy legitimizes it. Government manages consequences; democracy distributes power. Government provides order; democracy provides justification and restraint. This book begins from these distinctions because the descent it will document—week by week, minute by minute—is not only political, but structural. It concerns not merely what leaders do, but what government becomes when its purpose drifts.

A society cannot defend what it cannot name. Before confronting the forces reshaping American democracy, it must recall why government exists, why legitimacy matters, and why the experiment begun in Philadelphia remains both fragile and unfinished. Only then can the stakes of the present moment be understood: a moment when the inevitable fact of government and the fragile ideal of democracy are pulling apart.

CHAPTER 3
PROMISES AS CONSTITUTIONAL DESIGN

They had built a system without precedent. The Constitution was a design with no working model, created in a world where monarchies ruled, empires expanded, and revolutions devoured themselves. Its architects understood that invention alone was not enough. A republic without purpose would collapse under its own uncertainty. So before they debated structures or powers, they placed a sentence above everything else—a statement of what the new government owed its people, and what the people had the right to expect in return. That sentence became the Preamble, and the six promises within it became the conditions for the republic's survival.

These promises were not just ideals. They served as protections against the failures that had dismantled every republic the Founders studied. They understood the fate of ancient city-states torn apart by faction, republics overtaken by ambitious generals, confederations weakened by disunity, and nations where justice blurred with power. The Preamble was not merely decorative; it outlined performance standards. If the Constitution fulfilled them, the experiment could survive. If it failed, the document would be just parchment, not protection. In this chapter, we examine each promise as both origin and duty.

Union came first because nothing else could stand without it. The Articles of Confederation left the young nation fractured, unable to raise funds, enforce treaties, or function as a single entity. States issued competing currencies, pursued conflicting policies, and hoarded resources during war. The Founders feared that without union, the republic would follow the path of earlier confederations that withered from internal division. Union meant more than geography; it meant shared identity and coordinated purpose. Its modern test lies in whether a nation can still act together in the face of crisis or if fragmentation overwhelms the common good.

Justice promised a system of law that was neutral, equal, and independent of personal power. The Founders had lived under courts that served imperial interests, punishing dissent and privileging loyalty. They had seen how justice bends when judges serve rulers rather than principles. Justice became the republic's moral anchor: a safeguard against the concentrated power that had corrupted European courts and collapsed ancient republics. Over time, justice in America expanded—abolition, civil rights, and due process—but also contracted through slavery, segregation, and discrimination. Its fragility remains evident today. When justice becomes partisan or unequal, democratic legitimacy erodes long before institutions fall.

Tranquility meant internal peace secured not through suppression, but via trusted ways to resolve conflict. The memory of Shays' Rebellion had shown how quickly unrest could threaten a fragile union. The Founders understood that political competition without reliable channels for resolution leads to violence. They knew from history that republics fall when disputes move from assemblies to streets, and from streets to battlefields. Tranquility was not the absence of dissent; it was the presence of institutions strong enough to absorb it. The modern measure is whether citizens still believe that grievances can be resolved lawfully — or whether public faith has diminished enough to make disorder seem reasonable.

Defense ensured that the republic could survive in a world where stronger powers surrounded it. In 1787, the nation was bordered by Britain, Spain, and France, each with territorial ambitions. The Founders had no illusions about vulnerability. They remembered shortages of arms, fractured alliances, and the narrow margin by which independence had been won. Defense meant more than armies; it meant capacity, coordination, and credibility. Today, the concept includes cyber threats, infrastructure stability, biological risks, and domestic preparedness. The core truth remains the same: a nation that cannot protect itself will not last long enough to handle political disagreements.

Welfare, as defined by the Constitution, meant the "general welfare"—the shared goods essential for community life. Early forms included roads, ports, and public works, showing a belief that government should support prosperity beyond just the interests of elites. Over time, welfare grew to include public education, health protections, environmental safeguards, and social insurance —each acknowledging that a decent life needs more than private resources. The promise isn't luxury but basic conditions for dignity. When welfare declines, inequality rises, trust erodes, and the social fabric unravels. A government that ignores welfare breaks its fundamental promise.

Liberty was the culmination of the promises and the guarantor of the rest. It was protection from arbitrary power, foreign or domestic, and assurance that individuals could live without fear of rulers, mobs, or majorities. The Founders had witnessed how liberty collapsed when rights existed only at the pleasure of the powerful. They sought a system in which freedom would be secured by law and reinforced by civic culture. Liberty widened over generations as excluded groups claimed rights the Founders denied. Yet liberty remains vulnerable—not only to repression but to erosion, when rights exist formally but cannot be exercised meaningfully.

Taken together, the Six Promises form a coherent structure: a republic unified in purpose, governed by justice, restrained from violence, protected from threat, supportive of human flourishing, and anchored in liberty. None stands alone. Union without justice becomes coercion. Justice without liberty becomes rigidity. Welfare without tranquility becomes instability. Liberty without defense becomes weakness. These promises were designed to function as a system, not a menu. Break one link, and strain appears in the others.

Yet the promises, foundational as they were, had limits shaped by the assumptions of their age. They did not include every person in their protection. They did not anticipate the complexities of modern governance. They did not foresee the scale of economic inequality, the power of information systems, or the fragility of civic trust. Their aspiration was broad; their implementation was narrow. The republic would require continual effort to make the promises real for everyone, not just those imagined in 1787.

Throughout history, the Six Promises have acted as both goals and standards. When they were upheld, the nation moved forward—expanding rights, strengthening institutions, and increasing legitimacy. When they faltered, chaos ensued—civil war, economic failure, segregation, and disenfranchisement. Each period of challenge revealed a consistent truth: a republic thrives not by clinging to its beginnings but by renewing the commitments on which it was built. The promises last only when supported by institutions capable of upholding them.

In our era, the promises remain the measure of whether government serves the public or serves itself. A nation divided cannot meet shared challenges. A justice system perceived as partisan cannot preserve legitimacy. A society that resolves disputes through threat cannot sustain peace. A state unable to defend itself cannot navigate global risk. A government indifferent to welfare fosters distrust. A republic that treats liberty as optional abandons its foundation. The Six Promises remain the baseline against which the health of the democracy is judged.

The chapter that follows turns from founding promises to operational demands—from what the republic pledged to deliver to what it must continually do to uphold those pledges. If the Founders articulated the destination, the modern imperatives describe the machinery necessary for getting there. The promises define purpose; the imperatives define performance.

CHAPTER 4
THE SIX DEMOCRATIC IMPERATIVES

The Constitution was designed for its own era. Its authors understood the dangers of their time—monarchs with unchecked power, empires that swallowed weaker states, and factions that could tear apart fragile institutions. They didn't envision a continental republic connected to global markets, instant communication, and threats that develop faster than legislatures can respond. A strong democracy must carry its founding principles through today's conditions. Otherwise, the promises that anchored the early republic weaken, not because they become irrelevant, but because the system tasked with protecting them cannot keep up.

If the Six Promises define what a republic owes its people, the Six Democratic Imperatives specify the work needed to fulfill those obligations. They are not additions to the founding principles; they are the functions that must evolve as society changes. A democracy that cannot adapt, include, restrain power, protect dignity, maintain peace, or preserve knowledge is one that will eventually lose its legitimacy. These imperatives stem from two centuries of practice and conflict. Each is vital. None are optional.

Accountability is the first safeguard because it transforms authority into responsibility. The Founders aimed to achieve this through elections, separation of powers, and the lawful removal of officials who abuse the public trust. These mechanisms were important but incomplete. Political life introduces pressures—money that hides influence, information systems that distort consent, and private interests that can overpower public judgment. Today, accountability also needs transparency, enforceable ethics, and independent oversight strong enough to investigate wrongdoing without fear of retaliation. It also requires a public with the knowledge and capacity to judge performance. Without this foundation, elections become symbolic, and institutions tend toward impunity.

Adaptability protects a republic from brittleness. The Framers created an amendment process because they expected the nation to change, but they could not foresee the speed or scale of modern shifts. Economic crises arise in hours, not seasons. Viruses travel continents in days. Digital threats move at a pace that outstrips traditional lawmaking. A responsive democracy must anticipate risk, adjust policy before damage becomes irreversible, and modernize systems without abandoning core principles. Adaptability is not agility for its own sake; it is the capacity to protect accountability by keeping institutions functional under new conditions. A rigid system fails because it cannot correct course before consequences compound.

Inclusion broadens the scope of self-governance. At the nation's founding, that scope was limited—defined by race, gender, property, and religion. Over time, the country expanded participation through amendments, movements, and legislation. Each expansion enhanced legitimacy and stability. Conversely, each contraction—via suppression, intimidation, or unnecessary barriers—made the republic more vulnerable. Today, inclusion is not only a matter of justice but also of resilience. A system that excludes large segments of its population becomes easier to manipulate and more difficult to defend. Wide participation fosters diverse perspectives, distributes political power more evenly, and promotes accountability by ensuring leaders can be removed if they fail.

Dignity underpins the relationship between people and government. A democracy cannot survive if citizens expect only contempt, discrimination, or humiliation. In earlier centuries, dignity was protected for some and denied to many. The ongoing fight to make it universal—through emancipation, labor protections, civil rights, and disability rights—reveals how easily a republic can crack when institutions diminish human worth. Today, dignity demands systems that prevent abuse, safeguard civil liberties, and guarantee fair treatment. It is not just sentiment but a structural foundation. When dignity declines, inclusion becomes superficial, participation drops, and leaders who offer belonging through exclusion rather than equality gain ground.

Peace is the condition that allows disagreement to remain political rather than turn violent. The Founders aimed to resolve disputes without force—through courts, legislatures, and executive authority balanced by law. However, peace has always been fragile. It depends on a government strong enough to maintain public order but restrained enough to avoid treating its citizens as enemies. Today, peace involves limiting emergency powers, reducing political violence, and ensuring law enforcement protects rather than oppresses. When peace is maintained, society can adapt without crisis, and dignity can be preserved without strain. When peace breaks down, every other priority becomes much harder to sustain.

Knowledge forms the foundation of meaningful consent. The Founders recognized that an uninformed public is susceptible to manipulation, which is why they safeguarded a free press and promoted civic education. However, the modern information landscape introduces challenges that they could not have predicted. Deliberate falsehoods can spread more rapidly than corrections. Propaganda can be customized for individuals. Entire communities can be confined within constructed realities. A democracy cannot function without shared facts for deliberation. Today, knowledge relies on independent reporting, transparent records, scientific honesty, and public education that equips citizens to assess information critically. Without these elements, accountability becomes guesswork, and inclusion can be easily manipulated.

These six imperatives are not independent variables. They form a single operational system. Accountability without knowledge is blind. Knowledge without inclusion concentrates influence in the hands least likely to share it. Inclusion without dignity becomes performative. Dignity without peace is unstable. Peace without adaptability is fragile. Adaptability without accountability drifts into efficient corruption. A republic falters not when one imperative weakens, but when enough links break that the system can no longer repair itself. The danger lies not in sudden collapse but in gradual misalignment, when the machinery still exists yet no longer performs its intended function.

The promises of 1787 did not sustain themselves. They relied on institutions capable of fulfilling them as the world around us changed. The democratic imperatives show what is now needed to fulfill that work. They turn founding ideals into practical duties and give a clear way to measure if democratic structures still work as intended. When the imperatives are functioning together and strongly, the promises become real in everyday life. When they weaken, the promises shift from commitments to slogans, and public trust gradually declines.

A republic cannot endure on form alone. It survives through function—the daily, unglamorous work that keeps power limited, participation broad, dignity protected, conflict peaceful, institutions flexible, and truth knowable. These imperatives define what a democracy must be able to do, not what it hopes to do. They are the functional boundaries that keep power accountable, conflict peaceful, and truth visible. When they operate as a system, the constitutional promises gain force. When they fail, the promises become aspirational, and the public grows distant from its own government.

CHAPTER 5
THE SIX CIVIC DELIVERABLES

A democracy cannot survive on intention alone. The Six Founding Promises identify what a republic owes its people, and the Democratic Imperatives describe the machinery needed to fulfill those obligations. But a system is judged not only by its design or operation. It is judged by what it produces in the lives of its citizens. A promise is an aspiration. A deliverable is its proof. If democratic institutions function as intended, they generate conditions in which people can live securely, participate fully, and plan for a future not shaped solely by chance or privilege.

Throughout history, many governments have mastered administration without serving the public. Empires built roads to facilitate conquest, not mobility. Totalitarian states delivered efficiency but denied dignity. Even capable bureaucracies have failed to provide basic security or fairness for large portions of their populations. Function alone does not democratize power. A republic's legitimacy depends on whether its institutions produce outcomes that justify public trust. When people experience safety, opportunity, fairness, and continuity, the system strengthens. When they do not, the distance between institutions and those they govern widens, sometimes beyond repair.

The civic deliverables outlined here are not just abstract ideals. They are the tangible results a democracy must produce to maintain the consent that grants it authority. They define what citizens should expect from their government: compassion in hardship, education that fosters progress, safety and justice equally ensured, a sense of belonging that crosses identity boundaries, foresight that safeguards future generations, and continuity that sustains the republic. These deliverables create a system of outcomes. Their presence indicates health, while their absence exposes division.

Care must come first because everyone is vulnerable. No community can be stable when illness, disaster, or economic collapse leaves people without support. In earlier times, care appeared as public works, basic sanitation, and responses to epidemics. Over time, democratic societies realized that security must include access to healthcare, help during crises, and protection against poverty. Care is not paternalism; it is recognizing that citizens cannot enjoy freedom when their survival is at risk. Without care, fear takes over politics. That fear opens the door for leaders who promise protection while gaining more power.

Education and elevation are central to the second goal because knowledge fosters participation. Democracies depend on citizens who can evaluate information, make independent judgments, and contribute meaningfully to civic life. In the early republic, education was seen as a safeguard against tyranny, but access remained unequal for many years. The expansion of public schools, higher education, and vocational training increased opportunities and strengthened the system. Elevation goes beyond basic literacy or technical skills. It also includes the ability to rise through merit rather than birth or connections. When education suffers or becomes hard to access, the public becomes more vulnerable to manipulation, and the promise of equal citizenship diminishes.

Safety, justice, and freedom form a unified foundation because each depends on the others. Safety shields people from violence, whether from external threats, domestic crime, or abuse of state power. Justice ensures that laws are applied equally, restraining the powerful and protecting the vulnerable. Freedom maintains the space for dissent, creativity, and personal autonomy. These elements are inseparable. Safety without justice becomes coercion. Justice without freedom turns into rigidity. Freedom without safety leads to instability. A democracy must protect all three to maintain legitimacy. When any one is compromised, the others quickly weaken, and public trust diminishes along with them.

Belonging is crucial because a democracy can't function if large groups of people are treated as conditional members of the political community. The founding period left many out, and the fight to expand belonging has been a key part of American history. Today, belonging means more than just the absence of legal discrimination. It involves real inclusion in political, economic, and civic life. People who feel the system isn't made for them—whether because of race, religion, class, or origin—are less likely to participate, less likely to trust, and more likely to withdraw or resist. A republic breaks apart when belonging shrinks and grows stronger when it expands.

Foresight is the gift that protects those who are not yet born. Previous generations built infrastructure, conserved resources, and established institutions that outlasted them. A democracy must look beyond immediate concerns to protect the environment, invest in research, and prepare for emerging risks. Foresight requires addressing problems before they turn into crises and resisting political incentives that favor short-term gains at long-term costs. Nations that fail to plan invite instability. Those that maintain foresight create continuity. In a self-governing system, this responsibility is shared across generations and cannot be postponed indefinitely.

Endurance is the cumulative result of other contributions. A democracy endures not because it avoids conflict or change, but because it has established habits, institutions, and expectations that enable it to handle both without losing integrity. Endurance depends on peaceful transfers of power, a stable rule of law, and institutions capable of resisting corruption and external pressures.

It also relies on civic culture—trust, restraint, and a willingness to resolve disputes through lawful means. Republics that lose endurance often do so gradually, as small failures build up until the system can no longer correct itself. Endurance is maintained through ongoing effort, not occasional fixes.

These deliverables form a system rather than a list. Care without education traps people in dependency. Education without belonging leaves talent unused. Safety without foresight creates false stability. Belonging without justice becomes sentiment rather than structure. Foresight without endurance becomes planning without continuity. Endurance without care becomes the preservation of form rather than the protection of people. The strength of each deliverable depends on the strength of the rest. Weakness in one creates strain in the others, and widespread failure becomes visible not through sudden collapse but through steady erosion.

A democracy earns legitimacy when the public experiences these deliverables in their daily lives. The existence of constitutional rights or democratic procedures is not enough. Citizens judge the system by whether it protects them, educates them, includes them, plans for their future, and provides continuity across generations. When these conditions hold, trust grows, and the republic gains resilience. When they falter, trust recedes, and openings emerge for leaders who promise solutions without accountability or restraint. The health of a democracy can therefore be measured through the presence or absence of these outcomes.

These deliverables also define the responsibilities of democratic governance. They identify what citizens have reason to expect and what institutions have a duty to provide. They function as public standards against which performance can be judged, not in moments of crisis alone but in the ordinary course of civic life. A government that cannot produce these results may retain authority, but it will lose legitimacy—the foundation on which democratic power rests. The distance between authority and legitimacy is the distance between coercion and consent.

Ultimately, the civic deliverables outline the conditions for successful self-government. They are not guarantees; they are responsibilities. A democracy must continually work to fulfill them, not just to maintain order but to sustain the trust that enables collective decision-making. When these deliverables are present and strong, the system can correct itself and renew. When they fail, the republic loses the connection between people and government that makes democracy more than a mere formality. Once this bond is weakened, restoring it is difficult.

CHAPTER 6
THE MORAL FLOOR

The promises, the machinery, and the deliverables of democracy can all be in place, yet still fail if the people running the system have no baseline of ethics. The Founders gave us a structure, but they built it on an assumption—that those entrusted with its care would be people of honor. In their world, this was not a wild hope. Most had lived and fought alongside others for whom public trust was a charge, not a prize. They did not believe they needed to spell it out in the Constitution. What they did not see clearly enough was that ambition without restraint is not leadership. It is simply corruption waiting for its moment.

They viewed public office as a temporary act of service, not a career. It was to be bestowed by the people as an honor, mainly entrusted to the educated elite they believed would act for the common good. They designed it to be protected from the permanence of monarchy, though not necessarily from the quieter growth of an oligarchy drawn from their own ranks. In their view, the stability of the republic would depend as much on the quality of those in office as on the words written on parchment. This expectation was reflected in the choices of its first leaders. George Washington stepped down after two terms when he could have ruled for life. John Adams, despite bitter partisan rancor, accepted defeat and handed over power peacefully to Thomas Jefferson in the first peaceful transfer of power between rivals. These acts were not forced by law but driven by character, and for a time they set the tone. Early stability relied as much on these voluntary limits as on the written Constitution.

But the guardrails they imagined were not made of law—they were made of culture. And culture can erode. The shift did not happen all at once. Over generations, politics moved from an intermittent duty to a full-time career, from something one left to return to private life to something one clung to as identity and livelihood. As the stakes of policy and the spoils of office grew, so did the temptation to treat public power as personal property. Modern politics has stripped away the assumption of good faith. Parties now game the system at every turn, treating the law as the ceiling of constraint rather than the floor of expectation. Actions that once ended political careers now become fundraising pitches. The cultural guardrail of shame has splintered. In many quarters, the only standard that matters is whether something can be done, not whether it should be done. When the moral floor collapses, no number of written safeguards can keep a system honest. What remains is not a republic but a contest of raw power.

A working democracy depends on more than rules; it depends on a shared set of non-negotiable norms that both leaders and citizens uphold. At its most basic, this civic covenant demands truthfulness in matters of public consequence, the placing of personal gain beneath public duty, the acceptance of electoral defeat and the peaceful transfer of power, the rejection of state power as a weapon for personal or partisan revenge, the protection of opponents' rights even in the heat of disagreement, and the safeguarding of the institutions that allow fair contest and debate. These are not lofty ideals—they are minimum conditions. Breach enough of them, and you have authoritarianism in all but name.

Beneath those norms lie six essential traits without which the whole structure begins to tilt.

Character is the anchor—integrity, honesty, and humility that can resist both the seductions and the pressures of office. It is the inner compass that keeps a leader's words aligned with their deeds, and their deeds with the public interest.

Ethics is the chart—choices made for the public good rather than private enrichment, with firm boundaries between personal fortune and public duty.

Restraint is the brake—limiting one's own power even when the rules would permit expansion, knowing that unchecked authority corrodes the very legitimacy it seeks to consolidate.

Truthfulness is the bedrock—factual honesty in matters that shape public trust and policy, without which citizens cannot make informed choices or hold leaders to account.

Good faith is the connective tissue—respecting the spirit as well as the letter of democratic rules, refraining from sabotage simply because the rules allow it.

Stewardship is the long view—protecting institutions for the future, with reverence for the office and its traditions as part of that duty, knowing that one's time in power is temporary but the republic must endure.

History provides both warnings and encouragement. When the moral foundation remains, republics can endure significant shocks. Britain survived the Blitz with its parliamentary system intact, partly because its leaders refused to exploit wartime fear for personal gain. When it fails, even strong systems collapse quickly. The late Roman Republic saw ambitious men remove restraint, manipulate the law, and turn offices meant for service into tools for personal power, until civil war replaced civic life. More recent examples include governments that maintain elections and legislatures but weaken their integrity until nothing remains but an empty shell.

The absence of any one of the six traits weakens the others. A leader lacking character might still speak the truth, but without restraint, that truth can be used as a weapon. A leader without ethics might protect an institution only when it benefits personal interests. The loss of even one trait can gradually weaken the others in ways that aren't immediately visible but are ultimately destructive. This is why the civic covenant is so important: it serves as the cultural glue that holds the structure together. Without it, the pillars of self-government—promises, systems, and results—become unstable.

The Founders did not anticipate every threat. They knew how to guard against kings; they were less aware of how to defend against a political class willing to trade honor for power. They assumed the best and brightest would be selected, but the same closed circle meant to ensure quality could just as easily shield mediocrity or corruption. They wrote a Constitution that could limit a bad actor's influence, but not one that could guarantee that good actors held office. That, they believed, would be the responsibility of the people. And so it remains, though the cost of neglecting this is now higher than they might have imagined.

History's record is unflinching: republics almost always die from internal decay before they fall to external conquest. Decay begins when leaders discard the idea that they owe anything higher than their own ambition. It spreads when citizens accept that decay as normal, or excuse it as the price of victory. The Democracy Clock measures breaches in this moral floor because each breach speeds the collapse. If the test of a generation is whether it can advance liberty, the test of a republic is whether it can protect its own foundations. Our task now is to restore this baseline of civic ethics before the system is so degraded that only power, not principle, decides the hour.

The four pillars—**Promises, Imperatives, Deliverables,** and the **Moral floor**—are not separate structures standing apart from each other. They are a single architecture, each element bearing the weight of the others. The promises name what a republic exists to provide. The imperatives make it work in practice. The deliverables prove it is working in the lives of its people. The moral floor keeps those in power from twisting every part to their own advantage. Remove any one pillar and the rest begin to tilt.

Taken together, they embody what a robust democracy looks like at its strongest. They serve as the standard against which every breach, every backslide, and every act of corrosion must be measured. This is the "noon" of the Democracy Clock—not a perfect past we once had, but a full set of conditions we must uphold or restore if the republic is to endure.

From here, the task shifts. The model is built; now it must be tested against reality. That means asking what happens when these four pillars begin to crack, and naming the specific ways those cracks show. If we can see them clearly, we can measure how far the damage has gone—and how late the hour has grown.

CHAPTER 7
DIAGNOSTICS OF A FAILING REPUBLIC

The architecture of democracy can be described in promises, imperatives, deliverables, and ethics. But that is only half the picture. To measure how late the hour has grown, we also need to know what it looks like when that structure begins to fail. Democracies almost never die at once. They erode through a series of injuries—some spectacular, others barely noticed—until the core can no longer hold.

One breach may not seem decisive. A court bends to political pressure while the rest of the government seems intact. A free press survives, but its reach is drowned in propaganda. An election is held, but under rules quietly tilted to guarantee the outcome. Each of these may pass without crisis. Yet each leaves the republic weaker for the next blow.

The patterns are not new. Across history, republics, parliamentary governments, and young democracies have decayed in ways so consistent they can be named and counted. They have been documented under monarchies, dictatorships, one-party states, and regimes that still called themselves democracies long after the substance was gone. The details shift with time and place, but the patterns repeat.

The sixty traits that follow are not alarms for a single moment; they are diagnostics—the visible, repeatable patterns by which self-government is hollowed from within. None exists in isolation. A shift in one will often trigger movement in others.

No list is final. Another scholar might frame the dangers differently, or add traits drawn from a different era or culture. There are conditions we have chosen not to separate because they overlap so strongly with others. What matters here is the breadth of the net. Taken together, these sixty traits cover most, if not all, of the visible ways a democracy can fail. They are the traits we have selected for this book, this study, this record. They form a web, not a single chain. Weakness in any part of that web can spread quickly to the rest.

These traits were not chosen randomly. We tested them against six key aspects that determine the health of a democracy: the structure of power, how its institutions function, the predictability and fairness of its legal system, the distribution of economic benefits, the extent of civil liberties, and the beliefs people hold about their system. We also analyzed them through four common collapse mechanisms: impunity, where those in power evade accountability; co-optation, where systems are undermined from within; extraction, where public resources are diverted to elites; and demobilization, where citizens are rendered powerless or convinced their voices no longer matter. Together, these checks help ensure the list captures not only obvious threats but also subtle and less visible ones.

The sixty traits fall into five broad categories:

1. **Power and Authority**
2. **Institutions and Governance**
3. **Economic Structure**
4. **Civil Rights and Dissent**
5. **Information, Memory, and Manipulation.**

What follows is a record of each trait—its definition and its place in the larger pattern—followed by the history of how whole categories have been used to dismantle democracies.

Category I: Power and Authority

Concentration of political power is often the first and most visible warning sign of democratic decay. It rarely arrives all at once.

1. Executive power operates without effective oversight — Presidents, prime ministers, or ruling councils act without checks from other branches, issuing decrees or orders that bypass regular scrutiny.
2. Elections occur, but money and media guarantee elite outcomes — Contests still happen, but results are structurally skewed toward entrenched power through control of coverage, campaign finance, and access.
3. Term limits are repealed or circumvented in service of the regime — leaders extend their time in office through legal changes or reinterpretations, resetting clocks or removing caps entirely.
4. Law is a weapon of the state, not a limit on its power — Courts and prosecutors serve as instruments to protect allies and punish critics, erasing impartiality.
5. Emergency powers are normalized and permanent — Measures intended for crisis become the default mode of governance, suspending normal rights indefinitely.
6. Opposition parties are allowed but structurally weakened — Rivals exist only in form, stripped of resources, media access, or the ability to compete fairly.
7. Political appointments are awarded based on loyalty and wealth — Positions are filled with donors, family, or loyalists rather than competence or experience.
8. Dissent is reframed as disorder, treason, or terrorism —

Critics are painted as threats to national security, delegitimizing their participation.
9. Police and military are aligned with elite preservation, not public defense — Security forces serve the rulers' survival rather than the citizens' safety.
10. Foreign influence is welcomed if it supports regime interests — Strategic or economic arrangements are accepted when they entrench the ruling order, even at the cost of sovereignty.
11. Federal power is weaponized against disfavored states or localities — Central government punishes regions based on political loyalty.
12. Public tragedy is monetized by regime insiders — Crises become profit opportunities for those closest to power.

Throughout history, this category's traits have often been the first sign of decay. In Mussolini's Italy, legal decrees, loyalist appointments, and the harassment of opposition parties quickly solidified authority. Marcos' Philippines combined the suspension of term limits with martial law to maintain indefinite control. More recently, Orbán's Hungary has used media dominance, structural electoral advantages, and federal coercion to weaken opposition beyond recovery. Once these tools are in place, they can last for decades—long after the leader who first used them is gone—creating a political system where power stays within a closed circle.

Category II: Institutions and Governance
Even when power appears distributed on paper, democracies depend on institutions that function as intended: courts that rule without fear or favor, legislatures that deliberate rather than perform, and agencies that act in the public interest. When these systems are hollowed out, the form of democracy remains while its substance vanishes.

Diagnostics of a Failing Republic | 41

13. Courts issue rulings aligned with donor or elite preference — Judicial decisions consistently favor the powerful, reflecting influence rather than law.
14. Judicial independence is eroded through partisan appointments — Judges are chosen for loyalty to the ruling faction rather than legal integrity.
15. Legislatures function as performance, not deliberation — Parliaments or congresses meet and debate, but their role is symbolic, rubber-stamping executive will.
16. Administrative agencies are deregulated or captured by private interests — Regulators serve corporations or political patrons, abandoning public oversight.
17. Investigations into corruption are blocked, buried, or retaliated against — Efforts to expose wrongdoing are shut down, defunded, or weaponized as show trials.
18. Whistleblowers are prosecuted, not protected — Those who expose abuse face punishment rather than safeguards.
19. Inspectors general are fired or ignored — Internal watchdogs are removed or sidelined to prevent scrutiny.
20. Ethics commissions are defunded or toothless — Oversight bodies exist in name only, with no real investigative or enforcement power.
21. Transparency laws are weakened or unenforced — Access to public records is curtailed, delayed, or denied altogether.
22. Civil service roles are politicized or privatized — Appointments are made for loyalty or profit rather than competence, or essential functions are outsourced.
23. Civil courts are used to harass and silence critics — Defamation suits and legal threats target journalists, academics, or opponents.
24. Public funds are used for personal glorification and symbolic dominance — State resources are diverted to

monuments, parades, or propaganda celebrating the leader.
25. State power is outsourced to unaccountable private contractors — Core functions, including security and intelligence, are handed to for-profit actors beyond public oversight.

Authoritarian consolidation often depends on these traits to appear legitimate while maintaining obedience. In Turkey, after the 2016 coup attempt, mass judicial purges, partisan appointments, and the closing of independent agencies placed the courts and regulators firmly under executive control. In Hungary, constitutional amendments and court-packing have secured a series of rulings favoring the ruling party for a generation. The Soviet Union kept parliaments and courts in appearance but diminished them to ceremonial roles, disguising autocracy through procedural rituals. Once these patterns become ingrained, institutions serve as shields for power rather than checks on it.

Category III: Economic Structure

Economic arrangements are never politically neutral. In a healthy democracy, public policy mediates between competing interests, protects the common good, and limits concentrations of power. In a captured state, economic systems are designed to entrench the ruling class, turning markets into engines of political dominance.

26. Policy outcomes are driven by elite lobbying and financial contributions — Laws and regulations reflect the priorities of donors and corporate actors.
27. Access to lawmakers is bought through donations and influence networks — Decision-makers reserve their time and attention for financial contributors.

28. Former or future industry executives staff regulatory agencies — Oversight bodies are run by those with vested interests in the industries they police.
29. Wealth buys not only speech, but law — The affluent shape not just debate but the legal system itself to protect their position.
30. Entire industries are shielded from accountability through lobbying power — Whole sectors avoid regulation or oversight through political muscle.
31. Public goods (education, health, water, transit) are privatized for profit — Essential services are transferred to private ownership, often at public expense.
32. Tax codes are engineered to favor capital, not labor — Wealth, especially inherited or passive income, is taxed lightly while wages bear the burden.
33. Financial crimes by elites are unpunished or quietly settled — Fraud and misconduct by the powerful end in fines, not prison.
34. Economic monopolies are tolerated or encouraged — Competition is stifled in favor of large, politically connected firms.
35. Labor protections are eroded to keep workers atomized and dependent — Collective bargaining and workplace rights are weakened.
36. Inequality is not a flaw—it is a function of the system — Disparities in wealth and power are treated as inevitable or desirable.
37. Political risk is offloaded onto the public; profits are kept private — The costs of failure are socialized, while gains are privatized.
38. Crony capitalism becomes indistinguishable from governance — Business and politics merge into a single network of favors and immunity.
39. Economic data is selectively published, massaged, or

ignored — Statistics are manipulated to conceal poor performance or inequality.
40. Crisis becomes a profit opportunity for those closest to power — Disasters are exploited for private gain through contracts and concessions.

In many states, authoritarian rule has been solidified through economic control. In Russia, oligarchs linked to the Kremlin dominate energy, banking, and media sectors while facing little real competition. Under Pinochet, Chile's extensive privatizations and the weakening of labor rights transformed the economy, cementing elite dominance long after his dictatorship ended. South Africa's "state capture" period demonstrated how corporate actors could nearly dictate government policies when regulators and lawmakers are compromised. Once the economic system is captured, it becomes a silent force enforcing political power.

Category IV: Civil Rights and Dissent

The ability to speak, organize, protest, and vote is not incidental to democracy; it is its lifeblood. When these rights are narrowed or selectively enforced, the political system begins to suffocate.

41. Protest rights are abridged through zoning, permits, or "security" claims — Demonstrations are restricted to invisible or symbolic locations, or prohibited outright.
42. Journalists investigating the elite are surveilled or smeared — Reporters face harassment, intimidation, or character attacks for exposing misconduct.
43. Independent media is starved while state-aligned outlets thrive — Opposition voices lose funding or licenses while loyal outlets receive subsidies.
44. Universities are pressured to suppress dissent or lose funding — Academic freedom is curtailed through direct political pressure or budgetary threats.

45. Voter suppression is rationalized as election integrity — Legal or procedural barriers disproportionately disenfranchise disfavored groups.
46. Surveillance of ordinary citizens increases; elite crimes remain opaque — Public life is monitored while misconduct at the top is hidden from scrutiny.
47. Citizenship is stratified by wealth, ideology, and heritage — Legal status and rights depend on class, belief, or ethnicity.
48. Religion is co-opted as a tool of legitimacy and control — Faith institutions are harnessed to justify authority and suppress dissent.
49. Dissenters are labeled unpatriotic, subversive, or corrupt — Critics are branded as traitors or criminals to discredit their message.
50. Paramilitary violence is tolerated when it protects elite interests — Non-state armed groups operate with state blessing to intimidate or attack opponents.
51. Crimes committed by elite donors or allies are concealed, not prosecuted — The powerful enjoy impunity while the law is applied to the powerless.

The suppression of dissent is a common second step in democratic decline. In Nazi Germany, the Gleichschaltung process took control of all civic institutions, from universities to the press, under state authority. In apartheid South Africa, protest bans, media censorship, and violence by security forces made it possible to monitor, contain, or eliminate opposition. In modern Hungary and Turkey, using media control, criminal charges, and selective enforcement has drastically reduced the space for dissent, bringing it close to extinction.

Category V: Information, Memory, and Manipulation
Democracy relies on shared facts, an honest record of the past,

and the ability to challenge official narratives. When those are replaced by propaganda, selective memory, and engineered ignorance, the capacity for self-government collapses.

52. Elections are flooded with disinformation funded by elite actors — Campaigns deploy falsehoods to distort choice and protect those in power.
53. Chaos is used as a strategy to fragment focus and disable accountability — Multiple crises are stoked or staged to exhaust public oversight.
54. Data and algorithms are used to manipulate, not serve, the public — Information systems are weaponized to influence behavior without consent.
55. Civic education is hollowed out and replaced with market ideology — Training for citizenship is replaced by obedience or economic utility.
56. National history is rewritten to glorify conquest, not justice — Past abuses are reframed as triumphs, erasing victims from the story.
57. Textbooks and museums are altered to erase dissent and accountability — Cultural institutions are forced to reflect official narratives.
58. Government archives are sealed, sanitized, or destroyed — Records are hidden or purged to prevent investigation or reckoning.
59. Statues, portraits, and records of disfavored leaders are removed without process — Public memory is edited by executive order rather than democratic decision.
60. Memory is curated by power—what cannot be controlled is erased — Entire chapters of history are suppressed or obliterated.

Control of information often marks the final step in consolidating authoritarian rule because it guarantees that future generations will inherit only the regime's version of reality. Stalin's Soviet

Union rewrote history books, changed photographs, and erased political rivals from memory. In modern China, censorship of Tiananmen Square and control over school curricula prevent collective memory of dissent. Turkey's reinterpretation of its Ottoman and Republican past has been used to justify current power structures while sidelining alternative visions. When the state controls memory itself, resistance becomes not only dangerous but also easily forgotten.

The traits in this chapter are not isolated hazards. They are interconnected, often reinforcing one another across categories. An executive who governs without oversight (Trait 1) is more likely to pack the courts (Trait 14), which makes it easier to suppress protest (Trait 41) and manipulate public memory (Trait 56). Over time, the pattern becomes self-sustaining. Institutions cease to restrain power, economic systems serve the rulers, dissent is smothered, and truth itself is replaced with managed perception.

A single trait may be survivable; clusters are far more dangerous. When enough weaken or fail together, they form a new political order in which democracy exists in name but not in function. The promises, imperatives, deliverables, and moral floor describe what a healthy republic looks like. These sixty traits describe what happens when that health declines. They are not predictions; they are diagnostics—a record of when and how the republic begins to fail.

CHAPTER 8
TIME AS DEMOCRATIC EVIDENCE

The Democracy Clock is our tool for assessing the health of a republic. It is not just a metaphor but a diagnostic instrument, designed to monitor the gradual decline or sudden breakdown of democratic functions. Its measure is time, not because democracies operate on clocks, but because decline has a direction. Just as the Doomsday Clock translates nuclear threat into minutes to midnight, the Democracy Clock translates democratic danger into the same stark language. Midnights indicate the failure of a functioning republic and the inability to recover. Noons signify the ideal modern form of democracy — not the Founders' vision, nor any specific moment in U.S. history, but the fullest realization of the republic's promises, obligations, achievements, and moral standards, all reinforced by a civic commitment set in stone.

The clock's foundation consists of sixty traits of a failing republic — the structural and cultural failures that, together, threaten to end democracy. They are categorized into five groups: Power and Authority, Institutions, Law and Rights, Economics and Resources, and Civil Society and Culture. The clock's goal is to assess how many of these traits exist and how difficult they are to reverse. The result is a cumulative score that can be tracked over time, offering a continuous record of the system's stress.

Two measures determine each trait's weight. The first is presence, scored from zero to ten, where zero indicates the authoritarian tendency is absent and ten means it is fully present. The second is the difficulty of reversal, scored from zero to two; some damage can be undone with a change of leadership or a single law, while other changes require constitutional amendments, court reversals, or decades of cultural work. The higher the difficulty, the more entrenched the damage. These two numbers combined give each trait a score out of twelve.

This system is cumulative. A single trait at full strength might not topple a democracy, but clusters of traits matter greatly. When enough traits appear together—especially those with high difficulty scores—they reinforce each other. Power consolidates, accountability diminishes, and public belief in self-governance wanes. The movement of the clock not only indicates whether damage exists but also whether it is spreading, accelerating, or being repaired. Direction is as important as level.

The sixty traits are not isolated from the positive framework of a healthy republic. They are its inversions. Every promise in the Preamble has corresponding traits that weaken it. Every modern imperative—the functional requirements of democracy—has traits that obstruct or disable it. Every outcome—the actual functioning of a republic—has traits that diminish it. When all three layers are compromised, the civic covenant itself collapses. The clock measures this entire dynamic, not just one side.

The promises, imperatives, outcomes, and civic covenant define the republic's intended form and function. The traits reveal its failure modes. If the positive elements are like a blueprint, the traits are like stress points. The Democracy Clock reads both: the erosion of what should be preserved and the entrenchment of what should not. This dual perspective ensures we measure not just loss but also healing—since the clock can move in either direction, it can return toward health.

Each trait is scored twice. Presence is rated from zero to ten. A score of zero indicates the authoritarian tendency is absent; ten signifies it is fully present—and entirely harmful to democracy, as it negates, distorts, or dismantles one or more of democracy's promises, imperatives, deliverables, or core norms. The difficulty of reversal is scored separately from zero to two, based on how challenging it would be—both structurally and institutionally—to undo the damage. The lowest score, +0.5, applies to actions a president can reverse alone. Scores increase with each additional institutional actor needed: one chamber of Congress, both chambers, multiple state legislatures, or a high court. The maximum score, +2.0, applies when reversing would require overturning a Supreme Court ruling, repudiating a controlling precedent, or amending the Constitution itself.

The full range of mechanisms includes appointments and removals, executive orders and memos, Senate confirmations and refusals, congressional hearings and resolutions, state and federal legislation, court rulings and appeals, shadow docket interventions, and constitutional amendments. The higher the combined score, the more deeply entrenched the damage—and the closer the clock moves to midnight. Each step up the scale marks a deeper lock on power.

Noon was chosen for its symbolism—the sun at its peak, light reaching every corner, activity in full swing. It's the moment when nothing is hidden and the day's work is possible. Midnight carries the opposite weight: total darkness, minimal movement except for predators, and a natural urge to withdraw. Between these poles lies every possible state of a democracy, from the warmth and visibility of noon to the fear and stillness of midnight—and it is in describing midnight that the dangers become clearest. The end state reveals what is at stake.

At midnight, chaos is absent. It isn't a fragile democracy on life support. It's the moment when democracy no longer exists — in practice, and often even in name. Some regimes maintain superficial forms for show, staging elections with fixed results or allowing legislatures that cannot truly legislate. Others abandon the façade entirely, abolishing elected bodies, dissolving courts, and ruling by decree. What remains is a different political order, one that no impartial observer would call a democracy. The entire blueprint of a healthy republic — promises, obligations, deliverables, covenant — has disappeared. Power flows from the top; the people have lost their voice.

At midnight, the six promises are either abandoned or redefined to serve the regime. Justice becomes punishment for enemies. Domestic tranquility is maintained through surveillance and fear. The common defense protects the regime, not the people. The general welfare is redirected to a loyal elite. Liberty is reduced to the freedom to obey. Posterity is secured only for those in power. This isn't disorder. It's a stable, engineered order that prevents self-government.

At midnight, the modern imperatives also disappear. Controlled outcomes replace free and fair elections. A single pyramid of authority replaces a functioning separation of powers. Rights enforcement collapses; the rule of law is replaced by rule by law. Institutions are not independent actors but loyal departments. Civic participation is seen as dangerous. A culture of propaganda replaces a culture of truth. Every deliverable is stripped down to its core.

At midnight, the core promises of the nation — caring for people, education, safety and justice, belonging, preparing for the future, and maintaining democratic foundations — are effectively lost if not in name. Hospitals exist but do not serve everyone equally. Schools promote obedience. Streets are policed, but not necessarily for safety. The state is controlled by a faction. Future planning is replaced by immediate looting. And the covenant — the belief that the state exists by and for the people — is broken.

In a healthy republic, noon marks the peak of a functioning democracy in a modern society, limited by human capacity. All six promises are sincerely upheld: justice is fair, peace is genuine, defense is collective, welfare is public, liberty is broad, and future generations are considered. This is not utopia; it is a functioning system that continuously self-corrects, fixing faults before they become permanent. Self-correction is its key characteristic.

Here, the modern essentials are fully in effect. Elections are truly free and fair, and participation is universal. Powers are separated, checked, and balanced. Rights are enforceable and protected. Institutions are independent yet accountable. Civic engagement is protected and encouraged. Public discourse takes place in a culture of truth, not propaganda. The system is not immune to challenges, but it responds with resilience rather than suppression.

The deliverables are clear in this context. Care for the people is universal and fair. Education lifts up every citizen. Safety, justice, and freedom are real and widely shared. The nation belongs to all, not just a small part. Preparing for the future is an ongoing duty. Democratic stability is not an assumption but a deliberate effort at upkeep. It requires work, done openly. Beneath everything, the civic agreement remains alive. The people believe—and can see—that government exists by and for them. Leaders understand that their authority comes from the consent of the governed, and that holding office carries an unshakable moral duty to serve the public good. The parties choose, and the people elect, expecting their leaders to have integrity, act ethically, stay responsible and answerable to their constituents, and hold themselves—without exception—to the highest standard of morality and honesty. The oath of office is spoken and accepted as a serious vow, not just a formality, binding the leader to both the Constitution and the people. Public trust is not blind; it is earned, tested, and renewed. Public service is honorable, granted, and earned. This covenant is the living foundation on which every promise, obligation, and deliverable depends.

The clock's poles represent symbolic ideals, not destinations we expect to reach. Noon serves as a goal to strive toward, yet a living democracy will always have more to accomplish — new ways to fulfill its promises, new expressions of its imperatives, and evolving forms of its deliverables as changes in technology, population, climate, and other forces reshape public life. Debate over priorities isn't a flaw but a sign of vitality. Midnight, in turn, need not be inevitable. It can be kept forever out of reach if the people — and the representatives who still love democracy — act with the courage, persistence, and sometimes heroism required to turn the clock back when danger gathers. The clock is not fixed. It can move forward toward midnight or back toward noon. Authoritarian traits can emerge, grow stronger, and become entrenched; they can also weaken, disappear, or be dismantled. Democratic health can improve as well as decline. The point of the clock is to measure both directions, so that we do not mistake short-term fixes for structural recovery, or temporary gains for permanent security. It serves as a warning against wishful thinking.

Understanding the extremes is important, but most republics exist somewhere in between. The weekly readings from the clock capture subtle yet significant movements within that range — shifts toward concentrating power or dispersing it, toward eroding rights or strengthening them. These changes might be nearly invisible in a single week, but they accumulate over years or decades into transformations no one intended. The measure allows us to see which way we're headed while there's still time to change course, long before reaching the destination.

With the clock defined, we can now turn to history. The United States has never stood at noon, nor yet at midnight. Its time has moved forward and back, sometimes within a single presidency. By reading its history through the Democracy Clock, we can see patterns hidden in the daily noise — eras of repair, periods of entrenched damage, and turning points that pushed the hands faster than anyone realized at the time.

CHAPTER 9
INTERLUDE: FROM INHERITANCE TO MEASUREMENT

America was founded with two opposing forces: a hope for self-government and exclusions so deep that this hope required struggle to grow. From the moment the first colonial assemblies met under the shadow of empire, the nation carried both the promise of popular sovereignty and the contradictions that challenged it. The clock started ticking long before there was a clock to measure it.

Every era in the republic's history changed the timing. Independence shifted authority from a monarchy to a people still defining who "the people" were. The Constitution created machinery to support a republic but also left large areas of unaccountable power. Slavery entrenched authoritarian traits at the country's core; abolition ended the system but not the habits it fostered. At every stage, democratic advances coincided with democratic setbacks—and neither fully replaced the other.

Reconstruction moved the hands toward noon more rapidly than any other sustained period of democratic expansion in American history, and its violent undoing pushed them back just as quickly. Jim Crow formalized minority rule over millions, cementing traits that would take a century to confront. Industrialization created new centers of power that bypassed voters. Progressive reforms and later the New Deal built new protections and institutions, shifting time toward midday—while the country simultaneously tolerated or supported anti-democratic structures elsewhere. The clock never moved in only one direction.

The mid-20th century saw a rare convergence: courts expanding rights, mass movements increasing participation, and institutions asserting limits on power. The civil rights era brought the nation closer to democratic equality than it had ever been. These gains, however, were met by counter-movements that developed quietly at first—in economic doctrine, media infrastructure, campaign finance, and partisan identity. Watergate temporarily reasserted restraint, but the structural vulnerabilities it exposed were never fully addressed.

Beginning in the 1980s, the national political landscape reorganized around concentrated wealth, polarized information, deregulated institutions, and increasingly winner-take-all elections. These forces strengthened over decades, weakening the safeguards that once slowed democratic decline. The end of the Cold War removed external discipline; partisan media fractured a shared factual foundation; and the erosion of cross-party coalitions reduced incentives for restraint. By the early 2000s, democratic progress had already significantly regressed. The post-9/11 expansion of executive power, combined with a judiciary increasingly willing to tolerate partisan advantage, accelerated that decline. The financial crisis widened inequality; the Senate abandoned norm-based governance; state legislatures gerrymandered themselves into permanence; and social media platforms amplified disinformation and grievance. The conditions for a democratic setback were in place long before they were widely recognized.

When Donald Trump entered politics, he did not create these traits. He activated them.

His first presidency pushed the country dangerously close to a point where democratic correction became uncertain—not because every action was unprecedented, but because the surrounding system had lost its ability to restrain him. The safeguards that once resisted executive excess had been weakened by decades of structural change. When he returned to power in 2025, he inherited a nation already deep into its democratic evening—closer to twilight than at any time since Reconstruction. This position reflected not one man's choices, but a long accumulation of judicial entrenchment, institutional decline, economic concentration, disinformation networks, and a political culture increasingly tolerant of rule-breaking when it benefits its own side.

That is why the clock started where it did.

Not because of catastrophe, but because of cumulative neglect.

Not because democracy collapsed overnight, but because—week by week, trait by trait—damage accumulated until what once would have shocked the nation blended into background noise.

This period of reflection exists for one purpose: to make clear that Trump's second term did not emerge from nowhere. The groundwork was laid long before he assumed office, through decisions and patterns that reshaped how power, rights, and information operate. The Democracy Clock indicates where that long history left the country at the moment he resumed office—and why the fifty-two weeks that follow must be measured with care.

PART II
THE RECORD

CHAPTER 10
READING DEMOCRATIC TIME: A NOTE ON METHOD

What follows is a chronological record, not a narrative arc. It does not assume inevitability, predict outcomes, or impose drama on events that may not appear dramatic at first glance. It proceeds week by week because democratic erosion—and democratic repair—rarely occur all at once. They accumulate. The purpose of this section is to explain how that accumulation is measured, how weekly movement is assessed, and how the reader should interpret what follows.

Each entry in Part II covers a single week of governance. Weeks are used not because they represent natural political units, but because they strike a balance between detail and stability. Days are too short; months are too broad. Weeks allow patterns to appear without losing track of individual actions. They also reflect how modern governments usually operate: through ongoing decisions, procedural changes, enforcement choices, and institutional responses that happen gradually rather than all at once.

The Democracy Clock does not react to headlines or public opinion. It shifts only when underlying democratic conditions change. Some weeks feature events that are highly visible and widely reported. Others involve procedural changes, administrative decisions, or institutional failures that attract little attention at the time. Both are important. Democratic decline is rarely caused by spectacle alone. More often, it progresses through quiet normalization—small changes that once would have faced resistance but now pass with little notice.

Clock movement is cumulative. A single action rarely shifts democratic time on its own. Instead, actions reinforce or counteract existing conditions. A week may include developments that weaken democratic safeguards alongside actions that restore or defend them. In such cases, the clock reflects net movement, not isolated incidents. Many weeks will therefore show limited change. Some will show none at all. This is not a flaw in the method; it is evidence that the measure is not designed to dramatize routine politics.

Not every abuse advances democratic time toward midnight, and not every defense reverses it. The framework distinguishes between symbolic conflict and structural change. Rhetoric matters only when it alters enforcement, precedent, or institutional behavior. Likewise, legal or procedural victories matter only when they produce durable constraint rather than temporary delay. The clock is calibrated to reflect condition, not intent.

Readers should not expect symmetry. Democratic damage is often easier to inflict than to repair. Structural erosion can occur quickly; restoration usually requires sustained effort across multiple institutions and over extended periods. As a result, forward movement toward midnight may occur in sharper increments than backward movement toward noon. This asymmetry reflects historical reality, not editorial choice.

The clock also does not assume linear progression. Some weeks reverse earlier movement. Others reveal that prior gains were less durable than they appeared. Still others expose vulnerabilities that had gone unnoticed. Part II should therefore be read as a continuous assessment rather than a directional march. The question each week is not "what happened," but "what changed."

Interpretation within each weekly entry follows a consistent discipline. Events are assessed against the principles established in

Part I and the democratic conditions they affect. Where evidence is incomplete, uncertainty is acknowledged. Where effects are indirect, they are described as such. Where developments are ambiguous, that ambiguity is preserved rather than resolved by assertion. The method favors restraint over certainty.

This approach means that Part II will not always feel urgent. That, too, is intentional. Democracies do not fail because every week feels catastrophic. They fail when warning signs accumulate without sustained attention, when breaches become routine, and when corrective mechanisms lose their force. A calm record of change is therefore more useful than a heightened one. Alarm is a poor measuring instrument.

The companion volume to this book provides the complete record of governmental actions on which weekly assessments are based. That record exists to allow independent review, replication, and disagreement. The Democracy Clock does not ask the reader to accept conclusions on trust. It invites scrutiny of the evidence and the reasoning applied to it.

Part II begins at the point where the Interlude ended: the moment Donald Trump resumed office in January 2025. The starting position of the clock reflects the cumulative condition of American democracy at that moment, as established in Part I. What follows does not re-litigate that history. It measures what comes next.

The weeks ahead should be read patiently. Their significance lies not in any single entry, but in the pattern that emerges over time. Democratic condition is revealed through accumulation. This section exists to make that accumulation visible.

CHAPTER 11
WEEK 1: EMERGENCIES AS OPERATING SYSTEM

> *In Trump's first week back in office, overlapping emergencies, purges, and decrees turn the presidency into a central engine of unilateral rule.*

The second Trump inauguration did not unfold as a single break with the past so much as a rapid rewriting of what counted as normal. Within hours of the oath, the presidency was no longer just an office changing hands; it became the central engine of a dense, overlapping series of decrees. Immigration, energy, foreign aid, civil rights, and the internal machinery of government were all pulled into the orbit of one person's will. The week's pattern was not drift or improvisation. It was a deliberate use of familiar tools—executive orders, emergencies, personnel decisions—to redraw the boundaries of power. It felt coordinated, not chaotic.

At the close of the prior period, the Democracy Clock stood at 7:31 p.m. By the end of Week 1, it read 7:39 p.m., a net movement of eight minutes. The shift captured how quickly the formal architecture of a constitutional republic can be bent without a single statute being repealed. Trump's early actions concentrated authority in the presidency, normalized emergency rule, and weakened the institutions meant to constrain him. At the same time, they stratified citizenship, rewarded loyal violence, and invited moneyed allies—domestic and foreign—into the heart of governance. Courts, states, and civil society did respond, but always a step behind the pace set from the White House. The center of gravity moved toward unilateral rule.

Trump's second term began with a speech that repeated familiar falsehoods about a stolen election and a corrupt justice system. The words mattered less than what followed. Almost immediately, he declared a national emergency at the southern border, despite low crossings, and ordered active-duty troops to support enforcement. A parallel "energy emergency" framed fossil fuel expansion as a crisis response. These declarations were not just policy choices; they unlocked special powers and justified bypassing Congress and existing regulatory safeguards. Immigration and energy, two vast policy domains, were recast as matters of presidential emergency management. Ordinary politics gave way to permanent crisis.

At the same time, Trump moved to change who inside government could say no. He reinstated and expanded Schedule F, reclassifying thousands of civil servants into a category that stripped them of job protections and made them easier to fire. The order reached deep into policy roles that had been insulated from partisan swings, turning expertise into a conditional privilege. Independent regulatory agencies were told to align their budgets and priorities with White House approval, narrowing the space for arm's-length rulemaking. The creation of the Department of Government Efficiency—DOGE—inside the Executive Office, with a favored private-sector ally at its helm, embedded presidential teams across agencies and centralized control over digital systems and payments. Loyalty, not independence, became the organizing principle.

These structural moves were paired with open defiance of statutory limits. Trump ordered the Justice Department not to enforce a congressionally mandated TikTok divest-or-ban law for

75 days, even though courts had upheld it. His budget director announced plans to challenge the Impoundment Control Act, which bars presidents from unilaterally withholding appropriated funds, while the White House froze disbursements under the Inflation Reduction Act and the Bipartisan Infrastructure Act. In each case, the message was that laws passed by Congress were suggestions, subject to presidential timing and preference. Statute remained on the books, but compliance became optional.

Internal oversight was thinned in parallel. Trump fired at least a dozen inspectors general across agencies in a single sweep, without the usual notice or cause. These watchdogs, designed to investigate waste and abuse, were replaced or left vacant, sending a clear signal to those who remained. The first woman to lead a U.S. military branch, Coast Guard Commandant Linda Fagan, was removed over alleged overemphasis on diversity, and the TSA administrator was fired while the Aviation Security Advisory Committee was disbanded. These firings were framed as management decisions, but they stripped professional leadership from key security institutions and warned others that adherence to equity or independent judgment could cost them their jobs. Fear, not norms, did the work of control.

If the first development concentrated power inside the executive, the second turned that power outward against a defined set of people and places. Trump's immigration orders went far beyond prior enforcement debates. He suspended asylum and refugee admissions, shut down key processing tools, and ordered mass deportations under the language of "invasion." ICE and CBP were authorized to conduct aggressive raids, including in churches, schools, and hospitals, and to detain migrants without release. Expedited removal was expanded nationwide, shrinking due-process protections for non-citizens and heightening fear in immigrant communities. Everyday life for millions became more precarious.

The most direct constitutional test came with an executive order aimed at ending or restricting birthright citizenship for many

U.S.-born children of non-citizen parents. By attempting to narrow the Fourteenth Amendment's guarantee through unilateral decree, Trump treated constitutional membership as an administrative category he could redraw. Within days, coalitions of states and cities sued, and federal judges in Washington and Washington State issued temporary restraining orders, calling the move "blatantly unconstitutional." For the moment, the courts halted implementation, but the attempt itself marked a new willingness to treat core constitutional provisions as negotiable. The line between amendment and edict was put under strain.

Enforcement machinery was not only expanded; it was pointed at those who resisted. The Justice Department was directed to investigate and potentially charge state and local officials who maintained sanctuary policies, escalating a long-running conflict over immigrant protections into the realm of criminal exposure for elected leaders. In Mississippi, a state legislator introduced a bill to create an "Illegal Alien Certified Bounty Hunter Program," paying civilians to help deport undocumented people. Together, these moves blurred the line between public enforcement and deputized vigilantism, and they made local resistance to federal immigration policy a personal risk. Opposition was allowed, but structurally weakened.

Federal power was also used to punish disfavored regions. Trump threatened to withhold wildfire aid from California unless the state adopted voter ID requirements and changed water policies, tying disaster relief to unrelated political demands. He floated plans to abolish or radically shrink FEMA and created a review council to examine its impartiality, raising the prospect that future disaster response could be conditioned on political alignment. In Ohio, a new law allowed high fees for access to police body-camera footage, making it harder for residents and journalists to scrutinize law enforcement. These choices signaled that geography and politics would shape access to federal protection and transparency. The map of risk began to track the map of partisanship.

The third development inverted the traditional role of law. On his first day, Trump issued mass pardons and commutations for more than 1,500 January 6 defendants, including violent offenders, and ordered pending prosecutions dropped. He described them as "hostages," recasting an attack on Congress as a cause for mercy. At the same time, he restored the federal death penalty and urged prosecutors to seek aggressive capital sentences, including by challenging Supreme Court precedents that had limited its use. The combination of sweeping clemency for those who used violence in his name and a harsher punitive posture elsewhere marked a shift from rule of law to rule by law. The law's edge turned outward, not upward.

Civil-rights enforcement was frozen. The Justice Department's Civil Rights Division was ordered to halt all cases and block new filings, pausing federal action against discrimination in voting, housing, policing, and employment. The national database tracking police misconduct was dismantled, removing a key tool for identifying abusive officers and patterns of excessive force. Victims of state and private discrimination retained formal rights, but the federal government's capacity and willingness to enforce those rights were sharply reduced. Rights on paper no longer guaranteed remedies in practice.

Selective mercy extended beyond January 6. Trump pardoned anti-abortion activists convicted under the FACE Act, which protects access to reproductive health clinics, and allies in Congress introduced legislation to repeal the statute altogether. At the same time, he paused enforcement of the Foreign Corrupt Practices Act, signaling leniency toward Americans accused of bribing foreign officials. Taken together, these moves created a two-tier system: violence and financial misconduct aligned with regime causes were excused or rewarded, while vulnerable groups lost federal protection and opponents faced the threat of investigation. The justice system remained intact on paper, but its priorities had been turned upside down. Law became a weapon, not a limit.

A fourth development unfolded in the realm of culture and identity. Trump ordered the termination of all federal diversity, equity, and inclusion programs and offices, dismantling structures built to address discrimination and representation across agencies. He rescinded dozens of Biden-era executive actions on racial equity, LGBTQ+ protections, climate, and public health in a blanket revocation. The Department of Education was instructed to begin dismantling its federal role, threatening national standards and civil-rights enforcement in schools. These steps removed institutional supports that had made equality more than a slogan. The floor under many communities dropped.

At the same time, Trump narrowed legal recognition of sex and gender. An order redefined federal recognition to two biological categories "at conception," with broad implications for civil-rights enforcement and health policy. Separate directives barred federal coverage of gender-affirming care for minors and banned transgender athletes from women's sports by reinterpreting Title IX. These changes did not abolish transgender people, but they made their access to care, education, and public life more precarious, signaling that their rights were contingent on the preferences of those in power. Identity itself became subject to decree.

Reproductive rights were also tightened. Trump reaffirmed and strengthened the Hyde Amendment's ban on federal funding for elective abortions, reinstated the global gag rule cutting aid to foreign organizations that provide or discuss abortion, and revoked Biden-era protections for reproductive health access. An executive order enforcing Hyde and related measures reoriented federal health programs toward more restrictive policies at home and abroad. These legal moves were framed as restoring moral order, but they shifted the burdens of unwanted pregnancy and limited care onto women and low-income communities. The costs were borne by those with the least leverage.

Religion was drawn into politics as both shield and sword. Trump created a taskforce to end perceived anti-Christian bias in government, elevating one faith's grievances into federal policy. When the Episcopal bishop of Washington preached a sermon at the National Cathedral urging mercy for immigrants and LGBTQ+

people, he denounced her as a "radical left hater," casting religious advocacy for marginalized groups as partisan hostility. In this climate, Christianity, or at least a particular version of it, became a tool to justify policy and delegitimize dissenting moral voices. The combined effect of these moves was to enforce a narrower social order through law, bureaucracy, and symbolism. Conscience itself was sorted into loyal and disloyal camps.

Control over information formed the fifth major strand. Late in the week, Trump ordered HHS, CDC, and FDA to halt health advisories, scientific reports, and many external communications, including on avian influenza. Scientific meetings were paused, and new research and data releases were subject to political review. These gag orders did not erase existing knowledge, but they choked off the flow of updated information from trusted public-health institutions, centralizing narrative control over health risks in the White House. The public saw less and later.

Transparency in law enforcement was also reduced. The dismantling of the federal police-misconduct database removed a national record that journalists, advocates, and local officials had used to track abusive officers. DOGE, the new efficiency department, operated with alleged violations of transparency and record-keeping rules, prompting lawsuits that argued it functioned as an unregulated advisory committee. At the same time, Trump signed an order framed as restoring "freedom of speech" and ending federal censorship, barring agencies from certain content-moderation partnerships and launching investigations into past efforts to curb disinformation. The rhetoric of free speech was used to justify scrutiny of those who had tried to manage harmful content, while the administration itself restricted the flow of neutral data. Information was curated, not shared.

Symbolic and media moves reinforced this pattern. Trump ordered the renaming of Denali back to Mount McKinley and the Gulf of Mexico to the Gulf of America, using executive power to reshape national geography in a triumphalist, nationalist key. A "one flag" policy barred non-U.S. flags, including pride and Black

Lives Matter flags, from embassy flagpoles, narrowing the symbolic space for representing diversity abroad. The Federal Communications Commission, under a chair aligned with Trump, reopened campaign complaints against major television networks and entertained rhetoric about revoking MSNBC's license. Meanwhile, Trump repeatedly made false claims about Biden's clemency record and the 2020 election, and misrepresented state policies and international arrangements. With scientific and law-enforcement data constrained, these narratives had fewer official counterweights. The story of the country tilted toward a single voice.

The sixth development lay in the fusion of economic policy with personal and allied enrichment. Trump ordered the creation of a U.S. sovereign wealth fund, subject to congressional approval, and a strategic bitcoin reserve funded by forfeited assets. These structures would centralize large pools of public capital under executive influence and tie federal asset-forfeiture policy to speculative digital holdings. At the same time, he launched and promoted personal cryptocurrencies—TRUMP and MELANIA coins—with large insider allocations, using the presidency's visibility to drive speculative demand. Major exchanges facing SEC scrutiny listed and promoted the $TRUMP coin, apparently betting on a friendlier regulatory climate. Public office and private bets moved in tandem.

Family and business networks moved in parallel. Jared Kushner's Saudi-backed fund, Affinity Partners, secured a $2 billion investment from the kingdom's sovereign wealth fund despite internal objections, raising concerns that foreign governments were rewarding a former senior official in ways that could influence U.S. policy. New Trump-branded real-estate projects on government-linked sites abroad, such as Trump Tower Belgrade, created channels for foreign elites to enrich the president's business interests while he held office. The Trump Organization expanded merchandise tied to his return to the White House, monetizing the presidency through branded goods. The line between emolument and policy preference grew thin.

Broader economic policy reinforced these patterns. Trump closed the de minimis loophole on Chinese imports and imposed broad reciprocal tariffs, reshaping trade flows and risking retaliation. He expanded fossil fuel extraction on federal lands and in Alaska, rolled back electric-vehicle targets, and rescinded flood-protection standards for federally funded infrastructure, aligning land and climate policy with industry interests. The freeze on Inflation Reduction Act and infrastructure spending threatened long-term industrial and clean-energy investments, while DOGE's centralization of federal payments increased executive and private-sector influence over how public funds were disbursed. In this landscape, wealth did not just buy access; it helped write the rules. Crony capitalism became a governing method.

A seventh development returned to the internal machinery of the state, this time with a focus on politicization and outsourcing. Schedule F's reclassification of thousands of civil servants stripped many policy roles of tenure protections, making them vulnerable to removal based on perceived loyalty. DOGE's mandate to embed teams across agencies and centralize digital and payment systems gave a favored private-sector figure, Elon Musk, unusual influence over core state functions. A separate order directed comprehensive regulatory reviews across agencies, with DOGE involvement, to identify and roll back rules inconsistent with administration priorities. The bureaucracy was treated as a platform to be re-coded.

These changes did not go unchallenged. National Security Counselors and other plaintiffs sued, arguing that DOGE functioned as an unregulated federal advisory committee that violated transparency and record-keeping laws. The National Treasury Employees Union filed suit to block Schedule F, claiming that converting career civil servants into at-will appointees violated due process and civil-service statutes. Yet while these cases began their slow path through the courts, the administration continued to fire inspectors general, reorganize FEMA under a review council, and advance nominees like Pete Hegseth for Secretary of Defense despite serious allegations. The cumulative effect was to replace neutral expertise and internal checks with a loyalty-based apparatus and a partially privatized operational core. Capacity remained, but its purpose shifted.

The eighth development unfolded on the international stage. Trump ordered the United States out of the Paris climate agreement, again, reversing prior commitments to multilateral climate governance and signaling volatility in treaty adherence. He withdrew from the World Health Organization and halted contributions, reducing U.S. influence in global health and undermining shared infrastructure for pandemic preparedness. Participation in UNRWA and the UN Human Rights Council was ended, cutting support for refugee services and stepping back from multilateral human-rights forums. Foreign aid was broadly suspended for review, centralizing control over long-term development commitments in the White House. The country turned inward while keeping its power.

Symbolic foreign-policy moves reinforced this retreat. The embassy flag order narrowed the range of values U.S. missions could visibly endorse, while the renaming of geographic features projected a nationalist narrative outward. Yet the vacuum left by federal withdrawal did not remain empty. Michael Bloomberg and philanthropic partners pledged to cover U.S. Paris contributions privately, and ongoing CHIPS and IRA-driven investments in semiconductors, batteries, and solar manufacturing continued under prior law. These countercurrents suggested a fragmented foreign-policy landscape in which billionaires and subnational governments improvised around federal retrenchment, raising questions about democratic accountability for international commitments. Foreign policy became multi-track and uneven.

The final development of the week came from the remaining centers of resistance. State governments, unions, civil-rights groups, and federal judges moved quickly to blunt some of Trump's most aggressive actions. Coalitions of states and cities sued to block the birthright citizenship order, and federal district judges issued temporary restraining orders halting its implementation. Litigation challenged DOGE's legality and transparency, and the NTEU suit sought to defend civil-service protections against Schedule F. Pro-democracy civil-society organizations organized coordinated legal challenges and public campaigns against the executive orders, treating the courts as the primary arena for contesting the new agenda. The legal system became a crowded front line.

At the state level, California implemented a $20 minimum wage for fast-food workers, strengthening labor standards in a large low-wage sector even as federal labor protections were eroded. North Carolina civic groups prepared to pack legislative galleries and lobby against budget priorities expected to favor the wealthy, while Indiana considered using tax policy to hold non-profit hospitals accountable for overcharging patients. The National Labor Relations Board approved a union election at an Amazon warehouse in North Carolina, advancing a major organizing effort at a dominant employer. In the closing hours of his term, Biden had used clemency to commute Leonard Peltier's sentence and to protect relatives and officials targeted by MAGA Republicans, and he and Vice President Harris had inaccurately declared the Equal Rights Amendment to be law—an example of executive symbolism that, while flawed, contrasted with Trump's more structural uses of power. The contrast underscored how the same tools can serve different ends.

These responses showed that institutional and civic resistance remained active. Courts could still draw lines, as they did against the birthright order. Unions and advocacy groups could still organize, sue, and bargain. States could still set higher floors on wages and rights. But the tempo and centralization of executive action outpaced these checks. Each lawsuit, regulation, or protest addressed a single order or policy, while the White House moved across dozens of domains at once. The week's movement on the Democracy Clock reflected this imbalance: power consolidated quickly at the center, while resistance, though real, operated on a slower, case-by-case timescale. The gap between action and response widened.

In the arc of Trump's second term, Week 1 marked the beginning of a new story rather than a continuation of the old. The tools used—emergencies, executive orders, personnel purges, symbolic renamings—were familiar, but their density and coordination approached a constitutional hard break. Executive constraint, equal citizenship, rule of law, and the nonpartisan civil service all came under pressure at once. The erosion did not depend on a single spectacular act. It advanced through accumulation: a border emergency here, a birthright order there, a sovereign wealth fund, a gag on health agencies, a mass pardon, a fired inspector general. Each step altered what institutions could reliably guarantee. Rights and procedures remained on paper, but using them now required greater persistence and carried a greater cost. That is what the eight-minute movement on the Clock recorded: not the end of democracy, but the speed with which its guardrails could be bent when a determined executive chose to test them all at once.

CHAPTER 12
WEEK 2: LAW AND MEMORY AS WEAPONS

In Trump's second week back in power, pardons, purges, and data erasure turned law, citizenship, and information into tools of loyalty and fear.

The second week of Trump's second term did not unfold as a series of isolated shocks. It read instead like a plan moving from sketch to execution. Across agencies, courts, and streets, the same pattern appeared: neutral structures were bent toward loyalty, law was turned inward to protect those closest to power, and whole classes of people found their status more precarious than it had been seven days before. The surface language was managerial—efficiency, security, patriotism—but the effect was to redraw who counted, who decided, and who remembered. That was the point.

At the start of Week 2, the Democracy Clock stood at 7:39 p.m. By the end of the week it read 7:45 p.m., a net movement of 5.4 minutes. The shift came from the convergence of several arcs: a coordinated effort to erase January 6 accountability, a purge and politicization of the civil service and oversight bodies, an aggressive turn toward tiered citizenship enforced through raids and detention, and a broad campaign to control information and memory. Courts and civil society did act—blocking the funding freeze, pausing the birthright order, filing suits over raids and politicized hiring—but these were defensive moves against a presidency that now treated constraint as an obstacle to be managed, not a boundary to be respected. The imbalance was stark.

The clearest line ran through the justice system. Early in the week, the White House issued mass pardons and commutations for roughly 1,500 January 6 defendants, including Oath Keepers leader Stewart Rhodes. Clemency on this scale did more than shorten sentences. It recast the Capitol attack as forgivable, even honorable, conduct. When a federal court later lifted supervision conditions on Rhodes in light of the commutation, it showed how a single presidential signature could ripple through judicial orders, loosening what remained of formal restraint on a convicted insurrectionist. The signal reached far beyond one man.

At the same time, the administration moved to ensure that such prosecutions would not recur. Trump ordered the firing of dozens of Justice Department prosecutors and FBI agents who had handled his own cases or January 6 investigations. Senior FBI officials were pushed out or told to retire. A special DOJ "review" project was launched to revisit remaining January 6 cases, opening the door to downgrades or dismissals under the guise of internal reassessment. These were not abstract threats. They were personnel decisions that told every investigator where the new lines lay.

The legal record itself was then thinned. The Justice Department removed its public database of January 6 cases, eliminating a centralized record of charges, pleas, and sentences tied to the attack on Congress. In parallel, prosecutors closed cases against Trump's co-defendants in the classified documents probe, cutting off a potential source of testimony and detail about how sensitive materials had been handled. Combined with the pardons, these steps did not just alter outcomes; they obscured them. Citizens, journalists, and historians were left with fewer tools to reconstruct what had happened and how the state had responded. That loss was by design.

Taken together, these moves turned law from a check into a shield. Pro-regime violence and allied misconduct were not only forgiven; they were lifted out of the ordinary channels of accountability and memory. Those who had enforced the law in the prior term were removed. Those who had broken it in service of the president were restored. The message was plain without needing to be spoken: the risk of crossing the regime now lay in investigating it, not in attacking its opponents. Law still spoke in legal terms, but its direction had flipped.

If the justice system was being hollowed from the top, the civil service and oversight architecture were being stripped from the inside. Trump ordered the firing of at least eighteen inspectors general across major departments, some reportedly removed with little or no notice. These were the internal watchdogs charged with investigating waste, fraud, and abuse. Their removal in a single sweep, in defiance of protections enacted after the first Trump term, left large swaths of the federal government without independent eyes. Members of Congress from both parties expressed outrage and demanded explanations, but no immediate remedy followed. The firings stood.

At the same time, the White House revived and expanded a Schedule F-style project under a new "Schedule Policy/Career" directive. Large numbers of civil servants were reclassified into categories with fewer employment protections, and more than a thousand EPA employees were placed on probationary status. The Office of Personnel Management, now influenced by Musk-aligned aides, sent mass emails offering deferred resignation deals and buyouts to nearly the entire federal workforce, hinting at future layoffs. The offers were structured in ways that raised questions about their legality, but their practical effect was clear: encourage nonpolitical staff to leave and create vacancies that could be filled with loyalists. Fear did the rest.

Control over information about the workforce itself shifted as well. Political appointees directed agencies to gather detailed data on career staff and route it to a private Musk associate, blurring the line between official human-resources work and political vetting. Later in the week, civil servants were locked out of key HR data systems, concentrating access in the hands of a small circle of political aides. A class-action whistleblower lawsuit challenged this covert data collection, and federal courts began to hear arguments about privacy and politicization. But for the moment, the data sat where the White House wanted it: outside normal checks, available for use in future purges.

Labor-rights enforcement bodies were not spared. Trump ordered the firing of leaders at the National Labor Relations Board and the Equal Employment Opportunity Commission before their terms expired, despite statutory protections. Disbanding the EEOC by executive order removed a central federal mechanism for enforcing workplace civil-rights law. Removing NLRB leadership weakened the board that adjudicates disputes between workers and employers. Together with the inspector general purge and civil-service reclassification, these moves stripped away much of the neutral infrastructure that had once stood between presidential preference and the daily lives of public workers. The state's internal referees were being sent home.

While the internal state was being remade, the administration also tested how far it could reach into Congress's power of the purse. Trump and the Office of Management and Budget issued sweeping directives freezing almost all federal grants, loans, and financial assistance, as well as infrastructure funds and large portions of foreign aid. The orders halted disbursement of money that Congress had already appropriated, pending ideological review for alignment with administration priorities. Medicaid portals experienced outages linked to the freeze, threatening access to health coverage for millions of low-income residents. Universities, nonprofits, and state agencies scrambled to understand whether their programs would suddenly lose support.

Courts responded quickly. Federal judges in several jurisdictions issued emergency stays and restraining orders, keeping funds flowing while lawsuits proceeded. Nonprofits and states challenged the freeze as an unlawful attempt to bypass Congress's budget authority. In the face of mounting injunctions and political pressure, Trump rescinded the core funding-freeze memo later in the week. The rescission restored program flows, but it did not undo the lesson: a single executive order could throw trillions in planned spending into doubt, even if only for days. The chaos itself became a form of leverage.

Around this drama, other signals pointed to a broader effort to rewire federal spending and disaster response. House Republicans and the president floated the abolition of FEMA, raising the prospect of shifting catastrophe response onto states and private actors. A senator called for eliminating the Transportation Security Administration and handing airport security to airlines. At the same time, the Senate advanced Russ Vought's nomination to lead OMB, despite a Democratic boycott, placing a close Trump ally at the center of budget oversight. The combination suggested a long-term project: weaken or dismantle neutral service-providing agencies while consolidating discretionary control over money in the executive branch.

The most visible human cost of the week's decisions fell on immigrants and those whose status could be made conditional. Trump declared a national emergency at the southern border and signed sweeping enforcement orders that authorized aggressive raids and deportations, including in schools and churches. Long-standing protections against immigration arrests in "sensitive locations" such as classrooms, houses of worship, and hospitals were lifted. ICE set high daily arrest quotas and staged large-scale raids in cities, sometimes with the homeland security secretary present in tactical gear for cameras. Community groups expanded ICE watch programs to monitor these operations, but the immediate effect was fear: parents weighing whether to send children to school, congregants wondering if worship would bring arrest.

The geography of detention shifted as well. The administration ordered the Pentagon and DHS to prepare a 30,000-person migrant facility at Guantánamo Bay, extending civil confinement into an offshore military site long associated with indefinite detention and limited due process. At the same time, Trump invoked the Alien Enemies Act to target undocumented immigrants he linked to crime, using disputed claims of a "crime wave" to justify treating a domestic population as enemy outsiders. Temporary Protected Status and deportation protections for hundreds of thousands of Venezuelans were revoked, exposing them to removal after years of provisional safety. The line between "here" and "enemy" grew thinner.

Legal status at birth came under direct attack. Trump signed an executive order attempting to end birthright citizenship for children of noncitizens, challenging a core reading of the Fourteenth Amendment. Federal courts moved quickly to issue injunctions, temporarily preserving existing protections while litigation proceeds. But the order itself marked a structural shift: the presidency was now asserting authority to redefine who is a citizen without a constitutional amendment or statute. In Oklahoma, the state board of education voted to require proof of citizenship or immigration status for public school enrollment, threatening to exclude undocumented children from classrooms in defiance of long-standing Supreme Court precedent.

Political expression became another axis of vulnerability. Trump ordered the deportation of international students who joined pro-Palestinian campus protests, tying immigration status directly to protest participation. The Laken Riley Act, passed by Congress and signed into law, expanded mandatory detention and deportation authority for undocumented people charged with certain crimes, strengthening the tools available to hold noncitizens in custody. Reports emerged of Puerto Rican U.S. citizens wrongfully detained in immigration sweeps, and Indigenous people questioned or held during operations near the border. Brazil protested the degrading treatment of shackled deportees. These incidents showed how a system built for speed and spectacle could sweep up citizens and allies along with its intended targets.

Alongside these structural shifts, the administration launched a broad offensive against diversity, equity, and inclusion efforts and LGBTQ+ protections. Trump signed executive actions dismantling federal DEI and affirmative-action programs across the government, revoked contractor nondiscrimination rules, and ordered the closure of all DEI offices. The Equal Employment Opportunity Commission was disbanded by executive order, removing a central enforcement body for workplace civil-rights law. Agencies were instructed to scrub DEI language from documents and websites; the IRS and other offices deleted references to equity and inclusion from handbooks and online materials. What had been framed as commitments became liabilities.

Military and intelligence culture were reshaped in the same direction. The Air Force removed historical content on the Tuskegee Airmen and Women Airforce Service Pilots from training materials, erasing recognition of Black and women pilots' contributions. Trump barred transgender people from serving in the armed forces, issued an "excellence" order that redefined medical standards to exclude those with gender dysphoria, and dismantled military DEI structures. The Defense Intelligence Agency suspended observance of MLK Day, Holocaust Remembrance Day, Juneteenth, and Pride, signaling an official deprioritization of histories tied to oppression and resistance. At the same time, service members discharged for refusing COVID-19 vaccines were reinstated with back pay, suggesting that adherence to prior public-health orders could be overridden by later political decisions.

Education policy became a central battleground. Trump revived the 1776 Commission and ordered an "Ending Indoctrination Strategy," directing agencies to identify and defund programs deemed ideologically radical. Executive orders on "educational freedom" tied federal funds to school choice and to restrictions on teaching about race and gender. Schools were threatened with funding cuts if they taught critical race theory or "gender ideology." An antisemitism order expanded federal involvement in policing campus speech, with uncertain boundaries between civil-rights enforcement and academic freedom. Another order targeted transgender students' rights in schools, including bathroom access and participation in activities, narrowing civil-rights protections for a specific minority group.

Carceral policies for transgender people hardened. The administration ordered trans women in federal prisons transferred to men's facilities and ended gender-affirming treatment in custody. A separate executive order restricted federal support for gender-affirming care for minors and dependents, centralizing contested medical decisions in the presidency. These moves did not abolish rights on paper, but they made access to safety and care contingent on political favor, especially for those already under state control. Vulnerability became a policy tool.

As personnel and policy shifted, the leadership of security institutions changed as well. The Senate confirmed Kristi Noem as secretary of homeland security and Pete Hegseth as secretary of defense, placing close Trump allies with strong ideological profiles at the helm of immigration and military agencies. Confirmation hearings for Kash Patel as FBI director, Tulsi Gabbard as director of national intelligence, and Pam Bondi as attorney general underscored the trend: nominees who would not affirm the 2020 election result, would not rule out targeting political opponents, or had close personal ties to Trump were poised to lead key law-enforcement and intelligence bodies.

These appointments quickly translated into practice. ICE raids were staged with the DHS secretary in tactical gear, turning enforcement into televised spectacle. The Pentagon reallocated press-corps seating to favor pro-Trump outlets over established media such as NPR and the New York Times, altering who could regularly question defense officials. Within the military, bans on transgender service and DEI programs, combined with symbolic gestures like reinstating anti-vaccine troops, signaled that loyalty to the president's cultural agenda mattered as much as traditional notions of readiness or cohesion. Abroad, Trump lifted holds on large bomb deliveries to Israel, invited Benjamin Netanyahu—wanted by the International Criminal Court—to be the first foreign leader to visit the White House, and demanded that NATO allies raise military spending to five percent of GDP. Security policy thus served not only strategic aims but also ideological narratives and personal alliances.

Running through these developments was a deepening fusion of public office and private gain. Shortly before taking office, Trump launched a personal cryptocurrency branded $Trump; by week's end, his media company announced a major expansion into crypto investments via Truth.Fi. These ventures raised the prospect that regulatory and monetary policy could be shaped to benefit the president's own assets. At the same time, Trump secured a $25 million settlement from Meta over his suspension from its platforms, after a period of political pressure. The settlement, and a related First Amendment-linked case involving government influence over content moderation, showed how a powerful officeholder could extract concessions from private firms that regulate online speech.

Around the president, other insiders positioned themselves to profit from policy. Jared Kushner's investment firm held stakes in Gaza redevelopment projects that could gain from U.S. support for large-scale relocation of Palestinians. The Trump Organization pursued a Trump Tower project in Belgrade on land owned by the Serbian government, despite an ethics pledge about foreign government business, exposing gaps in emoluments safeguards. Elon Musk's role extended beyond commentary: his associates at OPM and Treasury sought access to sensitive payment infrastructure and personnel systems, prompting at least one senior official's resignation. Public opinion registered discomfort; an AP/NORC poll showed broad disapproval of billionaire-driven policymaking. But the structural direction was clear: policy outcomes and regulatory choices were increasingly entangled with the financial interests of a small circle around the president.

Information and memory were shaped to fit this new order. The removal of the January 6 prosecutions database, combined with mass pardons, curated public understanding of the insurrection. Records related to the police killing of Manuel Paez Terán at the "Cop City" site were withheld and then selectively released, allowing the Justice Department to control the narrative around a controversial use of force. Climate-crisis web pages and resources were taken down from USDA sites, limiting public access to scientific information communities use to plan for environmental risks. DEI-related training courses at the State Department's Foreign Service Institute were suspended, narrowing the lens through which diplomats are trained to see the world.

At the same time, misinformation and symbolic gestures filled the space left by erased data. Trump falsely claimed that the U.S. military had intervened in California's water system, dramatizing executive power and blurring fact and fiction in federal-state relations. He repeated a debunked story that Biden had funded condoms for Gaza to justify foreign-aid cuts. After a deadly aviation crash, he blamed diversity policies without evidence, then signed orders renaming FAA staffing priorities and rolling back DEI-oriented hiring, using tragedy to delegitimize inclusion efforts. Within the Defense Intelligence Agency, suspending observance of MLK Day, Holocaust Day, Juneteenth, and Pride, and at the White House, renaming the Gulf of Mexico as the "Gulf of America" and launching a monument-focused 250th-birthday task force, shifted official symbolism toward leader-centric, nationalist themes.

Not every institution moved in the same direction. Federal courts emerged as key brakes, even if only in a defensive posture. Judges issued emergency stays blocking the federal funding freeze, preserving grants and loans while challenges proceeded. Other courts temporarily halted the birthright-citizenship order, maintaining constitutional protections for U.S.-born children of noncitizens pending full review. Lawsuits were filed against ICE raids in churches and schools, against loyalty-based civil-service changes, and against covert data collection on career staff. Quaker congregations turned to the judiciary to defend religious sanctuaries; disability-rights advocates challenged anti-camping rules that criminalized unhoused people with disabilities; civil-rights groups mobilized to protect tens of thousands of votes in a North Carolina judicial race.

States and local actors also asserted countervailing norms. Illinois's governor banned January 6 participants from state employment, using hiring rules to reinforce that insurrection is incompatible with public service. Community organizations expanded ICE watch programs and launched initiatives to support Indigenous people affected by immigration sweeps. Public broadcasters and major media outlets, though under investigation and facing defamation suits, continued to report on these developments. The Federal Election Commission held open meetings and adjusted campaign-finance limits as part of its routine work, and the National Archives sought public comment on records schedules and maintained internal oversight boards. These actions did not reverse the week's structural shifts, but they showed that not all levers of accountability had been captured.

No major scheduled decision loomed at the close of the week beyond the ongoing litigation and confirmation processes already in motion: court hearings on the funding freeze, birthright order, and civil-service lawsuits; Senate consideration of controversial nominees; and the early stages of implementing the Laken Riley Act and Guantánamo expansion orders. Each of these would carry forward the tensions opened in Week 2 between executive ambition and the remaining checks around it. The next moves would test how much strain those checks could bear.

In the arc of the term, this week marked an early consolidation rather than a tentative experiment. The tools glimpsed in the first days—executive orders, personnel moves, symbolic gestures—were now applied across nearly every domain at once. Law was bent to protect allies and erase inconvenient history. The civil service and oversight bodies were reshaped to reward loyalty and punish dissent. Immigration and citizenship policy moved toward a tiered system enforced through raids and detention. Information and memory were curated to support the new order and blur its costs. Resistance existed, in courts, states, and communities, but it was reactive and fragmented, addressing individual blows rather than the coordinated project behind them. The Democracy Clock's movement captured that imbalance: the formal shell of democracy remained, but the institutions that once gave it depth and resilience were being stripped for parts.

CHAPTER 13
WEEK 3: SYSTEMS AS SPOILS

In Trump's third week back in office, executive power fused with private wealth, hollowing out oversight while courts and unions fought rearguard actions.

The third week of Trump's second term did not hinge on a single spectacular order or televised clash. Its shape emerged instead from the way power moved inside the state: who could spend, who could investigate, who could speak, and who could be erased from the record. The pattern was one of fusion—between executive authority and private wealth, between domestic law and foreign policy, between information systems and political control. What had been signaled in earlier weeks as intent now began to harden into structure.

At the close of Week 2 the Democracy Clock stood at 7:45 p.m. By the end of Week 3 it read 7:46 p.m., a net shift of one minute. The numerical change was small, but it captured a week in which the presidency tested the outer edges of its reach over money, borders, and memory, and found that many of those edges could be pushed back. Courts, unions, and states won important injunctions and partial rollbacks. Yet the center of gravity moved toward a presidency that could freeze aid, purge watchdogs, and hand core systems to private allies faster than any check could fully reverse.

The week opened with a shock to the global aid system. Trump ordered a 90-day freeze on most foreign assistance, including roughly $60 billion in USAID funding, and moved to fold USAID into the State Department. Staff were locked out of their own headquarters while the agency's website and social media went dark. The move concentrated control over humanitarian aid in the White House and State, sidelining an institution whose value had long rested on a degree of professional distance from day-to-day politics. At the same time, a separate executive order attempted to freeze a vast swath of federal grants, loans, and payments, testing whether the president could, in effect, impound money Congress had already appropriated.

Those domestic moves were paired with a new use of emergency powers in trade. Trump invoked national emergency statutes to impose sweeping tariffs on imports from Canada, Mexico, and China, citing opioids and migration as justifications. Business groups warned of price spikes and supply-chain disruption. The U.S. Postal Service briefly halted parcels from China and Hong Kong before restoring service, a small but telling sign of how quickly routine commerce could be disrupted when emergency framing was applied to trade. Regulatory agencies, under a White House freeze, delayed environmental and health rules, extending comment periods and pushing back effective dates. On paper, process remained. In practice, the president's reading of "emergency" now reached deep into ordinary economic life.

Abroad, the administration signaled a sharp break with multilateral norms. Trump announced plans for the United States to "take over and develop" the Gaza Strip, a proposal widely described as a blueprint for ethnic cleansing. He threatened to "take back" the Panama Canal or take unspecified powerful action, invoking coercive options against a treaty partner. He kept "all options on the table" against Mexican drug cartels after designating them terrorist organizations, normalizing talk of cross-border military strikes.

These statements were not yet operations, but they pulled the language of occupation and force into the center of U.S. foreign policy.

At the same time, the White House turned away from international legal and human-rights bodies. Trump ordered sanctions on International Criminal Court officials over investigations touching U.S. and Israeli personnel, using national emergency powers to shield allies from external accountability. He withdrew the United States from the UN Human Rights Council and UNRWA and ordered a review of support for international organizations more broadly. Aid to South Africa was halted, and the country was added to a de facto enemies list over disputed land policies, while a companion order promoted resettlement of Afrikaner farmers in the United States. Foreign assistance and threat designations were now openly tied to racially charged narratives and regime preferences, rather than to stable treaty or rights frameworks.

If foreign policy showed the outward reach of executive power, the Justice Department and FBI revealed how law itself was being bent inward. Acting leaders at DOJ ordered the firing of prosecutors and sought lists of FBI agents who had worked on cases involving Trump and the January 6 attack. DOJ withdrew prosecutors from election-fraud cases involving Republican lawmakers, signaling that some officeholders would no longer face the same scrutiny as others. Rank-and-file FBI employees responded by suing to block the release of their names, turning to the courts to protect themselves from retaliation by their own department. The stakes were personal and immediate.

These personnel moves were framed by a new narrative: that prior investigations were themselves abuses. Pam Bondi's confirmation as attorney general, over unified Democratic opposition, cemented that shift. Bondi launched a Weaponization Working Group to review prosecutions of Trump and January 6 cases, while Trump ordered DOJ to produce a report on the "weaponization of the federal government," explicitly including special counsel matters. At the same time, Trump issued blanket pardons for more than 1,500 January 6 participants, signaling that violence on his behalf would be forgiven. DOJ scaled back civil-rights enforcement and halted consent decrees in cities like Louisville and Minneapolis, while reinstating the federal death penalty and prioritizing certain capital cases. The state's harshest tools were revived even as accountability for allies was withdrawn.

Oversight bodies that might have checked these shifts were themselves cut down. Trump removed inspectors general from at least twelve major agencies in a single sweep, sharply weakening internal watchdog capacity. He attempted to oust Federal Election Commission chair Ellen Weintraub while complaints involving his own conduct were pending, threatening the independence of the agency charged with enforcing campaign-finance law. DOJ dismantled foreign bribery and kleptocracy units and scaled back enforcement of foreign lobbying and white-collar crime, easing pressure on transnational corruption networks. Efforts to remove members of the National Labor Relations Board left that body's quorum in doubt, prompting lawsuits from former officials. Courts responded with a series of injunctions—blocking the grants freeze, pausing the birthright-citizenship order, halting trans prisoner transfers, and extending the deadline on a coercive federal-worker buyout—but these were defensive actions against a broad campaign to turn law enforcement into a shield for the regime.

Beneath these headline moves, the state's administrative "plumbing" was being handed to a small, private network. Through a series of decisions by Trump and Treasury Secretary Scott Bessent, Elon Musk's DOGE team gained access and partial control over Treasury payment systems that disburse more than $5 trillion annually. A DOGE-aligned figure was installed over federal payment operations after a career official was forced out. An executive-order-driven outage in the National Science Foundation's payment gateway halted grant funding to scientists and nonprofits, demonstrating how control over payment infrastructure could be used to pressure research and civil society.

DOGE's reach extended beyond Treasury. At the Office of Personnel Management and the Small Business Administration, Musk associates obtained extensive access to federal HR and small-business data systems, and an unvetted server was installed outside normal procurement and privacy review. Millions of employees and entrepreneurs were exposed to new privacy risks. A mass "deferred-resignation" program, promoted through government email lists, offered federal workers paid time off in exchange for future resignations, but the fine print allowed agencies to require work, deny rescission, and bar legal recourse. The effect was to encourage exits and weaken job security, while giving managers a tool to thin out perceived opponents.

Regulatory gatekeeping shifted in parallel. At the Securities and Exchange Commission, staff lawyers were told to obtain political approval before opening investigations, centralizing enforcement decisions in the hands of appointees. The Consumer Financial Protection Bureau paused rules that would have kept medical debt off credit reports, preserving leverage for debt collectors and credit bureaus. At the Environmental Protection Agency and Interior, leadership drawn from industry lobbyists and attorneys moved to delay or undo rules on toxic chemicals, PFAS, and national monuments, while more than 160 environmental-justice employees were placed on leave. The agencies' formal missions did not change, but their capacity to act in the public interest was hollowed out.

DOGE's IT access reached into the information systems that underpinned these agencies. Musk operatives accessed and, in some cases, altered data at NOAA, CMS, the Department of Education, and USAID. Climate data disappeared from NOAA databases. Student-aid and health-care systems were exposed to unvetted actors. USAID's online presence vanished during the attempted merger and leadership purge. Treasury granted DOGE read-only access to coded taxpayer and payment data, prompting privacy lawsuits and protests from unions. Under legal pressure, the administration proposed narrowing DOGE's access to some Treasury systems, excluding Musk himself, but the basic precedent—

that a private team could be embedded inside core state infrastructure—remained.

The same logic of control and exclusion played out in the treatment of civil servants and inclusion frameworks. At USAID, State, Education, EPA, and other agencies, staff who resisted unauthorized access or worked on DEI and environmental justice were placed on administrative leave, offered buyouts, or had their contracts terminated. USAID staff were physically barred from their building while Musk's shutdown attempt received presidential backing. Across government, pronouns were banned from email signatures and DEI and affinity groups were disbanded, cutting off support structures for LGBTQ+ and minority employees. Trump revoked a 60-year-old equal-opportunity order and contractor nondiscrimination rules, weakening protections for minorities and small businesses that relied on federal work.

Executive orders went further, targeting DEI programs and gender-affirming care across federal institutions. Agencies were told to dismantle diversity initiatives and cut funding to hospitals providing gender-affirming care to youth. The Centers for Disease Control and other health agencies removed or altered webpages on contraception, gender-affirming care, STIs, and HIV to comply. In the military, transgender service members were purged and DEI-related clubs at West Point were disbanded. In the prison system, an order directed that trans women be medically detransitioned and moved to men's facilities, until courts intervened. These moves did not simply change policy; they redrew the boundaries of who could serve, who could be safe, and whose identity the state would recognize.

Immigration and citizenship policy became another arena where executive power and identity hierarchy met. An order effectively suspended U.S. asylum law, routing up to 30,000 migrants to detention at Guantánamo Bay. Humanitarian protections for hundreds of thousands of immigrants from Venezuela, Cuba, Haiti, and Nicaragua were revoked or undermined, exposing them to deportation and instability. Migrant detention operations at Guantánamo expanded, placing immigration enforcement further from routine judicial oversight. Domestically, ICE conducted aggressive raids in farm communities while manipulating public information about enforcement: old deportation press releases were re-dated so they would appear current in search results, gaming Google to project a constant sense of crackdown.

At the level of status itself, Trump attempted to end birthright citizenship for children of undocumented immigrants by executive order, challenging the 14th Amendment's guarantee. Courts quickly enjoined enforcement, but the move signaled a willingness to test constitutional limits on who counts as a citizen. Attorney General Bondi ordered an end to federal funding for sanctuary jurisdictions and sued Chicago and Illinois over their sanctuary laws, using fiscal and legal tools to punish localities that limited cooperation with federal crackdowns. States added their own layers: North Carolina criminalized road-blocking and mask-wearing at protests, while Louisiana used emergency powers and police threat to forcibly relocate unhoused people to an unheated warehouse, restricting press access. In each case, law and logistics were used to narrow who could move, speak, or simply exist without fear.

Civil and human rights more broadly were redrawn along lines of gender, race, religion, and punishment. An executive order banned trans women and girls from women's sports and conditioned visas on compliance, extending domestic culture-war rules into immigration decisions. A separate order on antisemitism directed agencies to explore deporting foreign student protesters, linking campus speech to immigration enforcement. At the same time, Trump created a DOJ-led task force and a White House Faith Office to combat perceived anti-Christian bias, embedding a favored religious identity into enforcement and advisory structures. DOJ retreated from civil-rights enforcement and police-reform agreements, while the federal death penalty was reinstated and tied, in part, to cases involving police killings. Another order linked seized oligarch assets to funding new detention facilities, blending punitive foreign policy with domestic carceral expansion.

On the ground, these shifts translated into concrete harms and fears. Wyoming Republicans advanced a bill redefining health care in ways that could broadly restrict abortion and other treatments. California community leaders demanded investigation into delayed wildfire evacuation orders that devastated a Black neighborhood, raising questions about racial inequities in disaster response. Courts heard class-action claims over abuse of incarcerated women by a prison gynecologist and ruled on racial bias in death sentencing. These cases showed that litigation could still surface and sometimes remedy structural discrimination, even as the federal executive moved in the opposite direction.

Information itself became a contested field. Health agencies removed or sanitized public-health guidance on sensitive topics. DOGE's access to NOAA, CMS, Education, and USAID systems allowed private actors to reshape or erase official records, including climate data. An HHS report on private equity's harms in health care briefly appeared, then its news release vanished from the agency's site. ICE's manipulation of press-release timestamps distorted the public record of enforcement. The Pentagon introduced a media rotation program that replaced major outlets with ideologically aligned or nontraditional ones like OANN and Breitbart in limited press spaces, shifting access toward friendlier media.

Regulators and the White House applied pressure to specific outlets. The FCC canceled POLITICO subscriptions, reinstated a long-dormant news-distortion complaint, and opened an investigation into a local station's immigration reporting. Trump publicly called for CBS and 60 Minutes to be terminated over editing of a Kamala Harris interview, attacking press freedom norms. Lara Trump moved from RNC leadership to hosting a Fox News weekend show, underscoring the revolving door between partisan politics and influential media. On social platforms, Musk used control of X to delete a post and suspend an account that listed DOGE employees, framing it as criminal leaking. DOGE and Treasury used federal email lists to push the deferred-resignation offer to all civil servants. The CIA sent a list of recent hires, including analysts, to the White House via unclassified email, exposing sensitive personnel to potential targeting. Across these episodes, state and private levers combined to curate what the public could see and to protect those aligned with the regime.

Against this backdrop, resistance did not disappear. Federal judges in multiple districts blocked or paused some of the most aggressive executive actions: the grants freeze, the birthright-citizenship order, the trans prisoner transfer policy, and the deadline on the federal-worker buyout. Courts heard challenges to the asylum suspension and USAID cuts, testing whether the executive could unilaterally rewrite statutory humanitarian obligations. FBI agents, employee unions, and former labor officials sued to restrict DOGE's database access, contest the deferred-resignation scheme, and challenge removals from the National Labor Relations Board. In North Carolina, a lower-court attempt to overturn a state supreme court election by discarding tens of thousands of votes drew scrutiny and appeals, highlighting the stakes for judicial independence.

States and legislators also moved. California appropriated $50 million to fund litigation against federal policies and to support immigrants with legal services, positioning itself as an institutional counterweight on climate, immigration, and civil rights. Senate Democrats and House leaders used filibusters, all-night protests, and bills like the ELON MUSK Act to oppose Russell Vought's budget role and Musk's influence over Treasury. Local activists organized demonstrations against cabinet nominees and DOGE's reach. Federal election and assistance commissions continued to hold public meetings under the Sunshine Act, and agencies published environmental impact statements that preserved formal channels for public input. Texas expanded solar power installations, and global markets shifted solar exports toward developing countries, hinting at economic currents that did not run through Washington.

These efforts won real, if partial, victories. DOGE's access to some Treasury systems was narrowed. Immigration court support programs saw funding restored after lawsuits. Some vulnerable groups gained relief through court rulings on racial bias and abuse. Yet the scale and speed of federal consolidation outpaced these checks. Inspectors general remained fired. Mass pardons for January 6 participants stood. DOGE's presence inside the state's core systems persisted. The week's resistance was fragmented and reactive, while the administration's moves were coordinated and structural.

Crony capitalism threaded through many of these developments. Trump family members expanded ventures in conservative venture capital, crypto, and foreign-funded private equity, including a Saudi-backed fund and joint projects with controversial investors. Donald Trump Jr.'s role at 1789 Capital positioned him to steer capital toward ideologically aligned firms. A senior DOJ nominee held undisclosed multimillion-dollar holdings linked to a Chinese company accused of forced labor, raising conflict-of-interest concerns at the heart of law enforcement. Sovereign wealth fund orders directed Treasury and Commerce to design a vehicle that could buy high-profile assets like TikTok, concentrating large pools of public capital under presidential influence. Industry-aligned EPA leadership, regulatory rollbacks, and pauses or suppression of consumer-protective rules and reports all pointed in the same direction: public resources and legal frameworks bending toward the interests of those closest to power.

What to watch from this week's record are the cases and reviews already in motion. Federal courts have before them challenges to the asylum suspension, USAID dismantling, DOGE's access to core systems, and the attempted birthright-citizenship order. The Supreme Court is considering a case that could revive the nondelegation doctrine and sharply limit agency authority. State-funded litigation, especially from California, is queued up against immigration and climate moves. The outcomes of these proceedings will determine how far the executive–oligarch nexus can extend its reach before running into hard legal limits.

In the arc of Trump's second term, Week 3 deepened the pattern of consolidation without open rupture. Executive orders reached into foreign aid, trade, asylum, and citizenship. Oversight bodies were thinned or removed. The civil service and regulatory agencies were reengineered around loyalty and private access. Information systems were treated as assets to be curated, not as public records to be preserved. Courts, unions, states, and civil society still had the capacity to slow and sometimes block these moves, but they did so case by case, often after the fact. The week's small forward movement on the Democracy Clock reflects that tension: formal structures endured, yet the cost of relying on them rose, and the space in which they could operate narrowed.

CHAPTER 14
WEEK 4: DOGE AS PARALLEL STATECRAFT

Trump and Musk quietly converted the federal bureaucracy into a pliable, privatized instrument, using money, law, and memory to tilt power inward and downward.

The fourth week of Trump's second term did not hinge on a single decree or spectacle. Its shape emerged from many decisions, scattered across agencies and domains, pointing in the same direction. Power moved inward, toward the presidency and a small circle around it. Expertise, procedure, and memory were pushed outward, treated as obstacles or raw material. The result was not yet a closed system, but the outline of one: a state that still bore the forms of a constitutional republic while its inner wiring was being rerun through private networks and personal will.

At the close of Week 3, the Democracy Clock stood at 7:46 p.m. By the end of Week 4, it read 7:50 p.m., a net shift of 4.2 minutes. The movement reflected an acceleration rather than a rupture. Trump and Elon Musk's Department of Government Efficiency moved from concept to operational control. Executive orders turned into mass firings, funding freezes, and data grabs. Law enforcement tools were redirected to shield allies and pressure enemies. At the same time, courts, inspectors general, state officials, and civil society forced partial reversals and exposed some of what was being done. The clock moved because the balance between those two forces tilted further toward unchecked executive power, even as resistance remained visible.

The clearest expression of that shift was the rise of DOGE as a parallel executive state. An order repurposed the U.S. Digital Service into a Musk-run unit with authority to cancel payments, suspend programs, and fire employees across the government. A second order, the "workforce optimization regime," placed DOGE operatives over hiring and firing decisions, turning what had been a technical service into a choke point for personnel and budgets. In a few strokes, a lightly accountable team aligned with a single billionaire gained levers that had once been dispersed among career managers, inspectors general, and Senate-confirmed officials.

Those new levers were used quickly. The administration initiated mass layoffs and buyouts at the Departments of Education and Energy, the Small Business Administration, the Consumer Financial Protection Bureau, and the General Services Administration. Another directive ordered agencies to fire nearly all probationary employees. At Energy and Veterans Affairs, more than 275,000 workers were dismissed, including staff at the National Nuclear Security Administration. These were not isolated cuts. They were a coordinated purge that hollowed out technical capacity, weakened unions, and sent a clear message to remaining staff: your job depends on political favor, not professional merit.

Courts tried to draw lines around this purge, but their rulings were uneven. Judges first blocked and then, on standing grounds, allowed mass buyout schemes and the "Fork in the Road" deferred resignation plan to proceed. Unions were told they lacked the right to challenge structural downsizing. At the same time, the Senate confirmed Russell Vought, a long-time advocate of shrinking and demoralizing the civil service, as director of the Office of Management and Budget. He joined DOGE in driving layoffs and in moves to starve the CFPB of funds. The formal architecture of oversight remained, but the people and programs that made it real were being stripped away.

DOGE's reach extended beyond personnel into science and security. It claimed to have identified over a billion dollars in cuts in three weeks, targeting NIH cancer research, National Science Foundation grants, and National Oceanic and Atmospheric Administration budgets. It placed the Social Security Administration under review, raising the specter of benefit disruptions. DOGE staff met with Pentagon officials to review defense spending, and then published classified National Reconnaissance Office budget and personnel data on their website. Musk's associates obtained unprecedented access to federal HR databases at the Office of Personnel Management. A quasi-private unit now touched both the files of individual civil servants and the inner workings of national security, while its own operations remained largely opaque.

If DOGE was the new machinery, money was the fuel Trump used to steer the state. The White House froze large portions of federal science funding, including NIH grants, and halted Home Energy Rebates and LIHEAP disbursements. FEMA grants for firefighting equipment and port security were stopped. In Alabama, an energy order that paused federal assistance triggered $100 surcharges on low-income households' utility bills. These decisions were framed as efficiency or review, but their effect was to shift risk and cost onto the poorest residents and to bypass Congress's choices about who should be protected.

The same pattern appeared in targeted moves against disfavored jurisdictions. The administration seized funds from New York City accounts, according to the city comptroller, while suing the state over its immigrant-friendly driver's license law and sanctuary policies. Tariff policy followed a similar logic. Trump ordered 25 percent tariffs on steel and aluminum imports and pushed for broad reciprocal tariffs, while quietly exempting low-value Chinese packages. Chinese counter-tariffs on U.S. energy and equipment followed. The burden of these choices fell on manufacturers, exporters, and consumers, even as the administration advanced a budget blueprint that slashed Social Security, Medicare, and food aid while expanding tax cuts for the wealthy.

Trump's rhetoric around federal debt added a layer of brinkmanship. He suggested the United States might not honor some Treasury bond obligations due to alleged irregularities and signaled potential halts in bond payments during DOGE reviews of payment systems. Former Treasury secretaries published a joint warning that such moves threatened constitutional spending rules and market stability. Judges ordered the restoration of frozen funds and the disbursement of impounded foreign aid, and Pennsylvania's governor sued to compel release of over $3 billion in withheld money. These interventions underscored that the constitutional power of the purse still had defenders, but they also revealed how much damage could be done before courts could act.

While DOGE and fiscal tools reshaped the administrative state, the justice system itself was being bent toward regime needs. The most vivid example was the corruption case against New York City Mayor Eric Adams. Justice Department leadership ordered prosecutors to drop the bribery charges in order to preserve Adams's cooperation on deportations and immigration enforcement. Line prosecutors resigned in protest. The decision linked prosecutorial discretion directly to policy bargaining, signaling that cooperation with the administration could buy legal leniency.

At the same time, Trump signed an order pausing enforcement of the Foreign Corrupt Practices Act, weakening anti-bribery rules for U.S. companies abroad. Federal investigations into Musk's companies, including Tesla and SpaceX, were reportedly halted. The administration abolished the FBI's Foreign Influence Task Force and a Justice Department unit targeting Russian oligarchs. Together, these moves reduced scrutiny of foreign interference and elite financial crime while preserving and expanding tools for aggressive immigration raids and domestic crackdowns.

Internal watchdogs were also under attack. Trump fired the director of the Office of Government Ethics and USAID's inspector general, adding to earlier mass IG dismissals. Eight former inspectors general sued for reinstatement under the IG Act. A federal judge ordered Hampton Dellinger reinstated as head of the Office of Special Counsel after his firing, restoring a key whistleblower-protection office. The Government Accountability Office reported that its oversight had saved $70.4 billion in a single fiscal year, a reminder of what was at stake. Yet the administration's response was not to strengthen such bodies, but to threaten them. Representative Eli Crane drafted articles of impeachment against Judge Paul Engelmayer for blocking DOGE's access to Treasury systems, and Elon Musk amplified personal information about a judge's daughter to his vast online audience. The American Bar Association and other legal groups issued statements condemning these attacks as violations of the rule of law, but the pattern was clear: law was being treated as a weapon and a shield, not a limit.

Alongside these structural shifts, the administration moved to dismantle the knowledge infrastructure that underpins modern governance. NIH announced cuts to cancer and other research, capped indirect costs on grants, and maintained a funding freeze even after two federal injunctions. Internal NIH memos later admitted the freeze was illegal and ordered grants to resume. DOGE cut National Science Foundation and NOAA budgets, threatening basic research, weather forecasting, and climate services. The Social Security Administration was placed under review, raising fears of payment disruptions for millions of beneficiaries.

Courts pushed back on some of these moves. Judges blocked NIH indirect cost caps and ordered the agency to resume grant funding, finding that the administration had violated prior orders. Chief Judge John McConnell ruled that the executive had defied a restraining order on a broader funding freeze and ordered immediate restoration of billions in frozen funds. These rulings enforced appropriations law and statutory grant frameworks, but they did not prevent the administration from trying again in other forms.

The attack on expertise extended to training and education.

Trump eliminated the Federal Executive Institute, a long-standing leadership school for senior civil servants, weakening institutional memory and professional development. Mass buyouts and layoffs, combined with the "Fork in the Road" resignation program, signaled that public service was now precarious work. The administration announced plans to close the Department of Education altogether, a radical step that would strip the federal government of a central role in schooling and civil-rights enforcement. At NASA, executive orders dismantled diversity offices and DEI policies, raising concerns about workforce culture and safety in a high-risk technical agency.

Education and health were also reshaped through personnel. The Senate confirmed Robert F. Kennedy Jr., a prominent anti-vaccine activist, as Secretary of Health and Human Services. Louisiana's health department stopped promoting mass vaccination, framing it as a matter of personal choice even amid outbreaks. Trump signed an order halting federal funding to schools and universities with COVID-19 vaccine mandates, pressuring institutions to relax public-health protections. In the Pentagon's school system, libraries were closed for a compliance review targeting books on gender and equity, cutting off students' access to a wide range of material. These moves did not ban inquiry outright, but they redirected it, privileging ideological narratives over evidence-based practice.

The week also saw a deepening of stratified citizenship and identity-based exclusion. Trump issued an order prioritizing asylum for Afrikaners from South Africa, a white ethnic group, on contested persecution grounds. ICE conducted heavily armed raids in Denver-area apartments, arresting dozens with media present, while nationwide operations netted more than 8,200 people in late January. Border Czar Tom Homan criticized those numbers as too low and called for more aggressive enforcement, including against non-criminal immigrants and sanctuary cities. The administration sued New York over its "green light" driver's license law and sanctuary policies, reopened an ICE office at Rikers Island jail, and sought to transfer Venezuelan immigrants to Guantanamo Bay before courts intervened.

At the same time, the White House pursued executive orders to end birthright citizenship, ban transgender people from serving openly in the military, and restrict gender-affirming healthcare for minors. Federal judges quickly blocked the birthright and trans-health orders, preserving constitutional and civil-rights baselines for the moment. Another order barred trans individuals from joining or serving openly in the armed forces, formalizing discrimination in a key public institution. Local actors pushed back where they could. Denver Public Schools sued to keep ICE out of schools. A new progressive caucus in the North Carolina legislature introduced bills to limit immigration enforcement in sensitive locations like hospitals and churches. But the direction of federal policy was plain: belonging, safety, and access to services were being sorted by race, nationality, gender identity, and ideology.

Information, memory, and culture were reshaped to match this new order. Trump signed an order directing health agencies to scrub diversity-related terms and content from their websites and research proposals. Federal agencies systematically removed or altered thousands of pages on DEI, LGBTQ health, and climate change. The National Security Agency conducted a "Big Delete" of internal and public content containing 27 banned words, including "privilege" and "inclusion." NASA and other agencies dismantled DEI structures and erased related content. These actions narrowed what the public could see and what civil servants could even name inside their own systems.

Education and cultural institutions were drawn into the same project. Pentagon school libraries suspended access to books while staff reviewed titles on gender and equity. Trump unilaterally purged Kennedy Center trustees and declared himself chair, asserting personal control over a national cultural institution. The National Park Service, acting under a sex-definition order, removed references to transgender people from the Stonewall National Monument website. A separate directive from the White House ordered the Park Service to erase trans contributions from Stonewall's official narrative. At the National Archives, senior leaders were fired while they oversaw investigations into Trump's records handling. Courts ordered health agencies to restore deleted HIV testing and contraception pages, and a judge compelled the FBI to search its records in response to a FOIA request on Trump's classified documents. These rulings showed that legal tools could still force some restoration, but the broader trend was toward a curated official memory in which inconvenient groups and histories simply disappeared.

Control over information also meant control over who could tell the story. The White House barred Associated Press reporters from press events and then banned AP journalists from the Oval Office and Air Force One after the outlet refused to adopt the term "Gulf of America." Access became a reward for compliant language and a punishment for editorial independence. Musk used his platform to amplify personal information about a judge's daughter, increasing the risk of harassment and signaling that judicial scrutiny could carry personal costs. ICE and the administration released daily deportation numbers without context, allowing them to frame operations as focused on criminals while obscuring broader impacts. DOGE's website featured metrics from the Competitive Enterprise Institute that labeled regulations "unconstitutional," recasting complex legal questions as simple anti-regulatory scores.

Foreign policy and national security were drawn into the same orbit of personalization and private influence. Trump announced a plan to seize and hold Gaza, relocating Palestinians elsewhere, and later declared an intention to invade and "own" the territory. These statements treated foreign land as property and displaced people as obstacles, discarding international law and congressional war powers. An executive order centralized control over foreign relations and the Diplomatic Corps in the White House, reducing professional diplomatic autonomy. Another order compelled the CIA to disclose the identities of everyone it had hired over the past two years, exposing intelligence personnel to risk and signaling that internal loyalty mattered more than security norms.

At the institutional level, the Senate confirmed Tulsi Gabbard as Director of National Intelligence despite bipartisan concerns about her views, and confirmed RFK Jr. at HHS. The administration abolished the FBI's Foreign Influence Task Force and a Justice Department unit targeting Russian oligarchs, even as it courted Vladimir Putin and hinted at sanctions relief. DOGE met with Pentagon staff to review defense spending and then leaked classified NRO data. Trade and energy policy were run through the same lens: tariffs, a National Energy Dominance Council, and environmental impact statements for LNG and mining projects were framed as tools of national strength, but they also aligned with the interests of fossil-fuel and extraction industries close to the administration.

Beneath these headline moves, federal power and economic policy were used against specific communities and regions. Halts to Home Energy Rebates, LIHEAP, and FEMA grants hit poor and disaster-prone areas hardest. New York City faced both fund seizures and legal attacks on its efforts to integrate undocumented residents into basic services. ICE crackdowns intensified, prompting protests and arrests in New York. In Fremont, California, the city council passed an ordinance criminalizing camping on public property and even "aiding and abetting" homeless encampments. Civil-rights advocates warned that the law criminalized poverty and mutual aid, chilling humanitarian work. At the same time, the administration moved to undo consumer protections on overdraft fees and medical debt, and to defund the CFPB by starving it of resources. Tariff choices raised costs for many while sparing some imports, and disaster in a historically Black neighborhood became an opportunity for rapid, above-asking real-estate sales. Inequality was not an accident of policy; it was its design.

Against this backdrop, resistance remained real but fragmented. Federal judges blocked the attempted shutdown of USAID, stopped DOGE from accessing Treasury payment systems and ordered the destruction of downloaded data, and issued temporary orders preventing Venezuelan immigrants from being sent to Guantanamo. Courts restored immigrant legal orientation programs, enforced prior funding orders, and blocked the birthright-citizenship and trans-healthcare executive orders. They reinstated the head of the Office of Special Counsel and compelled the FBI to conduct a full FOIA search on Trump's classified documents. Eight fired inspectors general went to court seeking reinstatement. Pennsylvania and other plaintiffs sued over impounded funds, and Judge Amir Ali ordered the release of frozen foreign aid.

Professional and civic actors added their own forms of pushback. The American Bar Association and broader legal community criticized rule-of-law violations and DOJ interference. Civil servants and FBI agents shared personal stories of their work to counter "deep state" rhetoric. Denver schools and the North Carolina progressive caucus used lawsuits and legislation to shield immigrants from enforcement in schools and other sensitive spaces. Activists in North Carolina organized events to highlight tens of thousands of disenfranchised voters and raised alarms about interference in a key state Supreme Court race. A detailed report titled "Trump Lost. Voter Suppression Won." documented ongoing suppression tactics. Constituents flooded congressional phone lines with tens of millions of calls opposing Trump and Musk's plans. Abroad, hundreds of thousands marched in Munich against a far-right party backed by Musk. Senators moved to codify Denali's name in law after a Trump renaming order, defending Indigenous heritage. These actions did not stop the week's structural changes, but they showed that institutional and civic muscles had not atrophied.

Some scheduled confrontations were already on the calendar. North Carolina Democrats planned a rally at the state legislature to oppose what they described as anti-democratic bills. Environmental impact statements for major energy and mining projects were opened for public comment. Ongoing lawsuits over DOGE's authority, impounded funds, and inspector-general firings awaited further hearings and rulings. Each of these processes promised to test, in specific venues and on set dates, how far the new executive structures could be pushed back.

In the arc of Trump's second term, Week 4 marked an early consolidation rather than a dramatic turn. DOGE's ascent, the civil-service purge, the use of funding as leverage, and the engineering of information and memory all deepened patterns that had been visible in outline. What changed was scale and confidence. Executive power was exercised more openly against courts, watchdogs, and disfavored populations. Law was invoked more selectively, as shield for insiders and sword against the vulnerable. At the same time, judges, inspectors general, state officials, and ordinary citizens continued to assert the old rules, often successfully in the short run. The week's movement on the Democracy Clock captured that tension: a measurable loss in the reliability of institutions, offset but not reversed by the stubbornness of those still trying to hold the line.

CHAPTER 15
WEEK 5: THE STATE AS PERSONAL INSTRUMENT

Mass firings, data seizures, and cultural erasures turned the federal government into a more personal, less accountable tool of rule in a single dense week.

The fifth week of Trump's second term read less like a series of disputes and more like a coordinated test of how much of the state could be bent at once. The same names and tools recurred across domains: executive orders, emergency language, a Musk-led efficiency project, and a Justice Department willing to lean on its own lawyers. Agencies that once stood apart from day-to-day politics were pulled into the orbit of a single project. The pattern was not subtle. It was dense.

At the close of the previous period, the Democracy Clock stood at 7:50 p.m. By the end of Week 5, it had moved to 7:51 p.m., a net shift of 1.3 minutes. The numerical change was small, but it captured a week in which the tools of government were reconfigured rather than merely used. Mass firings, spending freezes, and data seizures widened the space for unilateral action. Courts and Congress still appeared, but more often as background conditions than as active checks. The movement came from the way power was rearranged inside the state.

The clearest expression of that rearrangement was the rise of DOGE, the Department of Government Efficiency, as a parallel center of authority. Trump's order empowering a Musk-led DOGE committee to shrink the federal workforce delegated sweeping reduction powers to an unelected body, outside normal confirmation and civil service channels. That order did not just authorize cuts. It changed who decided which public functions mattered, and it did so without the usual layers of oversight that accompany such choices.

The consequences spread quickly through health and safety agencies. The administration announced mass layoffs in federal health agencies, including an entire class of Epidemic Intelligence Service officers at CDC and staff at HHS. These were the people trained to track outbreaks and manage crises. At the same time, USDA and FDA leadership fired about twenty staff involved in oversight of Neuralink, a company closely associated with Musk. The pattern was not random austerity. It was targeted removal of expertise in places where public health and private power intersected.

DOGE's reach extended into transportation and environmental stewardship. Large layoffs hit the Forest Service and National Park Service, thinning the ranks of those who manage public lands and wildfires. Hundreds of FAA technical employees responsible for air traffic control systems were terminated, even as SpaceX representatives were invited into the FAA command center to review air traffic systems. The same week, OSHA rescinded contractor protections and the administration canceled collective bargaining agreements with federal unions, then fired thousands of probationary federal employees and pressured mass resignations with buyout offers. The workforce that remained was smaller, less secure, and more exposed to political direction. It was easier to bend.

Foreign aid and global health capacity were also pulled into the purge. USAID was allowed to furlough over 2,000 workers after a federal judge declined to block the reductions, weakening development programs at a moment of global instability. Across agencies like USAID, USDA, and CDC, layoffs fell on veterans, early-career staff, and specialized personnel. There was one partial retreat: planned firings of more than 300 employees at the National Nuclear Security Administration were reversed after backlash, a reminder that even in a purge, some lines could still be pushed back. But the overall direction was clear. Courts upheld Musk's voluntary buyout scheme and refused to halt mass firings, while only occasionally stepping in to protect a narrow set of DEI-linked intelligence staff.

These moves did more than trim budgets. They politicized who could serve and hollowed out the state's ability to carry out basic tasks. Civil service protections, already fragile, were weakened by judicial deference to executive claims of efficiency. The winners were those closest to the DOGE project and the White House. The losers were the agencies that manage disease, air safety, forests, and foreign aid, and the public that depends on them.

Alongside the personnel purge came a more direct assertion of unilateral control over money and rules. Trump imposed a federal spending freeze on congressionally appropriated funds, despite statutory obligations to spend them. The freeze functioned as an illegal impoundment, allowing the White House to reshape policy by withholding money rather than by changing law. A companion DOGE deregulatory order invited agencies to declare existing rules unconstitutional or overbroad and to stop enforcing them, effectively letting the executive branch reinterpret statutes on its own.

The same logic appeared in an order bringing independent regulatory agencies under White House review. Bodies that had been designed to sit at some distance from presidential politics were told to submit their rules to OIRA and accept presidential oversight. Plans to disband the USPS governing board and shift control of the Postal Service to the Commerce Secretary pointed in the same direction: quasi-independent institutions were to be folded into the executive chain of command. Trump also targeted entities like the U.S. Institute of Peace and development foundations for downsizing or elimination, shrinking the parts of government that support diplomacy and long-term development.

These structural moves were reinforced by defiance of the judiciary. The administration continued contested policies despite injunctions on birthright citizenship limits and funding freezes, pushing toward a constitutional confrontation over compliance. At the same time, the Justice Department appealed to the Supreme Court for permission to fire the head of the Office of Special Counsel, framing protections for whistleblowers as an impermissible check on presidential power. A federal judge declined to block DOGE's access to Education Department data systems, citing efficiency, even as other courts temporarily protected the whistleblower watchdog and halted the firing of some DEI staff in intelligence agencies. Appeals courts twice refused to revive an executive order ending birthright citizenship for many children of noncitizens, affirming the Fourteenth Amendment's guarantee. These rulings felt like islands in a larger sea of executive assertion.

Emergency language and industrial policy were folded into this pattern. The administration announced plans to fast-track hundreds of fossil fuel permits under an "energy emergency," allowing developers to bypass environmental review and public input. Funding for EV subsidies and CHIPS Act implementation was frozen, undercutting congressionally approved efforts to support electric vehicles and semiconductor manufacturing. In each case, the White House used control over timing and implementation to redirect policy without changing the underlying statutes. Congress's power of the purse and the courts' authority to interpret law remained on paper, but their practical grip weakened.

If DOGE and impoundment reconfigured the machinery of administration, the Justice Department's choices reshaped the meaning of law itself. Inside DOJ, leadership coerced Public Integrity lawyers to drop a corruption indictment against New York mayor Eric Adams. Prosecutors were told to dismiss the case or face removal. Several resigned rather than comply. The head of the

Criminal Division, Denise Cheung, also resigned after refusing to open a politically driven investigation into a Biden-era contract. These departures marked a shift from independent prosecutorial judgment to overt political direction.

At the same time, Trump ordered the firing of all remaining Biden-appointed U.S. attorneys in one sweep, further aligning federal prosecution with presidential loyalty. The move came as the administration unlawfully fired pro-worker NLRB member Gwynne Wilcox, weakening labor enforcement. On the other side of the ledger, the criminal justice system in New York charged five people with depraved-indifference murder in the killing of transgender man Sam Nordquist, showing that in some venues, serious crimes were still pursued. The asymmetry was stark. Corruption cases against politically useful figures were dropped, while enforcement tools were sharpened against immigrants, workers, and critics.

The clearest signal of how the regime viewed political violence came at CPAC. Trump issued mass pardons for January 6 Capitol attackers and celebrated them from the stage. Those who had used force against Congress were recast as honored guests. The message was that violence in service of the regime would not only be forgiven but praised. Combined with DOJ's selective enforcement posture and the push to fire oversight officials, this celebration of January 6 lowered deterrence for future attacks on democratic institutions.

Immigration enforcement became another arena where law served as a weapon rather than a limit. Trump threatened to revoke protections for Ukrainians under the Uniting for Ukraine program and ordered a review of Temporary Protected Status for about a million people, putting lawful residents' status at risk. An order restricting federal benefits for undocumented immigrants hardened a tiered system of access to public goods based on legal status, later echoed in a $175 billion deportation budget and benefit cuts that entrenched a punitive regime.

The administration briefly stripped legal aid from unaccompanied immigrant children in immigration proceedings, only to reverse course after backlash, illustrating how executive discretion could abruptly curtail due process for the most vulnerable. ICE agents detained immigrants at courthouses and mandatory check-ins, including DACA recipients, weaponizing enforcement against those who complied with legal processes. The Justice Department fired more than two dozen immigration judges and candidates amid a heavy case backlog, and ICE leadership was reshuffled to accelerate deportations. The Equal Employment Opportunity Commission moved to dismiss gender-identity discrimination cases, narrowing protections for transgender workers. Together, these actions deepened a stratified system in which immigration status and identity shaped access to rights, even as courts blocked attempts to end birthright citizenship.

The week also saw a more direct challenge to the norm of limited presidential tenure. Trump publicly mused about running for a third term and questioned constitutional limits, normalizing the idea of extended personal rule. At CPAC, Steve Bannon and allied figures went further, promoting a constitutional change to allow Trump a third term. What had once been speculative talk became an organized project. This push unfolded against the backdrop of a 2023 law requiring congressional approval or a Senate supermajority for any withdrawal from NATO, a guardrail Congress had erected in anticipation of executive overreach on alliances. That earlier law showed that some institutions had tried to anticipate threats. The third-term project suggested that those guardrails were now being tested in more direct ways.

The same CPAC stage that hosted calls for term-limit changes also hosted the celebration of January 6 pardons. The pairing was telling. Extending personal rule and rewarding anti-democratic violence were presented as part of the same political vision. The winners in this vision were those loyal to Trump and aligned media and activist networks. The losers were the norms of peaceful rotation of power and the expectation that attacks on Congress would be punished, not honored.

Control over information and data formed another pillar of the week's developments. The White House and Trump administration banned Associated Press journalists from the Oval Office, Air Force One, and key briefings after AP refused to adopt the term "Gulf of America" for the Gulf of Mexico. AP responded with a federal lawsuit challenging its exclusion, arguing that access could not be conditioned on adopting official language. Elon Musk added to the pressure by publicly calling for imprisonment of 60 Minutes journalists who were critical of the administration, contributing to a climate of intimidation around investigative reporting.

At the same time, DOGE and its allies moved to seize control of sensitive data. DOGE representatives gained access to CDC and CMS payment and contracting systems, blurring the line between private actors and state data control. The department pushed for access to IRS taxpayer systems, framed as an anti-waste measure, and the White House defended this access with unsubstantiated claims of massive savings. Senators Ron Wyden and Elizabeth Warren demanded details from the acting IRS commissioner, seeking to clarify whether tax databases were being weaponized. Within the Social Security Administration, acting commissioner Michelle King resigned rather than grant DOGE access to beneficiary data, and General Services Administration staff quit rather than enable a Musk ally's request for Notify.gov access, a system capable of texting the public en masse.

Courts did not consistently restrain these moves. A federal judge declined to block DOGE's access to Education Department data systems, citing efficiency, even as other institutions raised alarms. Operation Whirlwind, run under new D.C. U.S. Attorney Ed Martin, sent letters to lawmakers and launched investigations into "threats" against officials, including criticism of Musk and DOGE. By linking criticism to potential criminal conduct, the operation blurred the line between protected speech and prosecutable threats. In this environment, RFK Jr., serving as HHS Secretary, promoted anti-vaccine rhetoric and questioned the childhood schedule, while Congressman Nick Begich amplified false DOGE claims about Social Security beneficiaries and supposed fraud. Regime-aligned disinformation filled the space created by weakened independent media and concentrated data power.

Beneath these immediate fights lay a broader project to rewrite civic education, culture, and public memory. In Department of Defense schools, the education authority ordered curriculum changes and book removals targeting materials on gender, sexuality, Black history, and transgender figures. Students at a DoD middle school in Germany walked out during a visit by Defense Secretary Pete Hegseth to protest DEI purges, signaling youth resistance to top-down ideological control. OSHA leadership ordered the destruction of eighteen workplace safety publications, many flagged simply for containing words like "diversity" or "gender," reducing access to guidance that protects workers. The loss was quiet but real.

The National Park Service removed transgender references from Stonewall National Monument webpages, narrowing public memory of the uprising and erasing the role of trans people in LGBTQ+ history. Protesters in New York City demonstrated against the removal of LGBTQ+ references from Stonewall materials, defending visibility against federal attempts to rewrite queer history. Elsewhere, the administration scrubbed mentions of Black people from some federal websites during Black History Month, undermining recognition of Black Americans' contributions. The National Endowment for the Arts canceled DEI-focused grants and banned programs that promote DEI or "gender ideology," redirecting cultural funding away from marginalized communities.

High culture was not spared. The administration took over the Kennedy Center, replacing its board with Trump allies and appointing an unqualified president, politicizing a major arts institution. Trump asserted power to rename major geographic features by executive order, declaring "Gulf of America Day" and claiming unilateral authority to rename the Gulf of Mexico and Denali. He misrepresented the Fourteenth Amendment on social media, falsely claiming it applied only to formerly enslaved people, to support efforts to curtail birthright citizenship. State Department directives canceled non-mission-critical media subscriptions worldwide, limiting diplomats' access to diverse information sources. Across websites, curricula, monuments, and grants, references to climate, DEI, Black history, and LGBTQ+ people were scrubbed. Public commentary, including reflections on presidential honesty and disinformation on Presidents Day, tried to place these changes in historical context, but the structural direction was one of narrowing stories and curated memory.

Economic policy during the week reinforced these shifts in power and memory by redistributing burdens downward. House Republicans advanced a budget blueprint with deep cuts to Medicare, Medicaid, and nutrition programs while extending tax breaks for the wealthy. Trump endorsed a competing House budget that added trillions in tax-cut-driven deficits and mandated large benefit cuts. The administration proposed further reductions to Social Security, Medicare, Medicaid, and food aid, often justified by inflated or misleading claims of waste and fraud. DOGE and the White House touted supposed savings from contract cancellations, misreporting an $8 million contract as $8 billion to claim $16 billion in savings. These numbers were debunked, but they served their purpose in public messaging.

Climate and industrial policy were rolled back in tandem. Environmental protections were weakened and fossil fuel expansion promoted through early-term orders to increase drilling and cut safeguards. The "energy emergency" fast-track allowed hundreds of fossil projects to bypass environmental review and public input. Climate-related research grants were cut, and the word "climate" was scrubbed from programs, weakening the knowledge base for policy. Funding for EV subsidies and CHIPS Act implementation was frozen, undercutting efforts to build domestic manufacturing and clean energy capacity. The administration moved to revoke federal approval for New York City's congestion pricing plan, using federal leverage to block a local environmental and revenue policy. Elon Musk called for defunding the International Space Station after a dispute with an astronaut commander, highlighting how private actors sought to redirect public resources toward their own ventures.

Trade and foreign policy took on a transactional, extractive cast. The administration proposed that the United States gain access to half of Ukraine's mineral resources in exchange for support, framing security assistance as a resource deal with a vulnerable ally. Plans for new tariffs risked a trade war, and consumer confidence dropped sharply, with survey researchers linking the decline to tariff policies. At the same time, the administration considered repealing tariffs on China in exchange for purchase promises and floated halving U.S. and Chinese military spending, despite opaque Chinese budgets. These moves risked weakening U.S. capabilities in ways that favored authoritarian rivals. State-level climate superfund laws in Vermont and New York, which sought to charge fossil fuel firms for damages, faced immediate lawsuits from red-state attorneys general and oil trade groups, illustrating how even modest efforts to rebalance costs from the public to polluters were contested.

Against this backdrop, resistance emerged but remained fragmented. Democratic leaders and activists organized nationwide protests against DOGE budget cuts, rallying outside congressional offices and Tesla dealerships. Federal workers and Representative Alexandria Ocasio-Cortez led protests outside SpaceX, with more than a thousand employees highlighting fears of privatization and billionaire capture of public policy. Large, diffuse demonstrations across the country decried perceived attacks on democracy and alliances. At Stonewall and in DoD schools, localized actions—protests over LGBTQ+ erasure and student walkouts against DEI purges—showed that the cultural project of rewriting memory was contested.

Inside institutions, some officials chose resignation over compliance. Michelle King left the Social Security Administration rather than hand over beneficiary data to DOGE. GSA staff resigned rather than grant Notify.gov access to a Musk ally. Denise

Cheung and other DOJ lawyers walked away rather than pursue baseless or politically driven cases. Unions sued over mass federal workforce reductions and the cancellation of collective bargaining agreements. AP went to court over its exclusion from White House venues. Senators Wyden and Warren pressed the IRS on DOGE's access to taxpayer data. Federal judges temporarily blocked the firing of DEI staff in intelligence agencies and preserved the whistleblower watchdog's position, while the National Archives and FOIA Advisory Committee scheduled a public meeting to maintain a venue for transparency. The Environmental Protection Agency continued to issue technical corrections, comment extensions, and environmental impact notices, keeping some procedural integrity alive.

Yet these efforts, while real, did not cohere into a force capable of reversing the broader drift. Courts more often deferred than intervened. Congress was locked in brinkmanship over budgets shaped by the White House. Protests were large but scattered across issues and geographies. Resignations removed pockets of resistance from inside agencies, sometimes leaving the structures they opposed easier to capture. The week's changes to staffing, spending, data control, and public memory moved faster than the mechanisms available to contest them.

In the arc of the term, Week 5 deepened the sense that the struggle was no longer over single policies but over the shape of the state itself. The tools of administration—who is hired and fired, which funds flow, what data is seen, what history is told—were used to entrench a more personal, less accountable form of rule. Rights and procedures remained on paper, and pockets of resistance showed they still had life. But using them now demanded more courage, more coordination, and more time than the week allowed. The erosion advanced not through a single rupture, but through the steady normalization of a government that serves power first and the public only as an afterthought.

CHAPTER 16
WEEK 6: BUREAUCRACY AS PATRONAGE ENGINE

> *A week of quiet decrees turned the civil service, immigration system, and information sphere into instruments of loyalty, wealth, and curated memory.*

The sixth week of Trump's second term did not hinge on a single decree or spectacle. It unfolded as a series of managerial moves, budget drafts, executive orders, and access decisions that, taken together, redrew the map of who holds power inside the American state. The pattern was not new, but its confidence was. Fiscal levers, personnel rules, immigration tools, and the information sphere were all pulled in ways that favored loyalty, wealth, and ideological alignment over neutral administration or equal protection. The center of gravity shifted. Again.

At the start of Week 6, the Democracy Clock stood at 7:51 p.m. By the end of the period, it read 7:52 p.m., a net movement of 0.2 minutes. The numerical shift was small, but it captured a week in which executive power widened its reach over money, people, and memory, while the cost of resistance rose. Courts and civil society did win some injunctions and carve-outs. Yet the dominant story was of a presidency learning how to use the machinery of government as an extension of personal and factional will, and of institutions struggling to keep pace.

The most visible change in the machinery of state came through the Department of Government Efficiency, or DOGE, and its alliance with Elon Musk. Early in the week, Musk, working through the Office of Personnel Management, ordered federal workers to email weekly "accomplishments" under threat that silence would be treated as resignation. Health Secretary Robert F. Kennedy Jr. instructed his staff to comply, even as other agencies and unions challenged the directive. The order looked like a management tool. In practice, it turned a private tech executive into a gatekeeper of civil-service job security, signaling that continued employment now depended on responsiveness to a politicized, extra-statutory demand.

Courts moved quickly to test that boundary. Lawsuits in California and elsewhere challenged Musk's ultimatum, and judges issued orders blocking the use of the email scheme to force mass resignations. A separate ruling halted OPM's authority to direct sweeping reductions in force, finding that the agency likely lacked legal power to order the kind of mass firings the White House envisioned. These injunctions did not restore normalcy. They did, however, show that civil-service protections still had some purchase in law, even as the executive branch probed for ways around them.

The White House responded not by retreating, but by shifting terrain. An executive order centralized oversight of contracts, grants, and loans under DOGE, and imposed a 30-day freeze on government credit cards. In one stroke, day-to-day spending power moved from line agencies to a Musk-linked node inside the executive. Agencies that once controlled their own travel, small purchases, and routine payments now had to route decisions through a central structure whose leadership did not answer to Congress. At the same time, OMB and OPM directed agencies to prepare mass layoff and reorganization plans by mid-March, turning the threat of large-scale purges into an organizing principle of internal planning.

The impact on the scientific and technical state was immediate. DOGE oversaw large-scale firings at NOAA, CDC, NASA, and related agencies, terminating hundreds of probationary staff. These were not headline positions. They were the analysts, modelers, and technicians who make weather forecasts, track disease, and maintain satellites. Their removal hollowed out capacity in ways that are hard for the public to see and easy for political appointees to steer. At the same time, DOGE posted a "wall of receipts" touting billions in supposed savings from these cuts, only to quietly delete inflated figures after media scrutiny. The numbers changed. The centralization did not.

Musk's role deepened through infrastructure as well as personnel. The Federal Aviation Administration signed a contract to use SpaceX's Starlink system for communications, embedding a Musk-controlled platform into critical aviation networks at the very moment his team was gaining control over federal payments and layoffs. Internal warnings at Health and Human Services that responses to Musk's accomplishment emails could be exposed to foreign actors underscored the data-security risks of this arrangement. The Federal Election Commission, for its part, canceled an open meeting and limited detail about closed sessions, reducing transparency over campaign-finance oversight just as DOGE's reach expanded. The result was a state whose purse strings, payroll, and pipes increasingly ran through a private, politically aligned hub.

While the administrative core was being reshaped, the administration turned immigration into a proving ground for executive power and stratified citizenship. Trump announced what he called the largest deportation operation in U.S. history, pledging to remove millions of undocumented residents. Orders followed to deport large numbers of unaccompanied migrant children, some of the most vulnerable people in the system. At Guantánamo Bay, a military prison complex was repurposed to hold up to 30,000 migrant detainees. Reports described shackling, cages, strip searches, and isolation. A facility once associated with wartime detention now housed civilians in conditions that blurred the line between immigration enforcement and punitive confinement.

On the mainland, the administration built the infrastructure of a surveillance-deportation state. Undocumented immigrants aged fourteen and older were ordered to register and provide fingerprints, expanding biometric tracking over a population already at risk. The State Department imposed permanent visa bans on transgender athletes who "misstated" their sex on applications, turning immigration law into a tool of cultural exclusion. In parallel, Trump proposed a $5 million "gold card" path to citizenship, offering expedited legal status to those who could pay. Together, these moves created a hierarchy in which some people were marked for removal, others for constant monitoring, and a wealthy few for purchase of rights.

The propaganda layer matched the policy. The White House posted an "ASMR deportation flight" video showing shackled migrants as a kind of entertainment content, trivializing their suffering and normalizing state cruelty. Foreign-aid decisions extended this logic beyond U.S. borders. The administration cut or froze major streams of assistance, including USAID contracts, refugee health services along the Thai-Myanmar border, and funding for UNAIDS, the UN's HIV/AIDS program. Courts did issue injunctions halting some refugee suspensions and ordering certain loan and grant flows to resume, and a ruling barred ICE from conducting enforcement in churches and religious sites. These were partial checks. The broader direction was clear: basic protections for non-citizens, and for poor communities abroad, were treated as discretionary.

A third front opened against transgender people and diversity, equity, and inclusion programs across government, schools, and culture. Trump signed an executive order banning transgender athletes from women's sports nationwide, and warned governors he would cut federal funding to states that refused to comply. Maine's governor publicly defied the order, saying the state would follow its own laws, and federal courts issued nationwide injunctions blocking some of Trump's anti-DEI directives. Another ruling protected trans women in prison from being transferred to men's facilities. These acts of resistance showed that the new campaign was contested from the start.

The administration pressed ahead anyway. The State Department's visa bans on trans athletes, the Pentagon's orders to identify and discharge transgender service members, and a memo implementing Trump's directive to remove trans troops unless they obtained waivers all used national-security and immigration tools to exclude a class of people from public life. Inside domestic agencies, the Social Security Administration closed its Office of Civil Rights and Equal Opportunity, weakening internal channels for discrimination complaints. At NIH, DEI-related grants remained frozen despite a court order, redirecting public-health resources away from equity-focused research. The Department of Education launched an "End DEI" reporting portal inviting citizens to flag diversity initiatives in schools, and the White House prepared an order to abolish the Education Department altogether, offering buyouts to staff and planning a major restructuring of SSA and deep cuts to the EPA.

These moves were accompanied by efforts to expand surveillance and narrow reproductive autonomy. In Missouri, a Republican lawmaker introduced a bill to create a registry of pregnant women deemed at risk of abortion, extending state monitoring into intimate medical decisions. Nationally, the administration shut down the National Law Enforcement Accountability Database, which had tracked police misconduct, and scrubbed DEI and climate references from federal research institutions' materials. Teachers' unions and civil-rights groups sued the Education Department over anti-diversity guidelines and funding threats, and educator coalitions challenged new civil-rights guidance in court. A 24-hour "economic blackout" organized by People's Union USA and allied groups protested cuts to DEI and social programs. The week thus recorded both a coordinated assault on equality infrastructure and the first organized attempts to blunt it.

Money and law converged in a separate but related development: the bending of regulation and enforcement to favor donors and regime-aligned business. The Securities and Exchange Commission dropped its lawsuit against Coinbase and paused a fraud prosecution of Justin Sun, both major pro-Trump donors. Coinbase had poured tens of millions into political spending, graded politicians, and hired Trump allies; Sun had funneled over $50 million into a Trump-backed venture. The timing of SEC retreats raised sharp questions about whether regulatory risk could now be bought down through political investment. The idea that wealth buys not only speech but law moved from abstraction to practice.

Jared Kushner's ventures illustrated the same pattern on the foreign-policy side. His firm, Affinity Partners, had raised $4.6 billion from foreign sovereign funds, including Saudi Arabia, while he remained close to Middle East policy. In Gaza, Kushner and the administration promoted redevelopment plans tied to private real-estate interests, including a "Trump Gaza" project marketed through an AI-generated resort video featuring a statue of Trump. These schemes linked U.S. policy toward a war-torn territory to potential profits for politically connected actors. At home, House Republicans advanced budget frameworks that paired deep cuts to Medicaid and other safety-net programs with large tax reductions for wealthy individuals and corporations, and the Senate moved a border-focused budget resolution emphasizing enforcement over social investment.

Trump pressed the Federal Reserve to cut interest rates as part of this broader tariff and tax-cut agenda, risking politicization of monetary policy. New tariffs on China, Canada, and Mexico threatened higher consumer prices and retaliatory measures, while a Canadian boycott of U.S. products signaled economic backlash from a key ally. Meanwhile, the administration removed online applications for several student loan repayment plans, complicating access to relief for borrowers without passing new law. Abrupt firings of poultry-disease staff during a bird-flu outbreak, followed by hurried attempts to rehire them, showed how austerity in technical agencies could undermine crisis response. A DoorDash settlement over misused delivery worker tips, secured by New York's attorney general, stood out as a rare instance where state enforcement still protected low-wage workers. The overall direction, however, was toward a system in which policy outcomes tracked the interests of capital and connected insiders, while ordinary people absorbed the risks.

Executive power also asserted itself against legal limits and foreign-policy norms. Trump pardoned Enrique Tarrio, the Proud Boys leader, and about 1,500 January 6 participants, removing legal consequences for political violence against Congress. The message was plain: those who act on behalf of the regime in future confrontations could expect similar impunity. At the same time, the administration defied a court order by blocking NIH peer-review panels and freezing billions in research grants, and ignored injunctions requiring certain foreign-aid and loan payments. Chief Justice John Roberts issued administrative stays that delayed enforcement of lower-court orders on USAID and foreign aid, giving the executive more time to resist mandated spending.

The gutting of USAID and foreign-aid flows reinforced this pattern. Most USAID staff were placed on leave, with plans to eliminate about 2,000 positions, sharply reducing U.S. development capacity and centralizing discretion in the White House. Funding for UNAIDS and refugee-focused health programs was terminated or frozen, withdrawing life-saving assistance from marginalized populations. In foreign policy, Trump directed officials to negotiate Ukraine peace terms directly with Russia without Ukraine present, sidelining a democratic ally in decisions about its own war. The AI "Trump Gaza" resort video, and the underlying redevelopment push, framed territorial and human-rights questions as opportunities for elite deal-making. Against this backdrop, U.S. ambassador David Pressman publicly criticized Hungary's democratic backsliding, calling Viktor Orbán's system one that served a narrow elite. His remarks underscored the gap between traditional democratic rhetoric abroad and the administration's own practices.

Domestically, national-security tools were turned inward. Trump suspended security clearances for lawyers who had represented former special counsel Jack Smith, signaling a willingness to punish legal adversaries by cutting off their access to classified work. He canceled key CDC and FDA vaccine-related meetings during a severe flu season, overriding routine scientific processes that guide immunization policy. Senator Angus King warned Congress that Trump's funding refusals and spending freezes amounted to an unconstitutional power grab, an attempt to alter laws by refusing to execute them. His appeals framed the week's events not as isolated disputes, but as a structural challenge to the separation of powers.

Alongside these shifts in money and force, the administration moved to bring the information space and culture under tighter political control. The most emblematic episode was the renaming of the Gulf of Mexico. Trump signed an executive order declaring it the "Gulf of America," and the White House conditioned press access on outlets' willingness to use the new term. Associated Press and Reuters were barred from events after refusing to comply. The administration seized control of the press pool from the White House Correspondents' Association, deciding which reporters could cover the presidency. Federal courts declined AP's request for emergency restoration of access, leaving the retaliatory ban in place.

Cultural institutions felt similar pressure. The Kennedy Center canceled LGBTQ-related performances, including the International Pride Orchestra, labeling them "anti-American propaganda." The Department of Education's anti-DEI reporting portal encouraged citizens to flag diversity efforts in schools, while New York's governor ordered the removal of a Palestinian studies job posting at CUNY, using executive influence to shape academic hiring. Trump attacked MSNBC and specific journalists as threats and racists, threatened to sue authors and publishers, and floated laws against "defamatory fiction." At The Washington Post, Jeff Bezos reoriented the opinion section toward themes of "personal liberties" and "free markets," prompting the opinion editor's resignation and highlighting how concentrated media ownership can narrow mainstream debate.

The administration also cultivated a parallel propaganda ecosystem. Attorney General Pam Bondi selectively released Epstein-related documents to far-right influencers rather than to Congress or independent investigators, and the White House hosted closed-door briefings for pro-Trump online personalities, feeding them sensitive material. Musk smeared a CNN legal analyst as part of a crime family without evidence. AI tools were used both by the administration, in the Gaza resort video, and by protesters, who hacked HUD building screens to display an AI satire mocking Trump and Musk. Local courts contributed to the narrowing of public visibility by denying livestreaming of a high-profile Greenpeace trial over pipeline protests and by forcing venue fights that raised concerns about juror ties to the fossil-fuel industry. Across these domains, access, language, and narrative were treated as levers of power.

Beneath the headline fights over media and culture, the week saw a quieter dismantling of civil-rights infrastructure and an expansion of tools to surveil and punish dissent. The shutdown of the National Law Enforcement Accountability Database removed a national record of police misconduct, making it easier for abusive officers to move between departments without scrutiny. The closure of SSA's civil-rights and equal-opportunity office weakened internal mechanisms for addressing discrimination in a core benefits agency. Together, these steps reduced the state's capacity to police its own abuses.

At the same time, the climate for dissent grew more hostile. Bomb threats invoking "Emperor Trump" forced the evacuation of the Principles First summit, a conservative anti-Trump gathering, using the specter of violence to intimidate critics. In Huntington

Beach, police arrested former NFL player Chris Kluwe after he delivered an anti-MAGA speech at a city council meeting, charging him with disruption. The Education Department's DEI-reporting portal invited citizen-on-citizen surveillance of educators, while CIA and Treasury officials grappled with an unclassified layoff-related email that had exposed identities of undercover officers, illustrating how politicized downsizing could create new security risks. Congressional oversight tried to respond: Representative Gerry Connolly launched an investigation into the U.S. attorney in Washington, D.C., over alleged abuse of office in targeting media critics of Musk and DOGE, and the FEC's curtailed transparency drew criticism. But these efforts lagged behind the pace of change.

Courts, finally, emerged as a mixed arena of resistance and accommodation. On one side, federal judges issued injunctions blocking Trump's anti-DEI orders, restraining DOGE's access to sensitive personal data, halting mass firings ordered through OPM, and enjoining freezes on refugee admissions, foreign aid, and certain loan and grant flows. Rulings barred ICE from conducting enforcement in churches and extended protections for trans women in prison. The Supreme Court overturned Richard Glossip's death sentence after finding prosecutors had withheld exculpatory evidence, and declined to revisit precedent upholding protest buffer zones around abortion clinics. These decisions showed that due-process and civil-liberties concerns still had force in parts of the judiciary.

On the other side, the Supreme Court's administrative stays on USAID and foreign-aid payments gave the administration room to resist appropriations, and oral arguments in a "reverse discrimination" case signaled potential changes that could make it easier for majority-group plaintiffs to sue, with implications for DEI and employment law. Courts refused to grant emergency relief restoring AP's White House access, effectively endorsing, at least temporarily, a retaliatory exclusion of a major news outlet. Local judges limited public visibility into protest-related litigation by denying livestreaming and leaving venue questions unresolved. The net effect was a judiciary that could still draw lines, but did so unevenly, with some decisions reinforcing executive preferences and donor impunity.

Against this backdrop of consolidation, resistance took varied and sometimes improvised forms. Civil servants and protesters resigned or demonstrated against Musk's role and mass firings, staging actions at Tesla dealerships and within DOGE itself. Teachers' unions and educator coalitions went to court to defend DEI practices and equal-opportunity norms in schools. Maine's governor publicly refused to enforce the trans athlete ban. People's Union USA organized a nationwide economic boycott to protest anti-DEI policies and social-program cuts, while Canadians and Canadian businesses launched their own boycott of U.S. products in response to tariffs and Trump policies. Inside the United States, House Republican leaders advised members to avoid or tightly control town halls after facing constituent anger over cuts, a small but telling sign that public backlash was being felt and, in turn, prompting further insulation from direct accountability.

Diplomatic and symbolic acts also marked the week's countercurrents. Ambassador Pressman's criticism of Hungary's illiberal model offered a reminder of democratic standards even as U.S. practice drifted. The hacked AI video at HUD dramatized both the vulnerability of government communication systems and the creativity of dissenters using new tools to challenge official narratives. These gestures did not reverse the structural shifts underway. They did, however, trace the outlines of an emerging opposition that spanned courts, unions, state governments, foreign consumers, and digital activists.

In the arc of Trump's second term, Week 6 deepened the pattern of a patronage autocracy built on a hollowed-out civil service, captured law enforcement, and a curated information space. The week's movement on the Democracy Clock was modest in minutes, but dense in content. Executive authority reached further into spending, personnel, and foreign policy. Law bent more visibly toward donors and allies. Citizenship and rights were sorted more sharply by wealth, identity, and loyalty. At the same time, injunctions, protests, boycotts, and public warnings showed that institutional and civic resistance remained possible, though under growing strain. The story of the week lies in that tension: a state being refitted for personal rule, and a society still searching for ways to insist that power answer to law.

CHAPTER 17
WEEK 7: TOOLS AS HABIT, NOT EXCEPTION

> *Executive orders, mass layoffs, and curated information flows turned once-extraordinary tools into routine methods for rewarding allies, disciplining dissent, and thinning the state.*

The seventh week of Trump's second term did not hinge on a single decision or crisis. It unfolded instead as a series of moves inside the machinery of government, each framed as management, efficiency, or security, that together shifted who could act, who could resist, and who would bear the costs. The pattern that emerged was not improvisation. It was a more confident use of tools already at hand: executive orders, budget instructions, personnel moves, and selective enforcement. What changed was the reach of those tools and the ease with which they were used. The tools came out faster.

At the end of Week 6, the Democracy Clock was at 7:52 p.m. It remained at the same public time through Week 7, with a net change of half a minute. The clock face did not seem to change, and the hands moved barely at all. However, the underlying calculation showed a deeper entrenchment of practices that make reversal more difficult: unilateral control over foreign aid and military posture, a civil service reshaped around loyalty and outsourcing, and a justice system that bends more easily for donors than for law. Courts and some oversight agencies pushed back visibly, blocking aid freezes, illegal firings, and research cuts. Their resistance slowed the drift but did not stop it. The small numerical shift this week reflected ongoing tension: structural damage building up, limited at the edges by institutions that still work. The strain was visible, even if not yet decisive.

The first development played out at the intersection of foreign policy, war powers, and legal accountability. On the opening day of the period, Secretary of State Marco Rubio invoked emergency authorities to send $4 billion in arms to Israel without prior congressional approval. The move used a statutory exception meant for urgent threats to bypass the legislature on a major weapons transfer. It concentrated war-making discretion in the executive branch and treated Congress's role as optional. The justification was speed. The effect was to treat emergency channels as routine policy tools.

At the same time, the White House attempted to freeze nearly $2 billion in congressionally approved foreign aid, including funds for Ukraine. The administration framed the impoundment as a review. Courts saw it as a challenge to the power of the purse. Federal judges, and ultimately the Supreme Court, rejected the freeze and ordered payments to continue. The rulings reaffirmed that once Congress appropriates money, the president cannot simply refuse to spend it. Compliance was grudging and delayed. The episode showed both the reach of unilateral action and the judiciary's remaining capacity to enforce spending laws. The law still spoke, but only after a fight.

Security policy followed a similar pattern. President Trump ordered U.S. Cyber Command to halt planning and operations against Russia, redirecting attention to other priorities. The order reoriented national defense posture by fiat, downgrading a documented cyber threat without public debate. In parallel, the administration paused over a billion dollars in military aid and broader assistance to Ukraine, voted against a UN resolution condemning

Russia's aggression, and scaled back intelligence and imagery support to Kyiv. These choices signaled a realignment away from traditional democratic allies and toward a more accommodating stance toward Moscow, driven from the Oval Office rather than from a shared interbranch strategy. Congress watched more than it shaped.

The same willingness to bend legal structures appeared in matters closer to the president's personal interests. Trump retrieved boxes of classified documents from the Department of Justice that had been seized at Mar-a-Lago, an extraordinary step for a subject of an investigation. The act raised questions about special treatment and the integrity of evidence handling. Courts also had to step in to protect the head of the Office of Special Counsel, ruling that he could not be removed before his term expired, and to manage an emergency application seeking to block the firing of the Special Counsel in another case. These decisions preserved some internal checks on executive abuse, but they did so amid impeachment threats against judges and public calls, including from Elon Musk, to remove jurists who ruled against the Department of Government Efficiency. The law remained a limit on paper. In practice, it was increasingly treated as a weapon to be aimed or evaded.

The second development unfolded inside the federal bureaucracy. The Department of Government Efficiency and allied officials implemented mass layoffs and buyouts across Education, Social Security, the IRS, the Department of Veterans Affairs, USDA, State, and other agencies. Reduction-in-force directives and voluntary separation packages were presented as cost-saving measures. In reality, they hollowed out the professional civil service and impaired the delivery of statutory programs. At Social Security, regional offices were consolidated and staff were cut, threatening delays and errors in the delivery of benefits to millions of retirees and people with disabilities. At the VA, plans to cut roughly 80,000 employees raised the prospect of longer waits and de facto privatization of veteran care. The safety net thinned in real time.

Regulatory and oversight capacity suffered similar blows. The administration shuttered 18F, the in-house digital team that had built tools like IRS Direct File, weakening the government's own technical leverage and increasing reliance on contractors. At the Consumer Financial Protection Bureau, leadership under Russell Vought placed nearly all staff on indefinite administrative leave and instructed them to ignore legally mandated supervision work, even as the agency told courts it remained operational. The move effectively disabled a congressionally created watchdog while misrepresenting its status to the judiciary. At the Inter-American Foundation, the White House installed Peter Marocco as sole board member and head, placed most staff on leave, and took the agency's website offline. A foreign-aid body designed to be independent and transparent was reduced to a one-man operation aligned with the president.

The postal and communications infrastructure was also drawn into this restructuring. The administration prepared to dissolve the USPS board of governors and place the Postal Service under the Commerce Secretary, threatening the quasi-independent governance of a core public service. A $42.5 billion rural broadband program was overhauled to favor cheaper satellite technologies over fiber, a shift that risked entrenching uneven digital infrastructure while advantaging specific private providers. Inside Social Security, employees were banned from accessing news websites on work devices, limiting their ability to stay informed and signaling a preference for internal information control over open awareness. Even routine work became more insulated.

These moves did not go entirely unchecked. The Merit Systems Protection Board ordered temporary reinstatement of nearly 6,000 fired USDA probationary employees, suggesting that mass terminations likely violated civil-service protections. The Centers for Disease Control and Prevention reversed prior firings of 180 employees and instructed them to resume work, acknowledging problems in earlier cuts. Federal courts blocked mass firings at the Department of Education and cuts to medical research funding as likely unlawful, and a judge ordered CFPB's chief operating officer to testify about alleged false declarations regarding agency operations. Lawmakers requested a GAO investigation into mass firings and the risks of privatization. Yet even with these interventions, the net effect was clear: capacity at key agencies shrank, neutral expertise was displaced, and future administrations would face a thinner, more politicized state. The damage was partly slowed, not undone.

The third development tied economic policy, law enforcement, and personal enrichment into a single architecture. President Trump announced and then formalized the creation of a federal crypto-strategic reserve and a digital asset stockpile. The reserve was designed around specific tokens, including those favored by politically connected investors. David Sacks served as crypto czar while his venture firm held interests aligned with assets in the reserve. Ripple and allied donors made large political contributions as XRP, their token, was included in the proposed national holdings. The structure channeled public resources into volatile assets closely linked to allies, blurring the line between public policy and private gain. Public risk underwrote private bets.

At the same time, the administration halted the fraud prosecution of Chinese crypto magnate Justin Sun after he heavily invested in Trump-linked memecoins. It also suspended enforcement of a Biden-era anti–money laundering rule aimed at shell companies, making it easier to hide illicit funds. Combined with the effective shutdown of CFPB supervision, these steps signaled that wealthy benefactors could expect leniency, while ordinary consumers lost protection. Financial crimes by elites became less likely to be prosecuted and more likely to be quietly settled or ignored. The threat of law tilted sharply by income.

Tariff policy added another layer of volatility and selective benefit. The White House and Commerce Secretary Howard Lutnick imposed, adjusted, paused, and partially exempted sweeping tariffs on imports from Canada, Mexico, and China. Duties were tied to executive determinations about drug enforcement readiness and other administrative judgments. The rapid oscillations disrupted trade expectations, raised consumer prices, and triggered retaliatory measures from key partners. The Federal Reserve Bank of Atlanta and market indicators reported a projected economic contraction and declines in stocks and manufacturing linked to the tariffs. Commentators warned that the administration might manipulate federal economic statistics to obscure the damage. Control over data became another lever of power. Numbers themselves were now suspect.

Wealth also shaped governance through more familiar channels. Billionaire donors, including Elon Musk and others, poured millions into state legislative and judicial races to influence policy on abortion, education, labor, and elections. Musk and allied PACs spent heavily to support Brad Schimel in the Wisconsin Supreme Court race and to oppose Susan Crawford, underscoring how moneyed interests can shape the composition of the court. State Street rolled back board diversity requirements and disclosure expectations for companies in its index funds, reducing private-sector pressure for representative corporate governance. The Senate confirmed Linda McMahon, a political ally and major donor, as Secretary of Education despite her limited background and stated goal of shrinking the department. An executive order revised Public Service Loan Forgiveness eligibility to exclude organizations engaged in disfavored activities, using student debt relief as a tool to pressure civil-society employers. Policy outcomes and personnel choices converged around the interests of capital.

The fourth development concerned immigration and citizenship, where the administration deepened a tiered system of rights based on origin and status. Trump mobilized federal law enforcement agencies and the U.S. military to conduct mass deportations, blurring civilian–military lines and deploying coercive power against a vulnerable population on a sweeping scale. The government reopened a migrant family detention center in Texas, reversing a prior policy to end family detention and expanding confinement for asylum-seeking parents and children. In a separate case, Immigration and Customs Enforcement detained a German tourist indefinitely after denying her entry, placing her in solitary confinement despite her visa-waiver status. The incident showed how broad detention powers could be applied arbitrarily, with little due process. Status became a trigger for confinement.

Structural moves reinforced these signals. An executive order designated English as the official language of the United States and revoked prior language-access requirements, reducing practical access to government services for non-English speakers and stratifying participation in public programs. Plans for a renewed travel ban targeting countries such as Afghanistan and Pakistan signaled continued use of nationality-based restrictions that limit mobility and family unity for targeted populations. The administration threatened to revoke temporary legal status for about 240,000 Ukrainians in the United States, then reversed under pressure. The threatened mass loss of status underscored how humanitarian protections could be used as leverage in foreign and domestic politics.

Beyond U.S. borders, the government pressured Central American countries to act as holding areas for migrants through threats over the Panama Canal and tariffs, externalizing detention and limiting access to U.S. protection. It suspended most foreign aid to South Africa under an order citing discrimination against white Afrikaners, using U.S. leverage in ways that could undermine broader equality and health programs. Symbolic acts carried the same message. Trump signed an executive order renaming Anahuac National Wildlife Refuge after Jocelyn Nungaray, a crime victim in a case involving undocumented immigrants, embedding an anti-immigrant narrative in public space. In speeches, he celebrated clampdowns on immigration and asylum and called for more funding to expand border crackdowns, framing restrictive measures as core achievements. Citizenship, in this landscape, was not a stable status but a hierarchy, with rights and protections contingent on origin, race, and political usefulness.

The fifth development focused on civil equality and the rights of marginalized groups. In Iowa, state legislators advanced a bill to remove civil-rights protections for transgender people, prompting mass protests. At the federal level, the administration transferred transgender women to men's prisons and restricted gender-affirming care despite court rulings, endangering trans prisoners and signaling executive resistance to judicial enforcement of their rights. These actions treated court orders as obstacles rather than binding law. Vulnerable groups bore the risk.

A broader campaign targeted diversity, equity, and inclusion infrastructure. The administration and its allies mounted coordinated attacks on DEI measures across federal programs and private entities. An interim U.S. Attorney threatened Georgetown University and Georgetown Law with hiring blacklists if they continued DEI programs, conditioning DOJ employment on universities abandoning inclusion efforts. The Department of Justice opened a Title VII investigation into the University of California system over alleged antisemitic hostile work environments, scrutinizing campus responses to Gaza-related protests. The administration cut off $400 million in federal grants to Columbia University over alleged failures to combat antisemitism, using research and program funding to pressure internal governance.

Reproductive autonomy came under similar pressure. In Alabama, the attorney general sought authority to prosecute people who help women travel out of state for abortions, prompting a federal challenge. The case tested how far states could criminalize assistance for out-of-state procedures and restrict interstate travel. At the state level, Republican legislators in Oklahoma and Idaho introduced measures to privilege heterosexual marriage and urge reversal of Obergefell v. Hodges, challenging settled Supreme Court precedent on marriage equality. In Texas, a pronoun-free communications order led to the firing of an employee who refused to comply, constraining expression for LGBTQ and allied workers.

Cultural fronts were no less active. John Amanchukwu, backed by Turning Point USA and other donors, led a national book-banning tour targeting school curricula, disrupting school board meetings with inflammatory rhetoric and demanding removal of

LGBTQ content. The campaign showed how private money could shape local educational norms and stigmatize queer themes. Yet resistance persisted. Senate Democrats blocked a federal bill that would have banned trans athletes from women's sports, maintaining existing protections against categorical exclusion. In Montana, Republican lawmakers joined Democrats to defeat bills banning drag shows and Pride marches and removing trans children from parents. California Black lawmakers introduced a package of state reparations bills based on a taskforce report, and a legislator advanced a bill to ban leaded fuel at racetracks in large cities to address health harms in urban communities. These efforts used legislative tools to expand, rather than contract, equality.

The sixth development turned to universities and campuses, which became central battlegrounds for speech control and punishment. During the week, Trump threatened to cut federal funding and expel or arrest students at colleges that allowed what he called illegal protests. The threat used federal leverage to chill campus dissent and academic freedom, recasting student activism as criminal disorder. The administration followed through on its willingness to use money as a weapon by cutting $400 million in grants to Columbia University, citing alleged failures to combat antisemitism. The move targeted a single institution with a sweeping financial penalty tied to its handling of protest and speech. Funding became a disciplinary tool.

Immigration tools were deployed in the same arena. The administration launched an AI-assisted program to revoke visas of foreign students flagged as Hamas supporters based on social media, blurring lines between protected expression and security threats. Automated screening of online speech became a gatekeeper for who could study and speak in the United States. DOJ's threats to Georgetown over DEI and the Title VII investigation of the UC system fit into this pattern: universities were told that hiring pipelines, federal scrutiny, and funding would hinge on aligning with the administration's preferred narratives about antisemitism, diversity, and protest.

Outside higher education, similar pressures reached down into schools. The book-banning tour and disruptions at school board meetings, amplified by viral videos and claims of persecution, sought to narrow acceptable curricula and stigmatize inclusive materials. Funding for these campaigns underscored how private donors could shape local governance. In Congress, the removal and censure of Representative Al Green for protesting during Trump's address, combined with House budget resolutions that launched reconciliation to extend tax cuts while cutting Medicaid and other low-income benefits, showed how legislative and fiscal tools could be used to discipline dissent and reorder priorities. Against this backdrop, grassroots protests, the 50501 movement's nationwide demonstrations, and Bishop William Barber's planned march from St. Mark's Episcopal Church to the Supreme Court signaled that civil society still contested the narrowing of space for debate. The streets remained a counter-stage.

The seventh development concerned information, propaganda, and control over memory. Trump's nationally televised address to Congress became a central event. The speech was filled with false claims on immigration, Ukraine aid, and the economy, and it was staged with curated guests meant to dramatize narratives on crime, transgender issues, and government cuts. A constitutional ritual of reporting to the legislature functioned as a campaign rally and a broadcast platform for debunked stories. The performance framed critics of immigration and Ukraine policy as un-American or complicit in crime, casting dissent as disloyalty.

Media and information channels were reshaped to support this narrative. The White House restricted Associated Press access to presidential events after AP refused to adopt mandated terminology like "Gulf of America," pressuring a major wire service to echo official language. Inside the security apparatus, the administration deprioritized monitoring of Russian cyber threats and fired or reassigned officials at FBI and CISA who worked on election protection and foreign disinformation, weakening institutional capacity to detect and respond to information threats. The Inter-

American Foundation's website was taken offline amid leadership changes, limiting public insight into foreign-aid projects. Education authorities canceled large-scale research contracts and undermined NCES data collection, making it harder to assess student outcomes and equity gaps.

Control extended to archives and symbols. The administration delayed release of a report on Jeffrey Epstein, limiting access to information about elite misconduct and official handling of the case. Trump requested that the Declaration of Independence be moved to the Oval Office, seeking physical control over a foundational national document. An executive order renamed a wildlife refuge to highlight a crime by undocumented immigrants, altering public commemorative space to embed an anti-immigrant story. A Pentagon spokesperson tweeted comments disputing Leo Frank's innocence that echoed white supremacist narratives about an antisemitic lynching, lending official weight to revisionist history.

Economic data and internal information flows were also at risk. Commentators warned that the administration might manipulate or obscure negative economic statistics related to tariffs, and fears of data massaging underscored the vulnerability of official numbers to political interference. The Social Security Administration banned employees from accessing news websites on government devices, constraining staff awareness of external developments. Together, these moves curated what the public and civil servants could see and remember. Against this trend, a few countervailing events stood out: Honda publicly refuted Trump's claim that it was building a new plant in Indiana, and Newsmax agreed to pay $40 million to Smartmatic to settle a defamation lawsuit over false 2020 election claims. The settlement showed that courts could still impose costs for election-related disinformation, but it was notable precisely because it was rare.

The eighth development returned to the courts and legal oversight, where pressure and resistance coexisted. Representative Eli Crane filed articles of impeachment against federal judge Paul Engelmayer after his ruling against the Department of Government

Efficiency, and Elon Musk publicly urged Republicans to impeach judges who ruled against DOGE. These calls signaled a willingness to punish the judiciary for independent review of executive programs. Trump signed an executive order targeting law firm Perkins Coie by suspending clearances and directing agencies to cut ties, penalizing a specific firm that had represented political opponents. He also signed a memo urging agencies to require upfront fees from people suing the administration, a move that risked pricing many individuals and groups out of court and weakening judicial review of executive actions. Access to justice itself became contested ground.

Professional and institutional actors pushed back. The American Bar Association issued a statement condemning intimidation of judges by the president and his allies, highlighting growing threats to judicial independence. Federal courts ruled that Trump's firing of NLRB member Gwynne Wilcox was illegal and ordered her reinstated, reaffirming statutory protections for independent labor adjudication. Judges protected the OSC head's fixed term, blocked unlawful education layoffs and research cuts, and enforced congressional control over foreign aid. The Merit Systems Protection Board and CDC reinstatements added administrative weight to these legal boundaries. Yet the Department of Justice's decision to place two Manhattan prosecutors on leave while they handled a corruption case against New York Mayor Eric Adams raised fears of political interference in local accountability processes.

Money continued to shape the legal landscape. Musk and other billionaires' spending in judicial races, especially in Wisconsin, underscored how donor interests could influence who interprets the law. At the same time, election administration and voting rules moved quietly in the background. Congressional leaders scheduled votes on the SAVE Act, which analysts warned would disenfranchise many voters, especially women who had changed names. The Election Assistance Commission sought public comment on the National Mail Voter Registration Form, and the Federal Election Commission scheduled a closed Sunshine Act meeting on compliance and civil matters. These procedural steps would help determine how easily citizens could register and how transparently campaign rules would be enforced. The legal system remained a site of contest, with its future shape uncertain.

The ninth development returned to Congress and public life as arenas of partisan theater. During Trump's address to a joint session, Representative Al Green protested from the floor. He was removed from the chamber and later censured by the House, a formal punishment that reinforced majority control over acceptable modes of legislative dissent. The incident showed how decorum rules could be used to police opposition inside the legislature. Trump's threats against campus protesters, combined with the choreographed guest list and the House's budget instructions, turned the evening into a demonstration of executive dominance and partisan discipline rather than deliberation. The chamber served as a stage.

Outside the chamber, dissent took other forms. The 50501 movement organized nationwide protests against policies seen as undermining democracy and human rights. Constituents confronted Republican lawmakers at events over DOGE-driven cuts and the treatment of Ukraine, signaling voter willingness to challenge representatives directly. Bishop William Barber and allied groups organized a march from St. Mark's Episcopal Church to the Supreme Court, calling for moral resistance to injustice. These actions showed that public life had not yet been reduced to stage-managed events, even as the risks of protest grew.

Informal power and spectacle threaded through these scenes. Musk suggested that Trump should consider pardoning Derek Chauvin, the former police officer convicted of murdering George Floyd, a proposal that risked signaling tolerance for excessive force when aligned with regime narratives about crime and order. House Speaker Mike Johnson removed Representative Mike Turner from the Intelligence Committee after he contradicted administration claims on Russia, weakening independent congressional oversight of security policy. Trump told cabinet secretaries that they, not

Musk, were in charge of their departments, a statement that sought to reassure on formal lines of authority while acknowledging unease about outside influence. An executive order established a White House task force for the 2026 FIFA World Cup, centralizing coordination of a major international event and blending governance with spectacle. Meanwhile, service cuts at agencies like Social Security and VA quietly reshaped everyday life for beneficiaries, far from the cameras.

No single event in Week 7 set a clear future date for resolution, though several processes—GAO investigations, court cases on abortion travel and trans prisoners, EAC form reviews, and scheduled votes on the SAVE Act—were already in motion. Their outcomes would determine how much of the week's drift could be slowed or redirected. The calendar held many small tests, not one decisive reckoning.

Taken together, the week deepened an erosion that had begun earlier in the term. Executive power widened through emergency authorities and selective enforcement. The civil service was thinned and repurposed toward loyalty and privatization. Economic and legal systems bent more readily to the interests of donors and insiders. Immigration and civil-rights policy hardened into a hierarchy of belonging. Information and memory were curated to fit the regime's stories. Courts, inspectors, and civil society still pushed back, sometimes successfully, but often only enough to delay rather than prevent change. The significance of the period lay not in a dramatic break, but in the ease with which these methods were applied and the growing cost of resisting them. The clock's still face masked a system settling into new habits.

CHAPTER 18
WEEK 8: CITIZENSHIP AND SERVICE AS LEVERAGE

> *A week of quiet decrees and targeted enforcement hollowed institutions, stratified belonging, and turned law and budgets into tools of loyalty and fear.*

The eighth week of Trump's second term did not hinge on a single shock. It unfolded instead as a dense layering of decisions that altered who counts, who serves, and who remembers. Immigration rules, civil service structures, university budgets, and media funding all shifted in ways that looked technical when taken alone. Together, they traced a sharper outline of a state that answers more to personal power and aligned wealth than to law, expertise, or equal citizenship.

At the start of Week 8, the Democracy Clock stood at 7:52 p.m. It ended the week at the same public time, with a net movement of 0.2 minutes. The face did not change; the mechanism did. The small shift captured how much of the week's work took place inside existing tools—executive orders, emergency declarations, budget choices, and enforcement discretion—rather than through open breaks. Executive power widened, law bent more easily toward friends and against critics, and the line between citizen and outsider grew more conditional, even as courts and civil society mounted visible, if partial, resistance.

The first major development ran through the machinery of government itself. Early in the week, Trump and Elon Musk's Department of Government Efficiency moved to "greatly expand presidential control" by centralizing cost-cutting and management authority in a White House–aligned unit. DOGE gained effective veto power over agency operations and spending, including a requirement that the Environmental Protection Agency seek DOGE approval for any expenditure over $50,000. What sounded like coordination in practice meant that technical agencies could not act on their mandates without passing through a political gatekeeper.

Trump then used executive orders to reshape the state's footprint without new laws. One order dismantled non-statutory components of several agencies, including the U.S. Agency for Global Media and minority business offices, under the banner of reducing bureaucracy. Another broad rescission order wiped away multiple Biden-era directives across health, labor, climate, and security policy, underscoring how much substantive protection now rested on a single signature. These moves did not abolish agencies outright; they hollowed them, stripping away programs and offices that had given them independent policy capacity.

On the ground, the restructuring took concrete form. The Education Department fired more than 1,300 employees, effectively halving its workforce and crippling its ability to administer aid or enforce civil-rights protections in schools. The Veterans Administration planned to cut about 80,000 jobs, many held by veterans, while forcing therapists to conduct mental-health sessions in open cubicles after ending remote work, trading privacy and quality for managerial control. DOGE announced the termination of 793 federal office leases, closing physical sites that had anchored service delivery, even as courts ordered Musk and his office to produce documents and staff identities about these cost-cutting operations.

Other agencies felt the same pressure. USAID's operational capacity was dismantled through cuts and mismanagement, weakening the main U.S. development arm. Science funding across multiple fields was reduced, and industrial policies that had supported a factory construction boom were canceled, shifting risk from federal budgets to workers and regions. DOGE's own choices revealed priorities: cuts that reduced basic services for U.S. employees abroad while funding office luxuries, and inflated claims of tens of billions in savings that later proved largely unverifiable.

Judicial oversight did not disappear, but it lagged behind the pace of change. A federal judge ruled that DOGE must comply with transparency laws and release internal records, and another ordered Musk's office to disclose staff identities and documents related to cost-cutting authority. These rulings pushed back against the emergence of a shadow administrative structure, but they did so case by case, after decisions had already reshaped the civil service. The balance of power tilted toward a White House–Musk axis that could act quickly, while courts and the public struggled to see, let alone reverse, what had been done.

If the first development focused on who governs, the second focused on who belongs. Late in the week, Trump issued an executive order ending birthright citizenship for U.S.-born children of non-citizens, challenging a long-standing interpretation of the Fourteenth Amendment. During the same period, the administration declared a national emergency at the southern border and prepared to invoke the Alien Enemies Act to arrest and deport certain non-citizens without following normal due process. Emergency and wartime powers, once used only for rare crises, were being prepared as tools for mass status changes.

These structural moves sat atop a series of targeted enforcement actions. Immigration and Customs Enforcement detained Palestinian green card holder Mahmoud Khalil using a rarely invoked Cold War–era authority, blurring the line between immigration law and punishment for political speech. Agents arrested

Khalil at Columbia-owned housing, tying his detention to campus protest activity, and later revoked another Columbia student's visa over alleged Hamas support, prompting self-deportation. In a separate sweep, ICE detained naturalized U.S. citizen Jensy Machado despite valid identification, exposing how aggressive operations can make even citizenship feel contingent.

The administration also revived family detention at private facilities in Texas, repurposing Fort Bliss army base as an immigrant detention center and deporting immigrants—including children and nationals of adversarial states—to detention sites in Panama and Costa Rica. One deportation removed the non-citizen parents of a ten-year-old U.S. citizen child who had recently undergone brain surgery, illustrating how rigid enforcement could override humanitarian considerations. Plans to revoke visas and green cards of people deemed to support Hamas, combined with the suspension of the U.S. refugee resettlement program, signaled that nationality and perceived allegiance now shaped access to safety and legal protection.

At the border and in detention, the human costs were stark. Three migrants died crossing Otay Mountain in a storm, despite distress calls to Border Patrol. A New Hampshire green card holder alleged torture during interrogation at Logan Airport, including violent questioning, sleep deprivation, and denial of medication. Meanwhile, immigration arrests and detention surged, including many people without criminal convictions, as expanded 287(g) agreements deputized local law enforcement. The pattern was clear. Formal citizenship and legal status no longer guaranteed stable rights; they were subject to reinterpretation under emergency logic and ideological suspicion.

A third development concerned how law itself was used. Trump pardoned individuals convicted for the January 6 attack on the Capitol, recasting participants in an assault on the transfer of power as allies rather than threats. The pardons weakened deterrence against future political violence and signaled that loyalty could outweigh the gravity of the offense. In the same week, the

Justice Department, under political pressure, dismissed a corruption case against New York Mayor Eric Adams, and Trump signed an executive order targeting the law firm Paul Weiss with clearance reviews and contract bans after it had opposed his allies.

These headline actions sat within a broader pattern of selective enforcement. The administration dropped an environmental-justice lawsuit against Denka's Louisiana plant, which had emitted carcinogens in a majority-Black community, and the Securities and Exchange Commission abandoned high-profile suits against major crypto exchanges Kraken and Coinbase. Financial enforcement softened further as the government signaled tolerance for money laundering through weaker oversight. At the same time, investigative power turned toward disfavored groups: the Justice Department subpoenaed a New York migrant shelter for detailed resident information, risking the conversion of social services into enforcement pipelines, and a North Carolina judge sought to discard over 65,000 ballots on technical grounds after losing his election.

The result was a legal landscape where risk flowed downward and protection clustered upward. Allies in politics and business saw cases dropped, rules relaxed, or rights restored, while critics and vulnerable communities faced subpoenas, raids, and ballot challenges. Law remained on the books, but its application became uneven, guided less by neutral criteria than by proximity to power and usefulness to the regime.

Universities emerged as a fourth arena where federal power and political priorities met. The administration canceled $400 million in federal grants and contracts to Columbia University, citing antisemitism findings, and linked those cuts to expectations about how the university should handle pro-Palestinian protests. Columbia responded by expelling, suspending, or revoking diplomas of students involved in a 2024 protest, decisions taken under clear federal pressure. The Department of Education issued warnings to 60 colleges over alleged antisemitism, signaling that campus speech and discipline would be closely tied to civil-rights investigations.

Immigration tools reinforced this pressure. Khalil's arrest at Columbia housing and the visa revocation of another student over alleged Hamas support showed how status could be used to chill activism among non-citizens. Plans to revoke visas and green cards for perceived Hamas sympathies extended that threat beyond a single campus. When Jewish Voice for Peace and allied protesters occupied Trump Tower to demand Khalil's release, nearly 100 people were arrested, illustrating both the vitality of civil society and the readiness of authorities to respond with criminal charges in a politically symbolic venue.

The effect on academic freedom was structural. Universities faced a choice between protecting open debate and risking massive funding losses or immigration consequences for their students. Federal civil-rights enforcement, a tool once used to expand inclusion, now doubles as leverage to narrow the range of acceptable political expression. Campus governance became a proxy battlefield for national ideology, with administrators caught between legal obligations, financial dependence, and student demands.

A fifth development centered on DOGE's austerity campaign and the stories told about it. DOGE oversaw the termination of hundreds of federal leases, shrinking the government's physical presence in communities. It imposed a spending veto over EPA operations and drove mass layoffs at the Education Department and the Veterans Administration. TSA employees lost union protections, and the Social Security Administration changed overpayment rules to allow 100 percent benefit withholding, regardless of fault, giving the agency sweeping leverage over vulnerable beneficiaries.

At the same time, DOGE and Musk framed these cuts as heroic savings. The DOGE website removed detailed data that had previously allowed independent verification of budget claims, and Musk's office overstated savings by tens of billions of dollars. Musk appeared on Fox Business to describe Social Security as a Ponzi scheme and called for workforce cuts, using his quasi-official platform to shape public perceptions of core social insurance programs. When the Musk Watch DOGE Tracker, launched by Popular Information, documented that most touted savings were unverifiable, Musk attacked the watchdog rather than addressing its findings.

This combination of centralized cost-cutting power and manipulated fiscal narratives shifted both substance and perception. Essential services—such as veterans' care, school nutrition, local food purchasing, and in-person access to benefits—were reduced or made more difficult to access, while the public was told that waste had been painlessly trimmed. The civil service became more precarious and politicized as job security and union protections eroded, and the data needed to challenge these changes became scarce.

The sixth development advanced in a related direction but concentrated on rights and protections. The Education Department's Civil Rights Division eliminated more than half of its offices through layoffs, significantly reducing federal capacity to investigate discrimination in schools. The broader Education workforce was cut in half, and federal diversity programs across the government were ended by executive order. These institutional changes were reflected in policy: Trump ordered transgender women in federal custody to be transferred to men's prisons despite prior court rulings, and the Wyoming legislature passed multiple bills limiting transgender rights in sports and public facilities. Labor and social protections also weakened alongside civil rights enforcement. TSA employees lost their collective bargaining rights, making it easier for management to discipline or reassign frontline security staff. The Social Security Administration's new overpayment rules allowed for full benefit recoveries, and cuts to school and food-bank programs reduced access to nutrition for children and low-income families. Medical research and teacher training funds experienced deep cuts, including canceled grants to Johns Hopkins and planned reductions to teacher preparation that were only temporarily blocked by court order.

These actions did not completely eliminate equality or unionism. Instead, they dismantled the structures that made rights enforceable and protections effective. With fewer investigators, offices, and legal tools, individuals facing discrimination or unfair treatment had less institutional support. The state's role shifted from being an active defender of civil rights and labor standards to a more detached, and sometimes hostile, manager.

Environmental and climate policy became a seventh battleground. The Environmental Protection Agency announced 31 rollbacks of regulations, including those on electric vehicles and coal, favoring fossil-fuel interests. The administration moved to review the 2009 greenhouse gas endangerment finding, threatening the legal basis for many climate regulations. Support for renewable energy and climate resilience initiatives both inside and outside the country was cut back, while a permit for a major liquefied natural gas export project off Louisiana was extended, solidifying carbon-heavy infrastructure.

Congress and agencies reinforced this tilt. Hearings were held to consider weakening the Endangered Species Act and Marine Mammal Protection Act, and Congress used the Congressional Review Act to overturn an EPA methane waste emissions rule and a Bureau of Ocean Energy Management regulation protecting marine archaeological resources. Funding for federal cybersecurity initiatives, including election-support programs, was cut, increasing the vulnerability of critical infrastructure. At the same time, the Justice Department dropped the Denka environmental justice case, signaling a reduced willingness to confront pollution in marginalized communities.

Courts again provided limited checks. Judges ordered the administration to justify the abrupt cancellation of billions in climate research grants, enforcing a requirement that agencies give reasons when reshaping scientific agendas. But these interventions came after rollbacks had already advanced. The structural direction was clear. Environmental and climate protections were being dismantled in favor of short-term industrial and fossil-fuel interests, with long-term public health and planetary stability treated as secondary.

An eighth concern involved information, media, and memory. The administration cut funding to the U.S. Agency for Global Media, including Voice of America and other broadcasters, removing resources from congressionally chartered outlets that had provided independent reporting abroad. At USAID, leadership directed staff to shred or burn agency records despite laws requiring preservation, a direct move to erase documentation of how foreign aid decisions were made. At the same time, the Education Department's civil-rights layoffs and the cancellation of medical research grants limited the production and enforcement of knowledge about discrimination and public health.

Public health information also faced difficulties. During a measles outbreak, Health and Human Services Secretary Robert F. Kennedy Jr. spread misinformation about vaccine safety and effectiveness, while HHS planned clinical trials of unproven alternative measles treatments and the National Institutes of Health reduced funding for studies on vaccine confidence. These actions shifted focus and resources away from evidence-based approaches, weakening trust in immunization efforts. International watchdogs responded by placing the United States on a global human rights watchlist, signaling external recognition that domestic policies were diverging from democratic principles and human rights standards.

The information environment was further destabilized by a major cyberattack on Musk's social media platform X, which caused long-lasting outages and fueled speculative blame-casting and conspiracy theories. A State Department official deleted past abusive tweets about the Secretary of State after assuming a high-profile public diplomacy role, raising questions about selective self-censorship and the integrity of the public record. While courts compelled DOGE to comply with transparency laws and ordered the release of internal records, other agencies moved in the opposite direction: the Federal Election

Commission canceled a scheduled open meeting at the last minute, reducing transparency around election-regulation decisions in the near term. The overall effect was a contested, shrinking public record, with key information channels either defunded, politicized, or hidden.

The final development of the week involved norms, religion, and electoral legitimacy, where erosion and resistance coexisted. Trump repeated false claims that the 2020 election was rigged and called for the imprisonment of unnamed perpetrators, further undermining trust in election results and portraying political opponents as criminals. Paula White, director of the White House Faith Office, encouraged legal challenges to the separation of church and state to reintroduce prayer and Bibles in public schools, signaling an official effort to merge religious authority with state power.

At the same time, efforts to restrict voting continued. In North Carolina, Judge Jefferson Griffin sought to discard over 65,000 ballots after losing his election, citing technical registration issues. The long shadow of Shelby County v. Holder remained visible, as researchers documented widening racial turnout gaps in Alabama after the loss of federal preclearance. Against this backdrop, Representative Terri Sewell and House Democrats reintroduced the John R. Lewis Voting Rights Advancement Act, an attempt to restore federal oversight of discriminatory voting changes and rebuild institutional safeguards for equal participation.

Dissenters faced delegitimization and surveillance. Trump publicly defended Elon Musk and labeled Tesla protesters as "domestic terrorists," using presidential rhetoric to recast peaceful corporate critics as security threats. DHS used polygraph tests to hunt for leakers about immigration raids, and internal surveillance tools were deployed to identify staff contacts with journalists. Yet civil society mobilized: Senator Bernie Sanders and allies held a national tour and mass protests against oligarchy and anti-science policies; North Carolina Democrats and allied groups organized rallies, gallery pack-ins, and protests at Tesla dealerships; and Democratic organizations launched "People's Town Halls" and empty-chair events in Republican-held districts to restore direct constituent dialogue. The struggle over democratic norms thus unfolded on both sides of the ledger—erosion from above, organizing from below.

There were no major scheduled turning points embedded in this week's record. The most consequential future-oriented elements were implicit: pending court responses to the birthright-citizenship order and the planned use of the Alien Enemies Act, ongoing discovery into DOGE's operations, and the reintroduced voting-rights bill awaiting legislative action. Each pointed toward arenas where the trajectory set in Week 8 could be either entrenched or checked, but their outcomes lay beyond the period's close.

In the broader scope of the period, Week 8 did not see a sharp decline but rather a deepening of existing patterns. Executive power and a parallel DOGE structure increasingly acted with confidence, using current tools to weaken institutions, redefine membership, and control information. Law enforcement and clemency were applied more selectively, while environmental, civil rights, and public health systems were cut back. Meanwhile, courts, journalists, and organized citizens demonstrated that resistance still existed, though often reactive and slower. The week's modest shift on the Democracy Clock reflected this tension: formal structures remained intact, but the reliance on them grew more costly, and the gap between legal promises and real protections widened.

CHAPTER 19
WEEK 9: EMERGENCY POWERS AS ROUTINE GOVERNANCE

In Trump's ninth week back in office, wartime statutes, deportation flights, and agency purges turned law and bureaucracy into pliable tools of executive will.

The ninth week of Trump's second term did not turn on a single order or speech. It unfolded as a series of moves that, taken together, showed law, information, and institutional design being bent toward the will of the executive. Immigration, education, media, and regulation all became arenas where power was exercised less as a shared framework and more as a personal instrument. The pattern was not subtle. It was insistent.

At the start of Week 9, the Democracy Clock stood at 7:52 p.m. By the end of the week, it read 7:56 p.m., a net movement of 3.3 minutes. The shift reflected the way emergency powers were folded into routine governance, courts were defied and attacked, and core state functions were reassigned to loyal units and private allies. Opposition still acted, and judges still ruled, but their ability to bind the executive narrowed. The change in time captured that gap between formal limits and effective power.

The clearest expression of that gap came in the administration's use of the Alien Enemies Act. An eighteenth-century wartime statute, long dormant in domestic life, was invoked to deport alleged members of the Tren de Aragua gang and broad categories of Venezuelan and Salvadoran migrants. The law's original context —foreign enemies in declared war—was recast into a standing tool for peacetime immigration enforcement. With that move, the president claimed the right to expel noncitizens on his own judgment, without the usual immigration hearings and protections.

On the ground, this authority was applied with blunt instruments. Tattoos and vague allegations of gang ties became enough to mark people for removal. LGBTQ+ migrants and asylum seekers with no criminal records were swept into the same net as violent offenders. ICE and CBP officers detained and mistreated people who, under prior practice, would have had a chance to contest the charges. A German green-card holder, a Canadian worker, and a child with brain cancer all appeared in reports of harsh treatment and denial of care. The line between "enemy" and neighbor blurred.

When Judge James Boasberg issued a temporary restraining order halting the deportation flights, the executive branch did not stop. Planes continued to leave for El Salvador, carrying shackled, shaved deportees whose images were later broadcast as a warning. The Department of Justice argued that Boasberg's orders did not apply once aircraft left U.S. airspace, as if jurisdiction evaporated at the coastline. The judge, unconvinced, demanded explanations for apparent noncompliance and pressed the government to account for its actions. The question was no longer only what the law allowed. It was whether the executive felt bound to obey.

The administration did not hide what it was doing. It turned the deportations into spectacle. Footage of migrants in El Salvador's harsh prisons—shaved heads, crowded cells, rows of shackled bodies—was shared by both governments as proof of toughness. A deportation video set to a popular song, used without permission, framed expulsions as a kind of dark entertainment.

The message was simple. The state could reach across borders, strip people of dignity, and present the result as a political victory.

At the same time, the president ordered airstrikes in Yemen without seeking congressional authorization. The use of force abroad, like the use of force at the border, moved further from shared deliberation and closer to unilateral command. Plans emerged for a militarized buffer zone along the New Mexico border, staffed by active-duty troops with detention authority. And in a single stroke, the administration revoked parole-like protections for more than 530,000 immigrants from Cuba, Haiti, Nicaragua, and Venezuela, exposing them to deportation after years of lawful presence. Emergency logic—exceptional powers for extraordinary threats—was becoming the baseline.

The legal and rhetorical frame around these actions made the underlying view of law plain. In a Justice Department speech that was nominally about policy, the president used the occasion to celebrate his own legal victories and air grievances about cases that had gone against him. The distinction between personal interest and neutral enforcement blurred. Soon after, he declared that President Biden's pardons were void because they had been signed by autopen, despite archival clarification that this was standard practice. The suggestion was that a sitting president could retroactively strip legal protections granted by a predecessor, not through statute or court ruling, but by assertion.

When courts pushed back on deportations, the confrontation sharpened. The Department of Justice sought to remove Judge Boasberg from the case and to narrow his authority over flights that had already taken off. The president called for his impeachment after adverse rulings, and Representative Brandon Gill introduced impeachment articles that echoed those demands. The White House press secretary went further, attacking Boasberg and his family in public statements, portraying him as a partisan actor and highlighting his spouse's donations. Bomb threats against judges who blocked Trump policies followed from supporters and allied media rhetoric that dismissed harms to innocent deportees as a "tough break."

Yet the judiciary did not simply absorb these blows. Chief Justice John Roberts issued a rare public rebuke, defending impeachment standards and the role of appellate review. Other federal judges, in at least a dozen cases, ruled key Trump orders illegal, including the misuse of the Alien Enemies Act and attempts to claw back climate grants. Courts blocked the dismantling of USAID as likely unconstitutional, halted a transgender military ban, and barred deportation of specific activists and academics while their cases proceeded. The formal structure of judicial review held. The practical question was whether rulings would be enforced, or whether they would be met with delay, reinterpretation, and political punishment.

Immigration policy became the main laboratory for this new relationship between law and power. Beyond mass deportations, the administration used visas, detention, and status revocations to target pro-Palestinian activists and academics. Mahmoud Khalil and Badar Khan Suri faced detention and deportation threats tied to their speech and scholarship. Long-time activist Jeanette Vizguerra was again placed at risk. Visa revocations and arrests on or near campuses sent a clear signal: political expression could carry immigration consequences. Courts intervened in some cases, issuing orders that protected individuals while litigation proceeded, but the chilling effect spread more widely.

At the same time, ICE intensified raids on Chinese immigrants nationwide, including in sanctuary cities. Reports described operations that left communities fearful and uncertain, with little clarity about who might be targeted next. Legal residents and workers found themselves detained for minor paperwork issues or mistaken identity. The revocation of parole and TPS-like protections for hundreds of thousands of people from Cuba, Haiti, Nicaragua, and Venezuela turned previously stable lives into precarious ones overnight. Citizenship and legal presence no longer functioned as firm shields. They became contingent, especially for those from disfavored countries or associated with disfavored causes.

The administration's approach to detention and punishment reinforced this stratification. Images of migrants in El Salvador's prisons, circulated by both governments, normalized extraterritorial punishment as an extension of U.S. policy. Plans for a militarized buffer zone on the southern border blurred the line between civilian law enforcement and military deployment. Within the United States, Tesla property damage by protesters or vandals was labeled domestic terrorism, with talk of twenty-year sentences in foreign prisons. Meanwhile, a January 6 participant, pardoned earlier, filed to run for the U.S. Senate on a hardline platform. The contrast between how different forms of lawbreaking were treated was stark.

Education and universities became another front where law and funding were used to reshape civic life. Through a series of executive orders, the president moved to dismantle the Department of Education, a congressionally created department, and to reassign its functions by decree. Student loan management was ordered to shift to the Small Business Administration, an agency with a different mission and oversight structure. Disability education and civil-rights enforcement functions were slated for reassignment as well. Online applications for income-driven repayment plans disappeared from government websites, leaving borrowers without clear paths to relief that remained on the books.

The American Federation of Teachers responded by suing the Department of Education over halted income-driven repayment processing, arguing that statutory options could not be frozen by administrative choice. At the same time, the administration announced that the SBA would take over the federal student loan portfolio, a massive public finance system, without a clear plan for borrower protections. Courts granted the Justice Department extra time in mifepristone litigation, opening space for potential policy shifts on medication abortion access. Regulatory levers—forms, deadlines, agency assignments—became tools for narrowing substantive rights without explicit repeal.

On campus, federal power was used more directly. The administration withdrew $400 million in federal funding from Columbia University and tied its restoration to demands about protest management, departmental structures, and policing. At the University of Pennsylvania, $175 million in funding was frozen over policies on transgender athletes in women's sports. An antisemitism taskforce and broad investigations into universities were announced, framed as civil-rights enforcement but closely linked to pressure on pro-Palestinian speech and scholarship. At UCLA, Gaza solidarity protesters entered litigation over alleged wrongful arrests and excessive force, raising questions about how universities and police handled politically charged demonstrations.

These moves did not occur in isolation. The Department of Veterans Affairs announced a phaseout of gender-affirming care for veterans, narrowing access to established medical services. Federal courts lifted prior blocks on executive orders dismantling diversity, equity, inclusion, and accessibility programs across the government, reshaping employment norms and internal culture. Together, these actions signaled a shift away from inclusive policies and toward a more constrained vision of who belonged in public institutions and on campus. Civic education, in both formal and informal forms, was being hollowed out and replaced with market and security logics.

Behind these visible battles, the machinery of the administrative state was being hollowed out and repurposed. The Department of Government Efficiency, or DOGE, emerged as a central instrument. Through executive orders, DOGE secured sweeping access to unclassified federal records and software systems, consolidating data and procurement authority in a lightly accountable unit. New orders on procurement, data sharing, and mineral production prioritized extractive industries and centralized contract decisions in the executive branch. The language was one of efficiency and anti-waste. The effect was to concentrate informational and economic power.

Concrete cuts followed. Deep staff reductions at the IRS led to mass firings and office closures, undermining tax collection and enforcement. The administration falsely claimed that thousands of employees had been fired for poor performance, despite internal warnings to the contrary. At the Federal Trade Commission, Democratic commissioners were fired, leaving the agency without a quorum and effectively paralyzing antitrust and consumer-protection work. The National Nuclear Security Administration faced staff freezes that threatened its technical capacity. The Department of Agriculture reduced inspection teams for plant and food imports, increasing risks from pests and unsafe products.

DOGE's reach extended into peacebuilding and culture. The administration removed the board of the U.S. Institute of Peace and asserted control over the institution, undermining its statutory independence. DOGE teams moved to eliminate the Institute of Museum and Library Services, canceling grants and voiding contracts that supported libraries and museums across the country. A contract tracking Russian abductions of Ukrainian children was terminated, signaling a deprioritization of certain human-rights investigations. USAID operations were frozen or redirected, though federal courts later blocked the full shutdown as likely unconstitutional and ordered restoration of staff and systems.

Judges also intervened to limit DOGE's push into Social Security data. Courts blocked the unit from accessing Social Security systems in what they described as a fishing expedition, ordered deletion of collected personal data, and criticized the broad fraud rationale offered by the government. New Social Security identity rules and a freeze on automatic SSN issuance for noncitizens, however, still went forward, straining field offices and delaying benefits for elderly, disabled, and immigrant claimants. The full-year appropriations law, passed with Democratic divisions and signed by the president, kept agencies funded but also locked in many of these restructuring priorities, reducing Congress's near-term leverage.

Within this reconfigured state, a small circle of corporate allies gained unusual prominence. Elon Musk and his companies stood at the center of this pattern. Reports described FAA contracts moving from Verizon to Starlink, while Starlink installed donated internet infrastructure across the White House campus. DOGE and the administration embraced land and mining initiatives that opened protected federal lands for housing and extraction, alongside a clean coal initiative and moves to restart coal plants. Tariffs that raised consumer costs and threatened jobs were justified as tools of national strength, even as they aligned with certain industrial interests.

Dissent around Musk and his firms was treated as a security matter. Property damage at Tesla facilities was labeled domestic terrorism, with officials floating the possibility of twenty-year sentences in foreign prisons. Representative Jasmine Crockett and allied organizers planned nationwide nonviolent protests at Tesla dealerships, urging divestment from the company; these actions tested how far protest rights would be respected when aimed at a favored corporate ally. Musk, for his part, called for prosecution of alleged Pentagon leakers who disclosed his planned briefing on China war scenarios, signaling hostility toward whistleblowing about his role in national security planning.

The administration's treatment of other actors reinforced the sense that law was being applied with an eye to loyalty. Democratic-aligned law firms were targeted with executive orders and public attacks, then saw punitive measures lifted once they agreed to policy changes and neutrality commitments. Security clearances were revoked from prominent political and legal opponents, including Joe Biden, Kamala Harris, and Liz Cheney, using access to classified information as a tool of punishment rather than a judgment about risk. Secret Service protection was stripped from Biden's adult children, suggesting that personal security could be granted or withdrawn based on political rivalry.

Information and memory were reshaped to support this new order. The White House restricted Associated Press access to the Oval Office and Air Force One over disputes about naming conventions, signaling that press access depended on editorial compliance. The administration dismantled the U.S. Agency for Global Media and shut down Voice of America and related broadcasters, eliminating a major source of U.S.-funded journalism that had operated with some independence. In their place, more tightly controlled outlets and feeds were poised to carry regime-aligned content.

On government websites, key guidance and historical material disappeared. A Surgeon General advisory framing gun violence as a public-health issue was removed from Health and Human Services pages. The Department of Justice deleted eleven ADA-related business guidance documents, including those on COVID and masking, under the banner of deregulation and inflation relief. The Pentagon removed and then partially restored online content about Code Talkers, Black veterans, and women pilots, rebranding them as "DEI" material before selective restoration. These changes did not erase history outright. They recast it, narrowing the official record of harm and struggle.

Propaganda filled some of the space left behind. Deportation imagery, including the El Salvador prison footage, was used to celebrate harsh treatment of migrants. A deportation video set to a familiar song turned expulsions into a shareable clip. Judges, campus protesters, and Tesla vandals were portrayed as radical or terrorist threats in public statements and allied commentary. Claims that Biden's autopen-signed pardons were invalid persisted even after the National Archives explained standard practice. Misrepresentations about IRS firings and other staff cuts framed deregulatory moves as housecleaning. At the same time, the administration released thousands of JFK assassination files and issued environmental impact statements for public comment, gestures of transparency that stood in tension with the broader trend.

Security and legal tools were increasingly personalized. Beyond the clearance revocations and Secret Service changes, the president's attempt to void Biden's pardons suggested that even settled acts of clemency could be reopened for political reasons. Terrorism charges were deployed against Tesla vandals, while some January 6 participants moved into electoral politics. Judges who ruled against the administration faced impeachment calls, smears, and threats. Whistleblowers, like FBI agent Johnathan Buma, were arrested rather than protected. The message to officials and citizens alike was that exposing misconduct or resisting directives could carry serious personal cost.

Opposition did not vanish. Democratic attorneys general filed multiple lawsuits and secured temporary restraining orders against firings, funding pauses, and other directives. They held community impact hearings that gathered testimony on job losses, deportations, and funding cuts, linking affected communities to legal challenges. Federal courts protected transgender service members, blocked some uses of the Alien Enemies Act, and shielded targeted activists and academics from immediate deportation. Local institutions, such as a New York village government confronted by a man falsely claiming to be mayor, resisted extra-legal power grabs. These acts showed that institutional muscle remained.

Environmental and public-health protections formed another contested field. EPA Administrator Lee Zeldin proposed rolling back thirty-one environmental regulations on air, water, and climate, shifting priorities toward short-term cost savings for industry. A clean coal initiative and moves to restart coal plants aligned energy policy with high-emission fuels. Protected federal lands were slated for housing and mining, favoring development and extraction over conservation. USDA inspection cuts, NNSA staff freezes, and tariffs that raised consumer costs all pointed in the same direction: long-term collective goods were subordinated to immediate economic and political aims.

Within this deregulatory push, technical rule changes accumulated. EPA approved state air plan revisions and stayed sanctions in

California and Sacramento, extended greenhouse gas reporting deadlines, delayed removal of a gasoline volatility waiver, and withdrew a coal waste rule after adverse comments. New pesticide tolerances and exemptions were set. The FDA updated medical device standards and revoked emergency authorizations for certain COVID-19 tests. OSHA renewed information collections for workplace safety, and TSA maintained data requirements for airport security. These actions showed that routine governance continued, even as the overall trajectory favored weaker protections and looser oversight.

No single development in Week 9 resolved the contest between executive ambition and institutional constraint. Courts asserted limits but struggled to enforce them against an administration willing to test the edges of compliance. Congress kept the government open but, in doing so, bankrolled much of the restructuring it opposed. Universities, journalists, and civil-society groups turned to litigation and protest, only to find that the costs of resistance were rising. The week's movement on the Democracy Clock captured this deepening erosion: not a collapse, but a steady shift in which law, memory, and state capacity were refashioned to serve power rather than restrain it.

CHAPTER 20
WEEK 10: VOTER ROLLS AS LEVERAGE

A quiet executive blitz rewired elections, immigration, law, and information systems to make the state more tool than commons, with courts mostly reacting at the edges.

The tenth week of Trump's second term did not hinge on a single shock. It unfolded as a dense layering of moves that, taken together, made the state feel less like a shared instrument and more like a personal tool. Elections, immigration, law, media, and public health were all touched, not by sweeping constitutional change, but by orders, appointments, and funding decisions that shifted who counted, who was watched, and who could push back. The pattern was one of tightening control over the channels through which citizens enter, vote, speak, and learn what their government is doing. It felt coordinated rather than random.

At the start of Week 10, the Democracy Clock stood at 7:56 p.m. It ended the week at the same public time, with a net movement of 0.2 minutes. The face of the clock did not change, but its gears did. The small shift captured how much of the week's damage was structural rather than spectacular: a major executive order on elections, a deepening use of immigration tools to punish dissent, new bargains that turned law into a currency for elites, and steady pressure on media and records. Courts and civil society registered resistance, but mostly in reaction, and mostly at the margins. The balance of power moved further toward a presidency that acts first and answers later, if at all.

The clearest expression of that shift came in a single executive order that reached into the heart of the electoral system. Trump signed a nationwide directive requiring documentary proof of citizenship for federal voter registration forms and pressuring states on how and when to count ballots. The order did not emerge from evidence of widespread noncitizen voting; it emerged from a narrative he had long advanced and now embedded into federal rules. States that failed to adopt strict proof-of-citizenship standards faced threats to their federal funding, turning what had been a state-managed gateway to the franchise into a lever of presidential discipline. The winners were those in the executive orbit who could now shape the electorate from Washington. The losers were eligible voters—especially the poor, the young, and naturalized citizens—whose ability to prove their status on paper would now determine whether they could participate at all.

Behind the order stood a new institutional actor: the Department of Government Efficiency, or DOGE, which sought broad access to state voter lists under the same directive. DOGE had already tried to centralize sensitive data inside the federal government, pushing for access to private information at several agencies until a judge temporarily blocked it. Now, with voter rolls in its sights, the department's mandate expanded from internal "efficiency" to external control. Centralizing voter data under an executive-controlled agency created the capacity for algorithmic targeting, selective purges, and fine-grained manipulation of turnout, all under the banner of integrity. The move did not abolish elections; it changed who could shape their inputs. It made the electorate itself more malleable.

The same week, the administration moved to expand surveillance of vulnerable groups while dimming the lights on domestic extremism. It considered using confidential tax data and social media screening to track immigrants and voters, even as it cut funding for a national database that tracked domestic terrorism, hate crimes, and school shootings. The IRS and ICE edged toward an agreement to share confidential tax records to locate undocumented immigrants, repurposing a fiscal institution built on trust into an enforcement arm. Social media accounts of green card and citizenship applicants were slated for inspection for "hostile attitudes" or "terrorist sympathy," blurring the line between security screening and ideological vetting. At the same time, defunding the violence-tracking database and shifting sensitive discussions onto encrypted apps narrowed the official record of threats and decision-making. The state watched downward more closely and watched itself less.

Pressure on states that resisted the administration's broader agenda reinforced the same pattern. Trump publicly demanded an apology from Maine's governor for refusing to implement a federal trans athlete ban, framing her stance as unlawful defiance of federal authority. The demand was symbolic, but it echoed the threats embedded in the election order: governors who diverged from his culture-war and power agenda could expect public shaming and, where possible, financial or regulatory punishment. Federal power, once a shared resource, became a stick to be wielded against disfavored regions and officials. The message was that autonomy would carry a price.

Immigration and citizenship policy formed the second major front, where structural tools and concrete abuses met. The week opened with a large-scale reassignment of federal agents from other duties to focus on undocumented immigrants, redirecting public safety resources away from other crimes and signaling that immigration enforcement would dominate the enforcement agenda. In parallel, the administration moved toward sharing confidential tax data with ICE and inspecting immigrants' social media, building a layered apparatus of surveillance that treated noncitizens and applicants as permanent suspects. These were not isolated tweaks; they were the background machinery that made later, more visible acts possible. The system was being rewired in advance.

Those acts came quickly. Federal immigration officers attempted to deport Columbia student Yunseo Chung for participating in pro-Palestinian demonstrations, linking her immigration status directly to her campus activism. In Massachusetts, masked officers arrested Turkish student Rumeysa Ozturk despite a court order barring her removal, showing open disregard for judicial protection. Homeland Security Secretary Kristi Noem then threatened to send more immigrants to a Terrorism Confinement Center in El Salvador, using the prospect of offshore detention in a harsh foreign facility as a tool of intimidation. Together, these moves signaled that immigration law could be used not only to police borders but to punish dissent and bypass domestic legal safeguards. Protest and status were now bound together.

Legal doctrine was bent to support this posture. The administration invoked the state secrets privilege in litigation over its use of the Alien Enemies Act, blocking disclosure in a deportation case and limiting judicial and public scrutiny of an expansive reading of wartime authority. Green card processing, including for approved refugees, was quietly paused without clear justification, creating uncertainty for people who had followed every rule. Fraud allegations were expanded against an immigrant based on disputed ties to an international agency. Each step widened executive discretion over who could stay, who could leave, and on what grounds, while making it harder for courts and the public to see or challenge the underlying reasoning. Emergency-style tools seeped into routine governance.

Courts did push back at the edges. A federal appeals court ruled that the administration could halt new refugee approvals but had to admit those already conditionally accepted, preserving some expectations while affirming broad power to close the door going forward. Another appeals court rejected the Justice Department's bid to lift a block on using the Alien Enemies Act for deportations, limiting the statute's expansion into routine enforcement. Chung sued over the attempt to deport her for protesting, testing whether judges would protect political expression from retaliatory immigration action. These decisions and lawsuits showed that judicial and civil-society resistance remained, but they did not reverse the trend. The architecture of stratified citizenship—where rights and vulnerability depended on status, ideology, and origin—grew more entrenched.

A third development unfolded in the realm of law and elite justice, where the presidency used targeted orders, settlements, and clemency to turn legal outcomes into negotiable favors. Trump signed an executive order aimed at a law firm associated with the Mueller investigation, suspending its security clearances and federal contracts. The order did not set a general policy; it singled out a specific firm for past work that had displeased him. Shortly afterward, Paul Weiss, another elite firm, agreed to provide $40 million in pro-bono services after facing a similar targeted order, and Trump publicly warned that law firms must "behave themselves." The message was clear: firms that crossed him could face punitive use of state power, and those that made themselves useful could buy relief. Law became a field of personal risk management.

The pattern repeated with Skadden. The administration extracted a $100 million pro-bono commitment from the firm in exchange for dropping a planned punitive order. These arrangements blurred the line between settlement and extortion, channeling vast amounts of legal work into administration-aligned causes under the shadow of executive threat. Wealthy firms could negotiate bespoke deals; smaller or less connected actors could not. At the same time, Trump pardoned Devon Archer, a former business partner of Hunter Biden convicted of defrauding a Native American tribe, and floated the idea of a government compensation fund for pardoned January 6 insurrectionists. Clemency and public money were thus directed toward politically salient allies and participants in an attack on the transfer of power, signaling that loyalty could erase or even reward serious wrongdoing.

Personnel choices reinforced the same logic. Trump installed Alina Habba, a close personal loyalist with a history of sanctions, as interim U.S. attorney for the District of New Jersey, placing a key prosecutorial office under the control of someone whose primary credential was allegiance. Retired Judge J. Michael Luttig, a conservative jurist, published an op-ed warning that Trump was declaring war on the judiciary and provoking a constitutional crisis. His warning did not stop the appointments or the deals, but it documented how they looked from inside the legal tradition: not as routine politics, but as an assault on neutral legality. In this environment, law became less a limit on power and more a weapon and a bargaining chip, with access and money determining who faced its full force. Justice tilted toward those closest to the throne.

The struggle over the civil service and federal agencies formed a fourth strand of the week's story. Trump filed an emergency appeal to the Supreme Court to continue firing thousands of probationary federal workers, seeking to preserve a mass firing campaign through extraordinary judicial channels. A federal appeals court upheld an order requiring the administration to rehire those workers, pushing back against the attempt to purge and reshape the workforce along political lines. The clash showed both the ambition of the executive project—to turn the civil service into a loyal apparatus—and the capacity of courts, at least for now, to defend basic protections. The stakes were the neutrality of the state itself.

At the same time, DOGE's attempted data grab and the judge's temporary block on its access to private agency data highlighted a parallel effort to centralize information power. The department's push to control personnel and operational data, combined with its new role in voter lists, pointed toward a future in which a single executive-controlled node could see and sort much of the federal state. Civil society groups sued to stop the dismantling of the Department of Education, and faculty and unions sued over the cutting of $400 million in public health research funding at Columbia University, using the courts to resist the hollowing out and reorientation of major agencies. House Speaker Mike Johnson floated the idea that Congress could eliminate some federal courts before later downplaying the remark, adding rhetorical pressure on the judiciary's very existence. Each of these moves, whether blocked or not, normalized the idea that agencies, data, and even courts themselves were subject to presidential will.

Public goods and research funding were pulled into the same orbit. The Department of Health and Human Services hired vaccine skeptic David Geier to lead a federal study on immunizations and autism, placing a discredited figure in charge of work that would shape public understanding of vaccine safety. HHS also announced it would retract over $11 billion in COVID-19 funds from state and local public health departments, weakening infrastructure built to manage ongoing and future health crises. The administration froze federal funding for Planned Parenthood and other family-planning organizations pending a diversity, equity, and inclusion review, using administrative scrutiny as leverage over providers' internal policies. It prepared to cut USAID funding for an organization supplying critical vaccines to poor countries, signaling a retreat from global public health support. The net effect was to steer health policy toward ideological and donor-aligned goals.

These choices did more than shift money. They redefined which risks the state would measure and address. Cutting funding for a national database tracking domestic terrorism, hate crimes, and school shootings reduced the capacity to monitor extremist threats at home. The Yemen Data Project reported that more civilians were killed in the first week of Trump's Yemen bombing campaign than in the prior twelve months of U.S.-UK strikes, challenging official narratives about precision and proportionality. Lawsuits like Columbia's, and the broader pattern of health and research cuts, showed how data and inquiry that might embarrass or constrain the administration were being defunded or sidelined. Over time, this reorientation of funding and personnel made it harder for the public to see where harm was occurring and to demand a response. What was not counted could more easily be ignored.

Media and information space came under direct and indirect pressure. Trump called for cutting taxpayer funding to NPR and PBS, labeling them biased, and the administration attempted to terminate funding for Radio Free Europe/Radio Liberty before a federal judge blocked the move. The injunction preserved an independent international broadcaster, but the attempt itself signaled an intent to narrow the information space by starving public and international media. At the same time, Trump attacked 60 Minutes and the New York Times on his social platform, accusing them of fabricating interview content and seeking to discredit investigative reporting. These smears did not change libel law—indeed, the Supreme Court declined to revisit New York Times v. Sullivan in a separate case, preserving strong protections for press criticism of public figures—but they chipped away at public trust in watchdog outlets.

Information control extended to how decisions were made and recorded. Senior officials, including Pete Hegseth, used an encrypted Signal group chat to discuss classified military plans for Yemen strikes, bypassing formal channels and risking unrecorded decision-making on major actions. A watchdog group sued over this practice, seeking to enforce federal records laws and prevent sensitive business from disappearing into encrypted apps. Trump then asked his national security adviser to investigate Signal's security, raising questions about whether the probe was about genuine vulnerabilities or about controlling communications channels that had just been used to leak. Combined with cuts to domestic terrorism data and attempts to centralize agency and voter information under DOGE, these moves pointed toward a government that wanted to know more about its subjects while leaving fewer traces of its own choices.

Rhetoric and enforcement against dissent formed another thread. Florida Attorney General Pam Bondi went on national television to call pro-Palestinian student protesters "domestic terrorists," framing campus dissent as a security threat rather than political expression. She then warned Representative Jasmine Crockett to "tread very carefully" about her comments on Elon Musk, accusing the congresswoman of threatening lives. The warning came not from a pundit but from a top law enforcement official, suggesting that sharp criticism of a powerful figure could be treated as incitement. In the same week, immigration officers targeted Yunseo Chung for deportation because of her protests, and masked agents arrested Rumeysa Ozturk despite a court order. Trump's attacks on major media outlets fit into this pattern, casting critics as dishonest or dangerous.

These moves did not outlaw protest or opposition. Students still marched. Members of Congress still spoke. Journalists still published. But the cost of doing so rose, especially for those without citizenship or institutional power. Universities faced increased pressure to curb activism to avoid legal and immigration repercussions. Noncitizen students had to weigh the risk that a demonstration could trigger detention or deportation. Elected officials had to consider whether criticizing a favored billionaire might draw a public warning from a state attorney general. The line between dissent and danger was redrawn by those who controlled enforcement, not by any change in statute.

Beyond domestic policy, Trump wielded economic and military tools abroad with similar unilateral confidence. He announced a 25 percent tariff on oil and gas trade with countries buying from Venezuela, using U.S. economic power to punish foreign energy choices without clear public deliberation. He followed with a 25 percent tariff on imported cars and car parts from certain countries, reshaping global supply chains by decree. These tariffs affected markets, jobs, and diplomatic relations, but they were framed as simple assertions of national strength. In Yemen, the bombing campaign's surge in civilian casualties, as documented by independent researchers, underscored the human cost of his military assertiveness and the gap between official assurances and on-the-ground reality. Congress and the public had little visibility into the targeting logic or strategic aims.

Some scheduled and ongoing actions promised further tests of these dynamics. The emergency appeal over mass civil service firings awaited Supreme Court response. Lawsuits over DOGE's data access, the dismantling of the Department of Education, Columbia's research funding cuts, and the use of Signal for military planning moved through the courts. Advocacy groups and unions pressed their cases, and judges issued injunctions and rulings that, in some instances, checked executive ambitions. These processes did not halt the administration's agenda, but they kept open channels through which future accountability might still be sought. The legal system remained a site of struggle rather than a settled shield.

In the arc of Trump's second term, Week 10 marked not a break but a deepening. The tools on display—executive orders framed as technical fixes, immigration powers used as political weapons, law turned into a currency for elites, media and data pressured into alignment—were not new. What changed was their reach and coordination. Voter access, citizenship, law, information, and public goods were all pulled a little further into the orbit of personal rule. Rights and procedures remained on paper, but using them demanded more courage and carried greater risk. The erosion of democratic safety did not announce itself with a single event. It accumulated in the ease with which authority advanced and the quiet with which it was absorbed.

CHAPTER 21
WEEK 11: CHAOS AS METHODICAL GOVERNANCE

Emergency economics, bureaucratic purges, and weaponized federal leverage advanced together, deepening structural erosion even as the Democracy Clock barely moved.

The eleventh week of Trump's second term unfolded as a study in saturation. Power was not asserted in one dramatic stroke but through a dense field of moves that reached into trade, bureaucracy, immigration, universities, media, and elections at once. Each action had its own justification—efficiency, security, integrity, patriotism—but together they described a government more willing to rule by decree, to punish dissenting institutions, and to treat law as a flexible tool rather than a binding limit. The pattern was not new. What changed was the confidence with which it was applied and the breadth of systems it now touched.

At the end of Week 10, the Democracy Clock was at 7:56 p.m. It remained at the same time at the end of Week 11, with a net shift of 0.4 minutes further into risk. The face didn't visibly change, but the internal mechanism shifted. The small numerical change reflected how much of the week's damage was structural rather than dramatic: emergency powers became normalized in economic policy, civil service capacity was hollowed out, universities and cities faced discipline through funding, and immigration and security tools were used more openly against vulnerable and dissenting groups. Resistance emerged—in courts, in state attorneys general, in a 25-hour Senate speech—but it was scattered and often reactive, struggling to keep up with the pace and scope of executive action.

The week's most visible assertion of unilateral power came through trade. Trump declared a national emergency and used it to impose a sweeping "reciprocal" tariff regime on imports, including a 25 percent tariff on cars and car parts. The White House framed this as "Liberation Day," a reclaiming of economic sovereignty from unfair foreign practices. In practice, it shifted core taxing and trade powers away from Congress and into the Oval Office, using emergency statutes that were never designed for long-term industrial policy. The tariffs landed not as a targeted tool but as a blunt instrument, applied across most trading partners with only a few notable carve-outs.

Markets reacted immediately. The announcement of the tariff package triggered sharp stock market declines, signaling investor concern about higher input costs, disrupted supply chains, and retaliation abroad. Cleveland-Cliffs, a major steel producer, announced layoffs of more than 600 workers, blaming tariff-driven disruptions in the auto sector. The Federal Reserve, under Jerome Powell, chose not to adjust interest rates in response, signaling a desire to remain an independent stabilizer amid political turbulence. However, it could not offset the basic fact that the executive branch had unilaterally changed the price structure of large parts of the economy.

Design choices within the tariff regime revealed whose interests mattered. Fossil fuel products and, effectively, Russia received exemptions from the broad tariff sweep, even as allies and rivals alike were affected. Commerce Secretary Howard Lutnick and other officials pushed the aggressive tariff stance despite internal economic concerns, while pro-tariff commentators and advisers argued that higher consumer prices were an acceptable cost for "reindustrialization." Public defenses of the policy minimized the impact on households and workers and framed the shock as a necessary correction, even as layoffs and market losses increased. Risk was shifted onto the public, and favored sectors and geopolitical partners were protected.

Institutional responses were tangible but fragmented. The Senate passed a bipartisan resolution condemning tariffs on Canadian products and introduced the Trade Review Act to restore congressional oversight of future tariff decisions. These actions signaled cross-party concern with emergency-based trade policy. However, Congress failed to revoke Trump's authority to impose the new tariffs, maintaining the emergency framework. A small Florida stationery company, Simplified, and its owner, Emily Ley, filed suit to challenge the legality of using emergency powers for broad tariffs, testing whether courts would set a limit. Meanwhile, the administration issued a carefully crafted formula for tariff rates after earlier misstatements about foreign tariffs, adjusting economic data to justify decisions already made. The overall effect was to strengthen presidential control over trade while wrapping it with only partial, after-the-fact oversight.

Beneath the headline tariffs, the administration pursued a quieter yet more far-reaching effort: transforming the federal bureaucracy. At Health and Human Services, Secretary Robert F. Kennedy Jr. announced mass layoffs and restructuring that would cut about a quarter of the workforce, including FOIA staff and public health workers. Bargaining rights were taken away from many remaining employees. The official words focused on efficiency and reform. In reality, this weakened the neutral public health capacity and made the department more responsive to political influence. The resignation of the FDA's top vaccine regulator, Dr. Peter Marks, over conflicts with anti-vaccine leadership highlighted how scientific expertise was being pushed out.

Environmental and climate capabilities faced similar pressures. The Environmental Protection Agency moved to eliminate over 1,100 scientific positions in its research office and tried to cut $14 billion in climate-related grants, even as a judge temporarily blocked some of these cuts. Trump froze clean-energy funding from the Inflation Reduction Act and halted approvals for wind and solar projects on federal lands and waters, slowing the energy transition and favoring existing fossil fuel interests. Meanwhile, the administration ended funding for several counter-terrorism and extremism research programs, reducing the evidence base for understanding domestic threats. These actions did not completely dismantle agencies but weakened them from within.

Foreign aid and social insurance were also pulled into this restructuring. The State Department announced plans to shut down USAID and fold its functions into the department, centralizing foreign assistance under tighter executive control and sidestepping Congress's original design for an independent aid agency. Elon Musk's Department of Government Efficiency, or DOGE, played a central role in driving federal job cuts and structural changes across agencies, despite being an extra-legal, privately anchored entity. DOGE's push for access to federal employee data was exposed and successfully challenged by the ACLU and labor unions, but not before it revealed how far an unelected actor had been allowed into the machinery of personnel decisions.

The Social Security Administration provided a glimpse of both the scope of this project and its limitations. Under DOGE's influence, SSA planned to close field offices and implement new in-person ID requirements that would have significantly increased demand at remaining locations, placing a burden on poor and disabled claimants. After public backlash, SSA reversed the closures and scaled back the rules, but then removed the original closure notices from its website, hiding the policy trail. At the same time, the administration canceled contracts that allowed Maine hospitals to enroll newborns for Social Security numbers and froze federal education funds in the state after a dispute with the governor. Basic administrative procedures became tools of punishment, turning national programs into instruments to discipline a disfavored state.

Leadership decisions reinforced the shift from neutral expertise to loyalty and private influence. Secretary of Defense Pete Hegseth hired his brother into a senior Pentagon advisory role despite anti-nepotism laws, blurring ethical lines in national security staffing. The Senate confirmed Dr. Mehmet Oz, a figure associated with health misinformation, to lead the Centers for Medicare and Medicaid Services, placing a politicized media personality in charge of a core social insurance agency. Cuts at the CDC and a hiring freeze at FEMA, imposed amid ongoing disease outbreaks and severe weather, further weakened the state's ability to protect vulnerable communities. The civil service still existed on paper, but its character was being changed.

Immigration and security tools, meanwhile, were more openly repurposed as instruments of control over dissenters and marginalized groups. The administration used rarely invoked immigration provisions and subjective criteria to deport pro-Palestinian activists and international students from Muslim-majority countries, treating political activity and origin as grounds for removal. A new legal authority, separate from the Alien Enemies Act, was invoked to send migrants to El Salvador, where they faced severe prison conditions. Venezuelans were deported to Salvadoran prisons based on tattoos, clothing, and a secret "Alien Enemies" point system that treated arbitrary symbols as evidence of gang ties. In one case, government attorneys admitted deporting a legally protected Maryland resident but argued that courts could not remedy the violation.

At the border, device searches were used to screen for political views, and travelers were denied entry for messages critical of Trump. The FBI shifted resources away from far-right domestic terrorism toward gangs, border task forces, and even vandalism of Tesla vehicles, focusing less on domestic terror threats and more on property and border enforcement. Inside DHS, the civil rights division was dismantled, removing an internal check on abuses in immigration and security operations. Secretary of Homeland Security Kristi Noem filmed a political video inside a Salvadoran prison holding deported Venezuelans, using incarcerated migrants as a backdrop for deterrence messaging. Detention became not just a policy tool but a public spectacle.

Courts did not stand aside entirely. Federal judges blocked or delayed several administration moves, including cuts to legal services for unaccompanied children in immigration court and the termination of Temporary Protected Status for Venezuelans. In some cases, courts ordered that detained immigrants could not be removed or must be returned, reinforcing that enforcement remained subject to constitutional and statutory limits. Yet these interventions were often narrow and case-specific, arriving after harm had begun. At the same time, CDC and FEMA cuts proceeded, and the broader architecture of deportation and detention grew more arbitrary. The line between security and punishment blurred.

Universities, museums, and local governments found themselves on the receiving end of federal leverage. The administration canceled $400 million in federal funding to Columbia University, citing its handling of pro-Palestinian activity, and then restored the money only after Columbia agreed to new restrictions on protests and external control over a department. Harvard faced a review of $9 billion in grants and contracts over antisemitism claims, and at least 60 other universities were warned that their funding could be at risk. An executive order directed the Smithsonian to remove exhibits deemed "improper" or "anti-American," targeting displays on race, American sculpture, and African American history. Money and content control were used together to reshape how institutions tell the country's story.

State and local institutions were drawn into the same pattern. A Chinese professor at New College of Florida was fired under a "countries of concern" hiring law, blending academic governance with security politics and chilling participation by immigrants in public universities. An executive order ended affirmative action at the U.S. Naval Academy, narrowing pathways for underrepresented groups into future military leadership. In Washington, D.C.,

Congress cut the city's budget by $1 billion in a federal spending bill, and Trump signed an order intensifying federal policing and immigration enforcement in the capital, overriding local preferences. In Maine, as noted, education funds and Social Security newborn contracts were frozen after a legal dispute with the governor. The message to universities and blue jurisdictions was consistent. Autonomy was contingent on alignment.

Courts sometimes amplified this weaponization. The Supreme Court stayed lower-court orders and allowed the administration to freeze diversity-focused teacher-training grants, including Teacher Quality Partnership and SEED programs, pending appeal. The Department of Education moved to terminate these grants, shifting education policy away from federally supported training and equity efforts. While some judges elsewhere blocked funding cuts or deportations, the high court's decision signaled that executive discretion over equity programs would receive a sympathetic hearing. Cultural and educational institutions that once saw themselves as semi-independent now faced a choice between compliance and financial risk.

Elections and voting rules were another front. The administration advanced an executive order tightening proof-of-citizenship requirements and mail-ballot deadlines nationwide, while House Republicans prepared to vote on the SAVE Act, which imposed strict ID rules and penalties around noncitizen voting. Both were framed as measures to protect election integrity. In practice, they threatened to disenfranchise naturalized citizens and others lacking ready paperwork, especially in communities already facing bureaucratic hurdles. A coalition of 19 Democratic attorneys general sued to block the executive order, asserting state control over election rules and warning of federal overreach.

Judicial decisions added to the pressure. In North Carolina, the Court of Appeals ruled in favor of a Republican candidate in a Supreme Court race, a decision that could discard more than 65,000 ballots, raising the prospect of an election outcome changed by judicially sanctioned disenfranchisement. Against this backdrop, Trump publicly mused about possible methods to obtain a third presidential term, floating workarounds to the Twenty-Second Amendment and testing elite and public tolerance for term-limit erosion. He also unilaterally delayed enforcement of a law targeting TikTok and other "foreign adversary" applications, asserting broad discretion over when statutory controls on digital speech would apply. The rules of the game—who could vote, whose votes would count, and how digital platforms would be governed—were treated as pliable.

Money and narrative saturated the electoral field. Elon Musk spent more than $20 million to influence the Wisconsin Supreme Court election and backed a million-dollar voter giveaway scheme that the state attorney general challenged as illegal. The administration and its allies promoted narratives about noncitizen voting and third-term possibilities, feeding a disinformation-rich environment. In Congress, House Republican leadership halted floor voting after a rule defeat tied to proxy voting for new parents, turning representation into a stage for internal power struggles. Senate Democrats warned against accounting gimmicks to hide the deficit impact of Trump's $4 trillion tax cuts, defending fiscal transparency even as the broader tax code tilted further toward capital. The legislative branch functioned, but often as performance rather than deliberation.

Media, information, and memory came under tighter control. Trump and the FCC launched investigations into NBC, NPR, and PBS, banned reporters from Associated Press, Reuters, and HuffPost from certain events, and filed a $10 billion defamation suit against CBS. These actions, combined with a separate defamation case involving John Oliver's coverage of Medicaid practices and the quiet removal of a restricted media adjudication item from an FCC agenda, created a hostile environment for independent journalism. Regulatory probes and mega-lawsuits did not shut outlets down. They raised the cost of scrutiny.

At the same time, the administration moved key decisions into darker corners. HHS fired FOIA staff as part of its broader layoffs, reducing capacity to respond to information requests. DOGE and SSA removed online notices about planned field office closures after reversing course, erasing evidence of earlier decisions. National security officials used personal Gmail and encrypted Signal chats for official business, including discussions of an impending strike in Yemen; when a leak from that chat emerged, no punishment was announced. A federal judge ordered participants to preserve their messages, a reminder that records law still applied, but the norm of conducting state business on durable, accessible channels had already been weakened.

Memory of past wrongdoing was also curated. In the New Orleans clergy abuse bankruptcy case, Judge Meredith Grabill removed survivors from a key committee and sealed a Department of Justice investigative report, limiting public understanding of institutional failures and chilling future whistleblowing. The Smithsonian order, combined with funding threats to universities and cuts to arts and humanities grants, signaled a broader effort to decide which histories and narratives would remain visible. Museums, textbooks, and archives were not abolished. They were edited.

National security and law enforcement leadership were reshaped around loyalty and political interference. The White House pressured the Department of Justice to drop a corruption case against New York Mayor Eric Adams, reportedly as part of a bargain over immigration enforcement, leading to resignations inside the DOJ. Trump fired six National Security Council officials after meeting with far-right activist Laura Loomer and removed General Timothy Haugh as head of U.S. Cyber Command and the NSA, reportedly over perceived disloyalty. These purges, combined with the earlier nepotistic Pentagon hire and the sidelining of counter-terrorism research and far-right threat monitoring, shifted security institutions toward regime protection rather than impartial defense.

The pattern extended into clemency and intimidation. Trump granted clemency to Ozy Media co-founder Carlos Watson, erasing a major fraud conviction and financial penalties for a well-connected media figure. State attorneys general formed a coalition urging law firms to resist administration intimidation, after Trump threatened punitive executive orders against firms representing his opponents. House Republicans displayed "Wanted" posters targeting federal judges who had ruled against Trump, escalating pressure on the judiciary. In a separate moment, Representative Victoria Spartz told constituents they were not entitled to due process when raising rule concerns, a small but telling sign of how basic rule-of-law norms were fraying among elected officials.

All of this unfolded within a deliberate atmosphere of churn. The administration's own actions created overlapping crises—tariffs and market shocks, mass layoffs and agency closures, immigration crackdowns and deportations, media wars and cultural fights—such that no single development could hold public attention for long. A composite event in the record described this explicitly: simultaneous shocks across trade, agencies, immigration, and media made it harder for citizens to track and respond to any one policy, diffusing accountability. Chaos was not an accident. It was a method.

Yet the week also recorded pockets of resistance and partial retreats. Public backlash forced SSA to reverse planned field office closures and scale back in person ID rules. The ACLU and unions blocked DOGE's access to federal employee data. Federal courts restored NIH grant funding after the administration acknowledged injunctions and halted some deportations and funding cuts. State attorneys general sued to block the election-overhaul executive order, and a small business challenged the emergency tariff regime. Senator Cory Booker used Senate rules to deliver a 25-hour speech warning of democratic backsliding, turning procedure into a platform for alarm. Bipartisan interest in curbing tariff powers surfaced in the Senate, even if it did not yet translate into binding law.

Even Trump's discretionary delay of the TikTok foreign-adversary applications law underscored how enforcement itself had become another lever of power. By unilaterally pausing a statute aimed at a major platform, the president signaled that digital speech rules would be applied when and how he chose. The law remained on the books. Its force depended on one person's calculation.

In the arc of the term, Week 11 did not bring a single break with the past. It deepened existing grooves. Emergency economics, civil service hollowing, weaponized federal leverage, targeted immigration enforcement, and curated memory all advanced together, with only partial and uneven checks. Rights and procedures still existed, and institutions continued to push back. But using them now demanded more persistence, more resources, and greater personal risk. The erosion of democracy in this period lay not in the absence of formal structures, but in the growing gap between what those structures promised and what they could reliably deliver.

CHAPTER 22
WEEK 12: EMERGENCY POWERS AS ROUTINE GOVERNANCE

> *Tariffs, deportations, and funding threats fused into a single method of rule, tightening executive control while leaving formal institutions visibly intact.*

The twelfth week of Trump's second term did not hinge on a single shock. It unfolded as a dense layering of moves that, taken together, made the state feel less like a shared instrument and more like a set of levers in one man's hands. Economic policy, immigration enforcement, education funding, and even the national story about history and faith were all pulled into a common pattern. Power was centralized, dissent was made costly, and the line between public duty and personal or factional interest grew thinner.

At the close of Week 11, the Democracy Clock stood at 7:56 p.m. It ended Week 12 at the same public time, with a net movement of 0.4 minutes deeper into danger. The face of the clock did not change, but its mechanism did. The week's small numerical shift captured a broad consolidation rather than a rupture: emergency tariff powers used as a personal economic weapon, immigration law stretched into a mass-deportation machine, universities and law firms disciplined through money and law, and information about climate, race, and foreign influence selectively withheld or rewritten. Institutions still acted, sometimes with courage, yet more often they were bent, bypassed, or absorbed. That is how a system shifts without a single headline break.

The most visible expression of this consolidation came through tariffs. Early in the week, Trump invoked the International Emergency Economic Powers Act to impose sweeping global tariffs, treating a Cold War statute as a standing license to reorder trade without Congress. New duties on China and dozens of other countries were announced, raised, and recombined in rapid succession, with effective rates on some Chinese imports climbing into triple digits. What would once have been the product of long negotiation and legislative debate now arrived as a series of presidential declarations framed as "Liberation Day" for American industry. Trade policy became a personal lever.

Markets and analysts reacted in real time. Major banks raised their estimates of recession risk, citing tariff shocks as the central driver. Indices swung sharply as investors tried to price in the new costs and the uncertainty around what might come next. Unusual trading patterns around tariff announcements prompted calls for insider-trading investigations, suggesting that those closest to power could profit from volatility that ordinary workers and consumers would simply have to endure. Tesla's decision to halt orders for certain models in China showed how quickly export-dependent firms could be squeezed by reciprocal measures abroad. The pain spread fast.

Foreign governments did not wait. China, the European Union, Canada, and others announced retaliatory tariffs and countermeasures, deepening the trade war and threatening sectors far from the original targets. Yet corporate America, which might once have been a loud brake on such policy, remained largely silent. Reporting suggested that major firms feared regulatory retaliation if they spoke out, a silence that itself marked a shift in the balance between private economic power and the presidency. The White House, meanwhile, insisted that iPhones would soon be made in the United States, despite industry skepticism, and used press events to misstate historical economic policy and sell the tariff campaign as a patriotic correction. The message was loyalty, not candor.

As the damage mounted, the president abruptly announced a 90-day pause on parts of the plan. The partial retreat did not come with a clear explanation or a new framework. It underscored instead how personalized and unpredictable economic governance had become: a single decision could crash markets, and another could ease them, with little input from the institutions that traditionally manage tax and trade. Congress and the courts tried to reassert themselves. Senators from both parties introduced bills to reclaim tariff authority and require legislative approval for future measures. A civil-liberties group sued, arguing that emergency economic powers could not stand in for Congress's taxing role. Yet House leaders aligned with the president used procedural rules to block a floor vote on disapproving the tariff emergency, turning the lower chamber into a stage for partisan performance rather than a forum for checking executive overreach.

The tariff story was also an information story. The White House refused to release the list of seventy-five countries it claimed were seeking trade deals, making it impossible for the public to verify the president's boasts. Trump reposted a fabricated video suggesting that Warren Buffett endorsed his market-crashing strategy, injecting disinformation into the official economic narrative. In this way, emergency economic rule, opacity, and falsehood reinforced one another. The more policy was made by decree, the easier it became to surround it with unverifiable claims.

If tariffs showed how economic power could be centralized, immigration enforcement showed how state coercion could be widened and deepened. Across multiple agencies, the week marked a shift from targeted enforcement to a system that treated status as contingent and revocable, even for those who had followed the rules. Immigration and Customs Enforcement expanded arrests and detention of people with Temporary

Protected Status, asylum seekers, and migrants who had dutifully appeared for check-ins. The message was clear. Compliance no longer guaranteed safety.

Legal tools were stretched to fit this posture. The administration leaned on the Alien Enemies Act, an eighteenth-century wartime statute, to deport Venezuelan migrants, often on the basis of tattoos or thin gang allegations. Visas and legal status for South Sudanese nationals and CBP One parolees were revoked en masse, turning lawful presence into a privilege that could be withdrawn by policy memo. Social Security numbers for some immigrants with temporary status were canceled, pushing them out of the workforce and toward "self-deportation" without formal hearings. Rights on paper became fragile in practice.

Data and bureaucracy became central instruments of this regime. The IRS agreed to share undocumented taxpayers' confidential records with DHS for enforcement, prompting resignations from agency leaders who saw the move as a breach of legal and ethical lines. ICE and Palantir-linked systems used large databases to identify immigrants for deportation based on physical and financial attributes, while DHS announced social-media surveillance of visa holders and applicants for "antisemitism." A new efficiency office inside the White House, the Department of Government Efficiency, was drawn into deportation data work, further entwining technocratic tools with political priorities. The machinery of the state turned inward on the people it tracked.

The human cost of this system surfaced in scattered cases. A British tourist and an Australian worker were wrongfully detained or deported despite valid status. Erroneous removal notices went out to U.S. citizens and lawful residents, exposing systemic flaws that could upend lives with a letter. Border Patrol custody saw a suicide and medical neglect of a detained student, underscoring how detention conditions could endanger health and life. Immigration agents attempted to enter Los Angeles elementary schools to locate young students, only to be rebuffed by administrators, a scene that captured how enforcement was pressing into spaces once considered off-limits. Fear spread beyond those directly targeted.

At the same time, the infrastructure of deportation was being privatized and expanded. The administration contracted a low-cost carrier to operate deportation flights and committed tens of billions of dollars to new, lower-standard private detention facilities. Coercive state power—arrest, confinement, expulsion—was thus increasingly exercised through for-profit entities with limited transparency. While federal courts issued injunctions that temporarily preserved some protections, such as a major parole program for Cubans, Haitians, Nicaraguans, and Venezuelans, the overall direction was toward a data-driven, error-prone system in which rights varied sharply by origin and perceived loyalty. Citizenship itself became stratified.

The courts themselves occupied an uneasy middle ground between resistance and accommodation. On one track, the Supreme Court issued emergency orders that allowed deportations under the Alien Enemies Act to proceed, narrowing collective legal remedies and pushing challenges into more executive-friendly venues. In another case, the Court stayed and later overturned lower-court rulings that would have required rehiring sixteen thousand purged federal probationary workers, enabling the administration's mass dismissals to stand and weakening the independence of the civil service. Deference to executive claims carried real institutional cost.

Yet in the case of Kilmar Abrego Garcia, a lawful resident wrongfully deported to El Salvador, the judiciary asserted its authority. A district judge declared his removal unlawful and ordered his return. The Supreme Court then spoke with unusual clarity, issuing a unanimous directive that the government facilitate his return. The administration's response was halting. It delayed, withheld information, and failed to comply promptly, raising a stark question: what happens when even a 9–0 Supreme Court order cannot secure swift obedience from the executive branch?

Other rulings showed similar tension. Federal courts blocked or limited executive orders targeting law firms that represented political rivals, preserving their ability to practice and signaling that legal advocacy could not be punished so easily. An appeals court reinstated members of independent boards like the Merit Systems Protection Board and the National Labor Relations Board, reaffirming statutory limits on presidential removal. A judge halted efforts to terminate a humanitarian parole program, and another allowed the Exonerated Five's defamation suit against Trump to proceed, underscoring that even presidents could face civil accountability for their words. At the same time, internal discipline within DOJ fell on lawyers who admitted wrongful deportations, and a senior White House aide smeared a judge as a "Marxist" for enforcing immigration law, sending a clear signal that candor and independence carried professional risk.

Beyond the courts, the administration turned its attention to institutions that produce knowledge and organize dissent. Columbia University was threatened with the loss of hundreds of millions of dollars in federal funding over its protest and security policies, a threat later withdrawn but not forgotten. Cornell, Northwestern, and other universities saw large research and program grants frozen or canceled over diversity initiatives and campus protests. Hundreds of international students and activists had their visas revoked or were arrested, using immigration status as a lever against campus speech. Student journalists covering Palestine-related issues faced pressure that led to takedowns and self-censorship. The campus became a test site for controlled debate.

Law firms and lawyers were drawn into the same orbit. Executive orders targeted firms that represented political adversaries, restricting their access and clearances. The administration sent letters attacking diversity-oriented hiring and secured agreements from firms to drop race-conscious practices. Immigration attorneys and other advocates were pressured over their client choices, with some firms steered into pro bono work aligned with administration priorities. Courts intervened at points, blocking some of the most direct attacks on firms and upholding the right of the Associated

Press to attend presidential events after the White House tried to condition access on adopting the term "Gulf of America." But the pattern was clear. Access to money, clients, and platforms was increasingly tied to political compliance.

Nonprofits and advocacy groups were not spared. Climate organizations, civil-rights groups, and other NGOs faced investigations and defunding when their work cut against the administration's agenda. Cultural institutions saw their budgets threatened, prompting lawsuits from library and museum workers who argued that cuts would harm public access to knowledge. Even a children's entertainer became the subject of a push for foreign-agent investigation over Gaza-related posts, illustrating how legal tools could be used to intimidate expressive activity online. Against this backdrop, civil society still moved: mass "Hands Off" protests against the Trump–Musk agenda drew crowds in hundreds of locations, Medicaid and SNAP recipients marched on Capitol Hill to oppose safety-net cuts, and labor leaders warned that the effective nullification of union contracts for 700,000 workers was an attack on workplace democracy.

While these pressures mounted, Trump worked to reshape the symbolic and structural foundations of executive power. He publicly speculated about serving a third term, normalizing talk that would once have been unthinkable under the two-term limit. On the southern border, he authorized the military to take control of public lands and created a buffer zone in which active-duty soldiers could detain migrants on U.S. soil, blurring the line between civilian law enforcement and military power. In Washington, he announced plans for a large military parade centered on himself and proposed a record Pentagon budget, even as domestic agencies faced cuts. Spectacle and force moved to the foreground.

Inside the Pentagon and the defense industrial base, executive orders restructured procurement, foreign sales, and maritime policy, centralizing decisions that had long been subject to more diffuse oversight. The Senate confirmed a less-qualified chair of the Joint Chiefs of Staff after waiving usual requirements, raising concerns that loyalty was displacing professional criteria at the top of the military. At the same time, the White House created a faith office and a task force to eradicate "anti-Christian bias," directing the State Department to catalog such bias under the prior administration. These moves gave one religious constituency privileged access to federal power and framed policy disputes through a lens of religious grievance.

The administrative state that might have balanced these forces was itself being hollowed out and repurposed. The Department of Government Efficiency, closely tied to Elon Musk, drove restructuring that cut staff at agencies like the Social Security Administration and steered contracts toward Musk-linked firms. A plan to restrict phone claims at SSA, later abandoned amid warnings of a "death spiral," showed how administrative tweaks could ration access to core benefits. The federal student loan program was moved from the Department of Education to the Small Business Administration, reframing higher education finance as a business product and straining an agency ill-equipped for the task. Public service was recast as a set of transactions.

Regulatory and enforcement capacity eroded in parallel. Budgets at the Food and Drug Administration and other health and safety agencies were cut, weakening oversight of food and drugs. The Justice Department disbanded its National Cryptocurrency Enforcement Team, relaxing scrutiny of a sector prone to abuse. Scientific research grants in areas labeled "woke"—AIDS, trans issues, climate—were slashed, politicizing the questions that could be studied with federal support. Targeted cuts to Maine's corrections programs over the housing of a trans woman in a women's prison used fiscal levers to enforce ideological positions on incarceration and gender.

Privatization extended beyond deportation flights and detention centers. Public goods and coercive functions alike were increasingly delivered through contracts with firms that operated under weaker transparency and accountability rules. Within the Federal Election Commission, senior positions were designated as policy-making or confidential under a Trump executive order, reshaping which roles were insulated from turnover and how election-oversight staff could be managed. A Republican budget framework in the House paved the way for large tax cuts and deep future spending reductions, locking in fiscal choices that would constrain social programs and, with them, the material basis for equal participation.

Some in Congress tried to push back on the most blatant conflicts. A senator introduced a bill to bar contracts to companies owned by special government employees like Musk, targeting self-dealing in procurement. Another released a report on weakened enforcement of the Foreign Agents Registration Act and proposed a Sovereign Wealth Fund Transparency Act, highlighting gaps in guarding policy from foreign money. Yet the Attorney General moved in the opposite direction, limiting FARA prosecutions and thereby reducing pressure on foreign influence operations aligned with the administration. High-dollar fundraising dinners with domestic and Saudi donors during the tariff-driven market turmoil underscored how access to the president and policy influence remained closely tied to wealth.

Voting rights and election legitimacy came under renewed strain. The House passed the Safeguard American Voter Eligibility Act, requiring documentary proof of citizenship—passports, birth certificates—to register or vote and threatening officials with penalties for non-compliance. In practice, such rules risked disenfranchising millions of eligible voters who lacked ready access to these documents, especially among marginalized communities. In North Carolina, courts ordered recounts and ID verification for tens of thousands of ballots in a state supreme court race, then demanded that overseas and military voters prove eligibility after casting their ballots, raising the prospect of discarding lawful votes under shifting post-election standards.

These measures were justified by a familiar narrative. Trump renewed baseless claims that the 2020 election had been rigged and demanded restrictive voting rules, including paper-only, same-day voting and strict citizenship proof. Data and algorithms used by DHS and Palantir-linked systems to identify immigrants for deportation were also deployed in voter-fraud checks, further entwining enforcement and electoral administration. At the same time, some electoral machinery still functioned: Wisconsin certified a state supreme court election in which a Trump- and Musk-backed candidate lost decisively despite heavy spending, and the Election Assistance Commission renewed advisory committees on voting systems and best practices. These pockets of normalcy, however, existed within a broader trend toward making the franchise more contingent and bureaucratized.

Control over information and memory formed the backdrop to all of this. An executive order directed the Smithsonian and other research entities to purge "improper" or "anti-American" ideology from their content, turning national museums into potential vehicles for state-approved narratives. The Pentagon ordered a "digital content refresh" to remove diversity, race, and LGBTQ-related terms from its platforms. The National Park Service edited an Underground Railroad webpage to remove Harriet Tubman and slavery references, then partially restored them under scrutiny, a small episode that nonetheless revealed active federal shaping of how racial history is told.

Scientific knowledge was targeted as well. Funding for the U.S. Global Change Research Program and the national climate assessment was terminated, curtailing the production of authoritative climate data. Grants for research on AIDS, trans issues, and climate were cut under the banner of fighting "woke" science. At the state level, the Mississippi Library Commission deleted race relations and gender studies databases from public access, aligning library content with anti-DEI laws and narrowing the range of perspectives available in schools and libraries. These moves did not ban inquiry outright. They made it harder, costlier, and less visible.

Transparency about power and influence eroded in parallel. The White House's refusal to release its claimed list of trade-partner countries, the scaling back of FARA enforcement, and sanctions on cooperation with the International Criminal Court all reduced the flow of information about foreign influence and war-crimes investigations. Press access was conditioned on adopting executive rebranding of geographic terms, and only a court order restored the Associated Press's place in the briefing room. Corporations, wary of retaliation, stayed quiet about tariffs that harmed their own interests. In this environment, data and algorithms were used not to illuminate public choices but to target individuals for enforcement and to justify policies whose full contours the public could not see.

Law and security tools sat at the center of this landscape. Trump ordered DOJ to investigate former officials Miles Taylor and Chris Krebs and to strip their clearances, a direct use of prosecutorial and security powers to punish internal critics. In a televised Oval Office event, he signed executive orders aimed at political opponents, turning the act of punishment into spectacle. The administration sought to reimburse pardoned January 6 defendants for restitution payments, further insulating them from consequences for attacking democratic institutions. At the same time, it limited enforcement of foreign-influence laws and sanctioned International Criminal Court collaborators, shielding some forms of elite wrongdoing while targeting those who pursued accountability.

Internal and external checks persisted, but in narrowed form. Courts blocked some executive orders against law firms, restored AP access, and allowed high-profile civil suits to proceed. Congress held hearings on judicial power and summoned the vaccine-skeptical health secretary to account for a deadly measles outbreak, exercising oversight over public health leadership and misinformation. Senate investigators documented weakened FARA enforcement even as the Attorney General moved to limit it further. These actions showed that institutional muscle remained, but they also revealed how much effort was now required to secure what had once been routine.

No single development in Week 12 transformed the system. The clock's face did not jump. Instead, the week deepened an existing pattern: emergency powers used as normal tools, law bent toward friends and against foes, universities and agencies steered by threat and reward, and the informational ground under citizens' feet made less stable. Resistance appeared—in courtrooms, on campuses, in the streets—but it was reactive, often confined to individual cases or narrow domains. The structure of power continued to tilt toward a presidency that governs by decree, backed by a security and information apparatus increasingly aligned with its interests.

In that sense, the week marked not a turning but a settling. The methods of the early term—tariff shocks, immigration crackdowns, funding threats, narrative control—were applied with greater confidence and less visible hesitation. Rights and procedures remained on paper, but invoking them demanded more courage and carried higher cost. Democratic safety eroded not through open rupture, but through the steady normalization of what had once been extraordinary.

CHAPTER 23
WEEK 13: LOYALTY AS DAILY GOVERNANCE

In Trump's thirteenth week, deportation, civil rights law, and information itself were methodically repurposed to reward loyalty and raise the cost of dissent.

The thirteenth week of Trump's second term didn't rely on a single order or speech. Instead, its shape came from how power was exercised across many fronts at once: in courts and prisons, on campuses and trading floors, inside agencies and newsrooms. What connected these actions wasn't noise but method. Law, money, and information were directed toward the same goal—making loyalty safer than dissent and turning the costs of resistance into a quiet, everyday reality.

At the end of Week 12, the Democracy Clock was at 7:56 p.m. By the end of Week 13, it read 7:57 p.m., a net change of 0.2 minutes. The move was small in size but significant in meaning. It reflected not a coup or a single disruption, but the gathering of choices that made executive orders harder to challenge, deportations harder to undo, and elections easier to sway while still appearing lawful. Courts, states, and civil society responded visibly. Yet, the week's balance of power shifted further toward an executive willing to see law as a tool rather than a limit.

The clearest test of whether courts still constrained the presidency was seen in the fate of Kilmar Ábrego García and others detained under the Alien Enemies Act. The administration had already admitted that Ábrego's deportation to El Salvador was wrongful but still left him in a large foreign prison designed for mass detention. Meanwhile, it used the Alien Enemies Act to deport Venezuelan migrants to the same facility, often without proof of a specific threat. In this scheme, deportation was not just removal from U.S. territory; it was a transfer into a harsher, more hidden system where American law was supposed to fade.

The Supreme Court's response was remarkably clear. In a 9–0 decision, it ordered the government to facilitate Ábrego's return, emphasizing that a wrongful deportation does not exempt it from U.S. law. Lower courts issued fact-finding orders, sworn declarations, and set deadlines. A district judge demanded explanations for the lack of compliance and initiated discovery to determine who made which decisions. Meanwhile, another judge found probable cause for criminal contempt against officials who had ignored an injunction related to Alien Enemies Act deportations, indicating that such defiance could lead to personal legal risks.

The administration responded not with compliance but with delay and misdirection. Public messaging misrepresented the Supreme Court's ruling as a victory, even as officials failed to act. The deportation agreement with El Salvador, which governed the very prisons where Ábrego and others were held, was classified, shielding its terms from Congress, courts, and the public. When contempt findings loomed, the government hurried to file emergency motions to block proceedings, claiming that foreign-affairs powers protected its choices. The legal fight shifted from one man's return to whether the executive could place its detention decisions beyond meaningful review.

Behind the litigation, the White House directly coordinated with President Nayib Bukele. Reports from that week showed the two leaders discussing not only keeping Ábrego in El Salvador despite court orders but also the possibility of sending U.S. citizens labeled "homegrown criminals" to the same mega-prisons. That conversation crossed a line. It treated a unanimous Supreme Court ruling as a political input rather than a binding command and regarded the liberty of residents and citizens as bargaining chips for executives. The contempt findings, emergency motions, and the edited New York Times front page that removed the word "wrongly" from Ábrego's description all pointed in the same direction. Court orders would be ignored, spun, and, where possible, evaded.

The same logic—treating law as a weapon rather than a limit—pervaded the administration's use of immigration and citizenship tools against dissenters, students, and even citizens. In Louisiana, an immigration judge ordered Mahmoud Khalil deported based on his political views and associations, relying on a memo rather than criminal conduct. On campuses, Palestinian and other scholars and students saw visas revoked, bail denied, and status stripped in response to activism or speech. More than 1,300 international students lost legal status en masse, with litigation left to determine whether any individualized process was required. The pattern was clear.

Errors and overreach did not stop at noncitizens. A U.S.-born man was detained under a state immigration law, and a citizen lawyer received an erroneous notice ordering him to leave the country. At the border, Customs and Border Protection officers stopped and searched the phone of a lawyer representing a pro-Palestinian protester, blurring the line between security checks and surveillance of legal advocacy. At the policy level, the administration froze an automated Social Security number program for noncitizens, forcing in-person visits that strained field offices and made lawful work harder to start.

New scrutiny tools extended beyond physical borders. The State Department announced social-media vetting for visa applicants who had visited Gaza, effectively linking entry to a review of online speech and associations. Meanwhile, federal courts heard challenges to mass visa revocations and expedited deportations to third countries without fear screenings, while the Supreme Court agreed to hear arguments on Trump's birthright-citizenship executive order. The legal battleground expanded, but the pattern remained consistent. Lawful presence, and even the meaning of citizenship itself, were being made dependent on ideology, origin, or perceived alignment with the regime.

Civil rights enforcement, once designed to protect those most at risk of discrimination, was turned inward and upside down. The president signed an executive order eliminating disparate-impact liability across federal civil rights enforcement, instructing agencies to deprioritize cases where policies had discriminatory effects without explicit intent. That single move hollowed out decades of doctrine that had allowed plaintiffs to challenge systemic racism in housing, education, and employment. It did not repeal statutes on paper. It removed the main way those statutes had been made real.

At the same time, the administration targeted transgender people through both law and leverage. A nationwide executive order barred transgender women from women's sports, while the Justice Department sued Maine and threatened to cut education funds unless the state banned transgender girls from girls' teams. Federal litigation over Title IX interpretation placed courts at the center of defining sex discrimination, but the immediate signal from Washington was blunt. Access to federal money would depend on excluding a vulnerable minority from full participation in school life.

The leadership and mission of the Justice Department's Civil Rights Division shifted to match this new landscape. Under Harmeet Dhillon, the division rewrote its mission statements to emphasize voter fraud and the protection of white people from discrimination, while downplaying traditional priorities like enforcing the Voting Rights Act and guarding marginalized communities. In parallel, the administration froze Title X family-planning funds, proposed deep cuts to health agencies, and moved to terminate Head Start funding, steps that would fall hardest on low-income and minority communities. Civil rights groups sued over anti-DEI policies and book bans in Pentagon schools, but they were now litigating against a federal apparatus that had been repurposed to police them rather than protect them.

Voting rules and election administration were reshaped under the banner of integrity. From the White House, an executive order required documentary proof of citizenship to vote, a standard that many eligible voters—especially naturalized citizens, students, and low-income residents—would struggle to meet. In Congress, the House passed the Save Act, which demanded similar proof to register and curtailed mail and online registration. Republican-controlled state legislatures introduced matching bills, building a coordinated framework that would narrow the electorate while claiming to guard against fraud.

Courts and election authorities in North Carolina showed how these rules could play out in practice. In a close state supreme court race, hundreds of ballots were invalidated based on residency challenges backed by the losing candidate. Subsequent moves sought to restore some of those votes, but appellate courts also endorsed broad eligibility challenges after the fact. The message was that election outcomes could be contested not only at the ballot box but through legal maneuvers aimed at disqualifying voters. Against this backdrop, the Civil Rights Division's new focus on voter fraud and white discrimination claims meant that federal enforcement would likely reinforce, rather than restrain, these trends. The Federal Election Commission's routine setting of dates and reporting rules for a Texas special election offered a glimpse of normal, neutral administration. It sat in the shadow of a much larger shift.

Universities, long seen as semi-autonomous spaces for research and debate, faced direct financial and regulatory pressure. The clearest example was Harvard. After the university refused to comply with federal demands on governance, speech, and hiring, the administration froze $2.3 billion in federal funding, including research grants. DHS cut security-related grants and demanded detailed records on international students, while threatening the school's authority to certify visas. Harvard's leaders publicly rejected these conditions, defending academic freedom and institutional independence, but did so while core funding and student status remained at risk.

The pressure extended beyond one campus. The administration revoked visas and legal status for over 1,300 international students across multiple institutions, often linked to activism or perceived political risks. The freeze on the Social Security Enumeration Beyond Entry program forced noncitizens to make in-person visits to obtain basic documentation, complicating academic and professional pursuits. In military and Pentagon-run schools, hundreds of books on slavery, civil rights, and the Holocaust were removed under anti-DEI directives, even as extremist texts remained available. Civil rights groups sued over these bans, arguing that they deprived students of access to essential history. The stakes for academic freedom were no longer just theoretical.

Transparency and data around universities and public programs were also curtailed. The administration removed a public tracker of federal spending and climate and environmental justice webpages, prompting lawsuits from advocacy groups seeking to restore statutory transparency tools. These deletions made it harder for universities, researchers, and communities to see how money and environmental burdens were distributed. Taken together, funding freezes, visa threats, book bans, and data removals signaled that higher education and knowledge production would be tolerated only when aligned with the regime's narratives.

Economic policy and regulatory structure moved further toward crony capitalism and agency capture. The week opened with sweeping tariffs—universal and country-specific—announced and then partially paused in rapid succession. The administration ended the de minimis rule for low-value Chinese imports, imposed a 21 percent tariff on Mexican tomatoes, and triggered capital flight and market turmoil. China retaliated by halting exports of key rare earths and Boeing aircraft purchases, exposing U.S. dependence on foreign inputs and jobs. California sued, arguing that the president was using emergency trade powers to bypass Congress, but in the meantime, businesses and workers bore the cost of policy whiplash.

Inside the regulatory state, key watchdogs were hollowed out or redirected. Executive orders rolled back National Environmental Policy Act procedures, making it easier to push through major projects without full review. The Justice Department terminated an environmental justice settlement in Lowndes County, Alabama, leaving a poor, majority-Black community without federal oversight of sewage and health protections. Crypto enforcement was effectively shut down as the administration deregulated the sector and disbanded a DOJ task force, even as Trump family investments in cryptocurrency expanded. At the Consumer Financial Protection Bureau, plans were set in motion to fire nearly 90 percent of staff after a court allowed downsizing, threatening the agency's capacity to police abusive financial practices. Later judicial intervention would pause some of these moves, but the intent was clear.

Direct financial entanglement between policy and private gain became more visible. Trump Media and Technology Group launched investment accounts designed to profit from the president's policy agenda, including tariff decisions, turning public choices into a revenue stream for his company. The administration urged the SEC to investigate a hedge fund's short position in Trump Media stock, risking politicization of securities oversight. Donors with tax problems retired the campaign debt of Billy Long shortly after his nomination to lead the IRS, raising questions about whether regulatory appointments were being shaped by those seeking favorable treatment. Proposed cuts to the State Department and health budgets, the cancellation of labor rights grants, and the planned termination of Head Start funding all shifted resources away from public goods and toward a landscape where concentrated private power faced fewer constraints. Federal Reserve Chair Jerome Powell's refusal to cut interest rates despite presidential pressure, and court blocks on some CFPB layoffs, showed that some guardrails still held. They did so against a rising tide.

Beneath these headline policies, the civil service and security apparatus were reshaped to serve presidential directives more directly. A new at-will category was created for roughly 50,000 federal workers, who could now be fired for vague offenses like "subversion of presidential directives." This change did not abolish agencies. It altered the incentives of those who staffed them, making career officials think twice before slowing or questioning orders. Across DHS and other departments, polygraph tests were deployed to hunt for leakers, reinforcing a climate of internal surveillance that discouraged whistleblowing and honest dissent.

Security tools were used against critics and truth-tellers. The administration stripped former officials Christopher Krebs and Miles Taylor of security clearances, both of whom were public critics of the president, and ordered investigations into them. At the Justice Department, the lawyer who had admitted in court that Ábrego's deportation was wrongful was fired, sending a message that honesty about government mistakes could end a career. The Department of Government Efficiency, led by Elon Musk, tried to embed staff inside a justice-reform nonprofit that received federal funds, blurring the line between oversight and political monitoring of civil society. On the southern border, the president authorized the U.S. military to control federal land for immigration enforcement and detention, further militarizing an area where migrants and border communities already faced increased coercive power. Routine rulemakings and data collections continued in the background, but the framework around them was being restructured to prioritize loyalty over neutral administration.

Information, media, and public memory were managed with increasing boldness. The White House blocked Associated Press journalists from accessing the Oval Office despite a court order, directly defying judicial protection of press freedom. The president called for CBS to lose its broadcasting license and urged the FCC to punish the network over critical reporting. Official communications attacked NPR and PBS as radical propaganda and grifts, framing public broadcasters as illegitimate. Behind the scenes, allies and regulators were used to pressure CNN and other outlets, with reports of offers to avoid lawsuits in exchange for favorable coverage.

At the same time, the transparency infrastructure was dismantled. The administration removed a congressionally mandated federal spending tracker and key climate and environmental justice webpages, prompting lawsuits from groups like Protect Democracy and the Center for Biological Diversity. These sites had allowed the public and Congress to see where money flowed and where pollution and climate risks fell. Their removal did not just hide data. It narrowed the range of questions that could be asked and answered about government choices. The State Department closed its Counter Foreign Information Manipulation and Interference office, eliminating the last dedicated hub for tracking foreign disinformation campaigns even as domestic disinformation grew.

Official narratives were rewritten at the source. Covid.gov, once a public health portal, was replaced with a site promoting the lab-leak theory and attacking scientific institutions, turning a government resource into a vehicle for a contested origin story and institutional distrust. The White House social media team posted an edited New York Times front page about Ábrego's case, removing the word "wrongly" and adding "who is never coming back," directly contradicting the Supreme Court's ruling. Book bans and content restrictions in Pentagon schools and a Texas school district removed works on slavery, civil rights, and the Holocaust, and even banned the Virginia state flag and seal from an online platform over nudity concerns. Civil rights lawsuits challenged these moves, but the cumulative effect was clear. The state was curating what citizens could see, study, and remember, while closing the office meant to guard against foreign manipulation of the same information space.

Across these developments, the moral floor of governance sagged further. Character and restraint were strained by retaliatory funding cuts to universities, the targeting of critics through clearances and deportation tools, and the willingness to defy unanimous court orders. Ethics blurred as tariffs, deregulation, and agency decisions aligned with insider financial stakes. Truthfulness eroded under misrepresentations of Supreme Court rulings, economic consequences, and public health science. Good faith in democratic rules weakened as immigration and voting systems were used to narrow who counted, and stewardship suffered as oversight mechanisms, archives, and civic education were dismantled or sanitized. Courts, states, universities, and civil society did respond—with lawsuits, refusals, and some successful injunctions—but their actions were largely reactive, arriving after the executive had already moved.

No single case or order defined Week 13. Its significance lay in the way familiar tools were used with greater confidence and less hesitation. Deportation powers became levers for offshoring people beyond the reach of law. Civil rights statutes were left on the books but emptied of their most effective remedies. Voting remained formally open, yet the path to the ballot grew narrower and more contingent on paperwork and status. Agencies continued to issue notices and collect data, even as their missions were bent toward donor and regime interests. Reporters still published, but under threat of license loss, access denial, and regulatory reprisal.

The week's modest movement on the Democracy Clock captured this pattern of deepening erosion without open rupture. Institutions still stood. Elections were still scheduled. Courts still issued orders, some of which bit. Yet using those institutions now required more persistence and carried greater risk, especially for those without wealth, status, or political protection. The distance between formal rights and lived security widened by another small but measurable step.

CHAPTER 24
WEEK 14: UNIVERSITIES AND BORDERS AS LEVERS

A near-still Democracy Clock masks a week in which the White House tightened control over courts, campuses, and civil rights while testing the limits of law.

The fourteenth week of Trump's second term did not hinge on a single order or speech. It unfolded instead as a dense layering of moves that tightened control over institutions, narrowed who could rely on the law, and blurred the line between public power and private interest. The pattern was not new, but its reach widened. Universities, courts, civil-rights frameworks, and the civil service all found themselves pulled into a common orbit: comply, or be punished.

At the start of Week 14, the Democracy Clock stood at 7:57 p.m. It ended the week at the same public time, with a net movement of 0.2 minutes. On the surface, the display did not change. Underneath, the small shift captured a week in which the executive branch pressed harder against legal limits, used money and regulation to discipline opponents, and rewrote rules that once protected the vulnerable. Courts and civil society answered in places, but the balance of power moved further toward a presidency that treats oversight as optional and law as a tool.

The sharpest edge of that clash appeared in immigration. For months, the case of Kilmar Ábrego García, wrongfully deported to El Salvador, had wound its way through the courts. This week, trial and appellate judges, backed by a unanimous Supreme Court, ordered the administration to facilitate his return and examined whether officials should be held in contempt for noncompliance. On paper, the rulings were clear: the executive had violated the law and must repair the harm. In practice, the president signaled he would ignore the Supreme Court's order, turning a single deportation case into a test of whether judicial commands still bind the White House.

Congressional Democrats tried to fill the gap. A delegation traveled to El Salvador, met with García, and spoke publicly about his case and the administration's defiance. Their trip did not change the president's stance, but it showed legislators using oversight travel and media to defend both an individual and the authority of the courts. The scene—members of Congress abroad, urging compliance with a Supreme Court order their own government was resisting—captured how far the separation of powers had drifted from its usual channels.

The same week, the Supreme Court temporarily halted deportations of Venezuelan detainees under the Alien Enemies Act, insisting that removals pause while the legality of this expansive use of an old statute was reviewed. A federal judge in California blocked the administration from withholding funds from sanctuary jurisdictions, rejecting an attempt to coerce local immigration policy through fiscal threats. On the docket, these were routine exercises of judicial review. In context, they were acts of resistance against an executive who had already shown a willingness to treat adverse rulings as suggestions.

On the ground, immigration enforcement grew harsher and less reliable. Border Patrol, ICE, and CBP wrongfully detained multiple U.S. citizens, people who could prove their status but were nonetheless swept into custody. A Milwaukee judge was arrested and charged with obstruction over actions related to an ICE arrest, signaling that local officials who resisted aggressive deportation tactics could themselves become targets. The administration considered, then stepped back from, invoking the Insurrection Act at the southern border, a near-miss that underscored how extraordinary domestic military powers now sit within reach. Together, these episodes described a system in which the law's formal protections remained, but their force depended increasingly on the president's willingness to honor them.

If immigration courts were one front, universities were another. The week opened with the administration cutting and freezing more than $2 billion in federal grants and contracts to Harvard University and threatening its tax-exempt status. The message was blunt: change your governance and response to campus protest, or lose core funding and fiscal privileges. An antisemitism task force layered on conditions, tying restoration of money to measures like mask bans and expanded arrest powers at protests. Security language provided the cover; the effect was to make continued dissent financially and legally costly.

Executive orders followed. One targeted higher-education accreditation, pressing accreditors to treat diversity, equity, and inclusion standards as suspect and to reframe "equity ideology" as a threat to quality. Another bundled foreign-funding transparency requirements with selective support for historically Black colleges and universities, while attacking DEI-linked programs. On their face, these moves spoke the language of accountability and merit. In practice, they inserted federal ideology into the criteria that determine which institutions can grant recognized degrees and receive federal aid.

Universities did not accept this quietly. Harvard and other plaintiffs filed lawsuits challenging the withdrawal of education and relief funds as unlawful, arguing that the executive could not unilaterally rewrite the terms of congressionally appropriated programs. More than 150 college and university presidents signed a joint statement denouncing federal interference in higher education as unprecedented overreach. Their words carried institutional weight, but they were issued under duress: grants frozen, tax status threatened, and students detained.

Immigration tools were woven into this pressure. In Florida, the administration and state officials pushed universities and campus-linked law enforcement into ICE's 287(g) program, effectively turning local officers into federal immigration agents and making international students more vulnerable to deportation over minor infractions. Tufts graduate student Rümeysa Öztürk was detained in harsh conditions without criminal charges, prompting congressional calls for her release and raising fears that immigration custody was being used to intimidate campus activists. Across the country, more than 700 demonstrations organized by the 50501 movement protested deportations and administration policies. Campuses served as both targets of federal leverage and hubs of civic resistance.

Beneath these visible conflicts, the legal framework of civil rights changed. The president signed an executive order removing the liability of disparate impact from federal civil rights enforcement. For decades, disparate impact allowed plaintiffs to challenge policies that disproportionately affected protected groups, even without proof of explicit intent. Its removal limited the tools available to fight systemic discrimination, especially in housing, education, and employment, and indicated a federal government less focused on outcomes and more on formal neutrality.

Simultaneously, Congress and the administration began significantly cutting Medicaid and disability-related services. Republican lawmakers pushed plans to reduce the federal share of Medicaid expansion funding and proposed cutting the program by nearly a third over the next decade. The Department of Health and Human Services, under Robert F. Kennedy Jr., suggested major cuts in disability-related education, research, and support services. Collectively, these actions threatened millions of disabled and low-income individuals with reduced access to care and support, not as an emergency but as a deliberate fiscal decision.

Disability policy became a site of surveillance and austerity. HHS halted autism research related to diversity, equity, inclusion, and accessibility, limiting the questions scientists could explore about disparities and inclusive practices. Simultaneously, the National Institutes of Health started collecting private medical records from multiple databases for an autism study, and HHS planned a large-scale registry to monitor autistic Americans using federal and commercial health records. These actions raised significant privacy concerns for a stigmatized group, implying a future where disabled people would be more closely tracked even as their support systems were cut.

Environmental justice faced a similar setback. The administration ended a civil rights settlement that had required Alabama to address raw sewage pollution in majority-Black Lowndes County, removing a federal tool that had begun to fix longstanding health risks. Officials rebranded the agreement as an "illegal DEI initiative," integrating it into the broader campaign against diversity programs. Residents continued to deal with failing septic systems and exposure to disease; their ongoing struggle was dismissed as ideological excess.

Immigration and detention policies connected these issues. The administration closed two important oversight offices for immigration detention: the Office for Civil Rights and Civil Liberties and the detention ombudsman. These offices had provided channels for complaints about healthcare, abuse, and conditions in facilities where the state holds people forcibly. Their closure removed institutional advocates for detainees and made it harder for Congress, courts, or the public to see inside the system.

On the enforcement side, patterns of wrongful detention continued. Citizens were arrested and held by immigration authorities despite valid proof of their legal status. Indonesian student Aditya Wahyu Harsono saw his visa revoked retroactively over an old misdemeanor and remained in custody despite his family's needs. Palestinian activist Mahmoud Khalil, a lawful resident, was denied permission to attend his child's birth and was ruled eligible for deportation because of his political beliefs, blurring the line between security policies and punishment for speech. Student detentions and visa revocations, including the Florida 287(g) program and the later reversal of a policy that had revoked student visas over minor infractions, showed how quickly legal status could be weaponized and how much effort it took to regain even partial protections.

Identity-based exclusions went beyond immigration. The administration asked the Supreme Court to reinstate a ban on transgender individuals serving in the military, seeking judicial approval for a categorical bar that would label a minority group as unfit for a fundamental public institution. At the Department of Veterans Affairs, a new reporting system encouraged staff to flag perceived anti-Christian bias through a dedicated taskforce, favoring one religious identity within a federal agency and raising the possibility that neutral enforcement of nondiscrimination rules could be replaced by grievance politics. Against this background, a small counter-movement emerged in Colorado, where a new law required counties to provide in-person voting access for eligible people held in jails and detention centers, modestly expanding voting rights for a group often effectively disenfranchised by custody.

Inside the executive branch, the administration's machinery was being reshaped. At the Department of the Interior, Secretary Doug Burgum signed an order consolidating control over personnel and budget under a politically connected assistant secretary with energy ties. This centralization diminished internal checks on public-lands management and raised constitutional questions about appointments and influence. At the State Department, Secretary Marco Rubio announced a broad reorganization with significant staff and bureau cuts, targeting offices focused on democracy, human rights, and global issues. The firing of USAID official Peter Marocco, a figure involved in dismantling the agency, suggested internal factional maneuvering rather than a straightforward effort to restore development capacity.

The administrative infrastructure showed the same pattern. The administration moved to replace the SmartPay government expense card program—a functional, in-house system—with a contract for Ramp, a private firm linked to senior allies. A core payment system for federal operations would now be run through a politically connected company, raising concerns about crony contracting and the privatization of essential government functions. Overseeing much of this, either formally or informally, was the Department of Government Efficiency, led by Elon Musk, which asserted aggressive control over federal employees through weekly reporting requirements and public clashes with Cabinet officials. Allowing a private billionaire to direct staff and pressure agencies blurred the line between public authority and private influence.

Personnel rules were revised to solidify these structural changes. An executive order extended probationary periods and made it easier to remove federal employees, requiring agencies to confirm probationary staff and easing dismissal rules. This theoretically aimed to improve accountability for poor performance. In reality, it boosted executive power over the civil service, making it simpler to dismiss employees who weren't loyal and signaling that job security depended on political loyalty. Policy actions reflected these new shifts. The administration increased coal mining to power data centers while cutting funding for miner health and safety agencies and delaying a silica dust regulation, trading worker protections for energy production. It halted federal dairy quality control programs after staff reductions in food safety divisions, weakening safeguards against contamination and shifting health risks onto consumers. The Department of Education abruptly ended pandemic-related school relief funding and liquidation extensions, risking nearly $3 billion in district support to help fund extensions of 2017 tax cuts. Tariff policies caused layoffs and gloomy outlooks at major companies like Cleveland Cliffs, GM, Volvo, and

Howmet Aerospace, while twelve states sued over the tariffs, claiming they fueled inflation and economic harm. Chinese importers canceled large U.S. pork orders and warned against unfavorable trade deals, highlighting how trade conflicts could target politically sensitive sectors. Treasury officials and the former president touted an expected trade deal with South Korea despite an existing free trade agreement, using symbolic announcements to claim victories that did little to change the core issues.

Emergency reasoning became a default justification for these decisions. The president used a claimed "energy emergency" to push Interior to fast-track fossil fuel and mining permits, reducing permitting times to 28 days and weakening environmental reviews and public input. A separate executive order aimed to "unleash" offshore critical minerals and resources by speeding up seabed development, prioritizing strategic resources and industry interests over environmental protections. On Earth Day, the White House promoted expanding oil, gas, and mineral extraction on federal lands and waters as a form of stewardship, reversing the day's usual meaning. The coal and data center expansion, combined with weaker protections for miners, followed the same pattern: emergency and competitiveness language used to justify long-term environmental and health damages that are hard to reverse. Information about these policies and the state itself became less reliable. DOGE claimed $160 billion in federal spending cuts on its website, but only $12.6 billion could be verified. Official fiscal reporting shifted from transparent accounting to a political tool. These exaggerated savings figures were used in fundraising emails suggesting Americans could get $5,000 rebate checks—promises with no legal basis but used to raise donations and influence voters. The same system that managed internal data now served as a platform for public deception.

The president's relationship with independent information sources continued to worsen. The White House dismissed credible reports that it was searching for a new Secretary of Defense as "fake news," which added to confusion about defense leadership and weakened trust in the media. After the Supreme Court blocked deportations, the president attacked judges on social media, blaming past leaders for current issues and trying to undermine judicial checks. He also called on Rupert Murdoch to fire Fox News's pollster after receiving an unfavorable approval rating, showing a dislike for independent measurements of public opinion and encouraging partisan control over data.

Meanwhile, security protocols inside the Pentagon also broke down. Secretary of Defense Pete Hegseth shared sensitive details about U.S. military strikes in Yemen in private Signal chats with family and associates, bypassing official channels used to handle defense secrets. He had an unsecured "dirty line" installed in his Pentagon office to access blocked websites, sidestepping security protocols in a secure facility. The Pentagon inspector general launched an investigation into his use of Signal and his handling of classified information, trying to see if watchdogs could enforce rules against a senior political appointee. Hegseth responded by publicly threatening criminal charges against former Defense Department employees accused of leaking information, a move that could discourage internal whistleblowing even while his own conduct was being examined.

Media institutions faced direct pressure. The administration shut down Voice of America and related news services, congressionally mandated broadcasters, until a federal judge ordered their restoration, reaffirming that the executive could not unilaterally abolish agencies created and funded by Congress. At the same time, the president issued a memorandum directing the attorney general to investigate ActBlue, a major opposition fundraising platform, for alleged foreign and straw donations. The order was based on disputed factual claims and risked weaponizing federal law enforcement against political rivals, blending legal process with partisan narrative.

Against this backdrop, some institutions still held their ground. A federal judge blocked the president's order adding a proof-of-citizenship requirement to the federal voter registration form, safeguarding congressional control over election rules and preventing a change that could have disenfranchised many eligible voters. Another judge ordered the restoration of Voice of America, as mentioned, reinforcing the separation of powers. A federal jury ruled against Sarah Palin in her retrial against the New York Times, reaffirming the "actual malice" standard and maintaining strong press protections under the First Amendment. Courts also secured a major opioid settlement with Walgreens over unlawful prescription filling, highlighting that some corporate health harms still resulted in significant penalties, even if resolved through civil payments rather than criminal convictions.

In the realm of political accountability, a federal court sentenced former Representative George Santos to prison for fraud and identity theft involving donor funds and personal enrichment. The custodial sentence demonstrated that at least some elite financial crimes face real punishment, modestly countering the broader pattern of impunity. Colorado's jail voting law, the routine regulatory work of agencies like OSHA, the DEA, and the Federal Election Commission, and ongoing updates to technical standards in areas like workplace safety and controlled substance licensing all represented the quieter maintenance of democratic infrastructure. These actions did not reverse the week's broader drift, but they showed that tools for constraint and repair remained available when structure and will aligned.

The week closed without a single dramatic rupture. Its significance lay in how familiar methods were applied with greater confidence and reach. Courts could still issue injunctions, and sometimes they did. Universities could still sue, and they did. Protesters could still march, and they did so in the hundreds of thousands. Yet each of these acts of resistance occurred in an environment where executive power was more centralized, oversight offices were fewer, civil rights doctrines were narrower, and state information was less reliable.

In that sense, Week 14 deepened the erosion rather than marking a new break. Executive defiance of court orders, the use of funding and accreditation to discipline universities, the dismantling of disparate-impact enforcement, and the capture and outsourcing of administrative agencies all pushed the system further from a model in which law limits power and closer to one in which power chooses which laws to follow. The Democracy Clock's near-stillness at 7:57 p.m. captured that paradox: little visible movement in time, and yet a steady, growing loss in what institutions can guarantee to those who depend on them.

CHAPTER 25
WEEK 15: EMERGENCY RULE AS ROUTINE GOVERNANCE

> *In Trump's fifteenth week back in office, emergencies, executive orders, and data systems quietly rewired law, citizenship, and information into tools of regime protection.*

The fifteenth week of Trump's second term didn't depend on a single major event. Instead, it involved a coordinated use of existing tools: emergency declarations, executive orders, budget plans, and internal directives. Each action could be justified as lawful, even standard. Together, they showed a government learning to govern by exception routinely and to use state mechanisms to protect itself.

At the end of Week 14, the Democracy Clock was at 7:57 p.m. By the end of Week 15, it read 7:59 p.m., a movement of 1.9 minutes. This change didn't come from a coup, a canceled election, or a major crisis. Instead, it signaled the normalization of emergency powers, law enforcement targeting allies and enemies, the decline of independent media, and the slow building of a layered social hierarchy. Courts and civil society pushed back at the edges, but the week's power balance shifted further toward an executive that acts first and leaves others to respond.

The clearest sign of that consolidation was the creation of paired national emergencies. Trump declared crises at the southern border and in energy production, using them to expand immigration enforcement and fossil-fuel drilling without needing Congress's approval. The border emergency framed deportation and detention within the context of national security. The "energy emergency" did the same for drilling, coal extensions, and deep-sea mining. Both turned what had been extraordinary powers into tools policymakers could use whenever the White House wanted to act quickly and unilaterally.

Those declarations were not isolated. They built upon a broader overhaul of the government's internal structure. The president reclassified many federal employees into a Schedule F-style category, making it easier to remove them and turning many career roles into de facto political appointments. Job protections that previously shielded analysts, lawyers, and program managers from partisan shifts were weakened. Neutral administration became more dependent on loyalty. Simultaneously, independent agencies like the SEC and FTC were ordered to submit their policy priorities to the White House for approval. The independence that had been established over decades was rolled back under direct presidential oversight.

Into that newly centralized structure, the administration added a new entity: Elon Musk's Department of Government Efficiency. DOGE was expanded to oversee contracts, grants, loans, and payment systems across the government. Its staff embedded at FAA and HUD under nondisclosure agreements, rewriting communications and regulatory processes with the help of AI tools. What used to be public functions—procurement, rule drafting, benefit delivery—were now routed through a quasi-private efficiency office aligned with the president, operating with less transparency than traditional departments.

The same pattern appeared in how entire departments and fiscal tools were managed. Trump issued orders to dismantle the Department of Education, transferring its functions and signaling that a cabinet-level protector of federal education policy could be eliminated by executive order. Another order shifted more disaster relief costs onto states, clearly indicating that aid could be conditioned on policy compliance. Emergencies and appropriations, once shared responsibilities, became tools for discipline. States that opposed policies on immigration, climate, or social issues faced the risk of bearing more of the burden when storms or fires struck.

Congress did not disappear this week, but its role narrowed. Republican leaders promoted a budget framework that enabled deep cuts to social spending to proceed with limited bipartisan debate, aligning the legislature's fiscal stance with the executive's agenda. House Republicans changed rules to block resolutions of inquiry into Defense Secretary Pete Hegseth's use of encrypted messaging, blocking a traditional oversight route. In the Senate, Republican leaders refused to limit unilateral tariff powers, leaving emergency trade authority largely unchanged. There were gestures of resistance—articles of impeachment filed by a Democratic representative, a tariff-repeal bill from a libertarian Republican, marathon speeches warning of authoritarian drift—but these were symbolic. The structural changes in budget procedures, trade authority, and oversight rules persisted.

Within the bureaucracy, the same pattern emerged in staffing and scope. The Justice Department's Civil Rights Division lost about 70 percent of its attorneys following leadership changes and shifts in priorities. Senior managers in the voting section were removed, and active voting rights cases were dropped. At the National Park Service, a workforce reduction aimed to eliminate around 1,500 positions, reducing capacity for conservation and public access. The Agriculture Department withdrew a salmonella safety rule for poultry after industry lobbying. On paper, agencies continued issuing technical rules and collecting data, but their ability to enforce civil rights, environmental, and public health protections was being effectively undermined.

If the first development of the week concerned decision-making authority, the second centered on who belongs. Immigration and citizenship policies hardened into a shape resembling an ethnonational, quasi-militarized regime. The administration used the Alien Enemies Act—an 18th-century wartime law—to detain and deport migrants from Venezuela and other countries under suspicion of security threats. Deportations were carried out through obscure arrangements with third countries like El Salvador, where some deportees vanished or were imprisoned. Plans moved forward to build a large migrant detention center at Guantánamo Bay, placing tens of thousands of people offshore and out of reach of usual courts and oversight.

On the ground, the border took on a military look. A buffer zone along the U.S.–Mexico border was treated as a militarized strip, and migrants crossing it faced prosecution. Civilian law enforcement assumed military-like roles. Meanwhile, ICE used welfare and sponsorship data to target unaccompanied children and their sponsors, turning child-protection systems into enforcement channels. Legal residents and green-card holders with past convictions were detained and scheduled for deportation. Families were separated abruptly, including those with medically fragile children. The message was clear: status could be revoked and presence made uncertain.

Alongside these enforcement actions, the legal notion of citizenship was also reshaped. Trump signed executive orders aiming to end or restrict birthright citizenship for children of certain noncitizens, challenging a century-old interpretation of the Fourteenth Amendment. The refugee resettlement program was halted, with admissions limited to case-by-case "national interest" exceptions. A broad directive ended unspecified federal benefits for undocumented immigrants, threatening access to essential services. English was declared the official language of the United States, and language rules for commercial drivers were tightened, raising obstacles for non-English speakers trying to work and communicate with the government.

These moves faced strong opposition. Federal courts issued rulings blocking or restricting deportations of Venezuelan immigrants under the Alien Enemies Act, ruling that the law could not be stretched to include peacetime mass removals. Judges defended specific individuals like Javier Salazar and Mohsen Mahdawi on grounds of due process and free speech. Appellate courts upheld injunctions limiting DOGE's access to Social Security records, thereby restricting the administration's data-mining efforts. Despite these rulings, Trump publicly criticized "radical-left judges," called for Supreme Court intervention, and allies in Congress even suggested arresting judges. The conflict between an expanding executive branch and a cautious judiciary deepened, even as enforcement on the ground continued.

A third part of the week's story involved the Justice Department and the president's use of clemency. Trump directed the DOJ to investigate ActBlue, a major Democratic fundraising platform, and law firms associated with his critics. Federal law enforcement, which is supposed to operate independently of partisan politics, focused on a political rival's infrastructure and disliked the rival's attorneys. At the same time, the administration paused enforcement of the Foreign Corrupt Practices Act and shut down the DOJ's cryptocurrency unit. Anti-bribery prosecutions and crypto investigations were halted, reducing legal risks for multinational companies and digital-asset firms, many of whom are donors or allies.

Clemency power was used heavily. The president issued pardons and commutations that erased over a billion dollars in fines and restitution owed by white-collar offenders and a cryptocurrency exchange. He also pardoned January 6 defendants and ordered related prosecutions dismissed. Those who attacked the Capitol on his behalf and those who committed major financial crimes had their legal burdens lifted. The pattern was clear: the law was strict on perceived enemies and protesters, but lenient or nonexistent for those close to power.

Inside the DOJ, this approach became institutionalized. A "weaponization working group" was formed to portray investigations of Trump as political persecution, framing oversight as illegitimate. The department dropped investigations and lawsuits against

89 corporations, many of them donors, and intervened in court to stop state climate lawsuits against oil companies in Michigan and Hawaii. Puerto Rico, observing these actions, voluntarily dismissed its own climate suit. Civil rights and voting rights enforcement were weakened by staff layoffs and case dismissals. Simultaneously, protections for journalists were rolled back: policies shielding reporters from subpoenas were revoked, and the threat of jail for those who refused to reveal sources returned. In a televised interview, Trump falsely claimed photoshopped tattoo evidence to justify a deportation, insisting on a false gang affiliation even when challenged. In this context, law became less a limit and more a weapon.

In Week 15, economic policy combined trade shocks, climate rollback, and personal gains into a single strategy. The government implemented sweeping tariffs, including a 145 percent duty on Chinese goods and broad reciprocal tariffs on imports from Mexico and Canada, often justified by vague security reasons. The small-value import loophole was closed, impacting small importers and Chinese exporters. Auto tariffs were adjusted quickly to support some domestic companies. High tariffs were also imposed on solar panels from Vietnam, Cambodia, and Malaysia, increasing the costs of clean-energy projects. Meanwhile, Amazon was pressured not to show tariff effects on prices, reducing consumer awareness of rising costs caused by the policy.

The economic effects were clear. Reciprocal tariffs and sector-specific duties contributed to declines in manufacturing and tourism. UPS announced layoffs of about 20,000 workers and the closure of 73 facilities due to reduced volume from tariffs. Initial unemployment claims reached their highest point in months. The Bureau of Economic Analysis reported a 0.3 percent drop in GDP in the first quarter of 2025, the first decline in three years. Trump, in a televised cabinet meeting, blamed his predecessor for the downturn. The risk structure was obvious: policy shocks were decided at the top, while workers and small businesses bore the brunt.

On climate and energy, the administration diverged from global trends. It accelerated fossil fuel extraction through fast-track permits, coal-plant extensions, deep-sea mining, and declared an energy emergency. Meanwhile, renewable energy permitting on federal lands and waters was halted, and tariffs on imported solar panels worsened the situation. Environmental justice programs and offices targeting pollution in marginalized communities were shut down. The U.S. withdrew from the Paris climate agreement, the UN climate loss-and-damage fund, the World Health Organization, and the UN Human Rights Council, reducing support for global public goods and weakening cooperation on climate and health crises.

These policy choices were linked to more obvious forms of crony capitalism. The $TRUMP cryptocurrency contest and the Executive Branch club offered access to the president and senior officials in exchange for token purchases and membership fees. Trump family members invested in an AI company just before deregulation favored that sector, raising conflict-of-interest concerns. The administration dropped investigations into 89 corporations, many of which donated to Trump's inaugural fund. A sovereign wealth fund and a strategic bitcoin reserve were announced, consolidating control over large pools of public money in the executive branch. Work requirements for Medicaid and SNAP advanced, while the federal minimum wage remained unchanged, and a plan to end the tax on tips provided relief that would miss many low-income workers. A farmer bailout was also prepared to offset tariff damage, socializing some costs while maintaining the trade course. In each case, profits and protections increased; risk and austerity decreased.

Civil-rights infrastructure, already strained by economic and enforcement choices, was further dismantled. Diversity, equity, and inclusion programs across federal agencies were terminated, and similar rollbacks were encouraged in the private sector. Environmental justice offices were closed. The Pentagon's Women, Peace, and Security program was ended, decreasing women's participation in security decision-making. Refugee protections were narrowed, with discussions about allowing only Christian Afghan refugees to stay after broader safeguards were revoked. Funding for UNRWA and the UN Human Rights Council was cut, weakening international mechanisms that support vulnerable groups.

Domestically, specific groups faced targeted restrictions. Federal funding and insurance coverage for gender-affirming care were limited, and gender transitions for minors were banned. A federal report recommended therapy instead of medical treatment for youth with gender dysphoria, contradicting major medical associations and justifying state-level restrictions. Transgender athletes were barred from women's sports, with some federal funds contingent on compliance. LGBTQ Pride events at the Kennedy Center were canceled. The Education Department launched investigations into race-conscious programs like Chicago's Black Student Success Plan and Harvard Law Review's editorial practices, signaling skepticism toward targeted equity efforts. In Maine, a politically charged freeze on child nutrition funds over transgender athlete policies ended with a settlement that restored funding but highlighted how essential programs could be used as leverage.

Courts again provided some counterbalance. Federal judges restricted deportations under the Alien Enemies Act and upheld injunctions against DOGE's access to Social Security records. Democratic state attorneys general coordinated efforts to challenge Trump's early executive orders. However, these legal victories were reactive and limited in scope. The broader trend—dismantling DEI and environmental justice systems, selective enforcement, and international withdrawal—remained steady, creating a foundation for a stratified social order.

Religion and nationalist symbols moved closer to the heart of government. The president created a Religious Liberty Commission and increased the policy influence of the White House Faith Office. During a National Prayer Day event, he described national renewal as a return to religion in public life, linking the country's future to a specific faith story. In Oklahoma, education officials adopted a curriculum that greatly increased references to Christianity while removing the separation of church and state. Social studies standards included discredited 2020 election fraud claims, requiring students to analyze conspiracies as if they were legitimate civic issues.

Symbolic control extended beyond schools. Trump ordered the renaming of the Gulf of Mexico and Mount Denali to politically meaningful names, asserting executive authority over geographic memory. The administration removed Doug Emhoff and other Biden-era appointees from the U.S. Holocaust Memorial Museum board, reshaping the leadership of an important institution of historical remembrance. Selective declassification of MLK and JFK assassination files increased transparency on one hand, while leaving motives and framing up to the current administration. These actions curated which histories were highlighted and which were marginalized, aligning national stories with the regime's self-image.

Information control intensified in more direct ways. Trump launched White House Wire, a government-run site that only shared positive coverage of his administration, blurring the line between official communication and propaganda. An executive order ended federal funding for NPR and PBS through the Corporation for Public Broadcasting, threatening the financial foundation of non-commercial news and educational programs, especially in rural and underserved areas. The FCC, led by officials appointed by Trump, began investigations into NPR and PBS that could justify further cuts. At the same time, the administration hosted alternative press briefings featuring right-wing influencers who echoed its narratives, raising loyalist voices above traditional reporters.

The cost of essential journalism rose. DOJ rescinded policies that protected reporters from subpoenas, opening the door to jailing those who refused to reveal sources. Trump publicly criticized individual journalists as biased and untalented. The White House Correspondents' Association withdrew comedian Amber Ruffin's invitation to its annual dinner after sharp criticism of the administration, a small but telling concession. AI tools were used to assist in drafting executive orders, including justifications for major tariff policies, making legal language less transparent and harder to trace back to human writers. Climate science agencies lost contributors, and the U.S. missed greenhouse gas reporting deadlines after withdrawing from international frameworks. Health policy was reshaped by a vaccine-skeptical Health and Human Services secretary who changed testing and surveillance protocols and delayed the approval of a new COVID-19 vaccine. The framework that enables the public to understand risk and hold power to account has weakened.

Education and protest spaces became highly contested. The administration threatened or froze funding to universities over alleged antisemitism and diversity policies, using federal money as leverage against campus speech and governance. The FBI raided the homes of pro-Palestinian students in Michigan, seizing electronics in a vandalism investigation that could chill political expression. Yale withdrew recognition from a student group that organized a protest against an Israeli minister. Swarthmore suspended students involved in a pro-Palestinian encampment without completing full conduct procedures. The Education Department's investigations into race-conscious programs added more pressure.

At the state level, Oklahoma's curriculum process was taken over by ideological actors. The legislature failed to vote on a resolution that would have sent controversial social studies standards back for review. The curriculum committee was filled with right-wing activists instead of educators. Last-minute changes and misleading deadlines were used to push the standards through the state board. Debunked election claims and Christian-nationalist themes entered public education not via open debate, but through procedural maneuvering. At the federal level, Trump's order to dismantle the Department of Education threatened to remove a national check on such state-level experiments.

Yet civic space was not entirely closed. Harvard University refused to comply with administration demands to change governance and admissions in exchange for funding, defending its institutional autonomy. Illinois's governor organized and led mass protests against Trump's policies that affected marginalized communities. Democratic leaders staged a 12-hour sit-in at the U.S. Capitol to protest budget cuts to social programs. Senate Democrats delivered marathon floor speeches to warn of authoritarian tendencies. These acts did not change policy, but they indicated that resistance remained in legislatures, campuses, and streets.

Behind the visible conflicts over tariffs, refugees, and public media, a quieter change occurred in how law and surveillance operate. AI systems were used to draft executive orders and to rewrite regulations at HUD under DOGE's guidance. DOGE staff embedded in agencies, working under nondisclosure agreements, reshaped processes that decide who gets contracts, how rules are interpreted, and how benefits are distributed. The administration sought emergency Supreme Court approval for DOGE to access Social Security records, aiming to mine nationwide benefits data in the name of efficiency. Federal courts blocked that access, at least temporarily, highlighting the risks of mass data mining by a politicized efficiency office.

These domestic actions took place within a global context where data and synthetic media were already being used to manipulate politics. Reports from abroad described deepfake videos used in election campaigns and stolen surveillance data resold by officials. At home, the rollback of journalist protections and the expansion of citizen surveillance, combined with impunity for elite financial crimes, pointed to a system where ordinary people were more vulnerable while those in power became more hidden. Algorithms and databases, instead of laws alone, increasingly determined who was seen, who was targeted, and who could challenge decisions.

No single event in Week 15 closed a door that had been open the week before. Rights still existed on paper. Courts continued to issue injunctions. Agencies still issued rules and gathered comments. But the week revealed a pattern where emergency powers became routine, law enforcement served the regime's interests, economic shocks were used to benefit insiders, and the systems of information and education that might have checked these trends were under pressure. The movement of the Democracy Clock reflected this buildup: a small numerical change that signified a larger shift in what institutions could reliably guarantee, and in how much effort it now took for citizens, judges, and civil servants to oppose these trends.

CHAPTER 26
WEEK 16: STRATIFIED RIGHTS AS ROUTINE GOVERNANCE

With the clock frozen at 7:59 p.m., immigration, media, and the civil service are quietly retooled to sort who is protected, heard, and expendable.

The sixteenth week of Trump's second term didn't hinge on a single order or spectacle. Instead, it played out as a week where existing tools were used more confidently and in more places to categorize people, institutions, and information into favored and disfavored groups. Immigration law, civil service rules, media regulation, and public funding all stayed in place. What changed was how they were enforced and to whom. The pattern that formed was one of stratification: of rights, access, and voice.

At the end of the previous period, the Democracy Clock read 7:59 p.m. By the end of this week, it was still at 7:59 p.m. The stillness in the clock didn't mean a pause in activity. It reflected a balance between increasing erosion and scattered resistance. Executive power pushed harder on immigration, media, and the civil service. Courts, state governments, and professional groups pushed back in specific cases. The week didn't push the hands further toward democratic midnight, but it added layers to the terrain where future movements will occur.

Immigration became the clearest example where emergency tactics turned into routine practices. The administration used the Alien Enemies Act and extensive foreign-affairs powers to deport Venezuelans based on disputed intelligence about gang connections, including some who had been legally present and followed all the rules. Deportation flights were justified as national security actions rather than standard enforcement. Simultaneously, emergency-style deportations to El Salvador targeted migrants who had complied with the rules, signaling that legal status no longer guaranteed fair treatment. The message was clear: status could be revoked at will.

Detention policy shifted similarly. A new rule required headquarters approval for any release from ICE custody, effectively freezing releases nationwide. Overcrowding resulted not by chance but as an expected outcome of making detention the default. Local discretion—once a minor check on central policy—was eliminated. The same headquarters controlling releases also approved a budget plan to increase ICE's detention funding by more than threefold and its removals budget by fivefold, positioning it as the best-funded law enforcement agency in the federal system. Scale became its own argument.

Coercion didn't always involve bars and handcuffs. The administration offered undocumented immigrants $1,000 and airfare if they agreed to self-deport, presenting this as a humane option while downplaying the long reentry bans that would follow. The program depended on unequal access to legal information: those most likely to accept were also least able to get legal counsel. Meanwhile, thousands of agents from other federal agencies—DEA, FBI, IRS, and others—were deputized to assist ICE, blurring the lines between specialized law enforcement and immigration control. The result was a migration system that resembled less ordinary law enforcement and more a standing emergency. It was designed to last.

Individual cases demonstrated both the reach of this system and its occasional limitations. An Irish green card holder, Cliona Ward, was detained for seventeen days over decades-old convictions until a state court vacated them, illustrating how rigid enforcement could disrupt settled lives and require diplomatic intervention. A Turkish student, Rümeysa Öztürk, was detained after writing a critical op-ed; federal courts ordered her transfer and subsequent release, affirming that immigration powers could not be used as punishment for protected speech. These rulings were significant, but they represented exceptions within a broader trend. That larger current continued to flow.

The administration's own rhetoric veered toward more explicit suspension of legal safeguards. Stephen Miller, speaking for the White House, said the team was considering suspending the writ of habeas corpus to limit court challenges to detention. The idea did not become law, but its public discussion signaled a willingness to treat one of the oldest protections against arbitrary imprisonment as negotiable. In the same week, an executive order established a large National Center for Warrior Independence to house homeless veterans, funded partly by redirecting resources from services for undocumented immigrants. Support for one vulnerable group was linked to the exclusion of another, making status and origin the key factors in redistributive decisions. Who belonged determined who would receive help. That week also saw senior officials question the universality of due process itself. President Trump publicly questioned whether everyone in the United States was entitled to due process, casting doubt on a core constitutional guarantee. Before a House appropriations subcommittee, Homeland Security Secretary Kristi Noem refused to affirm that the Constitution's protections applied to all persons, not just citizens. These were not slips of language. They were statements made under questioning, in settings where the meaning of the law is meant to be clarified, not muddled. The doubt was deliberate.

This mindset was evident in how the law was applied to friends and enemies. The president pardoned Enrique Tarrio, the Proud

Boys leader convicted of seditious conspiracy for his role in January 6, and his administration settled in principle with Ashli Babbitt's family. Both actions indicated leniency toward those involved in attacking Congress. Meanwhile, Trump's border czar threatened Wisconsin's governor with arrest for advising state workers to seek legal counsel before responding to ICE requests, and federal agents arrested Newark's mayor while he protested outside an ICE detention center, claiming local jurisdiction. Protest and legal advice by officials were regarded with suspicion; violence aligned with the president's movement was forgiven or compensated. Loyalty, not law, defined the boundary.

Courts offered partial counterbalances. In the Öztürk case, judges insisted that immigration detention could not be used to retaliate against speech. In another case, a federal judge ordered prosecutors and senior officials to avoid prejudicial public comments in a high-profile murder trial, safeguarding the defendant's right to a fair trial from politicized rhetoric. But other signals pointed in the opposite direction. Federal judges criticized Department of Justice lawyers for poor performance defending administration policies, raising doubts about whether the department was willing or able to subject executive actions to real scrutiny. And while the president signed an order instructing agencies to reduce criminal regulatory offenses—presented as relief from overcriminalization—this easing of liability occurred alongside proposals to suspend habeas corpus and ramp up enforcement against migrants and protesters. Decriminalization was selective.

The boundary testing extended into civil rights protections. The General Services Administration rescinded federal workplace nondiscrimination guidance on gender identity, rolling back protections for LGBTQ+ employees and narrowing official definitions of sex. This change did not draw much attention, but it shifted the baseline for how federal workers could expect to be treated. Taken together with the selective pardons, threats, and arrests, the week's actions suggested a legal order where the force of law increasingly depended on alignment with the regime. Protection itself became conditional.

Beneath these headline moves, the machinery of government itself was being reshaped. The Department of Government Efficiency (DOGE) oversaw a mass firing of tens of thousands of probationary federal workers in a Valentine's Day purge. An executive order expanded discretion to fire probationary employees, weakening job protections and making it easier to remove staff who might resist political directives. The Supreme Court's intervention in litigation over reinstatement complicated efforts to bring purged workers back, while lower courts largely blocked the most sweeping aspects of the purge. The Office of Special Counsel, after a leadership change, dropped its inquiry into the legality of the mass firings, signaling that an internal watchdog would not press the issue. Oversight bent, then stepped aside.

The purge was not limited to one agency. The Labor Department saw a 20 percent staff exodus and major cuts to international labor grants, weakening enforcement of labor standards and research. The administration announced plans to cut thousands of jobs at the CIA and other intelligence agencies, eliminating diversity programs and analytic capacity in national security institutions. A federal hiring freeze, including for air traffic controllers, was implemented despite known shortages; Newark's airport experienced severe delays and safety concerns as understaffing continued. An independent review of air traffic control oversight, launched after a deadly collision, was halted by the administration, reducing outside evaluation of systemic risks. Safety was also affected as scrutiny diminished.

Regulatory and expert bodies were similarly reduced. The Environmental Protection Agency's staffing was cut, and its Office of Research and Development was dissolved, undermining independent environmental science and shifting the agency toward political influence. The Consumer Product Safety Commission began to be dismantled, reducing oversight of product safety and increasing consumer risk. NASA faced a proposed 25 percent budget cut even as Mars initiatives were shielded, threatening broad scientific programs while prioritizing high-profile projects. USAID staff and grants were cut through DOGE-driven reductions, leading to expired food and medicine and lapses in health programs abroad, weakening U.S. support for global public goods and democratic resilience. Expertise was treated as expendable.

Information and oversight channels were also reconfigured. The FBI director delayed submission of the bureau's budget to Congress past the legal deadline and was reported to be disengaged from duties, impeding legislative oversight of a powerful law enforcement agency. DOGE consolidated personal data on millions of people, prompting at least 11 lawsuits alleging massive violations of the Privacy Act. A secure messaging app used for sensitive government communications was suspected to have been hacked and suspended, exposing vulnerabilities in channels meant to protect national security information. At the same time, an executive order directed the modernization of the Office of the Federal Register to speed publication of rules, potentially allowing regulatory changes to take legal effect more quickly, with less time for public or congressional response. Speed favored the center.

Media and information systems came under direct pressure. An executive order cut NPR and PBS off from federal funding, threatening the viability of noncommercial news and educational programming, especially in rural areas dependent on public broadcasting. Voice of America and its parent agency, USAGM, were dismantled by order; more than 1,000 staff were kept off the job while litigation proceeded, and 1,300 were placed on leave as VoA was taken off the air. Grants to sister outlets were canceled. In place of VoA's own journalists, leadership contracted One America News to provide newsfeed and video services, aligning a government-funded outlet with a hard-right partisan network. A public voice was swapped for a loyal one.

Regulatory tools were used to control private media. The Federal Communications Commission launched an unprecedented "news distortion" investigation into CBS News after a 60 Minutes interview with the president, echoing Trump's own lawsuit. A senior producer resigned following corporate intervention in Trump coverage, as Paramount Global leadership reviewed political content amid pending merger talks. The company scaled back DEI efforts and adjusted political initiatives to avoid regulatory backlash, showing how ownership and licensing power could suppress editorial independence. A pattern emerged: regulatory scrutiny of content and corporate structure created incentives for self-censorship in exchange for merger approval and regulatory peace. Silence became a strategic business choice.

Legal and rhetorical pressure on journalists increased. Attorney General Pam Bondi rolled back press protections in leak investigations after critical reporting, raising the risk that national security tools would be used to intimidate reporters. Director of National Intelligence Tulsi Gabbard criticized the Wall Street Journal for stories about Greenland intelligence activities, accusing the paper of politicizing and leaking classified information, and framing investigative reporting as a threat to democracy and security. A VoA journalist sued over the defunding order, claiming it violated press freedom and congressional appropriations, but the broader trend was clear: independent and public media were being starved or co-opted, while state-aligned outlets thrived. The scope of oversight narrowed.

The administration also experimented with new forms of narrative control. President Trump posted an AI-generated image of himself dressed as the pope on official channels during a papal transition, using religious symbolism for personal branding and blurring the line between satire and official messaging. Economic data were presented in ways that obscured responsibility: the Bureau of Economic Analysis and economic media described a GDP dip as caused by imports, reinforcing a misleading shorthand that imports are a "subtraction" from growth. Trade officials and the president made inconsistent statements about who pays tariffs and the scope of trade deals, contributing to confusion about economic policy and accountability. Data and algorithms were not falsified outright, but they were used in ways that shaped perception more than they informed. Confusion itself became a tool.

Universities and cultural institutions found themselves at the intersection of funding and ideology. The administration froze billions in federal research grants and aid to Harvard University and threatened its tax-exempt status over its handling of campus protests, using economic power to pressure governance and speech. In Congress, hearings and legislation on campus antisemitism and protests put universities under intense scrutiny, with the implicit message that failure to police certain speech could cost them money and standing. On campuses, protest was met with policing: Columbia University requested NYPD intervention to clear an occupied library, leading to the arrest of about seventy-five pro-Palestinian protesters; Swarthmore College called local police to disband an encampment and arrest activists; the University of Washington used law enforcement to clear an occupied engineering building and charge student protesters. Spaces for dissent shrank.

Prosecutorial responses to protests were uneven. In Michigan, Attorney General Dana Nessel dropped charges against seven university encampment protesters amid concerns about conflicts of interest and bias, while continuing vandalism cases against others. A related hearing highlighted tensions between political relationships, prosecutorial discretion, and equal treatment of demonstrators. At the same time, the National Endowment for the Arts terminated many grants and reoriented funding toward projects reflecting "American heritage," moving away from diversity-focused work. Public arts funding became a tool to privilege certain narratives in cultural memory. In Congress, a bill advanced to rename the Gulf of Mexico as the "Gulf of America," a symbolic gesture that sought to recast geographic memory along nationalist lines. Names and grants pointed in the same direction.

The fusion of public office with private enrichment and foreign entanglements deepened. Freight Technologies announced plans to buy $20 million in Trump-branded cryptocurrency explicitly to influence trade policy, treating a presidentially linked asset as a channel for lobbying. A $2 billion investment in Binance, backed by Abu Dhabi's MGX, was structured through a Trump family stablecoin, creating a path for foreign-government-linked capital to flow into ventures tied to the president. The Trump Organization launched a new hotel and tower project in Dubai with a Saudi-linked firm and entered a $5.5 billion deal to build a golf club in Qatar with a state-owned company, despite an ethics pledge against direct foreign-government business. The border between state and firm blurred.

Domestic capital followed similar patterns. Institutional investors significantly increased their holdings in Trump Media despite the company's losses, suggesting that political goodwill, not financial fundamentals, might be the main driver of returns. Reports indicated that big-oil donors received tariff exemptions and that Trump businesses pursued foreign-government deals, highlighting how economic policy and access could be influenced by personal and donor interests. Tariff policy itself was unstable: high tariffs on auto parts and other imports raised costs for consumers and industries; a threatened 100 percent tariff on foreign films, later partially withdrawn, used national security language to justify cultural trade measures; sweeping "Liberation Day" tariffs on multiple trading partners caused market declines; and unilateral tariff cuts for China before negotiations weakened U.S. leverage. Treasury Secretary Scott Bessent dodged congressional questions about who actually paid these tariffs, hiding the burden on households. The costs were visible but obscured.

Regulatory decisions seemed friendly to connected industries. An executive order promoted domestic production of critical medicines by easing environmental and regulatory checks on pharmaceutical manufacturing. The Federal Aviation Administration approved a fivefold increase in SpaceX launches from Boca Chica despite previous environmental damage, finding no significant impact and signaling a permissive attitude toward a politically connected company. In each case, the language of national security or competitiveness accompanied choices that shifted risk onto the public while protecting profits and flexibility for influential firms. Risk was socialized; gains were not.

Protest and dissent faced tighter policing and surveillance. Beyond campus arrests and the detention of the Newark mayor, DOGE's consolidation of personal data on millions of people raised concerns that information gathered for administrative purposes could be repurposed for political control. The breach of secure messaging showed how fragile official secrecy infrastructure could be, even as the administration moved to centralize communications and regulatory timing. Abroad, China's widespread electronic surveillance and AI to repress dissent served as a warning of what such tools can lead to when combined with authoritarian motives. Within the U.S., rescinding gender-identity workplace guidance and strict immigration enforcement against long-term residents made certain groups more vulnerable to state power. Vulnerability was patterned, not random.

Yet resistance was not absent. About 1,500 lawyers and supporters gathered outside the Manhattan federal courthouse to protest in defense of the rule of law, signaling organized professional concern about attacks on judicial independence. The American Bar Association sued the administration over the termination of federal grants and threats to its accreditation role, asserting its independence against retaliation tied to diversity and rule-of-law positions. Federal courts in North Carolina ordered certification of Allison Riggs as the winner of a close state supreme court race, rejecting retroactive ballot disqualifications and protecting voters from post hoc rule changes. Other judges largely blocked DOGE's attempt to purge civil servants en masse, preserving contractual protections for many workers. These acts were significant.

There were also instances where federal agencies and legislators reaffirmed legal boundaries. The Department of Agriculture settled with Maine to restore frozen school meal funds, limiting the use of federal grants to coerce state social policies. Senator Susan Collins used an appropriations hearing to criticize administration cuts to biomedical research and health agencies, reminding executive officials of Congress's power of the purse. Judge Beryl Howell permanently struck down an executive order that had targeted a specific law firm, Perkins Coie, for exclusion from federal work and buildings, reinforcing constitutional protections against retaliatory use of executive power. Justice Ketanji Brown Jackson publicly warned about political attacks on judges, a rare occasion of a sitting Supreme Court justice explicitly defending judicial independence. The guardrails flexed but held in some places.

State governments pursued their own public-interest agendas despite federal turbulence. Hawaii raised tourist taxes to fund climate resilience, using targeted levies to finance environmental protection and adaptation. New York's budget approved middle-class tax cuts, inflation refund checks, and universal free school meals, easing household burdens and making access to nutrition less dependent on income. Indiana enacted a law threatening nonprofit hospitals' tax-exempt status over high prices, using state tax powers to discipline influential health systems. These actions did not reverse federal trends but showed that subnational governance could still move differently. Other paths remained open.

The week ended without a dramatic shift, but not without consequences. Executive power continued to expand through interpretation and administration rather than through new laws. Oversight bodies were weakened or redirected. Media and cultural institutions were pressured to conform or punished for dissent. Meanwhile, courts, professional associations, and state governments showed that resistance still existed, although it was often reactive and uneven. The Democracy Clock did not advance because the week did not introduce a new kind of threat; it deepened existing ones. The story of this period lies in that deepening: in how ordinary tools were used to sort, reward, and punish, and in how much now relies on the scattered actors still willing to say no.

CHAPTER 27
WEEK 17: CITIZENSHIP AS LEVERAGE

A week of near-static clock time in which law, borders, and money were quietly retooled to sort belonging and shield power from consequence.

The seventeenth week of Trump's second term was shaped by a series of choices rather than a single order or speech. It revealed a pattern focused on who matters, who is protected, and who can resist. Immigration laws, foreign funds, and the flow of information were all part of this pattern. Instead of tearing apart existing systems, the week saw a tighter framework for law and politics, making the boundaries narrower.

At the start of Week 17, the Democracy Clock read 7:59 p.m. It stayed at the same time by week's end, with just a 0.1-minute change. The clock's hands barely moved, but the mechanisms behind them did. This small change shows that formal institutions still functioned—courts issued injunctions, hearings were held, agencies followed notice-and-comment procedures—yet they were manipulated to serve executive power. Authority was exerted more forcefully against migrants, critics, and independent agencies, and more openly in favor of private and foreign interests, even as some resistance slowed or limited the impact.

The most direct pressure was on habeas corpus and due process rights for migrants. Early in the week, a White House adviser suggested suspending the writ of habeas corpus, and the Department of Homeland Security considered labeling migrant crossings as a "rebellion" or "invasion." This wasn't just rhetoric. It was an effort to find legal grounds to treat migration as an emergency similar to war, allowing the administration to bypass standard procedures that require judicial review before detention. Simultaneously, DHS shut down the CBP One app, cutting off a key legal route for asylum appointments and pushing more people into irregular crossings, where it's easier to treat them as security threats rather than rights-based applicants. The message was clear.

On the ground, enforcement followed the same logic. The administration ended Temporary Protected Status for Afghans, declaring conditions improved despite Taliban rule, and moved to use the Alien Enemies Act—an eighteenth-century wartime law—to deport Venezuelans accused of gang ties. A federal judge in Pennsylvania allowed that use of the law, provided there was notice and an opportunity to challenge, while another judge refused to block the Internal Revenue Service from sharing immigrant tax data with ICE. At the same time, the FBI was ordered to shift a third of its resources from white-collar crime to immigration enforcement. The combined effect was to expand the tools for rapid removal and to concentrate investigative power downward, away from elite misconduct and toward vulnerable noncitizens.

Yet the courts did not simply accept this. The Supreme Court issued an injunction halting deportations of Venezuelans under the Alien Enemies Act due to lack of due process, and in a separate 7–2 decision, it ruled that alleged gang members could not be deported without proper procedures. Federal judges ordered the release of detained students and scholars whose activism on Gaza had been viewed as a security threat, and one judge in South Dakota blocked the deportation of an Indian PhD graduate over a minor traffic violation. These rulings did not reverse the administration's strategy, but they forced it to operate within narrower limits and reaffirmed that even in immigration matters, constitutional protections still apply. The brakes still worked, but only under strain.

The president's words pushed in the opposite direction. By the end of the week, he was publicly questioning whether people in the United States even have a right to due process. That statement, along with Stephen Miller's habeas trial balloon and DHS's "invasion" memos, signaled an executive willing to test the outer limits of constitutional boundaries. Deportations already underway in defiance of some court orders, and a request for 20,000 National Guard troops to assist with immigration enforcement, demonstrated how quickly these ideas could be put into action. The legal system remained present, but it was now reacting to an administration that viewed rights as obstacles to bypass rather than limits to respect.

The same enforcement tools were directed inward against dissenters and critics. ICE agents arrested Newark's mayor, Ras Baraka, at a protest outside a private immigration detention facility, sending a clear message that even elected local officials risked detention if they challenged federal authorities. Homeland Security spokespeople went further, threatening that Democratic members of Congress could be arrested if they attempted oversight visits at the same site. In Tennessee, traffic-stop sweeps resulted in over a hundred people being taken into immigration custody, sparking accusations of racial profiling. Inside the Capitol, disability rights activists protesting Medicaid cuts were arrested in a committee room, and Ben Cohen was detained during a Senate hearing after criticizing the Gaza blockade and domestic spending cuts. Protest was treated as a law enforcement issue.

Universities also became another battleground. At Columbia, student protesters were arrested and student journalists briefly suspended as campus authorities and New York police tried to control Gaza-related demonstrations. Behind the scenes, ICE and federal prosecutors obtained a warrant under allegedly misleading pretenses to target Columbia students for "harboring" violations, using that pretext to search their residences and devices. The State Department directed university officials to report international students involved in protests considered antisemitic or terrorist-related, effectively turning campus administrators into extensions of immigration surveillance. For foreign students, the line between political speech and deportation risk grew thinner.

High-profile critics and legal figures were not spared. Customs and Border Protection questioned commentator Hasan Piker extensively at the border, focusing on his views of Trump and Gaza, blurring the lines between security screening and ideological vetting. The Secret Service and DHS launched a threat investigation into former FBI director James Comey over an ambiguous Instagram post, indicating that even prominent critics could face formal scrutiny for their speech. In Wisconsin, a state judge was indicted for allegedly helping an undocumented immigrant evade ICE in her courtroom, and she moved to dismiss the case on the grounds of judicial immunity. At the federal level, Justice Department officials prepared investigations into prosecutors who had filed cases against Trump, while a new "weaponization" working group announced plans to publicly "name and shame" political opponents who could not be charged. The focus of the law was shifting outward.

Courts and civil society resisted where they could. Judges ordered the release of detained students and scholars, and a federal court temporarily prevented the administration from canceling grants to the American Bar Association for training lawyers in domestic and sexual violence cases, citing potential retaliation. Another court maintained ABA funding even as the administration sought new authority to revoke nonprofits' tax-exempt status if they were labeled "terrorist-supporting," a designation easily stretched to disfavor advocacy groups. Bruce Springsteen used a concert to criticize attacks on due process and ideological pressures on universities, showing how cultural figures tried to keep democratic norms visible in public life. However, the enforcement pattern—

border screening, warrants, threat investigations—was now clearly aimed at chilling protest and dissent, especially for those with uncertain status.

Beneath these enforcement actions lay a deeper reshaping of citizenship and belonging. The administration granted refugee status to a group of white South Africans, framed as victims of "genocide," even while it maintained a broader halt on refugee resettlement. At the same time, it ended Temporary Protected Status for Afghans, claiming conditions had improved enough to send them home despite ongoing repression under the Taliban. New executive orders authorized the deportation or exclusion of non-citizens based on their political and cultural views, including broad definitions of antisemitism that could include pro-Palestinian speech. These moves indicated that humanitarian relief and entry rights would be granted or revoked not only based on danger abroad but also on how well they aligned with the administration's ideological and cultural priorities.

The core of citizenship was also challenged. The Supreme Court heard consolidated cases challenging Trump's executive order limiting birthright citizenship for U.S.-born children of non-citizens, scrutinizing guarantees under the Fourteenth Amendment. While some justices showed skepticism, the fact that the Court considered the order reflected how far the debate had shifted. In South Carolina, the state's high court upheld a six-week abortion ban, narrowing reproductive rights and reinforcing a vision of rights that varied greatly by jurisdiction. In the military, Pentagon leaders ordered academies to ignore race, ethnicity, and sex in admissions, while maintaining athletic preferences, and ordered the removal of hundreds of books on diversity and gender from military and base school libraries worldwide. These actions reshaped who would lead the armed forces and what ideas would be available to service members and their families.

Economic policy deepened inequality. House Republicans pushed a tax bill that changed the child tax credit, leaving many low-income and undocumented families without full benefits and reinforcing the link between economic support and citizenship. Executive orders on immigration permitted the deportation or exclusion of non-citizens based on their views, while a flawed analysis was used to justify an FDA review of mifepristone rules, risking access to abortion medication through politicized science. The same state that secured the release of the last living American hostage in Gaza—showing its ability to protect citizens abroad—was also shrinking the number of people at home who could claim full membership and bodily autonomy. Protection became conditional.

Foreign money and personal gain influenced the week's decisions. At the center was Qatar. The president planned to accept a $400 million luxury jet from the Qatari royal family for use as Air Force One and later as his presidential library, blurring the line between state asset and private gift. Simultaneously, the Trump Organization signed a $5.5 billion deal to build a Trump International Golf Club in Qatar with Qatari Diar, a state-owned firm, and Dar Global. These projects occurred alongside a large defense and aviation package with Qatar, linking arms sales and economic cooperation to the same entity offering the jet and hosting the golf course.

The legal basis for these arrangements was kept deliberately unclear. The Justice Department and White House counsel issued emoluments opinions approving the jet and related deals, but the reasoning wasn't made public. Senate Democratic leader Chuck Schumer responded by blocking Justice Department nominations until the administration clarified the Qatar jet deal, using confirmation powers to enforce constitutional safeguards. However, the deals continued, and the administration's willingness to accept such gifts signaled to foreign governments that influence and favor could be bought through co-branded projects and luxury gifts.

Qatar was not alone. SpaceX secured a $6 billion Pentagon contract as part of a proposed "Golden Dome" missile shield, a project whose inspector general had been fired earlier in the term. Business leaders who had once boycotted Saudi Arabia attended a high-profile investment lunch there alongside Trump, highlighting how economic opportunities and arms deals could override human rights concerns. In Serbia, a $500 million Trump-branded hotel project in Belgrade was halted after a forged demolition document surfaced, raising questions about corruption and governance in cross-border deals tied to presidential associates. Across these cases, foreign policy and national security decisions were intertwined with the president's private business interests, making it difficult to distinguish public strategy from personal gain.

Inside the justice and security system, the same pattern of self-protection and loyalty over law played out. The Justice Department announced plans to investigate prosecutors who had brought cases against Trump, turning the investigative focus back on those who had tried to hold him accountable. Judge Aileen Cannon dismissed the Mar-a-Lago classified documents case on novel grounds, ruling that the special counsel had been unlawfully appointed, thereby removing a major legal threat to the president. The indictment of a Wisconsin judge over her handling of an immigrant arrest in her courtroom served as a warning to the judiciary: decisions that frustrate federal enforcement could now carry personal criminal risk.

At the same time, the capacity of the state to enforce civil rights protections was being weakened. The Justice Department's Civil Rights Division experienced a mass exodus, with reports that 70 percent of attorneys had left; leadership asked departing staff to reconsider, but the scale of loss highlighted deep politicization. The administration nominated Casey Means, an unlicensed, anti-vaccine figure, as surgeon general, prioritizing ideological alignment over medical expertise. It fired the head of the U.S. Copyright Office soon after she issued a cautious report on AI and copyright, signaling intolerance for independent expert judgment in a key knowledge governance role. National Intelligence Director Tulsi Gabbard removed the chair and deputy of the National Intelligence Council after a report contradicted Trump's claims, politicizing intelligence assessment and narrowing the space for inconvenient facts.

Congressional oversight struggled to keep pace. The House Judiciary Committee's Republican majority summoned former special counsel prosecutor Jay Bratt to testify about Trump prosecutions, signaling a willingness to pressure prosecutorial decisions. FBI Director Kash Patel appeared at a Senate Appropriations hearing without a required budget plan, impairing lawmakers' ability to scrutinize spending. Homeland Security Secretary Kristi Noem refused to answer basic questions about deportations of U.S. citizens and immigration practices. FAA officials declined to disclose how many air traffic controllers had left since Trump took office, even as Newark Airport faced severe staffing shortages that caused major delays and raised safety concerns. Judges Amy St. Eve and Robert Conrad requested increased funding for judicial security amid rising threats, and conservative jurist J. Michael Luttig publicly warned that Trump was weaponizing the federal government, but their appeals highlighted how exposed the remaining pockets of independence felt.

Information and memory became contested terrain. The White House launched "White House Wire," a government-run news website featuring AI-generated imagery and videos of deportation flights, designed to dramatize its immigration agenda. These tools allowed the administration to bypass independent media filters and present emotionally charged narratives directly to the public. At the same time, it excluded wire service reporters from Air Force One during a presidential trip, using access as leverage to punish or sideline outlets that might offer critical coverage. Control of the story became a governing tool.

The most dramatic move came at Voice of America. In defiance of a court order, the administration fired nearly 600 contractors, most of them journalists, gutting a major U.S.-funded international broadcaster. Many of those dismissed were immigrants or refugees from authoritarian states whose immigration status depended on their employment. The firings weakened independent reporting to foreign audiences and raised fresh rule-of-law concerns about compliance with judicial directives. Combined with the creation of a state-run news site, the VOA purge marked a shift toward a media environment where state-aligned outlets thrive while independent voices are starved.

Universities and libraries were drawn into the same struggle over what could be seen and studied. The Pentagon and the Department of Defense Education Activity ordered the removal of DEI and gender-related books from military and base school libraries worldwide, narrowing the range of perspectives available to service members' families and reshaping civic education in a more nationalist, less equality-focused direction. The administration cut an additional $450 million in federal grants to Harvard University amid a First Amendment lawsuit, using funding levers to pressure a leading academic institution that had challenged its policies. The State Department's directive that universities report international students involved in certain protests turned campus administrators into reluctant participants in surveillance, with obvious chilling effects on research and debate.

The administration's approach to information went beyond censorship and pressure; it also embraced spectacle. DHS considered a reality TV show where immigrants competed for U.S. citizenship, degrading legal status into entertainment. Economic messaging followed a similar pattern of manipulation and volatility. The president announced a 100 percent tariff on all foreign-made movies, combining cultural protectionism with trade policy. Over fifty tariff policy changes, including sharp hikes on Chinese goods followed by a 90-day pause that reduced rates from 145 percent to around 30 percent, created a volatile trade environment. Executive orders on drug pricing promised to link U.S. prices to the lowest abroad while threatening foreign negotiators. Moody's downgraded the U.S. sovereign credit rating for the first time since 1917, citing widening deficits and stalled fiscal reforms, even as official rhetoric painted a positive economic picture.

Behind these moves was a fiscal and regulatory agenda that favored defense and elite interests over social welfare and public health. The administration proposed a $1.01 trillion military budget with significant cuts to non-defense spending, solidifying a model that prioritized contractors and the Pentagon over education, environment, and health. House Republicans advanced coordinated plans to extend the 2017 tax cuts, impose new work requirements, and cut Medicaid and SNAP by hundreds of billions of dollars, while phasing out key green tax credits from the Inflation Reduction Act after 2031. Environmental and health protections were rolled back: the Department of Energy eliminated 47 appliance efficiency standards, and the administration moved to rescind limits on four toxic PFAS chemicals in drinking water. Newark's air traffic controller crisis, driven by staffing cuts and reorganization, demonstrated how austerity and deregulation could weaken critical infrastructure and safety.

Not every institution moved in the same direction. Courts approved a $750 million settlement with victims of gynecologist Robert Hadden and imposed new safety policies on Columbia University and NewYork-Presbyterian Hospital, holding powerful institutions accountable for decades of sexual abuse. The FBI launched a nationwide investigation into an online group coercing minors into sexual content and self-harm, demonstrating federal capacity to address digital exploitation. Agencies continued routine but important work: the EPA published environmental impact statements and proposed Superfund cleanup settlements; the FDA updated drug and biologic patent review periods, approved new food color additives, and sought input on infant formula standards; the Election Assistance Commission refined voting system reporting forms and financial worksheets for election grants. Harvard Law School confirmed that a long-held document was an original 1300 Magna Carta, a reminder of the deep historical roots of due process and rule-of-law principles.

These pockets of normal governance and occasional resistance did not cancel out the broader pattern of the week. They showed that institutional muscle memory for rule-bound practice still exists and that some judges, civil servants, and civil-society actors are willing to assert it. But they also revealed how much strain those muscles are under. Judges asked for more security as threats increased. Independent experts were fired or sidelined. Agencies that continued to follow notice-and-comment procedures did so in an environment where major decisions about war, migration, and money were increasingly made through opaque opinions and personal relationships.

Week 17 thus marked not a dramatic plunge but a deepening of the same grooves already cut. Law was used more openly as a weapon against migrants, protesters, prosecutors, and judges. Foreign money and personal business interests were woven more tightly into the fabric of state policy. Citizenship and protection were sorted more explicitly by race, origin, and ideology. Media, universities, and libraries were pressured to align or pay a price. Courts and some state actors pushed back in specific cases, preserving islands of due process and accountability, but the tide of executive overreach and institutional capture continued to rise around them. The clock's face stayed still; the machinery behind it did not.

CHAPTER 28

WEEK 18: INEQUALITY AS OPERATING SYSTEM

A reconciliation megabill, weaponized borders, and captured institutions hardwire hierarchy into law while the Democracy Clock's hands barely seem to move.

The eighteenth week of Trump's second term did not depend on a single dramatic event. Instead, it was a week in which the fundamental concepts of belonging and security were reshaped through laws and daily practices. Policies on finance, immigration enforcement, and the treatment of universities and media all shifted in the same direction: away from equal citizenship toward a system where status, safety, and influence are based on wealth, loyalty, and alignment with the regime's narrative about the country.

On the Democracy Clock, the change was nearly invisible. The previous period ended at 7:59 p.m., and this week also ended at the same time, with only a 0.1-minute difference. The clock hands didn't jump forward because no single institution collapsed. Instead, they moved because the week reinforced existing trends: law used as a tool rather than a boundary, fiscal policies favoring capital and punishment, and the gradual transformation of independent institutions into instruments of control. The small numerical change hides the significance of what was put into place.

The centerpiece of the week was the One Big Beautiful Bill, a reconciliation mega-bill pushed through Congress on an accelerated schedule. House leaders advanced an 1,100-page package through overnight hearings and narrow votes, using expedited procedures that left little time for public scrutiny or internal debate. The bill permanently extended the 2017 tax cuts, cut deeply into Medicaid and SNAP, and funneled money into deportation, detention, and border infrastructure. In form, it was a budget. In substance, it rewrote the social contract.

The tax provisions secured lower rates for corporations and high earners while reducing resources available for healthcare and food assistance. Provisions to impose work requirements and tighten eligibility for Medicaid and SNAP meant that millions faced the risk of losing coverage or benefits. At the same time, the bill funded detention capacity for at least 100,000 people and expanded budgets for CBP and ICE, embedding a carceral approach to migration in the federal ledger. The state's generosity flowed upward and outward. Its discipline flowed downward and inward.

Other fiscal moves reinforced this pattern. The administration cut IRS enforcement funding by nearly a third, a change expected to ease life for high-income tax evaders while shifting the burden onto compliant or less wealthy taxpayers. Provisions in the bill and related proposals slashed support for clean energy, electric vehicles, and advanced vehicle programs, while Congress and the administration rescinded the methane waste emissions charge for oil and gas systems. Fossil-fuel incumbents gained relief. Climate and public health bore the cost.

At the same time, Oregon counties diverted addiction treatment funds into prosecutors' offices and police equipment, turning a health-focused grant stream into a tool of punishment. The administration cut USAID contracts in ways that left food aid rotting in warehouses, harming both American farmers and foreign recipients. Plans to re-privatize Fannie Mae and Freddie Mac, floated amid rising mortgage rates and a Moody's downgrade of U.S. sovereign debt, threatened to increase borrowing costs for homeowners under the guise of ideological preferences. The downgrade itself, citing large tax cuts and governance risks, indicated that outside observers viewed fiscal choices as undermining long-term stability.

Corporate behavior reflected these shifts. Major firms associated with anti-hunger work—AT&T, Comcast, T-Mobile, Uber, United—publicly supported the reconciliation bill despite its deep cuts to SNAP. Their support highlighted how lobbying priorities can differ from public messaging: tax and regulatory gains took precedence over concerns about food insecurity. Together, the bill and its related measures solidified a fiscal order where policy outcomes are driven by elite money, tax codes favor capital over labor, and inequality is seen less as a problem than as a designed system.

If Congress served as the vehicle, the presidency provided the engine. Inside the executive branch, the week saw a further shift toward a unitary presidency. The Department of Justice moved to allow U.S. Attorneys to indict members of Congress without prior review by the Public Integrity Section, weakening an internal safeguard meant to prevent politicized prosecutions of legislators. Simultaneously, the Supreme Court stayed lower-court rulings in Trump v. Wilcox and related cases, effectively permitting the president to remove independent agency heads while appeals are pending. Although this stay did not officially change doctrine, it acted as a green light for purges of quasi-judicial regulators.

The Court also approved the administration's urgent request to end Temporary Protected Status for about 350,000 Venezuelans. By supporting the executive on TPS, the justices reinforced presidential control over humanitarian protections and indicated that sudden loss of status for large groups of noncitizens would face little judicial challenge at the highest level. In another emergency order, the Court restored voting rights for a censured Maine lawmaker in the state house, intervening in internal legislative discipline without explanation. A 4–4 deadlock over an Oklahoma religious charter school left a lower court's decision in place but offered no clear guidance. The pattern at the top was one of volatility and sensitivity to executive interests.

However, below the Supreme Court, other judges pushed back. Federal courts blocked efforts to disband agencies and education programs, stopping attempts to reduce the Department of Education and end desegregation grants in southern schools. Judges ordered the government to halt deportations to South Sudan and to return or keep custody of certain migrants, after finding officials violated injunctions against third-country removals. Another court temporarily prevented DHS from ending international students' legal status while litigation over Harvard's visa revocation continues, protecting thousands from sudden expulsion.

In a separate case, a district court reinstated two members of the Privacy and Civil Liberties Oversight Board who Trump had fired, defending the independence of a key surveillance watchdog. Judge John Bates in Washington invalidated an executive order that had suspended a law firm's clearances and access because it involved Trump investigators, calling the retaliation unconstitutional. Yet even as these rulings preserved pockets of independence, the Federal Election Commission canceled several Sunshine Act meetings, reducing transparency around campaign finance enforcement, and Congress used the Congressional Review Act to overturn environmental rules. The overall picture was one of imbalance: presidential power over agencies and immigration expanded, while judicial resistance remained fractured and reactive.

Inside the bureaucracy, the week's changes were mostly structural. The administration proposed a plan to reclassify about 50,000 civil servants into a new "policy/career" category, making them easier to dismiss for vague performance reasons. This change threatened the neutrality of federal expertise, especially in statistical and economic roles that produce inconvenient data. At the

Consumer Financial Protection Bureau, leadership attempted to dismiss most staff and revoked dozens of consumer protection guidelines, including limits on medical debt in credit reports. Three commissioners at a consumer product safety agency were removed, paving the way for more compliant replacements.

The Department of Justice's Civil Rights Division shifted away from its traditional focus on protecting marginalized communities. Negotiations for consent decrees in Minneapolis and Louisville, initiated after the killings of George Floyd and Breonna Taylor, were ended despite prior findings of systemic violations. About 70 percent of Civil Rights Division staff reportedly resigned in protest as the division moved to investigate alleged "anti-white" discrimination in Chicago and Harvard. The Department of Government Efficiency pressed forward with efforts to dismantle the U.S. Institute of Peace and other congressionally established agencies, although courts later invalidated some of these actions.

Service agencies also faced challenges. FEMA admitted it was unprepared for hurricane season and indicated plans to shift responsibilities back to states, even as it failed to deliver timely aid to tornado-affected communities in Mississippi and St. Louis. At the Department of Veterans Affairs, staffing reductions, unit closures, and contract cancellations disrupted veteran care under DOGE guidance. USAID contract cuts left food aid unused in storage. In Oregon, addiction treatment funds were diverted to law enforcement. The overall impact was a weakened administrative state that still had enforcement powers but less capacity and will to protect consumers, civil rights, or vulnerable groups.

Funding levers became tools of discipline. The administration cut federal grants to Harvard over contested claims of anti-white and anti-Asian discrimination, using financial pressure to influence hiring and diversity practices. Senate hearings revealed concern that an IRS commissioner nominee might be reluctant to resist threats to Harvard's tax-exempt status. Senators questioned agency heads about cuts to programs for lead poisoning prevention, ALS research, childcare, disaster aid, and human rights, but their oversight occurred after decisions were made and within a budget already set by the executive. Congress recognized the shift in mission. It struggled to reverse it.

The most visible consequences of these shifts appeared in immigration and policing. The administration ended Temporary Protected Status for Venezuelans and began deportations, exposing hundreds of thousands to sudden loss of legal status and potential harm. ICE coordinated arrests around immigration courts, discouraging attendance and undermining access to legal processes. In one case, officials deported eight men to South Sudan despite a court order, prompting a federal judge to condemn the government's actions. Bhutanese Nepali refugees were sent to countries where they lacked citizenship, leaving them effectively stateless.

Detention practices also showed a lack of regard for dignity. A detained Palestinian activist, Mahmoud Khalil, was denied contact with his newborn son despite standards allowing such visits. Plans emerged to redirect $250 million in foreign aid to repatriate Ukrainians, Haitians, and others to conflict zones, turning development funds into a tool for deportation. Meanwhile, the administration rapidly approved entry for white South African refugees citing alleged discrimination, even as it restricted other humanitarian options. This highlighted a hierarchy of belonging based on race and perceived ideological affinity.

Policing and protests followed a similar pattern. Georgia prosecutors pursued RICO charges against dozens of Cop City protesters, treating a decentralized movement as a criminal enterprise. In Atlanta, a civil rights lawsuit claimed that a woman was left topless in a squad car during a SWAT raid linked to the same controversy, showing the human toll of aggressive tactics. At the federal level, DOJ sought to end consent decrees in Minneapolis and Louisville, weakening tools to combat abusive policing in heavily policed communities. Immigration enforcement and domestic law enforcement aligned around a model where security forces protected power and property more than people.

Criminal law also became a tool for disciplining oversight and opponents. A sitting member of Congress, Representative LaMonica McIver, was charged with assault after a confrontation during an ICE facility visit, sparking fears that legislators could face prosecution for aggressive oversight. In Newark, trespassing charges against Mayor Ras Baraka related to his presence at an immigration facility were dismissed, and a judge criticized DOJ's conduct as a "worrisome misstep." The Department of Justice opened a criminal investigation into Andrew Cuomo's congressional testimony about nursing home deaths, a move that, in context, seemed less like neutral enforcement and more like selective scrutiny of a high-profile Democrat. During Senate testimony, DHS Secretary Kristi Noem publicly misdefined habeas corpus as a power to remove people from the country, exposing gaps in constitutional knowledge at the top of an agency that controls people's liberty.

While the state hardened its stance on migrants, protesters, and oversight-minded officials, it also extended leniency and access to those with wealth or strategic importance. The most striking symbol came from abroad. President Trump accepted a jumbo jet from Qatar for use as Air Force One, a high-value gift that blurred constitutional limits on foreign emoluments. Administration defenders compared the jet to historic public gifts, downplaying the personal benefit and the leverage such a gift could provide. The acceptance and subsequent public defense of the aircraft indicated that foreign governments could influence U.S. officials through material benefits.

At home, Trump hosted high-dollar cryptocurrency investor events at his properties. Attendees spent hundreds of millions on a Trump-linked token, some while under regulatory investigation. The gala and dinner provided proximity and prestige in exchange for speculative investments, merging personal gain with political fundraising. Regulatory leverage was evident elsewhere too. Verizon's acquisition of Frontier proceeded as the company ended its DEI programs and removed related content from its website, a change reportedly linked to FCC conditions. Senators questioned whether Paramount's efforts to settle Trump's defamation lawsuit over a CBS interview were tied to regulatory approvals, raising concerns that media companies might trade editorial independence for business advantages.

The administration also pressured law firms to align their pro bono work with its interests. After an executive order targeting Jenner & Block for representing Trump investigators was struck down, other firms faced implicit warnings about the costs of taking on clients who challenged government policies. Trump threatened Walmart over tariff-related price increases, using the bully pulpit to intervene in private pricing decisions for political optics. Broad tariffs, including a 10 percent universal import rate and a 30 percent China-specific rate, were maintained even as the president threatened new 50 percent tariffs on EU goods and 25 percent on iPhones unless production moved to the United States. Trade policy became a stage for brinkmanship and leverage, with markets and allies adjusting to the whims of a single actor.

Information and memory were carefully managed. The White House adopted an influencer-focused strategy, flooding the media with pro-Trump content, boosting partisan voices, and marginalizing critical outlets. Trump repeated false claims that the 2020 election was rigged and that he won by millions of votes, providing rhetorical cover for restrictive voting and immigration policies. He reposted a "Clinton body count" conspiracy video and other disinformation, normalizing baseless accusations against opponents. DHS spokesperson Tricia McLaughlin falsely accused House Democrats of "bodyslamming" ICE officers during an oversight visit, a claim contradicted by video but used to smear critics.

Legal and security measures were employed to regulate speech. The administration threatened to sue the parent company of Business Insider and ABC News over unfavorable stories, using the threat of litigation to suppress investigative reporting. DHS and the Secret Service launched an investigation into a cryptic Instagram post by former FBI Director James Comey as a possible threat to Trump, deploying security resources against symbolic expression by a critic. At the Pentagon, new rules limited reporters to specific areas and required escorts for movement, tightening credential requirements under the guise of leak prevention. These restrictions reduced transparency around defense policy at a time when military decisions carried significant consequences.

The broader information landscape revealed its own vulnerability. Congress enacted the TAKE IT DOWN Act, establishing new rules for removing certain online content and reshaping platform responsibilities, which could impact speech and privacy. The Chicago Sun-Times published an AI-generated summer reading list with nonexistent books, exposing how automation without strong fact-checking can undermine media credibility. House Republican leaders delayed installing a Capitol plaque honoring January 6 officers, despite prior approval, diminishing institutional memory of the attack and downplaying sacrifices that complicate pro-Trump narratives. Each action, small alone, contributed to a landscape where facts were challenged, archives were curated, and memorialization was driven by political motives.

Education and identity became explicit battlegrounds. In Oklahoma, State Superintendent Ryan Walters mandated that public schools teach debunked claims about the 2020 election and integrate the Bible into U.S. history curricula. These directives politicized civic education and blurred church-state boundaries, embedding partisan myths and sectarian frames into the classroom. Trump's renewed fraud claims and his questioning of Joe Biden's cancer diagnosis, followed by brief expressions of sympathy, folded even personal health information into narrative warfare. Abroad, administration officials promoted a "white genocide" narrative about South Africa to President Cyril Ramaphosa, exporting racially charged conspiracy theories into diplomacy.

Federal rules began to reflect a narrower view of identity. The Transportation Security Administration replaced "gender" with "sex" terminology across its regulations, aligning with an executive order and signaling a shift in how the state records and recognizes people. Corporate and institutional histories were rewritten in parallel. Verizon removed DEI content from its website as it ended those programs. Oil-company sponsorships of museums and youth groups, revealed through congressional subpoenas, showed how cultural institutions could be used to launder reputations and shape public narratives about climate and energy. A California court's decision to halt a vague ban on critical race theory in Temecula schools offered a counterpoint, preserving space for race-related instruction and underscoring the stakes of curricular fights.

Universities and legal-intellectual infrastructure faced direct federal retaliation. DHS Secretary Noem revoked Harvard's authority to host foreign exchange students, threatening thousands of international students and sending a message to a prominent critic of the administration. The Trump administration cut federal grants to Harvard on contested discrimination grounds, while DOJ Civil Rights opened investigations into alleged anti-white bias at Harvard Law Review. In Senate hearings, lawmakers pressed the IRS commissioner nominee about Trump's threats to Harvard's tax-exempt status, highlighting the use of fiscal tools as a cudgel.

Courts again provided partial checks. Federal judges prevented DHS from ending the legal status of international students during ongoing litigation and reinstated members of the Privacy and Civil Liberties Oversight Board whom Trump had dismissed. Senate oversight hearings examined misstatements and issues across agencies, and law firm challenges to retaliatory executive orders succeeded in some instances. Nevertheless, the overall environment sent a message that universities, watchdog groups, and law firms faced the risk of losing visas, grants, and tax benefits if they opposed the regime. Formal opposition remained legal, but the costs of dissent increased. Some scheduled events were already certain. The implementation of the One Big Beautiful Bill's tax and spending provisions, ongoing litigation over Harvard's visa authority and TPS termination, and upcoming agency budget hearings all awaited, testing how much the new fiscal and institutional framework could endure and how much resistance courts and Congress could still muster.

Throughout the term, Week 18 did not introduce new control methods; it reinforced existing ones. Fiscal policy, immigration enforcement, administrative restructuring, and narrative shaping moved together toward a more unified, patronage-driven, and stratified state. The modest progress on the Democracy Clock reflects not a slowdown in erosion but the normalization of practices once deemed crises. Institutions still function, courts continue issuing orders, and elections are still in sight. However, the conditions under which they operate—who can safely dissent, rely on protections, or have their stories taught and remembered—shifted further away from equal citizenship toward a system where power, wealth, and loyalty determine the rules.

CHAPTER 29
WEEK 19: INSTITUTIONS AS INSTRUMENTS OF LOYALTY

A week of near-static clock time but deepening campaigns to bend immigration, universities, media, and law itself toward executive preference and profit.

The nineteenth week of Trump's second term wasn't defined by a single order or speech. Instead, it unfolded as a series of connected campaigns, each targeting a different institution that once stood between the presidency and unchecked power. Immigration courts, universities, public broadcasters, museums, and school boards all found themselves pulled into the same conflict: whether laws and policies would serve the public broadly, or cater to the preferences and grievances of one leader and his allies. The pattern was straightforward. It was methodical.

At the end of Week 18, the Democracy Clock was at 7:59 p.m. It remained at the same time as Week 19 concluded, with a net change of 0.2 minutes. On the surface, nothing changed hour-wise. But beneath, the week intensified existing trends: executive orders replaced legislation, humanitarian protections were stripped from migrants, universities and the media were punished for dissent, and clemency and settlement were used to shield elites. Courts, state officials, and civil society responded with injunctions, lawsuits, and protests. That small numerical shift reflected a bigger reality. The system's structure stayed the same, but the power balance within it shifted further toward the executive.

Immigration was the most obvious example where this shift was visible. The administration moved to revoke humanitarian protections and parole programs that had allowed hundreds of thousands of migrants from Cuba, Haiti, Nicaragua, and Venezuela to live and work in the U.S. A Supreme Court order lifting lower-court blocks enabled the government to end these programs quickly, turning legal security into a temporary favor that could be revoked at any time. The decision wasn't just about paperwork. It turned lives into uncertain contingencies.

At the same time, Homeland Security officials ordered immigration agents to triple daily arrests to 3,000, turning enforcement into a numbers game. Quotas of that scale left little room for judgment. They encouraged sweeps and shortcuts, and they increased the risk that citizens and lawful residents would be caught up in the dragnet. That risk was not theoretical. In Alabama, a U.S. citizen filming a worksite raid was detained when his Real ID was dismissed as fake. In Georgia, a college student was arrested under a local-federal program and spent weeks in detention. In another case, a gay asylum seeker had to be ordered back to the United States by a federal judge after an unlawful deportation.

The human impact of these policies showed in smaller stories as well. Humanitarian parole for a critically ill four-year-old Mexican girl was revoked, despite her need for life-saving care. Visas for a Mexican singer and his band were canceled before a U.S. concert, cutting off a cultural exchange that posed no security threat. Along with the mass rollback of parole and temporary protected status, these decisions marked a shift from case-by-case mercy to blanket exclusion, with origin and category replacing the law's original intentions. The message was clear.

The administration also turned the visa system into a tool of surveillance and control. Student visa interviews worldwide were halted so that new social media vetting could be implemented. Consular officers were instructed to review applicants' online lives as a condition of studying, and visitors to certain institutions faced additional scrutiny. These measures blurred the line between security checks and monitoring viewpoints. They sent a message to foreign students and scholars that entry to the United States depended not only on their qualifications but also on what they said online.

Courts did not stand aside entirely. Federal judges ordered "reasonable fear" interviews before deportations to third countries and stopped at least one deportation flight to South Sudan that violated prior orders. In another case, a judge required the government to facilitate the return of the wrongly deported asylum seeker. These rulings reaffirmed that due process still had force. Yet the administration's open defiance of some immigration orders, and its willingness to push ahead until stopped, showed how far executive practice had moved from routine compliance. The law remained on the books. Its effect depended increasingly on the speed and reach of judicial intervention.

If immigration policy was the laboratory for exclusion, Harvard University became the test case for how far the executive would go in punishing institutions seen as disloyal. The week began with an order revoking Harvard's ability to enroll foreign students and a demand for detailed information about campus protests. The message was clear: access to international students and federal recognition would depend on cooperation with federal scrutiny of dissent. Within days, the administration terminated all federal contracts and grants with the university, canceling roughly $100 million in research and clinical funding. The response was swift.

These actions were coupled with a push for more detailed surveillance. Officials sought lists of Harvard's foreign students, even though federal databases already contained that information. Plans were advanced for mandatory social media screening of all foreign student visa applicants, and additional screening was ordered for visitors to Harvard itself. The tools used were bureaucratic—forms, interviews, data requests—but their goal was political. They transformed immigration and funding mechanisms into tools for disciplining a specific campus.

Harvard and its peers did not accept this silently. A federal district court in Massachusetts issued a temporary restraining order blocking the foreign-student ban, and later extended its injunction to protect the university's ability to host international students while litigation continued. Harvard filed suit against the administration and organized a coalition of more than two hundred college leaders, who characterized the federal demands as assaults on academic freedom and institutional independence. The legal battle did not eliminate the threat. However, it showed that universities, when treated as opponents, could respond as litigants and organizers rather than helpless supplicants.

The campaign against universities reflected a wider attack on public media and independent information sources. An executive order stopped the use of federal funds for NPR and PBS, effectively ending congressionally approved support for public broadcasters. The order did not point to errors in coverage or misuse of funds. It followed a pattern where critical outlets were punished while allies were rewarded. NPR, PBS, and Colorado public radio stations responded by filing federal lawsuits, claiming that the funding ban was retaliatory and unconstitutional. The stakes were clear.

Meanwhile, the White House communications office stopped publishing and removed official transcripts of Trump's speeches from searchable databases. This didn't silence the president; his words still reached audiences through rallies and preferred networks. However, it made it harder for journalists, researchers, and citizens to verify what was said and when. The State Department shut down its office of analytic outreach, which connected government analysts with outside experts. Across agencies, decisions about which records to keep, release, or hide became more driven by politics than by neutral archival practices.

Trump's actions reinforced this trend. Reports showed him

rewarding loyal media, law firms, and universities with access and contracts, while targeting critics with threats and orders to cut funding. The closure of analytic offices, removal of transcripts, and retaliatory actions against disliked groups created a pattern: power controlling memory and information. A federal judge's order requiring the administration to release previously withheld funds to Radio Free Europe/Radio Liberty was a rare exception. It affirmed Congress's authority over funding and supported a broadcaster operating in authoritarian countries abroad, even as similar pressures grew at home.

While information was restricted, the justice system leaned toward loyalty and wealth. Over the week, Trump issued a series of pardons and commutations that revealed a clear hierarchy of whose crimes mattered. He pardoned Scott Jenkins, a former sheriff convicted of selling badges and favors. He granted clemency to reality TV figures Julie and Todd Chrisley, convicted of bank fraud and tax evasion. He pardoned nursing home executive Paul Walczak after tax crimes, saving him from prison and restitution. He commuted the sentence of Larry Hoover, a former gang leader serving life, and then announced a broader package of clemency for twenty-five people, including former officials and other elites.

In each instance, the formal power to pardon was unquestioned. What changed was how it was used. Financial crimes, public corruption, and high-profile offenses linked to donors or political allies were often granted mercy. Meanwhile, immigration enforcement became more aggressive, and low-status offenders faced quotas and raids. This contrast suggested that the law was not a neutral constraint but a resource to be allocated: leniency for the powerful, severity for others. That is how hierarchies become rigid.

Corporate accountability followed a similar pattern. Boeing reached a non-prosecution agreement over the 737 MAX crashes, despite violating a prior deferred prosecution deal. The company avoided trial for systemic safety failures that had cost lives. Its extensive political and contracting ties to the administration—large defense contracts, lobbying, and representation—raised questions about whether its treatment was based on legal merits or access. The transfer of a former deputy convicted in a separate high-profile case to a halfway house highlighted how officials who abuse power can expect relatively lenient outcomes. For ordinary defendants, such results were rare.

Economic policy itself became a tool for personal and political gain. Trump announced a 50 percent tariff on European Union goods and threatened a 25 percent tariff on iPhones unless production moved to the United States. He extended deadlines and used looming tariff hikes as leverage over allies and companies. Courts later ruled that much of his emergency tariff regime—the so-called "Liberation Day" tariffs—was unconstitutional, finding that he had exceeded statutory and constitutional authority. Yet the administration filed emergency appeals to keep the tariffs in place while litigation continued, maintaining the economic pressure and the image of toughness.

Foreign policy and private business interests intertwined in ways that were difficult to separate. Vietnam expedited approval for a Trump-branded golf complex and tower, bending its rules and offering unusual concessions during tariff negotiations. Reports suggested that Trump's financial interests influenced foreign policy decisions more broadly. At home, Trump Media & Technology Group raised $2.5 billion to buy Bitcoin as a corporate treasury asset, while Truth Social launched investment accounts aimed at profiting from administration tariffs and "Made in America" policies. These products exploited insider knowledge of policy directions and linked investor returns to the success of a single political project.

The broader fiscal agenda pointed in the same direction. A comprehensive tax-and-spending package known as the One Big Beautiful bill extended earlier tax cuts, added new deductions, and funded mass deportations while cutting safety-net programs. The Federal Reserve chair met with Trump after the president publicly demanded lower interest rates, then insisted that decisions would remain data-driven. The exchange underscored both the pressure on independent economic institutions and their fragile resolve to resist. Meanwhile, analysts reported a sharp decline in international tourism linked to U.S. trade and immigration policies, and extremist propagandists used Trump's tariffs in recruitment narratives abroad, framing them as signs of Western instability.

Behind these specific policies, there was a broader shift in how executive power was exercised and limited. Reports noted that Trump had signed a record 152 executive orders since returning to office, shifting policymaking from Congress to the stroke of a pen. Stephen Miller, serving as deputy chief of staff, proposed suspending the writ of habeas corpus, one of the oldest protections against arbitrary detention. Trump criticized judges in a Memorial Day post, calling them "USA hating" and suggesting they helped criminals. This rhetoric was intentional. It portrayed an independent branch of government as an enemy of the people.

The judiciary responded with a mix of resistance and adaptation. Federal courts had issued at least 177 decisions pausing administrative initiatives, from unlawful firings to rollbacks of transgender protections. In the Garcia rendition case, a judge denied the administration's request for more time, insisting on timely accountability. Other judges allowed states' lawsuits over the Department of Government Efficiency and Elon Musk's role to proceed, and struck down an executive order targeting the Wilmer-Hale law firm for its past work. These rulings protected legal actors from direct retaliation and reinforced limits on creating powerful executive entities without proper authorization.

Yet, the strain on the judiciary was clear. Federal judges and the Judicial Conference's security committee considered establishing an independent armed security force for judges, reflecting deep concern about their safety and the politicization of existing protection. Democratic state attorneys general prepared and filed multiple lawsuits to counter potential overreach, using federalism as a tool for accountability. Congress, for its part, passed a tax-and-spending bill funding a massive Golden Dome missile defense system, committing long-term resources that would influence future oversight and budget debates. A federal judge's order to release funds to Radio Free Europe/Radio Liberty, despite executive hesitation, showed that separation of powers disputes now extended even to foreign-facing media.

While formal institutions grappled with these pressures, the administration and its allies worked to reshape culture, education, and identity. Trump signed an executive order targeting diversity, equity, and inclusion programs at military academies, leading to the disbanding of student groups and removal of materials. He wore a campaign hat while speaking at West Point graduation and delivered partisan speeches at West Point and Arlington National Cemetery, blurring the line between state ceremonies and campaign events. These actions linked the military's public image to a specific political movement.

Elsewhere, the Department of Justice launched an investigation into California's law allowing trans girls to participate in girls' sports, using civil rights enforcement tools to restrict rather than protect participation. State legislatures in Utah, Idaho, and Montana enacted bans on displaying LGBTQ+ flags at government buildings and schools, limiting symbolic expression and signaling official disapproval. Federal hostility toward DEI initiatives and trans rights dampened corporate support for Pride events, reducing resources for public LGBTQ+ visibility. Within the federal workforce, new Merit Hiring Plan guidelines discouraged considering race or gender and emphasized loyalty to the executive, signaling a politicized civil service.

Education policy became a key battleground. In Oklahoma, the state superintendent imposed a social studies curriculum infused with election conspiracies and Christian nationalism, despite expert objections. Parents, grandparents, and teachers sued state officials, challenging the curriculum on procedural grounds and arguing that standard review processes had been bypassed. A parent group used a parental opt-out law—originally designed to protect conservative values—to shield children from politicized lessons. These actions demonstrated how statutes could be repurposed to oppose, rather than promote, indoctrination.

Cultural institutions were also affected. Trump removed the director of the National Portrait Gallery because of her support for DEI, extending ideological loyalty tests into museums and public memory. Meanwhile, Virginia's General Assembly took a different approach by passing a constitutional amendment to protect abortion rights and putting the issue to voters. This contrast showed that while the federal government tried to limit identity and inclusion, some states used their power to expand rights and maintain diversity.

Civil society responded to these changes with widespread, decentralized protests. A grassroots movement called 50501 organized protests across the country against authoritarianism and oligarchy, with actions in all states. Other campaigns targeted specific centers of influence: Fox Takedown protests focused on Fox News stations over perceived propaganda; Purge Palantir activists demonstrated against a surveillance company viewed as enabling government overreach; Tesla Takedown organizers held showroom protests and boycotts to reduce a tech leader's political influence by hitting his economic base. These efforts combined street protests with consumer pressure, aiming to change behavior by increasing reputational and financial consequences.

At the same time, extremist groups kept marching. Patriot Front held a white nationalist rally in Kansas City, highlighting the ongoing threat to minority communities. Trump posted a meme depicting himself on a mission from God after a tariff ruling, using imagery linked to QAnon to frame his conflict with courts and critics in a quasi-religious way. Crime data told a different story from the one often used to justify crackdowns: reports showed notable drops in violent crime and mass shootings. The gap between improving public safety and increasing state coercion raised questions about the true reason for expanded powers.

The information landscape itself was changing. Islamic State propagandists used Trump's tariffs in recruiting stories, portraying

U.S. trade conflicts as signs of Western decline. The FBI reopened investigations into the 2023 White House cocaine incident and the Dobbs draft leak, and announced stepped-up probes into the January 6 pipe bomber and COVID-19 origins. These high-profile actions aimed to reassure the public but also placed the Bureau in contested political narratives about past crises. A new investigation into AI-enabled impersonation of the White House chief of staff highlighted emerging threats from deepfakes, where false messages could be inserted into decision-making processes.

Private control over communication infrastructure has deepened. Elon Musk's AI company acquired X, formerly Twitter, consolidating an AI firm's influence over a major social network and its data. Elsewhere, the National Archives and its FOIA Advisory Committee announced a public meeting to discuss reforms and implement transparency laws, marking a modest but meaningful effort to preserve access to government records amid broader secrecy trends. Outside the United States, World Bank researchers reported strong learning gains from low-cost AI tutors in Nigeria, signaling how technology could expand educational opportunities if used for public benefit rather than manipulation.

Across these areas, the week's changes were gradual rather than sudden. Humanitarian protections were rolled back while arrest quotas increased. Universities and public media were told that their funding and students depended on cooperation and deference. Clemency and settlements favored those with access, while migrants and marginalized groups bore the brunt of enforcement. Executive orders increased, and suspending habeas corpus was even floated as a possible option. Courts, state officials, universities, parents, journalists, and protesters pushed back, often successfully in the short term. However, each victory required more effort, coordination, and risk than before.

In that sense, Week 19 was not a break but a deepening. The formal structure of democracy—elections, courts, legislatures, a free press—remained intact. However, the ways those institutions functioned changed further. Law was used more openly as a weapon than as a limit. Citizenship and access became more sharply divided by origin, wealth, and ideology. Information and memory were curated more tightly by those in power. Resistance persisted, and in some areas, grew more inventive. The cost of that resistance and the ease with which authority advanced when unchecked were what the clock recorded.

CHAPTER 30
WEEK 20: SURVEILLANCE AS EVERYDAY GOVERNANCE

In a week of near-still clock time, immigration raids, data centralization, and partisan clemency showed power consolidating quietly inside a more permissive order.

The twentieth week of Trump's second term did not hinge on a single rupture. It unfolded as a dense layering of actions that, taken together, showed a regime no longer testing the limits of the system but operating within a new, more permissive understanding of what power could do. Immigration raids, budget bills, court orders, and symbolic gestures all pointed in the same direction: a state that classifies people by origin and loyalty, rewards insiders, and treats dissent as a security threat. The pattern was not subtle; it was steady.

At the close of Week 19, the Democracy Clock stood at 7:59 p.m., ending Week 20 at the same public time with a net movement of 0.1 minutes. On the surface, the clock appeared to hold, but in reality, it indicated a slight further erosion in democratic safety. This small shift reflected that many of this week's actions deepened existing trajectories rather than opening new fronts. Courts that had been showing more deference moved a bit further; immigration enforcement that was already strict became more openly political; surveillance that had been expanding gained new tools. The danger this week lay more in consolidation than in novelty.

The clearest sign of that consolidation appeared in immigration enforcement, which moved firmly into the realm of political control. Immigration and Customs Enforcement and the Department of Homeland Security carried out aggressive raids that targeted individuals and also detained 'collateral" victims at workplaces and check-ins. Record numbers of arrests and warrantless detentions made vulnerability a constant threat. For noncitizens and mixed-status families, daily life became a landscape filled with risk. The law still spoke in terms of enforcement and public safety. Its real effect was to make entire communities easier to intimidate.

That intimidation was not limited to the margins. In Washington, federal agents from the Federal Protective Service and ICE entered Representative Jerry Nadler's office claiming it was for a safety check and handcuffed a staffer. The incident blurred the line between building security and political pressure on a senior opposition lawmaker. In California, SEIU state president David Huerta was arrested amid an immigration raid, with official accounts later contradicted by video evidence. These incidents showed enforcement spilling into the domestic political sphere, sending a message that even elected officials and union leaders were not immune from the machinery of raids and cuffs.

On campuses and in the streets, immigration status became a tool to suppress dissent. A student who wrote a Gaza opinion piece was arrested and seen as a security risk. Pro-Palestinian protesters faced detention using immigration as a pretext. When anti-deportation protests in Los Angeles grew, the government sent in National Guard units and Marines to try to break up what were mostly peaceful demonstrations. The decision to deploy military forces during a domestic protest marked a significant shift. Dissent was no longer just policed; it was treated as a semi-insurgent threat that justified armed response. The legal methods used against individual activists became more obscure and harsher. Palestinian activist Mahmoud Khalil was detained under a rarely invoked law, leading to a constitutional challenge. The combination of outdated legal authority and modern political speech sent a warning: the government was willing to use extensive legal measures to silence voices it saw as dangerous.

Meanwhile, structural changes made the system more rigid. The Supreme Court allowed the government to end humanitarian paroles for about half a million people, and the White House created an Office of Remigration to encourage deportations over protections. Wide-ranging travel bans and visa suspensions for specific institutions, including restrictions on foreign students at Harvard, centralized control over who could enter or study in the U.S. Some lower-court rulings ordered the return of deportees or halted removals, especially for families and LGBTQ asylum seekers. These instances were pockets of resistance in a broader system that now viewed origin and ideology as grounds for reducing rights.

If immigration enforcement demonstrated how the state could classify and punish, the courts and executive orders revealed how it could observe and control. The Supreme Court upheld Trump's decision to remove National Labor Relations Board chair Gwynne Wilcox, reinforcing a unitary executive theory that views independent regulators as extensions of the presidential will. In the same week, the Court lifted an injunction that had blocked the Department of Government Efficiency—an unelected, contractor-linked agency known as Doge—from accessing Social Security data and moving forward with "efficiency" measures. These emergency stays, issued on the Court's shadow docket, effectively authorized the administration and its private partners to mine sensitive records while union and privacy challenges were still unresolved. The message was clear: the president's influence over the bureaucracy was expanding.

Behind these orders was a broader data initiative. The administration issued an executive order to centralize federal personal data using Palantir technology to create a unified infrastructure across agencies. Along with Doge's new access to Social Security files, this established a surveillance-heavy state where an opaque entity could analyze the intimate details of millions of lives under the guise of fraud detection and cost savings. The same Court that opened this door also permitted the administration to cancel large-scale immigration paroles during litigation and agreed to hear a case that could restrict lower courts' ability to issue nationwide injunctions in rights cases. In other rulings, it dismissed Mexico's lawsuit against U.S. gunmakers, expanded religious tax exemptions, and eased reverse-discrimination claims, signaling a bench inclined to protect industries and majority plaintiffs.

Lower courts remained active in the story. Judges in various jurisdictions blocked or corrected deportations, ordering the return of migrants wrongly deported to El Salvador and Mexico, and halting removals for a gay asylum seeker and families in Colorado. The Court of International Trade declared Trump's broad metal tariffs illegal, reaffirming Congress's authority over tariffs, even though an appeals court stay kept the duties in place. A district judge allowed a lawsuit from fourteen states against Doge and the Social Security Administration to proceed, opening the possibility to review this new form of outsourcing. These acts of resistance were genuine. However, they were limited. Significant changes in labor rights, data access, and immigration status mainly came from the Supreme Court's emergency orders and the executive branch's willingness to enforce them.

While the legal framework leaned toward deference, the White House moved to redefine accountability itself. Trump issued blanket pardons and commutations for January 6 defendants and ordered related cases to be dropped. Participants in the attack on the transfer of power were portrayed as victims of overzealous prosecution rather than political violence perpetrators. Meanwhile, the president ordered investigations into Joe Biden's cognitive health and the pardons and clemency decisions of his predecessor. A key constitutional power, traditionally used for mercy and correction, was turned into a tool for partisan scrutiny. The message was that future presidents who used clemency in ways opposed by a successor could face retrospective investigations.

January 6 figures themselves joined this effort to invert the narrative. Enrique Tarrio and others filed a lawsuit challenging their prosecutions, trying to portray enforcement as persecution. In the information sphere, Trump amplified conspiracy theories claiming that Biden had been executed and replaced by clones or robots. These fantastical claims, broadcast by a sitting president, eroded shared reality and blurred the line between satire and state narrative. On Capitol Hill, the House Oversight Committee leadership pursued partisan inquiries into Biden's cognition and aides, while Democrats on the same committee demanded the full release of Jeffrey Epstein case files from the FBI and Justice Department. Oversight became a split screen: one side aimed at delegitimizing a predecessor, the other at exposing secrecy around elite misconduct.

On the ground, the pattern of who faced handcuffs and who received clemency was stark. Rev. William Barber and Moral Monday protesters were arrested in the Capitol Rotunda for peaceful protests against budget cuts in healthcare and social services. Newark Mayor Ras Baraka filed a lawsuit alleging false arrest and malicious prosecution by federal officials, claiming that criminal charges were used against a local critic. Along with the January 6 pardons, these cases illustrated a justice system that had been reoriented. Insurrectionists were forgiven; anti-austerity clergy and dissenting mayors found themselves in the dock.

Beneath these headline struggles, the administration and its congressional allies pushed forward a comprehensive overhaul of the safety net. The House approved the One Big Beautiful Bill and a Republican budget bill that significantly reduced funding for Medicaid, nutrition assistance, rental aid, preschool development grants, FEMA resilience programs, veterans' care, and NOAA and NWS capacities. Simultaneously, the bills maintained or expanded 2017-style tax cuts and blocked state regulation of artificial intelligence. This effectively shifted resources away from poor and working-class households toward higher-income taxpayers and corporations, embedding this change into law.

Targeted actions further reinforced this trend. The administration proposed deep cuts to NIH and other biomedical research funding, risking long-term medical innovation and public health infrastructure. It pushed plans to transfer veterans' care from VA facilities to private providers while reducing VA jobs and contracts, turning a core public service into a fragmented market. In reproductive health, the White House ceased enforcement of emergency abortion guidelines under EMTALA, leaving life-or-death decisions in emergency rooms more vulnerable to state bans and local prosecutors. A West Virginia prosecutor even suggested women should report miscarriages to police under an abortion ban, intensifying fears that pregnancy outcomes could lead to criminal investigation. The boundary between health care and law enforcement grew increasingly blurred.

Independent analysts warned about the costs. The Congressional Budget Office and the OECD released reports showing that Trump's tariffs and the omnibus bill would increase deficits, slow economic growth, and raise the number of uninsured people. Rising unemployment claims and concerns about the accuracy of inflation data, fueled by staffing shortages at the Bureau of Labor Statistics, added to economic stress. Yet when Senator Joni Ernst was asked about Medicaid cuts, she downplayed their impact and used religious language about mortality, framing the cuts as both manageable and morally justified. The administration asked Congress to rescind $9.4 billion in previously allocated funds, including money for public media and foreign aid, and threatened to cancel significant federal funding and rail grants for California. The risks and austerity measures were downplayed, while potential gains remained protected.

Along with the cuts, the week revealed how deeply economic policy had become intertwined with the interests of a few wealthy oligarchs. The GENIUS Act, pushed forward after substantial crypto donations, promised to regulate stablecoins, including

USD1, a token linked to the Trump family. A $2 billion investment by UAE-owned MGX into Binance used USD1 as the investment vehicle, transforming a private coin connected to the ruling family into a channel for foreign capital. Senator Elizabeth Warren released a report detailing Elon Musk's wealth increase and his influence over federal policy, highlighting how closely contractors like Musk were embedded in decisions on space, data, and infrastructure. Public policy and private financial interests are becoming increasingly difficult to distinguish.

The relationship between Trump and Musk, once mutually beneficial, spilled into an open feud. After Musk criticized spending bills and aspects of the administration's agenda, Trump publicly suggested terminating Musk's federal subsidies and contracts, including those tied to NASA and Doge. The president's threats linked the continuation of major federal contracts to personal loyalty rather than performance. At the same time, the two men clashed over Doge's role, ISS logistics, and media narratives, with their dispute amplified across platforms. Corporate power responded unevenly. Some firms cut ties with law firms that complied with Trump's anti-media order, signaling resistance to executive overreach. Others withdrew sponsorships from Pride events under political pressure, showing how business influence could also reinforce culture-war priorities.

Tariff policy and industrial strategy followed the same pattern of personalized, donor-sensitive decision-making. Trump doubled tariffs on steel and aluminum imports to 50 percent through executive action, reshaping trade conditions with limited congressional input. His budget director, Russell Vought, indicated plans to use impoundment and executive tools to reduce federal spending without full legislative approval. Meanwhile, the administration promoted policies that slowed industrial growth and cut support for battery and EV manufacturing, leading to canceled plants and weakening domestic capacity in strategic sectors. Economic levers were used with little concern for long-term stability but with a strong focus on political gain and the preferences of aligned industries.

Information, science, and memory were not passive in this process; they were targets. At the Department of Veterans Affairs, political leadership required doctors and scientists to obtain clearance before publishing or speaking, effectively routing research through appointees who could suppress inconvenient findings. Critics described a "war on science" as staffing cuts and communication restrictions undermined evidence-based debate about veterans' health. The administration issued an executive order on "Restoring Gold Standard Science" that, despite its name, empowered political appointees to punish or silence unwelcome research, centralizing control over what is considered authoritative evidence. The aim was not to improve science but to enforce compliant science.

Independent media faced similar pressures. The White House and its allies moved to defund NPR and PBS, claiming they conflicted with American interests, bundling those cuts into a rescission package that also targeted foreign aid. Public broadcasters responded by filing a lawsuit challenging Trump's order to cut funding to what he claimed were biased outlets, testing whether the executive could punish media financially based on perceived bias. At the Pentagon, briefing-room doors were locked, and regular press conferences were halted, reducing transparency about military policy. Economic data also became less reliable as BLS staffing shortages jeopardized the quality of inflation surveys, and White House officials misstated the deficit impacts of legislation. The informational foundation for citizens grew shakier.

The battle over memory and education took on a more symbolic yet equally significant form. The Department of Defense temporarily removed Jackie Robinson's biography from its website, and Trump ordered the renaming of the USNS Harvey Milk and other ships to highlight "warrior culture," erasing civil rights figures in favor of martial themes. Secretary of Education Linda McMahon gave ambiguous testimony on whether teaching Black history and the facts of the 2020 election violated federal DEI policies, which encouraged self-censorship in schools. Homeland Security Secretary Kristi Noem accused Harvard of promoting Chinese Communist Party priorities and espionage without evidence, framing a leading university as a foreign influence hub. DHS issued flawed lists of "noncompliant" sheriffs and sanctuary jurisdictions to shame local officials, then retracted them after pressure. These actions collectively showed an administration controlling which histories and facts could be officially recognized and using data as a weapon to enforce compliance.

Religion and civil rights activities were pulled into the same sphere. The Department of Justice's Civil Rights Division warned California schools that permitting trans girls in sports violated equal protection, while Trump threatened to impose hefty fines on the state over transgender athlete participation. Federal civil rights law, historically used to promote inclusion, was turned against a marginalized group. In reproductive policy, the rollback of EMTALA and miscarriage-reporting rhetoric indicated a readiness to involve police and prosecutors in highly personal areas of life. On the protest front, Moral Monday demonstrators were arrested in the Capitol, a traffic safety activist in Charlottesville was charged with vandalism for chalking a crosswalk, and a nationwide crackdown on organized retail theft demonstrated how property crime could be aggressively policed even as political violence was met with leniency. The hierarchy of what the state chose to punish was clearly displayed.

Religious rhetoric helped justify these decisions and delineate who belonged. Senator Ernst invoked Christianity when defending Medicaid cuts, framing suffering and mortality as matters of faith rather than policy choices. Representative Mary Miller criticized a Sikh prayer in Congress after misidentifying the faith of the leader, normalizing ignorance and bigotry in official discourse. In the private sector, political attacks on corporate diversity efforts contributed to withdrawals from Pride sponsorships, reducing the visibility and funding of LGBTQ events. A bipartisan anti-grooming law in Louisiana expanded tools against abuse but, within this climate, raised questions about how broadly such offenses could be interpreted. Overall, the result was a narrowing of who could fully participate in public life and a blending of policy with specific religious and cultural identities.

All of this unfolded amid a deliberate surge of action. Within just a few days, the administration doubled metal tariffs, announced plans for impoundment, issued broad orders on cybersecurity, drones, and supersonic flights, launched mass immigration raids, pushed for deep budget cuts, centralized data under Doge and Palantir, and spread conspiracies about Biden's supposed death and replacement. Economic indicators fluctuated: unemployment claims increased, inflation data became less reliable, and independent agencies warned of deficits and slower growth. DHS's shaming lists of sheriffs, later retracted, added chaos to enforcement efforts. The sheer volume and variety of these moves overwhelmed the capacity of the media, courts, and civil society to track and challenge them. Changes in surveillance, inequality, and institutional independence hardened, while attention shifted rapidly from one crisis to another.

Some counterforces persisted. Lower courts upheld due process in individual deportation cases. Public broadcasters challenged to defend their funding and independence. House Democrats demanded transparency regarding Epstein's records. The National Archives quietly invited public comment on records schedules, tending to the long-term integrity of government archives. Lawmakers such as Angus King and Jamie Raskin referenced historical warnings about demagoguery and conscience, and Senator Cory Booker called on citizens to hold fearful politicians accountable. Civil society groups organized protests and legal challenges, even as some leaders faced arrest. The guardrails bent but did not break.

Yet the balance of the week favored those who wielded power, not those who checked it. Executive orders and emergency stays expanded surveillance and data access more quickly than privacy advocates could respond. Budget bills and rescission packages moved through Congress with little genuine deliberation, embedding inequality and privatization into law. The Supreme Court's emergency docket became a quiet driver of structural change, aligning with executive and corporate priorities. Immigration enforcement and policing were used to intimidate opposition and vulnerable communities, while paramilitary-style political violence from January 6 was overlooked. The incentives were clear: loyalty was rewarded, and resistance carried increasing costs.

In that sense, Week 20 marked not a dramatic shift but a deepening of the existing trend. Citizenship was more sharply divided by wealth, ideology, and heritage. Law functioned more as a weapon than as a boundary. Surveillance became more widespread, even as elite dealings remained hidden. Universities, media, and scientific institutions faced pressure to conform or risk losing funding and access. The system still held elections, courts still issued rulings, and protests still took place, but the cost of engaging with those channels rose, and the rewards for loyalty to the regime increased. The almost-stillness of the clock revealed a sobering truth: the danger now was how normal this had begun to feel.

CHAPTER 31
WEEK 21: EMERGENCY POWERS AS ROUTINE GOVERNANCE

In Los Angeles and beyond, immigration raids, troop deployments, and cultural decrees showed how emergency tools can be normalized as everyday management.

The twenty-first week of Trump's second term revealed how emergency measures can become routine. Immigration enforcement, protest policing, and even public memory were unified into a single approach, with the presidency at its core. What once seemed extraordinary—federal troops in a major American city, welfare data accessed by deportation officials, monuments ordered by decree—was now framed as management, security, and patriotism. This pattern did not rely on a single breaking point but on repeated actions.

At the start of Week 21, the Democracy Clock was at 7:59 p.m. By week's end, it reached 8:00 p.m., a change of just 0.4 minutes. This small measure carried significant implications. It reflected the merging of immigration raids with military deployments in Los Angeles, the testing of legal boundaries on federalization of the Guard and election oversight, and the increased use of data, media regulation, and cultural policies to reward loyalty and punish dissent. Courts and civil society did not stand still. Their resistance was reactive and often partial, while executive power expanded in multiple directions.

The clearest display of that power occurred in California. Despite objections from Governor Gavin Newsom and every other Democratic governor nationwide, President Trump federalized thousands of California National Guard troops and deployed them to Los Angeles. The official reason was to support immigration enforcement and restore order during protests. However, the move effectively shifted a key state security function from Sacramento to the White House. Normally, the Guard reports to the governor for domestic issues, but in this case, they took orders from a president who described the city's protests as a "Migrant Invasion" and a potential "insurrection." That framing made a difference.

Along with the Guard, active-duty Marines were also deployed. Defense Secretary Pete Hegseth ordered hundreds into the Los Angeles area and indicated readiness to send more. Marines are trained for combat, not crowd control. Their presence in a domestic protest blurred the line between military and civilian policing—something previous generations considered a last resort. Here, these deployments were part of a planned immigration strategy rather than a response to an unexpected crisis. Later reports revealed that using troops for immigration enforcement had been in planning for months.

On the ground, ICE and DHS conducted large-scale raids across Los Angeles and other California communities. Agents searched workplaces and neighborhoods, often without warrants, using armored vehicles and flash-bang grenades. People with no criminal records were detained. Access to lawyers was delayed or denied. Conditions in detention facilities were poor. The raids extended beyond noncitizens. A deputy U.S. marshal was mistakenly arrested. Newark's mayor was taken into custody while observing an operation. A pregnant U.S. citizen was violently detained. These incidents demonstrated how a campaign targeting immigrants can affect citizens' rights when force becomes normalized.

Protesters opposing the raids and troop deployments faced similar treatment. Federal officers and Guard units used rubber bullets, flash-bang grenades, and other "less lethal" weapons against mostly peaceful crowds. One widely shared video showed an officer firing a round at close range at a woman near her home. Journalists covering the protests reported being hit with projectiles and briefly detained. Above, Customs and Border Protection flew Predator drones, capturing and sharing aerial footage of the city. The tools of foreign surveillance and warfare had become part of the visual language of domestic protest control.

Oversight efforts fared poorly in this environment. Members of Congress were turned away from detention centers in Los Angeles and New York when they attempted to inspect conditions during the raids. A senator, Alex Padilla, was dragged and handcuffed by federal agents while questioning DHS officials at a press conference about the deployments and arrests. The arrest of SEIU California's president, David Huerta, while he observed a raid, sent a similar message to labor. The law still recognized congressional oversight and union advocacy, but on the ground, both were treated as interference.

The human and financial costs of this militarized approach were significant. The Pentagon's comptroller estimated that federalizing the Guard and deploying Marines to Los Angeles would cost $134 million. ICE raids at plants like Glenn Valley Foods removed large portions of the workforce, disrupting food production and local labor markets. Even President Trump acknowledged that his immigration policy was hurting farmers by removing long-term workers. Yet the administration continued, with White House adviser Stephen Miller demanding arrest quotas of at least 3,000 people per day. Volume became a measure of success.

Public response increased in size and intensity. Anti-ICE protests in Los Angeles and other cities continued throughout the week, sometimes involving property damage but more often peaceful marches and vigils. As Trump prepared a military parade in Washington filled with tanks for his birthday, organizers supported by figures like Christy Walton launched "No Kings Day" and "No Kings" protests at around 2,000 locations. Millions of people planned and participated in protests that openly connected deportations, troop deployments, and the president's defiance of court orders. In several states, Republican governors and sheriffs activated or threatened to activate their own National Guard units and warned of harsh responses, including lethal force, if protests became unruly. Militarization and opposition fueled each other.

Immigration law became another contested field. In Texas, a federal court blocked the administration's attempt to use the Alien Enemies Act to deport people to El Salvador, holding that the wartime statute could not be repurposed for routine immigration removals and requiring a 30-day window for legal challenges. In New Jersey, Judge Michael Farbiarz ordered the release of a Palestinian activist whom the administration had detained as a supposed foreign-policy threat, limiting claims to hold noncitizens indefinitely without charges. Advocacy groups pursued suits to stop ICE from arresting immigrants at courthouses, arguing that such practices deterred people from seeking justice. These rulings did not dismantle the enforcement machinery. They narrowed some of its most aggressive edges.

Election administration also faced judicial review. Federal judges in Massachusetts and Washington, DC issued injunctions against Trump's executive order that required proof of citizenship to vote in federal elections and threatened to withhold funds from states that didn't comply. Another ruling highlighted that the Constitution gives no broad election-management power to the president, limiting efforts to centralize control over voting rules within the executive branch. These rulings reaffirmed that, officially, the structure of federal elections remains decentralized and resistant to unilateral overhaul.

Still, the same week, the executive branch responded against oversight actors. The Department of Justice indicted Representative LaMonica McIver for allegedly obstructing immigration officers during a detention-center visit, blurring the line between legitimate congressional oversight and criminal interference. Senator Padilla's rough treatment at a DHS event underscored this point. Inside the Pentagon, the inspector general launched an investigation into whether Defense Secretary Hegseth's aides had been instructed to delete encrypted Signal messages, raising concerns about record-keeping and accountability within the office responsible for domestic troop deployments. The formal oversight mechanisms still existed, but their personnel now faced legal and physical risks.

Courts remained active beyond immigration and elections. Judges temporarily blocked several administration efforts to defund or censor unfavored educational and research institutions, including orders targeting the American Bar Association, grants labeled as promoting "gender ideology," and funding tied to campus protest policies. An appeals court upheld a $5 million defamation award against Donald Trump in the E. Jean Carroll case, affirming that even a president can be held civilly liable for defamatory attacks on private citizens. At the same time, Congress considered protective legislation like the My Body, My Data Act, aimed at shielding reproductive health information from surveillance, and the Election Assistance Commission scheduled public meetings on voting system guidelines and a 2025 election data summit. The legal landscape was crowded, contested, and far from settled.

Immigration itself became a tool for ideological policing. ICE and DOJ targeted immigrants and activists for pro-Palestine speech, using arrests, visa denials, and surveillance to punish political expression. The State Department revoked visas for hundreds of international students involved in pro-Palestine protests, turning immigration status into a means of campus discipline. USCIS announced it would monitor immigrants' social media for "antisemitic activity" that could influence visa decisions, linking online speech to legal status in the country. These actions did not outright ban dissent but made it far more costly for those without citizenship.

The reach of enforcement expanded into welfare and health systems. The administration authorized the transfer of Medicaid enrollees' personal data, including immigration status, to DHS to support deportations. Information provided by people to access medical care now flowed into enforcement databases. This repurposing of welfare data undermined trust in social programs and blurred the boundary between service provision and policing. Local institutions responded as best they could. The Los Angeles Unified School District created safety perimeters and alternative viewing options for graduations to protect immigrant families from ICE presence, adjusting school operations to minimize exposure to raids.

The stratification of rights was clear even in smaller stories. A well-known influencer, Khaby Lame, was detained over an alleged visa overstay and agreed to leave voluntarily. The acting chair of the Equal Employment Opportunity Commission directed staff to stop processing gender-identity discrimination claims and removed nonbinary markers from intake forms, effectively denying trans and nonbinary workers equal access to federal civil rights protections. The Department of Health and Human Services proposed removing LGBTQ-specific counseling from the national 988 suicide hotline, reducing tailored support for a vulnerable community. These administrative choices did not change the actual civil rights laws but altered who could realistically claim their protections.

Media and information systems faced coordinated pressure. The Department of Justice reversed a previous policy and granted itself broader authority to subpoena journalists' records in leak investigations, not only for classified information but also for disclosures that could "undermine" Trump's agenda. This change, along with targeting lawyers and potential whistleblowers through security-clearance revocations, increased the personal risk of exposing wrongdoing. The FCC, led by Chairman Brendan Carr, opened investigations into unpopular outlets like CBS over editorial decisions, while the administration moved to dismantle the U.S. Agency for Global Media and limit Voice of America. Public broadcasters NPR and PBS faced potential defunding through both executive actions and a House rescissions bill.

Individual journalists felt the pressure of this environment. ABC News suspended and later fired correspondent Terry Moran after critical comments about Trump officials, following outreach from the administration. The White House retaliated against the Associated Press for using disliked terminology, removing it from press pools and restricting access even after a court found First Amendment violations. On the streets of Los Angeles, reporters were struck with rubber bullets and pepper balls, and press and civil-liberties groups documented what they called deliberate targeting. Meanwhile, the administration embedded Dr. Phil's TV crew inside ICE raids, turning coercive operations into curated content for sympathetic audiences. Independent reporting was limited. State-influenced narratives were amplified.

Control over culture and education progressed in tandem. Trump issued executive orders to restore removed monuments and establish a National Garden of American Heroes, using federal authority to promote a celebratory version of U.S. history in public spaces. He announced the reinstatement of Confederate names on Army bases, reversing efforts to confront the legacies of slavery and secession. At the Kennedy Center, he removed the chair and president in an attempt to combat perceived "wokeness," extending presidential influence into a major cultural institution. He also attempted to fire the director of the National Portrait Gallery over diversity initiatives, but the Smithsonian's Board of Regents refused, asserting its authority over personnel decisions and maintaining a degree of institutional independence.

Within government and military education systems, the administration ordered the removal of hundreds of DEI-related books and activities. Military academies and Defense Department schools eliminated titles on race, gender, and sexuality from their libraries and curricula. Federal agencies erased more than 250 DEI and gender-related terms from their websites under executive orders, limiting how government could describe marginalized groups and efforts toward equity. The Department of Education threatened to revoke funding from schools that taught about systemic racism. Grants for research involving disfavored gender-related terms were canceled. Fulbright projects exploring DEI themes required political approval, and some scholarships were denied.

These actions echoed in state and civil-society spheres. Florida officials threatened criminal prosecution of a school superintendent over library books labeled as pornography, even when legal standards did not support that label. When bills to remove certain books stalled in the legislature, the state board of education took similar restrictions administratively. Advocacy groups like Moms for Liberty and Citizens Defending Freedom organized campaigns to remove books and reshape curricula on race, LGBTQ issues, and sex education, occasionally reporting librarians to law enforcement. The Southern Baptist Convention endorsed a resolution calling for the repeal of same-sex marriage legalization. New York City adopted the IHRA definition of antisemitism for city agencies, raising concerns that criticism of Israel could be mistaken for hate speech. Pride flags were banned from federal offices and consular posts. Religion and morality were used to justify a narrower view of identity and belonging.

Within the machinery of government, politicization deepened. At the Department of Homeland Security, a 22-year-old recent graduate was appointed to lead its main terrorism-prevention center, raising questions about whether loyalty and optics had displaced experience and institutional memory. Health and Human Services Secretary Robert F. Kennedy Jr. dismissed all 17 members of the CDC's vaccine advisory committee and moved to replace them with controversial figures, politicizing a body whose value depended on scientific independence. Director of National Intelligence Tulsi Gabbard fired the acting counsel to the intelligence community inspector general and installed a direct adviser, undermining the IG's independence and concentrating control over internal investigations.

Civil-rights enforcement and revenue collection were similarly reshaped. The EEOC's sidelining of gender-identity cases and removal of nonbinary markers signaled that protections for trans and nonbinary workers would not be meaningfully enforced. The Senate confirmed Billy Long, a former congressman who had once sought to abolish the IRS, as IRS commissioner, aligning a key tax institution with anti-tax ideology and raising the risk of internal sabotage or demoralization. The Department of Government Efficiency's earlier hollowing out of USAID, now visible in impaired development capacity, showed how ad hoc executive entities could be used to weaken diplomacy and aid under the banner of cutting waste.

Ethical boundaries eroded. Congressman Mark Green accepted a private-sector job while remaining in Congress without disclosing his employer, highlighting weak enforcement of conflict-of-interest rules. The Department of Justice issued orders revoking security clearances from law firms representing Trump's opponents, using national-security tools to punish legal advocacy. Yet there were pockets of internal resistance. More than 90 NIH scientists signed a letter opposing administration policies they said undermined the agency's mission, defending scientific integrity and public health. The Pentagon inspector general's probe into deleted messages and the Smithsonian board's refusal to fire the Portrait Gallery director showed that some watchdogs and boards still asserted their roles.

Information and economic policy are closely linked. The administration suppressed or modified economic and climate data, delaying deficit reports, editing climate assessments, and reducing staff at statistical agencies. Commentators documented these practices, creating an alternative record. The Environmental Protection Agency worked to remove greenhouse gas limits and weaken toxic standards for power plants, shifting regulatory authority toward fossil-fuel interests. The National Park Service faced significant budget cuts, affecting programs that protect night skies and soundscapes. These decisions prioritized short-term industry gains over long-term public health and shared heritage.

Funding and regulation became tools for control. The administration withdrew grants from the American Bar Association after criticism of Trump, froze grants and threatened Harvard's tax-exempt status over hiring and admissions policies, and cut support for scientific projects that used banned terms. Universities allowing campus protests faced threats to their funding. Medical journals were accused of bias, and officials hinted at restricting government scientists' ability to publish in them. A broad budget reconciliation package, promoted by Republican leadership and the White House, known as "One Big, Beautiful Bill," proposed cuts to Medicaid and tax reforms favoring the wealthy, using budget procedures to implement extensive redistributive changes with limited debate. Analysts from the World Bank and others predicted Trump's trade war would cut U.S. growth in half, linking confrontational tariffs to broader economic costs.

All of this occurred amid a deliberate expansion of multiple fronts. Immigration raids, troop deployments, media conflicts, environmental rollbacks, book bans, and data manipulation didn't happen sequentially—they arrived together. Oversight bodies—courts, state officials, scientists, journalists—had to decide where to focus limited attention and resources. The administration used data systems for enforcement, from Medicaid transfers to social media surveillance, expanding monitoring of ordinary citizens while making elite decision-making more opaque. Chaos became a strategic approach, not an accident.

The week ended without a single decisive event. Instead, it left a layered record of how power was exercised and challenged. Executive authority expanded through federalization of troops, reinterpretation of laws, and control over information and culture. Oversight continued but was strained, with judges issuing injunctions that were quickly appealed, lawmakers facing indictment and harassment, and internal watchdogs being reshaped. Public resistance was large and visible, from "No Kings" marches to letters from scientists, yet it operated in an environment where the costs of dissent were increasing.

In the course of the term, Week 21 marked a deepening of existing patterns rather than a new shift. Emergency-style tools became normalized. Immigration served as a test case for rights erosion. Media, schools, and museums were pulled into the struggle over narrative and memory. The small movement of the Democracy Clock reflected this accumulation: not a collapse, but a tightening of the space where democratic institutions can operate and citizens can stand without fear.

CHAPTER 32
WEEK 22: CITIZENSHIP AS SORTING MECHANISM

> *A week of layered decisions that turned immigration, protest, markets, and memory into tools for ranking who belongs and who may be punished.*

The twenty-second week of Trump's second term didn't depend on a single order or speech. Instead, it involved a complex series of decisions that determined who could belong, protest, profit, and which stories the country is allowed to tell about itself. Immigration raids, court rulings, corporate withdrawals from civil rights commitments, and symbolic changes in the White House all pointed in the same direction: a state more willing to classify people by loyalty and usefulness, and less willing to accept limits on how that classification is carried out. The pattern became clearer and more difficult to ignore.

At the end of Week 21, the Democracy Clock read 8:00 p.m., and it remained at the same time after Week 22, with a net shift of 0.3 minutes. The clock face stayed the same, but the internal mechanism shifted. The small advance reflected a week in which executive power expanded in many areas—immigration, energy, tech, and public memory—while courts and parts of Congress managed to regain some ground in a few domains. The balance of power did not break, but the cost of resistance increased, and the hierarchy of who is protected versus exposed became more defined.

The clearest sign of that hierarchy appeared in the immigration system. Early in the week, Trump signed orders directing DHS and DOJ to target and defund "sanctuary" jurisdictions, using federal funding as leverage over local immigration policies. Simultaneously, he and adviser Stephen Miller set ambitious daily arrest quotas for ICE—3,000 arrests per day—and expanded enforcement to include large numbers of non-criminal migrants. Immigration law on paper remained the same, but the meaning of enforcement shifted. It became a volume-driven campaign, focusing as much on political geography as on individual behavior.

On the ground, this shift led to raids that invaded civic spaces. ICE teams carried out sweeps through Democratic-led cities, targeting swap meets, Home Depot parking lots, churches, schools, farms, and community centers in places like Lake Worth Beach, Florida. Citizens and non-citizens alike were caught in operations that blurred the line between targeted enforcement and mass policing. In Florida, the state attorney general continued to enforce a blocked immigration law until a federal judge held him in contempt. This episode showed how executive support and local enthusiasm could combine to override judicial boundaries.

As these raids increased, the administration moved to limit the oversight that could monitor them. DHS and ICE issued guidance requiring 72 hours' notice before congressional visits to detention facilities, despite laws written to allow unannounced inspections. Lawmakers kept oversight authority, but their ability to see conditions as they truly were—rather than as prepared for inspection—was sharply reduced. Meanwhile, DHS canceled about 30,000 asylum appointments booked through the CBPOne app, stranding families who had followed official instructions and relied on lawful pathways to seek protection. The message was clear: following the rules did not guarantee a hearing. The same system that closed doors for many opened them for a few. Trump announced exemptions from deportation for undocumented workers in agriculture and hospitality, sectors vital to donors and business allies. Commerce Secretary Howard Lutnick introduced a waitlist for a "Trump Card" residency program, offering permanent status to those able to pay $5 million. These moves made explicit what had been implicit: immigration status could be used as a punishment for disfavored communities and as a commodity for the wealthy. Courts did intervene at the margins—ordering the restoration of legal services for families separated under previous policies, blocking a Harvard-specific student visa ban, and releasing a Palestinian activist whose detention appeared punitive—but these rulings served as case-by-case relief within a broader pattern of stratification.

Beyond immigration, the presidency treated law and markets as flexible tools. Trump again extended the enforcement delay of the TikTok divestiture law by executive order, despite a statute and Supreme Court ruling that had set a clear deadline. In doing so, he claimed that his own judgment about timing could override both Congress and the Court in regulating a major platform. He also secured a golden-share arrangement giving him veto control over U.S. Steel's board decisions, an unprecedented combination of public authority and private corporate governance that raised obvious conflict-of-interest concerns. The line between state power and private gain grew thinner. Emergency language became a bridge between policy and profit. Trump ordered Michigan coal plants to stay open under a declared national energy emergency, overriding state climate law and long-planned closures. The Department of Energy was told to keep those plants running, shifting costs and health risks onto ratepayers and local communities while protecting fossil-fuel owners. In California, a separate dispute over federalization of National Guard units showed how security powers could be pulled upward. A district judge rebuked the administration's unilateral control, but the Ninth Circuit quickly stayed that ruling, leaving federal authority in place and signaling how fragile state control over its own forces had become.

Federal power was also used more directly against disliked regions. Trump threatened to withhold wildfire disaster aid from California over political disputes, turning life-safety funding into a bargaining tool. At the same time, he held a large military parade in Washington, D.C., linked to his birthday, and ordered the renaming of a Navy vessel that had honored Harvey Milk. The parade normalized leader-centered displays of force in civilian spaces. The renaming signaled ideological control over military symbols. Courts and Congress responded actively to these actions. Federal judges restored NIH and EPA grants that had been cut on discriminatory grounds, blocked mass firings at Education's Office for Civil Rights, and refused to let DOJ represent Trump personally in the E. Jean Carroll defamation case. Lawmakers introduced war-powers resolutions to limit unlawful actions against Iran and a crypto-corruption bill to address self-dealing. However, these checks were scattered, reactive, and often narrowly focused.

While power remained concentrated at the center, dissent grew in the streets. Millions participated in "No Kings" demonstrations across thousands of locations, protesting what they viewed as Trump's consolidation of authority. The protests were mostly peaceful, centered around a simple demand for limits on executive power. Yet, responses from state and local authorities often treated them as security threats. In Los Angeles, police declared unlawful assemblies, used teargas and projectiles, and imposed curfews. The tactics resembled riot control more than crowd management, blurring the line between maintaining order and suppressing political expression.

Elsewhere, officials' statements incited violence from below. In Florida, Governor Ron DeSantis said drivers could legally run over protesters if they felt threatened, framing vehicular attacks as possible self-defense. In Texas, credible threats linked to an anti-Trump rally prompted the evacuation of the state Capitol, disrupting legislative proceedings. In Salt Lake City, a confrontation involving an armed individual and volunteer peacekeepers at a protest ended with a protester's death, highlighting how the presence of firearms increased the risk of any misstep or provocation. The right to assemble now carried a more apparent danger.

The most chilling event occurred in Minnesota, where a gunman assassinated a Democratic state lawmaker and injured others. The attack was politically motivated, targeting elected officials rather than random victims. Federal and state prosecutors responded with extensive charges, and the state's congressional delegation issued a bipartisan statement condemning the violence as an assault on democracy itself. That response mattered. It reaffirmed, at least in words and charges, that political disputes should not be settled by force. Meanwhile, civil society and local institutions found ways to resist the broader climate of fear: the Los Angeles Dodgers refused ICE agents access to their stadium parking lots, the NAACP broke with tradition by declining to invite Trump to its national convention, and journalists and legal observers sued DHS and Secretary Kristi Noem over alleged protest suppression.

Information about these events did not spread in an unbiased environment. The administration and its allies worked to reshape both the channels and the content of public knowledge. At the media level, the Trump administration issued layoff notices to over 600 employees at Voice of America and the U.S. Agency for Global Media, effectively dismantling much of the country's independent international broadcasting capacity. Inside the Pentagon, a rapid response team used official social media accounts to attack reporters and critics, blurring the line between public information and partisan messaging. At the Social Security Administration, the White House pressured the commissioner not to contradict Trump's false claims about scam calls, subordinating factual guidance to presidential narratives. Facts were expected to be bent.

Public health information faced similar challenges. A senior CDC scientist responsible for hospitalization surveillance resigned, citing concerns about how vaccine data was being used. Former members of the Advisory Committee on Immunization Practices warned that their firing and broader staffing cuts were weakening the vaccine program. By week's end, the CDC had retracted $11.4 billion in COVID funding, fired key outbreak officials, and canceled a major H5N1 vaccine contract while imposing strict trial requirements. On paper, the agency continued to propose new data collections and surveillance systems. In reality, its capacity to generate and interpret data was steadily eroding.

The administration also sought to shape the symbolic landscape of national memory. At the White House, Trump removed the Martin Luther King Jr. bust from the Oval Office and replaced Hillary Clinton's official portrait with his own painting in a prominent display. At the Pentagon, officials directed a "passive approach" to Juneteenth messaging, instructing public affairs to avoid strong recognition of emancipation. The Navy removed Harvey Milk's name from a ship, erasing an LGBTQ rights pioneer from a visible part of military history. Outside Washington, the administration illegally froze congressionally approved funds for libraries, archives, and museums, as later documented by the Government Accountability Office. These institutions preserve records and stories. Cutting their resources limits what they can remember.

Disinformation and surveillance connected these actions. After the Minnesota assassination, right-wing media figures and social media influencers quickly spread false claims that the killer was a leftist "Marxist," blaming Democrats for the attack. Senator Mike Lee amplified those claims, posting and then deleting false statements about the suspect's ideology. The goal was to portray a right-leaning killer as a tool of the left, confusing public understanding of political violence and shifting blame away from those who had actually influenced the attacker's views. Confusion was not accidental. It was intentional.

At the same time, Trump renewed his call for a special prosecutor to investigate the 2020 election, again claiming it was riddled with fraud despite no evidence and the passing of years. He demanded a criminal inquiry into a settled result, keeping doubt alive and reinforcing the idea that disfavored votes are suspicious.

In immigration, the State Department required foreign students and scholars to provide access to their social media accounts for visa screening, with officials instructed to look for perceived hostility toward the United States or its allies. Australian writer Alistair Kitchen was denied entry and deported after questions about his protest coverage and political views. These actions showed how the same government that spread falsehoods about violence and elections also monitored and punished dissenting speech, especially from those without full citizenship protections.

Economic policy and enforcement aligned with these political priorities. In the crypto sector, the Securities and Exchange Commission dropped its civil lawsuit against Binance shortly after the exchange listed a Trump-linked token. The administration eased cryptocurrency regulations overall and paused several fraud cases, signaling that ventures tied to allies would face lighter enforcement. In environmental and gun regulation, EPA leadership instructed Midwest staff to halt enforcement against fossil fuel companies, while the Department of Justice planned to cut two-thirds of the staff inspecting federally licensed gun dealers. These choices reduced deterrence for powerful industries and shifted risk onto communities exposed to pollution and gun violence.

At the same time, the administration and Congress used the Congressional Review Act to disapprove an OCC bank-merger review rule and an EPA air-quality rule, reshaping how financial consolidation and major emitters are scrutinized. Trump's control over U.S. Steel through a golden-share, the launch of Trump Mobile as a branded telecom venture, and the $5 million Trump Card residency program all pointed to a governing style in which public office opened private markets. Corporate behavior adjusted accordingly. Target rolled back diversity, equity, and inclusion initiatives after the inauguration. Amazon and Verizon withdrew support for Juneteenth celebrations and DEI programs, moves reportedly linked to regulatory bargaining. In West Virginia, the governor ended state support and paid-holiday status for Juneteenth. Recognition of emancipation and racial justice became commodities to be traded or withdrawn in pursuit of other advantages.

Stratification by identity and status was not limited to economics. Legally, the week saw an attempted executive order to cancel birthright citizenship for children of undocumented immigrants, directly challenging constitutional guarantees of membership. The Supreme Court's Skrmetti decision upheld Tennessee's ban on gender-affirming care for minors, narrowing equal-protection interpretations and validating broad state restrictions on healthcare for transgender youth. Symbolically, the renaming of the Harvey Milk ship and the halt of a national LGBTQ-focused suicide hotline signaled that certain lives and histories were less worthy of honor or support. The law and these symbols pointed in the same direction.

Selective benefits reinforced this hierarchy. Undocumented workers in favored industries received de facto protection, while poorer migrants in Democratic cities faced increased raids and canceled asylum appointments. Wealthy applicants could buy a pathway to residency. Foreign students and scholars were screened for their online views, with those viewed as hostile excluded. Juneteenth and DEI retrenchment, along with the removal of civil rights symbols from the White House, narrowed the public space where histories of slavery, resistance, and queer struggles could be shared. Civil rights organizations responded where possible: the NAACP's decision not to invite Trump to its convention clearly signaled that, in its view, the administration's policies and rhetoric fell outside acceptable leadership bounds.

Against this backdrop, courts and Congress offered partial resistance. Federal judges not only restored NIH and EPA grants but also blocked the Education Department's civil rights office purge, halted the Harvard international student ban, and ordered the release of a Palestinian activist whose ICE detention seemed retaliatory. Judge Dana Sabraw enforced a settlement requiring legal services for families separated under earlier policies, reaffirming that the executive must fulfill its obligations. Another court refused to let DOJ shield Trump personally in the Carroll case, drawing a line between private misconduct and public office. These rulings did not reverse the overall trend but demonstrated that some guardrails still held.

On the legislative side, Senator Jeff Merkley and colleagues introduced the End Crypto Corruption bill to bar officials from profiting from crypto ventures, while Democrats opened inquiries into Trump's cryptocurrency dealings. War-powers resolutions from both chambers sought to reassert Congress's role over potential action against Iran, and Senator Tammy Duckworth pressed the defense secretary on the costs and effectiveness of Red Sea operations. The Government Accountability Office's finding that the administration had illegally frozen funds for libraries, archives, and museums documented an abuse of appropriations power, even if it did not immediately reverse the damage. Election administrators, meanwhile, continued the quiet work of democracy: the Election Assistance Commission sought data on local office staffing, and the FEC set filing dates for a special congressional election, even as it canceled an open meeting that would have offered more transparency.

Culturally, Juneteenth and civil rights commemorations turned into bargaining chips. West Virginia's withdrawal of state support, corporate withdrawals from celebrations, and the Pentagon's muted messaging all reflected a broader anti-DEI stance. In the White House and the Navy, the removal of the MLK bust, the portrait switch, and the renaming of Harvey Milk altered the visible story of who is recognized as a national hero. The illegal freezing of cultural and archival funds threatened the institutions that preserve the deeper record. Each move could be defended individually as a budget decision, a decor choice, or a naming preference. However, taken together, they signaled a coordinated narrowing of which histories would be celebrated and which would be allowed to fade away.

No single event in Week 22 rewrote the Democracy Clock. Instead, the shift resulted from accumulated actions: immigration raids serving as partisan punishment, executive orders treating statutes as suggestions, economic favors mixing governance and enrichment, and symbolic edits rewriting the civic narrative. Courts and lawmakers demonstrated that resistance still existed, but their responses were often reactive and limited to specific cases. Civil society mobilized in streets and institutions, yet faced a government increasingly willing to meet dissent with force, contempt, or silence.

In this way, the week reinforced an existing pattern rather than created a new one. Emergency powers became routine tools for energy and immigration policies. Law enforcement and security forces aligned more openly with preserving executive authority than protecting vulnerable communities. Information and memory were curated to support the regime's narratives, while those challenging them—journalists, activists, immigrants, even scientists—faced greater risks. The formal structures of democracy remained intact, but the lived experience of equal protection, open dissent, and shared truth grew more fragile.

CHAPTER 33
WEEK 23: SECRECY AS WAR-MAKING METHOD

> *Unauthorized strikes, militarized immigration raids, and curated intelligence fused into a week where executive power acted first and explained, if ever, later.*

The twenty-third week of Trump's second term unfolded as a demonstration of concentrated power. Across issues like war, immigration, courts, media, and education, authority moved upward and inward, drifting away from shared judgment toward a small circle around the president. This pattern did not rely on a single dramatic break. Instead, it resulted from repeated choices to view constraint as a barrier, not a safeguard, and to see disagreement as disloyalty rather than a normal part of democratic debate. This choice was made across every arena.

At the end of the previous period, the Democracy Clock was at 8:00 p.m. By week's end, it had shifted to 8:01 p.m., a modest change of 1.2 minutes. Although the numerical shift was small, it reflected a significant increase in the use and concealment of executive power. Unauthorized airstrikes, managed intelligence, militarized immigration raids, and systemic changes in courts and universities all moved in the same direction. They made it easier for those in power to act first and justify later, if at all. The week's main event was the decision to bomb Iran. On June 21, President Trump ordered large-scale airstrikes on three Iranian nuclear sites without congressional approval. The operation cost hundreds of millions and posed clear risks to global oil markets and shipping. It bypassed the War Powers Resolution and any formal declaration of war, treating the most serious decision a democracy can make as an executive matter alone. The strikes were portrayed as decisive and necessary. The process leading to them was intentionally kept opaque.

That opacity was intentional. Before and after the strikes, Trump publicly dismissed his own intelligence community's assessments that Iran had not decided to build a nuclear weapon and that its program had not been destroyed. Defense and intelligence agencies, including the Defense Intelligence Agency, reported that the operation had not eliminated Iran's capacity. Senior officials instead promoted a "spectacular success" narrative, comparing the strikes to historic atomic bombings and insisting that Iran's nuclear ambitions were over. The decision to reject internal assessments in favor of a more triumphant story showed how information itself had become a tool of war. Facts were shaped to fit the preferred narrative.

As criticism grew, the administration tightened control over information. A promised classified House briefing on the Iran operation was canceled without explanation. When senators were finally briefed, the White House removed the director of national intelligence, Tulsi Gabbard, from the lineup amid disputes over her assessment. Lawmakers were instead provided with officials more aligned with the president's narrative. After a damaging leak of a DIA report, Trump announced plans to restrict congressional access to classified information, using secrecy rules to punish oversight rather than protect national security. Simultaneously, he revoked the security clearances of several former senior officials. The circle of experienced voices capable of speaking with authority during a crisis shrank.

The administration's treatment of the press followed a similar pattern. Trump and Defense Secretary Pete Hegseth attacked media coverage of the Iran operation, accusing journalists of cheering against America. A criminal leak investigation was launched into the DIA report, indicating that revealing inconvenient facts could pose legal risks. Critical reporters were specifically targeted, with CNN's Pentagon correspondent Natasha Bertrand among them. The line between protecting secrets and suppressing scrutiny blurred. The presidency moved closer to a model where war is fought not only abroad but also against independent sources of information at home.

While bombs fell overseas, a different kind of force was being used inside the United States. Immigration enforcement became the main stage where the administration tested how far it could push the combination of security, punishment, and politics. ICE and DHS increased nationwide raids, especially in Los Angeles. Agents worked in masks and plain clothes, confronting people on the streets, pepper-spraying bystanders, and making arrests that caught not only undocumented immigrants but also U.S. citizens and local officials. Daily arrest quotas turned enforcement into a numbers game. Fear became the main tool.

The president intensified this approach by ordering the deployment and federalization of National Guard units and Marines to Los Angeles to support immigration raids, despite the state's objections. Thousands of troops were sent into a major American city to back civil enforcement efforts. This blurred the line between military and police, and between federal and local authority. It showed that resistance from state leaders could be overridden if it conflicted with the administration's immigration goals. The use of uniformed force against protesters and communities highlighted how security agencies were being aligned with maintaining federal power rather than protecting people.

Behind these visible operations, a vast detention infrastructure was being built. Plans progressed for a 5,000-bed migrant camp in the Everglades, called "Alligator Alcatraz," created through emergency seizure of 39 square miles of land. The facility, estimated to cost about $450 million annually and funded by FEMA, signaled a long-term commitment to mass confinement as a response to migration. Simultaneously, ICE signed a contract with private prison company CoreCivic to convert a shuttered California prison into the state's largest immigrant detention center, with 2,500 beds. Public funds flowed into carceral infrastructure, much of it managed by for-profit contractors with limited public accountability.

The human toll of this system was immediate. Abelardo Avellaneda Delgado died during transit under the care of a private transport contractor. Iris Monterroso-Lemus lost a pregnancy after being denied medical care in detention. A Honduran mother and her children, including a child with leukemia, were arrested at an immigration court hearing, turning the courthouse into a site of fear. U.S. citizen Andrea Velez and others were wrongfully detained during raids in Los Angeles. Pakistani journalist Jalil Afridi was briefly detained and had his press credentials seized after a State Department briefing. These cases highlight how aggressive tactics and outsourced operations increased the likelihood of errors and abuses. They also demonstrate how little recourse individuals had when caught in this machinery.

Policy changes reinforced the trend. The administration moved to quickly dismiss hundreds of thousands of asylum claims and to transfer prosecutorial authority from U.S. attorneys to DHS, streamlining deportations and weakening independent oversight of enforcement. Deals were explored with dozens of countries, including many with poor human rights records, to accept deportees. The Supreme Court stayed lower-court rulings and permitted deportations to third countries, including conflict zones, expanding executive discretion over removals. ICE imposed a 72-hour notice requirement for congressional visits to detention centers, despite laws allowing surprise inspections. One of the few direct oversight tools available to lawmakers was quietly weakened.

Citizenship itself became more uncertain for some groups than for others. DHS terminated Temporary Protected Status for more than half a million Haitians, giving them only a short grace period before losing lawful status. Simultaneously, the administration planned to resettle 1,000 Afrikaners from South Africa while continuing to bar refugees from travel-ban countries. These decisions highlighted a hierarchy of humanitarian concern shaped by race, origin, and ideology. Legal status was no longer just about law and need; it increasingly depended on where someone came from and how they fit into the administration's narrative of deservingness.

The Justice Department's approach toward courts and law added another layer to this picture. A whistleblower, DOJ lawyer Erez Reuveni, described being fired after resisting orders to mislead courts about deportation injunctions and to proceed with flights despite restraining orders. His letter and related reports alleged that senior official Emil Bove had urged ignoring court orders in immigration cases. At the same time, DOJ took the extraordinary step of suing the entire bench of federal judges in Maryland over an order requiring a one-day pause before deportations. These actions treated judicial oversight not as a co-equal function but as an obstacle to be challenged and, if possible, punished.

Bove's career demonstrated how such behavior could be rewarded. At his appeals court confirmation hearing, he denied encouraging defiance of court orders and defended his role in dropping a corruption case against New York City Mayor Eric Adams, a move critics saw as political bargaining to gain immigration cooperation. He also oversaw purges of prosecutors and FBI agents involved in January 6 cases, calling their work a "grave injustice." Elevating a nominee with this record to a lifetime judicial position indicated that loyalty to the administration's priorities could outweigh concerns about respect for courts and impartial enforcement. The judiciary itself became part of the political effort.

The Supreme Court's rulings during the week shifted the legal landscape in ways that favored executive and elite interests. In a series of emergency orders and decisions, the Court restricted lower courts' ability to issue nationwide injunctions against federal policies, including in a birthright citizenship case. This limited a key tool for quickly stopping potentially unconstitutional actions nationwide. The Court also ruled that Medicaid patients could not sue to enforce their right to choose providers, making it harder for low-income people to challenge state efforts to exclude clinics like Planned Parenthood. In immigration, the Court permitted deportations to third countries to continue despite safety concerns. These rulings did not eliminate judicial review but made it harder for vulnerable individuals to use courts to protect their rights.

There were pockets of resistance within the judiciary. The Second Circuit ordered the return of Jordin Melgar-Salmeron after ICE deported him in violation of a stay, insisting that the executive branch obey injunctions. Judges released Mahmoud Khalil and Kilmar Abrego Garcia from detention, citing weak evidence and lack of danger. A Florida panel heard claims that state senate districts had been racially gerrymandered, and a New Orleans jury awarded $2.4 million to a clergy abuse survivor under a revived civil window law. The Supreme Court disbarred former Trump lawyer Kenneth Chesebro for his role in efforts to overturn the 2020 election. These actions showed that some judicial capacity to check abuse remained, despite structural rulings and appointments skewing the system toward deference.

Control over information and narratives was fiercely contested. The administration moved to dismantle Voice of America and its parent agency, USAGM, firing 639 employees and attempting to defund the broadcaster. A federal judge rebuked the administration for not complying with an earlier injunction on VOA firings, but the mass layoffs proceeded, weakening an institution meant to provide independent news to foreign audiences. Simultaneously, watchdog group Media Matters filed a lawsuit, claiming that the Federal Trade Commission had been weaponized to retaliate against it for reporting on extremist content. The case implied that regulatory authority was being used against critics.

Individual journalists faced direct pressure. Besides the attacks on Bertrand, the administration detained Afridi and confiscated his credentials, sending a warning to foreign reporters that critical coverage could lead to immigration issues. Trump and his press team repeatedly accused journalists of lying about the Iran strikes and undermining national security. Vice President J.D. Vance mistakenly identified Senator Alex Padilla by the name of a notorious criminal during a news conference, blurring the line between political opposition and criminality. These incidents fostered an environment where investigative reporting and dissenting voices were viewed with suspicion. The cost of speaking honestly increased.

Civil courts became battlegrounds over media narratives. Trump filed a defamation lawsuit against CBS over alleged editing of election coverage, with a mediator proposing a $20 million settlement. California Governor Gavin Newsom also filed a major defamation suit against Fox News and Jesse Watters, seeking hundreds of millions of dollars over what he called deceptive editing and false statements. These cases tested how much public officials and powerful individuals could use litigation to influence or punish coverage. They also demonstrated that the tools of civil law, once considered neutral, had become part of a larger struggle over who gets to define reality.

Knowledge institutions beyond the media were pulled into the same orbit. Health Secretary Robert F. Kennedy Jr. dismissed members of the CDC's Advisory Committee on Immunization Practices and replaced them with ideological allies skeptical of vaccines. The reformed panel voted against thimerosal-based flu vaccines despite scientific consensus on their safety. A CDC presentation cited a non-existent study by an appointee with anti-vaccine ties, allowing misinformation to enter official channels. The Supreme Court upheld key provisions of the Affordable Care Act related to preventive services but confirmed that the health secretary could remove task force members and review recommendations, increasing political influence over expert bodies. Together, these actions shifted vaccine policy from evidence-based guidance toward a politicized framework.

Higher education and civic education faced similar pressures. Homeland Security Secretary Kristi Noem threatened to revoke Harvard's certification to host foreign students, citing alleged extremism, until a judge blocked the move. The Justice Department expanded investigations into university hiring and diversity, equity, and inclusion policies, and a settlement forced the University of Virginia's president to resign over diversity disputes. OMB recommended ending nearly all State Department pro-democracy programs worldwide, reducing U.S. support for civil society abroad. In K–12 education, the Supreme Court required public schools to permit religious opt-outs from LGBTQ-themed instruction, and the administration declared California's trans-inclusive sports policies a violation of Title IX, threatening enforcement. The Court also upheld Texas's age-verification law for pornography websites, endorsing a model of online regulation that could chill lawful speech. These actions limited what could be taught, researched, or supported under public policy.

Within this tightening environment, the boundaries of belonging were redrawn. Zohran Mamdani, a Muslim socialist advocating for a redistributive platform in New York City rent freezes, large-scale affordable housing, higher taxes on the wealthy, public groceries, free buses, universal child care—became a focal point. After his primary win, he faced Islamophobic and death threats, prompting hate-crimes investigations. Trump-aligned Representative Andy Ogles called for his denaturalization and deportation, claiming misrepresented ties and framing him as effectively tied to terrorism. Trump amplified these calls. The idea that a sitting American politician could be stripped of citizenship for their beliefs and background shifted from fringe ideas into mainstream political discourse.

The same logic appeared elsewhere. Wrongful detentions of citizens during immigration raids, arrests of families in court, and targeting of journalists and officials at ICE facilities all indicated that some people's rights were more fragile than others. The administration framed immigration and education debates in moralistic, culture-war terms—portraying trans-inclusive policies and DEI programs as threats to children or national identity—further linking religious and ideological conservatism with law enforcement priorities. Dissenters were accused of being unpatriotic or corrupt, and oversight was portrayed as sabotage.

The week also featured a clear act of political violence. In Minnesota, House Speaker Melissa Hortman and her husband were shot by a gunman disguised as a police officer, who also wounded another lawmaker and her spouse. The attacker's impersonation of police blurred the line between authority and extremism. Simultaneously, federal agents in masks arrested elected officials like New York City Comptroller Brad Lander and Newark Mayor Ras Baraka near ICE facilities, and charged Representative LaMonica McIver. Protesters at Palantir and Medicaid protests were detained for disorderly conduct. ICE's new policies made congressional oversight visits more difficult. Rhetorical attacks on lawmakers, including Trump's social media assaults on Alexandria Ocasio-Cortez and his criticisms of intra-party opponents of the Iran strikes, created an environment where holding office or protesting carried increasing personal risks.

Economic policy and self-interest underpinned these security and rights issues. The Senate moved forward with a significant budget reconciliation bill that included deep Medicaid cuts, increased deficit spending, and fossil-fuel tax breaks. The parliamentarian determined that several provisions violated Senate rules, and leadership chose not to overrule her, maintaining some procedural limits. However, Republican lawmakers called for her dismissal, indicating a willingness to politicize even neutral referees to push a partisan agenda. The bill's substance shifted burdens onto low-income populations while preserving advantages for corporations. Fiscal measures were used to reinforce inequality.

At the same time, elite actors benefited from the crisis environment. Stephen Miller held a financial stake in Palantir as it secured a $30 million contract with ICE for surveillance, raising clear conflict-of-interest concerns. Trump Media announced a $400 million share buyback, boosting the value of a politically influential media company closely tied to the president. Trump halted trade talks with Canada in retaliation for its digital services tax on U.S. firms, using trade policy to defend favored corporations. He publicly pressured Federal Reserve Chair Jerome Powell to cut interest rates, challenging central bank independence and signaling that monetary policy should align with presidential preferences. Public funds were channeled into detention infrastructure and, after court intervention, into EV charger programs. Alternative models existed—California's expansion of film and TV tax credits, Mamdani's redistributive platform—but they operated at the margins of a federal system increasingly geared toward crisis and corporate gain.

Amid these shifts, some elements of routine governance persisted. Federal regulators issued various technical rules and notices, from chemical risk evaluations and Superfund settlements to medical-device classifications and telecom data collections. The National Archives invited public comment on records disposition schedules, and EPA published environmental impact statements for review. The National Security Council began rehiring staff after earlier deep cuts, suggesting a partial restoration of capacity. Courts clarified AI copyright rules, holding that training models on lawfully purchased books was permissible, while using pirated texts was likely unlawful. These actions showed that not all institutional functions had been captured or hollowed out. They also risked projecting a sense of normalcy that could obscure the scale of ongoing democratic erosion.

Taken together, the week's developments moved the Democracy Clock forward not through a single catastrophe but through the steady thickening of a new normal. War could be launched without authorization and sold with curated intelligence. Immigration enforcement could be militarized, outsourced, and expanded into mega-camps. Courts could be reshaped to narrow remedies just as the executive tested the limits of obedience. Media and universities could be pressured, purged, or sued into alignment. Citizenship and safety could be stratified by origin, ideology, and identity, while those who protested or held office faced an increased risk of arrest or violence.

The moral baseline for public life weakened under this burden. Character, meaning aligning words with duty, gave way to narratives designed for personal gain. Ethics blurred as personal interests and public agreements became entangled. Restraint was rare in war-making and enforcement. Truthfulness was replaced by disinformation about Iran and elections. Trust in the process declined as rules were pushed to their limits. Care for institutions was sacrificed for short-term control. Yet resistance persisted. Judges issued rebukes and injunctions. Civil society organized protests and lawsuits. Some state and local actors pursued different economic and civic visions.

The week's significance lies in how these elements coexisted. Routine rulemaking and court decisions went on, giving the illusion of a functioning democracy. At the same time, the conditions necessary for that democracy to reliably check power, protect dissent, and treat citizens as equals became more limited. The passage of time highlighted this tension: a small change on the clock, but a big shift in how easily authority could act without proper oversight.

CHAPTER 34
WEEK 24: HARDWIRING INEQUALITY AS GOVERNANCE

A megabill, a compliant Court, and a militarized border quietly rewrote who counts, who pays, and who can still say no.

The twenty-fourth week of Trump's second term unfolded as a week of solidifying power. What had been hinted at in speeches and trial balloons earlier was now codified into laws, court decisions, and budget allocations. The pattern was not a single shock but a series of converging actions: a massive tax-and-spending bill, a Supreme Court inclined to protect the presidency and weaken rights, and an immigration and enforcement system enlarged and reshaped as a tool of authority. The surface language was familiar—growth, security, order—but the real work was to redefine who counts, who pays, and who can say no. That was the point.

At the start of Week 24, the Democracy Clock read 8:01 p.m. By the end, it was at 8:02 p.m., a net change of 0.3 minutes. The numerical move was small, but it marked a week in which executive power became more insulated from oversight, law was openly wielded as a weapon, and the fundamental ideas of citizenship and social protection tilted toward exclusion and hierarchy. Congress, courts, and agencies all played roles in this shift. Some judges and state officials pushed back at the margins, but the core of the shift moved toward a presidency less constrained by law and a state more focused on enforcement and inequality.

The main focus of the week's major structural change was the One Big Beautiful Bill. Trump and Republican leaders promoted it as a wide-ranging tax-and-spend package that, they claimed, would unleash growth and restore fiscal sanity. In reality, the bill made the 2017 tax cuts permanent and added new breaks favoring higher earners and capital owners. The Congressional Budget Office forecasted that the package would increase the deficit by at least $3.3 trillion, even as Treasury officials insisted, contrary to the data, that growth would cover the costs. The Senate adopted a "current policy baseline" that treated trillions in tax cuts as having no cost, hiding their true impact on the budget. The dollar experienced its worst first-half performance since the early 1970s, and the economy shrank by 0.5 percent in the first quarter, but these warning signs did not change the bill's direction. They were dismissed as noise.

On the spending side, the megabill cut back the welfare state. It proposed approximately $930 billion in Medicaid cuts, with estimates that 11.8 million people would lose coverage. It reduced SNAP by $186 billion and shifted costs to states, weakening the federal role in fighting hunger. It phased out expanded Affordable Care Act subsidies, accepting that millions more would become uninsured. Medicare faced over $500 billion in cuts over nine years, and the bill ended coverage for some legal immigrants who had paid into the system, explicitly linking access to their origin and status. Trump signed these measures into law, including provisions that ended Medicare for certain noncitizen seniors and imposed stricter work requirements on Medicaid and SNAP recipients. The result was to turn health and food security from a shared guarantee into a conditional benefit that could be revoked more easily.

Simultaneously, the bill directed large sums of money into the security state. Congress and the president approved an extra $158 billion for defense, pushing annual military spending past the trillion-dollar mark. New funds went to missile defense, ships, and nuclear weapons, reinforcing a military-industrial pattern with limited public debate on tradeoffs. Immigration enforcement received $172 billion, including $45 billion for new jails, and ICE's budget was raised to nearly Army levels. Trump signed bills that significantly increased detention capacity and hiring, diverted billions to border wall construction, and raised the debt limit by $5 trillion to support these priorities. The Federal Communications Commission, for its part, paused rules capping prison and jail phone rates until 2027, maintaining high costs and kickback arrangements that burden incarcerated individuals and their families. In foreign aid, researchers warned that USAID cuts in the fiscal package could cause over 14 million additional deaths worldwide by 2030, highlighting how domestic budget decisions affect global outcomes.

The massive bill also targeted specific institutions and services favored by disfavored groups. Trump signed a one-year Medicaid ban on Planned Parenthood affiliates, effectively defunding many clinics that provide reproductive and general care to low-income patients. He approved measures that withheld nearly $7 billion in K–12 funding for after-school, language, and adult education programs, and his administration had already cut over $1 billion in school-based mental health funds. These actions, combined with deep cuts to Medicaid and SNAP, shifted financial and social risks onto households and states while maintaining tax advantages and subsidies for corporations and high-income individuals. Policy decisions favored donor and corporate interests, with fossil fuel companies and defense contractors among the main beneficiaries.

If the bill was the substance, the way it moved through Congress was the method. The Senate used reconciliation to fast-track the package, advancing it through narrow procedural votes that limited debate. The parliamentarian initially ruled that several provisions violated reconciliation rules, underscoring that internal constraints still existed on paper. Trump responded by urging Republican senators to ignore the parliamentarian's guidance, and

Senate leaders obliged, bypassing both the parliamentarian and the Government Accountability Office on key questions about tax cuts and EPA waiver rollbacks. By adopting a baseline that treated permanent tax cuts as costless, they altered budget scoring norms, obscuring the true fiscal impact from the public. That was a choice. The final Senate vote on the budget bill was 51–50, with Vice President Vance breaking the tie. That razor-thin margin showed how slim majorities can implement far-reaching structural changes under reconciliation rules.

In the House, the Freedom Caucus initially criticized the bill's deficits, and some members hesitated at its size and content. But Trump and House leaders used intense pressure, warning of primary challenges and other consequences for dissenters. The House kept a procedural vote open for more than two hours—far longer than usual—while leadership worked the floor to flip holdouts. Representative Brian Fitzpatrick reversed his party's stance on a key vote and privately warned Trump about the risks of cutting Ukraine aid, but party operatives reportedly tried to locate and pressure him. Ultimately, the House accepted the Senate bill largely unchanged, and Congress passed the One Big Beautiful Bill and related legislation despite broad public opposition.

Alongside this extraordinary use of procedure, much of the administrative state continued to issue routine notices. EPA extended comment periods on major environmental impact statements, added contaminated sites to the Superfund list, and adjusted compliance deadlines for emission rules. The Food and Drug Administration processed patent determinations and information collections. The FCC and TSA updated paperwork requirements. These actions, which seemed normal, provided a background of continuity even as the central fiscal structure was being hollowed out and repurposed. The contrast underscored how authoritarian-leaning change can progress through the same channels that handle everyday governance. It can look like business as usual.

If Congress was being turned into a transmission belt, the

Supreme Court was reshaping the legal foundation of executive power. The Court issued a landmark ruling granting presidents absolute criminal immunity for official acts. This decision significantly weakened the chances of holding a sitting or former president criminally responsible for abuses committed under the guise of office. Simultaneously, the Court limited federal judges' ability to issue nationwide injunctions against presidential policies. In Trump v. CASA and related cases, it restricted lower courts' power to provide uniform relief, insisting that remedies be narrower and more localized. A subsequent decision further curtailed nationwide relief against presidential actions, making it more difficult for a single judge to block an illegal policy across the country.

These doctrinal shifts had immediate effects. When Trump issued an executive order to limit birthright citizenship, the Court allowed partial enforcement while banning nationwide injunctions. That meant the policy could be enforced in some areas but not others, splitting a key constitutional guarantee along geographic lines. In another case, the Court approved deporting eight men from a U.S. base to South Sudan despite concerns about torture, showing deference to executive deportation decisions even in life-or-death situations. At the same time, the Court agreed to hear a challenge to coordinated campaign spending limits supported by top Republican committees, indicating openness to further relaxing rules on political money. The Court's docket told a story.

The Court also took on more culture-war cases. In Mahmoud v. Taylor, it ruled that parents could opt their children out of LGBTQ+ themed lessons on religious grounds—a decision that risked fostering curricular censorship and marginalizing queer identities in public education. It agreed to hear appeals on state bans that prevent transgender students from participating in sports consistent with their gender identity, positioning itself to reshape civil rights protections for trans youth. These actions, along with the immunity and injunction decisions, pointed toward a judiciary more aligned with executive and donor interests and more willing to carve out exceptions from inclusive civic norms.

Not all judicial actions went in one direction. A federal district court struck down Trump's asylum ban and "invasion" proclamation, reaffirming statutory and constitutional limits on presidential power over immigration. Another judge temporarily blocked mass dismissals at the Department of Health and Human Services as arbitrary and capricious, shielding civil servants from political purges. Courts also halted the termination of Temporary Protected Status for up to 500,000 Haitians and rejected the administration's effort to detain a Georgetown scholar pending deportation. These rulings showed that pockets of judicial independence still existed. However, they operated within a new framework where the president enjoyed broad immunity, nationwide injunctions were limited, and the Court itself was shaping who could be protected and where.

Immigration and citizenship were the areas where these structural changes were most obvious and personal. The massive enforcement budget of the megabill solidified ICE as a quasi-military force, with a budget nearly matching that of the Army and tens of billions allocated for new jails and border infrastructure. Trump visited a new detention complex in the Florida Everglades—called Alligator Alcatraz—and promoted it as a flagship project. The facility, built in a remote wetland and operated by private contractors, drew protests from hundreds of demonstrators and a lawsuit from environmental and immigrant-rights groups. Democratic lawmakers were denied entry when they tried to inspect conditions, a direct rebuff to congressional oversight.

On the ground, ICE raids and detention practices reflected these new priorities. Agents conducted aggressive operations that targeted long-term residents, including family members of veterans. Reports described overcrowding, lack of basic necessities, and poor medical care in detention centers. In Los Angeles, ICE agents were caught on camera urinating on a high school campus before a raid, prompting calls for an investigation and exposing a culture of impunity. The administration attempted to deport a stateless Palestinian woman, Ward Sakeik, despite a federal court order, highlighting a willingness to ignore judicial authority in individual cases. Bhutanese refugees deported from the U.S. also found themselves facing removal from Nepal, illustrating how U.S. enforcement choices could strand people between legal systems.

Legal tools were modified to support this enforcement-heavy regime. The administration began sharing Medicaid data with the Department of Homeland Security to assist immigration enforcement, blurring the lines between health services and policing and raising fears that immigrants might avoid seeking care. A coalition of twenty state attorneys general sued to block this data-sharing, arguing it violated privacy protections and misused health systems. The Department of Justice issued guidance focusing on civil denaturalization cases in which targets lack a right to counsel, expanding the government's power to revoke citizenship with limited safeguards. Trump's team moved to end Temporary Protected Status for Haitians, threatening legal status for hundreds of thousands, though a federal injunction temporarily paused the effort.

At the same time, the administration tightened student visa rules by proposing more frequent renewal requirements that could disrupt international education flows and increase administrative burdens. Trump announced plans to end birthright citizenship by executive order, signaling a willingness to redefine a constitutional boundary unilaterally. He publicly floated the idea of deporting even U.S.-born citizens who commit crimes, blurring the line between citizenship and deportable status. Representative Marge Greene introduced a bill to conduct the census on a citizens-only basis for apportionment, a move that would reduce representation for diverse areas with many noncitizens. In Georgia, local authorities appointed an election denier to a county board of elections, embedding skepticism of multiracial electorates into the machinery of election administration.

These moves faced resistance. Judges blocked the TPS termination and pushed back against some detention demands. States sued over Medicaid data-sharing. Industry groups like the National Restaurant Association warned that immigration crackdowns were harming labor-dependent sectors and lobbied for targeted relief. But the overall trend was clear: immigration law and status were being turned into flexible tools of repression, creating a stratified citizenship system where origin, wealth, and political views influence one's security. Citizenship itself was being graded.

Law enforcement and security agencies were both empowered and politicized simultaneously. Trump issued an executive order protecting law enforcement officers, providing legal resources and new penalties for officials deemed obstructive. This shifted power toward security forces and away from local accountability mechanisms. The huge funding for ICE, detention, and defense in the megabill further solidified a security-state approach. Meanwhile, the administration cut funding to enforce contempt of court orders, weakening courts' ability to ensure compliance from officials and agencies.

On the ground, this resulted in a pattern of shielded force. ICE raids continued despite reports of abusive conditions. The Alligator Alcatraz facility opened amid concerns over rights and the environment, yet lawmakers were blocked from inspecting it. In Alabama, the state law enforcement agency refused to release body-camera footage related to the police killing of Jabari Peoples, limiting public scrutiny and eroding trust in investigations. The Department of Justice appointed a January 6 defendant as an adviser on alleged "weaponization" issues, and Trump nominated a conspiracy-promoting lawyer to lead the Office of Special Counsel, which is meant to protect whistleblowers and enforce ethics rules. These appointments indicated that loyalty and ideological alignment, rather than dedication to the rule of law, were the main criteria for key oversight roles.

Abroad, Trump's approach to force was equally personalized. He ordered large-scale airstrikes on Iranian nuclear facilities without clear congressional approval, emphasizing expansive war powers with limited democratic oversight. He later admitted that he allowed Iran to bomb a U.S. air base in retaliation, raising concerns about opaque command decisions with serious security implications. The Senate voted down a resolution that would have limited his ability to escalate war with Iran, leaving presidential authority largely unchecked in this area. In another context, Trump threatened to tie U.S. aid to Israel to how Benjamin Netanyahu handled his corruption trial, signaling a willingness to leverage national resources to influence foreign judicial processes for political gain.

Systems of information, science, and education were also manipulated for political control. At the Department of Health and Human Services, Secretary Robert F. Kennedy Jr. took direct control of the Centers for Disease Control and Prevention in the absence of a director and dismissed seventeen independent vaccine advisers. This move politicized public health guidance and weakened independent scientific input at a time when trust in vaccines and health institutions was already fragile. At the Environmental Protection Agency, plans were made to cut at least 1,000 scientists from the research division and replace it with a smaller team, even as the agency launched a lab animal adoption program that received positive attention. Hundreds of EPA employees, scientists, and academics signed a statement warning that agency policies were undermining its mission, an internal act of dissent that highlighted the high stakes involved.

The administration shut down the U.S. Global Change Research Program's public climate website, removing a key source of federal climate information from public view. This move, along with the adoption of budget baselines that concealed the costs of tax cuts, demonstrated how data could be curated or erased to support preferred narratives. In education, the administration withheld school-based mental health funds and K–12 grants, prompting a multistate lawsuit and raising concerns about politicized resource allocation vital to student well-being. A federal judge's injunction against mass layoffs at HHS showed that administrative law still held sway, but the broader trend indicated increased political control over knowledge-producing institutions.

Universities faced direct pressure as well. The House approved a budget that increased the endowment tax to 21 percent for wealthy institutions like Stanford, signaling a willingness to use tax policy to reshape higher education funding and independence. The administration sent a letter threatening Harvard with the loss of federal funding over disputed antisemitism claims, raising fears that civil rights enforcement was being used as a tool to influence campus governance and free speech. Separately, the University of Pennsylvania, under federal pressure, adopted guidelines that barred trans women from women's sports and removed Lia Thomas's records from its history. This decision linked educational policy and civil rights to federal leverage and showed how recent events could be rewritten to align with current political priorities.

The Supreme Court's rulings on parental opt-outs from LGBTQ+ curricula and its decision to hear trans sports bans reinforced this trend. Along with the UPenn agreement and the firing of a Catholic school teacher over his same-sex marriage, they signaled a shift toward a tiered rights system where LGBTQ+ inclusion and recognition could be limited through a combination of state power and institutional compliance. There were isolated countercurrents — the Privy Council in London upheld same-sex civil partnerships in the Cayman Islands, and Zohran Mamdani won a ranked-choice Democratic mayoral primary in New York City despite attacks from presidential candidates — but they did not change the overall direction.

Media, critics, and opposition figures faced a coordinated mix of legal, rhetorical, and financial pressure. Border Czar Tom Homan and DHS Secretary Kristi Noem urged the Department of Justice to investigate and possibly prosecute CNN over its coverage of an app that helped immigrants track ICE activity. Trump suggested that his administration might force reporters to reveal anonymous sources in a national security case, threatening a core protection for investigative journalism. He refiled a lawsuit against an Iowa pollster and newspaper in state court over unfavorable polling, continuing a pattern of using civil litigation to pressure media and election critics. Paramount agreed to pay Trump $16 million to settle a dispute over a critical 60 Minutes interview, prompting Senator Elizabeth Warren to call for an anti-bribery investigation into whether the settlement reflected the monetization of presidential influence over media. The White House also used its platform to smear political opponents. Press Secretary Karoline Leavitt falsely labeled Zohran Mamdani as a communist and antisemite from the briefing room, while Trump attacked him on social media as a "Communist Lunatic" and threatened to impose financial penalties and deport him over policy disagreements.

Trump called for investigations into opponents such as former DHS Secretary Alejandro Mayorkas, framing policy disputes as grounds for criminal inquiry. The Social Security Administration sent a misleading email claiming that Trump's tax bill eliminated Social Security taxes for seniors, an official communication that misrepresented policy and could confuse beneficiaries. Universities were again drawn into this web, with funding threats and endowment taxes used as tools to influence campus speech and governance. Oligarchic actors did not stand outside this system; they were both participants and targets. Elon Musk denounced the budget bill as "utterly insane," launched a new "America Party," and vowed to fund primary challengers against Republicans who supported the legislation. His wealth and media reach allowed him to shape narratives and electoral incentives around fiscal policy. Trump responded by suggesting that Musk should be deported and threatening to cut subsidies to his companies, demonstrating how immigration and economic levers could be used against even the most powerful critics. Meanwhile, Iran-linked hackers threatened to release stolen emails from Trump associates, highlighting foreign actors' ability to manipulate domestic narratives through cyber intrusions.

Across these areas, the moral baseline continued to decline. The president's unilateral decisions on war and immigration favored personal and partisan interests over public duty. Ethical boundaries between public office and private gain blurred, from the launch of a luxury Trump Fragrances line while in office to undisclosed dark-money payments to senior officials. Restraint was rare: executive orders and budget strategies pushed the limits of what rules technically permitted, and when norms or advisory bodies obstructed them, they were bypassed or dismissed. Disinformation about the megabill's impacts and immigration policies flowed from official channels, while civil society and some media outlets struggled to correct the record at scale.

There were, however, signs of resilience. Some congressional leaders and judges opposed unauthorized military actions, mass firings, and sweeping immigration orders. State attorneys general sued over Medicaid data-sharing and school mental health cuts. Election officials held open, livestreamed meetings on voting system certification, and EPA extended comment periods on major environmental projects. Civil society groups mobilized against Alligator Alcatraz and other enforcement expansions, and internal dissent at agencies like EPA and HHS showed that professional norms had not vanished. These actions did not undo the week's structural shifts, but they preserved avenues for contestation that might matter in future periods.

Week 24 was not a sudden break but a step toward consolidation. The One Big Beautiful Bill established a fiscal and enforcement system that favors capital and coercion over social protections. The Supreme Court's rulings expanded presidential immunity and reduced judicial oversight, especially in areas such as immigration and campaign finance. Immigration and citizenship were redefined as flexible tools for repression, with expanded enforcement powers and weakened legal protections. Law enforcement and security agencies were compensated and politicized, while systems of information, science, and education were manipulated for ideological control. Media and critics faced rising intimidation, and civil rights eroded along predictable lines of identity and alliances.

The slow clock movement reflected an ongoing pattern of

erosion without a clear break. Rights and procedures still existed, but now their use required more effort and posed greater risks. Oversight mechanisms remained on paper, but their actual influence waned. The significance of this week lay in how easily authority advanced and how much of that progress became embedded in lasting law.

CHAPTER 35
WEEK 25: IMMUNITY AS ARCHITECTURE OF POWER

A Supreme Court shield for presidents, a hollowed civil service, and militarized immigration enforcement converged to normalize emergency-style rule and partisan law.

The twenty-fifth week of Trump's second term did not hinge on a single shock. It unfolded as a coordinated tightening of power across law, bureaucracy, borders, and information. What distinguished this period was not novelty but convergence: the presidency, the courts, and the security apparatus moved together to expand executive authority, weaken neutral institutions, and raise the cost of dissent. Immigration, public health, and even churches and schools became tools in this effort. Each decision changed a small aspect of how power functions. Together, they redefined the landscape.

At the start of Week 25, the Democracy Clock read 8:02 p.m. By the end, it showed 8:06 p.m., a net shift of 4.7 minutes. This change reflected a week in which formal rules and daily practices aligned to weaken checks on the presidency, politicize the civil service, and normalize emergency-style rule in areas like war, trade, and domestic enforcement. Courts did not merely fail to oppose these moves; in key moments, they enabled them. Congress, where it acted, often did so mainly to support the president's agenda. Resistance came in scattered rulings and oversight letters, but it was reactive and lagging.

The clearest sign of this new balance was from the Supreme Court. In a landmark ruling, the justices declared that a former president has absolute immunity from criminal prosecution for core official acts and presumptive immunity for a broader range of conduct. Practically, this erects a barrier around much presidential behavior, making it much harder to hold a sitting or former president criminally liable for abuses. The same Court also limited lower courts' ability to issue nationwide injunctions, reducing a key tool judges used to pause contested federal policies nationwide. These doctrinal shifts didn't happen in a vacuum. They unfolded during a week when the president was already expanding his reach.

On the administrative front, the Court lifted an order freezing Trump's "workforce optimization" plan, which authorized widespread federal layoffs, and later cleared the way for a significant reorganization of the State Department. By staying injunctions and allowing these workforce reductions to proceed, the justices endorsed rapid restructuring of the civil service with minimal legislative involvement. The rulings provided legal cover for a president already moving to purge and reshape key agencies. They also signaled to lower courts that deference to executive decisions, even with major structural implications, would be the standard.

Freed from these limitations, Trump acted as if presidential power had expanded significantly. He ordered a military strike on Iran without seeking congressional approval, bypassing the legislature's constitutional role in war and peace decisions. More broadly in foreign policy, he issued an executive order claiming sole presidential authority over external relations, sidelining Congress's traditional roles in treaties, war powers, and oversight. At the same time, he limited lawmakers' access to classified information, reducing the raw material needed for meaningful oversight of national security decisions. This combination—unilateral military action, exclusive foreign policy claims, and restrictions on information—pushed the system toward a presidency that decides first and provides explanations, if any, afterward.

Economic policy followed a similar pattern of improvisational command. Trump declared a national emergency to impose tariffs, using crisis powers to reshape trade terms without congressional approval. Over the week, he announced, delayed, and then rescheduled tariff implementation dates, causing confusion for businesses and allies. New tariffs targeted copper, Canadian imports, South Korean goods despite a free-trade agreement, and several countries linked to BRICS or other perceived slights. A 50 percent tariff on Brazilian imports was explicitly tied to displeasure over Jair Bolsonaro's prosecution, and a Section 301 investigation into Brazil's social media regulation turned trade tools into leverage over another country's speech policies. Tariff policy became a constantly shifting threat, used as a loyalty test and personal tool rather than a stable policy framework.

The same disregard for statutory boundaries appeared in domestic governance. Trump blocked more than six billion dollars in congressionally approved education funds for after-school and summer programs, effectively treating appropriations as optional. He instructed the Justice Department not to enforce a TikTok ban law for seventy-five days, creating a gap between statute and practice based solely on executive preference. In each case, the president signaled that duly enacted laws and budgets were subject to his ongoing consent. As the Supreme Court narrowed injunctions and expanded immunity, the practical options for enforcing compliance diminished.

If doctrine and high-level actions set the framework, the week's second major development demonstrated how that framework was being filled out. Within the national security and foreign policy apparatus, loyalty and ideology displaced expertise. Trump fired the director of the National Security Agency and his deputy after receiving a social media influencer's list of allegedly disloyal officials. He then removed six National Security Council staffers on similar grounds. These were not routine rotations; they were purges driven by perceived personal loyalty, blurring the line between national security judgment and the president's political comfort.

Reports from within the NSC described a body blindsided by Pentagon decisions, with staffing cuts and dysfunction undermining coordination. In this weakened state, the administration announced a plan to cut roughly fifteen percent of domestic State Department staff under an "America First" reorganization. Within days, over 1,300 employees received layoff notices. The Supreme Court's rulings on workforce optimization and State Department layoffs meant there was little legal opposition to slow this hollowing out. Diplomatic capacity, institutional memory, and channels for dissent all diminished simultaneously.

The erosion went beyond foreign policy. FEMA leadership limited staff communication with Congress and local officials during active flood response, restricting the flow of information needed for oversight and effective coordination. A grant to improve National Weather Service communication with local authorities was canceled even as Texas faced deadly floods. At the same time, the administration and Congress cut funding for NOAA and the National Science Foundation, weakening weather forecasting and basic research. USAID budgets were slashed in ways that researchers warned would cause millions of deaths, especially among children abroad. These choices did not just trim programs —they reduced the country's ability to see, understand, and respond to crises.

Personnel decisions reinforced the ideological tilt. Trump nominated Nick Adams, a controversial commentator known for Islamophobic rhetoric, as ambassador to Malaysia, signaling that sensitive diplomatic posts could be used for culture-war messaging rather than professional representation. In the judiciary, he elevated Emil Bove, a loyal prosecutor facing whistleblower allegations that he advised ignoring deportation court orders, to a lifetime appellate seat. These appointments embedded partisan alignment and disregard for legal constraints into institutions meant to outlast any single administration. Meanwhile, Ukraine policy swung between pauses and partial resumption of weapons shipments, with disputed explanations about stockpile levels. A weakened interagency process made it easier for such shifts to reflect personal or factional impulses rather than coherent strategy.

Immigration policy served as the clearest example of these approaches. Structurally, the reconciliation law allocated $170.7 billion to immigration enforcement, including a 265 percent increase in ICE detention funding and major border wall investments. At the same time, the administration ended Temporary Protected Status for Honduran and Nicaraguan immigrants who had lived in the U.S. for decades, and moved to end TPS for other countries as well. These decisions stripped legal protections from long-settled communities, turning established lives into precarious arrangements vulnerable to sudden removal.

The Supreme Court expanded executive power by permitting deportations to third countries with no direct links to the migrants involved. A district judge in Massachusetts, bound by a recent Supreme Court clarification, refused to stop the deportation of men with weak ties to South Sudan despite safety worries. These rulings and policies together grew the state's ability to exile noncitizens to remote, potentially dangerous places, with little judicial oversight. Immigration law, once seen as having some humanitarian protections, has shifted toward nearly unrestricted removal authority.

On the ground, enforcement became more theatrical and militarized. In Los Angeles's MacArthur Park, ICE and allied agents carried out large raids with armored vehicles and support from the National Guard. No arrests were made, but the operation was filmed and broadcast as a display of power. Similar raids targeted cannabis farms and farms in California, where federal agents and Guard troops used tear gas and other chemicals; one farmworker died, and hundreds were detained. In San Francisco, an unmarked ICE SUV plowed through a crowd of protesters outside immigration court, with agents hitting people with batons and using pepper spray. These scenes blurred the lines between policing and military operations, turning immigrant neighborhoods and workplaces into stages for state power.

Detention conditions matched this imposing display. A remote Florida facility, called "Alligator Alcatraz," operated with inadequate water, food, and shelter, using geography and deprivation as means of control. Reports across the country described overcrowded, unsanitary ICE centers filled with unrest and fear. National Guard units and even Marines were deployed to run detention centers and assist ICE at the border, involving military forces in roles usually handled by civilian agencies. Meanwhile, the Department of Homeland Security shut down important oversight offices responsible for tracking detention conditions and civil rights, removing internal watchdogs just as arrests and detentions surged.

Individual cases showed how this machinery impacted lives. A Canadian mother was detained during her green card interview. A long-term resident who arrived as a child was arrested in front of her family. A farmworker activist was detained on an old deportation order, raising fears that immigration tools were being used to suppress labor organizing. A Palestinian activist filed a $20 million claim, alleging he had been falsely imprisoned and defamed as a security threat for his Gaza advocacy. A journalist saw local charges dropped but remained in ICE custody. Each story demonstrated how legal status, speech, and proximity to protest could intersect with a system now wielding more power and fewer checks.

The ideological framework surrounding this system was explicit. Trump used social media to praise ICE and promote "remigration," a term associated with ethnic cleansing, portraying aggressive deportation as patriotic defense. He described Democratic lawmakers who opposed his budget bill with the words "I hate them," personalizing political conflict and signaling that opposition was not just mistaken but loathsome. A senator accused an immigrant-rights group of aiding crime for monitoring ICE activities, stigmatizing civil-society watchdogs as illegitimate. An ambush on ICE agents in Texas, injuring a local officer, highlighted how this heated environment risked spilling into armed confrontation. In this context, immigration enforcement became both a tool and a symbol: a way to reshape the population and send a message about who truly belonged.

Beyond immigration, the administration and its allies pushed the boundaries of who counts as a full rights-bearing member of the nation. Historically, the Fourteenth Amendment and post–Civil War rulings expanded federal power to secure citizenship and equal protection, reversing earlier exclusions like Dred Scott. That trajectory was in the background as Trump launched efforts to undermine birthright citizenship, challenging the guarantee that anyone born on U.S. soil is a citizen. A federal district court in New Hampshire blocked his executive order and certified a nationwide class, preserving protections for now, but the litigation signaled that a core pillar of American membership was now being contested.

Reproductive rights, already reshaped by the Supreme Court's earlier decision overturning Roe v. Wade, faced new challenges. A Boston court temporarily blocked a provision that defunded Planned Parenthood from Medicaid reimbursements, and the organization filed a lawsuit to protect its clinics. However, the underlying law and the Court's previous willingness to return abortion regulation to the states had already created a patchwork of access. Trump suggested that states should decide whether to restrict birth control, implying that even contraception could be subject to the will of the majority. On the Court, Justices Clarence Thomas and Samuel Alito renewed criticism of precedents on contraception and same-sex marriage, signaling they might revisit those rights.

At the same time, cases involving elite-linked misconduct were contained rather than fully aired. The Justice Department and FBI released an unsigned memo concluding that Jeffrey Epstein died by suicide and that there was no "client list," while withholding most underlying evidence. Federal courts closed related investigations.

House Democrats pressed for Epstein files and a withheld volume of a special counsel report mentioning Trump, but DOJ resisted, controlling what Congress and the public could see. A whistleblower, former DOJ lawyer Erez Reuveni, alleged that senior officials had instructed attorneys to ignore court orders halting deportations; his texts surfaced in the Senate's consideration of Emil Bove's nomination. The pattern suggested an executive branch willing to defy judicial authority in sensitive cases, even as it elevated those implicated in such defiance.

Not all legal processes bent in the same direction. Federal courts upheld a $5 million civil judgment against Trump in the E. Jean Carroll case, showing that civil litigation could still impose consequences for personal misconduct. A district court blocked Trump's birthright citizenship order, and the Supreme Court refused to revive Florida's harsh immigration law criminalizing undocumented entry, affirming federal primacy over immigration enforcement. Medical groups sued over vaccine policy changes, and Planned Parenthood turned to the courts to contest targeted defunding. These actions demonstrated that institutional resistance remained possible. But they were exceptions in a week where the dominant pattern was law serving as a partisan instrument and elite crimes remaining opaque.

On the streets and in detention centers, security forces increasingly align with regime preservation rather than public defense. Trump seized control of California's National Guard despite the governor's objections to suppress immigration protests, deploying troops against mostly peaceful demonstrators. National Guard units and Marines were embedded in immigration detention and enforcement roles in Florida and at the border, normalizing military involvement in civilian policing. High-profile raids in MacArthur Park and on farms were staged as televised spectacles, with armored vehicles, chemical munitions, and no clear public safety rationale. An ICE SUV driving through protesters, the death of a farmworker during a raid, and inhumane conditions at "Alligator Alcatraz" all occurred without reported accountability.

Legislators attempted to respond at the margins. Democratic senators introduced a bill to prohibit masked ICE agents and require visible identification, aiming to curb tactics that resembled abductions. A coalition of eighteen states filed an amicus brief supporting lawsuits against militarized raids in Los Angeles. Yet these efforts faced an executive branch that framed dissent as disorder or treason. Trump's rhetoric toward opponents, his praise for Bolsonaro's actions during Brazil's 2022 election, and his willingness to describe foreign prosecutions and court orders as "witch hunts" or secret censorship all contributed to a narrative in which security forces stood between the people and corrupt elites—defined, in practice, as critics and independent institutions.

Economic and fiscal policies entrenched a parallel structure of inequality and dependence. The reconciliation law permanently extended the 2017 tax cuts for corporations and the wealthy while drastically cutting Medicaid and SNAP. It heavily increased ICE and border wall funding. Treasury officials defended these choices as promoting personal responsibility, framing social program cuts and tariff impacts as issues of individual virtue rather than structural design. Medicaid work requirements were tied to labor-market engineering, with the Department of Agriculture and the administration suggesting that beneficiaries could replace deported migrant farmworkers. Social rights were thus conditioned on labor needs, pushing low-income people into precarious work to retain healthcare.

At the same time, the Pentagon's budget exceeded one trillion dollars, with more than half of discretionary spending flowing to contractors. USAID cuts, expected to cause over fourteen million deaths worldwide—especially among children—highlighted how austerity and security priorities shifted life-and-death risks. An executive order ended subsidies and tax credits for wind and solar energy, shifting industrial policy away from renewables. Tariff volatility—on copper, allies' goods, and BRICS-aligned countries—created uncertainty that firms and consumers had to deal with, while defense contractors and some industrial sectors enjoyed steady profits. Political risk was transferred to the public. Profits stayed private.

Cronyism and captured institutions supported this order. The IRS and federal courts reinterpreted the Johnson Amendment, allowing churches to endorse political candidates while keeping tax-exempt status, even as other nonprofits remained restricted. This change created a tax-subsidized channel for partisan mobilization through religious institutions. In education, the White House launched an AI initiative with major tech firms, and the American Federation of Teachers accepted $23 million from AI companies to establish a National Academy for AI Instruction. OpenAI and Google provided free tools to students through institutional partnerships. These moves embedded corporate algorithms and platforms into classrooms, shaping how future citizens learn and interpret the world.

Market power and information manipulation reinforced each other. Amazon increased list prices before Prime Day and offered higher referral fees to media outlets, encouraging promotional coverage and exaggerating discounts. The administration claimed that the unpopular reconciliation law was "the most popular bill ever," misrepresenting public opinion to justify redistributive policies. Tariff threats and emergency powers were used to create overlapping economic crises and confusion, making it harder for the public and institutions to identify responsibility. In this environment, economic data and narratives were curated to support policies, rather than policies being guided by transparent facts.

Public health, science, and climate information were combined into a single narrative. Health and Human Services Secretary Robert F. Kennedy Jr. dismissed the CDC's vaccine advisory panel and replaced members with skeptics. He used national media to claim that measles infection was safer than vaccination, launched an autism research initiative based on a discredited vaccine link, and promoted vitamins and supplements as treatments for measles. Advisory processes were altered to include non-existent studies and fringe views. Funding cuts to health research and vaccination programs coincided with a record number of measles cases. Essentially, misinformation became part of federal health priorities.

Climate and disaster information experienced similar distortions. Cuts to NOAA and NSF weakened weather and climate research. During severe Texas floods, state officials criticized the National Weather Service for underestimating rainfall, while the Department of Homeland Security accused mainstream media of intentionally lying about the disaster. The administration ordered an EPA investigation into conspiracy theories claiming "Deep State" geoengineering caused the floods, lending official support to fringe narratives. FEMA's new spending-approval rules delayed response efforts, and a grant to improve NWS communication was canceled during the crisis. Congressional committees were urged to investigate these delays, and New Mexico sued the Air Force over PFAS contamination, but these actions occurred amid declining scientific capacity and growing distrust.

Foreign and domestic uses of power converged into a final pattern. Trump suggested federal takeovers of New York City and Washington, D.C., if voters elected left-wing mayors, implying he might override local election results. He announced plans to dismantle FEMA by the end of hurricane season, shifting disaster response responsibilities to states and private entities. Abroad, he linked 50 percent tariffs on Brazil to Bolsonaro's trial, initiated a trade investigation into Brazil's social media regulation, and cut democracy-promotion programs while increasing military budgets. Netanyahu's nomination of Trump for the Nobel Peace Prize helped frame controversial Middle East actions as peacemaking. At home, "remigration" rhetoric and church endorsements of candidates, combined with AI-driven educational partnerships, reshaped civic culture around loyalty, security, and market ideology.

Some federal actions moved in the opposite direction. Congress and the president enacted laws restoring municipal lands and settlement trust eligibility to Alaska Native villages, strengthening local self-governance. Agencies like the EPA, CDC, and FDA continued routine advisory processes on PFAS standards, tuberculosis, and tobacco regulation. The Office of Government Information Services held a public meeting on FOIA oversight. These steps showed that not every part of the state moved in lockstep with the executive's project. Yet, in terms of scale and direction of change, they were outweighed.

The week's movement on the Democracy Clock reflected this imbalance. Executive power grew more insulated from legal consequences and legislative control. The civil service and scientific infrastructure were thinned and politicized. Immigration enforcement and domestic security blurred into a system of notable cruelty and intimidation. Economic and religious institutions were drawn deeper into partisan alignment. Information about health, climate, and elite wrongdoing was curated or distorted. Rights that once seemed settled—citizenship by birth, reproductive autonomy, equal participation for LGBTQ+ and transgender people—were treated as open questions.

In this landscape, resistance did not disappear. Courts blocked some orders, civil-society groups sued and organized, and parts of Congress demanded documents and hearings. But the week showed how much more effort is now required to secure the same protections, and how often that effort arrives after the fact. The erosion of democratic safety was not a single collapse. It was the steady advance of authority through doctrine, management, and narrative, met by fragmented and delayed responses.

CHAPTER 36
WEEK 26: DATA AND FORCE AS GOVERNANCE

In a week without a single shock, immigration raids, civil service purges, and curated secrecy deepened a regime of control over bodies, data, and memory.

The twenty-sixth week of Trump's second term did not depend on a single shock. It instead unfolded as a week in which government tools were refined to better serve those in power. Immigration raids, staffing orders, budget cuts, and court rulings came as separate events. Together, they depicted a state learning how to confidently and less restrainedly use its influence over bodies, data, money, and memory.

At the end of Week 25, the Democracy Clock was at 8:06 p.m. It remained at the same time after Week 26, with no net change in minutes. This stillness did not indicate calm. It signaled a week in which the direction was already set, and the focus was on strengthening existing approaches. Executive power pushed further into civil service and the courts. Immigration enforcement intensified into a continuous emergency. Public resources were reduced, while private and partisan channels grew thicker. Resistance was visible —in courts, legislatures, and streets—but as friction, not reversal.

The most noticeable part of this week's story was in the fields and streets where immigration law was enforced. At licensed cannabis farms, ICE and local officers arrived with less-lethal weapons and tear gas, turning a workplace raid into a scene of violence that injured workers and left one person dead. The president had already authorized agents to use "whatever means" they considered necessary for self-protection and ordered the arrest of protesters trying to block operations. What might have once been seen as a last resort was now part of the standard stance of the state.

Behind these scenes of force, the legal ground shifted. A new policy ended bond hearings for many undocumented immigrants, moving decisions about release from judges to the Department of Homeland Security. Rapid deportation rules shortened notice and narrowed the window for legal challenge. ICE expanded its officers and detention facilities, while Title 42 and related measures continued to be used to turn back asylum seekers. The architecture of emergency—fast, opaque, and harsh—was becoming permanent, not as a declared state of exception but as the normal operation of the system.

Data became a second line of control. The IRS and ICE developed a system to share confidential tax records, including addresses, for deportation targeting. Medicaid and other health data on tens of millions of people were planned to be used in a similar way. Information once collected for civic purposes—paying taxes, seeking medical care—was repurposed as a tool for surveillance and removal. The message to mixed-status families and vulnerable communities was clear: every form filled out could lead to enforcement.

Individual cases gave this structure a human face. Agents arrested an Iranian chiropractor at his child's preschool, breaking a car window in front of children. An Irish tourist who overstayed a visa by three days was held for about a hundred days in criminal facilities. Deportations were planned to third countries such as Eswatini, where those being removed had no ties and little assurance of safety. At the "Alligator Alcatraz" detention site in Florida, more than 250 non-criminal detainees were held in overcrowded, unsanitary conditions. Each story was an outlier in its details and typical in its logic. The burden of error and excess fell on those with the least power to contest it.

By the end of the week, masked, often unidentifiable agents conducted mass deportation raids across communities, staging operations from Terminal Island, a site already marked in American memory by Japanese American incarceration. Protesters who interfered with ICE operations faced arrest. The line between law enforcement and paramilitary presence blurred. Courts did push back at the margins—a Los Angeles judge temporarily blocked raids based on racial profiling; federal judges protected some refugees and TPS holders; advocates filed class actions against courthouse arrests—but these were narrow rulings in a system whose default settings had shifted toward speed and severity.

While immigration enforcement hardened on the ground, the administration worked to reshape who controlled the levers inside the state. The centerpiece was an executive order creating Schedule G, a new category of excepted service for policy roles. Under Schedule G, thousands of positions that had been shielded by civil service protections could be filled and removed at presidential discretion. What had been a professional bureaucracy, with some insulation from politics, was opened to rapid turnover based on loyalty. The effects of that shift appeared across agencies. At the Department of Education, the Supreme Court granted a stay that allowed the administration to proceed with large-scale layoffs, despite lower-court findings and congressional funding for more positions.

At the State Department, more than 1,300 staff were cut, and the Bureau of Democracy, Human Rights, and Labor was closed, removing a key institutional voice for rights in foreign policy. At the National Institutes of Health, leadership moved to replace advisory panel scientists with politically aligned appointees, threatening the independence of scientific advice.

The Department of Justice became a focal point of this politicization. Attorney General Pam Bondi dismissed the department's senior ethics attorney, Joseph Tirrell, along with more than twenty other employees. Maurene Comey, a federal prosecutor who had worked on the Epstein case and other sensitive matters, was abruptly removed. Meanwhile, the administration bypassed a judicial panel that had rejected John Sarcone III as interim U.S. attorney by appointing him instead as "special attorney to the attorney general," granting him full U.S. attorney powers without Senate confirmation. These actions did not eliminate oversight on paper, but they shifted who would exercise it and on whose behalf.

Even agencies responsible for logistics and internal management were affected. The General Services Administration rescinded forty-one Federal Management Regulation bulletins, reducing guidance on handling federal assets and fleets. At FEMA, Homeland Security Secretary Kristi Noem required her personal approval for expenditures and contracts over $100,000 and allowed call-center contracts to lapse during Texas floods, sharply decreasing answered calls. The formal mission of disaster response remained, but the capacity and discretion to carry it out were centralized near a single political office.

The same logic of control and protection influenced the government's handling of the Epstein scandal. Early in the week, DOJ and the FBI announced they would not release further Epstein information and insisted that no incriminating client list existed. A formal memo concluded that Epstein had died by suicide and declined to provide additional data. The attorney general and FBI director framed the matter as closed. The president dismissed questions about the memo as unimportant in a cabinet meeting and urged the FBI to focus instead on voter fraud and corruption, redirecting investigative attention toward narratives more useful to him.

Yet, the evidence record itself raised doubts. DOJ released what it called "full raw" surveillance video from Epstein's cell, only for reporters to find nearly three minutes missing. The firing of Maurene Comey, whose work involved Epstein and other high-profile cases, added to the sense that those who probed too close to elite networks faced consequences. In Congress, House Rules Committee Republicans used procedural control to block Democratic amendments that would have forced the release of Epstein files, even as Speaker Mike Johnson later called publicly for transparency. The gap between rhetoric and votes underscored how information politics could be staged.

Outside government, pressure grew. Representatives Marc Veasey and Ro Khanna announced plans for a resolution and amendment demanding the release of Epstein records. Senator Ron Wyden pressed DOJ for banking records linked to Epstein's financial network. Senator Dick Durbin sought details on claims that 1,000 agents had been assigned to the case. Investigative outlets documented how the administration's selective disclosures and messaging managing fallout rather than informing the public fully, while high-profile figures on social media amplified criticism of the president over the unreleased files.

By week's end, DOJ moved to unseal redacted grand jury transcripts, and the president ordered Bondi to release Epstein grand jury testimony. On paper, these were steps toward transparency. In context, they seemed more like tactical concessions under pressure, coming after weeks of secrecy, retaliatory firings, and missing footage. The president's own online posts, calling the backlash a "hoax" and attacking former supporters, added chaos that made it harder to distinguish genuine transparency from narrative management. The net effect was to deepen public suspicion that crimes by elite donors and allies could be kept out of reach.

While scandal management unfolded in Washington, the rules of representation were being rewritten in the states and courts. In Florida, the state supreme court upheld a congressional map that dismantled a Black-influence district and diminished Black voters' power. At the federal level, rulings against affirmative action and related doctrines shifted legal standards away from race-conscious remedies. These decisions did not completely prevent minority participation but narrowed the tools available to turn participation into influence.

At the same time, partisan actors moved to influence district maps more directly. The president publicly called for a mid-decade redrawing of Texas congressional districts to increase Republican seats, involving the White House in what was once a state-level process. In Texas and California, competing redistricting plans showed both parties seeking structural advantage, although the federal government's support favored the president's allies. In Texas, Attorney General Ken Paxton threatened to arrest Democratic legislators who boycotted a redistricting special session, transforming a traditional minority tactic—denying quorum—into grounds for criminal sanctions.

Administrative rules offered a quieter route to similar goals. In North Carolina, the state board of elections voted to require extra registration data that could move about 100,000 voters to provisional status, effectively suppressing participation under the pretext of list maintenance. The Election Assistance Commission, on the other hand, announced a public meeting on updated voting system guidelines, a small but genuine act of transparent oversight. Outside these institutions, more than 1,500 "Good Trouble Lives On" demonstrations invoked John Lewis's legacy to rally citizens around voting rights. The battle over who counts, and how, was fought simultaneously in courtrooms, committee rooms, and streets.

Beneath these political battles, the foundation of democracy—its economic and informational systems—was being changed. A reconciliation bill removed support for renewable energy and the Low Income Home Energy Assistance Program, leading to higher projected power costs and worsening energy insecurity for poorer households. The administration cut $4 billion in federal funding for California's high-speed rail project, weakening long-term, climate-friendly infrastructure and signaling partisan use of federal funds against a disliked state. Tariffs of 30 percent on goods from the European Union and Mexico, along with a 17 percent tariff on

Mexican tomatoes, shifted costs onto consumers while giving certain domestic producers an advantage.

Congress and the White House then collaborated on a $9.4 billion rescissions package. The bill retroactively backed unilateral spending cuts, reduced foreign aid, and defunded PBS and NPR. Along with dismantling the U.S. Agency for Global Media, these cuts weakened public broadcasting and international news efforts, pushing information systems toward private and partisan outlets. Domestically, the Department of Housing and Urban Development prepared to end seven major investigations into housing discrimination and segregation, while the IRS sought to shut down its Free File tax program after meetings with tax software lobbyists. Enforcement against systemic discrimination and a public option for filing taxes both gave way to industry preferences.

Data collection was also reduced. The administration cut resources at the Bureau of Labor Statistics, increasing dependence on estimated prices in inflation reports. NOAA halted work on a project to predict extreme rainfall, decreasing the government's ability to prepare for climate-related disasters. NASA chose not to publish key climate change assessments on its website. These decisions did not erase facts but made them harder to find and easier to distort. When official statistics and scientific reports lack clarity, both citizens and policymakers are left to interpret narratives rather than evidence.

At the same time, the line between public office and private gain became more blurred. The administration lifted export controls on advanced chips and design tools for China, enabling U.S. companies to resume profitable sales even as it threatened broad secondary sanctions on countries trading with Russia. The Trump Organization announced Trump Tower Bucharest and lifted its self-imposed ban on foreign deals, reopening channels for foreign governments and firms to seek favor through the president's businesses. Large settlements from media lawsuits, sometimes up to $63 million, were directed to fund Trump's presidential library, blurring the boundaries between defamation lawsuits, political influence, and financing a presidential institution. Wealth did not just buy speech; it bought law and legacy.

The information environment that could have checked these actions was itself under strain. Reductions in funding for PBS and NPR, lawsuits against members of the Corporation for Public Broadcasting's board, and the dismantling of USAGM weakened independent public media. The Federal Election Commission canceled open meetings, limiting public oversight of campaign finance enforcement. NASA's withheld climate assessments and the BLS data cuts formed part of a wider pattern where inconvenient information was delayed, minimized, or kept off official platforms. A clearer picture emerged: fewer independent voices, less accessible science, and more opportunities for those in power to shape reality.

Private media and online platforms were not immune to this struggle. CBS announced the cancellation of "The Late Show with Stephen Colbert," removing a major platform for political satire. In Congress, a Republican representative proposed ending the House's subscription contract with The Wall Street Journal after critical reporting, indicating a willingness to use legislative tools to punish unfavorable outlets. The president used his own platform to post unsubstantiated claims of mortgage fraud against Senator Adam Schiff amid inflation driven by tariffs, shifting focus from policy impacts to personal attacks. Investigative journalists examining elite misconduct, including cases related to Epstein, faced smear campaigns and, in some instances, legal threats.

Within the justice system, the pattern of selective enforcement became clearer. DOJ dropped charges mid-trial against Dr. Michael Kirk Moore, who was accused of destroying Covid vaccines and issuing fake cards, weakening deterrence against undermining public health programs. In the Breonna Taylor civil rights case, the department requested a one-day sentence for former officer Brett Hankison, raising doubts about federal commitment to police accountability. At the same time, DOJ narrowed but continued a bribery prosecution against Representative Henry Cuellar, showing that corruption cases could proceed when they aligned with the administration's priorities.

Civil rights enforcement moved in the opposite direction. DOJ canceled a Biden-era settlement that required Alabama to address the Lowndes County sewage crisis, removing federal pressure to fix environmental injustice in a poor, mostly Black community. English-only guidance at DOJ limited multilingual services, making it harder for non-English speakers to navigate legal processes and assert their rights. The Office of Congressional Ethics found substantial evidence of ethical violations by former Congressman Alex Mooney, yet the House Ethics Committee left the issue unresolved before he left office. Formal structures remained, but their ability to impose consequences on elites was limited.

Not all uses of law followed this pattern. Federal courts blocked a refugee ban, protected Afghans' Temporary Protected Status, and granted a temporary restraining order in an ICE detention case. Environmental groups and states sued over FEMA resilience grant cuts and the Alligator Alcatraz facility, combining ecological and civil liberties arguments. Baltimore invested in community-based violence reduction programs and data-driven mediation, demonstrating how law and policy can be used to enhance safety without expanding coercive force. These examples did not outweigh the broader trend, but they showed that alternative models of governance still existed.

Civil society and some institutions pushed back against the new order, even as intimidation grew. Lawmakers who toured the Alligator Alcatraz facility reported overcrowded cages and poor sanitation, prompting public outrage. When Florida Democrats were denied access to the site, they sued to enforce their inspection rights. Environmental groups filed their own suit to halt the facility's operation. Nationwide, "Good Trouble Lives On" demonstrations honored John Lewis and mobilized citizens around voting rights and justice. Indivisible organized online training sessions to build local organizing capacity.

Inside the security apparatus, cracks appeared. DHS agents testified in court about unusual orders to arrest pro-Palestinian students and academics, saying they had questioned the legality of directives targeting specific political groups. In Texas, officials and residents involved in flood response faced death threats, showing how public service itself was becoming more dangerous. On Capitol Hill, repeated hearings on antisemitism in higher education put heavy pressure on universities to police speech, with the implied threat of funding consequences. The same week, Congress passed routine legislation on technical corrections, fentanyl control, and innovation, reminding us that normal lawmaking continued alongside more corrupt uses of power.

Across these areas, the moral baseline continued to fall. Character, meaning aligning words with public duty, was strained by mass layoffs at the State Department and the closure of a human rights bureau. Ethics became blurry as immigration enforcement and Epstein-related issues intersected with private interests and political protection. Restraint was replaced by maximum use of executive authority in immigration, trade, and staffing. Truthfulness declined amid disinformation about opponents and curated archives. Trust in procedures weakened as legislatures blocked transparency amendments and staged oversight shows. Stewardship suffered as oversight mechanisms were dismantled and agencies were pushed toward partisan goals.

Yet the Democracy Clock did not move this week because the overall direction was already set. Week 26 was less of a change than a deepening. The executive branch extended its reach over who serves, who is monitored, and what the public can access. Courts, legislatures, and civil society raised objections, sometimes forcefully, but mostly after damage had been done. The balance of power and accountability shifted further, not through one big event but through many small, coordinated acts that made the extraordinary seem routine.

CHAPTER 37
WEEK 27: DATABASES AND DETENTION AS GOVERNANCE

A week when immigration camps, crypto reserves, and AI propaganda showed how law, money, and information are being refitted to serve power first.

The twenty-seventh week of Trump's second term didn't hinge on a single order or speech. Instead, it played out as a series of changes in how the state perceives, categorizes, and controls people. Immigration raids, tax laws, campus settlements, and crypto regulations all advanced simultaneously, each presented as technical or necessary. Together, they painted a clearer picture of a system in which law, money, and information primarily serve power, with the public as a secondary effect.

At the start of the week, the Democracy Clock was at 8:06 p.m. By week's end, it read 8:09 p.m., a net shift of 2.6 minutes. This change came from a gradual buildup rather than a sudden break: a tax law that increased structural inequality, executive orders that made homelessness and campus protests federal issues, court rulings that eased mass layoffs, and a communication strategy that relied on AI-generated fake content and curated archives. The time shift showed how much harder, in just days, it became for ordinary people to rely on neutral institutions to hold power accountable or see themselves as equals before the law.

The most noticeable aspect of that change centered on immigration. The administration had already increased detention and enforcement efforts, but this week those efforts coalesced into something resembling a permanent internal security system. ICE's budget was tripled, and its authority expanded, with new tent facilities and a 5,000-bed complex at Fort Bliss funded through a $1.26 billion contract. These were not temporary surge sites; they represented long-term infrastructure designed to hold large numbers of people in remote, militarized environments.

Surveillance increased alongside expanding capacity. The Centers for Medicare and Medicaid Services granted ICE access to the personal data of nearly 80 million Medicaid recipients, turning a healthcare database into an enforcement tool. At the same time, ICE agents were allowed to wear masks during raids and courthouse operations, hiding their identities as they used this data to find and arrest individuals. The combination of masked officers and mined health records made it harder to identify those acting on the state's behalf and raised the risk of targeting communities that already feared government contact.

On the ground, these tools led to arrests and detention that blurred the lines between citizens and non-citizens, allies and enemies. Journalists like Mario Guevara, known for covering immigration enforcement, were detained and pushed toward deportation even after local charges were dropped. Asylum seekers who appeared in court as required were sometimes detained at or after hearings, showing that following legal procedures could itself lead to detention. Reports from Florida and other states described shackling, overcrowding, and medical neglect in ICE facilities, including the "Alligator Alcatraz" camp in the Everglades, where conditions were compared to torture.

Military support made the system feel less like civil administration and more like a domestic deployment. About 2,000 National Guard troops were mobilized to assist at detention centers, and

Florida highway patrol troopers were deputized to enforce federal immigration law. Courthouse and street sweeps in cities like Los Angeles and New York sometimes caught U.S. citizens, while teenagers in custody were asked if they wanted to "self-deport." The message was clear: immigration status, or even perceived status, could subject someone to a parallel legal system with fewer rights and more force.

Power in this domain was not entirely unchecked. A coalition of state attorneys general urged Congress to ban masked federal agents and require visible identification, warning that anonymity undermined accountability. Courts ordered the reinstatement of immigration judges' authority to appoint counsel for vulnerable immigrants and intervened in cases like that of Kilmar Ábrego García, blocking immediate deportation and requiring notice before removal. However, these rulings were narrow and reactive. The broader pattern was one of a security system designed to protect the regime's priorities, not the people within its reach.

The same Justice Department that allocated resources to immigration enforcement scaled back its oversight of local police. In the Breonna Taylor case, federal prosecutors requested a one-day sentence for former officer Brett Hankison, whose actions contributed to her death. A federal judge rejected that request and imposed a 33-month sentence, indicating that some courts were unwilling to treat civil rights violations as minor offenses. The difference between prosecutorial leniency and judicial firmness revealed a growing divide within the justice system.

This gap widened further when the administration ended investigations and consent decrees with more than twenty police departments, including cities with long histories of abuse. These agreements had been among the few tools available to enforce structural reforms in departments resistant to change. Their termination not only closed specific cases; it signaled that the federal government would no longer serve as a consistent safeguard against local misconduct. In the same week, a lawsuit concerning the death of Cornelius Taylor during an Atlanta encampment sweep highlighted how aggressive "cleanup" policies could transform poverty into a matter for armed intervention rather than social support.

On other fronts, courts and state actors tried to hold a line. A federal judge temporarily blocked a Mississippi law banning DEI programs in public education, preserving diversity initiatives while their constitutionality was tested. Another court ordered that mentally disabled immigrants must once again be able to receive appointed counsel, and multistate coalitions sued over restrictions on undocumented immigrants' access to federal programs. The Muscogee (Creek) Nation's decision to extend citizenship to descendants of enslaved people offered a rare example of an institution broadening inclusion rather than narrowing it. Yet these moves seemed like islands in a sea of federal retreat from civil rights enforcement.

At the highest level, law itself was increasingly treated as a weapon rather than a limit. Director of National Intelligence Tulsi Gabbard issued referrals urging treason investigations against former President Obama and his aides over long-settled questions of Russian interference. The Justice Department formed a "strike force" to pursue alleged Obama-era conspiracies, even as prior bipartisan findings had already established the basic facts. In parallel, the president and his allies circulated an AI-generated video depicting Obama being arrested and pushed a narrative that Democrats had "rigged" the 2016 election, blending prosecutorial power with propaganda.

The Epstein scandal became another arena where law and secrecy were bent toward self-protection. President Trump directed Attorney General Pam Bondi to seek the release of grand jury testimony in the case, a move that would normally be extraordinary. At the same time, DOJ refused to release most of its 100, 100,000 pages of Epstein files, even under intense public pressure. Senators like Dick Durbin questioned why agents were being reassigned en masse to review Epstein documents for references to Trump, raising the possibility that investigative resources were being used to manage political risk rather than pursue justice.

Congressional oversight remained divided along similar lines. Speaker Mike Johnson refused to schedule votes on bipartisan resolutions to release Epstein files and then shut down the House early, using parliamentary procedures to avoid a politically risky transparency fight. Nonetheless, the House Oversight Committee voted to subpoena Ghislaine Maxwell and the DOJ for documents, asserting its authority to investigate elite sex trafficking networks. Federal courts, for their part, rejected DOJ's requests to unseal grand jury materials, emphasizing confidentiality rules even as the administration pushed for selective disclosure. This resulted in a complicated mix of partial revelations, blocked votes, and sealed records, leaving the public with more questions than answers.

Information control extended beyond the courtroom. Trump filed multi-billion dollar defamation suits against the Wall Street Journal, Rupert Murdoch, and others over a published letter allegedly linking him to Epstein. A federal judge's dismissal of his separate $50 million suit against Bob Woodward showed that some legal protections for journalists still existed, but the magnitude of the new claims sent a clear message: critical reporting on the president's past could involve significant legal risks. When the White House then took control of press pool assignments and excluded the Journal from the pool, it turned access itself into a tool of discipline.

The administration also moved to reshape the broader media landscape. Kari Lake, appointed at the U.S. Agency for Global Media, locked the acting CEO out of systems and threatened the Voice of America director with removal, intensifying political control over government-funded broadcasting. The FCC approved the Paramount–Skydance merger only after commitments to drop DEI initiatives and address alleged newsroom "bias," blurring the line between competition policy and ideological pressure. A $9 billion rescissions package cut foreign aid and public broadcasting funds, weakening institutions that supported independent reporting and cultural memory.

Abroad, the United States withdrew from UNESCO, retreating from a body that had long promoted press freedom and heritage preservation. At home, the State Department altered its human rights reports to omit sections on reproductive health, LGBTQ+ rights, and minorities, narrowing the categories of abuse officially recognized. A DHS tweet echoing neo-Nazi rhetoric about genocide against Indigenous peoples suggested that even language of conquest and extermination might appear in official channels without immediate correction. These moves didn't just shift policy; they edited the record of whose suffering was deemed relevant.

At the same time, the administration leaned into AI and automation as tools for narrative control. An AI-driven bot network on X amplified pro-government messaging, creating the illusion of broad support for administration figures. The executive order banning "woke" AI in federal use mandated ideologically defined "neutrality" in automated systems, giving the White House leverage over how algorithms present facts and options. Coupled with deepfake-style videos and calls to revoke Pulitzer Prizes from outlets that reported on Russian interference, the effect was to delegitimize independent journalism and flood the public sphere with regime-friendly stories.

Beneath these information battles, the economic foundation of the state was being rebuilt to favor capital and insiders. A new tax law extended the 2017 tax cuts permanently, further reduced corporate taxes, and cut Medicaid and food stamps, adding an estimated $3.4 trillion to the debt while raising uninsured rates. Tariffs were increased to levels not seen since 1910, with average rates around 20.6 percent. General Motors reported a 35 percent drop in net income tied to automotive tariffs, and analysts documented higher food prices for households, effectively turning trade policy into a regressive tax.

Education and social services became bargaining chips. The administration froze roughly $6 billion in federal education funds, prompting lawsuits from school districts and nonprofits, then agreed to release most of the funds under pressure. The timing showed how control over disbursement could be used as leverage in policy disputes. A broader rescissions act canceled billions in foreign aid and public broadcasting, while the EPA rescinded a $20 million clean water grant, and USDA underwent restructuring with salary cuts and relocations. These choices shifted burdens onto rural, low-income, and farm communities while maintaining fiscal space for tax cuts and favored industries.

Crypto and AI policy sat at the intersection of personal enrichment and national strategy. Trump signed an executive order creating a Strategic Bitcoin Reserve and a federal digital asset stockpile, aligning the government's balance sheet with a volatile asset class closely tied to his allies. The GENIUS Act, shaped by industry lobbyists, provided a statutory foothold for stablecoins. Trump Media & Technology Group, majority-owned by the president, acquired $2 billion in bitcoin and pivoted into a crypto holding company, intertwining his personal wealth with federal crypto policy. A new SEC chair quickly dropped major enforcement cases, and ethics waivers allowed adviser David Sacks to keep undisclosed crypto investments while shaping regulation.

On the AI front, executive orders accelerated the development of data centers and AI infrastructure by relaxing environmental and permitting regulations, and exempting some laws like NEPA. Another order promoted AI exports and deregulation, aiming to strengthen U.S. dominance while reducing safety measures. These actions coincided with the EPA shutting down its research and development office and initiating widespread layoffs, and with the State Department and USDA facing major cuts and reorganizations. The Supreme Court lifted injunctions halting State Department workforce reductions and approved a stay allowing the removal of Consumer Product Safety Commission commissioners, boosting executive power over independent agencies. The pattern was clear: weaken unbiased science and diplomacy, empower allied industries, and let courts pave the way.

Universities felt this influence strongly. Columbia University reached a settlement with the administration that restored roughly $400 million in federal grants only after agreeing to speech-related conditions, receivership, and oversight. The settlement included restrictions on masks and pro-Palestinian speech and placed an academic department under external supervision. About eighty students were disciplined—suspended or expelled—under a new antisemitism definition critics argued equated criticism of Israel with hatred of Jews. Federal funding, once a support for research and education, became a tool to reshape campus governance and suppress dissent.

In the same week, the White House issued an executive order on "Saving College Sports," which limited third-party pay for athletes, bringing federal authority into discussions that had been moving toward increased athlete compensation. Along with the Columbia settlement, the order indicated a broader tendency to impose rules in areas traditionally governed by a mix of state law, institutional policies, and private negotiations. Universities were no longer just recipients of funds; they became instruments for enforcing ideological and economic policies.

The reach of executive power extended into public spaces and geographies as well. An order addressing homelessness mandated the removal of unhoused individuals from public areas into treatment or confinement, and directed the DOJ to seek overturning precedents that limited criminalization of outdoor sleeping. Civil commitment standards were relaxed, broadening the state's authority to confine individuals under the guise of public safety. The Atlanta encampment death lawsuit brought a human perspective to these policies, illustrating how they could lead to deadly force against those with nowhere else to go.

In Texas, Trump personally oversaw a redistricting process despite concerns from the DOJ about racial gerrymandering. Lawsuits challenging sanctuary city policies in places like New York City and federal appeals aimed at cutting off diversity-related grants were framed as issues of "election integrity" and equal treatment. Meanwhile, courts repeatedly declared Trump's executive order ending birthright citizenship unconstitutional, reaffirming the protections of the Fourteenth Amendment. The clash between presidential ambitions and constitutional limits was evident. Maps and citizenship rules were pushed to their limits, with the presidency exerting pressure and the judiciary holding some boundaries for now.

Across these areas, the moral foundation weakened. Character, meaning the alignment of words with duty, was strained by treason accusations against political opponents and by disinformation about Epstein and immigration. Ethics became unclear as personal and donor interests in crypto, media, and detention contracts intertwined with national policies. Restraint declined as executive orders were used aggressively to clear encampments, reshape college sports, and redraw districts. Truthfulness suffered as AI-generated arrest videos and curated archives became common. Trust and responsibility diminished as legislative procedures were exploited to dodge oversight, and agencies that once acted as neutral stewards of science, rights, and history were repurposed.

Yet, resistance persisted. Federal courts blocked DEI bans, reinstated TPS for Haitians, dismissed some lawsuits against sanctuary jurisdictions, and ordered the revival of a public spending tracker website. The National Archives sought public input on records schedules, inviting citizens into decisions on whether to preserve or delete records. State attorneys general sued over benefit restrictions and raid mask mandates. These actions didn't reverse the overall movement of the week but demonstrated that institutional strength still existed, even if it was under increasing strain.

The importance of the week lay more in how these different actions reinforced each other than in any one decision. Immigration enforcement became a testing ground for militarized, data-driven control. Economic policies shifted risks downward while boosting profits. Universities and media outlets learned that funding and access depended on compliance. Courts, while still able to say no, were increasingly asked to approve executive dismissals and structural changes. Information—what was accepted as fact, whose suffering was documented, and which histories were told—was curated to favor those already in power.

In that sense, the modest progress of the Democracy Clock reflected a deeper change. Rights and protections still existed on paper. Elections still took place. Courts still handed down unfavorable rulings. But exercising those rights, challenging those elections, and relying on those courts now required more courage, more resources, and more luck. The cost of dissent increased, the benefits of loyalty grew, and the space for ordinary people to stand outside the shadow of the state shrank slightly more.

CHAPTER 38
WEEK 28: CONFINEMENT AS GOVERNANCE

With no single shock, the administration deepened a regime where law, welfare, and information serve personalized power and stratified citizenship.

The twenty-eighth week of Trump's second term didn't bring any major events that grabbed the public's attention. Instead, it involved a complicated series of decisions and directives that, together, made the power structure more personal, more isolated, and more unequal. The pattern wasn't improvisation; it was a steady use of law, money, and memory to draw a clearer line between those who could be influenced and those who could act.

At the start of Week 28, the Democracy Clock was set at 8:06 p.m. It stayed at the same time by the week's end, with no net change in minutes. The stillness of the dial didn't mean that nothing was happening; it showed that the week's actions intensified an already fragile balance rather than creating a new one. Executive power kept expanding in areas like immigration, trade, and information. Courts and civil society showed resistance in some areas, but not enough to shift the overall balance. The moral floor, already weakened, sagged further under the weight of normalized lawlessness.

The most obvious example of that lawlessness was in immigration and detention. The administration relied on the Alien Enemies Act, an 18th-century law, to deport Venezuelan migrants without hearings. Flights continued even after a federal court ordered a stop to removals to El Salvador, signaling that judicial orders could be ignored when they conflicted with executive priorities. Similarly, immigration authorities used security and gang rhetoric to justify mass expulsions, portraying vulnerable people as enemy combatants rather than rights-bearing individuals.

Behind these headline actions, a new area of confinement formed. FEMA launched a $608 million grant program to build temporary migrant detention facilities, turning emergency management funds into a pipeline for cages and camps. In Florida's Everglades, the Alligator Alcatraz camp operated as a legal black hole. Detainees were held without charges, with no access to counsel, and courts were told they lacked jurisdiction to intervene. The camp's very design—remote, opaque, and framed as necessary for security—made it a model for extrajudicial confinement on American soil.

Conditions within this archipelago revealed what it meant to be outside the law. At CoreCivic's Cibola facility, reports detailed drug trafficking, fatalities, and torture-like treatment. In another center, a double-amputee detainee was placed in solitary confinement after refusing to enter a flooded area that would have damaged his prosthetics. A South Korean scientist with a green card was detained at San Francisco International Airport and denied access to an attorney, with his legal status offering no protection against arbitrary detention. These incidents were not isolated abuses; they served as case studies of a system where profit, secrecy, and fear took precedence over safety and due process.

The logic of confinement extended beyond the border. President Trump signed an executive order allowing mass detention of homeless individuals under a crime and disorder initiative, explicitly framing homelessness as a security threat. FEMA's detention grants and the homelessness order together expanded infrastructure and legal authority for sweeping up marginalized citizens as well as non-citizens. On the streets, a Florida citizen who filmed officers using chokeholds and tasers during an immigration stop was arrested and later sentenced, signaling that even witnessing and recording state violence carried personal risks. Simultaneously, Trump urged DACA recipients to "self-deport" despite no formal rule change, weaponizing uncertainty and fear to deport people without the need for legal procedure.

If the camps and flights demonstrated the harshness of power, the rhetoric and policies around citizenship revealed its ideological foundation. Vice President J.D. Vance publicly redefined American citizenship based on ancestry and place, emphasizing blood and heritage over shared principles. His remarks clashed with federal courts that upheld a nationwide ban on Trump's attempt to end birthright citizenship, maintaining a constitutional guarantee that has long supported egalitarian membership. The tension between Vance's vision and the courts' injunction highlighted a live conflict over who counts as fully American.

Policy actions moved in Vance's hierarchy. The administration ended the CHNV parole program and increased arrests targeting over a million immigrants, many of whom work within local economies. The Department of Justice requested detailed personal data on non-citizen voters from California counties, risking deterrence of participation and enabling targeted enforcement under the guise of fraud prevention. On welfare, the administration announced significant cuts and cost shifts in the SNAP food assistance program, including new limits for non-citizens, alongside historic Medicaid reductions, tax cuts, and deportation funding. These changes deepened economic instability for immigrants and the poor, framing social rights as contingent on status and ideology.

The same stratifying logic appeared in health and bodily autonomy. The administration pushed Congress to defund gender-affirming care and issued an order threatening funds for hospitals treating trans youth. Texas sought to export its abortion penalties into New York by targeting a doctor protected by a shield law, while New York defended its existing legal framework. Coalitions of states sued to block the transgender healthcare order and to protect Planned Parenthood funding, using federalism as a defensive tool. Yet, the need for such lawsuits highlighted how far the federal government had moved toward using health policy as a weapon against disfavored groups.

Voting and representation followed a similar pattern. In North Carolina, legislative leaders rescheduled sessions with little notice to override vetoes on anti-immigrant, anti-DEI, and anti-LGBTQ bills and to push a voter suppression bill, HB 958, while limiting public access. In Texas, Republican leaders released a congressional map expected to give their party five additional seats, drawing criticism for racial discrimination and partisan entrenchment. Missouri lawmakers moved to repeal voter-approved initiatives on Medicaid expansion and abortion rights. Overall, these actions treated popular will as a hurdle to be managed rather than a source of authority. In contrast, New Orleans' decision to launch a municipal ID program for residents without traditional documents, and state efforts to protect lawmakers after assassinations and threats, showed local attempts to increase access and preserve safety, even as higher levels of government narrowed the circle of belonging.

Meanwhile, economic governance shifted further toward rule by decree. The One Big Beautiful Bill Act's trillion-dollar Medicaid cuts, along with tax reforms and deportation funding, restructured federal health support in ways that weakened a core social right and favored enforcement and benefits for the upper class. President Trump signed a rescissions package that clawed back previously allocated funds, including those for education, and his budget chief considered pocket rescissions that would allow appropriated funds to expire unused. These moves blurred the line between executing and nullifying laws, weakening Congress's power of the purse.

Trade policy became a personal tool. The administration implemented a new tariff regime raising effective rates on imports from Europe, Japan, Britain, and other allies, shifting the country toward protectionist, leader-driven trade. Trump declared a national emergency over Brazil's conduct and imposed a 40 percent tariff on Brazilian imports, explicitly linking the move to Brazil's treatment of Jair Bolsonaro and alleged speech issues. He increased tariffs on Canadian goods from 25 to 35 percent and imposed a 40 percent duty on transshipped items, using trade to punish a close ally over drugs and foreign policy disputes. He also suspended duty-free de minimis treatment for low-value imports and repeatedly adjusted reciprocal tariff rates by executive order, all under standing emergency powers.

These actions occurred against a backdrop of rising inflation and conflicts with the Federal Reserve. Trump condemned a weak jobs report as rigged, dismissed the Bureau of Labor Statistics commissioner, and appointed a political loyalist. The Fed kept rates steady, but the president's criticism politicized an institution meant to provide technocratic stability. Courts examined challenges to Trump's use of emergency economic powers for broad tariff measures, but the administration continued, announcing new global tariff baselines just before a self-imposed deadline while its authority was under appeal. The message was clear: Act first, make other branches respond.

Domestic redistribution followed a similar pattern of centralization and favoritism. The administration cut more than half of federal community violence intervention grants, shifted SNAP costs onto states, and promoted "Trump accounts," which Treasury Secretary Scott Bessent described as a covert way to privatize Social Security. NIH research funding was temporarily frozen and then restored under pressure, illustrating how long-term scientific projects could be used as bargaining chips. The Environmental Protection Agency moved to revoke the greenhouse gas endangerment finding, removing a key statutory basis for climate regulation. Simultaneously, Trump accepted a luxury jumbo jet from Qatar to serve as Air Force One, financed its refit through an opaque nuclear modernization fund transfer, and announced a 90,000-square-foot White House ballroom funded by himself and private donors. Public assets and funds became intertwined with foreign benefactors and personal projects, blurring the line between state and leader.

Beneath these headline policies, the machinery of administration was reconfigured. The Department of Government Efficiency deployed an AI tool to generate a list targeting half of all federal regulations, centralizing discretion over which protections remained in a small executive unit. The process was opaque, with criteria hidden inside code, yet the outcomes were tangible: rules related to housing, consumer finance, and safety could disappear without public debate. The EPA's action against the endangerment finding and HHS Secretary Robert F. Kennedy Jr.'s removal of a key preventive health task force, replacing experts with vaccine skeptics, demonstrated how evidence-based guidance was being replaced by ideology.

The justice system was pulled into the same orbit. Department of Justice leaders manipulated interim U.S. attorney appointments by designating incumbents as acting just before their terms expired, preventing courts from installing independent interim prosecutors. In New Jersey, defendants challenged the legality of Acting U.S. Attorney Alina Habba's appointment, and cases were paused, reflecting concern that prosecutorial authority was being reshaped through irregular processes. The Senate nonetheless confirmed former Trump lawyer Emil Bove to a lifetime seat on a federal appeals court despite whistleblower allegations that he ignored court orders and misled lawmakers. Attorney General Pam Bondi filed a misconduct complaint against Judge James Boasberg over comments about the administration, and Chief Justice John Roberts reported escalating threats and intimidation against judges following rulings adverse to Trump policies. Together, these moves tilted the judiciary toward deference and self-censorship.

Even the basic staffing of emergency roles showed strain. The head of the White House Office of Pandemic Preparedness and Response Policy resigned after revealing he had never been formally appointed, exposing a governance gap at the heart of crisis management. Comparative reporting on Xi Jinping's loyalty-based appointments and selective anti-corruption purges in China offered a mirror: a model of how concentrated control over personnel and regulators can fuse economic and political power. In Washington, the same logic appeared in softer form, as civil service roles and legal posts were filled and managed for loyalty rather than competence.

Universities, schools, and civil society organizations found themselves under coordinated pressure to conform. The administration froze $108 million in federal research funding to Duke University over allegations of race-based discrimination and investigated its law journal's selection practices for its editor. Columbia University saw $1.3 billion in funding withheld, then restored only after a $221 million settlement and an agreement to abandon consideration of race and other factors in hiring. Mandated antisemitism trainings at universities, designed by pro-Israel groups and equating anti-Zionism with antisemitism, became conditions for federal support. The Department of Justice ordered federal grantees to ban diversity, equity, and inclusion programs, extending ideological control through funding contracts.

Federal scrutiny extended into campus governance and free speech. The administration reviewed George Mason University's pro-president resolution and demanded the preservation of related communications, indicating that even internal statements could attract official attention. In K–12 education, Oklahoma's superintendent announced a MAGA-aligned exam to certify teachers from liberal states, effectively politicizing professional licensing. These actions occurred in a broader climate where the CIA director refused to rule out treason charges against former intelligence leaders and a former presidential candidate, and the Department of Homeland Security displayed manifest destiny imagery and appropriated artwork to promote nationalist themes. Civic education and identity were being reshaped to support "America First" narratives.

Media, data, and archives were similarly manipulated. Trump called for revoking NBC and ABC broadcasting licenses, accusing them of partisanship. An FCC commissioner warned that such threats were already leading to self-censorship. The FCC approved a CBS–Skydance merger with conditions that limited civil-rights programming and required a political bias monitor, embedding ideological filters into corporate media. Axios published highly favorable coverage of Trump's second term, aligned with conservative sponsors and relying on administration sources, while minimizing negative impacts. The SEC approved a Trump Jr.–backed gun company for public trading shortly after the Trump-appointed chair attended events with him, raising concerns about regulatory favoritism.

Control over information extended to data and records that support public debate. Firing the BLS commissioner over an unfavorable jobs report undermined the independence of economic statistics. The FBI ordered Trump's name redacted from Epstein files released under FOIA and pressured a resistant records chief to retire, effectively sanitizing the archival record amid a major scandal. At the same time, watchdog groups sued DOJ to obtain the legal memo approving Trump's acceptance of the Qatari jet, testing whether emoluments issues could still be argued in court. Trump provided shifting accounts of his relationships with Jeffrey Epstein and Virginia Giuffre, and made exaggerated claims about ending wars and trade agreements during meetings with foreign leaders. In this environment, investigative outlets like Popular Information revealed biased Sinclair news practices, Social Security service cuts, and ballot miscounts later corrected, demonstrating that independent media could still force reversals—but only after damage had been inflicted.

Law and prosecution increasingly targeted political and cultural opponents, while elite allies perceived signs of leniency. Trump publicly called for the prosecution of Kamala Harris,

Beyoncé, Oprah Winfrey, and Al Sharpton over unfounded election claims, normalizing the idea that critics and rivals could be treated as criminals. CIA Director Ratcliffe's willingness to consider treason charges against former intelligence leaders and a former presidential candidate blurred the line between accountability and criminalizing dissent. Conversely, Trump floated the possibility of pardoning Ghislaine Maxwell after sending a senior DOJ official to interview her, hinting that the pardon power could be used to shield a convicted sex trafficker connected to an elite abuse network.

Neutral arbiters faced pressure. Trump criticized a Fox News commentator for supporting stricter gun laws, indicating even friendly platforms weren't safe from dissent. The ethics complaint against Judge Boasberg and threats against judges after unfavorable rulings demonstrated how legal and semi-legal tools could be used to intimidate judicial independence. In Congress, House Speaker Mike Johnson suddenly adjourned the chamber to prevent a vote on releasing Epstein files, using procedural tactics to block transparency. Meanwhile, other lawmakers pushed in the opposite direction: bipartisan subpoenas aimed at Maxwell's testimony, oversight leaders demanded the DOJ and FBI release Epstein-related files and evaluate counterintelligence risks, and committees sought Bannon's interview tapes. The contest over Epstein records highlighted a broader pattern of selective transparency designed to protect Trump while fueling conspiracy theories.

Across the states, federalism became a battleground rather than a safeguard. Republican-led legislatures in North Carolina, Texas, and Missouri pushed gerrymandering, voter suppression, and rollback of voter-approved initiatives, reinforcing minority rule and limiting avenues for peaceful change. Civil society responded with protests at North Carolina's rescheduled hearings and demonstrations at Senator Chuck Schumer's office that resulted in mass arrests, including elected officials, over Gaza policy. Democratic-led states turned to courts to defend transgender healthcare, reproductive rights, SNAP privacy, and funding for Planned Parenthood.

California's governor proposed changes to the state's independent redistricting commission in response to Texas's mapping. Local initiatives like New Orleans' municipal ID program and the Social Security Administration's reversal of phone service cuts after public backlash showed that at smaller scales, public pressure could still influence outcomes.

Religion and nationalist memory acted as unifying forces for this project. Trump ordered that federal employees be permitted to promote and recruit for their religious beliefs at work, blurring the separation between church and state within government workplaces and encouraging new pressures among colleagues. DHS's use of manifest destiny imagery and the appropriation of artwork for nationalist themes, Vance's ancestry-based citizenship rhetoric, mandated antisemitism trainings that equate anti-Zionism with antisemitism, and the MAGA teacher exam all pointed toward the same conclusion: a quasi-theological nationalism where dissenting views on race, history, or foreign policy could be dismissed as un-American or impious. Trump's exaggerated claims about ending wars and reshaping trade deals added a personal mythology atop this sacralized narrative.

No single event in Week 28 directly pushed the Democracy Clock forward. Instead, the week deepened a landscape in which law increasingly acts as a weapon rather than a limit; citizenship and welfare are divided based on ancestry, ideology, and economic utility; and knowledge institutions, media, and archives are controlled to protect the leader and his supporters. Executive power functioned with fewer effective checks, even as courts and civil society managed to secure narrow injunctions and reversals. The outcome was not stagnation but consolidation: a strengthening of existing patterns and a further decline in the moral standards underpinning the system.

CHAPTER 39
WEEK 29: LAW, MAPS, AND MEMORY AS CONTROL

In a week of consolidation rather than shock, law, representation, and information were tightened to favor power while formal democratic shells stayed intact.

The twenty-ninth week of Trump's second term did not hinge on a single shocking event. Instead, it involved a complex series of actions that collectively made the state feel less like a shared institution and more like a personal tool. Law, data, borders, money, and memory were all affected. Each change was presented as technical, managerial, or necessary. Together, they created a clearer picture of a government that expects institutions to bend to its will.

At the start of Week 29, the Democracy Clock showed 8:06 p.m. and ended there as well, with no net change in minutes. The clock's stillness did not indicate calm; it reflected a week in which existing threats intensified rather than appeared anew. The moral baseline continued to decline, but the actions taken that week extended existing patterns rather than crossing into new territory. Executive power was exercised aggressively, law was weaponized against investigators and migrants, and information was curated to serve the White House's interests. Courts and civil society showed resistance, but not enough to shift the overall balance. The overall direction remained downward.

The first major development centered on who controls facts. On the first day of the week, Trump dismissed Bureau of Labor Statistics commissioner Erika McEntarfer after a weak jobs report. The dismissal followed a series of public attacks where he claimed that BLS jobs data were "rigged" to favor Democrats. The firing was lawful on the surface. Its significance lay in the message: economic data that reflected poorly on the administration would not be tolerated. Staff within the statistical system now had to balance professional standards against the threat of personal retaliation. That threat was very real.

The assault on neutral measurement did not stop with jobs data. The administration moved to terminate two greenhouse-gas monitoring satellite missions at NASA, cutting off streams of climate information that regulators and scientists rely on. At Health and Human Services, Secretary Robert F. Kennedy Jr. canceled roughly half a billion dollars in mRNA vaccine research contracts while publicly casting doubt on mRNA effectiveness against respiratory infections. These decisions were framed as scientific course corrections. Yet, they closely aligned with ideological narratives and left long-term public health capacity weaker and more politicized. Evidence took a back seat to story.

Money and medicine intersected in Medicare. The Centers for Medicare & Medicaid Services delayed and revised rules on expensive skin-substitute products after a $5 million donation from a key manufacturer. A planned cost-cutting rule was replaced with a looser alternative that kept billions in billing for a favored firm. Officially, the change was about refining policy. In practice, it showed that well-timed contributions could influence coverage decisions for the country's largest public health program. Policy followed money. Against this backdrop, the FBI released 2024 crime statistics showing notable drops in violent and property crime. The data challenged political claims of a crime wave used to justify crackdowns and emergency deployments. Yet major outlets provided limited coverage of the report. The gap between actual trends and the stories reaching the public widened.

Meanwhile, the White House announced an AI action plan that loosened federal oversight of algorithms, and ICE prepared an "awareness saturation" campaign to flood social and streaming platforms with recruitment messages. Data and technology were directed more toward shaping narratives than promoting shared understanding. Facts were available but muted. The second development took place within the justice system. The Office of Special Counsel opened a Hatch Act investigation into former special counsel Jack Smith, who had previously prosecuted Trump. The probe suggested that pursuing a sitting or former president could be viewed as suspect political activity. Almost simultaneously, the Justice Department under Attorney General Pam Bondi convened a grand jury to investigate alleged "treason" related to discredited claims that Obama-era officials fabricated evidence against Trump in 2016.

Legal tools of criminal law were thus used to revive conspiracy theories and scrutinize those who had previously held the president to account. Law became a weapon, not a boundary. Retaliation extended beyond federal prosecutors. The Department of Justice subpoenaed New York Attorney General Letitia James in connection with her civil cases against Trump and the NRA, suggesting that a state official who had successfully pursued fraud and corruption claims could now face federal pressure. In immigration, a U.S. Court of Appeals panel vacated a contempt ruling against the Trump administration for violating a deportation freeze order to El Salvador. The decision limited the district judge's authority over executive defiance and demonstrated how appointees of Trump on appellate benches could weaken lower-court attempts to enforce limits. Checks were in place, but they had been weakened.

The ongoing story of Jeffrey Epstein unfolded throughout the week. The White House held high-level strategy meetings on handling Epstein's fallout, then canceled one after it leaked. Trump publicly defended a meeting between the Deputy Attorney General and Ghislaine Maxwell's lawyer, calling it routine. Meanwhile, House Oversight issued subpoenas to Bill and Hillary Clinton and former top law enforcement officials, demanding Justice Department files on the case. Outside Congress, journalists and advocacy groups fought to obtain FBI records, challenging the withholding of more than 10,000 pages. Federal courts slowly unsealed some related civil records while maintaining secrecy in key areas and even ordered devices wiped in a separate obscenity case. The pattern was clear: aggressive legal efforts targeted Trump's critics and investigators, while procedural opacity shrouded elite-linked abuse. Transparency was selective.

The third major issue concerned who has power and who determines it. In Texas, Republicans started mid-decade congressional redistricting at Trump's request, aiming to flip Democratic districts into Republican ones ahead of the 2026 elections. Texas House Democrats responded by leaving the state to deny a quorum, a drastic move that showed how badly normal legislative negotiations had broken down. Republican leaders responded by imposing daily fines and pursuing civil arrest warrants to force their return. Governor Greg Abbott and Attorney General Ken Paxton went further, threatening felony charges, removal from office, and declaring seats vacant. Lawmakers were treated as fugitives, not colleagues.

The standoff drew in federal authorities. Senator John Cornyn sought FBI help to locate the absent lawmakers, and Director Kash Patel agreed, blurring the lines between national security resources and partisan state conflicts. While Democrats hid in Illinois, a bomb threat forced them to evacuate their temporary quarters, adding physical danger to political pressure. The message to opposition legislators nationwide was clear: using procedural tools to resist redistricting could now carry legal, financial, and personal risks. Resistance had a cost.

The Texas dispute was part of a larger effort to redraw maps. Vice President J.D. Vance and the Trump administration encouraged Indiana Republicans to pursue their own mid-cycle congressional redistricting that favored the GOP. Democratic governors and party leaders prepared legal challenges and even created counter-maps in blue states, signaling an arms race in partisan gerrymandering. Some Republicans, including Representative Blake Moore, publicly opposed the Texas plan, while Representative Kevin Kiley introduced federal legislation to ban mid-decade redistricting nationwide. These efforts, along with protests inside the Indiana Statehouse, showed that resistance to gerrymandering still existed both inside and outside the ruling party. It was real, but outmatched.

At the federal level, Trump ordered work on a new census that would exclude undocumented immigrants from the count, directly challenging the constitutional requirement to count all persons. Such a census would shift representation and funding away from areas with high immigrant populations. Meanwhile, the Supreme Court heard a challenge to Louisiana's congressional map with two majority-Black districts, a case that could influence how far states can go in ensuring minority representation. Senate Democrats reintroduced the John R. Lewis Voting Rights Advancement Act to restore preclearance and beef up protections against discriminatory voting laws. Representation was being redesigned on multiple fronts, with counter-efforts struggling to keep up. The ground beneath voters continued shifting.

The fourth development linked the border and the streets. Inside the Department of Homeland Security, a memo drafted by Philip Hegseth proposed expanding military involvement in domestic immigration enforcement, deepening Defense Department roles in urban operations. Trump directed the Pentagon to prepare potential military action against Latin American drug cartels, turning criminal enforcement into a quasi-military mission. These steps blurred the lines between civilian policing and armed force, as well as foreign operations and domestic politics. Security became a flexible term.

On the ground, the administration accelerated mass deportation efforts. ICE staffing increased dramatically, and Congress approved tens of billions in new funding, including a $231.8 million contract to expand detention capacity at Fort Bliss and profitable deals for private prison operator GEO Group. Facilities modeled after "Alligator Alcatraz" multiplied, and new state-run sites were planned. A brief cash-bonus program for deporting people within days, later canceled after public backlash, revealed the underlying incentive: speed and volume over due process. A Home Depot raid in Los Angeles, carried out despite a court order against indiscriminate sweeps, showed how enforcement agents could disregard judicial limits. Courts could be ignored.

Reports from Senator Jon Ossoff's office documented hundreds of alleged human rights abuses in ICE detention, including deaths, denial of care, and obstruction of oversight. Grassroots groups protested outside immigration courts and alleged covert detention sites, only to see several demonstrators arrested. Meanwhile, the administration reallocated FEMA resources and emergency management capacity toward detention projects like Fort Bliss and Alligator Alcatraz, prioritizing immigration enforcement over disaster resilience. An executive order criminalizing public camping and mandating the institutionalization of unhoused people extended carceral logic into domestic social policy. Food assistance cuts, expanded detention, and crackdowns on homelessness formed a pattern: poverty and migration are treated as security threats to be contained. Vulnerability is met with handcuffs, not help.

The fifth development outlined how rights and status were sorted. The administration moved to block abortion services at VA hospitals nationwide, even in cases of rape or serious health risk, narrowing veterans' healthcare rights and deepening geographic disparities in access. The Air Force denied early retirement to transgender service members who had previously been approved, effectively pushing them out without benefits. These steps signaled that service to the country did not guarantee equal treatment if one's identity fell outside favored categories. Service did not secure rights.

Symbolic choices reinforced this hierarchy. The Army decided to restore a Confederate memorial at Arlington National Cemetery, spending public funds to reinstall a monument associated with slavery and rebellion. Simultaneously, migrant detention centers expanded, and mass deportation infrastructure became more entrenched. FEMA rules were revised so that certain boycotts of Israel would be treated as antisemitic discrimination in disaster aid, blurring the line between protected political expression and bias. Abroad, the State Department prepared human rights reports that downplayed abuses in countries like El Salvador, Israel, and Russia, softening or omitting references to killings, torture, and persecution of LGBTQ+ people. Official concern for rights became selective.

Economic and health policies amplified these divides. A spending bill cut food assistance for about 22.3 million families while preserving tax cuts, shifting burdens downward. The cancellation of mRNA vaccine and research contracts affecting COVID-19 and HIV projects risked worsening health inequities by slowing innovations that disproportionately benefit vulnerable populations. On campuses, federal directives demanded detailed admissions data to prove race was not considered, and funding freezes and curriculum mandates at Brown, Columbia, UCLA, and other institutions pressured universities to align with contested definitions of antisemitism. Harvard sued over multibillion-dollar funding cuts and visa restrictions, a rare institutional pushback. Across domains, access to bodily autonomy, education, and safety grew more dependent on identity and ideology. Equality became conditional.

The sixth development took place in the economy. Trump and Congress pushed a protectionist agenda that used tariffs as both policy and spectacle. An executive order changed tariff rates for dozens of countries, and a new wave of duties on imports from over sixty nations raised average U.S. tariffs to about 18 percent, the highest in nearly a century. Separate threats and actions targeted India over Russian oil imports and Spain over its choice of

European fighter jets, linking trade penalties to geopolitical loyalty and procurement decisions. These actions caused volatility in global supply chains and increased prices on everyday items like school supplies, effectively taxing consumers to support a political narrative of toughness. Households bore the cost.

At home, fiscal and regulatory choices shifted risk and reward. The same spending bill that cut food assistance also kept tax advantages for the wealthy. An executive order allowed 401(k) plans to include cryptocurrency and other alternative assets, putting workers' retirement savings at risk in volatile markets with limited oversight. The HONEST Act, sponsored by Senator Josh Hawley and supported by Trump, tightened stock-trading rules for officials but exempted the president from divestment, allowing him to hold conflicted assets. In Medicare, a donor-linked rule rewrite favored expensive, unproven products. Overall, these policies moved public systems toward private profit-making. Risk moved downward; profits moved upward.

Infrastructure and consolidation completed the picture. Banks and private credit funds increased their exposure to opaque lending for AI data centers, while Microsoft and Meta took on lease and loan obligations tied to speculative growth. The administration approved a merger between Paramount and Skydance Media shortly after canceling a high-profile critical show, further increasing concentration in entertainment and news. Con Edison cut power to over 88,000 New York City households during extreme heat while seeking an 11 percent rate hike, leaving many without electricity for extended periods. Essential services, from energy to information, operated on a profit-first basis, with regulators and grant rules increasingly aligning with White House priorities. Public need took a backseat.

The seventh development focused on how power was shown. Trump threatened to federalize Washington, D.C., in response to an alleged assault and ordered a seven-day federal crackdown on violent crime in the capital, despite FBI data showing declines. Federal officers were deployed in an emergency-style operation that emphasized strength over addressing a real crisis. The president also made nuclear threats and ordered submarine deployments in response to Russian rhetoric, using strategic weapons language that blurred the line between foreign policy and domestic political theater. Spectacle and security combined.

Abroad, tariff threats on India and Spain, along with a 25 percent duty on Indian imports of Russian oil, turned trade into a tool of personal diplomacy. Plans for a bilateral meeting with Vladimir Putin in Alaska, excluding Ukraine, indicated a willingness to sideline an affected ally in negotiations. At home, Trump publicly pressured Federal Reserve Chair Jerome Powell to resign over interest-rate policy, urged the Senate to eliminate the blue-slip tradition for judicial nominations, and pushed senators to cancel their August recess to speed up confirmations. These actions centralized appointment powers and treated independent institutions as obstacles to be bypassed. Norms became hurdles rather than guides.

Symbols and structures were mobilized for the same purpose. The announcement of a $200 million White House ballroom, styled after Trump properties and funded by opaque "patriot donors," turned the presidential residence into a stage for personal glorification. Executive orders increased oversight of federal grants to align with presidential priorities and framed bank compliance rules as partisan "debanking," instructing regulators to undo guidance. NASA was directed to focus on a nuclear power plant on the Moon with exclusion zones, blending technological ambition with unilateral claims over shared space. Executive authority and security forces were used not only to govern but to dramatize dominance. Governance became performance.

The eighth development centered on controlling information and memory. The White House removed official transcripts of Trump's remarks from public access on its website, reducing the record available for scrutiny. Meanwhile, the administration prepared human-rights reports that softened or omitted references to abuses by favored regimes, and planned to declare "no credible" violations in countries with documented killings and torture. The State Department's decisions signaled that the official U.S. account of global rights would be shaped by geopolitical preferences. Memory was edited at its source.

Within the archival state, the National Archives sought public comment on records disposition schedules that would determine which agency documents could be destroyed. The Library of Congress briefly removed, then restored, sections of the online Constitution Annotated, including provisions on habeas corpus and emoluments, citing a coding error. The episode demonstrated how technical decisions and errors could suddenly restrict access to foundational legal texts. At the Federal Election Commission, an open meeting was canceled while a closed compliance session continued, and a planned agenda item on broadband deployment was dropped, limiting public discussion of digital infrastructure and election-law enforcement. Public oversight diminished.

Universities became another battleground for narrative control. Trump and Education Secretary Linda McMahon ordered colleges to submit detailed admissions data to prove race was not considered, turning federal data systems into tools for ideological policing. Funding was frozen or conditioned at Brown, Columbia, UCLA, and other campuses over antisemitism claims, with mandated curriculum changes that steered teaching toward administration-favored narratives. Harvard sued over funding cuts and the loss of authority to host international students, asserting its autonomy in court. These pressures eroded civic education and replaced it with compliance to state and market priorities. Debate gave way to surveillance. Media and litigation completed the cycle. Trump filed a $10 billion lawsuit against Dow Jones and sought Rupert Murdoch's deposition over Wall Street Journal coverage of his Epstein ties, widely seen as an attempt to intimidate investigative outlets. The cancellation of Stephen Colbert's show, followed by approval of the Paramount–Skydance merger, raised doubts about how economic consolidation and political pressure might narrow critical voices. ICE's planned "awareness saturation" campaign and the administration's AI deregulation plan pointed toward a future where algorithms and targeted messaging would be used to shape public perception with fewer safeguards. Durham's unclassified annex, which challenged claims of an Obama-era conspiracy against Trump, and the underreported FBI crime declines showed that even when official records corrected politicized narratives, their influence depended on a media environment increasingly shaped by power. Truth existed, but it struggled to be shared.

The ninth development linked these threads to money and personal gain. Trump received a $400 million luxury jet from Qatar, a gift raising serious emoluments and influence concerns. At the same time, he pursued the privately funded White House ballroom, inviting "patriot donors" to support a $200 million project that merged public space with private patronage. The funding sources were unclear, and the benefits—both symbolic and practical—flowed directly to the president's image and network. Public office and private favor became intertwined.

Ethics rules were revised to fit the circumstances. The HONEST Act's stock-trading ban for officials was designed so that its divestment requirements would not affect the sitting president, allowing Trump to continue holding and benefiting from conflicted assets while tightening restrictions for others. Contracts at Fort Bliss and with GEO Group, along with revisions to Medicare rules and deregulation of 401(k)s, created profit streams for companies aligned with the administration's priorities. Public programs and crises became opportunities for insiders to extract value, while the line between public office and private gain became increasingly blurred. Corruption turned into a structural issue rather than an isolated problem.

There were scheduled moments of contestation on the horizon. The Supreme Court's upcoming decision on Louisiana's map, Harvard's lawsuit over funding and visas, and ongoing battles over FOIA and Epstein records all threatened to test how much institutional resistance remained. Filing deadlines set by the FEC for a

Tennessee special election and public comment periods at the National Archives presented narrower, procedural opportunities where rules could still be influenced openly. These were small but meaningful openings.

In the larger course of the term, Week 29 signaled consolidation rather than a breakthrough. Executive power was exercised more freely, law enforcement aligned more closely with the president's interests, and the institutions of representation, detention, and information moved further from neutral service to partisan preservation. The Democracy Clock did not advance, not because the threat diminished, but because the actions of that week intensified an already fragile situation rather than opening a new front. Rights, data, and memory still existed on paper. Using them now required more effort, carried greater risks, and faced a state more willing to respond with pressure.

CHAPTER 40
WEEK 30: EMERGENCY AS METHOD IN WASHINGTON

A manufactured crime crisis in the capital anchors a week of legal experiments, militarized governance, and quiet capture of neutral institutions.

The thirtieth week of Trump's second term didn't hinge on a single order or spectacle. It unfolded as a series of interconnected experiments testing the limits of power disguised as law, security, and management. The focus was on Washington, D.C., where the administration aimed to turn the capital into a testing ground for emergency rule and federalized policing, while simultaneous efforts in immigration, the military, the economy, and public memory revealed the same approach. Each area seemed separate, but together, they demonstrated a government more willing to see constraints as obstacles to be challenged rather than boundaries to be respected.

At the end of the previous period, the Democracy Clock read 8:06 p.m. By the end of Week 30, it still pointed to 8:06 p.m., with a net change of just 0.3 minutes. Public time remained unchanged, but the internal shift indicated a continued loosening of restraint. Executive power pushed aggressively against local self-governance in D.C., due process in immigration, neutrality in statistics and veterans' care, and pluralism in the armed forces. Courts, inspectors general, and state officials pushed back, causing some retreats in the capital and stopping a few excesses elsewhere. However, the pattern showed that when the White House tested the limits of law, others had to step in to pull it back, often after damage had already been done.

The most visible experiment took place in the nation's capital. The week began with the president turning his focus to Washington's streets, not as a resident but as a proprietor. He ordered homeless residents to leave the city under threat of federal enforcement, framing their presence as a stain on the seat of government rather than a social failure to address. Soon after, he announced a press conference to "remake" D.C. crime policy, depicting a city with falling violence as a place in crisis. Public attacks on the mayor and even the Federal Reserve chair blurred local governance and independent economic stewardship into a single image of supposed misrule. The stage was set for intervention. That intervention came in the form of an executive order declaring a crime emergency in Washington, D.C. The order did not respond to rising violence; it created a legal pretext.

By invoking emergency powers, the president took control of the Metropolitan Police Department and signaled plans to seek long-term congressional authority over the force. At the same time, he directed lawyers to explore legislation to overturn the D.C. Home Rule Act, which had granted residents the right to elect their own leaders. The capital's police and basic self-governance were thus treated as tools that the White House could seize when local decisions did not align with its interests.

D.C. officials and allies in Congress did not accept this silently. The District's attorney general filed suit challenging the takeover, arguing that the federal government had exceeded statutory limits on emergency powers. On Capitol Hill, Democratic lawmakers introduced a joint resolution to end the federalization of D.C.'s police, using Congress's authority over the District to counter the president's claim of necessity. These actions did not immediately restore the status quo but demonstrated that local and legislative actors still had ways to challenge unilateral control, even when the target was the city housing the federal government.

By the end of the week, the White House agreed to scale back its control over the D.C. police department. While this did not eliminate the earlier assertion of power nor remove the threat to Home Rule, it marked a partial retreat—a recognition that litigation and political pressure could still impose limits on overreach. In this way, D.C. served as a testing ground twice over—first for assessing how far emergency declarations could replace elected authorities, and then for gauging how much resistance remained when those authorities pushed back.

Meanwhile, while the capital's status was challenged in courts, the administration's approach to immigration revealed how law could be wielded less as a boundary and more as a weapon. Early in the week, Immigration and Customs Enforcement arrested the owner of a small business, Trump Burger, over visa issues, despite his long residence and community ties. Agents detained a lawful permanent resident and a student over a fourteen-year-old marijuana offense, and they took into custody a DACA recipient and organizer in El Paso. Each case involved individuals who had built their lives under existing rules. Their detention sent a message that even those who had complied could suddenly find their ground pulled out from under them.

The stakes increased further with reports that ICE had deported U.S. citizen children and their mothers to Honduras without proper hearings, including a child with cancer. A separate raid at a Home Depot in Los Angeles ended with a man fleeing and being killed by a vehicle, highlighting how aggressive tactics can turn routine enforcement into deadly risks. These were not abstract policy debates but tangible uses of state power against bodies and families, where due process seemed more like an afterthought than a fundamental principle.

At the same time, the Justice Department and the attorney

general worked to increase the cost of resistance. Federal lawyers sought severe sanctions against an immigration attorney for alleged misrepresentations in a deportation case, a move that risked discouraging zealous advocacy for clients facing removal. Attorney General Pam Bondi sent letters to dozens of sanctuary city leaders, threatening prosecution and loss of federal funds if they maintained policies that limited cooperation with ICE. The administration also warned that local officials could face criminal charges, and the White House itself threatened sanctuary jurisdictions with prosecution and defunding. Law, in these hands, became a tool to intimidate not only migrants but also the local officials and lawyers who supported them. Behind these individual stories lay a growing infrastructure of detention and profit. Local officials in Mason, Tennessee, approved converting a closed prison into a private ICE detention center, expanding for-profit immigration detention in a small town far from most detainees' homes and legal support. In Florida, the governor announced a new state immigration detention facility called a "deportation depot," deepening state-level investments in carceral responses to migration. These facilities did not arise in a vacuum; they were responses to federal enforcement priorities that promised steady demand for beds and contracts.

Oversight and community resistance tried to keep pace. A federal judge ordered ICE to improve conditions at a New York City holding facility, mandating better food, medical access, and legal visits. Democratic members of Congress sued over new rules requiring advance notice for visits to detention centers, arguing that the policy blocked unannounced inspections and sanitized oversight. Lawmakers reported being repeatedly denied entry under the notice regime, confirming that the executive was using procedural rules to keep eyes away from potential abuses. Outside government, groups like the DC Peace Team offered active bystander training for encounters with ICE, and activists in North Carolina launched a campaign to pressure an airline over its ICE contract. These efforts did not reverse the system, but they showed that civil society and some courts still contested a regime that combined fear, punishment, and profit. The same pattern of selective enforcement and militarization appeared in the broader security apparatus. Inside the FBI, Director Kash Patel deprioritized investigations of right-wing extremist groups, reassigning agents away from a threat that had proven deadly in recent years. This shift did not abolish the bureau's work on domestic terrorism, but it signaled that certain ideologically aligned actors would receive less scrutiny, even as other groups—immigrants, protesters, foreign gangs—were treated as urgent dangers.

On the streets of Los Angeles, the line between law enforcement and political intimidation became blurred. U.S. Border Patrol agents armed with rifles appeared at a public event with California Governor Gavin Newsom at a museum, a deployment that seemed less like routine security and more like a show of force aimed at a vocal critic of the administration. In the same city, federal troop deployments during immigration protests faced legal challenges. A U.S. district court heard California's case against the use of troops, and the state's governor and attorney general filed suit, accusing the deployment of National Guard and Marines alongside ICE in local arrests as unlawful. These cases challenged the reach of the Posse Comitatus Act and the limits on using military forces for domestic law enforcement without state approval.

Abroad and at the border, the administration further blurred the line between crime control and war. The president designated the Venezuelan gang Tren de Aragua as a terrorist organization, expanding his powers over immigration and detention by applying wartime laws to a criminal group. He instructed the Pentagon to use military force against certain foreign drug cartels, treating them as quasi-military targets rather than typical law enforcement issues. The Justice Department doubled the bounty on Venezuelan President Nicolás Maduro to $50 million, intensifying pressure in a way that combined legal indictments, regime change signals, and bounty hunting. These actions extended emergency and terrorism logic into areas where traditional criminal law long served, making it easier to invoke extraordinary measures against disliked groups.

If security forces were being repurposed, the Pentagon itself was being reshaped along ideological lines. Defense Secretary Pete Hegseth used his platform to repost and endorse a video opposing women's right to vote, giving cabinet-level weight to arguments against a fundamental democratic right for half the population. This was not a random comment. It aligned with a larger effort to redefine who qualifies as a full citizen-soldier and, consequently, as a full citizen.

Within the ranks, Hegseth banned transgender individuals from serving in the military and removed many minority and female officers, effectively resegregating parts of the armed forces. These purges did more than change personnel lists; they signaled that loyalty to a certain social order, rather than loyalty to the Constitution alone, was becoming a criterion for service. The message to LGBTQ troops and officers of color was clear: their place in the institution was conditional and could be revoked.

Symbolism strengthened this hierarchy. Hegseth reinstalled a Confederate memorial at Arlington National Cemetery, a monument that romanticizes the Confederacy and minimizes slavery. Restoring it used the nation's most sacred military ground to promote a Lost Cause narrative, portraying treason in defense of slavery as a form of honorable sacrifice. Meanwhile, Christian nationalist themes seeped into military recruitment and messaging, with sectarian language becoming a core part of service identity. Together, these actions harnessed religion and revisionist history to justify an exclusionary vision of the armed forces and, by extension, the nation. Beyond security and identity, the week also saw a steady erosion of neutral institutions and public services.

In economic data, the president fired the Bureau of Labor Statistics commissioner after an unfavorable jobs report and nominated a Heritage Foundation economist, EJ Antoni, to replace her. This was accompanied by broader staff replacements in federal statistical agencies with loyalists. These changes didn't immediately alter the data but threatened the independence of the information that underpins policy debates, market decisions, and public understanding of the economy. Courts played a mixed role in this institutional reshaping. A federal appeals court allowed the administration to cut billions in USaid foreign aid funding, upholding the executive's authority to withhold funds allocated by Congress and shifting budgetary power toward the White House. Another appeals court lifted a block on mass firings at the Consumer Financial Protection Bureau, clearing the way for layoffs of 1,500 staff at a key consumer watchdog. These rulings indicated judicial tolerance for executive restructuring of independent regulators, even when such moves weakened oversight of markets and foreign policy.

Veterans' healthcare served as a case study of how public services could be reduced and privatized. The Department of Veterans Affairs reduced staff and shifted toward privatized care, shrinking its workforce and steering veterans toward private providers. The VA ended labor agreements with health workers' unions, undermining collective bargaining and potentially worsening staff retention and care quality. In Congress, a House committee advanced legislation to increase veterans' access to private healthcare, further reorienting a core public service toward market delivery. An inspector general report documented severe staffing shortages across VA hospitals, confirming that policy-driven attrition was hollowing out capacity even as demand stayed high.

The same pattern of politicization and retaliation appeared in the Justice Department. Attorney General Bondi dismissed federal prosecutor Mike Gordon, known for his work on January 6 cases, amid a broader climate of pressure on those who sought accountability for the attack on the Capitol. The removal suggested that prosecutors who enforced the law against insurrectionists were now vulnerable to political retaliation, reinforcing the sense that enforcement priorities were being realigned to protect allies and punish critics. Economic governance more broadly shifted toward a state-capitalist model, where the executive negotiated directly with major corporations. Nvidia and AMD agreed to share 15 percent of

China-related chip revenues with the U.S. government in exchange for export licenses, blurring the line between taxation and licensing and deepening direct bargaining between the White House and powerful companies.

Analysts described U.S. economic policy under Trump as moving toward state capitalism, where political leaders guide markets through targeted deals rather than neutral rules. In energy and land use, the administration moved to open most of the National Petroleum Reserve–Alaska to oil and gas drilling, shifting control of a vast federal reserve toward extractive interests and weakening environmental safeguards and indigenous input. The president revoked a previous executive order promoting competition in the American economy, signaling a retreat from efforts to curb corporate concentration. He used executive authority to extend the suspension of additional tariffs on Chinese imports and issued orders to streamline commercial space launch approvals, including a draft order to exempt many launches from environmental review. These steps concentrated discretion in the executive branch, favored rapid industry growth, and sidelined environmental and local review processes.

At the other end of the economic ladder, Congress and the president expanded work requirements for SNAP benefits to include more vulnerable groups, such as older adults, parents, veterans, and homeless individuals. Tightening access to basic nutrition shifted economic risk onto those with the least power, even as the benefits of state–corporate deals flowed upward. The combination of personalized bargaining with firms, deregulation of extractive and high-tech sectors, and stricter conditions for the poor showed how policy outcomes were driven by elite lobbying and executive preferences rather than broad public debate.

Representation itself became the focus of an interstate partisan arms race. In Texas, Governor Greg Abbott called a second special legislative session focused on redistricting, using procedural control to keep lawmakers in Austin until Republicans could pass a new congressional map. Texas Democrats responded with a quorum break, leaving the chamber to deny the majority the numbers needed to act, and coordinated with allies in California. State Representative Gene Wu and others organized public opposition to the maps, framing them as an effort to rig electoral outcomes in a closely divided state.

On the other coast, California Governor Gavin Newsom warned President Trump to stop influencing redistricting in Republican states and criticized the Texas effort as an assault on democracy. He announced a conditional plan to redraw California's congressional districts if Texas proceeded, linking his state's representation to actions taken elsewhere. Newsom proposed a special election to authorize temporary redistricting if Texas moved forward, using direct democracy as a form of retaliation. These moves transformed redistricting from a state-specific process into a national partisan chess match, where maps in one state could trigger counter-maps in another.

Control over history, information, and identity became another battleground in the week's power struggle. The administration moved to review Smithsonian exhibitions for alignment with a celebratory national narrative, pressuring the institution to vet content for "American exceptionalism." An executive order and related directives aimed to ensure that museum exhibits reflected a prescribed vision of the country, threatening curatorial independence and seeking to standardize public history around a single political story. This effort coincided with Hegseth's restoration of the Confederate memorial at Arlington and his promotion of Christian nationalist messaging, tying military symbolism and museum content into a broader project of curated memory.

Intelligence and media were pulled into the same orbit. Director of National Intelligence Tulsi Gabbard declassified and released a highly classified report on 2016 Russian interference with presidential backing, allowing the executive branch to selectively reveal sensitive information in ways that could reshape public memory of past elections. The White House hosted right-wing podcaster Benny Johnson at a press briefing, giving official validation to a conspiracy-prone commentator with ties to Russian media. These actions did not create disinformation, but they used the authority and access of the state to amplify outlets and narratives aligned with the administration's interests.

Language and identity in official data were also adjusted from higher up. The Transportation Security Administration revised its passenger survey to replace the term "gender" with "sex," a seemingly technical change that reflected a choice to narrow the recognition of gender-diverse identities in federal records. On campuses, the Justice Department accused George Washington University of civil rights violations over antisemitism complaints, showing federal influence over how universities handle speech and protests. At the same time, a federal judge blocked Trump administration efforts to cut funding to schools over diversity, equity, and inclusion programs, protecting some space for educational institutions to support inclusion without the threat of financial retaliation.

Amid this, pockets of transparency and civil society pushback continued. A federal appeals court ordered the restoration of a public federal spending database, enforcing statutory transparency rules and reinforcing Congress's intent that budget decisions stay visible. Another judge ordered the release of frozen funds to the National Endowment for Democracy, reaffirming legislative control over foreign aid. Advocacy groups sued the Justice Department and FBI to force the release of Epstein-related records under FOIA, and the Environmental Protection Agency published notices of Environmental Impact Statements and extended comment periods, encouraging public participation in major environmental decisions. Outside government, the group Indivisible launched a Truth Brigade campaign to fight disinformation, organizing volunteers to identify and counter false narratives in the information ecosystem.

These acts of resistance did not reverse the week's overall direction, but they showed that the moral baseline had not completely collapsed. Courts enforced minimum standards in detention facilities, blocked some funding cuts driven by ideology, and dismissed overbroad terrorism charges against a "Cop City" protester for due process violations. Inspectors general documented the neglect in veterans' care. State officials in California and local activists across the country mobilized against what they described as an assault on democracy. The ongoing debate over who shapes the public record, who counts as a full citizen, and who controls the levers of force remained active, even as power shifted toward those willing to extend their reach.

In the midst of Trump's second term, Week 30 did not mark a sudden change. Instead, it intensified existing trends. Executive authority further extended into local policing, immigration, economic policies, and cultural memory, often justified by claims of emergency, efficiency, or patriotism. The law was more openly used as a tool to punish opponents and shield allies, while neutral institutions were staffed and directed to support regime narratives. The slight shift on the Democracy Clock showed this slow, steady erosion: rights and procedures still existed, but it took more effort to invoke them and carried greater risks. The story of the week was not about a single order, but about how easily authority moved forward and the increasing burden on those trying to resist.

CHAPTER 41
WEEK 31: EMERGENCY AS GOVERNING METHOD

> *In Washington, elections, immigration, and memory, the administration treated emergency powers and loyal law as routine tools of rule rather than rare exceptions.*

The thirty-first week of Trump's second term didn't hinge on a single order or speech. Instead, it unfolded as a series of decisions that, collectively, showed an administration increasingly viewing the machinery of the state as something to be bent to their will rather than kept in balance. Law enforcement, policing, immigration, data, and even museums were all used as tools to gain an advantage and suppress dissent. Although this pattern wasn't new, it had grown more confident. What began as experiments in stretching authority now resembled a governing strategy. That was the key shift.

At the start of Week 31, the Democracy Clock was at 8:06 p.m. By week's end, it read 8:07 p.m., a tiny gain of just 0.2 minutes. The change was small in measure but significant in impact. It reflected not a coup or sudden break, but the steady accumulation of power: a capital city placed under federal military control, elections manipulated through redistricting and voting rules, immigration used as an ideological tool, and civil service and data officials being purged or silenced. Courts and civil society showed some resistance but were increasingly strained and lacked shared authority. The balance of power had shifted.

The clearest sign of this new confidence was in Washington, D.C. Early in the week, the president declared a public-safety emergency in the capital and placed the Metropolitan Police Department under federal control, despite data showing that crime rates had fallen. The move was framed as a response to a crisis. In reality, it suspended local home rule and gave the White House direct authority over local law enforcement. This declaration was not meant to be temporary or tied to a specific event. It was an open-ended assertion that the executive could step into local policing whenever it wanted. This declaration was quickly enforced by force. National Guard units from Republican-led states were sent to D.C. to support the federal takeover, alongside federal agents. The city's streets, already familiar with heavy security, now saw armed troops patrolling under presidential orders. At the same time, the administration announced a broader "military-style crackdown" on crime in D.C., with hints that similar operations might be expanded to other cities. Ordinary public safety concerns were recast as reasons for a near-military occupation. Emergency powers could now be declared at will.

The line between civilian and military justice also blurred. The president ordered National Guard troops patrolling D.C. to carry their service weapons, increasing the danger of any encounter with residents. Twenty Defense Department JAG officers were assigned as special assistant U.S. attorneys in the city, integrating military lawyers into civilian prosecutions. Meanwhile, the new U.S. Attorney for D.C. directed prosecutors to pursue the most serious charges in new arrests while easing enforcement of some local gun laws. Severity was to be reserved for civilians on the street, not for certain types of weapons. That was the goal.

Data was used to justify this shift rather than to evaluate it. Even as crime statistics challenged claims of a surge, the Justice

Department launched investigations into whether D.C. police had manipulated crime data. Federal prosecutors were instructed to examine local reporting practices, and the administration publicly questioned the accuracy of the city's numbers. The same crime data previously used to shape policy were now regarded as unreliable when they conflicted with the president's narrative. The investigation itself became a tool to reinforce the story of an emergency and to justify ongoing federal control. Numbers were manipulated to fit the narrative.

The militarization expanded beyond the capital. The Pentagon launched a recruitment campaign to assign civilian Defense Department employees to Immigration and Customs Enforcement and Customs and Border Protection, embedding military-affiliated staff deeper into domestic enforcement. Marines and federalized National Guard troops were deployed to Los Angeles to respond to protests against immigration raids. In each case, institutions designed for external defense were pulled into internal law enforcement. The beneficiaries of this approach were the executive branch and its appointees, who gained new tools to police dissenting cities. The losers were local governments and residents, whose usual accountability channels were replaced by distant command.

While the capital was being transformed into a testing ground for permanent emergency measures, the law itself was being redefined. The week began with the president issuing mass pardons for individuals convicted or charged in the January 6 attack on the Capitol. By pardoning those sentences, he signaled that violence against electoral institutions could be excused when it benefited his agenda. Later, he publicly called for the release of Tina Peters, the Colorado election clerk convicted of tampering with voting systems, and threatened "harsh measures" if she remained imprisoned. Clemency and pressure were directed at loyal offenders whose crimes targeted the electoral process. Loyalty, not legality, determined the actions.

At the same time, the Justice Department concentrated on

enemies and predecessors. A grand jury was convened to investigate baseless claims of an Obama-era "treasonous conspiracy" related to the 2016 election, formalizing a theory long dismissed by investigators. Near the week's end, federal agents raided the home and office of former national security adviser John Bolton over classified documents, reopening scrutiny that earlier cases had effectively closed. The timing and targets revealed a clear pattern. Prosecutorial tools were being used to intimidate critics and to keep past political battles alive on the government's terms.

The handling of Jeffrey Epstein–related records showed a different aspect of the same approach. The Justice Department agreed to release investigation files to the House Oversight Committee, but only gradually and under strict executive control. It sought to unseal grand jury materials, a request federal courts rejected, and then selectively released Ghislaine Maxwell interview transcripts that tended to exonerate the president while halting broader disclosures. Congress demanded full, unredacted records, and the committee began planning their public release. Yet, the pace and framing of information remained largely controlled by the executive branch. Transparency became a curated performance rather than a neutral duty.

Not all legal actors followed the administration's lead. A federal judge ruled that Alina Habba, a former Trump lawyer, had been unlawfully serving as acting U.S. Attorney for New Jersey, highlighting the importance of proper appointment processes for prosecutorial independence. In New York, an appeals court overturned a $500 million civil fraud penalty against Trump as excessive while keeping fraud findings and business restrictions in place. And in Manhattan, the district attorney indicted a senior adviser to the city's mayor on bribery and conspiracy charges. These actions demonstrated that some courts and local prosecutors still enforced boundaries and policed corruption. However, they did so against a backdrop where the central government increasingly used law as a shield for allies and a weapon against critics.

Elections and representation changed in quieter but no less

important ways. In Florida, the state supreme court upheld a congressional map supported by Governor Ron DeSantis that reduced Black voting power in the northern part of the state, despite anti-gerrymandering rules. In Texas, the House approved a mid-decade congressional map engineered at the president's request, projected to shift five seats from Democrats to Republicans, favoring white and Republican voters. To secure a quorum, the Republican speaker required Democratic members to sign compliance statements and subjected them to state trooper monitoring and quasi-detention inside the Capitol. The chamber became a tightly controlled space.

Democratic lawmakers in Texas fought back using the tools still at their disposal. Some fled the state to prevent a quorum, then returned under threat of arrest to build a legal case against the map. Representative Nicole Collier refused to sign surveillance agreements, stayed overnight in the House chamber, tore up compliance statements, and later sued over her confinement. State courts issued restraining orders to prevent Beto O'Rourke's group from sending funds to Democrats outside Texas, and the attorney general used consumer-protection laws to challenge the group's fundraising. The legislature functioned more as a stage for enforced compliance and legal disputes than as a forum for debate.

Across the country, Democratic leaders responded similarly. In California, Governor Gavin Newsom and the legislature passed mid-decade redistricting legislation expected to favor their party, bypassing the independent commission approved by voters. A special election was called to approve the new maps, and Republican lawmakers sued to block the plan, claiming the rushed timeline and process violated redistricting norms. What was once a one-sided act of partisan mapmaking has now become openly reciprocal. Both parties see district lines as tools, and voters are invited to ratify the results. Parallel pressures also targeted national voting rules.

The president announced plans for an executive order to ban mail-in voting and voting machines nationwide, centralizing control over election methods in the presidency and overriding state authority. He reiterated calls for states to end mail-in voting and switch to paper ballots, often speaking to Christian audiences, and continued to spread false claims that mail ballots and machines are riddled with fraud. In the same week, he joked publicly about canceling the 2028 elections if the U.S. was at war, normalizing the idea that democratic transfers of power could be suspended under security pretenses. The groundwork was being laid. Outside the White House, allied organizations worked to restrict ballot access. America First Legal petitioned the Election Assistance Commission to require proof of citizenship for federal voter registration, a change that would burden naturalized citizens and low-income voters who lack passports or Real ID licenses. In North Carolina, lawmakers advanced a bill requiring full Social Security numbers on registration forms and reorganized the state elections board, likely deterring registrations and increasing partisan control over election administration. At the federal level, U.S. Citizenship and Immigration Services issued a memo tightening citizenship evaluations based on subjective "good moral character" standards, expanding the discretionary space for denials. Overall, these actions aimed to make participation more difficult and easier to restrict in the name of protecting election integrity.

Immigration policy has become a key tool for sorting and controlling disliked communities. Early in the week, the administration stopped issuing U.S. medical visas for children from Gaza, after pressure from a far-right influencer. This decision put lifesaving care for sick children secondary to ideological and security concerns. At the same time, Florida's governor announced building a new federal immigration jail at a closed state prison, deepening the state's role as a "deportation depot." Federal courts partially pushed back, ordering the closure of the notorious "Alligator Alcatraz" facility due to environmental violations and detainee conditions, but the state appealed, prolonging the conflict. The surveillance system expanded significantly. U.S. Citizenship and

Immigration Services increased social media screening of applicants for signs of "anti-American" activity, and the administration introduced continuous monitoring of all 55 million U.S. visa holders, including online speech. Additionally, more than 6,000 student visas were revoked, with officials citing alleged crimes and terrorism support without detailed proof. International students and campus activists experienced delays, revocations, and arrests. Immigration status transformed from a legal classification into a test of ideological loyalty, with lawful expression risking being deemed disqualifying.

Longtime migrants also saw their stability weaken. A federal appeals court allowed the administration to continue ending Temporary Protected Status for over 60,000 immigrants from Nicaragua, Honduras, and Nepal amid ongoing litigation, exposing residents to renewed deportation threats. A separate ruling limited the scope of the travel ban for certain visa applicants, offering limited relief. Meanwhile, the administration reached a temporary agreement with Uganda to accept third-country deportees, extending U.S. removal policies beyond direct returns and raising concerns about rights protections in receiving nations. The winners in this system were officials who gained influence over millions of lives. The losers were migrants whose futures could be altered by opaque algorithms and shifting political winds.

On the ground, enforcement grew increasingly militarized and privatized. ICE carried out raids that disrupted school attendance and targeted a Los Angeles teenager near his home, held migrant families in a Sheraton hotel despite corporate promises not to detain individuals there, and conducted a large workplace raid at a New Jersey warehouse using zip ties and visible worker sorting. The agency planned to acquire its own fleet of planes to expand deportations and spend millions on SUVs and custom "DEFEND THE HOMELAND" vehicle wraps through no-bid contracts. Social media campaigns featured militarized images and slogans. Hotels were used as detention sites and as accommodations for agents. Pentagon civilians were assigned to ICE and CBP. Deportation became a branded, permanent infrastructure—less visible to the public and less accountable to traditional oversight. Inside the federal workforce, protections and independence were stripped away.

Late in the week, the administration canceled union contracts for roughly 400,000 federal employees by executive order, eliminating collective bargaining rights for large segments of the civil service. The move sharply reduced organized labor's influence within government and increased executive control over hiring, firing, and workplace conditions. It also sent a message to individual workers: resistance would now be faced alone, without the backing of a union contract. Key data and intelligence agencies were reshaped along similar lines. After an underwhelming jobs report, the president fired Bureau of Labor Statistics commissioner Erika McEntarfer and nominated E. J. Antoni, a Heritage Foundation economist and January 6 participant, to replace her. This change threatened the independence of core economic statistics, which support everything from interest rate decisions to social program adjustments. Meanwhile, the Justice Department began investigations into D. C. crime statistics and publicly questioned local data that contradicted the administration's narrative of a crime emergency. Numbers that once anchored debate were now subject to political loyalty tests.

In the intelligence community, Director of National Intelligence Tulsi Gabbard revoked security clearances for 37 current and former officials accused of politicization or leaks and announced plans to cut the Office of the Director of National Intelligence staff by about half, including scaling back the Foreign Malign Influence Center. These steps risked punishing internal critics, deterring whistleblowers, and weakening analytic capacity—especially around foreign disinformation. That same week, the administration and its allies launched a coordinated campaign against Federal Reserve Governor Lisa Cook, with the president calling for her resignation, regulators referring allegations of mortgage fraud, and the Justice Department opening a criminal investigation. These combined pressures blurred the line between legitimate oversight and political targeting of an independent monetary policymaker.

Meanwhile, policy choices in education, health, and disaster relief deepened existing inequalities. A tax bill capped federal student loan borrowing and eliminated some graduate loan programs, shifting higher education costs onto individuals and likely reducing access for lower-income students. A budget reconciliation bill was projected to trigger nearly $1.5 trillion in automatic cuts to Medicare and Medicaid, shifting fiscal burdens onto seniors and low-income populations while maintaining other priorities. The Education Department proposed limiting access to Public Service Loan Forgiveness based on employers' perceived threats to national security or "American values," tying debt relief to ideological alignment.

Public health and social services were merged into the same pattern. The administration reclaimed over $12 million in federal grants from California's public health program due to alleged promotion of "gender ideology," using funding as leverage against unpopular social policies. It rolled back Obama-era guidance that required schools to support English learners, lowering obligations to provide language assistance for millions of children. FEMA ended paper payments and door-to-door outreach for disaster aid, requiring applicants to have an email address—a change that risked excluding elderly, disabled, and low-income survivors without reliable internet access. In environmental policy, the EPA moved to revoke the 2009 endangerment finding for greenhouse gases, weakening the legal basis for regulating climate pollution and aligning federal tools with fossil fuel interests.

These foreign moves intersected with domestic ideological battles. The halt of Gaza medical visas for children, the firing of a State Department press officer who drafted a statement opposing forced Palestinian relocations, and the Uganda third-country deportation deal all showed how human rights questions were subordinated to political narratives. Foreign policy became another arena where loyalty and optics outweighed consistent norms.

Vulnerable populations abroad—sick children, asylum seekers, civilians in conflict zones—bore the cost of decisions made to satisfy domestic constituencies and shield allies from scrutiny.

Against this broad trend of consolidation, resistance persisted. Federal courts ordered the closure of the "Alligator Alcatraz" immigration detention center and prevented its expansion, enforced Illinois' Right to Privacy in the Workplace Act against a federal challenge, and stopped a Texas law requiring Ten Commandments displays in public school classrooms. Another judge ruled that the State Department could not deny certain visas solely based on the travel ban, and the Supreme Court issued a divided emergency ruling that partially stayed the restoration of NIH grants while keeping the invalidated guidance in force. In Oregon, Grants Pass settled litigation by agreeing to provide at least 150 camping spaces and services for unhoused people with disabilities, even as a broader Supreme Court ruling allowed cities to criminalize camping.

Civil society and media actors also fought back. Rev. William Barber and allied activists organized Moral Monday protests across the South against a congressional funding bill supporting the president's agenda. Fifteen young climate activists sued Wisconsin over laws that prevent regulators from considering pollution in permitting fossil fuel plants, arguing that these statutes violate their constitutional rights. The ACLU filed a petition challenging ICE's detention of Atlanta journalist Mario Guevara as retaliatory, raising alarms about immigration powers being used to punish critical reporting. Newsmax agreed to pay $67 million to settle Dominion Voting Systems' defamation lawsuit over 2020 election falsehoods, demonstrating that courts can still impose real costs on media outlets spreading disinformation about voting systems.

Congress pressed the Justice Department over delays in producing Epstein files and scrutinized NIH grant decisions, seeking to reassert oversight. These actions mattered. They showed that judges, legislators, civil servants, and citizens still had tools to challenge overreach and to protect rights and truth. However, they were fragmented and reactive, often limited to narrow procedural issues or specific facilities. They did not form a unified counter-strategy capable of changing the course of power. The executive branch continued to operate on many fronts simultaneously—policing, elections, immigration, labor, data, foreign policy—creating overlapping crises and confusion that hindered sustained accountability. By the end of Week 31, the moral baseline had fallen further.

Character, ethics, restraint, truthfulness, good faith, and stewardship all showed serious breaches: pardons and threats concerning election offenders, manipulation of federal resources and appointments for political gain, aggressive use of emergency powers, disinformation about crime and voting, disregard for procedural norms, and the dismantling of oversight mechanisms. Courts and civil society provided important but partial support for stewardship and good faith. The overall trend, however, was downward. Executive power grew more unilateral, law more partisan, citizenship more divided, and information more curated.

The week's modest shift on the Democracy Clock reflected this paradox. There was no single disaster, no formal suspension of elections, no overt declaration of dictatorship. Rights still existed on paper. Institutions still operated. But leveraging them now required more persistence and entailed greater risk. The capital city had become a testing ground for militarized governance. Elections were being manipulated through maps and rules. Immigration and labor policies were intensifying a two-tiered society. Knowledge and memory were being rewritten to flatter those in power. The erosion did not announce itself overtly. It continued steadily and deliberately, in the space between what the rules allowed and what the oath of office once constrained.

CHAPTER 42
WEEK 32: EMERGENCIES AS EVERYDAY RULE

A half-minute shift on the Democracy Clock marks a week when emergency logic, lawfare, and economic patronage quietly deepen executive control.

The week did not revolve around a single order or speech. Instead, it unfolded as a series of actions that, together, demonstrated a government increasingly willing to govern by decree, treat opposition as a security threat, and categorize people into tiers of protection and risk. The pattern was familiar, but the confidence with which it was implemented across policing, elections, labor, and memory gave the period its seriousness. It felt coordinated, not accidental.

At the start of Week 32, the Democracy Clock showed 8:07 p.m. It finished the week at the same public time, with a net shift of half a minute further into danger. The clock face remained unchanged, but its hands moved slightly forward. This small change captured a week in which no single event dominated, yet the tools of emergency, law enforcement, and economic power were tightened in ways that will be difficult to undo. Courts, civil servants, and civil society showed resistance, but they did not change the overall trajectory.

The clearest sign of that direction was in Washington, D.C. On paper, the president declared a "crime emergency" in the capital and used it to take control of city policing. Crime rates were low, but the declaration allowed the White House to assume command of the Metropolitan Police Department and to frame the move as a response to chaos. Within days, an executive order expanded the emergency, increasing federal operational control and linking it to National Guard deployments. What appeared to be a temporary response began to look more like an occupation.

Congressional allies pushed to make that occupation permanent. Representative Andy Biggs introduced a bill that would turn six-month federal takeovers of D.C. policing into the default during declared emergencies. The proposal didn't eliminate local government; it simply ensured that, when the president invoked crisis, national control could continue. Simultaneously, the administration ordered a federal takeover of Union Station under the guise of "beautification," extending executive authority over a key transportation hub in the already-subordinated district. The capital became a testing ground.

The logic did not stop at the capital. After Maryland's governor criticized federal actions, the president threatened to send troops to Baltimore, blurring the line between public safety and personal retaliation. In Illinois, the White House floated National Guard deployments to Chicago, prompting Governor J.B. Pritzker to say the state was ready to sue over any unauthorized military presence. California's governor, Gavin Newsom, condemned the militarization of Los Angeles and other cities, framing the deployments as illegal power grabs rather than neutral security measures. Blue jurisdictions were put on notice.

Resistance grew not only in governors' mansions but also on the streets and in the courts. Organizers in Washington called for a September march demanding the withdrawal of federal troops from the district, while nationwide groups like Indivisible described the pattern as racially charged militarization of mostly-Black cities. A D.C. grand jury declined to indict a protester accused of throwing a sandwich at a federal officer, a small but significant refusal to endorse the most aggressive views of federal authority. Meanwhile, a federal judge blocked efforts to defund sanctuary jurisdictions, and an earlier congressional budget freeze had already caused a large shortfall in D.C.'s finances, showing how fiscal tools and emergency rhetoric now worked together to limit local self-governance.

If the capital showed how force could be centralized, the justice system demonstrated how the law could be manipulated. The week began with the arrest of Newark's mayor in a chaotic incident overseen directly by the deputy attorney general, an unusual level of senior involvement in a local matter. The charges did not hold, but the message remained: federal law enforcement could reach into city halls. Soon after, FBI agents raided the home and office of former National Security Adviser John Bolton over classified information issues, deviating from the usual procedures used with high-profile figures and signaling that prominent critics were not beyond the reach of dawn raids.

At the same time, the Department of Justice used coercive tactics against vulnerable defendants. In the case of Kilmar Ábrego García, prosecutors allegedly threatened deportation to a country where he faced greater risks to pressure him into a guilty plea in a smuggling case. The Federal Housing Finance Agency, under new leadership, analyzed detailed mortgage data to build fraud cases against outspoken critics of the president, like Senator Adam Schiff, New York Attorney General Letitia James, and Federal Reserve Governor Lisa Cook. Regulatory data, meant for neutral oversight, was turned into a tool for targeted legal pressure. Laws became weapons, not just limits.

The contrast with elite-linked cases was striking. When the House Oversight Committee subpoenaed records from Jeffrey Epstein's estate, the Justice Department responded with a limited production mostly consisting of already public documents, resisting real transparency about past non-prosecution decisions and possible ties to current officials. Ghislaine Maxwell, convicted of sex trafficking, was moved to a minimum-security facility, drawing criticism from victims who saw it as lenience for a high-profile offender. A whistleblower later revealed that a senior official had copied Social Security data for 300 million Americans onto an unsecured server, yet there was no immediate accountability at the top. Impunity flowed upward.

The president's own rhetoric reinforced this two-tier system. He threatened to reopen the Bridgegate scandal against former Governor Chris Christie, now a critic, and told the Justice Department to prioritize prosecuting American flag burners, despite Supreme Court rulings protecting such acts as free speech. The department also launched criminal investigations into former FBI Director James Comey and former CIA Director John Brennan over past testimonies, targeting officials who had once scrutinized the president. Law enforcement authority was not expanded by law; it was redirected by decision. The targets told the story.

Courts did not remain inactive, but their efforts were limited and challenged. Judge Paula Xinis blocked Ábrego's re-deportation and ordered that he be held near the court, citing due process limits on immigration enforcement. A federal court ruled that Alina Habba had not been lawfully serving as U.S. attorney for New Jersey, strengthening procedural limits on appointing loyalists to key prosecutorial roles. Another judge dismissed a groundbreaking lawsuit the administration filed against all Maryland federal district judges, upholding judicial immunity and defending the separation of powers. On a smaller scale, ordinary people also pushed back: a mother in Los Angeles filed a million-dollar claim against immigration agents over an arrest she described as racially motivated and violent. However, these acts of resistance took place in a landscape where the initiative mainly remained with the executive.

Alongside these legal actions, the administration aimed to redefine dissent as a form of disorder. One executive order directed the

Justice Department to punish jurisdictions that used cashless bail, threatening federal funding to override local criminal justice reforms. Another ordered prosecutors to prioritize cases involving flag burning, turning a symbolic protest into a criminal threat to the nation. Both orders treated policy disagreement and expressive acts as security threats to be eliminated rather than topics for debate. The scope of "acceptable" politics narrowed.

This same logic extended to the press and elections. The president urged the Federal Communications Commission to revoke the broadcast licenses of ABC and NBC, labeling them "threats to democracy" for their coverage. He publicly claimed record-high poll numbers despite low approval ratings, using disinformation to project an image of widespread support. Simultaneously, he announced that aides were drafting an executive order to eliminate mail-in voting nationwide, centralizing control over voting methods in the presidency and portraying this common practice as inherently suspicious. Democratic tools were redefined as dangers.

These actions occurred amid heightened fears and misinformation. Representative Nancy Mace spread a false report about a school shooter by posting a misidentified student's video, showing how elected officials could unintentionally fuel panic. Yet, civil society continued to organize. Labor and advocacy groups planned a Labor Day "die-in" to highlight the harms of a large federal bill they called the "One Big Ugly Bill," and protest organizers in D.C. prepared a march against troop deployments. A D.C. grand jury's decision not to indict the sandwich-throwing protester suggested that not all institutions accepted the administration's framing of protest as crime. Still, the overall effect of executive orders, threats, and prosecutions was to shrink the space in which dissent felt safe.

Nowhere was social stratification more evident than in immigration and social policy. The administration established a large immigrant detention center at Fort Bliss, Texas, on a military base, drawing comparisons to internment camps and raising questions about the rights and conditions of those detained. ICE agents arrested two firefighters from a wildfire crew during an operation, disrupting emergency responses and indicating that even essential workers were not protected from strict enforcement. An 18-year-old detainee was moved across state lines without prompt notice to his family, and another detainee, Luis Manuel Rivas Velásquez, was secretly relocated after complaining about conditions, hindering his access to legal counsel and loved ones. Vulnerability was used as leverage.

Emergency management showed a similar pattern of punishment for candor. Hundreds of FEMA employees sent a "Katrina Declaration" letter to Congress, warning that staffing cuts and policy changes had left the agency ill-prepared for disasters. In response, leadership placed some signatories on administrative leave, a clear signal that internal dissent would be met with professional risk. An executive order excluding additional federal units from standard labor-management rules on national security grounds further reduced collective bargaining rights for segments of the civil service. Those who were already vulnerable—immigrants, disabled people, internal critics—bore the brunt of these choices.

Even as leadership was purged, some formal processes continued. The CDC scheduled an Advisory Committee on Immunization Practices meeting on multiple vaccines, with public comment, preserving the appearance of evidence-based recommendations. The agency also sought input on a standardized data management plan template to improve transparency and reproducibility in health research. The Food and Drug Administration held meetings on staffing, patient experience, and manufacturing readiness. These efforts suggested that procedural normalcy still existed on paper, even as the institutions that housed it were being bent toward loyalty. Form endured while substance shifted.

Economic policy, meanwhile, moved further into the president's personal orbit. He announced that the U.S. government had taken a 10 percent equity stake in Intel, a major chipmaker, after personally demanding the arrangement. The administration floated a broader strategy of acquiring stakes in firms heavily reliant on federal contracts, signaling a shift toward state-linked corporate ownership negotiated at the top. The line between public authority and private enterprise blurred, with industrial policy increasingly shaped by insider conversations rather than open debate. Crony capitalism became a governing method.

Trade policy followed a similar pattern of centralized discretion. The administration imposed tariffs on small inbound packages by removing the long-standing de minimis exemption, prompting postal suspensions in many countries and disrupting low-value trade flows. A formal executive order later abolished the exemption entirely, raising costs for consumers and small importers while concentrating trade decisions in the White House. At the same time, the government canceled CHIPS Act-funded solar and wind projects in favor of fossil fuels, redirected public investment away from renewables, and proposed admitting 600,000 Chinese students to U.S. universities to help stabilize higher education finances. The Environmental Protection Agency granted numerous small refinery exemptions from biofuel blending obligations, weakening renewable fuel mandates. Sector after sector was realigned around executive preferences and favored industries.

Labor policy faced a coordinated attack. The president proposed eliminating federal minimum wage and overtime protections for childcare and home care workers, removing basic safeguards from millions in a low-paid, largely female workforce. He rolled back minimum wage protections for disabled workers, reducing economic security for a group already facing structural barriers. An order moved to rescind collective bargaining rights from about one million federal workers, representing the largest attempted rollback of federal union rights in recent history. Another directive cut the minimum wage for federal contractors from $17.75 to $13.30 per hour, directly lowering earnings for many performing public work. The wage floor itself was lowered.

These changes did not happen in isolation. The administration also cut over $800 million in public safety and crime-prevention grants, undermining community-based programs even as it emphasized punitive deployments and federal control. Together, the wage cuts, union rollbacks, and funding reductions weakened workers' bargaining power, increased economic instability, and diminished organized labor as a significant check on executive and corporate power. In response, labor and allied groups planned the Labor Day die-in against the "One Big Ugly Bill," using direct action to highlight the stakes of the new social contract.

Elections and representation were reshaped in quieter but equally impactful ways. The president's draft executive order to eliminate mail-in balloting nationwide threatened to centralize control over voting methods and to limit a practice widely used by the elderly, disabled, and those with inflexible work schedules. In Texas, lawmakers approved, and the governor signed a new congressional map estimated to give Republicans up to five additional U.S. House seats, raising concerns about partisan gerrymandering and the dilution of minority voting power. Civil rights groups, including the NAACP, sued, arguing that the map was a racial gerrymander in violation of the Voting Rights Act. The rules of representation were under challenge.

Elsewhere, courts pushed back. In Utah, a state court invalidated Republican-drawn congressional maps for violating a voter-approved independent redistricting commission requirement, ordering new maps by late September. The ruling strengthened judicial enforcement of anti-gerrymandering reforms. In Missouri, the governor called a special legislative session to redraw districts and change initiative rules, seeking a more Republican-favoring map and tighter constraints on citizen-led ballot measures. In Georgia, a Fulton County judge fined county commissioners daily for refusing to appoint two Republicans to the election board, enforcing state law on board composition but raising concerns about the compelled inclusion of election deniers.

Amid these maneuvers, some institutions worked to preserve integrity. The U.S. Election Assistance Commission scheduled a public meeting on voting system guidelines, supporting transparent, expert-driven oversight of election technology. Grassroots groups like Wake County Indivisible hosted municipal candidate meet-and-greets, fostering informed participation in local elections. Yet the broader pattern was clear: under the banner of "integrity," state and federal actors were redrawing lines and rewriting rules in ways that could lock in partisan advantage and weaken voters'—especially minorities and urban residents—ability to hold leaders to account.

Control over information and memory formed the final layer of the week's story. The president's call to revoke ABC and NBC licenses was paired with a $1.1 billion cut to the Corporation for Public Broadcasting. Public media stations, especially in rural areas, warned of severe service impacts, including reduced capacity for emergency alerts and civic information. Independent and noncommercial outlets, already operating on thin margins, faced a new wave of financial strain, while state-aligned voices remained untouched. The media landscape tilted.

At the same time, the administration moved to shape national symbols and historical narratives. An executive order mandated classical styles for new federal architecture, using building design to project a particular vision of American identity. The Pentagon decided to reinstall a portrait of Confederate General Robert E. Lee at West Point's library, reversing earlier efforts to remove such imagery and signaling a political re-centering of contested historical figures. The General Services Administration updated its Art-in-Architecture information collection to emphasize certain historical subjects, a bureaucratic adjustment that would influence which stories appeared in public art. Stone and canvas became tools of power.

Some transparency and accessibility efforts continued. The National Archives held a FOIA Advisory Committee meeting to discuss vexatious requests and reforms, while agencies issued notices of environmental impact statements, inviting public comment on major projects. The Federal Communications Commission asked for input on the accessibility of digital devices for people who are blind or visually impaired. Yet, these efforts unfolded in an environment where the loudest structural moves favored state-aligned narratives and symbols, and government archives in sensitive areas, such as the Epstein case, were being withheld or sanitized.

Looking ahead, several scheduled actions already cast their shadows. Utah's court-ordered redrawing of congressional maps by late September, the Election Assistance Commission's public meeting on voting system guidelines, and the planned September march in Washington against troop deployments all aimed to test, in concrete ways, how much space remained for legal correction and public protest within the tightening framework. Each would measure the remaining flexibility in the system.

During this period, Week 32 didn't introduce new tools of control but rather intensified their use. Emergency declarations became a routine method for federal takeovers of local policing. Law enforcement and regulatory data were more openly used against critics, while elite-linked cases stalled. Labor protections were rolled back in clusters, not as isolated reforms. Public health and emergency agencies were purged of independent leadership even as their formal processes persisted. Media funding and national symbols were adjusted to shape a specific narrative of the country. The week's modest progress on the Democracy Clock reflects this accumulation: rights and procedures still exist but now require more courage, organization, and willingness to face personal risk to be used.

CHAPTER 43
WEEK 33: AUTHORITARIAN POWERS AS POLICY

A week of near-stillness on the Democracy Clock masks how executive orders, security forces, and lawfare quietly consolidate personal rule and stratified citizenship.

The thirty-third week of Trump's second term did not depend on a single shock. Instead, it developed as a complex layering of decisions that, collectively, made the power structure more personal, more insulated, and more punitive. The week's events affected national security, immigration, labor, public health, and the information system, but the pattern remained consistent. Tools once used for broad public purposes were manipulated to fit the needs and narratives of the presidency.

At the end of the previous period, the Democracy Clock showed 8:07 p.m. It stayed at the same public time this week, with a tiny net change of 0.1 minutes—too small to be visible on the dial but still significant in substance. This apparent stillness reflected a balance between increasing executive overreach and pockets of institutional resistance, especially in the courts. The slight shift showed how much could change without a full break: executive orders bypassing Congress, security forces turning inward, and legal processes used as weapons rather than limits, partly countered by judges and state officials still enforcing boundaries.

The clearest statement of intent came directly from the president. In public remarks, he said he needed "authoritarian-style powers" to restore prosperity. The phrase was deliberate. It framed democratic constraints as obstacles to economic recovery and portrayed concentrated authority as a solution rather than a threat. This claim set the tone for a series of executive actions that viewed lawmaking and war powers as tools for personal rule, not shared governance.

One of the most notable moves was symbolic on the surface but deep in its implications. By executive order, the president renamed the Department of Defense as the Department of War. No law was changed. Congress did not debate the renaming. Yet, the order asserted unilateral control over the military's identity and language, at a time already marked by controversial uses of force. The new name highlighted aggression over defense and hinted at how future deployments—both foreign and domestic—might be justified. It was a change in words pointing toward a change in mindset.

Trade policy followed a similar route. The president issued an order establishing a new tariff framework under the United States–Japan Agreement, setting terms usually handled through congressional trade legislation. Another order revised reciprocal tariffs and procedures under a declared "national emergency," further embedding emergency-based control over economic relations. These decrees did more than adjust rates. They centralized tariff authority in the White House, even as appellate courts ruled that earlier emergency tariffs exceeded legal limits.

National security institutions were drawn closer to the president's personal circle. Under his directives, Director of National Intelligence Tulsi Gabbard publicly revealed and revoked the clearance of a senior undercover CIA officer. This action politicized a key safeguard of intelligence work and sent a signal that careers and safety could be sacrificed to demonstrate loyalty. Simultaneously, the administration increasingly used clearance procedures to sideline intelligence officers without clear reasons. A neutral security tool became a way to exert control.

Military power was also used in ways that blurred traditional boundaries. The administration dispatched naval forces and 4,000 troops off Venezuela's coast for a drug-interdiction mission, then later conducted a strike on a Venezuelan-linked boat, with legal grounds that members of Congress openly questioned. Representative Adam Smith and others raised concerns about war-powers oversight, but the deployment had already occurred. The pattern was familiar: act first under a security guise, then challenge the legislature or courts to respond.

Even decisions that seemed minor or technical bore the same pattern. The White House unilaterally canceled $4.9 billion in foreign aid approved by Congress, asserting control over spending powers that the Constitution grants to Congress. It also announced plans to move the Space Force headquarters from Colorado to Alabama after political lobbying, implying that decisions about where to base strategic assets could be driven by politics rather than operational needs. In a somewhat ambiguous move, the president signed an order establishing a new regime to designate foreign governments that wrongfully detain Americans. While the order ostensibly expanded tools to protect citizens abroad, it also centralized yet another aspect of foreign-policy authority in the executive.

If national security and trade demonstrated how power was centralized at the top, immigration policy showed how it spread into a vast security apparatus. The Department of Homeland Security argued that nearly all unauthorized border crossers were ineligible for bond and frequently appealed release orders, automatically staying judges' decisions. This approach turned bond hearings into formalities and limited immigration courts' discretion, making detention the default rather than the exception. As a result, freedom became the rare outcome instead of the norm.

At the same time, DHS launched a large recruitment drive for 10,000 ICE officers and 3,000 Border Patrol agents, lowering hiring standards and offering bonuses. The department also proposed paying salaries, benefits, and bonuses for local police who joined federal immigration enforcement efforts, blurring the line between community policing and deportation work. USCIS, which traditionally focused on benefits, expanded its role by adding law enforcement agents to carry out immigration arrests and warrants. These measures collectively built a larger, more aggressive enforcement system aligned with tough policies and less guided by professional norms.

The targets of this apparatus were not abstract. The administration suspended most visitor visas for Palestinian passport holders, restricted asylum for families targeted by gangs and domestic violence survivors through precedential rulings, and warned at least one asylum seeker that he would be deported to El Salvador even if he won his case. It attempted to deport about 600 unaccompanied Guatemalan children before a court blocked the move, and it used reunification appointments as enforcement traps by requiring parents to undergo ID checks that sometimes led to arrests. Each decision narrowed protection for specific nationalities and identities, deepening a tiered system of rights.

Detention conditions and local autonomy also came under pressure. A controversial Florida immigrant jail known as "Alligator Alcatraz" won a temporary reprieve from closure when an appeals court stayed a district judge's order, prolonging harsh confinement. The Justice Department sued Boston and Mayor Michelle Wu over sanctuary policies, seeking to force local cooperation with deportation efforts. An immigration raid at a Hyundai plant in Georgia swept up Korean workers and triggered diplomatic protests from Seoul, showing how aggressive enforcement could strain foreign relations. And the administration opened a criminal investigation into Federal Reserve governor Lisa Cook for alleged mortgage fraud, raising questions about whether prosecutorial power was being used as leverage over an independent economic policymaker.

Not all jurisdictions accepted this trajectory. The California legislature passed a bill requiring schools to alert communities when immigration agents were on campus, aiming to protect immigrant students' access to education and due process. The measure did not change federal policy, but it showed how states could still carve out pockets of safety and transparency within an expanding federal security regime. It was a small but concrete act of resistance.

Inside the domestic state, the same week saw a coordinated weakening of expert governance and internal dissent. In public health, the president ordered the firing of CDC director Susan Monarez, a newly confirmed scientist, and backed HHS Secretary Robert F. Kennedy Jr.'s reshaping of CDC leadership. The administration simultaneously cut CDC funding sharply and proposed reductions exceeding half the agency's budget, targeting programs on smoking, maternal health, and other core functions. In Florida, lawmakers advanced a proposal to eliminate all vaccine requirements for public school students, aligning state policy with federal anti-vaccine leadership.

These moves drew unusually broad resistance from within the health establishment. Nine former CDC directors published an op-ed warning that RFK Jr.'s policies endangered public health and urging Congress to intervene. Over 1,000 current and former HHS staff signed a letter demanding his resignation over vaccine misinformation and staffing decisions. Susan Monarez herself wrote that antivaccine rhetoric was being forced into CDC advisory processes. Senators on the Finance Committee held a contentious hearing with RFK Jr., pressing him on staff purges and vaccine cuts. The oversight was sharp, but it did not reverse the underlying changes.

Retaliation against internal critics extended beyond health. At the Social Security Administration, Chief Data Officer Charles Borges was forced out after he raised alarms about insecure uploads of millions of Americans' records, signaling that those who reported data breaches risked their jobs. At FEMA, reports surfaced that more than 30 employees had been suspended after warning Congress about agency problems, prompting calls for investigation from watchdog groups. At the Environmental Protection Agency, at least seven employees were fired for signing a dissent letter, punishing professional disagreement within the civil service.

Environmental and climate policy were rolled back in tandem. The EPA reversed impairment designations for an Iowa river and cut funding for a water pollution report, weakening oversight of agricultural runoff and reducing public visibility into contamination. The Departments of Energy, Interior, and Transportation withdrew or paused support exceeding $1.3 billion for major offshore wind projects, including advanced installations off the East Coast. The administration secured court approval to end more than $16 billion in climate change grants. Labor leaders criticized these moves as cuts that would harm working families and cost jobs, while the governors of Connecticut and Rhode Island coordinated efforts to preserve the nearly complete Revolution Wind project, asserting state-level resistance to federal reversals.

Media and information agencies were not exempt. The U.S. Agency for Global Media, under a politicized acting CEO, announced layoffs of over 500 employees at Voice of America and related broadcasters, and PBS cut staff after federal funding was reduced. These cuts weakened both international public diplomacy and domestic noncommercial news, leaving state-aligned and commercial outlets relatively stronger. The pattern across agencies remained consistent: dissenters were punished, budgets were slashed, and loyalists or ideologues were promoted, making the bureaucracy more compliant and less capable.

On the economic front, the week delivered a sharp blow to organized labor and clarified who benefited from recent policies. The administration canceled union contracts and stripped collective bargaining protections from roughly 450,000 federal workers, including many in the civil service. Announced around Labor Day, this move reversed more than a century of gradual recognition of public-sector worker rights. It increased worker precarity, gave managers greater unilateral control, and weakened one of the last major strongholds of union presence in the country.

Simultaneously, the Congressional Budget Office and other

analysts reported that the president's tax laws heavily favored millionaires while cutting supports for low-income families, including Medicaid and food aid. Survey data indicated that most Americans no longer believed that hard work would lead to upward mobility, reflecting waning faith in the fairness of the economic system. Overall, these findings underscored how fiscal policy has entrenched inequality and shifted risks downward.

Trade policy once again stood at the crossroads of law, economics, and narrative. A federal appeals court in Washington, DC, ruled that most of the president's emergency tariffs went beyond his legal authority, reaffirming Congress's dominance over trade. Bond markets experienced stress, and there were indications that the government might owe refunds. Companies like John Deere reported profit drops and layoffs tied to higher input costs from tariffs, illustrating how trade wars shifted pain onto workers and industrial communities. However, the White House responded by greatly exaggerating tariff revenue in a Labor Day statement, claiming $8 trillion when experts estimated about $115 billion, and sought Supreme Court review to uphold the contested tariffs. New executive orders on Japan and reciprocal tariffs extended this emergency-based approach rather than abandoning it.

Economic power was also wielded to control independent institutions. The administration froze nearly $800 million in research funds to Northwestern University, prompting the president's resignation and demonstrating how federal money could be used to influence academic governance. Conversely, a federal court ruled that the administration had unlawfully ended $2.6 billion in grants to Harvard University and ordered their reinstatement, reaffirming legal protections for academic independence. The different outcomes showed both the reach of executive pressure and the courts' ability to check it. Smaller examples illustrated how political loyalty and culture-war signaling had become economic tools. A Trump-associated crypto token launched with fanfare and quickly lost value, raising concerns about exploiting political allegiance for speculative schemes. Cracker Barrel reversed a logo change after backlash from conservative figures, including the president, suggesting that corporate decisions could be driven by partisan pressure rather than market judgment.

These incidents were minor but pointed to a broader fusion of politics and commerce. Elections and opposition politics were no longer left to ordinary competition. The president announced plans for executive orders to mandate nationwide voter ID requirements and sharply restrict mail-in voting, aiming to override state control over election rules under the guise of ensuring election integrity. He pressured Republican state legislators to redraw congressional districts to increase GOP seats, using presidential influence to shape House representation. At his direction, the Justice Department opened an investigation into ActBlue, the main Democratic fundraising platform, while leaving its Republican counterpart untouched, weaponizing federal law enforcement against an opposition tool.

Quieter administrative decisions also reduced participation. USCIS prohibited nongovernmental groups from registering new voters at naturalization ceremonies, removing a crucial entry point to civic engagement for new citizens. The Justice Department sued Boston over sanctuary policies, signaling that cities protecting immigrants could face federal legal and financial pressure. Prosecutors charged an ICE protester in Spokane with conspiracy, and the administration considered classifying being transgender as a mental illness to justify a firearms ban. Each action targeted different groups—immigrants, urban jurisdictions, protesters, trans individuals—but the common thread was the same. Law and policy were used to burden disliked groups and opposition-aligned actors without outright banning them. The treatment of dissent and the exposure of elite abuse showed how security language could be weaponized against critics. The FBI and Justice Department charged veteran Bajun Mavalwalla with conspiracy after an ICE protest, signaling a willingness to use serious criminal laws against demonstrators.

In Washington, DC, residents reported heavily armed National

Guard and federal patrols in neighborhoods, profiling and arresting people, including children. These patrols prompted calls for a national march and inspired community groups to hold ICE-watch trainings, but they also turned parts of the capital into de facto occupation zones. At the Capitol, survivors of Jeffrey Epstein's abuse held a press conference demanding justice and full accountability. As they spoke, a fighter jet flew overhead in a no-fly zone, disrupting the event and raising fears that military assets were being used to drown out critical speech about elite wrongdoing.

In Congress, Representatives Ro Khanna and Thomas Massie led bipartisan efforts to release Epstein-related files, organizing hearings and subpoenas. Yet the House Oversight Committee's eventual release of more than 33,000 documents mainly included material already public, allowing leaders to claim transparency without revealing new information. Further evidence suggested that elite figures were being shielded. A recording captured a Justice Department official discussing the possibility of redacting Republicans from Epstein files and easing Ghislaine Maxwell's prison conditions. The department later issued a statement that effectively confirmed controversial comments about her treatment. These revelations, combined with the partial document dump, indicated that crimes committed by donors and allies were being curated in the record rather than fully prosecuted. When Representative LaMonica McIver faced indictment and a censure effort stemming from oversight at an ICE facility, the House ultimately voted to dismiss the censure resolution, highlighting tensions over whether those who scrutinized enforcement would be punished or protected.

The information environment in which all this unfolded was itself being reshaped. Layoffs at Voice of America and other U.S. Agency for Global Media outlets, along with staff cuts at PBS after federal funding was cut, weakened independent and public media capacity. At the same time, the White House flooded the public sphere with misleading claims about tariffs and economic performance, and commentators documented gaps between official statements and underlying data. Susan Monarez's account of antivaccine rhetoric being forced into CDC advisory processes, and the Senate's grilling of RFK Jr., showed how scientific communication was being bent toward ideological narratives.

Congress became a stage for competing stories rather than a forum for shared fact-finding. House Republicans blocked a plaque honoring officers who defended the Capitol on January 6 while creating a new subcommittee to reinvestigate the attack, signaling an effort to recast its meaning in official memory. The administration's communications team met with lawmakers to rebrand an unpopular megabill, focusing on marketing rather than substance. Legislative time and symbolism were thus devoted less to deliberation and more to narrative control.

Behind many of these developments lay a quieter technological shift. The administration reinstated ICE's contract with Israeli spyware firm Paragon, restoring access to powerful phone-hacking tools capable of breaking encrypted communications. ICE expanded its use of such tools, increasing the state's ability to collect and analyze data on targeted populations. Combined with mass hiring of enforcement officers, financial incentives for local police to join federal programs, reunification appointments used as traps, and bond ineligibility tactics, the spyware contract deepened the reach of a surveillance regime that could be turned not only on immigrants but also on journalists and activists. Because these capabilities were outsourced to a foreign-linked private contractor, they were harder for courts, Congress, or the public to see and regulate.

No single court ruling or act of resistance reversed these trends, but some did mark real limits. The appeals court decision against emergency tariffs, the injunction blocking the deportation of Guatemalan children, and the order restoring Harvard's grants showed that parts of the judiciary still enforced statutory and constitutional boundaries. State legislatures and governors, from California to New England, used their own authority to protect immigrants, vaccines, and wind projects. These actions did not stop the week's erosion, but they prevented it from being absolute.

Taken together, the week intensified a pattern already evident earlier in the term. Executive orders replaced legislation. Security forces focused more on preserving power than on public defense. Law was used to intimidate critics and burden opponents. Whistleblowers and experts faced punishment, while elite misconduct was hidden rather than exposed. Public media shrank as disinformation grew. Still, courts, states, and parts of Congress resisted, preventing the system from fully shifting to rule by decree.

The Democracy Clock's near-stillness during this period reflected that tension. The basic framework of democracy remained intact: elections were held, courts operated, legislatures met, and agencies functioned. But the costs of using those structures increased, especially for those lacking wealth or institutional support. Rights could still be invoked, but doing so required more persistence and involved greater risks. In this way, the week didn't mark a new phase but confirmed the continuation of an existing one: a government that increasingly viewed constraints as problems to solve and dissent as threats to manage.

CHAPTER 44
WEEK 34: MILITARY GOVERNANCE AS ROUTINE

National Guard deployments, paramilitary immigration raids, and curated memory deepen an order where opposition persists but carries rising personal and civic cost.

The thirty-fourth week of Trump's second term did not rely on a single order or spectacle. It developed as a continuation of patterns already seen: force directed inward, law bending toward power, and information controlled so the public saw less and feared more. The surface appeared busy but familiar—raids, rulings, speeches, budget debates. Beneath the surface, the week deepened a structure in which opposition was tolerated but increasingly punished, and where tools of the state were aligned with partisan goals.

At the end of the previous period, the Democracy Clock stood at 8:07 p.m. It ended this week at the same time, with only a tenth of a minute of change. The clock face remained unchanged, but the gears behind it shifted. This small net change reflected a balance between ongoing erosion and scattered pockets of resistance: courts that still sometimes said no, governors trying to shield their residents, and civil society refusing to stay silent. Yet, the dominant movement pointed in one direction. Executive power faced little effective oversight, courts and Congress further leaned toward the president's agenda, and coercive tools were more openly used against disfavored communities and cities.

The clearest sign of this shift was the deployment of troops and federal agents inside American cities. In Washington, the president ordered about two thousand National Guard soldiers to assume control of policing, superseding local authority in the nation's capital. This occurred amid protests against his rule and militarized law enforcement. It turned the Guard into the primary face of public order in a city lacking full self-governance. Residents awoke to uniforms and armored vehicles where municipal police once stood. Chicago and Memphis soon experienced the same approach. In Chicago, the administration sent National Guard units and federal immigration agents into neighborhoods, claiming to target crime and immigration. In Memphis, the president announced plans to deploy Guard troops despite local opposition, again citing crime. These actions were not responses to insurrection or natural disasters. They were justified as routine governance tools, most aggressively used in Democratic-led areas. The line between civilian policing and military occupation became thinner. The effects on the ground were significant. In Chicago, ICE and Guard presence became part of daily life in neighborhoods already over-policed. One ICE operation ended with the shooting and death of Silverio Villegas-Gonzalez during a vehicle stop near the city. That same week, reports described troops gathered in Washington as protests persisted, turning the capital into a stage for power rather than a forum for dissent. Inside the Guard, internal documents criticized the Washington takeover for using fear and eroding trust, indicating that even within the security forces, there was discomfort at being used as a domestic political tool.

Local leaders attempted to resist. In Chicago and nearby Evanston, mayors and officials warned residents about federal agents and condemned the militarized approach. Illinois's governor met with immigrant community leaders to explain constitutional rights and to calm nerves. Protesters in DC and Chicago crowded the streets to oppose the deployments, insisting that their cities were not battlegrounds. Yet, the deployments continued. The balance of power favored the president, who could command troops and agents, while local officials were left to issue statements and organize resistance.

Immigration enforcement itself took on an openly paramilitary character. ICE launched a large raid at a Hyundai–LG battery plant in Georgia, detaining about 475 workers in one sweep. Many were foreign nationals; some were parents separated from their children with little warning. On the same day, agents raided a nutrition bar factory in New York, detaining over forty workers and again tearing families apart. These were not quiet audits. They were large operations that turned workplaces into scenes of sudden disappearance.

The pattern extended to sanctuary jurisdictions. Under the banner "Patriot 2.0," the administration targeted immigrants in Massachusetts who had been released from custody under local policies. The message was clear: federal power would be strongest where local governments tried to protect their residents. In Chicago, the combined ICE and Guard presence led to a fatal traffic-stop shooting and the detention of a Korean worker with a valid visa, who was pressured to leave. Legal status offered little protection when enforcement was driven by spectacle and fear.

Policy choices reinforced the same hierarchy. The administration issued orders excluding certain immigrants from federal programs, including Head Start, linking access to early education and health services to immigration status. Officials moved to restrict services for undocumented families more broadly, until courts intervened. They deported Guatemalan children while falsely claiming their parents had requested their return, then quietly retracted the claim when it could not be sustained. The narrative of benevolent enforcement masked a reality of coerced removals and fractured families.

Courts and local actors provided partial safeguards. Federal judges blocked some restrictions on immigrant access to Head Start and other services, and stopped an intrusive subpoena for trans patients' medical records from a Boston hospital. These rulings protected basic rights for vulnerable groups. Governors and mayors met with immigrant leaders, issued rights advisories, and publicly opposed militarized raids. Yet, other judicial decisions went the other way. A series of emergency orders from the Supreme Court allowed ICE to resume race- and language-based stops in Los Angeles, weakening equal protection in the name of enforcement. The same Court's shadow docket became a quiet driver of discriminatory policing.

The logic that treated immigrants as targets extended beyond the water's edge. In the Caribbean, the administration ordered a deadly strike on a Venezuelan boat in international waters, alleging gang activity. Pentagon lawyers were still seeking legal authority when civilians were killed. The operation was described as drug interdiction but resembled war more than law enforcement. At the same time, officials considered expanding military drug operations using Puerto Rico as a base, further blurring the line between foreign missions and domestic territory. Plans were also made to propose at the United Nations that asylum seekers be required to claim protection in their first country and that asylum be made temporary, tightening global norms in ways that would leave refugees with fewer safe havens.

Midweek, a different kind of violence occurred. At Utah Valley University, a gunman shot and killed Charlie Kirk during an outdoor event, wounding others before taking his own life. Law enforcement acted swiftly. A nationwide pursuit culminated in the arrest of Tyler Robinson in Utah, demonstrating the investigative capacity in a politically sensitive case. But the response from the presidency and allied networks transformed the killing from a crime into a political tool. From the Oval Office, the president blamed the "radical left" for Kirk's death, treating a broad political group as collectively responsible. He called for "quick trials" for the suspect, prioritizing speed over process in a case already soaked in politics. In another statement, he used the killing of a Ukrainian refugee in a separate incident to attack cashless bail and Democrats, linking individual tragedies to partisan narratives. The line between grief and campaign messaging disappeared. Around this, a punitive ecosystem developed. MAGA-aligned influencers organized campaigns to identify and get critics of Kirk fired from their jobs, scouring social media for offensive or mocking posts. Employers were pressured to dismiss staff, turning economic security into leverage against speech. A Texas university arrested and expelled a student for mocking Kirk's death online, combining campus discipline with criminal process over offensive but nonviolent speech. On cable news, MSNBC fired commentator Matthew Dowd after he criticized Kirk's rhetoric, a move seen as bowing to political pressure. Members of Congress joined the effort. Representative Clay Higgins called for lifetime social media bans and professional penalties for those mocking the assassination, openly threatening to use state power to police speech. Meanwhile, the president elevated Kirk to the status of martyr. He announced a posthumous Presidential Medal of Freedom for him, the nation's highest civilian honor. Allies in Congress requested a statue of Kirk in the Capitol. These honors were not neutral; they signaled who was considered a national hero.

Other symbols were treated differently. House leadership refused to implement a bipartisan law requiring a plaque honoring January 6 police officers who defended the Capitol, ignoring a statutory mandate. Outside the White House, police dismantled a peace vigil that had stood for forty years, detaining a volunteer and removing a longstanding symbol of anti-nuclear protest from public view. The contrast was stark: a dissenting vigil erased, defenders of Congress left unrecognized, and a partisan activist elevated to the pantheon. Public memory was being curated in real time.

The institutions meant to stand apart from politics moved closer to the president. The Supreme Court and lower courts allowed Trump to fire a Biden-appointed member of the Federal Trade Commission despite statutory protections for independent commissioners. Chief Justice Roberts, acting for the Court, permitted the removal while litigation was ongoing. A federal appeals court dismissed states' lawsuits challenging mass firings of probationary federal employees, limiting external checks on the administration's ability to reshape the civil service. Together, these rulings made it easier to purge regulators and staff who were not aligned with the president.

The Senate adjusted its own rules to match. Republican leaders lowered the vote threshold for considering presidential nominees to a simple majority, reducing minority leverage in confirmations. This change, combined with the courts' deference on firings, cleared a path to rapidly install loyalists across agencies and boards. The civil service, once buffered by tenure and merit protections, became more exposed to political winds. Careers that had depended on expertise and neutrality now depended more on favor.

Policy outcomes followed the new structure. A district court in Washington allowed the administration's termination of more than 1,600 National Science Foundation grants, worth over a billion dollars, to proceed. The cuts fell heavily on basic research and programs serving underrepresented groups in STEM. Federal appeals courts cleared the way for the administration to block Medicaid reimbursements to Planned Parenthood for a year, threatening clinic closures and reducing reproductive health access for low-income patients. These decisions did not simply interpret law; they enabled a social agenda that would have struggled to pass as standalone legislation.

Congress, for its part, often chose not to act. Republican leaders declined to assert oversight over unilateral military strikes and spending cuts, tolerating executive impoundment of congressionally approved programs. Reports described how Trump had been allowed to cut or delay multiple initiatives without strong challenge. At the same time, the administration filed emergency appeals to freeze billions in foreign aid that courts had ordered spent, and judges permitted a form of pocket rescission that expanded executive leverage over appropriated funds. The legislature's power of the purse, a core check in the constitutional design, was eroding through inaction and litigation.

There were still rulings that pushed back. A federal appeals court held that Trump had exceeded his authority in imposing sweeping global tariffs, affirming that trade powers have limits. Other courts invalidated deportation policies and a funding cut to Harvard, and the Supreme Court upheld an $83 million defamation verdict against Trump in the E. Jean Carroll case, confirming that presidential status does not erase personal civil liability. Judges temporarily blocked Trump's attempt to fire Federal Reserve Governor Lisa Cook and reinstated the Library of Congress's copyright chief, reinforcing some protections for independent officials. These decisions showed that the judiciary was not monolithic.

Yet overall, the week's legal landscape tilted toward deference to executive and donor-aligned priorities. The framework of elections and representation was reshaped in quieter ways. In Missouri, the legislature approved a congressional map that added a safe Republican seat and dismantled a Kansas City district with significant Democratic and minority populations. The map was designed to increase Republican representation and dilute urban and Black votes. It demonstrated how control over redistricting could be used to predetermine outcomes while maintaining the appearance of competitive elections. At the federal level, the House passed the Stop Illegal Entry Act, imposing mandatory minimum prison sentences for certain migrant reentry crimes. The law expanded criminal responses to immigration and would disproportionately impact noncitizens, many of whom lived and worked in communities with fragile political voices. In Michigan, a judge dismissed felony charges against fifteen of Trump's 2020 fake electors for lack of evidence of intent, limiting accountability for an earlier attempt to overturn election results. The decision weakened deterrence for future schemes that might test the boundaries of electoral law. Data and enforcement tools moved into position around the ballot box. Reports indicated that the Justice Department was building a national voting database, centralizing sensitive voter information inside an agency now closely aligned with the president. The project raised questions about who would control access and how the data might be used in future disputes.

The Supreme Court's shadow-docket decision allowing racial profiling in immigration enforcement signaled a willingness to endorse discriminatory practices through emergency orders, a method that could be used for other types of policing. Cleta Mitchell, a lawyer linked to Trump's earlier efforts to challenge elections, publicly suggested that the president could declare a national emergency to control federal elections, hinting at a way to override state-run systems under the pretense of a crisis. Oversight of election rules became more opaque. The Federal Election Commission canceled a scheduled open meeting and held a closed session on litigation matters, reducing public insight into how campaign finance and enforcement decisions were made. In Congress, Republicans cut $1 billion from Washington D.C.'s budget, using fiscal control over the disenfranchised capital to limit its services and send a message about the costs of political opposition. Each move was justifiable individually. Together, they formed an infrastructure where representation could be managed from above.

Information about elite misconduct and state actions was carefully managed. In the Epstein case, the Justice Department aimed to dismiss survivors' civil lawsuit over past federal inaction, resisting full disclosure of how earlier investigations had been handled. It asked courts to keep the names of two recipients of Epstein-related payments confidential and delayed responses to a key Freedom of Information Act request until November 2027. Lawyers for many survivors reported limited outreach. The combined effect was to push critical records and accountability beyond the current political horizon.

Other institutions filled parts of the gap, but on their own terms. The House Oversight Committee released estate records, including a Trump-signed birthday note to Epstein, then Republican lawmakers minimized their importance publicly. JPMorgan

Chase retroactively flagged 4,700 Epstein-related transactions totaling over $1.1 billion as suspicious, years after the fact. These steps recognized the scale of the network but also showed how financial and political actors could delay scrutiny until it was less immediate.

The intelligence community was not immune. Director of National Intelligence Tulsi Gabbard ordered the recall of a classified report on Venezuela, even though staff confirmed its accuracy. The recall suggested political discomfort with the analysis rather than technical flaws. In the economic sphere, the Bureau of Labor Statistics released a weak August jobs report following the firing of its director and a website outage. The president responded by dismissing the numbers and promising future growth driven by construction, framing the data as a temporary glitch rather than a warning. The leadership turmoil, technical problems, and political spin raised doubts about the independence of official statistics.

Across various areas, the administration relied on overlapping crises and quick actions to stretch the public's ability to follow events. In a short time, it launched a controversial military strike, oversaw mass raids, pursued emergency court actions on foreign aid and tariffs, cut science and health funding, and managed the fallout from a political assassination. Each development demanded attention. Together, they created information overload. In that environment, conspiracy theories thrived, and formal accountability channels struggled to keep up.

Public health, science, and climate policy were influenced by ideological and donor interests. In Florida, the surgeon general announced that the state would abandon mandatory childhood vaccination requirements, breaking with long-standing norms that had kept preventable diseases at bay. At the federal level, the administration planned to link COVID-19 vaccine access to unverified reports of child deaths and considered restricting access on that basis. A "Make America Healthy Again" report on children's health acknowledged concerns but avoided addressing pesticides and ultra-processed foods, reflecting deference to agribusiness and food industry interests.

Science funding and education faced similar pressure. The termination of more than 1,600 NSF grants, upheld by the courts, shifted federal priorities away from basic research and programs supporting underrepresented groups. The administration cut funding for disability education and colleges serving students of color, while a Republican tax-and-spending plan shifted costs onto state budgets, leading to cuts in services. In North Carolina, the legislature's failure to pass a full budget resulted in a $319 million shortfall in Medicaid funding, causing immediate coverage cuts for millions and shifting fiscal strain onto the most vulnerable.

Reproductive and global health were also impacted. The administration ordered the destruction of nearly $10 million in contraceptives for low-income countries, undermining family planning programs abroad. It used pocket rescission and litigation to cut or block foreign aid and democracy-promotion funds, weakening support for global health initiatives. At home, Medicaid defunding of Planned Parenthood, enabled by court rulings, threatened clinic closures and reduced access to reproductive care for low-income patients.

Climate and energy policy favored incumbent interests. The Environmental Protection Agency moved to rescind $7 billion in Solar for All grants intended to assist low- and middle-income families in accessing clean energy. It also announced plans to end the greenhouse gas reporting program for major polluters, a key source of data for climate policy. These actions favored fossil fuel and utility interests over environmental accountability. Some federal agencies continued routine tasks—issuing guidance on non-opioid pain treatments, updating hazardous waste rules, and reviewing new chemicals—but the overall trend was a rollback of protections and investments that serve broad public welfare.

Religion and symbolism were used to legitimize this order and marginalize dissent. In Texas, lawmakers implemented a school prayer law and vowed to appeal a ruling blocking Ten Commandments displays in classrooms, pushing Christian practices into public education. In Washington, the House held a hearing promoting an unpublished study critical of vaccines, giving anti-science narratives a formal platform. At West Point, a planned award ceremony honoring Tom Hanks was canceled after political pressure, demonstrating how even cultural recognition within military institutions could be politicized.

Within the armed forces, the line between faith, politics, and command blurred. Defense Secretary Pete Hegseth delivered a religious and partisan speech to troops in uniform, praising Charlie Kirk and blending Christian language with political loyalty. At the same time, the president signed an order renaming the Department of Defense as the Department of War, a symbolic shift that emphasized aggression over defense. Inside the White House grounds, the Rose Garden became the site of an exclusive "Rose Garden Club" dinner for loyal supporters, turning a public space into a quasi-private venue for patronage.

These gestures were reinforced by the curated treatment of monuments and memory. The dismantling of the White House peace vigil, the refusal to honor January 6 officers, and the push to honor Kirk with a Medal of Freedom and a Capitol statue all pointed in the same direction. They elevated figures aligned with the president's movement and erased or sidelined symbols of resistance and institutional defense. Public commentary by historians and former leaders noted how post–9/11 choices had already eroded democratic norms, situating the week's symbolic battles in a longer arc of memory shaped by power.

The information environment in which all this happened was flooded with propaganda tools. The president used an AI-generated militaristic image to threaten Chicago on social media, pairing it with a meme suggesting military action against the city. Right-wing influencer Ben Bergquam embedded himself with ICE agents during raids in Chicago, filming operations and confronting residents, turning enforcement into political spectacle. Tom Homan, the administration's border czar, claimed without evidence that immigration protesters were being paid and threatened legal action against their funders, casting grassroots dissent as corrupt.

These narratives were amplified by disinformation about crime and protest. Homan and allied media figures blamed liberal influences for Kirk's killer without evidence. The president politicized violent incidents to attack opponents and promote allied candidates. His Oval Office framing of Kirk's killing as the work of "radical left lunatics" fed a conspiratorial view of domestic politics. At the same time, the administration considered tying vaccine policy to unverified child death reports, risking further erosion of trust in public health.

Punishment for dissenting speech reinforced the message. Campaigns to get critics fired, threats of lifetime social media bans and license targeting, and the firing of a television commentator after criticism of Kirk's rhetoric all showed how economic and professional sanctions could be used to police opinion. The Federal Communications Commission's management of small TV station applications, including freezes and phased resumptions, shaped who could access broadcast spectrum in this environment. Overlapping crises and emergency actions, described earlier, added to the sense that events were too many and too fast to fully understand.

No single event in Week 34 marked a departure from what had come before. The week's importance lay in how familiar methods were used with greater confidence and reach. Military and immigration forces were employed as tools of domestic control. Courts and Congress, while not entirely under influence, more often enabled rather than restrained. Information about elite wrongdoing, foreign policy, and the economy was delayed, curated, or spun. Public health, science, and climate policy were directed to serve ideological and donor interests. Religion and symbolism were used to sanctify the project and to portray dissent as unpatriotic or impious.

The Democracy Clock's face did not visibly move, but the underlying situation worsened. Rights still existed on paper.

Protests still happened. Some judges still drew lines. Yet, claiming those rights now required more courage and came with higher costs. The tools available to those in power—to surveil, punish, distort memory, and determine who matters—became more sophisticated and normalized. In that sense, Week 34 was not a disruption. It was another layer in the sediment of an emerging order, one in which democratic forms persisted while their substance grew weaker.

CHAPTER 45
WEEK 35: SECURITY AS PRESIDENTIAL CLAY

National Guard deployments, immigration raids, and curated memory showed how ordinary tools of government were reshaped around one man's fears and advantage.

The thirty-fifth week of Trump's second term didn't rely on a single order or speech. Instead, it unfolded as a complex sequence of actions that used security, law, and memory as tools to be shaped by the presidency. National Guard deployments, immigration raids, media pressure, and economic decrees all moved through official channels, yet together they signaled a further shift toward a system where power responds less to institutions and more to one man's perception of threats and advantage. The story of the week lies in how ordinary government tools were bent to serve that purpose.

At the start of Week 35, the Democracy Clock showed 8:07 p.m. By the end, it read 8:08 p.m., a net change of 0.1 minutes. The small shift was because courts, state governments, and civil society still pushed back, sometimes effectively, to slow or block the administration's goals. But the overall direction was clear. Executive power was asserted over cities and agencies, law was used against critics, and the space for independent media and science shrank. The clock moved because resisting these trends became more costly, even as formal rights and procedures remained on paper.

The most visible display of power came on American streets. In Memphis, the president announced that National Guard troops would be deployed as part of a "Memphis Safe Task Force," despite the city's historically low crime rates. An executive order placed Guard units alongside federal agencies in local policing, turning what was once a civilian task into a joint military–law enforcement operation. The language described it as public safety. The effect was to normalize soldiers in the role of city police.

Plans didn't stop in Memphis. Within the administration, officials drafted proposals to use Louisiana's National Guard for routine urban law enforcement, encouraging governors to invite similar interventions. That same week, the president threatened to declare a national emergency to seize control of Washington DC's police department over disputes about immigration cooperation. Emergency rhetoric, once reserved for hurricanes or riots, became a tool to override local authority when cities pushed back against federal deportation efforts.

By week's end, the threat in Washington moved from talk to action. The president ordered a temporary federal takeover of the DC police department, supported by a National Guard deployment for a month, citing concerns about crime. This wasn't a response to an uprising or natural disaster. It was a political decision to put the capital's policing directly under presidential control. At the same time, federal agents and Guard units were used in both DC and Memphis under the guise of crime control, reinforcing a model in which security forces serve regime preservation rather than local accountability.

Congressional Republicans moved in unison. The House advanced and passed a series of "tough on crime" bills aimed at Washington, D.C., including measures to try 14-year-olds as adults and to reshape sentencing and policing despite local objections. These bills, combined with Guard deployments and a federal takeover, treated the district less as a self-governing community and more as a testing ground for punitive, federally driven criminal justice. The divide between civilian policing and militarized, centralized control grew narrower.

If Guard deployments demonstrated authority on the streets, immigration enforcement revealed how deeply coercion could penetrate homes, workplaces, and detention centers. In Los Angeles, ICE carried out large-scale, militarized raids across neighborhoods, targeting immigrants and perceived immigrants. Heavily armed teams swept through communities, spreading fear and raising concerns about racial profiling and due process. In Georgia, a raid at a Hyundai plant detained hundreds of Korean workers, many with valid visas, showing how aggressive, quota-driven enforcement could trap lawful residents and strain foreign relations.

Conditions after arrest were equally revealing. Reports from ICE facilities described overcrowding, deprivation, and abuse, including for children. The reopening of Angola prison's infamous Camp J as an ICE detention center—renamed Camp 57—blurred the line between criminal punishment and civil immigration detention. A unit known for harsh treatment in the criminal justice system was repurposed for those held on administrative grounds. The message was that immigration status, not conviction, could now land someone in some of the nation's harshest confinement.

Legal definitions shifted to bolster this stance. ICE and DHS announced that assaulting officers would be prosecuted as a federal felony under expanded standards, with "threats" now including acts like filming operations. A memo circulated by DHS and the FBI suggested that certain emojis might indicate affiliation with a South American gang, inviting surveillance and deportation based on flimsy digital signals. Simultaneously, the administration revoked visas for immigrants who posted online celebrating Charlie Kirk's death, directly tying legal status to political expression.

Courts provided limited checks. Federal judges upheld Temporary Protected Status for Venezuelans, blocked deportation of

Guatemalan minors, and ordered improved detention conditions in some facilities. A federal stay delayed the deportation of a pro-Palestinian activist whose removal order raised free speech concerns. Yet other rulings went the opposite way. An appeals court ordered the deportation of Mario Guevara, an Atlanta journalist known for immigration reporting, despite his prior bond and path to residency. Another judge's order against activist Mahmoud Khalil proceeded until higher courts intervened. The pattern was inconsistent: some vulnerable individuals received protection, others lost it, and the overall system leaned toward fear.

Additionally, the administration altered the terms of belonging through financial means. A presidential proclamation introduced a $100,000 annual fee for each H-1B visa, aiming to reshape skilled immigration and tech labor markets while testing the limits of executive fee-setting authority. Another executive order established a "Gold Card" visa available for $1–2 million, creating a pathway where residency could be purchased outright. In the U.S., Texas passed a law restricting real estate purchases by many Chinese, Iranian, Russian, and North Korean nationals. Alongside the end of ICE's "sensitive locations" policy for hospitals and schools, these actions deepened a tiered system in which wealth, nationality, and ideology determined not just opportunity but fundamental security.

The killing of Charlie Kirk, a controversial activist, became the emotional and symbolic focal point of the week's politics. After Utah authorities arrested a suspect and filed charges, the president ordered US flags lowered to half-mast and awarded Kirk a posthumous Medal of Freedom. The House passed a resolution honoring him and condemning political violence. These gestures elevated Kirk from a partisan figure to a national martyr, blurring the line between state remembrance and factional celebration.

Alongside these symbols, financial and forceful measures were introduced. The administration requested tens of millions in new security funding for top executive and judicial officials, and House Republicans included an $88 million increase for elite protection in a stopgap spending bill. DHS and ICE used Kirk's killing as a recruitment tool at a nearby career expo, emphasizing law enforcement careers in explicitly partisan terms. The tragedy thus justified both expanded security budgets and a narrative of embattled leadership under threat.

Rhetoric followed this same trajectory. The president and his allies intensified claims that Democrats and left-wing activists were responsible for political violence. Stephen Miller warned that law enforcement powers would be used against opponents labeled "domestic terrorists." Visa revocations targeted immigrants expressing joy at Kirk's death. Attorney General Pam Bondi told employers they had an obligation to fire workers who disparaged Kirk, turning private employment decisions into tools of political discipline. Vice President JD Vance appeared on Kirk's own podcast to spread unfounded claims about far-left violence, reinforcing a story in which criticism of a regime-aligned figure bordered on treason.

This atmosphere directly influenced media and cultural conflicts. The president threatened ABC correspondent Jonathan Karl with potential DOJ actions after tough questioning. Jimmy Kimmel's late-night show was suspended following remarks about Kirk's killing, after FCC Chair Brendan Carr signaled regulatory pressure. Nexstar, seeking approval for a major merger, aligned the cancellation with its business interests, while Sinclair and Nexstar affiliates replaced Kimmel's slot with a Charlie Kirk tribute. Commentators and advocacy groups characterized Disney's decision to pull Kimmel as corporate censorship driven by political pressure. The result was a broadcast landscape where satire critical of the president was replaced by programming that celebrated his ally.

Behind these headline fights, the machinery of law enforcement and justice was being reshaped. The administration and Attorney General Bondi considered using RICO statutes against protesters, including pro-Palestinian demonstrators, treating collective dissent as potential organized crime. In a separate case, they used civil rights law to justify a criminal investigation of an Office Depot employee who refused to print Kirk posters, turning protections meant for marginalized groups into tools against individual conscience. Inside the Justice Department and FBI, personnel and priorities shifted. The president pressured prosecutors to pursue mortgage fraud charges against New York Attorney General Letitia James, a political adversary, and attempted to fire US Attorney Erik Siebert when the evidence did not support the case. FBI leadership reassigned about 20 percent of agents, including domestic terrorism squads, to immigration enforcement, reducing their capacity to monitor violent extremism while increasing surveillance of immigrants. A lawsuit and criticism over the handling of the Kirk shooting investigation claimed that loyalty to Trump, not investigative competence, guided decisions.

Other watchdogs faced similar pressure. The Labor Department issued a memo threatening legal consequences for employees who spoke to the media about working conditions, chilling whistleblowing in a key regulatory agency. At the same time, the FBI director admitted not fully reviewing the Epstein files and declined to confirm whether the president appeared in them, fueling concerns about selective transparency involving powerful figures. These actions signaled that speaking out from within the system carried rising risk, while inquiries into elite wrongdoing could be slowed or steered.

Courts and Congress did not stay idle. The House and Senate Judiciary Committees scheduled and held oversight hearings with FBI Director Kash Patel, questioning him about the reassignment of agents and politicization of resources. A Fulton County judge dismissed broad RICO charges against "Cop City" protesters for lack of proper authority, limiting the use of organized-crime tools against demonstrators. Federal courts blocked the president's attempt to dismiss Federal Reserve Governor Lisa Cook, preserving central bank independence, and rejected his $15 billion defamation suit against the New York Times, denying an effort to weaponize libel law against a major newspaper. A federal judge ordered Rudy

Giuliani to pay over $1.3 million in legal fees related to his efforts to overturn the election, imposing tangible costs for attempts to subvert the 2020 result. Yet, other judicial decisions either enabled or left open ways for executive power to expand. The Supreme Court agreed to hear arguments on the legality of the president's global tariffs, a case that would determine how far emergency economic powers can extend without explicit congressional approval. Courts issued mixed rulings on immigrant protections and detention conditions, as noted earlier. The overall effect was a legal landscape in which some boundaries remained firm, while others were contested or quietly expanded.

If law and security were being bent, the information environment was being curated. The Kimmel affair was only one front. FCC Chair Carr launched investigations into NPR, PBS, and other media companies, tying merger approvals to their diversity and inclusion stances. House Democrats responded with oversight: opening inquiries into FCC and White House contacts with media executives, calling for Carr's resignation, and attempting—unsuccessfully—to subpoena him over Kimmel-related threats. These efforts showed that legislative concern about regulatory intimidation was real, but also how difficult it was to compel cooperation from entrenched appointees.

At the same time, the Department of Justice removed from its website a study showing far-right groups as the leading source of ideological homicides, obscuring evidence central to domestic terrorism policy. The Pentagon halted the release of key atmospheric and oceanic data to scientists and forecasters, citing cybersecurity, thereby concentrating environmental information inside the defense establishment. The administration ordered the removal of slavery-related exhibits and signs from national parks, directly editing the historical record presented to millions of visitors. Each action changed what the public could see and understand about violence, climate, and the nation's past.

Universities and schools felt similar pressure. At Texas A&M, a student complaint about "gender ideology" in the classroom led to the firing of faculty, cascading leadership resignations, and ultimately the president's departure. The episode revealed how political and ideological complaints could reshape university governance and chill academic freedom. The Education Department partnered with conservative groups to provide programming on patriotism and liberty, aligning official civic education with specific ideological organizations. Along with the park exhibit removals, these actions weakened critical civic education and replaced it with narratives more favorable to the regime.

Science and public health governance were not spared. Robert F. Kennedy Jr., serving as HHS Secretary, purged the CDC's Advisory Committee on Immunization Practices and reconstituted it with vaccine skeptics, politicizing a body whose value depended on scientific independence. The administration canceled a major Moderna bird flu vaccine contract and fired CDC Director Susan Monarez after clashes over vaccine policy, weakening institutional capacity during ongoing infectious disease risks. A presidential executive order on "restoring gold standard science" increased White House control over research grants, with a focus on diversity programs, centralizing funding decisions.

These top-down changes influenced policy. Florida's executive branch ended childhood vaccine mandates for diseases like measles and polio without normal legislative or scientific review, shifting risk onto children and communities. Under its new composition, ACIP reversed a prior vote to maintain Vaccines for Children coverage of the combined MMRV shot, risking reduced access for low-income families, and voted against a prescription requirement for Covid vaccines while emphasizing individualized decision-making, adding ambiguity and hurdles. Former CDC Director Monarez and Senator Doug Jones testified to Congress about these shifts, warning that political interference threatened evidence-based health decisions. In response, a coalition of West Coast states issued independent vaccine guidelines, trying to preserve science-based public health information at the state level.

Economic and environmental policies increasingly favored elite and corporate interests. The Labor Department announced nearly 150 deregulation initiatives, including ending wage and overtime protections for millions of domestic care workers—a workforce mainly made up of women and immigrants. Congress and the president passed a domestic spending bill that cut over $1 trillion from Medicaid and CHIP, shifting healthcare costs onto states and low-income families. Internationally, the administration reduced grants by $500 million to fight child and forced labor, diminishing US support for vulnerable workers abroad. These decisions weakened worker protections and the social safety net both at home and internationally.

Simultaneously, the administration approved a deal granting the United Arab Emirates access to advanced AI chips while investing $2 billion in a crypto firm linked to Trump, raising serious conflict-of-interest concerns. The EPA moved to rescind the greenhouse-gas endangerment finding and decreased its research activities, undermining the scientific basis for federal climate policies. The Justice Department aimed to invalidate Vermont's Climate Superfund Act, which sought to hold big polluters accountable for climate damage, and Republican legislators pushed defense bill provisions that delayed PFAS foam bans and reduced cleanup funding. Although some routine environmental and consumer-protection activities continued at agencies like EPA, FDA, and FCC, the overall strategic focus at the top favored deregulation and industry interests.

The human context for these policies was one of growing pressure. Americans faced the fastest decline in average credit scores since the Great Recession, driven by increasing costs and the resumption of student loan payments. The administration considered emergency assistance for farmers affected by climate change and tariffs, recognizing economic harm but reserving judgment on who would receive help. The FCC introduced new rate and reporting regulations for communications involving incarcerated individuals, modestly reducing exploitative prison phone charges, but such measures were exceptions amid a broader trend of shifting risk downward and profits upward.

Finally, the presidency continued to push the limits of formal authority. An executive order further delayed enforcement of a congressionally mandated TikTok ban, despite a Supreme Court decision, indicating that negative court rulings could be delayed when politically inconvenient. The attempt to remove Fed Governor Lisa Cook over disputed mortgage allegations challenged the independence of the central bank. A unilateral missile strike on a Venezuelan vessel in international waters, justified as anti–drug trafficking, bypassed congressional approval and expanded executive war powers. An emergency board intervened in a Long Island Rail Road labor dispute, shaping bargaining conditions under the cover of an investigation.

Symbolic and institutional glory marked these actions. The president announced plans for a new $200 million White House ballroom, directing public funds toward ceremonial space. He publicly suggested that TV networks could be punished or lose licenses for negative coverage, linking regulatory power to personal grievances. Budget brinkmanship over a seven-week continuing resolution, combined with Senate rejection of the House bill over healthcare cuts, raised the risk of a shutdown and highlighted how social programs had become bargaining chips. The Federal Election Commission quietly canceled two public meetings scheduled for November, slightly reducing transparency around election regulation.

Against this backdrop, elections and voting rules were reshaped under partisan pressure. Missouri approved a mid-decade congressional gerrymander designed to flip a Democratic seat, manipulating representation outside the normal redistricting cycle. The Justice Department sued Oregon and Maine over access to voter registration lists and ineligible voter information, raising concerns that federal litigation over "integrity" could be used to weaken state-run systems. In North Carolina, a bill criticized as rigging elections advanced through the House, adding to worries about structural barriers to fair representation. Throughout, the president repeated the false claim that he had won the 2020 election, keeping denialism alive as a background justification for these changes.

However, signs of resilience persisted. A House effort to censure Representative Ilhan Omar on disputed grounds narrowly failed, keeping her committee roles intact and signaling some resistance to using internal discipline as a weapon. Voters in Minnesota elected Democrat Xp Lee in a special election to fill the seat of slain state representative Melissa Hortman, restoring partisan balance and condemning violence as a way to gain power. Abroad, Brazil's Supreme Court convicted former President Jair Bolsonaro of plotting a coup and sentenced him to prison, offering an international contrast in holding those who try to overturn elections accountable. In Congress, lawmakers proposed legislation to remove broad passport-revocation powers and to protect anti-government speech from censorship, seeking legal defenses against executive overreach.

The week ended without any major breakthrough, but it reinforced existing trends: militarized domestic security, using immigration as a tool of stratified citizenship, laws favoring enemies and allies, media and memory curated by those in power, science subordinated to ideology, and economic policy tilted toward those closest to the regime. Courts, states, and civil society continued their resistance, sometimes successfully. But each act of resistance now faced a more centralized, more confident executive willing to test boundaries and accept only those limits it could not yet evade. The passage of time captured this imbalance: a small numerical shift and a deeper sense that the foundation of democratic life remains fragile.

CHAPTER 46

WEEK 36: LAW, HUNGER, AND SILENCE AS LEVERAGE

With the clock frozen, the administration deepened its use of law, security, and data to punish critics, coerce states, and narrow who counts as fully protected.

The thirty-sixth week of Trump's second term did not hinge on a single shock. It unfolded as a dense layering of moves that, taken together, made the state feel less like a common instrument and more like a weapon in partisan hands. The pattern was not new, but the confidence with which it was applied across law enforcement, information, and economic power gave the week its character. It was a week in which the tools of democracy were used to narrow who counted as a full participant in it.

At the end of Week 35, the Democracy Clock was set at 8:08 p.m. It stayed at the same time through Week 36, with no net change in minutes. The stillness in the measure didn't mean calm. It reflected a balance between increasing authoritarian tactics and pockets of institutional resistance. Courts blocked some grant conditions and defamation claims. States and civil society pushed for more transparency and oversight. But the core pattern continued: executive power was used to turn dissent into a threat, to skew justice in favor of allies and against critics, and to make access to protection and truth dependent on loyalty.

The most significant changes this week impacted the Justice Department. On paper, the department's mission stayed the same. But in practice, its capacity and priorities were reshaped. House Judiciary Democrats found that DOJ's Public Integrity Section, once staffed with thirty-six attorneys, had been reduced to just two. This quiet erosion mattered. It meant fewer lawyers to investigate bribery, conflicts of interest, and abuses of office. Even when evidence emerged, there were fewer people to push cases forward.

The Tom Homan bribery case showed what that meant concretely. Homan, Trump's border czar, was recorded accepting $50,000 from undercover agents. Yet DOJ leadership closed the investigation and publicly denied he had taken a bribe. Congressional Democrats launched oversight inquiries, demanding documents and explanations. A watchdog group filed a FOIA request for the tapes themselves. On the surface, the system still had channels for challenge. But the decision to shut the case down, despite recorded evidence, sent a clear message about who would and would not face corruption charges.

Meanwhile, the department acted aggressively against figures who had crossed Trump. Former FBI Director James Comey was indicted on charges of lying to Congress and obstruction, after an earlier office had declined to bring the case. The indictment came only after an acting U.S. attorney, who resisted the prosecution, was replaced by Lindsey Halligan, a Trump lawyer with no prosecutorial background. As the statute of limitations approached, Halligan's office hurried to file charges. Venue and personnel had been adjusted until the desired outcome seemed achieved.

Former CIA Director John Brennan faced a similar situation. DOJ opened a criminal investigation into his role in the 2016 Russia interference assessments, continuing a pattern of targeting intelligence officials who scrutinized Trump's campaign. Representative Dan Goldman warned that DOJ probes were being influenced by presidential demands. The pattern involved uneven enforcement—

some allies, like Homan, were protected, while critics, like Comey and Brennan, were pursued aggressively. Around these high-profile cases, Congress's handling of the Jeffrey Epstein files illustrated how scrutiny of elite networks could be limited. House Judiciary Committee Republicans voted against issuing subpoenas to major bank CEOs over Epstein-linked transactions. House Oversight leaders delayed releasing related records and blocked a floor vote on broader disclosures. FBI Director Kash Patel refused to answer questions about his own appearance in Epstein documents. Some Epstein schedules and files did reach the Oversight Committee, naming high-profile visitors and donors, but overall, the approach was slow and cautious.

There were counter-movements. A federal judge dismissed Trump's $15 billion defamation lawsuit against the New York Times, criticizing its inflammatory rhetoric and reaffirming limits on using civil courts to punish critical media. Other courts halted more than 100 administrative policies across 400 lawsuits, reinstating civil servants and restoring CDC funding. These rulings showed that parts of the judiciary still served as a check. However, the Supreme Court moved in the opposite direction on major issues of executive power, granting stays that allowed Trump to keep a removed FTC commissioner out of office and to pause congressionally allocated foreign aid. The overall effect was to weaken impartial enforcement of corruption laws while increasing presidential influence over regulators and spending. If the justice system was being manipulated, the security apparatus was being redirected as well. Trump signed executive orders designating Antifa as a domestic terrorist organization. The orders did not specify a single group but instead labeled a broad, diffuse movement.

That vagueness was intentional—it provided a framework to treat a wide range of protests and left-leaning activism as terrorism. Days later, a presidential memorandum directed investigations of domestic terrorism focusing on left-wing groups and nonprofits, framing them as part of a "terror network." Congress, meanwhile, approved a massive $170 billion allocation to ICE over four years to support deportations, aiming to remove one million immigrants annually. This funding reinforced a high-capacity enforcement machine. Data showed ICE was now detaining more immigrants without criminal records than those with convictions. A disabled detainee filed a habeas petition challenging prolonged detention and inadequate medical care. Nineteen detainees at Louisiana's Angola prison launched a hunger strike over brutal conditions, lack of services, and medical neglect. Their protest drew attention to the use of a former maximum-security prison as an immigration detention site.

The human toll of this system appeared through individual stories. ICE detained Des Moines school superintendent Ian Roberts on an outdated removal order, disrupting local education leadership and sending a message about how far immigration enforcement could reach into civic life. In New York, an ICE officer pushed a detainee's wife to the ground at immigration court; the incident was caught on video and led to the officer's removal. Farmworker activist Alfredo Juarez Zeferino was held under such harsh conditions that he ultimately chose voluntary departure. California officials launched an investigation into the death of a Mexican man in ICE custody, while a Los Angeles car wash owner filed a $50 million lawsuit over an ICE raid.

The security approach extended beyond immigration enforcement into protest policing. Police in Michigan and Los Angeles used teargas and other crowd-control chemicals on demonstrators, with reports of long-term reproductive health effects. Protesters at a small pro-Palestinian demonstration outside Benjamin Netanyahu's New York hotel were arrested, as security perimeters around diplomatic events narrowed the space for expression. Portland officials issued a notice of violation to an ICE detention facility for exceeding permit limits, an example of local government trying to control federal operations on its soil. But the larger pattern was clear: extraordinary powers justified in the name of terrorism and border security were being used to suppress dissent and make certain communities feel permanently at risk.

Federal authority also turned inward, against states, school districts, and voters. The Agriculture Department froze over $10 million in food assistance for Kansas because the governor refused to share beneficiary data, using hunger relief as leverage in a federal–state dispute. DHS withheld $65 million in grants from magnet schools over their trans-inclusive policies, punishing districts financially for maintaining protections for transgender and nonbinary students. These were not abstract conflicts; they impacted whether low-income families could buy food and whether schools could sustain programs.

Simultaneously, Trump ordered the Justice Department to sue multiple states over detailed voter rolls and personal information. DOJ filed lawsuits against six states, demanding extensive voter data under the guise of election oversight. The lawsuits increased federal involvement in election administration and raised fears that personal information could be misused for partisan motives. The president publicly justified these efforts as necessary for "integrity," even as they threatened to deter participation and intimidate local officials.

Shutdown brinkmanship became another tool of coercion. Trump canceled meetings with Democratic leaders on government funding as a shutdown loomed. His budget officials signaled they expected a shutdown and emphasized its impact on Democratic constituencies. The president went further, threatening to fire, rather than furlough, large numbers of federal employees during a funding lapse. OMB directed agencies to prepare for large-scale reductions in force, turning a budget impasse into an opportunity to purge programs and staff misaligned with presidential priorities. The House passed a continuing resolution to fund the government through late November, but the Senate rejected it, and the administration showed little interest in compromise.

Alongside these pressures, the administration moved to darken the data landscape. USDA canceled its annual food insecurity survey and ended its household food security report, erasing a decades-old series that tracked hunger trends. The Bureau of Labor Statistics postponed its consumer expenditures report after Trump fired its commissioner for unfavorable jobs data. The White House dismissed these measures as politicized. The effect was to remove key benchmarks for understanding inflation and hardship, making it harder for Congress, states, and the public to assess the impact of policy choices.

The National Archives illustrated how records themselves could be politicized. On one hand, NARA invited public comment on proposed federal records schedules, maintaining a formal process for deciding what information would be preserved or destroyed. On the other hand, it improperly released Representative Mikie Sherrill's nearly unredacted military records to an ally of her gubernatorial opponent. That release weaponized confidential service records in an election, undermining privacy protections and trust in archival neutrality. State Department staff, meanwhile, warned that ambassadorships were going unfilled and that personnel were being judged on "fidelity," suggesting that even internal data about performance and loyalty were being used to reshape the diplomatic corps.

Information control did not stop at data and records. It extended to the press and entertainment. At the Pentagon, reporters were required to sign pledges not to gather unauthorized information and were subject to new restrictions on their movement within the building. These rules curtailed independent reporting on military affairs and signaled that access could be conditioned on compliance. The Federal Communications Commission threatened ABC affiliates' licenses over Jimmy Kimmel's on-air criticism of Trump, using regulatory power to punish a broadcaster for unfavorable content.

ABC and its parent company, Disney, suspended Kimmel's show amid this pressure, then reinstated it after public backlash. Even after reinstatement, major station groups like Sinclair and Nexstar refused to air the program on their ABC affiliates, filtering political satire out of local airwaves. Trump himself called negative coverage and heckling "really illegal," urged prosecutions, and framed Kimmel's show as an illegal campaign contribution. The combined effect of presidential rhetoric, regulatory threats, and corporate caution narrowed the space for televised criticism.

The administration's approach to truth was on display at the United Nations. From the UN podium, Trump urged nations to close borders and expel foreigners, attacked the UK's green and migration policies with debunked claims, and repeated false narratives about sharia law in London and climate agreements. He portrayed an escalator malfunction at the UN as deliberate sabotage and a security threat, and demanded investigations into alleged efforts to undermine his speech and movements. These episodes turned a diplomatic forum into a stage for disinformation and personalized grievance.

At home, Trump promoted unproven claims linking acetaminophen and vaccines to autism, targeting pregnant women with anti-vaccine and anti-Tylenol rhetoric. These statements, amplified by state-aligned platforms, undercut evidence-based health guidance and deepened reliance on politicized narratives. The administration also introduced a "Presidential Walk of Fame" display that omitted Joe Biden's portrait, replacing it with an autopen image. This symbolic curation of recent history, combined with the misuse of archival records and suppression of inconvenient data, showed how memory itself was being shaped to flatter the incumbent and sideline disfavored figures.

Foreign policy and economic tools were used in similarly personalized ways. Trump ordered lethal strikes on Venezuelan vessels alleged to be drug smugglers without providing evidence to Congress or the public. He threatened Afghanistan with unspecified "bad things" if it did not return Bagram Airbase, using social media to issue warnings that bypassed normal diplomatic channels. He announced the end of military assistance to NATO countries bordering Russia and publicly questioned whether threats to European cities would trigger U.S. defense commitments. These moves weakened alliance assurances and signaled a more transactional approach to collective security.

Sanctions and tariffs became tools of retaliation. The administration imposed a 50 percent tariff on Brazilian goods in response to anger over Jair Bolsonaro's coup conviction and ordered sanctions on the wife of a Brazilian Supreme Court justice involved in that case. These actions politicized trade and human rights tools, punishing a foreign judiciary for domestic accountability. Domestically, Trump announced sweeping tariffs on pharmaceuticals, furniture, cabinets, and trucks, despite previous court limits on his tariff powers. He proposed using tariff revenue to bailout farmers hurt by his own trade policies, centralizing both the infliction of economic pain and the distribution of relief.

Aid and financial support were directed along ideological lines. The State Department moved to redirect $1.8 billion in foreign aid away from long-standing democracy and health programs toward "America First" projects. Treasury prepared a $20 billion support package for Argentina's government, an allied administration, outside normal appropriations processes. FEMA and Homeland Security expedited $11 million in disaster aid for a pier project in Naples, Florida, after a political donor's intervention. These decisions blurred the line between technocratic policy and patronage, making it harder to distinguish governance from reward.

Inside the government, the civil service and military were reshaped to align more closely with presidential preferences. Trump's threats to fire civil servants during a shutdown, combined with OMB's planning for reductions in force, turned job security into a tool of discipline. DNI Tulsi Gabbard revoked thirty-seven security clearances for intelligence officials and congressional staff without notifying the White House, disrupting oversight and demonstrating how access to classified information could be used punitively. At the Pentagon, Defense Secretary Pete Hegseth dissolved the advisory committee on women in the armed services and summoned hundreds of generals and admirals to an unusual mass meeting, signaling an effort to recast military culture through direct political messaging.

Agency missions were scaled back or reversed. HUD leadership reduced Fair Housing Act enforcement and issued gag orders to civil rights staff, weakening the federal ability to fight segregation and discrimination. The Energy Department returned $13 billion in green project funds to the Treasury, reversing climate investments and favoring fossil-fuel industries. Congress's large increase in ICE funding, along with DHS reforms to prioritize higher-paid H-1B visa applicants and Trump's sudden $100,100,000 fee per H-1B worker, shifted immigration and labor policies toward wealthier employers and away from lower-status workers.

Outside Washington, some institutions pushed back. California's governor signed a law banning most law enforcement officers from covering their faces while on duty, aiming to boost transparency and accountability in policing. Renton, Washington prosecutors charged suspects in a violent attack on a trans woman under hate-crime statutes, using existing law to defend a targeted community. Young climate activists filed a human rights petition against the U.S. government over support for fossil fuels, turning to international forums to challenge domestic policies. These actions did not reverse federal trends, but they showed that alternative models of rights enforcement and stewardship still existed.

The week also saw an escalation in how opposition was portrayed. Trump publicly pressured the attorney general to prosecute named political enemies, called negative coverage "really illegal," and signed a memo targeting lawyers who had litigated against his administration for professional discipline. DOJ planned investigations into a Soros-funded group at his urging. In Arizona, state representative John Gillette used social media to call for Representative Pramila Jayapal to be "tried, convicted and hanged" for supporting non-violent protest. That language was not from the fringe alone; it echoed a broader framing in which critics and left-wing activists were portrayed as criminals, traitors, or terrorists.

There were upcoming decision points. The House's short-term funding bill set a new deadline of November 21 for government funding, ensuring that shutdown threats would return. DOJ's voter data lawsuits against six states began progressing through the courts, with hearings and rulings upcoming. The Supreme Court's stays on foreign aid and regulatory appointments indicated that further decisions on executive power over spending and independent agencies were imminent. Each of these processes would test whether the institutional resistance seen this week could hold.

During Trump's second term, Week 36 signified not a jump but a deepening. Emergency rhetoric about terrorism and border security became normalized and extended into domestic politics. Law enforcement and prosecution were increasingly influenced by personal and ideological motives. Economic and foreign policy tools were used to reward allies and punish enemies, both at home and abroad. Information, such as hunger statistics and military records, was curated to support the incumbent's narrative. The clock didn't move forward because the balance between decline and resistance held, but the direction of pressure was evident. Rights and protections still existed, yet calling on them required more courage and came with higher costs. The institutions that might have once contained and corrected abuses were themselves being manipulated, one procedural decision at a time.

CHAPTER 47
WEEK 37: SHUTDOWN AS QUIET PURGE

> *A nearly motionless clock masks a week in which shutdown brinkmanship, militarized enforcement, and deepfakes quietly rewired power, rights, and public memory.*

The week did not unfold with a single shock. It progressed as a series of moves that, collectively, demonstrated a government more willing to leverage every tool—money, law, force, and narrative—to reward loyalty, punish opposition, and reduce the neutral space where democracy usually exists. What shifted was not the formal structure of institutions but the way power moved within them: who remained, who left, who received payment, who was targeted, and whose version of events was accepted. The pattern was consistent, not sudden.

At the end of Week 36, the Democracy Clock stood at 8:08 p.m. By the end of Week 37, it stayed at 8:08 p.m., a slight net change of 0.1 minutes. The public time did not shift, but the underlying dynamics did. The week deepened the use of shutdowns as a weapon, expanded the reach of militarized politics, and reinforced a tiered system of rights and safety. Courts, unions, and some state actors pushed back in certain areas, but their resistance slowed rather than stopped the drift. The apparent calm of the clock concealed an ongoing erosion of restraint, honesty, and accountability.

The most noticeable change occurred within the federal workforce itself. The administration's Deferred Resignation Program, already underway, led to the departure of over 100,000 federal employees within days. These were not typical retirements. Employees were told to resign now or face potential firing later under uncertain conditions. This resulted in a hollowing out of agencies' memory and capacity, especially among those least willing to serve under direct political pressure. What remained was a leaner, more cautious civil service.

At the same time, the White House directed agencies to prepare for significant layoffs connected to the funding lapse. Planning documents described the cuts as a response to budget shortfalls, but the context made clear that the shutdown was also an opportunity. In internal memos, the administration acknowledged that a prolonged closure would cause substantial GDP loss and job reductions, yet the president publicly framed the situation as a chance to make "irreversible" cuts to medical and social programs. The message to public workers and beneficiaries was that their security could be sacrificed in a fiscal standoff. That message resonated.

Unions attempted to draw a line. Federal labor groups sued to block the mass layoffs, arguing that the Deferred Resignation Program and layoff plans violated civil-service protections and collective bargaining rights. Their lawsuits emphasized that the fight was not merely about salaries but also whether the executive could unilaterally reshape the bureaucracy under the cover of a shutdown. Even as these cases progressed, the damage was already done: tens of thousands of experienced staff had left, and those remaining feared that their jobs depended on political loyalty. Fear became a management tool.

The same week, the administration used the budget crisis to redraw the map of federal investment. The Office of Management and Budget canceled nearly $8 billion in climate and clean-energy funding, much of it in Democratic-led states, and froze billions more in infrastructure money for New York City and Chicago. A $2.1 billion transit grant for Chicago was halted under the banner of opposing race-conscious contracting. Tunnel and transit projects in New York were similarly stalled. These decisions were framed as technical reviews or civil rights concerns, but the pattern was clear: jurisdictions that resisted the president's agenda saw their long-term projects put at risk.

Shutdown mechanics also became a tool for obscuring the consequences of these choices. The government allowed the funding lapse to delay the monthly jobs report and other key economic data, depriving the public and markets of timely information about the labor market. An internal White House memo estimated steep economic losses from a prolonged shutdown, yet the administration pressed on. At the same time, a large bailout for Argentina continued uninterrupted, insulated from the domestic freeze. Foreign commitments and politically important farm bailouts moved forward, while climate projects, transit upgrades, and homelessness programs at home were cut or stalled. The priorities were unmistakable.

Oversight and information channels narrowed in parallel. The Federal Election Commission canceled several open meetings while proceeding with a closed one, reducing public visibility into campaign-finance enforcement. The administration withdrew a controversial nominee to lead the Bureau of Labor Statistics after bipartisan concern, averting one overt politicization of economic data, but then used the shutdown itself to halt the flow of statistics. Federal agencies, from Housing to Education, turned their websites and email systems into partisan billboards, inserting blame for the shutdown into automatic out-of-office replies. Voice of America, the government's international broadcaster, was suspended and its journalists furloughed, even after a court had ordered hundreds of them reinstated. The shutdown thus served not only to starve programs and staff, but to reshape who could speak and what the public could see.

If the shutdown was one front, immigration was another. The administration fired more than 100 immigration judges and replaced them with 600 military lawyers, many lacking the usual qualifications for such roles. This was not a marginal adjustment. Immigration courts are where the state decides who may stay, who must leave, and on what terms. By purging experienced judges and importing officers from the military justice system, the White House shifted a key adjudicative arena toward a culture of command and loyalty. The move dovetailed with a broader shift in Justice Department priorities away from drug trafficking and money laundering and toward immigration prosecutions. The system's center of gravity moved.

On the ground, that shift resulted in harsher outcomes for those with the least leverage. Long-standing Southeast Asian refugees with old convictions were deported, despite decades of residence and the United States' own role in the conflicts that brought them here. Dozens of Iranians were removed under a bilateral deal, even as rights groups warned about conditions in the receiving country. The administration moved to end Temporary Protected Status for Venezuelan and Haitian nationals; the Supreme Court granted an emergency stay allowing the policy to proceed while legal challenges continued, exposing thousands to the risk of removal before their claims were fully heard. Protection became more fragile.

Conditions in detention highlighted the human cost of these choices. At the Dilley family facility, run by a private contractor, court filings described poor treatment and prolonged confinement of parents and children. Elsewhere, aggressive raids and warrantless arrests swept up U.S. citizens alongside noncitizens, leading to lawsuits and settlements. A Justice Department rule conditioned victim aid for sexual assault and domestic violence on immediate proof of immigration status, prompting a coalition of twenty states to sue, warning that survivors would be discouraged from seeking help. In each case, immigration enforcement logic seeped into social services and public safety, making access to protection dependent on legal status.

Courts and states pushed back at the margins, but the overall direction favored enforcement. The Justice Department sued Minnesota over its sanctuary policies, challenging local efforts to limit cooperation with federal immigration authorities. A federal court held that immigration stops could be based partly on race so long as citizens were released once they proved their status, weakening equal-protection norms. In the high-profile case of Kilmar Ábrego García, a Salvadoran asylum seeker publicly vilified as a gang member without convictions, immigration courts applied strict filing deadlines to deny reopening his claim, while other federal judges, in separate cases, ruled that deporting pro-Palestinian scholars for their speech violated the First Amendment. The result was a patchwork: some rulings defended speech and process, but the system as a whole tilted toward speed, suspicion, and removal.

Alongside these legal shifts, the president and his team reshaped domestic politics in the language of war. In a speech at Quantico, Trump urged the use of combat troops in U.S. cities to confront what he called an "invasion from within," and warned generals that they could be dismissed if they did not comply with his directives. He then ordered Defense Secretary Pete Hegseth to deploy federal troops to Portland over state and local objections, treating protest and crime in a single city as a national security problem. The administration declared an armed conflict with drug cartels and labeled them terrorist organizations, expanding war powers into what had long been a law enforcement domain.

Abroad, the president announced plans for military strikes against alleged traffickers in Venezuela, again without clear congressional approval. At home, he signed an executive order labeling Antifa—a loosely defined protest movement—as a major terrorist organization. He also ordered wide-ranging investigations of activists and nonprofits linked to domestic terrorism. These actions blurred the line between external enemies and internal opponents. Tools designed for foreign conflict—terrorist designations, war rhetoric, and the promise of combat troops—were used domestically against cities, protesters, and civil society groups.

Chicago exemplified how this war framing played out locally. Under Operation Midway Blitz, heavily armed ICE teams executed a large-scale immigration raid in a neighborhood. A multi-agency nighttime raid on an apartment complex left residents, including children, restrained outside for hours. When protesters tried to block government vehicles and oppose the raids, federal agents used tear gas and pepper balls to disperse them. The tactics resembled counterinsurgency more than routine law enforcement. The city felt occupied rather than served.

Economic pressure accompanied the show of force. That same week, the administration froze $2.1 billion in transit funding for Chicago, citing concerns over race-based contracting. The freeze threatened long-planned upgrades to the city's transit system and sent a message: resistance to federal priorities could come at a cost in safety and infrastructure. The deportation of Mario Guevara, a long-time resident and journalist arrested while reporting on protests and later deported to El Salvador after charges were dismissed, added another layer. It signaled that documenting these operations could itself become grounds for expulsion.

Chicago was not alone. The Justice Department's FACE Act lawsuit against pro-Palestinian activists who disrupted a synagogue event, and the aggressive prosecution of pregnancy-related offenses across states, demonstrated how laws originally meant to protect access and safety could be repurposed to punish certain protests and behaviors. Along with the Ábrego García case and the deportations of refugees and Iranians, these actions turned immigration and protest spaces into testing grounds for a harsher, more politicized form of governance. The experiments were already underway.

Within the legal system, the week's pattern was one of selective pressure and uneven resistance. The firing of acting U.S. attorney

Michele Beckwith after she insisted that Border Patrol agents obey a court order sent a clear message: prosecutors enforcing judicial rulings against executive preferences could lose their jobs. The New York City Bar Association's public criticism of the indictment of former FBI Director James Comey as politically motivated underscored broader concern that prosecutorial power was being used for personal scores. Simultaneously, the administration pursued a FACE Act case against synagogue protesters and oversaw a surge in pregnancy-related criminal prosecutions, including homicide charges, following Roe v. Wade's reversal. Laws meant to safeguard clinics and lives were being used to criminalize dissent and women's actions.

Courts did not simply give in. A federal judge ruled that Trump's acting U.S. attorney in Nevada was not validly in office, enforcing statutory limits on temporary appointments. Other courts blocked the administration's attempt to redirect FEMA disaster funds away from twelve Democratic states, sharply criticizing its legal reasoning and reinforcing that emergency funds could not be weaponized for political purposes. The Supreme Court temporarily allowed Federal Reserve Governor Lisa Cook to stay in her position while reviewing Trump's effort to remove her, protecting central bank independence for now. The Federal Trade Commission unanimously filed an antitrust lawsuit against Zillow and Redfin over an advertising deal, indicating that some competition enforcement continued.

Yet these acts of resistance existed alongside rulings that expanded executive power and restricted rights. The Supreme Court's emergency stay on TPS terminations favored the administration's schedule over protecting vulnerable communities. A federal court's acceptance of racial profiling during immigration stops—so long as individuals could later secure release—normalized discriminatory enforcement. The Justice Department declined to release additional Epstein investigation files even as House Democrats published new estate documents, keeping key aspects of elite misconduct hidden. Defense Secretary Hegseth announced a review of the Pentagon Inspector General's office and records policies while under scrutiny, fueling fears that internal watchdogs were being reshaped to limit oversight. The acting inspector general of the National Archives began an investigation into the release of Representative Mikie Sherrill's largely unredacted military records, examining whether archives were being used as tools against political opponents.

Alongside these institutional actions flowed a steady stream of manipulated information. The president posted, then deleted, an AI-generated message claiming fictional "medbed" hospitals for all Americans, blurring the lines between official policy and conspiracy theories. He spread false claims that hundreds of FBI agents had incited violence on January 6, contradicting established investigations and undermining accountability for the Capitol attack. Unverified medical advice about Tylenol and vaccination schedules was shared, and the White House communications office issued a misleading press release misrepresenting studies to claim that Tylenol use during pregnancy causes autism. These messages did more than just mislead; they emanated from the highest levels of government, making it harder for the public to discern trustworthy guidance.

The White House also embraced synthetic media as a political tool. Racist AI-generated deepfake videos depicting Senate Majority Leader Chuck Schumer and House Minority Leader Hakeem Jeffries making fabricated statements circulated and were shown in official spaces. Other AI-created content was incorporated into narratives about healthcare and immigration. Meanwhile, agencies used their channels to assign blame for the shutdown along partisan lines. HUD, the VA, Education, and other agencies sent emails and posted notices that blamed Democrats. Education officials even altered automatic replies from furloughed employees to include political messaging, effectively turning civil servants' personal communications into part of a coordinated propaganda effort.

Independent and critical voices faced new restrictions. Voice of America's broadcasts were suspended during the shutdown, shortly after a court reinstated hundreds of its employees, implying that funding tools could be used to bypass judicial protections for journalism. Apple removed ICE-tracking apps from its store after administration pressure, limiting digital tools used by communities to monitor enforcement. A class action lawsuit challenged the administration's collection of personal data across federal agencies, alleging privacy and voting rights violations and raising concerns that centralized information systems could be exploited for surveillance or electoral interference. Within the Department of Energy, leaders instructed staff to avoid terms like "climate change" and "decarbonization," restricting the language experts could use to describe their work and, by extension, what the public could hear.

Taken together, the week's developments showed a government leaning more heavily on chaos as a method. Shutdown brinkmanship, mass resignations, troop deployments, foreign strikes, deepfakes, and archival diversions unfolded at once, creating overlapping crises and distractions. Each move could be defended in isolation as a response to budget constraints, crime, foreign threats, or campus conflict. In sequence, they made it harder for any single abuse to hold public attention long enough to be checked. Oversight bodies were not abolished, but they were strained, bypassed, or repurposed. Rights were not formally repealed, but their exercise became more costly and uneven.

The Democracy Clock's near-stillness in Week 37 reflects this paradox. On the surface, there was no single constitutional rupture. Elections still loomed, courts still issued rulings, and Congress still met. Yet the moral floor continued to sink. Character gave way to loyalty tests; ethics blurred as public resources and private interests intertwined; restraint eroded under the pressure of war rhetoric and shutdown leverage; truthfulness faltered amid deepfakes and pseudoscience; good faith receded as procedures were bent to defeat their own purpose; stewardship suffered as watchdogs were weakened and the civil service was thinned. The week did not close a chapter. It deepened a pattern in which power advanced quietly, through the very systems meant to contain it.

CHAPTER 48
WEEK 38: SHUTDOWN AS WEAPONRY

In a week of near-still clock hands, immigration crackdowns, shutdown tactics, and politicized prosecutions quietly tightened executive power and thinned democratic constraint.

The thirty-eighth week of Trump's second term unfolded amid pressures from multiple directions. Immigration raids, shutdown tactics, prosecutions, and propaganda arrived not as a single shock but as concurrent streams, each presented as part of routine governance, each shifting the balance of power and its use. While this pattern was not new, it was now more confidently displayed: law inclined toward loyalty, force encroached into civil spheres, and the cost of resistance increased further.

At the end of Week 37, the Democracy Clock showed 8:08 p.m. It remained at the same time after Week 38, with only a tenth of a minute's movement. The hands did not leap, but they did not stay still. This slight change indicated the deepening of ongoing trends rather than a sudden rupture: executive power extended further, law enforcement grew more partisan, and oversight became thinner, even as governors, judges, and civil society pushed back in visible yet limited ways. The clock held because pockets of resistance persisted within the system, but the overall trajectory was toward concentrated power and diminishing checks. The most vivid scenes emerged from Chicago and Portland, where immigration enforcement was used as a pretext for domestic displays of force. In Chicago, federal agents deployed tear gas, pepper balls, and aggressive tactics against protesters and journalists at immigration demonstrations, blurring the line between crowd control and battlefield conduct. Reports surfaced that agents made false 911 calls and that a woman, Marimar Martinez, was shot during an operation, raising fundamental questions about honesty and proportionality in federal policing.

These issues were not isolated mistakes but part of a broader decision to treat dissent and migration as security threats warranting militarized responses. In this context, the White House ordered 300 Illinois National Guard troops into Chicago to support immigration enforcement, while Texas Governor Greg Abbott sent his Guard units into Illinois and Oregon at federal request. What had once been state-controlled forces, used sparingly for disasters or emergencies, now served as tools in a federal campaign focused on Democratic-led cities. These deployments turned urban neighborhoods into testing grounds for how far the president could extend military presence into civil spaces despite local opposition. Courts and governors did not accept this quietly. In Oregon, U.S. District Judge Karin Immergut issued orders blocking the federalization and deployment of National Guard troops to Portland, reaffirming that the president's authority over state forces had limits. California's governor and Oregon officials sued to prevent California Guard units from being sent into Portland, leading to a court compromise: federalization of the Oregon Guard could proceed, but they could not be deployed into Portland itself. In Chicago, Judge April Perry's rulings on Guard deployments evolved over the week, reflecting active judicial scrutiny of federal claims that unrest was a "rebellion," while still allowing some room for executive action.

On the ground, local officials tried to reclaim space for civil life.

Chicago's mayor signed executive orders barring ICE from using city-owned property for operations, asserting municipal authority to shield residents from federal raids. Protesters organized a large, peaceful march that shut down Michigan Avenue, showing that mass assembly was still possible even under heavy federal presence. Journalists and unions filed lawsuits over the use of extreme force at protests, and Judge Sara Ellis issued a preliminary injunction in northern Illinois limiting federal agents' use of crowd-control weapons and requiring them to identify themselves, a direct judicial check on anonymous, militarized policing.

Yet even as these constraints were asserted, the enforcement machine kept running while its internal brakes were loosened. DHS maintained most ICE operations fully staffed during the shutdown but furloughed the Office of Detention Oversight, prioritizing coercion over inspection. The controversial Alligator Alcatraz detention facility in Florida remained open despite due process concerns and limited access to counsel, with appeals judges allowing operations to continue while litigation over attorney access played out. FEMA's decision to reimburse Florida more than $600 million for that complex effectively federalized its financial base, making it harder to argue that the facility lay outside federal responsibility. Governors from Illinois and California urged their peers to oppose federal troop deployments and even threatened to leave the National Governors Association, while a Republican governor in Oklahoma publicly criticized Texas's decision to send Guard troops into Illinois. The resistance was real, but the structure of enforcement—troops on the streets, detention centers funded, oversight furloughed—remained largely intact.

Beyond the city streets, senior officials worked to expand the legal framework for using force, both domestically and internationally. The Department of Justice issued a memo treating suspected drug-trafficking boats as part of an armed conflict, effectively recasting traffickers as enemy combatants. On that basis, Defense Secretary Pete Hegseth ordered a strike on a boat off Venezuela, stretching the legal justification for lethal action without fresh congressional approval. Reports that a separate strike mistakenly hit a Colombian vessel underscored the risks of highly personalized command over force: a misidentification at the top could trigger an international incident with little transparency about how the decision had been made.

The legal profession took note. The New York City Bar Association condemned the Venezuelan boat strikes as illegal summary executions and urged Congress to reassert its war powers. Their statement did not halt operations, but it documented a professional judgment that the executive was going beyond legal bounds. Inside the White House, aides led by Stephen Miller discussed invoking the Insurrection Act to send troops into U.S. cities, and Miller publicly claimed that the president held plenary authority to deploy the military against domestic unrest. These assertions did not yet produce a formal Insurrection Act order, but they normalized the idea that protest and disorder could be treated as war, with the president as sole decider.

Congress had an opportunity to limit this authority and chose not to. The Senate voted against a measure that would have required presidents to seek congressional approval before using deadly force against drug cartels, preserving broad unilateral discretion for targeted killings. At the same time, the president hosted a roundtable on criminalizing flag burning, a form of speech long recognized as protected, and issued an ultimatum to Hamas to accept his Gaza peace plan by a fixed deadline. He also announced a large currency swap framework with Argentina shortly before its midterm elections. Each move tied security or economic tools to personal timelines and narratives, reinforcing a pattern in which the presidency, rather than institutions, set the terms for war, peace, and leverage.

If force was stretched at the edges, law at home was bent at the center. The Justice Department under Attorney General Pam Bondi faced sharp questioning in Senate hearings over dismantled integrity units and politicized prosecutions. Senators pressed Bondi on why the Public Integrity Section had been stripped of staff and authority, why corruption probes had been dropped, and how her work for Qatar as a foreign agent intersected with decisions that favored Trump's interests. Meanwhile, 282 former DOJ officials issued a public letter warning that the department's integrity was being eroded by court violations, targeted prosecutions, and the weakening of anti-corruption efforts.

Concrete examples demonstrated what this meant in practice. DOJ closed an investigation into border czar Tom Homan despite an undercover recording allegedly capturing a bribe offer related to immigration enforcement contracts. Democracy Forward had to sue the FBI and DOJ under FOIA to get records about the case, yet agencies continued resisting disclosure. Conversely, U.S. Attorney Lindsey Halligan secured indictments of former FBI Director James Comey and New York Attorney General Letitia James, both well-known critics of Trump, after career prosecutors had initially found no grounds for charges or chose not to proceed. The sequence—Durham's earlier conclusion that Comey should not be charged, followed by a new indictment under different leadership—highlighted how prosecutorial decisions could shift based on politics rather than evidence.

Within the FBI, leadership fired or reassigned agents involved in Trump-related investigations, signaling that certain inquiries posed career risks. The Civil Rights Division pressured Portland authorities over charges against conservative influencer Nick Sortor, with federal officials threatening to investigate local police for anti-conservative bias; those charges were subsequently dropped. Simultaneously, the White House ordered a crackdown on supposed "leftwing terrorism" targeting major Democratic donors and liberal groups, while DOJ planned a multi-agency probe into the finances of liberal organizations. Donors like George Soros and Reid Hoffman were portrayed as potential terror financiers, blurring the line between political donations and violent extremism.

Secrecy and selective transparency reinforced this weaponization. DOJ and the FBI released curated records from Special

Counsel Jack Smith's earlier investigation into Trump, including subpoenas of Republican senators' phone data, in ways that fed partisan narratives while leaving the broader evidentiary record unclear. Agencies failed to comply with FOIA requests about Homan's alleged bribery, leading to litigation. In the separate Epstein files saga, Attorney General Bondi and FBI leaders withheld client records, supposedly ordered agents to flag references to Trump, and Congress blocked votes on the Epstein Files Transparency Act. House leaders kept the chamber in recess and delayed seating Representative-elect Adelita Grijalva, partly to avoid a transparency vote. The outcome was a system where elite-linked cases were shielded from scrutiny, while law enforcement tools were used against opponents.

The government shutdown became another tool in this power restructuring. The Office of Management and Budget, under Russ Vought, canceled energy and transportation projects in Democratic-led areas during the funding lapse and announced plans to use the shutdown to impose large cuts on infrastructure and climate initiatives linked to political opponents. The president openly framed the shutdown as an opportunity to cut "Democratic programs," making clear that control over federal operations was being used to punish disliked constituencies rather than to manage a neutral budget.

At the same time, OMB reinterpreted statutory back-pay protections for furloughed federal workers. Guidance memos cast doubt on whether all furloughed employees would receive back pay, and the administration quietly revised public guidance to narrow guarantees. The president raised the idea that not all furloughed workers should be made whole, signaling a willingness to leverage livelihoods. For rank-and-file employees, this turned a legal right into a political issue. For the executive, it created a new tool: the ability to reward or punish parts of the civil service based on how shutdown pain was distributed.

Congress, which could have countered this, instead acted theatrically. The House and Senate repeatedly failed to pass funding bills, prolonging the shutdown's impact on airports, national parks, and basic services. House Speaker Mike Johnson kept the chamber in recess during the crisis and delayed Grijalva's swearing-in, limiting the body's capacity to vote on transparency or funding measures. Democrats introduced a Federal Worker Childcare Protection Act to reimburse childcare costs caused by the shutdown, a mitigation effort that highlighted how the burden of political conflict fell on workers and families rather than the officials behind the standoff. Meanwhile, enforcement agencies like ICE remained open, while detention inspectors were furloughed, deepening the imbalance between coercion and oversight.

The shutdown also intersected with longer-term policy shifts. The administration pushed plans to cut Affordable Care Act tax credits, Medicaid, and other social programs, shifting costs onto lower-income households and deepening inequality. Officials explored selling parts of the federal student loan portfolio to private markets, which would move borrowers from public to profit-driven oversight and reduce accountability in higher education finance. In this way, a temporary funding crisis became a vehicle for lasting changes in who bore risk and who wielded power.

Immigration and detention policies were fundamentally restructured. The administration removed or transferred 139 immigration judges, mostly those with high asylum grant rates, indicating an effort to tilt rulings against migrants. Deportations to African countries, including Eswatini, increased, reflecting a tough stance with significant consequences for noncitizens' safety and family unity. The Alligator Alcatraz facility continued operations despite reports of inhumane conditions and limited legal access, now supported by significant federal reimbursement. Oversight staff in the Office of Detention Oversight were furloughed while enforcement activities persisted, leaving detainees more vulnerable.

These institutional changes were reflected in individual cases. Activists from the Global Sumud Flotilla, including Greta Thunberg, were deported amid reports of harsh detention conditions, indicating that humanitarian actors and political protesters at the border were treated as security threats rather than rights-bearing individuals. A Rutgers professor and anti-fascism scholar, Mark Bray, was prevented from boarding an international flight after Trump's threats against antifa-linked academics, suggesting that travel and security measures could be used to silence critical voices. Inside DHS, a liaison faced misconduct allegations involving a coerced hotel-room sharing arrangement, and the informant feared retaliation, demonstrating how politicized agencies left civil servants vulnerable when seeking redress.

There were partial countermeasures. U.S. District Judge Rudolph Contreras temporarily stopped ICE from automatically detaining immigrant youth in adult facilities at age 18, upholding previous protections. Federal courts, including the Supreme Court, rejected efforts to end birthright citizenship and declined Ghislaine Maxwell's appeal, leaving some high-profile criminal rulings in place. However, these decisions coexisted with the broader tightening of enforcement and reduced oversight, and they did not change the overall trajectory of the system.

As legal and administrative tools focused inward, the president's rhetoric turned outward against critics and opponents. Trump publicly called for the arrest of Illinois Governor J.B. Pritzker and Chicago Mayor Brandon Johnson over policy disputes, using the threat of criminal charges to intimidate officials. He demanded the removal of New York Attorney General Letitia James, who had pursued civil fraud cases against him, and shortly afterward, she was indicted on bank fraud and false statement charges widely seen as politically motivated. These actions, along with Comey's indictment, sent a clear message: independent legal actors challenging the president could face federal prosecution.

The targeting expanded beyond officeholders. The administration ordered a crackdown on alleged "leftwing terrorism," instructing federal law enforcement to investigate major opposition donors and liberal groups. House Republican leaders and the

White House labeled upcoming "No Kings" protests as terrorism or "hate America" rallies, equating anti-authoritarian demonstrations with support for foreign enemies. Texas Attorney General Ken Paxton announced arrests and charges against a midwife and others under strict abortion laws, while federal courts handled trials of anti-abortion activists accused of invading clinics. Across these areas, dissent—whether in reproductive health work, protests, or philanthropy—was portrayed as suspicious, if not criminal.

Security tools were used to monitor and discipline critics within the state itself. The Pentagon investigated nearly 300 employees for online comments critical of conservative activist Charlie Kirk, blurring the line between private speech and punishable conduct. New restrictions on defense reporters and leak crackdowns raised the stakes for those who might expose internal disagreements or abuses. The Pentagon Press Association warned that the new rules could criminalize routine journalism. In this climate, Trump's attacks on media figures like Rev. Al Sharpton, NBC, and Comcast's chair, coupled with hints at license reviews, carried more than symbolic weight; they suggested that regulatory power could be turned against disfavored outlets. Information control and symbolic politics tied these strands together. The White House altered the process for selecting reporters in the press corps, risking a tilt toward friendlier outlets and fewer adversarial questions.

At the Pentagon, leak crackdowns and new restrictions on reporters tightened secrecy around military policy. At the same time, DOJ and OMB quietly revised public guidance on federal worker back pay and released selective records from Jack Smith's investigation, shaping what the public could see and when. The administration used overlapping crises—the shutdown, troop deployments, vaccine-policy shifts, and tariff announcements—to create a dense environment in which each move was harder to scrutinize. Disinformation came from the top. Trump posted a video depicting political opponents as zombies, a piece of presidential propaganda that dehumanized rivals and cast politics as a struggle against monstrous enemies. He repeated a debunked claim that he had warned about Osama bin Laden before 9/11, attempting to rewrite his own record. From the Cabinet table, he and HHS Secretary Robert F. Kennedy Jr. promoted disproven links between vaccines and autism and pursued studies to "prove" them, even as the CDC altered childhood immunization schedules and removed certain combined vaccine recommendations. Six former Surgeons General publicly condemned RFK Jr.'s mismanagement and misinformation, warning that public health was being steered away from evidence-based practice.

The administration also worked to fix a particular story of the nation in law and symbol. Trump formalized Columbus Day as a national holiday on the second Monday of October, elevating a celebratory narrative of conquest at a time when many communities had moved toward Indigenous Peoples' Day. Treasury advanced plans to mint a dollar coin featuring Trump's image while he remained in office, bending statutory and customary limits on currency design. The White House criticized the Nobel Committee for awarding the Peace Prize to Venezuelan opposition leader María Corina Machado rather than to Trump, framing an independent international body as biased. An announcement of a Qatari Air Force base in Idaho, against the backdrop of Trump's business ties to Qatar, raised questions about how strategic narratives and alliances were shaped by both private interests and policy.

Against this backdrop, pockets of institutional and civic resistance stood out, not because they reversed the week's movement, but because they showed that the system had not yet fully yielded. State and local officials ordered reviews of federal raids, challenged voter-file seizures, and sued to block Guard deployments. Judges limited the use of force at protests, enforced protections for immigrant youths, and required the Pentagon to disclose information about Elon Musk's security clearances. Professional associations—from the New York City Bar to the Pentagon Press Association and the former Surgeon Generals—issued public warnings about executive overreach and misinformation. Civil-society groups like

Democracy Forward turned to FOIA litigation to pry loose records that agencies refused to release.

These acts of resistance were real, but they were reactive and fragmented. They came after troops had been deployed, after prosecutions had been launched, after guidance had been quietly changed. They often depended on individuals willing to bear personal risk: judges whose homes were targeted after blocking voter-file releases, whistleblowers whose allegations about bribery or record-handling were met with closed investigations and stonewalling, civil servants who feared retaliation for reporting misconduct.

The moral floor for those in power—character, ethics, restraint, truthfulness, good faith, stewardship—continued to erode, while the burden of upholding democratic norms shifted onto those with less formal authority.

In economic policy, the presidency's reach extended into markets and corporate decisions, blurring public and private interests. The administration announced or imposed major new tariffs on Chinese goods and Italian pasta, triggering market volatility and reshaping trade relationships. The Commerce Department's 92 percent tariffs on Italian pasta manufacturers illustrated how trade remedies could be used to reorder international markets. At the same time, the White House struck a most-favored-nation drug-pricing deal with AstraZeneca tied to relief from threatened tariffs, centralizing complex pricing decisions in direct bargaining between the president and a single firm. Abroad, a large currency swap framework with Argentina, timed just before its midterm elections, showed how financial tools under executive control could influence foreign democratic outcomes.

Viewed together, Week 38 did not introduce a new method of rule. It deepened existing ones. Law was used more openly as a weapon against critics and a shield for allies. Military and paramilitary forces moved further into domestic life under the banners of immigration control and public safety. The shutdown, once a sign of legislative failure, became a deliberate tool for restructuring programs and weakening the civil service. Information was curated, delayed, or distorted to support these moves, while symbols and holidays were reshaped to center the leader and a narrow national story.

The Democracy Clock's near-stillness in public time masked this accumulation. The week did not bring a single break with the past so much as a tightening of the pattern: authority widened through interpretation, oversight thinned through delay, and dissent was recast as disorder or treason. Rights and procedures remained on paper, but using them demanded more persistence and carried greater cost. Whether the scattered acts of resistance recorded this week can harden into durable checks, or whether they will be absorbed into the new normal, remained an open question as the week closed.

CHAPTER 49
WEEK 39: SHUTDOWN AS WEAPONIZED GOVERNANCE

With Congress stalled, the White House turned budgets, law enforcement, and public memory into tools for punishing opponents and narrowing democratic space.

The thirty-ninth week of Trump's second term did not hinge on a single shock. Instead, it unfolded as a complex layering of actions that, taken together, made the state feel less like a shared tool and more like a weapon controlled by one faction. Power was exercised through budgets, hiring, raids, lawsuits, and even holidays. Each action could be justified as technical or routine, but their pattern could not.

At the start of Week 39, the Democracy Clock read 8:08 p.m. and ended the week at the same time, with a slight inward shift of less than a minute. The face stayed still, but the mechanism changed. This reflected a deepening of trends already underway: Congress stalled while the executive improvised with appropriations; law and immigration powers were used against critics and immigrants; information channels and public memory were narrowed. Courts, unions, and states pushed back in some places, but their efforts were reactive and scattered. The week signaled not a new decline but a consolidation of an emerging order.

The shutdown set the stage for the week. In the Senate, leaders failed nine and then ten cloture votes to reopen the government, ending each in a stalemate. In the House, Speaker Mike Johnson canceled sessions and kept the chamber adjourned into a fourth week, even as agencies exhausted their funds. The building meant for debate and decision went dark instead. Representation existed on paper, but members could not legislate, question, or even be sworn in. In that vacuum, the White House stepped in. Using the shutdown as cover, the administration froze or canceled over $27 billion in federal funds, mostly affecting Democratic-led regions. Funding for the Gateway Tunnel between New York and New Jersey was withdrawn, halting a long-planned rail link under the Hudson River. Grants for other blue-state infrastructure and services were similarly stopped. The message was clear in effect if not in words: the appropriations passed by Congress were now dependent on political alignment with the president.

The pattern extended beyond transportation. In Kipnuk, an Alaska Native village, a $20 million flood-protection grant was cut just before a deadly typhoon, leaving a poor Indigenous community more vulnerable to rising seas and storms. Meanwhile, the administration reduced National Weather Service funding, degrading storm forecasting and weakening this basic public service. Risks shifted downward to those with the least power, while the core retained control over who would be protected and who would not. The burden moved, but the power did not. The most significant display of fiscal power was in how the military payroll was handled. As the shutdown persisted, President Trump claimed authority to pay furloughed troops by redirecting future-year Pentagon research and development funds without new legislation. He announced that FY2026 RDT&E appropriations would be repurposed to cover current salaries, and his administration carried out this plan. Congress's traditional power of the purse, long seen as a strict boundary, was circumvented by the executive in real time.

Courts did not accept every maneuver. Federal judges blocked some attempts to coerce states by tying FEMA and anti- terror grants to immigration cooperation, ruling that the administration could not revoke New York City transit security funds or condition disaster aid on local enforcement choices. Later in the week, a group of former intelligence officials under the "Steady State" banner released a report warning that such patterns—shutdown brinkmanship, selective funding freezes, and improvised budget reallocations—were pushing the United States toward competitive authoritarianism. Their critique did not stop the practices, but it placed them in a larger context.

While money was being redirected, the people who run the government were being reshaped. Early in the week, the administration began mass layoffs of more than 4, 4,000 federal workers under the cover of the shutdown. Reduction- in- force notices went out across agencies, signaling that job security for civil servants now depended on political winds. Unions representing federal employees, including AFGE and AFSCME, quickly went to court for emergency restraining orders, arguing that the layoffs were unlawful and retaliatory. Fear spread rapidly among employees.

Judges responded quickly. In several cases, including one before U. S. District Judge Susan Illston, courts issued injunctions blocking the layoffs, at least temporarily. These rulings did not restore full security, but they showed that the judiciary still recognized limits on using a fiscal crisis to purge the bureaucracy. For a moment, the neutral civil service had defenders with the power to say no. That mattered.

The administration's response was not to back down but to alter the rules. President Trump signed an executive order that imposed a broad hiring freeze on federal civilian positions and centralized staffing decisions in new strategic committees under White House influence. Entry into the civil service now required passing through narrower, more political gates. At the same time, the administration dismissed independent inspectors general and purged career officials deemed "disloyal," including plans to install Trump allies in key IRS investigative roles. Watchdogs who once had authority to investigate abuse were removed or sidelined.

The Office of Population Affairs provided a clear example of what this meant in practice. Nearly all staff in the office, which manages family-planning programs, were dismissed. With its internal capacity severely reduced, the government's ability to develop and oversee reproductive health policy diminished overnight. Decisions that once relied on expert knowledge were now influenced by a small group of political appointees. The same reasoning was applied to domestic troop deployments. When the administration later dispatched military forces into U.S. cities as part of a "domestic security" strategy, it did so through a security bureaucracy increasingly driven by loyalty rather than independence.

Immigration and security authority became another area in this week's story. The administration granted USCIS agents expanded law-enforcement powers, including arrest authority and the ability to seek warrants. A benefits-focused agency that traditionally processed applications was partly transformed into an enforcement tool. In Chicago, Border Patrol and ICE agents conducted a military-style raid on an apartment complex, breaking down doors without apparent warrants. Residents woke to armed officers in their hallways, and fear spread well beyond those directly targeted.

The human toll became evident in smaller, quieter cases. ICE agents revived a seldom-used law requiring legal residents to carry registration documents at all times, fining a longtime resident for failing to do so. In Arkansas, a mistaken drug arrest over perfume led to visa revocation and immigration detention for Kapil Raghu, whose life was disrupted by a series of errors and profiling. In Louisiana, queer and trans detainees at a processing center reported sexual abuse, medical neglect, and coercion into labor, revealing a system where vulnerability led to exploitation. These were not just abstractions—they were lives.

At the policy level, National Security Presidential Memorandum 7 redefined certain beliefs—being "anti-Christian," criticizing migration, or supporting specific movements—as signs of potential violence. These ideological markers fueled expanded social media surveillance of visa holders and other noncitizens. When the administration revoked visas of foreigners who criticized Charlie Kirk after his killing, it showed how speech could lead to immigration consequences. Labor unions sued to block this new surveillance system, arguing it chilled online expression and violated privacy rights, though the surveillance infrastructure was already in place.

Courts again set some boundaries. In Illinois, judges prohibited ICE from making warrantless arrests and halted federal efforts to send National Guard troops into the state, protecting due process and state authority against aggressive tactics. A federal district court ordered immigration officers in Chicago to wear body cameras during operations, responding to past abuses and creating a record for future challenges. Another court allowed Palestinian activist Mahmoud Khalil to travel freely within the U.S. while fighting deportation, reaffirming that immigration proceedings do not erase basic movement rights. These rulings did not dismantle the overall enforcement system, but they demonstrated that some parts of the judiciary still upheld constitutional procedures.

As these tools expanded, the administration and its allies worked to redefine who was considered a threat. Early in the week, President Trump signed a memo designating Antifa as a domestic terrorist organization, despite its loose structure and lack of a clear statutory basis. He and adviser Stephen Miller threatened to cut funding to groups labeled "anti-American" or terror-linked, signaling that civil society organizations on the left could lose grants or contracts based on ideology. The Department of Justice opened a RICO investigation into George Soros's Open Society

Foundations, using criminal law to stigmatize a major philanthropic network associated with liberal causes.

Against this backdrop, activists organized "No Kings" protests to challenge gerrymandering and what they saw as authoritarian drift. The rallies, planned in cities across the country, became a focal point for the week's rhetoric. House Republican leaders branded them "Hate America" events. MAGA-aligned media outlets called them "pro-Antifa hate America rallies." The White House press secretary described Democrats' base as "Hamas terrorists, illegal aliens, and violent criminals." Peaceful protest was recast, in official language, as a security problem.

Security measures followed these statements. The administration used National Guard units and federal agents in immigration crackdowns around protest sites, blurring the line between crowd control and political intimidation. Vice President JD Vance said the administration was considering invoking the Insurrection Act to deploy Guard units in Democratic-led cities. Later in the week, troops were deployed to U.S. cities as part of a domestic security strategy. At the Broadview ICE facility in Illinois, at least fifteen protesters were detained amid physical confrontations with state police. DHS officials spoke of coordinated narcoterrorist and extremist plots against immigration officers, narratives that supported more aggressive surveillance and force.

Information control and academic pressure formed a parallel track. At the Pentagon, new media rules required reporters to seek preapproval for reporting and to sign non-solicitation pledges, with the threat of expulsion for violations. Defense Secretary Pete Hegseth's department framed the guidelines as order and security. Major outlets saw them as censorship. In response, they returned their press badges and walked out, choosing to lose access rather than accept conditions they viewed as unconstitutional. President Trump publicly endorsed the restrictions as "common sense," signaling that the White House backed a narrower, more compliant press corps inside the defense establishment.

In Chicago, a federal judge issued a temporary restraining order protecting journalists from arrest or the use of riot-control weapons absent probable cause during immigration operations. The order underscored that, at least in one jurisdiction, courts still recognized the press as a distinct actor entitled to protection when covering state power. Yet the broader trend pointed the other way. Independent media were being pushed out of key spaces, while state-aligned outlets that accepted the new rules retained their foothold.

Universities faced their own version of this squeeze. The administration launched a "Compact for Academic Excellence" that linked federal funding to ideological conditions: limiting diversity, equity, and inclusion programs and cutting back international student enrollment. Leading institutions such as Brown and MIT refused to sign the compact, choosing to risk financial penalties rather than accept federal interference with campus values. In Indiana, a university administration ordered the student newspaper to stop print publication and fired its media adviser, actions widely condemned as censorship of student journalists. Shared governance further declined in Texas, where a new law dissolved faculty senates at public universities and concentrated power in administrators and political appointees.

National media outlets were not spared. President Trump refiled and expanded a $15 billion defamation lawsuit against the New York Times and several reporters, after an earlier version was dismissed. The enormous size of the claim and its persistence used the threat of devastating damages to pressure a leading investigative organization. Meanwhile, Citizens for Responsibility and Ethics in Washington sued DHS and the National Archives over missing text-message records, warning that failures to preserve digital communications were erasing parts of the historical record. Government communication channels were exploited for partisan narratives: automated out-of-office emails blamed Democrats for the shutdown, and Homeland Security Secretary Kristi Noem produced videos for airports and transit systems portraying the crisis as the opposition's fault, although many public authorities refused to air them.

The rules of electoral competition were also being rewritten. In North Carolina, Republican legislative leaders announced plans to redraw congressional maps mid-decade to add an extra GOP seat. The state Senate's elections committee scheduled a meeting to advance the controversial plan, moving quickly toward maps expected to diminish minority and opposition representation. At the national level, the Supreme Court heard arguments in Louisiana v. Callais, a case that could narrow the scope of Section 2 of the Voting Rights Act and make it more difficult to challenge racially discriminatory redistricting.

Representation within Congress itself came under strain. Speaker Johnson's decision to keep the House adjourned effectively delayed the swearing-in of Adelita Grijalva, an elected Democrat from Arizona. State Attorney General Kris Mayes demanded that Johnson seat her and then sued to enforce it, arguing that constituents were being denied their rightful voice in the chamber. The case highlighted how procedural control over the calendar could be used to withhold representation without formally canceling an election.

Outside these official spaces, citizens organized themselves. The "No Kings" rallies were one example of this, explicitly linking gerrymandering and executive overreach. Democratic governors from fifteen states formed a public health alliance to coordinate disease tracking and vaccine access in response to federal funding cuts, creating an alternative network of governance. In California and elsewhere, state-level vetoes and bills influenced how environmental and racial justice issues were addressed, sometimes reinforcing and sometimes resisting national trends.

Economic and foreign policy decisions during the week were heavily influenced by private financial interests. The administration approved a $20 billion bailout for Argentina, then moved to double it to $40 billion, despite internal acknowledgments that the package would not significantly benefit the United States. The deal was widely seen as helping a hedge fund ally with extensive Argentine holdings. Senator Elizabeth Warren and colleagues introduced legislation to block the bailout, aiming to restore congressional control over such large commitments, but the executive branch had already set the course.

In the Gulf, a similar pattern appeared. A United Arab Emirates state fund, MGX, completed a $2 billion pre-issuance purchase of a Trump-linked stablecoin through World Liberty Financial. Shortly after, the administration made favorable decisions on chip exports that benefited the same foreign partner. Saudi Arabia agreed to invest heavily in Trump-connected ventures, and simultaneously, the U.S. approved a nearly $142 billion arms sale to the kingdom. President Trump issued an executive order extending NATO-like security guarantees to Qatar, a country whose elites had provided him with significant gifts, including a private jet. Foreign policy commitments, defense exports, and personal business interests intersected in ways that blurred the line between public service and private gain.

Domestic economic policy reflected the same influence. The administration threatened 100 percent tariffs on Chinese imports, then granted exemptions for the AI sector, favoring a strategic industry with close ties to capital and the executive. IRS enforcement plans were reshaped to facilitate criminal investigations into left-leaning groups and donors, turning tax enforcement into a possible tool for selective punishment. Meanwhile, the costs of these decisions were borne by ordinary people. Canceled infrastructure projects, degraded weather forecasting, and cutbacks on climate resilience in places like Kipnuk shifted risks onto communities with little influence over these choices.

Beneath these headline moves, the national story and public space were being rewritten. For Columbus Day, President Trump issued a proclamation celebrating Christopher Columbus as an "original American hero," framing conquest and colonization as the foundation of a proud, white Christian nation. The administration used the occasion to attack critical histories that emphasized Indigenous dispossession and violence. At the same time, it moved to sell the Wilbur J. Cohen Federal Building, home to murals celebrating the Social Security Act and the broader welfare state. The sale, embedded in a water bill, combined material and symbolic rollback of New Deal-era commitments.

The president openly spoke of shifting away from the Social Security model toward "rugged individualism," portraying social insurance as a mistake rather than an achievement. Plans were unveiled for a triumphal arch in Washington, D.C., funded by private donors but designed as a prominent monument near key national symbols. A lavish new White House ballroom was also proposed. These projects used public space and quasi-public funds to promote leader-centric imagery and nationalist narratives, while spaces that commemorated social equality and shared risk were devalued or sold off.

Within the governing coalition, struggles over identity and extremism appeared in smaller incidents. A swastika-modified U.S. flag displayed in a congressional office spurred investigation by Capitol Police and raised concerns about hate symbols in official spaces. Leaked racist chats among young Republican leaders resulted in the disbanding of a state youth group, even as some senior officials, including the vice president, downplayed the messages as youthful indiscretions. These incidents demonstrated how the boundaries of acceptable rhetoric were being tested and, in some areas, stretched.

Despite this broad consolidation, resistance persisted through lawsuits, injunctions, and alternative institutions. Courts ordered ICE to remove an unlawful fence blocking access to a detention facility, reopening a public street and restoring space for protests and oversight. They limited warrantless immigration arrests, blocked federalized Guard deployments in Illinois, and mandated body cameras for immigration officers in Chicago. Judges halted some of the layoffs implemented during shutdowns, safeguarding civil servants from immediate dismissal.

Civil society groups and business organizations joined the fight. The U.S. Chamber of Commerce sued to block the new $100,000 H-1B visa fee, arguing that it violated law and harmed firms relying on skilled foreign labor. CREW's litigation over missing DHS text messages aimed to enforce record-keeping laws and maintain the digital record of government decisions. Residents of Gloster, Mississippi, filed suit against a biomass company over air pollution, raising environmental justice claims in a low-income community. Survivors of clergy and county-employee abuse secured substantial settlements in New Orleans and Los Angeles, forcing powerful institutions to reckon with past harms.

State leaders demonstrated different norms. Illinois Governor JB Pritzker released detailed tax filings, including gambling winnings and income, as a gesture of financial transparency. Democratic governors' public health alliance built capacity for disease tracking and vaccine distribution outside federal channels. Prosecutors pursued hate-threat cases, such as the man who pleaded guilty to threatening an LGBTQ+ Pride event, signaling that some forms of targeted intimidation still received strong legal responses. These actions did not reverse the national trajectory, but they showed that not all centers of power aligned with the regime's goals.

Looking ahead, several processes already underway promised to shape the next phase. The North Carolina Senate's scheduled meeting on redistricting would decide whether the proposed gerrymander became law. The Supreme Court's eventual ruling in Louisiana v. Callais would clarify how much protection Section 2 of the Voting Rights Act still offered against discriminatory maps. Arizona's lawsuit to force the swearing-in of Adelita Grijalva would test whether procedural control in the House could be used to deny representation. And the Steady State group's warning about competitive authoritarianism would either be heeded or ignored.

In the course of Trump's second term, Week 39 marked a deepening of existing patterns rather than a break. Executive power continued to extend into areas once guarded by Congress, inspectors general, and neutral civil servants. Law and immigration tools were used in ways that made dissent and noncitizen status more vulnerable. Information channels and public memory were curated to favor a nationalist, leader-centered narrative. Yet courts, unions, states, and communities still found ways to resist, even if only marginally. The week's small movement on the Democracy Clock reflected this tension: the structure of democracy became more fragile, but it had not yet failed.

CHAPTER 50
WEEK 40: BALLROOM AS BLUEPRINT

A demolished East Wing, weaponized clemency, and engineered representation show how personal rule advances without a single formal break in the system.

The fortieth week of Trump's second term revealed how a democracy can be subtly distorted without an obvious break. Power shifted through institutions, budgets, courts, and screens. The presidency used public spaces as private stages, law as a flexible tool, and crises as opportunities to reward allies. Meanwhile, streets filled with people demanding that the country was not ruled by kings. The conflict between those two visions—personal rule and shared governance—pervaded every major event of the week and continued nonstop.

At the end of the previous period, the Democracy Clock showed 8:08 p.m. By the close of Week 40, it read 8:11 p.m., a total shift of two and a half minutes. This change didn't result from a coup or a dramatic order. Instead, it stemmed from demolishing a historic part of the White House, issuing pardons and payouts that turned justice into favoritism, altering maps and procedures to weaken elections, and openly discussing a third term. Each step shifted the reliability of institutions and for whom they served. In sum, these actions reinforced a pattern where the presidency treated constraints as suggestions and public trust as disposable.

The week's most visible—and most literal—act was the president's ordering the demolition of the White House East Wing. Crew moved to tear down a central section to make space for a privately funded ballroom named after him. This project proceeded without the usual planning review and preservation process that normally protect national landmarks. It wasn't an upgrade to improve functionality; it was a redesign of the people's house to fit one man's tastes and political spectacle, as if the building were his personal property. The symbolism was unmistakable.

Around the demolition, the administration maintained a veil of secrecy. The Treasury Department advised employees not to share photos of the East Wing being reduced to rubble. Staff were instructed to keep their phones away, ensuring no informal images leaked to the public. What would normally be announced, debated, and documented was instead treated as a private construction project. The order did more than hide dust and debris; it signaled that the public's right to see what was happening to its symbols now depended on the president's comfort.

A similar mindset showed up in the digital realm. The administration removed Federal Trade Commission blog posts that warned about the dangers and risks of artificial intelligence. These weren't partisan opinions; they were expert analyses meant to inform the public and industry about a rapidly evolving technology. Removing them narrowed official memory of what regulators had once communicated. It made it harder for citizens, journalists, and courts to understand how policies had changed and why. Whatever remained on the site reflected the current stance; anything conflicting with it was quietly erased.

Even as the White House was being reshaped and records were reduced, senior officials found new comforts. During the ongoing government shutdown, when many federal workers went unpaid and essential services were strained, the Department of Homeland Security bought two Gulfstream private jets for top officials. The timing was striking. While agencies furloughed staff and veterans worried about delayed benefits, luxury aircraft joined the fleet. The purchase highlighted a hierarchy of concern: austerity for ordinary workers, luxury for those near power.

If the East Wing demolition showed how physical space could be used for personal glory, the week's clemency and legal maneuvers showed how law itself could be bent to benefit insiders. The president commuted former congressman George Santos's sentence after less than three months in prison for serious financial fraud. Santos had lied to voters and donors, then faced federal conviction. By sharply reducing his punishment, the president signaled that political allies could expect mercy even when they had misused public trust. The pattern was obvious. Soon after, he pardoned Changpeng Zhao, the billionaire founder of Binance, after a money-laundering conviction. Zhao's company had faced major sanctions violations. His wealth and ties, including connections to Trump-linked ventures, now coincided with a complete erasure of legal consequences. In both cases, clemency did not seem as an act of mercy toward the powerless. It appeared as a reward for proximity and usefulness. The message to the wider elite was clear. With the right relationships, even serious financial crimes could be washed away.

The president also moved to make the Justice Department a source of personal money. He demanded about $230 million in compensation from the DOJ for past investigations into him, framing lawful inquiries as wrongful persecution. The claim was to be evaluated and paid by officials he had appointed. Later reports indicated that DOJ funds were, in fact, used to satisfy his demand. If true, prosecutorial resources—intended to enforce law on behalf of the public—were converted into a private settlement for the president himself. The line between the state's funds and his personal grievances blurred almost completely. Simultaneously, federal prosecutors targeted prominent critics. New York

Attorney General Letitia James, who had led aggressive civil actions against Trump, faced a federal mortgage fraud indictment that career prosecutors reportedly opposed. Former FBI Director James Comey, long an opponent of the president, was caught up in a criminal case marked by disputes over leaks and claims of selective prosecution. House Republicans referred former CIA Director John Brennan to the DOJ for alleged false testimony. Each case had its own legal details, but together they suggested that prosecutorial efforts favored perceived enemies over well-connected allies.

Even court orders faced resistance. A whistleblower inside the Justice Department revealed that deportation flights continued despite a federal injunction. Venezuelan migrants were being sent to El Salvador's mega-prison in defiance of a judge's order. When the facts came to light, US District Judge James Boasberg ordered the flights to stop. This episode highlighted both sides of the justice system during this period: an executive branch willing to ignore legal limits, and a judiciary still capable, in some cases, of insisting its rulings be followed. The tension was ongoing.

While law and clemency were being repurposed, the government itself was undergoing restructuring. The Senate moved forward with confirming Douglas Troutman, a longtime chemical industry lobbyist, to lead the Environmental Protection Agency's toxics office. The very person paid to weaken chemical safety rules was about to oversee them. Regulatory capture, long a concern in Washington, shifted from risk to reality at one of the most sensitive public health agencies. Industry interests and oversight were merging. In the executive branch, the president created an interagency task force aimed at removing perceived "Deep State" opponents from the federal workforce. The goal was clear: identify and remove neutral civil servants and replace them with loyalists. Simultaneously, the Supreme Court overruled injunctions that had temporarily halted large-scale federal layoffs. Lower courts had tried to slow down mass firings related to the shutdown. The Court's decision paved the way for a swift overhaul of the bureaucracy, weakening job protections that support a nonpartisan civil service.

Shutdown tactics became a tool in this restructuring. The administration issued furlough notices to most civilian staff at the National Nuclear Security Administration, even as budget disputes continued. Critical national security functions were used as bargaining chips in partisan standoffs. Elsewhere, the EPA canceled a $20 million climate resilience grant for the Alaskan community of Kipnuk, which faces severe erosion. The decision shifted the costs of climate change onto a small, vulnerable population and freed up funds for other priorities. The future of the Education Department was also uncertain. The president considered moving a $15 billion disability education program out of the agency as part of a broader plan to dismantle it. Such a move would not only disrupt services for students with disabilities but also weaken a cabinet department responsible for enforcing education rights nationwide. Unions responded by suing over executive orders that eliminated collective bargaining rights for federal workers. Their lawsuits served as a reminder that not all institutions accepted the new order, even as the balance of power tilted against them.

Representation, the core promise that votes translate into voice, came under pressure from multiple directions. In North Carolina, the Republican legislature passed a congressional map intended to turn a 10–4 Democratic advantage into an 11–3 Republican majority, despite a closely divided electorate. Senate Bill 249 limited the governor's power to veto the map. The redistricting diluted Black and opposition representation and solidified partisan gains for years to come. It was a textbook example of how gerrymandered lines can do what no speech or slogan can: predetermine election outcomes. In Washington, House Speaker Mike Johnson used procedural control similarly. He refused to seat Adelita Grijalva, a duly elected representative from Arizona, during the shutdown. Without being sworn in, she couldn't sign a discharge petition that might have forced a vote to reopen the government or release sensitive files. Her constituents were left without representation in a crisis. The House itself remained adjourned for much of the summer, conveniently delaying action on releasing the Epstein files. Time, in this context, became a tool of power. Arizona's attorney general, Kris Mayes, and Grijalva herself sued the House and the Speaker to force her swearing-in. Their case asked the courts to uphold fundamental constitutional guarantees of representation against the internal practices of another branch.

Meanwhile, the Senate failed to pass the Shutdown Fairness Act, which would have guaranteed pay for essential federal workers and troops during the stalemate. In North Carolina, the General Assembly failed to pass a state budget even as federal Medicaid and SNAP cuts loomed. Across various levels of government, legislative bodies operated less as forums for debate and more as instruments for stalling, protecting, or entrenching power. Security forces and emergency tools were drawn deeper into domestic politics. The president publicly discussed invoking the Insurrection Act and deploying National Guard troops to Democratic-led cities, including San Francisco. He talked about using military force not in response to an actual uprising but to manage protests and urban unrest. In Texas, Governor Greg Abbott preemptively deployed the National Guard ahead of the nationwide "No Kings" protests, warning of unrest that hadn't yet happened. Seeing soldiers in place before any violence sent a clear message about how dissent would be handled. Immigration enforcement grew more militarized. Immigration and Customs Enforcement increased its weapons spending by over 600 percent compared to the previous year. The agency conducted aggressive raids resulting in arrests and injuries to U.S. military veterans protesting deportations. In one case, a student was handcuffed after an algorithm misidentified them. Venezuelan migrants were deported to El Salvador's megaprison, a facility designed for mass incarceration. U.S. citizens were also swept up in immigration raids. These actions suggested that security forces aligned more with the regime's narratives about threats than with public safety.

Courts again provided partial counterweights. Federal judges issued rulings that limited or scrutinized Guard deployments and immigration tactics. One appellate court ordered body cameras for ICE officers in certain operations. The Court of Appeals for Veterans Claims rejected the VA secretary's request to pause nearly all veterans' disability cases during the shutdown, ensuring timely access to benefits. However, other decisions, such as a Texas judge's order blocking the Keeping Families Together policy, moved in the opposite direction, abruptly stripping protections from mixed-status families. The legal landscape was uneven, with rights defended in some courts and curtailed in others.

Information itself became a contested field. The president posted AI-generated videos depicting himself as a crowned fighter pilot dropping waste on protesters and naming opponents. The imagery was cartoonish and cruel. It portrayed dissenters as targets to be humiliated from above. The use of AI blurred the line between satire and deepfake, between political messaging and digital spectacle. Musician Kenny Loggins demanded that his song be removed from the video, objecting to its unauthorized and politicized use. His protest underscored how cultural works could be co-opted into propaganda without consent.

At the Pentagon, Defense Secretary Pete Hegseth oversaw the replacement of the traditional press pool with a new media corps dominated by far-right outlets operating under restrictive rules. Mainstream reporters walked out rather than accept censorship and limited access. The Defense Department, one of the most powerful institutions in the country, now funneled information through ideologically aligned channels. At the White House, press secretary Karoline Leavitt attacked a reporter on social media as a partisan hack after critical questioning. The combined effect was to delegitimize independent media while elevating friendly voices.

Inside the justice system, information was both leaked and erased. Lindsey Halligan, the interim US attorney for the Eastern District of Virginia, used auto-deleting encrypted messages to share grand jury details with a reporter. Public watchdog groups warned that such practices might violate federal records laws. Auto-delete features meant that key prosecutorial communications could vanish without a trace, undermining transparency and accountability. At the same time, the FBI and Department of Homeland Security allowed an unsubstantiated rumor about Venezuelan gang threats to spread widely before quietly correcting it internally. No public correction followed. The rumor helped justify harsh policies against immigrant communities, even after officials knew it was mistaken.

Outside government, the information environment was further muddied. Popular podcasts, including those hosted by Joe Rogan, spread false claims about antidepressants, vaccines, soy, immigration, and conspiracy theories like Pizzagate. Research by journalists and European broadcasters documented high error rates and sourcing problems in AI chatbots' news answers. These tools, already used by millions, frequently hallucinate facts or misattribute sources. The risk was clear. As citizens turned to automated systems and high-audience shows for news, they entered an environment where truth and falsehood were increasingly difficult to distinguish.

Some state leaders tried to build counterweights. Illinois Governor J.B. Pritzker created the Illinois Accountability Commission to document abuses by federal agents operating in his state. The commission's mandate was simple: gather evidence where federal transparency had failed. Its existence acknowledged that traditional oversight channels were faltering. If the federal government would not reliably record and disclose its own actions, states would try to do so themselves.

Over the week, economic policy revealed how closely governance had become tied to family and donor interests. The administration announced and upheld sweeping tariffs, including threats of 100 percent duties on Chinese goods and reciprocal tariffs of 10–40 percent on Southeast Asian countries. These actions disrupted supply chains and increased consumer prices. A coalition of businesses petitioned the Supreme Court to overturn the global tariffs, labeling them an illegal multitrillion-dollar tax, and arguing that the president had overstepped Congress's authority over trade. The case questioned whether economic shock could be imposed unilaterally from the Oval Office.

Abroad, the president and Treasury Secretary Scott Bessent organized a $20–40 billion bailout and swap lines to stabilize Argentina's peso. Reports suggested these arrangements favored a hedge fund connected to Trump. Simultaneously, the administration pushed for increased beef imports from Argentina despite opposition from domestic ranchers. Trade policy thus served two purposes: opening markets that benefited foreign partners and investors, and undermining U.S. producers lacking similar access. Risks were shifted onto taxpayers and workers; gains were concentrated among the president's inner circle.

Defense spending followed a similar pattern. The Army awarded a major drone components contract to Unusual Machines, a company in which Donald Trump Jr. held a significant stake. The deal blurred the lines between procurement and family enrichment, implying that military hardware decisions could also serve as investment opportunities for the president's relatives. In Nevada, the administration canceled approval for a large clean energy project, while elsewhere approving a massive liquefied natural gas export hub. Fossil fuel interests and connected firms gained, while long-term climate and infrastructure goals were sidelined.

In the private sector, leading AI firms—including Nvidia, OpenAI, CoreWeave, AMD, Oracle, and xAI—entered into large, circular investment and purchasing agreements for chips and cloud services. These deals concentrated financial power and technical capacity within a tight corporate network. Though not a direct government action, this consolidation intersected with public policy. The same companies shaping digital infrastructure now appeared poised to benefit from regulatory choices and procurement decisions made by an administration already inclined to favor large, aligned players.

Despite these developments, civic resistance persisted. On

October 18, the 50501 Movement and allied groups organized "No Kings" protests across all 50 states and abroad. Demonstrators gathered under a simple banner: the presidency was not a throne. The protests remained largely peaceful. They demonstrated that assembly and speech rights, though under pressure, were still being exercised on a broad scale. Days later, the movement held a national organizing call to transform protest energy into sustained campaigns, including mutual aid, boycotts, and a planned "Remove the Regime" convergence.

Inside the Senate, Jeff Merkley used floor time to warn that Trump's actions threatened democracy. His speech placed the week's events in constitutional context, arguing that the accumulation of small abuses could amount to a larger breach. Public opinion data pointed in the same direction. A survey by the Public Religion Research Institute reported that a majority of Americans viewed Trump as a dangerous dictator whose power should be limited. The language was stark. It suggested that concern about authoritarian drift had moved from activist circles into the mainstream.

Yet even as alarm grew, the president's allies spoke openly about extending his rule. Steve Bannon claimed that Trump would run for an unconstitutional third term and hinted at a plan to bypass the Twenty-Second Amendment. The statement did not come from a fringe figure. It came from a close confidant with a large audience. His words marked a shift from vague talk of "staying in power" to explicit contemplation of term-limit evasion. In the same week that protesters marched under "No Kings," a leading ally floated the idea of a president for life in all but name.

Some state leaders tried to mitigate federal harms while this struggle played out. California Governor Gavin Newsom deployed the National Guard and volunteers not to police protests but to support food banks during the shutdown. His move highlighted a different use of state power: cushioning residents from federal dysfunction. Pritzker's accountability commission served a similar purpose on the information front. These actions did not reverse the week's trends. They did show that federalism still offered pockets of resilience.

The week closed without a single decisive confrontation. Instead, it left a layered record: a wing of the White House gone, a ballroom rising in its place; pardons and payouts that told elites the law could be bent; maps and procedures that dulled the force of elections; soldiers and agents positioned against protesters and migrants; AI videos and a curated press corps shaping what the public saw; tariffs and bailouts that enriched those closest to power; and crowds in the streets insisting that the country was not meant to be ruled this way. The movement of the Democracy Clock captured that accumulation. It marked a deepening erosion, not yet a collapse, in which the habits of personal rule grew more confident and the work of resistance grew more urgent and more costly.

CHAPTER 51
WEEK 41: SHUTDOWN AND BALLROOMS AS RULE

A fourth week of shutdown, militarized immigration, and donor-funded monuments showed power consolidating quietly as law, welfare, and truth bent around one man's needs.

The forty-first week of Trump's second term did not depend on a single shock. Instead, it played out as a complex layering of decisions that, together, made the state seem less like a shared institution and more like a set of tools under one man's control. Shutdowns, immigration raids, nuclear tests, pardons, and propaganda all occurred at the same time. Each action had its own reasoning, but the pattern became clear in how they reinforced each other.

At the start of the week, the Democracy Clock showed 8:11 p.m. It ended at the same visible time, but with a net movement of 0.3 minutes further into danger. The small numerical change hid a deepening of existing trends. Congress drifted further from real governance. Executive power increasingly extended into war, welfare, and law enforcement. Wealth and loyalty gained access to contracts, clemency, and even the physical appearance of the White House. Courts and civil society pushed back in some areas, but mostly in response, not control. The clock moved forward because resisting power became more costly while options for opposition shrank.

The most noticeable issue was the government shutdown, now in its fourth week. Federal workers remained unpaid, and core services operated with limited resources. Meanwhile, the House was adjourned, and the Senate failed to pass a short-term funding bill. The shutdown no longer simply represented a bargaining failure; it had become a way of governing. The deadlock over healthcare subsidies and spending cuts was real, but it also masked a deeper shift: using fiscal crises to reshape the government.

This was especially clear in how food assistance was handled. The administration refused to use billions in contingency funds for SNAP, even as 42 million people faced losing benefits. Officials decided to suspend November payments and later removed online guidance that explained how those reserves could be accessed during a shutdown. On the USDA website, a partisan banner labeled the situation a "Radical Left Democrat shutdown," turning a neutral service portal into a propaganda tool. The policy choice was severe, and the way information was shared made it harder for states and families to find alternative options.

The economic effects were immediate and local. Analysts warned that SNAP cuts would impact grocery stores, farm suppliers, and low-wage jobs in small towns and cities. At the same time, air traffic controllers and TSA agents were ordered to keep working without pay, straining safety systems and clogging airports. The largest federal workers' union urged passing a stopgap bill to restore pay. The message to workers was direct: the government could force them to work without wages and treat basic protections as bargaining chips.

The shutdown also became a pretext to reshape public health. At the Centers for Disease Control and Prevention, leadership enacted a reduction in force that eliminated a quarter of the staff, including legal and ethics offices. The Washington liaison office that briefed Congress was closed. On paper, these were budget-driven cuts. In reality, they diminished the agency's ability to advise lawmakers, police conflicts of interest, and oversee research. A key institution for managing collective risk was weakened just as emergency-style governance was becoming routine.

Courts did not remain entirely passive. Federal judges in Rhode Island and Massachusetts ordered USDA to continue SNAP payments, blocking the planned suspension. Other judges halted mass layoffs of federal employees and later determined that some CDC terminations were unlawful, allowing unions to challenge broader purges. These rulings did not end the shutdown or restore normal budgeting. However, they set boundaries that the executive could not cross without openly defying court orders. Even then, the president left the country for an Asia trip while 1.4 million federal workers went unpaid, signaling how little the hardship affected his movements.

If the shutdown revealed how fiscal tools could be used inwardly, immigration policy showed how security tools could target specific communities and critics. Within ICE, at least a dozen field office directors were reassigned. Border Patrol officials known for hardline enforcement were promoted to push deportations toward a target of 3,000 arrests per day. On city streets, 1,500 agents conducted helicopter raids in places like Chicago and Los Angeles, using tear gas and masked detentions. A Honduran immigrant, José Castro Rivera, died in a crash while fleeing an ICE operation. A Halloween parade saw tear gas deployed on civilians. The border had shifted into the interior.

Behind the visible raids lay a more secretive infrastructure. Lawsuits described individuals held for days or weeks in short-term ICE detention rooms meant to be temporary, with limited access to lawyers and family. Advocates in Illinois sued over conditions at the Broadview facility, alleging coerced signatures and blocked attorney visits. Plans emerged to privatize deportation transport in Texas, assigning armed contractors responsibility for moving detainees. Each step reduced public accountability and increased profit's role in the machinery of removal.

State officials tried to lessen the damage at the margins. Illinois Governor JB Pritzker urged DHS and ICE to suspend raids over Halloween weekend to spare children from the trauma of seeing parents taken away. His plea highlighted a widening gap between federal tactics and local understandings of public safety. Yet, the deeper policy direction was set elsewhere, in the White House and at the State Department, where Stephen Miller coordinated secret daily calls directing visa revocations and deportations of specific critics.

Those calls were part of a broader ideological sorting of who could belong. The administration restructured State's migration bureaus, creating an "office of remigration" and appointing fellows aligned with its anti-immigration agenda. Visas were revoked for thousands, including students and outspoken critics, while refugee policy was rewritten to favor white South Africans. The annual refugee cap was cut to 7,500, and broad country bans were imposed on immigrants from nineteen nations. Humanitarian protection, once based on need and risk, was recast along lines of race, ideology, and perceived loyalty.

The same logic extended beyond borders. Trump ordered lethal maritime strikes on boats in the Caribbean and Eastern Pacific, killing dozens of alleged traffickers. A carrier strike group, the USS Gerald R. Ford, was deployed off Venezuela for counter-narcotics operations. The line between law enforcement and power projection blurred. The UN High Commissioner for Human Rights called for investigations into the strikes, citing concerns about legality and civilian casualties. At home, Democrats were barred from briefings on these operations, weakening Congress's ability to oversee the use of force conducted in the nation's name.

While immigration and security policies were being pushed toward ideological goals, economic and legal tools were used to reward allies and strengthen a patronage economy. The Pentagon awarded a drone contract to Unusual Machines, a company tied to Donald Trump Jr., even as he influenced defense hiring and spending. The Trump family's crypto venture, World Liberty Financial, reported an $864 million windfall, and Trump-linked tokens gained expanded trading on Binance US. Shortly after a major investment in those tokens, Trump pardoned Binance founder Changpeng Zhao, who had been convicted of money laundering. Seven senators questioned the pardon, but the sequence of investment, clemency, and profit sent a clear message. Aligning with the president's financial interests could potentially lessen or eliminate legal consequences.

Inside the United States, the physical seat of the presidency itself became a venue for cronyism. Trump ordered the demolition of the historic East Wing of the White House to build a new ballroom, funded by major tech and telecom corporations. The project repurposed a core national symbol for personal prestige and donor recognition. At the same time, he fired all members of the federal Commission of Fine Arts, clearing the way for loyalists to approve Trump-branded monuments like the proposed "Arc de Trump." Senate Democrats demanded a full list of ballroom donors, seeking to reveal any quid pro quo between corporate funders and government decisions. Their oversight letters highlighted how little formal ethics enforcement limited conflicts of interest.

The reliance on private and foreign capital during crises deepened the sense that public goods depended on elite favor. As troops went unpaid during the shutdown, megadonor Timothy Mellon contributed $130 million to cover a few hours of military payroll. Treasury Secretary Scott Bessent arranged a $40 billion bailout and currency swap for Argentina, stabilizing foreign bondholders while domestic programs like SNAP faced cuts. Trade policy swung between punitive tariffs and targeted relief: new tariffs on Canadian goods and chocolate raised consumer prices, while deals with China adjusted access to rare earths and soybean purchases, increasing U.S. dependence on Chinese decisions. Energy and trade choices that hurt Iowa's farmers and manufacturers, and drove up electricity bills, impacted regions and workers with little leverage the most.

Law, in this environment, became less a boundary and more a

weapon. The Department of Justice charged former FBI Director James Comey and indicted New York Attorney General Letitia James, both prominent Trump critics. In a separate move, Trump filed a $230 million claim against DOJ under the Federal Tort Claims Act, seeking damages for what he framed as persecution by previous investigations. The claim would be decided by officials he had appointed. These actions blurred the line between personal grievance and institutional accountability, pressuring legal personnel to align with the president's interests.

The pattern extended to electoral politics and protests. Federal prosecutors indicted congressional candidate Kat Abughazaleh for participating in protests at a Chicago ICE facility, signaling that direct action against federal enforcement could carry career-ending legal risks. DOJ demanded 2020 election records from Fulton County, Georgia, reopening a settled contest and extending Trump's narrative of a stolen election into federal law enforcement. Inside the security apparatus, Stephen Miller and allies compiled lists of FBI agents who worked on January 6 and Mar-a-Lago cases, for possible purges. The threat of being targeted for past investigations threatened to chill future investigations into elite wrongdoing.

Media and cultural institutions faced similar pressure. Corporate leaders at Paramount urged 60 Minutes to avoid controversial coverage of Gaza and Trump, narrowing the range of stories reaching the mass audience. A Trump-appointed media regulator allegedly threatened ABC, contributing to Jimmy Kimmel's suspension after critical monologues. On campus, George Mason University ordered the removal of a Students for Justice in Palestine video, citing the IHRA definition of antisemitism. These actions did not ban dissent outright but raised the costs of expressing it, especially when it involved the president or his favored causes.

Courts again offered some counterweights. A federal judge issued a gag order on DOJ and DHS in a specific case to protect a defendant's right to a fair trial, restricting the government's ability to influence public perception of the prosecution. Another judge blocked a Trump executive order provision that would have required proof of citizenship on federal voter registration forms, maintaining easier access to the voter rolls. In Chicago, Judge Sara Ellis ordered a senior Border Patrol official to wear a body camera and give daily updates on raids, an unusual step to enforce constitutional limits on militarized immigration enforcement. The Seventh Circuit later limited that oversight, reflecting the ongoing tension within the judiciary.

The information environment in which all this unfolded grew more distorted. Official channels like the USDA website carried partisan blame and stigmatizing language about "illegal aliens" and trans people. Trump claimed, falsely, to have brought $20 trillion of investment into the U.S. economy and misrepresented Ronald Reagan's views on tariffs to justify his own trade agenda. Guidance about SNAP contingency funds was altered or removed, obscuring the fact that cuts were policy choices, not fiscal inevitabilities. Meanwhile, overlapping crises—the shutdown, tariff wars, foreign bailouts, nuclear testing, immigration crackdowns—were rolled out in quick succession. The effect was to fragment public focus. It became harder to sustain scrutiny of any single policy when each day brought a new front-page conflict.

Against this backdrop, pockets of resistance persisted. Letitia James launched a public portal for reporting illegal or unconstitutional actions by federal authorities, creating a state-level channel for documenting abuses. Senate committees questioned the CZ pardon and demanded ballroom donor lists. Civil rights lawyers pressed cases against racial gerrymanders and abusive detention conditions. In New Orleans, survivors of clergy sexual abuse secured a $230 million settlement that included commitments to release internal church files, a rare instance of institutional transparency. California supported Planned Parenthood clinics with $140 million in state funding after federal cuts.

Abroad, Japan pursued structural reforms to reduce electricity prices, modernize corporate culture, and attract greenfield investment, offering a contrasting picture of how a democracy might use policy to expand, rather than restrict, opportunity. These efforts were genuine but also fragmented and reactive. They came from state governments, unions, advocacy groups, and individual judges more than from the national institutions meant to balance the presidency.

The House remained largely idle during the shutdown. The Senate swung between gridlock and occasional bipartisan checks on tariffs and pardons. Courts protected SNAP, voting access, and some labor rights, yet higher benches also limited oversight of immigration raids and left key questions about Guard deployments unresolved. The burden of defending norms shifted downward and outward, onto those with fewer tools and less time.

In moral terms, the week deepened a pattern already visible: character subordinated to grievance, ethics to gain, restraint to impulse, truth to narrative, good faith to procedural maneuver, stewardship to spectacle. The demolition of the East Wing for a donor-funded ballroom, the use of hunger as leverage, the targeting of critics through immigration and prosecution, and the casual talk of a third term all pointed in the same direction. Institutions still functioned. Rights still existed on paper. But claiming them now required more courage, more resources, and more willingness to take personal risks.

The week did not mark a dramatic turning point. It marked consolidation. Shutdown as strategy, raids as theater, pardons as currency, and chaos as cover all became more settled features of the landscape. The Democracy Clock's slight movement captured this slow tightening: not a leap, but another notch in a system where power flows more easily to the top, and the paths for holding it to account grow narrower and. steeper.

CHAPTER 52
WEEK 42: HUNGER AND PARDONS AS POWER

A week of shutdown brinkmanship, militarized enforcement, and pay-to-play clemency showed law, welfare, and knowledge bent to serve executive will.

The forty-second week of Trump's second term did not rely on a single shock. Instead, it was a complex layering of decisions that saw law, welfare, and knowledge as tools to be bent rather than limits to be respected. Across different areas, the same pattern appeared: rules were exploited for advantage, institutions were steered toward loyalty, and those on the margins bore the consequences. Resistance arose in courtrooms, in state policies, and in civil society, but it was met with a presidency more willing to ignore, delay, or work around constraints. That willingness became more evident.

At the end of the previous period, the Democracy Clock read 8:11 p.m. It remained at the same public time at the week's close, with only a slight internal shift. The clock's face stayed the same, but the mechanisms behind it changed. The week's actions deepened executive defiance of courts, expanded the use of emergency and war powers, and blurred the line between public policy and private gain, even as judges ordered compliance and some voters sought more inclusive paths. This apparent stillness reflects a balance of forces: rapid erosion met with pockets of resistance strong enough to prevent a clear lurch but insufficient to halt the overall direction. The strain on the system increased even as the hands stayed in place.

The most immediate arena where power and law collided was the federal shutdown and the fight over food assistance. Early in the week, Trump announced he would not comply with a federal court order requiring full November SNAP benefits during the shutdown. He framed the refusal as fiscal prudence and constitutional hardball, insisting that keeping the country "liquid" justified withholding food aid. Officials at the Department of Agriculture moved partial funds, but the president's public stance made clear that, in his view, judicial rulings were suggestions to be weighed against political leverage, not commands to be obeyed. Hunger became a bargaining chip.

Federal judges pushed back. In Rhode Island, Judge McConnell ordered the administration to pay full November SNAP benefits, criticizing earlier noncompliance and emphasizing that statutory obligations to low-income households do not disappear in a budget standoff. Another district court reiterated that withholding food aid for political gain was unlawful. The administration responded not by conceding but by appealing these rulings, turning the question of whether the executive can ration subsistence benefits into a prolonged legal contest. The courts asserted their authority, while the White House treated their orders as another bargaining tool. The rule of law was slowed down.

Congress's behavior reinforced the sense that basic welfare had become hostage to partisan strategy. Senate Republicans blocked a Democratic resolution to fully fund SNAP during the shutdown, and the chamber rejected a broader government funding package for the fourteenth time, prolonging the closure. Each failed vote kept agencies partially shut and left millions of families uncertain about their next month's groceries. The legislature became more of a stage for blame rather than a forum for resolution. In that vacuum, the president's willingness to defy court orders carried more weight. The cost was borne by those with the least cushion.

The shutdown's effects rippled across the country's infrastructure. The Federal Aviation Administration warned that unpaid controllers were overworked and started planning to slow air traffic. By midweek, the agency announced a ten percent reduction in flight capacity, cutting thousands of flights daily to handle staff shortages. What started as a political standoff in Washington turned into delayed travel, strained safety systems, and financial losses for airlines, workers, and travelers. Meanwhile, Trump threatened federal workers with firing and withheld back pay, using the payroll of a neutral civil service as another tool in his fight. Ordinary federal employees became pressure points.

Economic messaging tried to soften the blow. Officials claimed that inflation and grocery prices were falling, while blaming the shutdown for broader economic problems. The narrative downplayed policy choices—like tax cuts, tariffs that rattled manufacturers, and the deliberate use of SNAP as leverage—and described the crisis as an unfortunate result of necessary toughness. In North Carolina and elsewhere, defying SNAP orders was framed as a constitutional stand against Democrats, framing legal noncompliance as patriotism. The most affected—low-income families relying on food assistance—were portrayed as pawns in a larger battle. Their hardship was viewed as collateral damage.

Beyond domestic issues, there was an effort to expand the president's authority to use force. The Department of Justice issued a memo stating that lethal airstrikes on boats did not count as "hostilities" under the War Powers Resolution. By redefining the term, the memo allowed ongoing bombings to continue without triggering the law's reporting and approval requirements. This legal move didn't create new weapons; it loosened the constraints on existing ones, reducing Congress's ability to demand oversight over when and where American forces fight. Words on paper shifted the scope of war.

Trump's rhetoric went even further. He said he would consider using the Insurrection Act to deploy the Army or Marines against domestic unrest, and claimed such deployments would be beyond judicial review. The suggestion that no judge could challenge troop deployment inside the U.S. signaled a willingness to treat the military as a domestic police force under his personal command. Abroad, he threatened military action against Nigeria over violence targeting Christians, ordered preparations, and hinted at possible operations inside Mexico against drug cartels. He speculated about war with Venezuela and predicted Nicolás Maduro's downfall, keeping intervention options open in public discussion. Force was presented as a first choice.

Congress and the courts tried to define boundaries, but their efforts were inconsistent. The Senate rejected a war powers resolution that would have required approval for strikes in Venezuela, leaving those operations with fewer legislative limits. Simultaneously, senators passed a mostly symbolic measure to nullify Trump's reciprocal tariffs, asserting Congress's constitutional role over taxation even as House inaction limited its impact. The Supreme Court heard arguments on the legality of tariffs imposed under the International Emergency Economic Powers Act, testing whether presidents can effectively levy taxes through emergency authority. The fact that the Court took up the case signaled concern, but until rulings are made, the executive continues using trade tools as quasi-war instruments. The emergency frame became a permanent justification.

Within the defense establishment, oversight channels shrank. Defense Secretary Pete Hegseth ordered that all Pentagon contacts with Congress go through a central office, placing political appointees between lawmakers and military professionals. What was once a web of direct relationships—commanders briefing committees, analysts answering technical questions—was consolidated into a single, controlled pathway. Meanwhile, Trump urged Republicans to eliminate the Senate filibuster to pass restrictive voting measures and accelerate his agenda, treating procedural rules as obstacles to be removed when they hindered partisan goals. The combined effect was to sideline both branches that might check the presidency: Congress, with its war powers and internal rules, and the courts, in reviewing domestic force. Power shifted further toward the Oval Office.

The fusion of force and fear was especially evident in immigration enforcement. On Halloween and during Día de los Muertos events in Chicago and Los Angeles, federal immigration agents, backed by troops and masked personnel, conducted raids that resembled military operations more than routine policing. Pepper spray and arrests disrupted community celebrations. In Chicago, agents stormed areas where families gathered; in Los Angeles, they moved through public spaces with overwhelming force. The timing and tactics sent a clear message: even everyday civic life in immigrant neighborhoods could be disrupted at will. No gathering felt safe.

Individual cases revealed the human toll behind the spectacle. ICE deported Randall Alberto Gamboa Esquivel while he was in a vegetative state after months in detention; he later died abroad. In Chicago, agents arrested a daycare worker inside a childcare center, allegedly using excessive force in front of children. In Los Angeles, they detained a U.S. citizen father during a parking lot raid and drove off with his toddler, leaving bystanders stunned. These were not isolated errors; they reflected a pattern of aggressive enforcement that ignored due process, family integrity, and community trauma. The law's sharp edge fell hardest on the most vulnerable.

The machinery behind these actions became more complex and less transparent. ICE considered hiring private bounty hunters to track immigrants, proposing to pay profit-driven contractors to locate people for enforcement. The agency also announced a 24/7 call center in Nashville to help law enforcement find unaccompanied migrant children using data tools, expanding surveillance over one of the most vulnerable populations in the system. Congress, for its part, passed legislation allocating $45 billion to expand ICE detention centers, including facilities for children. The funding solidified a detention-centered approach to migration, with new beds and buildings that will outlast any single policy debate. Concrete and contracts fixed a set of choices.

State-level decisions reinforced this stratification. The Texas Department of Public Safety suspended issuing commercial driver's licenses to non-citizens, including DACA recipients, cutting off lawful work opportunities in a key economic sector. A major ICE raid at a Hyundai-LG battery plant in Georgia detained and deported over 300 South Korean workers, disrupting a significant manufacturing project and unsettling foreign investors. Together, these actions signaled that immigration status and national origin could determine not only one's risk of raids and detention but also one's access to basic economic participation. Work itself became dependent on status.

Beyond immigration, the week's decisions deepened a hierarchy of citizenship and rights. The Supreme Court allowed the administration to enforce a passport policy that limits sex markers to sex at birth, preventing transgender and non-binary people from accurate identification on federal documents. The conservative majority's order reinstated a rule that affects travel, safety, and recognition for these communities. Meanwhile, the Court considered whether to hear Davis v. Ermold, a case that could reopen questions about nationwide same-sex marriage rights. Even the possibility of revisiting settled precedent unsettled LGBTQ+ protections, indicating that established rights were once again uncertain. Security of status became provisional.

Domestic social policy moved similarly. In Utah, state officials advanced plans to build a large facility to involuntarily confine unhoused individuals under a rehabilitation model. The shift from housing-first approaches to locked "campuses" reframed homelessness as a moral failing to be corrected through confinement rather than a condition to be addressed with housing and services. The policy risked criminalizing poverty and weakening the rights of unhoused people to move and assemble. Meanwhile, Trump froze $100 million in federal funds for tribal climate relocation projects, halting promised support for communities facing rising seas and environmental displacement. The decision used executive control over appropriations to stall aid for some of the country's most vulnerable residents. Vulnerability met delay, not relief.

Other institutions made decisions that increased inequality. The Federal Communications Commission voted to raise allowable rates for prison phone and video calls, shifting more costs onto incarcerated individuals and their families, even while it reinstated a ban on kickbacks in prison phone contracts. An Oklahoma judge approved a youthful offender plea deal with minimal punishment for an eighteen-year-old convicted of multiple rapes, raising questions about whose crimes are met with leniency. In this context, Colorado voters approved a tax increase on high earners to fund universal school meals and raises for cafeteria workers, presenting a different approach where fiscal tools are used to expand, rather than restrict, basic security.

This contrast showed that alternative paths still existed. If the social order was becoming more stratified, the economic system was being rewritten to benefit those close to power. The administration and Congress passed a major tax cut bill that primarily favored wealthy individuals and corporations, shifting fiscal benefits upward and limiting resources for public programs. Simultaneously, the White House ordered the demolition of the East Wing to build a $300 million ballroom, replacing traditional public-service spaces with an area dedicated to presidential prestige. The physical seat of government itself transformed into a platform for personal glorification. Public architecture was molded to support one man's image.

The ballroom project was more than symbolic. Extremity Care, a health-care company selling costly skin substitutes, secretly donated $2.5 million toward construction, channeling the money anonymously while benefiting from a delayed Medicare rule that would have restricted coverage of its products. The administration postponed the cost-control rule and later proposed a payment cap that still allowed coverage of unproven, expensive treatments. The company's CEO attended an exclusive donor dinner with Trump amidst these favorable decisions. The sequence—regulatory delay, secret donation, high-level access—demonstrated how policy could be shaped by those able to buy proximity to power. Pay-to-play shifted from suspicion to pattern.

Regulatory capture also appeared in other sectors. The FCC's decision to raise prison phone rate caps favored telecommunications providers over incarcerated families. NASA's administrator, Jared Isaacman, was reappointed after pressure from Elon Musk, highlighting how major scientific appointments could be influenced by private interests rather than independent evaluation. The Federal Reserve injected $125 billion in short-term liquidity into the banking system to stabilize funding markets during economic stress, socializing risk while profits remained private. Tariff policies hurt manufacturers like Toyota and Stellantis, leading to layoffs and economic anxiety in rural communities, even as the administration maintained export controls on advanced chips to China and escalated a trade war that cut soybean exports and restricted rare-earth minerals. The gains and losses reflected lines of power.

Within this economic landscape, wealth did not just buy access; it bought law. Trump pardoned Binance founder Changpeng Zhao after his money-laundering conviction, despite the firm's ties to his family. He later admitted he had granted clemency without fully understanding who Zhao was, highlighting the arbitrary and self-interested use of the pardon power in high-stakes financial cases. The president also pardoned Michael McMahon, a former police officer convicted of acting as an agent for China in an intimidation plot, and approved a lenient plea in a serious rape case. These decisions fit alongside the tax cuts and regulatory favors as part of a broader pattern where elite financial and political crimes avoided real punishment. Accountability bent around wealth and connections.

The week's most sweeping act of impunity came with mass pardons for seventy-seven people involved in efforts to overturn the 2020 election. Issued while shutdown fights, tariff litigation, and immigration raids dominated headlines, the clemency orders removed federal accountability for key figures in a scheme of democratic subversion. A technical glitch briefly posted seven pardons online with nearly identical signatures, later replaced, raising questions about whether clemency had been reduced to an administrative bulk process rather than a case-by-case constitutional act. The timing and manner of the pardons suggested both confidence and carelessness: confidence that such acts would stand, and carelessness about the appearance of individualized justice. The signal to future plotters was unmistakable.

At the same time, the Justice Department's choices and congressional maneuvers worked to hide elite wrongdoing. Representative Jamie Raskin accused DOJ of a "gigantic cover-up" in abruptly ending the Epstein co-conspirator inquiry, highlighting concerns that abuse cases involving powerful figures were being shielded from full investigation. In the House, Speaker Mike Johnson delayed swearing in Adelita Grijalva for more than six weeks after her special election win, preventing her from voting and from signing a discharge petition that would have forced the release of Epstein-related records. Arizona's attorney general sued the House over the delay, arguing that withholding the oath violated constitutional representation. The combined effect of closing the investigation and blocking procedural steps was to keep sensitive files out of public and congressional view. Memory itself was controlled from above.

Courts showed flashes of skepticism toward politicized prosecutions, but within a system already tilted. In the case against former FBI director James Comey, a magistrate judge ordered prosecutors to turn over all grand jury materials and later demanded complete transcripts after an incomplete submission. The rulings signaled judicial concern that the indictment might reflect retaliatory use of the Justice Department. Yet even as some judges pressed for transparency, DOJ launched an investigation into California's redistricting referendum while Trump labeled it a "GIANT SCAM," casting doubt on a voter-approved measure and spreading disinformation about fraud. House Republicans explored using the Fourteenth Amendment's insurrection clause to block Zohran Mamdani from becoming New York City mayor, signaling a willingness to call opponents illegitimate rather than accept electoral outcomes. Law became a weapon more than a limit.

Media and oversight figures operated under pressure in this environment. CBS paid Trump $16 million to settle a lawsuit over editing his 60 Minutes interview while the network sought approval for a merger, suggesting that major outlets might temper editorial decisions to avoid political retaliation and secure business deals. Within the FBI, Director Kash Patel forced out senior aviation official Steven Palmer after scrutiny of the director's personal jet use, a move that appeared like retaliation against internal oversight. These actions reinforced a climate where watchdogs and independent voices—whether inside agencies or in the press—faced financial and professional risks for challenging those in power. The cost of speaking out increased.

The administration also aimed to reshape knowledge institutions and civic narratives. Cornell University reached a settlement restoring federal funds in exchange for sharing data and adopting the administration's civil rights interpretations, including campus climate evaluations under federal standards. The White House proposed a broader "compact" offering universities preferential funding if they promoted a conservative agenda and rolled back diversity initiatives. Combined, these measures tied research funding and institutional stability to ideological conformity, pressuring higher education to align with the ruling bloc's cultural and legal priorities. The classroom became another battleground.

Information management extended beyond campuses. Economic officials and spokespeople selectively framed data, claiming improvements in inflation and prices while downplaying the administration's role in economic hardships. The SNAP defiance in North Carolina was portrayed as a matter of constitutional principle rather than lawbreaking. The FBI planned an open advisory meeting on national crime information systems, even as ICE built a data-driven call center to track unaccompanied minors. These developments showed how data systems could be used both to manage populations and influence perceptions, depending on who controlled the definitions and the flow of information. Numbers became tools for narrative as well as policy.

Religion and security narratives were woven into this fabric. Trump's threat to invade Nigeria to protect Christians abroad invoked faith as a justification for force, blending foreign policy with sectarian appeals that could marginalize other groups. At home, FBI Director Patel publicized an alleged Halloween terror plot by young gamers, a claim that defense lawyers challenged. The incident raised concerns that ordinary behavior could be exaggerated into extremism, justifying broader surveillance and enforcement. In each case, identity—religious, sexual, national—became a lens through which the state claimed the right to act more aggressively. Categories of belonging influenced exposure to power.

Amid these pressures, some institutional routines persisted. The Census Bureau sought approval to continue collecting the demographic data for the Current Population Survey. The Environmental Protection Agency issued rules on chemical uses and pesticide residues. The Food and Drug Administration scheduled an advisory committee meeting on a heart device. Senate committees held hearings on veterans' disability benefits reporting. These actions maintained parts of the administrative state's normal operations, but they occurred alongside, and often beneath, the more significant shifts in how power was exercised and whom it served. Normalcy endured in pockets.

Looking ahead from this week, several processes were already underway. The Supreme Court's pending decisions on emergency tariffs and its review of a same-sex marriage case would determine how much executive authority and civil rights could be extended. Appeals over SNAP funding would test whether courts could enforce welfare obligations against a resistant White House. The new ICE detention funding and Utah's plans for a homelessness facility would move from approval to construction, solidifying physical infrastructures of confinement. University agreements and settlements would start to influence curricula and campus policies. The decisions made this week will have lasting effects in brick, paper, and digital forms.

In the course of Trump's second term, this week signified a deepening of existing patterns rather than their beginning. Executive defiance of courts, the routine use of war and emergency powers, the merging of public office with private gain, and the stratification of citizenship all advanced further. Meanwhile, judges ordered compliance, voters chose redistributive policies, and civil society actors sued to enforce representation and expose cover-ups. The overall effect was not stagnation but tension: democratic processes still functioned, yet they operated within a system increasingly designed to absorb, delay, or punish their signals. The moral standards further declined, even as parts of the system struggled to hold.

CHAPTER 53
WEEK 43: MEMORY AND LAW AS WEAPONS

> *A settled pattern emerges as the executive bends welfare, enforcement, and even museums to its will while courts and Congress mount scattered, fragile checks.*

The week did not hinge on a single order or speech. Instead, it unfolded as a series of decisions that, taken together, revealed a government more willing to deploy every available lever—funding, law enforcement, data, and even museums—to protect itself and punish those outside its circle. The pattern was not new, but it was more settled. What once appeared as improvisation now seemed intentional.

At the end of the previous period, the Democracy Clock stood at 8:11 p.m. By the end of Week 43, it remained at 8:11 p.m., reflecting a net change of minus 0.3 minutes. The hands did not jump, but they did not pause. The small backward shift captured a week during which the executive expanded its control over law and administration, while courts and parts of Congress achieved a few narrow wins for transparency and due process. The balance of power tilted further toward a presidency that viewed constraints as problems to be solved rather than principles to uphold.

The most visible sign of this imbalance was the record-length government shutdown. After forty-three days, Congress and the president agreed on a temporary funding measure that reopened agencies, restored back pay, and reversed some planned layoffs. The Senate passed the bill with bipartisan support, and the House adopted the same framework. When the president signed it, the spectacle of shuttered offices and unpaid workers ended. However, the core dispute over health care subsidies and food assistance remained unresolved. Earlier Democratic proposals to extend Affordable Care Act premium credits and protect SNAP had been set aside. The deal reinstated movement without resolving the fundamental fight over basic welfare.

Within the shutdown episode, Congress showed both its weakness and its capacity for self-correction. A little-noticed rider in the House version of the funding bill would have allowed senators to sue the Justice Department for damages if they were improperly surveilled, creating an opportunity for individual lawmakers to profit from institutional misconduct. The provision passed once, tucked into the larger package. Only after public criticism—from members like Representative Sean Casten and outside observers—did Speaker Mike Johnson commit to repealing it. Ethics, in this case, emerged as a reaction, not a guiding principle.

Meanwhile, the executive treated the shutdown as a stage to demonstrate control. The president threatened air traffic controllers who refused to work without pay, promising bonuses to those who complied and penalties for those who did not. Essential workers became pawns in a budget dispute. At the same time, he ordered national parks kept open despite furloughed staff, maintaining the illusion of normalcy while shifting risk onto visitors and fragile landscapes. The message was clear: public services could be manipulated to serve political ends, even when the law technically permitted it.

If the shutdown showed how the president used fiscal stress to influence behavior, immigration enforcement demonstrated how he relied on force and fear. The week started with scattered incidents that, taken alone, might have seemed like excesses: an ICE arrest in Massachusetts where a man collapsed while holding a child; reports of agents pepper-spraying an Illinois couple, their baby, and a relative during a stop; an officer in California pointing a gun at a woman filming him until local police intervened. In North Carolina, local law enforcement cooperated with ICE to trap undocumented workers. Each incident blurred the line between targeted enforcement and intimidation.

Policy changes widened that blur. The administration shut down the CBP One app, which had been a legal pathway for asylum seekers to schedule border crossings. Instead, there was more discretionary enforcement and mass deportation. New biometric rules for Canadian visitors required photos upon entry and exit, and registration for longer stays, increasing surveillance of regular travelers. These actions reduced rights-based access and boosted the government's ability to track and remove.

The clearest example was in Chicago. Under Operation Midway Blitz, ICE and CBP carried out large-scale raids, detaining about 1,300 people and turning immigrant neighborhoods into what residents called ghost towns. Advocates claimed that the operation broke a court order against warrantless arrests. Families stayed indoors, schools and workplaces emptied. The raids weren't just about who was taken; they were about making people feel law enforcement could arrive at any door, at any time.

Outside U.S. borders, the government pushed enforcement into rougher areas. It sent 252 Venezuelan men—many low-level or uncharged—to a notorious prison in El Salvador, labeling them irregular warfare operatives. This move blurred the line between immigration control and extraterritorial punishment, outsourcing custody to a foreign facility with fewer protections. At home, detainees at a privately operated ICE center in California filed a class-action lawsuit, alleging medical neglect, poor sanitation, and limited legal access, highlighting the dangers of delegating coercive power to for-profit contractors.

Courts didn't completely stay silent. Federal judges in Illinois blocked efforts to deploy National Guard troops for immigration enforcement, reaffirming the divide between military forces and domestic policing. Judge Sara Ellis issued a restraining order limiting ICE agents' use of force in Chicago. Judge Jeffrey Cummings ordered bond hearings and prohibited pressure for "voluntary" deportations, upholding due-process rights against mass arrests. Another court found the detention of daycare worker Diana Santillana Galeano unlawful and ordered a prompt bond hearing. While these rulings didn't stop the raids, they helped re-establish some legal limits on how they could be carried out.

The same pattern—assertive executive action, partial judicial brake—appeared in the way law and clemency were used. Early in the week, the president pardoned Binance founder Changpeng Zhao, known as CZ, after a major stablecoin deal tied to a Trump family business. The move signaled that financial crimes by well-connected actors could be washed away when they intersected with presidential interests. Clemency, in this case, was not a tool for mercy or correction; it was a reward.

At the same time, the president instructed the Justice Department to investigate named Democrats over their ties to Jeffrey Epstein. Federal law enforcement, which is supposed to enforce laws neutrally, was directed toward political opponents. DOJ also joined Republican lawsuits challenging California's congressional map and, according to activists, pursued false 2020 election fraud claims in Georgia. These actions made law seem like a weapon to be used, not a rule to follow.

Inside the prison system, the treatment of Ghislaine Maxwell raised similar concerns. Reports detailed preferential conditions for the high-profile inmate and the firing of staff who leaked her emails to Congress. House Judiciary Committee Democrats subpoenaed those emails to see if she had received special treatment. The fight over her correspondence was about more than one prisoner; it was about whether information that could embarrass powerful people could stay hidden.

Financial regulators and watchdogs also faced pressure. At the

Consumer Financial Protection Bureau, the Justice Department claimed that the agency's funding—coming from Federal Reserve earnings—was illegal. The Office of Legal Counsel issued an opinion that negative Fed earnings prevented CFPB funding. White House budget director Russell Vought announced plans to shut down the bureau within three months. On paper, these were technical disputes over funding and laws. In reality, they appeared to be a coordinated effort to weaken a watchdog created to police financial abuses.

Housing finance experienced a similar story. Federal Housing Finance Agency director Bill Pulte was accused of politicizing his role, attacking perceived enemies, and pressuring the Federal Reserve chair. At Fannie Mae, many employees were fired under the guise of ending diversity, equity, and inclusion programs, but the layoffs seemed targeted at oversight staff too. Leadership and FHFA officials were involved in leaking confidential mortgage pricing data to a competitor, and those who questioned the leak were pushed out. When the Justice Department and FHFA leadership removed ethics officials amid an investigation into improper access to political mortgage files, it suggested that those asking difficult questions were being pushed aside.

Not all legal processes moved in the same direction. In Georgia, after District Attorney Fani Willis was removed from the Trump 2020 election interference case, prosecutor Pete Skandalakis took over, keeping the case going. A federal bankruptcy court approved a $7 billion settlement to restructure Purdue Pharma into a nonprofit, extracting funds from the Sackler family while maintaining some capacity for treatment. A former aide to California's governor was indicted for campaign fund fraud. These actions showed that, in some areas, the law still worked as a check on power and a means of justice.

Below these headline conflicts, the machinery of administration was being redirected. USDA, armed with a Supreme Court stay, ordered states to recover November SNAP benefits and warned of financial penalties for noncompliance. Emergency food payments to 42 million people were withheld or reversed during the shutdown. The memo to states was written in bureaucratic language, but its effect was clear. Low-income households would shoulder the cost of fiscal and political strategy.

At the Environmental Protection Agency, a proposed rule would ease reporting requirements for PFAS, a class of toxic "forever chemicals." Many low-concentration, byproduct, imported, and research uses would be exempt from disclosure, reducing transparency about substances linked to serious health risks. Elsewhere in the agency, one-third of surveyed museums reported losing federal grants or contracts, forcing cuts to educational programs serving students and vulnerable groups. Although the funding decisions did not carry explicit ideological labels, they aligned with a broader effort to weaken institutions that foster critical civic understanding.

Other EPA actions appeared more routine: extending comment periods on a D4 chemical risk evaluation, postponing a science advisory meeting disrupted by the shutdown, giving non-federal labs more time to comply with methylene chloride safety rules, and publishing environmental impact statements for projects such as a Texas ship channel expansion. The agency also approved Texas's authority over Class VI carbon sequestration wells. These steps showed that technical rulemaking and cooperative federalism continued to function. However, they were overshadowed by high-impact choices favoring industry convenience and limiting public oversight.

Abroad and at the border, security tools were employed in ways that blurred policy and punishment. The case of Sami Hamdi, a British commentator, illustrated this. After criticizing Israel, his visa was revoked and canceled. ICE detained him at San Francisco International Airport and expelled him from the country, labeling him a security threat without charges. His treatment suggested that dissenting foreign voices could be cast as threats rather than participants in debate.

That same week, the United States continued supporting Israeli military actions in Gaza and the West Bank that critics described as genocidal. The USS Gerald R. Ford was deployed to Latin American waters under an anti-drug banner, escalating military presence near Venezuela. Britain, uneasy about lethal U.S. strikes in the Caribbean, suspended intelligence sharing amid fears of being complicit in unlawful operations. These moves strained alliances and raised questions about how far the administration would go in using force without transparent legal justification.

In Europe, the administration reduced aid to Ukraine and other allies, weakening a frontline democracy facing Russian aggression. New tariffs on European imports used U.S. market power as a bargaining chip, while a favorable tariff break for Switzerland followed soon after the president received gold gifts from Swiss industry leaders. In these instances, trade policy appeared less as a neutral tool of national interest and more as a field where personal and political relationships could influence outcomes.

Domestic economic policy followed a similar pattern of spectacle and selectivity. The president proposed a $2,000 tariff-funded dividend for most Americans, framing it as a populist alternative to extending ACA subsidies. He floated the idea of abolishing private health insurance in favor of small direct government payouts. The administration announced plans for 50-year FHA mortgages that would lower monthly payments but increase lifetime interest and slow down equity growth. Each proposal offered immediate relief or cash but shifted long-term risk onto households and away from the government.

The informational foundation supporting these policies was also destabilized. A senior economic adviser admitted that the Bureau of Labor Statistics had been hollowed out and that inflation and employment data might be fabricated. The president claimed China had agreed to relax rare earth export restrictions, despite conflicting reports. When official data and statements become unreliable, citizens lose a vital tool to judge performance and hold leaders accountable. Markets and policymakers also face challenges navigating without trusted benchmarks.

Cronyism intertwined with these decisions. Trump-branded wine and cider began appearing in Coast Guard-run exchanges, tax-advantaged stores on military bases. The line between public facilities and a sitting president's private business blurred. The Swiss tariff break, following gold gifts from Swiss industry leaders, reinforced the sense that foreign economic actors could buy favorable treatment. Meanwhile, corporate sponsors like Beam and Eight Sleep continued funding Tucker Carlson's podcast even after he platformed white supremacist Nick Fuentes, channeling private money into extremist media. Only after public scrutiny did one sponsor, Rocket Money, withdraw.

Information itself became a contested space. In New York City's mayoral race, Andrew Cuomo's campaign shared AI-generated videos depicting opponent Zohran Mamdani in racially charged ways, while Eric Adams's campaign used AI robocalls and dystopian imagery to dramatize urban decline. At the national level, the former president posted an AI-generated video of himself flying a jet and attacking Americans during protests. These synthetic images and voices did not merely entertain; they normalized a political language in which the line between real and fabricated visuals was intentionally blurred.

Right-wing outlet The Blaze published and amplified an unverified story claiming a former Capitol Police officer as the January 6 pipe bomber, based on speculative gait analysis. Legal threats forced a pause, but the damage to the individual's reputation and to public understanding of the unresolved attack was done. The president threatened to sue the BBC for $1 billion over a misleading edit in a January 6 documentary, using the threat of massive litigation to discourage critical coverage. Meanwhile, reports that DOJ was investigating debunked Georgia fraud claims suggested that institutional weight might be used to support narratives already discredited.

Against this backdrop, Congress and abuse survivors pushed in opposite directions on a key case: Jeffrey Epstein. House Oversight Committee Democrats released 23,000 subpoenaed documents, including emails that seemed to challenge the president's claims of ignorance about Epstein's crimes; one message stated that he "of course... knew about the girls." Republicans on the committee released 20,000 pages detailing Epstein's efforts to hide negative coverage and manipulate search results. The disclosures revealed how a wealthy offender shaped public narratives to avoid scrutiny and how elite networks intersected with his operations.

Inside the House, Representative Adelita Grijalva and a bipartisan group of members completed a discharge petition to force a vote on the Epstein Files Transparency Act, requiring the Justice Department to release sealed records. Survivors and family members delivered a letter demanding that the vote proceed. Speaker Johnson, despite personal opposition and pressure from the former president on allies like Lauren Boebert and Nancy Mace to withdraw support, scheduled the vote. The move bypassed leadership control and required a recorded roll call, preventing members from quietly sidestepping a decision on whether to open the files.

The debate over Epstein records coincided with a broader effort by the executive branch to shape public memory. An executive order directed the Smithsonian to remove "improper, divisive, or anti-American" content, with a particular focus on exhibits at the National Museum of African American History and Culture. Administration reviews targeted displays that depicted U.S. history critically, especially regarding race and injustice. Combined with the loss of federal funding for many museums, these actions pressured cultural institutions to sanitize their narratives. What remained visible to the public was what those in power found acceptable.

Courts and local agencies offered modest counterweights. A federal judge approved a settlement of over $3 million and an apology for the police raid on the Marion County Record, a small Kansas newspaper, signaling judicial disapproval of law enforcement actions that chill press freedom. In Georgia, the state election board settled a lawsuit over members' use of private email for official business, agreeing to use official accounts and avoid ephemeral messaging. These steps strengthened transparency norms in specific areas of the system, even as larger forces moved in the opposite direction.

Universities and campuses became another battleground over speech, protests, and power. Two professors at the University of Texas at Dallas sued the institution and state officials, claiming they were arrested during a peaceful protest and then barred from campus in retaliation. In California, tenured professor Ramsi Woodcock challenged his ban from teaching after making anti-Israel remarks, raising questions about how Title VI, antisemitism concerns, and academic freedom should be balanced. These cases asked courts to define the boundaries between civil rights enforcement and constitutional protections in academic environments.

Local authorities responded to hate incidents using existing tools. At Mississippi State University, a student was arrested and charged with disturbing the peace after antisemitic taunts and coin-throwing at a public event featuring media figure Dave Portnoy. The arrest demonstrated that the law could be used to address harassment without new speech-specific statutes. Simultaneously, the Anti-Defamation League announced an initiative to monitor mayor-elect Zohran Mamdani for antisemitism, illustrating how civil society groups can influence political reputation and debates over what constitutes legitimate criticism versus hate.

These campus and civic disputes occurred against a backdrop of polarized foreign policy. The U.S. stance on Israel and Palestine, the deployment of military assets in Latin America, and the reduction of aid to Ukraine fueled domestic debates about loyalty, security, and dissent. Immigration status, funding, and access to platforms became tools in these debates, used to reward agreement and punish deviation.

Looking ahead from Week 43, the scheduled House vote on the Epstein Files Transparency Act served as a concrete test. With a discharge petition already in place and survivors demanding action, the question was not whether the bill would reach the floor, but how members would vote and whether the Justice Department and other agencies would fully comply if the bill passed.

Overall, the week reinforced an existing pattern rather than starting a new one. Executive power extended further into law enforcement, welfare administration, foreign policy, and cultural memory, often without effective oversight. Congress showed moments of independence on transparency and ethics but mostly accepted the president's leverage on key social protections. Courts, particularly at the district level, enforced due process in immigration cases, blocked some military deployments, and upheld press freedom and open records in specific disputes. However, these acts of resistance were scattered and reactive, not yet forming a coherent counterweight.

The moral baseline of governance weakened under the weight of self-interested pardons, retaliatory investigations, and admissions that official data could no longer be trusted. Character, ethics, restraint, truthfulness, good faith, and stewardship all suffered visible blows. Yet, the fact that lawsuits were filed, discharge petitions completed, and injunctions issued showed that the architecture of accountability still existed and could be utilized. The Democracy Clock's near-stationary reading captured that tension: a system not yet broken but increasingly strained, where the cost of exercising rights and institutions rose even as their formal existence remained.

CHAPTER 54
WEEK 44: BELONGING REDRAWN BY FORCE

Immigration raids, anti-trans decrees, and secrecy fights hardened stratified citizenship while Congress and courts mounted partial, fragile checks on executive power.

The forty-fourth week of Trump's second term did not depend on a single order or event. Instead, it was a complex series of actions that changed who is seen by the government, who is protected by it, and who can use its force. Immigration raids, anti-trans policies, foreign agreements, and legal strategies appeared as separate incidents. When viewed together, they revealed a pattern of governing: using power to redraw boundaries of inclusion and decide what the country is allowed to remember about those outside the mainstream.

At the end of the previous week, the Democracy Clock read 8:11 p.m. By the end of Week 44, it still read 8:11 p.m. This stagnation did not mean calm. It reflected a week where already high risks were reinforced rather than sharply increased. Executive power continued to extend across law enforcement, identity, and information, while Congress and the courts showed signs of resistance. The balance between erosion and pushback remained stable, but the strain on the system deepened.

The most visible display of federal force came through immigration enforcement. The Department of Homeland Security launched Operation Charlotte's Web after local police in North Carolina refused to honor immigration detainers without judicial warrants. That refusal was an act of loyalty to due process. DHS saw it as defiance. The operation involved Customs and Border Protection and Border Patrol teams conducting large-scale interior raids in Charlotte and nearby areas—not at the border but in neighborhoods and workplaces where people had built lives.

In Charlotte, agents searched homes and streets, detaining immigrants and, in some cases, U.S. citizens. Reports described property damage and questions about warrants. The raids weren't targeting serious criminals. Court records from a similar Chicago operation, Midway Blitz, later showed most people arrested there had no criminal convictions. The pattern was clear: enforcement power was being broadly used against ordinary residents, with security language masking a large-scale sweep that treated presence itself as a threat.

Communities responded. Charlotte residents and local groups organized large protests outside a DHS office, demanding an end to the raids and respect for warrants. Federal officers arrested at least two protesters outside the facility, turning a protest over enforcement tactics into another example of those tactics. In Raleigh–Durham, as agents moved into the region, community organizations formed witness teams and hotlines to monitor encounters and support families. The right to assemble and observe the state at work was under pressure when it was most important.

The federal government also expanded its use of uniformed force. The administration sent National Guard troops into several U.S. cities without local approval, citing unrest and immigration enforcement needs. Guard units, trained for war and disaster, now patrolled streets across the country despite objections from mayors and governors. The move blurred the line between police work and military action. It made an emergency stance seem normal as a routine tool of governance, especially in areas that resisted federal priorities.

Some institutions pushed back. In Chicago, a federal court reprimanded a Border Patrol official for attacks on peaceful protesters, highlighting that even in tense situations, federal agents are still bound by constitutional limits. In another case, a court hearing in Castañon Nava v. DHS revealed the arrest records from Midway Blitz, showing how few detainees had criminal histories and challenging official justifications. On the West Coast, the San Diego City Council moved forward with an ordinance requiring federal agents to get warrants before entering non-public areas of city facilities, reasserting judicial oversight over federal presence in local spaces. These actions did not stop the raids or the Guard deployments. However, they set boundaries that some local and judicial authorities were still willing to establish.

If immigration enforcement demonstrated how the administration used force against communities and regions it disfavored, its treatment of transgender people showed how it used law and bureaucracy to redraw the map of citizenship itself. In just one week, the White House issued Executive Order 14183, banning most transgender people from military service and ending gender-affirming care for those who remained. Service members who had built careers under previous rules now faced exclusion or the loss of promised medical coverage. A lawsuit by transgender Air Force members seeking early retirement pensions and benefits they believed were unlawfully denied became one of the first legal tests of this new regime.

The military order was only part of the picture. Executive Order 14168 and related guidance reversed federal recognition of gender identity across documents and systems. The administration removed the "X" gender marker from passports and limited the ability to update gender markers, narrowing whose identities the state would acknowledge. It removed LGBTQ health pages, suicide-risk data, and trans-related terminology from federal records, including health guidance. Where data once highlighted increased risks and needs, there are now gaps. Harms that cannot be measured are easier to ignore.

Downstream systems followed the same logic. A separate order threatened funding for hospitals providing gender-affirming care for youth, pressuring health systems to cut services even where families and doctors agreed they were necessary. Housing guidance pushed shelters to exclude transgender women from women's spaces based on "biological sex," raising the risk of homelessness and violence for a group already at high risk. New prison rules directed that trans women be transferred to men's facilities and that solitary confinement be used as a default response to threats, trading safety for isolation. The administration also cut funding for the 988 suicide hotline's LGBTQ youth dedicated option, removing a tailored support line just as policy-driven stress was rising.

Education and culture were not spared. Federal directives removed LGBTQ- and race-related books and guidance from military-base schools and discouraged social transition support, limiting what children in government-run schools could learn about themselves and their peers. The administration characterized these moves as "restoring biological truth" and promoted "exploratory therapy," which critics compared to conversion practices. This language framed recent progress in recognition and protection as deviations from reality and labeled supporters as extremists. Following these federal signals, more than twenty-five states enacted or advanced laws restricting gender-affirming care for minors, demonstrating how national cues can spur state-level rollbacks.

Individual acts of resistance emerged within the system. An FBI employee, David Maltinsky, sued the Bureau and the Justice Department, claiming he was wrongfully fired for displaying a Pride flag, raising concerns about viewpoint discrimination within a major security agency. Transgender service members turned to courts to defend their pensions and status. Yet, the overall policy direction was clear. Across military, healthcare, housing, prisons, education, and documentation, transgender people faced increasing marginalization, with their existence progressively erased from official records.

While identity-based stratification hardened, a parallel struggle unfolded over whether law would limit or uphold power. Congress, in an unusual display of near unanimity, passed the Epstein Files Transparency Act. The House voted 427–1 to require the Department of Justice to release unclassified records related to Jeffrey Epstein. The Senate approved the measure by unanimous consent. After months of delay, ordinary members forced a vote through a discharge petition, overcoming leadership hesitation and executive opposition. The House then officially transmitted the resolution to the Senate and, after passage there, to the president.

Trump signed the bill, officially establishing a legislative check on executive secrecy in a case involving powerful networks. Simultaneously, his administration moved to weaken its impact. The president ordered a new investigation into Epstein-related links that could be used to justify withholding records, creating a pretext to invoke "ongoing investigations" as a shield. The White House and Attorney General Pam Bondi tried to withhold files despite the new law, citing broad national security and investigative exemptions. House Oversight Democrats and media outlets warned publicly that records might be destroyed or hidden, and Ranking Member Robert Garcia cautioned DOJ against tampering with the archive.

The fight over the files became a test of whether transparency laws would be truly binding or merely obstacles to be bypassed. The Epstein issue did not happen alone. The House Oversight Committee released more than 20,000 documents from Epstein's estate, revealing networks that had long avoided scrutiny. Ethics investigators reported that former Representative Matt Gaetz likely paid a 17-year-old for sex, emphasizing both the need for strong oversight and the limits of criminal accountability for powerful figures. A Senate Finance Committee report found that JPMorgan Chase underreported over a billion dollars in suspicious Epstein-linked transactions, showing how major banks can shield elite misconduct when compliance systems are weak or conflicted. Senator Ron Wyden called for a deeper investigation into the bank's handling of those transactions.

Elsewhere in the justice system, patterns of impunity and weaponization appeared. The Department of Justice entered settlement talks with Michael Flynn over his $50 million claim against the government, a move that hints at preferential treatment for a pardoned former official. Trump pardoned white-collar offender Charles Scott after minimal jail time, and a January 6 participant he had previously pardoned, Andrew Paul Johnson, was arrested on new child sexual abuse charges—reigniting debate over whether clemency had been granted to individuals who posed ongoing risks. In the James Comey case, a federal magistrate judge found government misconduct and ordered grand jury materials to be turned over to the defense. Prosecutors admitted they had failed to present a revised indictment to the grand jury and submitted an unauthorized charging document. This episode revealed a serious breach of charging procedures in a politically sensitive case.

Other enforcement tools showed signs of politicization. A grand jury opened an inquiry into whether Federal Housing Finance Agency Director Bill Pulte and DOJ prosecutor Ed Martin had appointed unauthorized individuals in mortgage probes targeting Trump critics. Workers at a Utah business sued former state attorney general Sean Reyes, alleging he had used false information in a televised trafficking raid that damaged their livelihoods. Along with Trump's directive to Attorney General Bondi to investigate named Democratic figures using Epstein materials, these cases demonstrated how investigative power could be manipulated to target enemies and protect allies.

Beneath these headline conflicts, the machinery of administration further shifted toward loyalty, patronage, and personal gain. At the FBI, Director Kash Patel waived standard polygraph exams for senior officials needing access to sensitive information, weakening internal vetting in one of the country's most powerful security agencies. He also assigned an FBI security detail to his girlfriend, Alexis Wilkins, diverting specialized protection resources to a private relationship. These decisions signaled to staff that rules could be bent for insiders and that closeness to the director was more important than neutral standards.

At the Department of Homeland Security, Secretary Kristi Noem oversaw a $220 million anti-immigration advertising campaign that mostly benefited a politically connected Delaware firm without competitive bidding. The contract blurred the lines between public procurement and partisan messaging, turning a core agency into a tool for both ideology and patronage. At the Department of Veterans Affairs, officials abruptly ended an agreement to provide medical care for ICE detainees without a replacement system, resulting in detainees losing access to dialysis, chemotherapy, and other critical treatments. A class-action suit followed, alleging systemic denial of care, and a FOIA lawsuit by CASA sought records on how the VA handled detainee medical claims. The collapse revealed how life-and-death functions could be disrupted by opaque decisions faced with little internal oversight.

The human toll of these shifts was significant. In one case, Border Patrol improperly deported Britania Uriostegui Rios, a transgender woman, to Mexico despite a court order recognizing her risk of torture there. This deportation showed how enforcement agencies could override judicial protections and basic safety for marginalized individuals. More broadly, the VA–ICE breakdown and the anti-trans policies in prisons and shelters placed vulnerable people at the mercy of systems increasingly driven by ideology and expedience rather than a duty of care.

Other institutions related to security and emergency response also showed strain. Acting FEMA Administrator David Richardson resigned amid criticism and plans to downsize the agency, raising concerns about the federal government's capacity to manage disasters. Six former service secretaries and retired four-star officers issued a report warning about politicization of the U.S. military, citing domestic deployments and leadership purges as signs that the armed forces' apolitical character was deteriorating. Defense Secretary Pete Hegseth dismissed several senior officers, including the chair of the Joint Chiefs of Staff, as part of a broader reshaping of the military's top ranks. These actions suggested that high-level positions were being filled with a focus on political alignment rather than professional merit.

The pattern of pressure extended into civil society. The State Department moved to suspend thirty-eight universities from its Diplomacy Lab program over diversity, equity, and inclusion hiring practices, using access to a federal research partnership as leverage over campus governance. In Texas, Governor Greg Abbott unilaterally designated the Council on American-Islamic Relations and the Muslim Brotherhood as terrorist organizations under state law, despite terrorism designations being a federal authority. The step stigmatized Muslim civil rights advocacy as a security threat and signaled that religious identity could be used as a tool of political control.

Against this backdrop, Trump's own rhetoric took a darker turn. After a group of Democratic lawmakers released a video reminding military personnel of their duty to refuse unlawful orders, the president called for their execution. He repeated the threat the next day, portraying them as traitors deserving death. These were not offhand remarks. They were public statements by the head of state, aimed at elected officials, whose message was rooted in constitutional oaths. The effect was to normalize eliminationist language against political opponents and to warn those who might resist unlawful commands that they could be cast as enemies of the nation.

The threats fit into a broader pattern of coercion. Trump publicly criticized and withdrew support from Republican lawmakers over their stance on Epstein files and redistricting, using his influence to enforce loyalty and discourage independent judgment. He threatened to "strongly oppose" Indiana legislators who refused to gerrymander districts to his liking. Shortly after he attacked Indiana Senator Greg Goode over redistricting, Goode was targeted in a swatting incident—a false emergency call that brought armed police to his home. The sequence illustrated how heated rhetoric could translate into dangerous intimidation of elected officials, even if the perpetrators remained unknown.

Media and cultural figures also came under pressure. Trump announced his intention to sue the BBC for billions over coverage of his role in the Capitol riot, signaling a willingness to use civil courts to intimidate a public broadcaster. He attacked NBC host Seth Meyers for critical commentary, and FCC Commissioner Brendan Carr amplified calls for Meyers's firing, hinting at regulatory disfavor. When female reporters pressed him about foreign business ties, Trump suggested that ABC News should lose its license.

These moves did not immediately silence critics. They raised the cost of critical coverage and reminded media employers that regulatory power could be turned against them. Civil society responded in its own ways. Epstein survivors held press conferences at the Capitol, standing alongside supportive lawmakers to demand the release of the files and accountability for those who had enabled Epstein's abuse. The Removal Coalition and allied activists organized a large, peaceful mobilization in Washington, D.C., calling for transparency and democratic norms. Their presence underscored that, despite intimidation and legal uncertainty, organized dissent remained active and visible.

Foreign policy and private business interests intertwined as the administration deepened its ties with Saudi Arabia. Trump announced plans to sell F-35 fighter jets to the kingdom despite security objections from within the U.S. government and allies. He named Saudi Arabia a major non-NATO ally and announced significant economic deals, elevating an authoritarian partner to a privileged strategic status. In a meeting with Crown Prince Mohammed bin Salman, he praised the prince's record and downplayed the U.S. intelligence community's findings on Jamal

Khashoggi's murder. Human rights concerns and expert assessments were secondary to geopolitical and financial interests.

Simultaneously, the Trump Organization began talks to develop a Trump-branded property in a Saudi government real estate project and advanced plans for a tokenized luxury resort in the Maldives with Dar Global. These ventures stood to benefit from the relationships the president was cultivating in his official capacity. The overlap between public decisions and private gain was clear. It was presented as economic opportunity but raised fundamental questions about whether foreign policy decisions served the public interest or the president's personal network.

The broader security economy reflected similar dynamics. Congress contemplated a 2026 military budget nearing $1.045 trillion, with projections showing four major arms contractors receiving over a quarter of Pentagon contract dollars. These firms had channeled significant public funds into shareholder dividends. The concentration of defense spending in a few companies underscored how war and preparation for war could entrench corporate power over security policy. Meanwhile, Russia increased its bombardment of Ukrainian cities, drawing limited effective response from Trump, and analysts urged improvements in U.S. industrial policy to boost domestic drone production amid China's dominance of the drone supply chain. Security decisions were being made in a landscape where private profit, foreign influence, and public risk were closely intertwined.

Economic policy at home followed a similar pattern, with risks shifted downward and accountability blurred. The administration's Liberation Day tariffs on intermediate goods increased costs for manufacturers and contributed to rising unemployment and inflation, particularly in goods-producing sectors. Under pressure, the White House partially rolled back some tariffs through complex exemptions, but the overall regime remained. Workers in manufacturing and transportation bore the worst of the disruption. Meanwhile, Trump used executive authority to lift certain contested tariffs on key imports to address rising prices, highlighting how trade powers could be wielded unilaterally for short-term political gain rather than through broader discussion.

The administration's economic team promoted a "Golden Age" narrative, blaming former President Biden for beef price spikes and broader issues despite data indicating tariff-driven disruptions. Public statements downplayed job losses and inflation, contradicting industry reports and macroeconomic indicators. The result was an information environment where citizens found it difficult to connect policy decisions to real-world outcomes. Holding officials accountable for economic performance became more challenging when the official story diverged sharply from the evidence.

Elsewhere, other actors attempted to address structural imbalances. Commentators like Noah Smith argued that U.S. housing policy and zoning laws disadvantaged younger generations by keeping housing scarce and costly, highlighting how regulatory choices could reinforce intergenerational inequality. The City of Chicago settled a lawsuit with DoorDash for $18 million over pandemic-era practices that listed restaurants without consent and inflated prices, demonstrating how local governments can use litigation to curb exploitative platform behavior. However, these efforts operated at the margins within a national policy environment that increasingly treated inequality as an inherent feature rather than a flaw.

Beneath and around these developments, the struggle over information and memory intensified. The same executive orders that removed recognition and protections for transgender people also deleted LGBTQ health pages, suicide-risk data, and trans-related terminology from federal records. Passport systems were modified to eliminate non-binary markers and restrict updates. Military-base schools were ordered to remove books and guidance regarding marginalized groups. These actions did more than alter policy; they rewrote the documentary record of who exists and the harms they face.

The administration's handling of the Epstein files followed a similar rationale. Although Congress mandated disclosure, the

White House and DOJ cited national security and ongoing investigations to limit release. Warnings from lawmakers and journalists about potential destruction or withholding of records highlighted how fragile archives can be when they involve powerful networks. The attempt to use exceptions to bypass transparency laws revealed how such laws could be hollowed out without formal repeal.

Meanwhile, official voices aimed to control the media environment. Attacks on Seth Meyers, threats of multibillion-dollar lawsuits against the BBC, and suggestions that ABC should lose its license indicated that critical coverage might face regulatory or legal retaliation. The administration also exploited overlapping crises—tariff changes, anti-trans orders, Epstein maneuvers, and heated rhetoric about lawmakers—to dominate the agenda. Each event demanded attention, but together they fragmented it. Chaos became a strategy to make sustained scrutiny difficult.

Outside the United States, China offered a clear example of where such control can lead. The Chinese government cracked down on social media content seen as overly pessimistic, censoring online expressions to influence public sentiment and silence criticism. It integrated social-media manipulation into its military and cohesion strategies, viewing information systems as tools for both internal control and external influence. Meanwhile, Beijing guided its economy through campaigns against "involution," subsidies to struggling electric-vehicle companies, and efforts to stabilize a declining real estate market. This combination of economic management and digital mood regulation illustrates a model where the state shapes both material and informational realities.

Within the American system, some institutions continued to follow more traditional norms. The Federal Communications Commission scheduled an open meeting to discuss spectrum, relay services, outdated rules, and cybersecurity, reflecting ongoing procedural governance of communications infrastructure. The FCC and other agencies sought public comments on rules related to information collection, confidentiality, and communications involving incarcerated individuals. Federal regulators and courts issued routine decisions on environmental and public health issues, including air quality, pesticides, medical products, and industrial pollution.

In New York City, mayor-elect Zohran Mamdani appointed former FTC chair Lina Khan to his transition team, signaling an intention to scrutinize private-equity influence over local services. The week also included the public resummoning of Abraham Lincoln's Gettysburg Address, a speech reaffirming democratic principles of equality and popular sovereignty. These elements did not reverse the larger trend of the week but showed that not all parts of the state had yet converged on the same pattern.

No major hearings or votes were scheduled for the week that would decisively change these trajectories, but several processes were already underway. Courts were preparing to handle the Epstein transparency law's implementation, the detainee medical class action, and lawsuits from trans service members and federal employees. Congress had enacted the Epstein mandate and promoted a discharge petition to restore federal workers' union rights. State and local entities, from San Diego's city council to Indiana's Senate, had taken procedural steps to resist certain pressures. These pending actions represent a narrow line of future tests for the system's remaining checks.

During Trump's second term, Week 44 was not a dramatic plunge but a deepening rut. Executive power continued to operate with limited oversight, bending law enforcement, identity policy, and information systems to serve elite interests and punish dissent. Meanwhile, Congress, courts, and civil society showed that resistance was still possible, even if often reactive and partial. The Democracy Clock did not move forward because the balance between erosion and pushback, already fragile, stayed the same. However, the buildup of layered citizenship, curated memory, and normalized coercion weakened the foundation of democratic life and made standing on it more difficult.

CHAPTER 55
WEEK 45: LAW AS SORTING MECHANISM

A week of static clock hands but deepening habits, as law, borders, and information are used to decide who counts and who may speak.

The forty-fifth week of Trump's second term did not depend on a single shock. It unfolded as a complex layering of actions that challenged law, borders, information, and memory simultaneously. The pattern was not new, but its confidence was. Law was skewed against enemies and in favor of allies. Immigration rules and security agencies were used to determine who belonged. Data, books, and broadcast licenses became tools in the same struggle. This week's story is less about a new decline than about the normalization of a way of governing.

At the end of the previous period, the Democracy Clock showed 8:11 p.m. It remains at 8:11 p.m., a zero-minute change. This stability does not mean inaction in the field. It reflects a balance: significant new damage to the moral foundation and institutional independence, offset by pockets of judicial resistance and civil opposition strong enough to prevent movement, but not to change course. The week reinforced existing patterns rather than creating new ones.

The clearest path of that pattern ran through how dissent was handled. Six Democratic veteran lawmakers released a video reminding service members of a core rule: they must refuse unlawful orders. In a healthy system, such a statement would be unremarkable, even expected from those who had worn the uniform. Here, it became the spark for a campaign. Trump condemned the video as "seditious," called for the lawmakers' arrest, and suggested their actions were punishable by death. The language of treason and execution, once reserved for the most serious betrayals, was applied to routine oversight speech.

Institutions responded accordingly. At the Pentagon and the newly renamed Department of War, officials launched investigations that could recall Senator Mark Kelly to active duty for court-martial over his involvement in the video. Military law, designed to regulate conduct in uniform, was stretched to punish civilian political speech. At the Justice Department, the FBI's counterterrorism division opened investigations into the six lawmakers, viewing their reminder about illegal orders as a potential security threat. The machinery built to track terrorists was turned toward elected representatives. It was a sharp shift.

At the same time, the president used his formal powers to erase consequences for those who had attacked the electoral system on his behalf. He issued a sweeping pardon whose language appeared broad enough to cover many 2020 election-related offenses, signaling that loyalty in that effort could secure immunity. In Georgia, prosecutors and courts dismissed the last racketeering case over Trump's 2020 interference after the elected district attorney was disqualified. A central avenue for legal reckoning over the attempt to overturn an election simply vanished.

Inside the Justice Department, the structure adapted to these new realities. Thousands of lawyers left or were pushed out, especially in civil rights, voting, and public integrity sections. The public integrity unit was shrunken to two lawyers and diverted from corruption cases. Voting-rights enforcement was steered to favor maps that benefited Republicans and oppose those that could help Democrats. The department, once claiming neutrality, was reshaped to protect the regime and harass its critics. Law became less about limits and more about tools.

Courts did not move uniformly. A federal judge dismissed prosecutions of James Comey and New York Attorney General Letitia James, ruling that the interim U.S. attorney who filed the cases had been appointed illegally. The decision reaffirmed constitutional appointment rules and blocked an obvious attempt to criminalize two Trump opponents. The Eleventh Circuit upheld nearly a million dollars in sanctions against Trump and his lawyer for a frivolous racketeering suit, sending a message that some courts would not allow their dockets to be weaponized. However, these pockets of resistance sat alongside Georgia's dismissal and other rulings that eased pressure on the president and his allies. The result was inconsistent law: strict for some, lenient for others.

The same week, Trump announced a pardon for former Honduran president Juan Orlando Hernández, convicted in U.S. courts of major drug trafficking. The move disregarded years of transnational anti-corruption efforts and signaled to foreign elites that ties to the White House could outweigh U.S. court verdicts. Trump also called for the release of Tina Peters, a Colorado election official convicted of compromising voting equipment to support his fraud claims, portraying her as a whistleblower instead of a saboteur. Those who broke the law on his behalf were recast as victims or heroes.

If law was being reshaped, so too was the presidency's unilateral power. Trump moved to cancel all executive orders signed by autopen during the Biden administration and planned to void most of his predecessor's directives. The official reason was technical—questioning the use of a mechanical signature—but the impact was broad. It claimed the power to retroactively invalidate prior presidential actions on a new basis, destabilizing legal continuity and implying that one president's signature could erase another's work.

This was part of a larger trend in 2025 executive orders that exceeded traditional limits. Orders challenged the independence of the Federal Reserve, threatened media outlets, and pressured courts. They were framed as necessary corrections or urgent responses, but together they shifted decision-making inward, toward the Oval Office, and away from shared institutions. Management speak masked where power truly resided.

Emergency powers, originally reserved for rare crises, became part of routine policy. The administration declared a national energy emergency to compel Consumers Energy to keep a Michigan coal plant operating despite plans to retire it and objections from the state. This order transferred an estimated $113 million in costs to regional ratepayers and increased local pollution. It justified overriding state policy by citing the plant's profitability and its role in the grid, and used emergency law to settle what was a regulatory and economic issue. Abroad, the Office of Legal Counsel issued a memo justifying lethal boat strikes in the Caribbean as collective self-defense that didn't require congressional approval. The opinion expanded the president's ability to use force without Congress by interpreting existing authorizations and self-defense doctrines broadly. War powers were gradually extended through interpretation, not new laws.

Other executive actions added to this trend. Trump launched the Genesis Mission, centralizing federal AI development and data use under his control. While promising efficiency and innovation, it also concentrated power over advanced tools capable of shaping surveillance, policy modeling, and information flow. He designated certain Muslim Brotherhood chapters as foreign terrorist organizations—a unilateral move with far-reaching implications for foreign policy, sanctions, and domestic surveillance. He ended Temporary Protected Status for Myanmar nationals and ordered broad reviews of refugee statuses, affecting legal residency based on shifting political considerations.

Economic policy followed similar unilateral and selective patterns. The administration canceled the release of the third-quarter GDP advance estimate, depriving the public and markets of an important economic indicator during a severe affordability crisis. Despite reports of nearly 10% annual price increases and widespread hardship, the data were withheld. Simultaneously, the White House announced a $12 billion bailout for farmers harmed by its own trade policies, socializing the costs of tariff policies while maintaining the strategy. Emergency orders and subsidies became tools to reward favored sectors and allies, embedding crony interests into infrastructure and energy decisions that would be difficult to undo. Immigration and citizenship policy also took a central role. Trump threatened to denaturalize immigrants he labeled as "non-compatible with Western civilization," implying citizenship could be revoked based on cultural or ideological grounds. DHS and USCIS increased asylum case reviews, re-examined green cards, and halted processing of Afghan residency applications, including those who aided U.S. forces. Ending Temporary Protected Status for Myanmar nationals and reviewing TPS for Somalis, following political promises to terminate it, further reflected this approach. Humanitarian protections once considered stable were recast as contingent favors.

On the ground, enforcement became harsher and more prone to errors. ICE increased detention of immigrant children in federal shelters, often after family separations, using custody practices that discouraged migrants from asserting rights or seeking protection. Agents detained a seventeen-year-old U.S. citizen student in Oregon during his lunch break, despite his claims of citizenship. They detained Bruna Ferreira, a Brazilian mother with deep U.S. family ties, over a visa overstay, and Maher Tarabishi, a longtime resident and caregiver, as a suspected criminal alien despite no criminal record. In another incident, ICE officers detained Native American actor Elaine Miles after deeming her tribal ID fake, blurring the line between tribal sovereignty and immigration enforcement.

Deportation logistics revealed another layer of complexity. ICE continued deportation flights under contentious contracts while facing a legal challenge from CSI Aviation, highlighting how removal operations were embedded in lucrative private arrangements that could outlast policy shifts. Airport protests, retail boycotts, and consumer campaigns targeted companies profiting from ICE work, showing civil society's efforts to curb coercive practices through market pressure. Yet the flights persisted.

Fear was not limited to noncitizens. In North Carolina, masked Border Patrol agents conducted street operations described by residents as kidnappings. People stayed home from work and school. Protests followed, but the immediate effect was to suppress everyday movement and, by extension, political participation. In Georgia, ICE raided a South Korean-owned battery factory, seemingly driven by arrest quotas, triggering a diplomatic incident and raising questions about who set enforcement priorities. The display of force served both domestic politics and broader strategic aims.

In Indiana, the tools of intimidation extended into the legislature itself. As Trump pushed for mid-decade redistricting to secure more GOP-leaning districts, state senator Michael Bohacek publicly opposed the plan, citing Trump's insults toward people with disabilities. Around the same time, lawmakers reluctant to endorse the maps were targeted with swatting attacks—false emergency calls that sent armed police to their homes. Police unwittingly became instruments in a campaign to increase the personal cost of resisting partisan gerrymandering. The message was clear: even fundamental rules of representation would be decided under pressure.

Against this backdrop, lawsuits and rights claims attempted to establish limits. Coalitions of states and the District of Columbia sued to block SNAP eligibility restrictions for certain legal immigrants and challenged HUD homelessness program changes that harmed trans and nonbinary people. Chicago faith leaders filed a First Amendment suit over clergy access to detained immigrants, arguing that DHS could not block spiritual support. These cases did not reverse the broader trend, but they kept alive alternative interpretations of law and responsibility.

Information and memory were fiercely contested. The cancellation of the GDP report was one issue, and another occurred at the

Centers for Disease Control and Prevention, where Health and Human Services Secretary Robert F. Kennedy Jr. directed edits to vaccine–autism web content that contradicted scientific consensus. These edits, later acknowledged, politicized core public health messaging and risked eroding trust in evidence-based guidance. National reading and math test results were released, revealing large numbers of students below basic levels, even as school districts and universities adopted no-zero grading and eliminated standardized tests. This created a strange landscape: stark data showing decline alongside policies that made honest performance measurement more difficult. Media and cultural institutions felt direct pressure. Trump again threatened to have the FCC revoke ABC's license over unfavorable coverage, despite lacking the authority, continuing a pattern of using regulatory language to intimidate critical outlets. He verbally attacked female reporters during a press conference, adding gendered abuse to the cost of asking tough questions.

The FCC, for its part, opened inquiries into how national programming affects local stations' public-interest duties and sought comment on E-Rate paperwork, modest steps that at least acknowledged structural strains on local news and school connectivity. In entertainment, political pressure led to Jimmy Kimmel's suspension, prompting millions of Disney and Hulu subscribers to cancel their services in protest. The episode demonstrated how regulatory intimidation could distort media markets, but also how consumers could push back. A poll showed that more than half of Americans would avoid buying Tesla for political reasons, illustrating how corporate political activity influenced consumer choices and, indirectly, the distribution of economic and communicative power.

The fight over memory was even more explicit in Tennessee. Secretary of State Tre Hargett ordered 181 public libraries to review and remove LGBTQ-themed books under anti-DEI and "gender ideology" rules. The directive imposed viewpoint-based censorship on local institutions, erasing some identities from public collections and signaling that state power would decide which lives could appear on the shelves. In North Carolina, the House Oversight Committee summoned the Chapel Hill School District over pronoun use and DEI policies, using the threat of sanctions to police inclusive practices and pressure educators to suppress support for transgender students.

At the federal level, the State Department moved to exclude universities that use DEI hiring from its Diplomacy Lab program, leveraging its partnership power to shape internal academic policies. Trump met cordially with New York City mayor-elect Zohran Mamdani after earlier threatening to withhold funds if he won, demonstrating how federal resources could be dangled or withdrawn based on local political choices. Together, these actions embedded culture-war enforcement into education and municipal governance, narrowing the space for pluralism.

The week's foreign-policy and security decisions reflected influence from external authoritarian powers and domestic elites. U.S. officials promoted and contested a 28-point Ukraine peace plan reportedly drafted with Russian input. Conflicting statements and leaks rebranded Russian-influenced terms as American proposals, making it unclear who was actually guiding U.S. policy. Simultaneously, the administration leaked false claims of a completed peace deal, manipulating media narratives and creating confusion among allies and the public.

The State Department designated Venezuela-linked Cartel de los Soles as a terrorist organization, broadening legal means for action against Caracas and raising concerns of escalatory steps with limited congressional oversight. Trump's order labeling certain Muslim Brotherhood chapters as foreign terrorist organizations similarly expanded unilateral security designations, affecting diplomacy, sanctions, and domestic surveillance. These classifications, while presented as counterterrorism measures, also served broader ideological and geopolitical objectives.

Private infrastructure played a key role in some of these decisions. Elon Musk's company xAI relied on Chinese-made transformers for a military-linked AI supercomputer, revealing supply-chain vulnerabilities in a system vital to national security. A lawsuit claimed that a Russian-linked subcontractor compromised data center security by photographing and sharing images of the facility. The Genesis Mission's centralization of federal AI and data under executive control, combined with these private vulnerabilities, created a landscape where foreign and domestic elites could influence both security policies and infrastructure for profit.

Economic hardship provided the backdrop for all these developments. Analysts documented rising electricity prices and increased power outages linked to grid upgrades for data centers, showing how infrastructure investments shifted costs onto vulnerable households. The affordability crisis worsened, with little policy to mitigate it. Public risk was transferred to ratepayers and taxpayers, while profits and strategic gains flowed to those closest to power.

Courts offered a mixed picture once again. A federal appeals court blocked the expansion of a rapid deportation policy for recent immigrants, affirming due process protections and checking executive overreach in immigration enforcement. A federal court temporarily halted Texas's mid-decade congressional redistricting that added Republican-leaning districts, preserving existing lines until the Supreme Court reviews, and slowing a key part of Trump's plan to secure House control. The Florida Supreme Court ruled that Marsy's Law did not automatically guarantee anonymity for police officers involved in fatal incidents, thereby strengthening transparency in use-of-force cases. Meanwhile, the Ohio Supreme Court issued split decisions, reflecting ongoing disagreements over the same issue.

Judges also ordered the Justice Department to speed up FOIA processing related to Epstein, and, together with DOJ, moved to unseal grand jury materials and investigation files. These actions increased public access to information about elite abuse networks, countering secrecy surrounding powerful figures. However, in North Dakota, the state supreme court reinstated a felony abortion ban with limited and vague exceptions, reducing reproductive rights and aligning with conservative legislative preferences. The dismissal of the Georgia election case, already acknowledged, removed a major avenue for holding Trump accountable. The judiciary remains a battleground, not a fully settled institution.

Amid these cross-currents, some actors tried to shed light on the landscape. Social media platform X introduced a transparency tool revealing the foreign origins of prominent MAGA accounts, exposing cross-border influence operations in U.S. politics. The move did not resolve the disinformation ecosystem, but it provided users with more context about the sources of polarizing content. In a week when the administration itself leaked misleading stories about Ukraine and discussed restrictions on speech after Charlie Kirk's assassination, any added transparency carried weight.

No single scheduled event overshadowed the week, but several ongoing processes were already underway: the pending Supreme Court review of the Texas maps, ongoing state and faith-leader lawsuits over SNAP, HUD, and detention access, and internal timelines for Genesis Mission build-out and emergency generation at coal plants. Each of these will influence future rulings, budgets, and infrastructure decisions based on the choices made during these days.

Taken together, Week 45 marked not a pause in deterioration but a consolidation of approach. Executive orders and emergency claims expanded unilateral power. Law enforcement and military tools were directed against lawmakers and migrants, while pardons and dismissals sheltered allies. Borders and citizenship became tools for sorting who could live without fear. Data, science, books, and broadcasts were curated to favor the regime's narrative. Courts and civil society pushed back in some places, enough to keep the Democracy Clock steady, but not enough to regain ground. The system still bore the marks of democracy, yet using them now required more courage and involved greater risk.

CHAPTER 56
WEEK 46: IMPUNITY AS OPERATING SYSTEM

A week of layered decisions turned clemency, immigration, security, and information policy into tools of faction, family, and fear rather than into instruments of public trust.

The forty-sixth week of Trump's second term did not hinge on a single shock. Instead, it unfolded as a complex series of decisions that, taken together, made the state feel more like a tool of faction and family than a guardian of shared public trust. Issues like law, borders, money, and memory were all affected. Each move was defensible within its narrow context. These actions showed a government increasingly willing to sort people by origin and loyalty, to manipulate institutions for private gain, and to treat force and secrecy as routine tools of control. The pattern was hard to miss.

At the beginning of Week 46, the Democracy Clock showed 8:11 p.m. It ended the week at the same time, with only a tiny shift of 0.0.1 minutes deeper into danger. The clock face stayed the same, but the structure behind it changed. The actions of the week revealed how far existing powers could be stretched: clemency became a shield for corrupt elites, immigration law a sift that sorted by heritage, security forces tools of political will, and economic policies vehicles for insiders. Courts and Congress showed some resistance but not enough to alter the trend. The drift persisted.

The clearest sign of this pattern was the president's use of clemency. Within a few days, he pardoned former Honduran president Juan Orlando Hernández, convicted in the U.S. for major drug trafficking; commuted and pardoned financier David Gentile, who faced a $1.6 billion fraud sentence; and granted clemency to executive Tim Leiweke, indicted for rigging a public university arena bid. He also pardoned Representative Henry Cuellar while he faced foreign bribery charges. These were not minor figures- they were political insiders and foreign power brokers whose crimes affected public trust, public funds, or both.

The volume of clemency matched its symbolism. Reports indicated that over 2,000 pardons and commutations had been granted in 2025, mostly to allies and corrupt actors. This turned the Constitution's safety valve into a patronage operation. The message was clear: proximity to the president could erase even serious financial and political crimes. For those outside that circle, the law remained strict and unforgiving. For those inside, it was negotiable.

Alongside these actions, the president attempted to manipulate perceptions of history. By declaring that all documents signed by President Biden using an autopen were invalid, he cast doubt on numerous previous executive actions, including pardons. Though lacking a clear legal basis, the move served a political purpose. It implied that legality depended on who held office and that a successor could retroactively invalidate lawful acts of their predecessor. The stability of law, which relies on signatures as institutional rather than personal symbols, was jeopardized. The foundation of established decisions shifted. The same week revealed how legal instruments were wielded against perceived enemies. A Reuters-reported campaign of retaliation targeted at least 470 individuals and organizations for actions the president disliked.

This was not a single prosecution or an isolated threat; it was a systematic use of state power—investigations, regulatory actions, and other means—against critics. In this context, clemency for allies and pressure on opponents became parts of the same strategy: law as both weapon and shield, used based on loyalty. Justice as equality diminished. However, the justice system did not collapse everywhere. Federal courts invalidated two unlawful U.S. attorney appointments used to prosecute politically sensitive cases. The Third Circuit Court of Appeals upheld the disqualification of Alina Habba as interim U.S. attorney for New Jersey, reaffirming that Senate confirmation cannot be bypassed. Another case saw a federal court declare Lindsey Halligan's appointment as U.S. attorney unlawful and dismiss her prosecutions. In Virginia, a grand jury refused to re-indict New York Attorney General Letitia James after a judge had already found the earlier case against her unlawful. While these rulings did not overturn the entire pattern, they demonstrated that some judges and jurors still upheld basic limits. The guardrails held in certain areas.

If clemency and appointments exposed how the law could be manipulated for insiders, immigration policies revealed how it could be hardened against disfavored groups. The week began with the president threatening to strip citizenship from certain naturalized immigrants, framing denaturalization as a tool to deal with individuals he deemed unworthy. In Oval Office remarks, he called Somali immigrants "garbage" and later condemned them as undesirable. Stephen Miller publicly argued that Afghan immigrants should be judged collectively, not individually, implying they brought problems from their home country. A Department of Homeland Security spokesperson declined to correct the president's language, instead citing unproven claims of "widespread fraud" among Somalis. Words indicated who belonged and who did not.

These words were not empty rhetoric. They sat atop sweeping policy moves. The president ordered USCIS to pause the adjudication of all pending asylum applications, halting roughly 1.5 million cases. He instructed a suspension and re-review of immigration benefits for nationals of nineteen "high-risk" countries, making country of origin a basis for retroactive suspicion. Homeland Security Secretary Kristi Noem announced plans to expand the travel ban to over thirty countries, further restricting entry based on nationality. These measures shifted the system from individual assessments to group-based exclusions. Heritage became a proxy for risk.

On the ground, enforcement followed the same patterns. ICE and DHS carried out mass raids on car washes in Los Angeles, arresting hundreds of workers. Strike teams intensified deportation efforts against Somali immigrants in Minnesota, even as the president's rhetoric about that community grew more hostile. In New Orleans, Operation Catahoula Crunch sent 250 agents into a Democratic-led city with the goal of thousands of arrests, amid reports of racial profiling and even the detention of citizens. In one case, ICE deported a long-time resident and student, Any Lucia López Belloza, despite a federal court's emergency stay order. The legal protections that remained on paper proved fragile in practice. Court orders did not always reach the streets.

The surveillance infrastructure expanded alongside these raids. The Department of Veterans Affairs created an internal database on non-citizen workers, meant for sharing with enforcement agencies. A health-focused institution was repurposed as an immigration enforcement node, increasing the vulnerability of those who served veterans. In Texas, a new law authorized private lawsuits with large statutory damages against anyone involved in providing abortion pills, including out-of-state actors. Though not an immigration measure, it reflected the same logic of extraterritorial control and citizen enforcement, turning civil litigation into a tool of ideological policing. Private suits became a form of state reach.

Economic and social consequences followed. Commerce Secretary Howard Lutnick acknowledged that mass deportations were hurting private-sector job growth, even as he tried to deflect blame. A private payroll report from ADP showed the U.S. losing 32,000 private-sector jobs in November, marking the fourth consecutive negative month. Major consumer brands reported sales declines in Latino neighborhoods, attributing them to deportation fears that kept customers away. Simultaneously, the Federal Communications Commission implemented new rate caps for incarcerated people's phone and video services, a small measure that eased some economic pressure on marginalized families even as broader federal policies intensified it. Relief appeared in narrow forms.

The security policy advanced simultaneously, broadening the use of force both domestically and abroad. A clear example was the narco-boat strike campaign. Reports surfaced that Defense Secretary Pete Hegseth had allegedly ordered a second deadly attack on a drug boat with instructions to "leave no survivors," targeting individuals who were shipwrecked after an initial strike. The White House defended the legality of the contested second attack but declined to provide evidence. During a cabinet meeting marked by erratic behavior and false claims about policy successes, the president praised the strikes and presented them as a display of toughness. By the end of the week, he directed the Pentagon to continue lethal maritime operations against suspected traffickers, authorizing at least twenty-two such strikes and effectively treating drug smuggling as an armed conflict. The line between policing and warfare blurred.

On the streets, the line between protest and disorder narrowed. In Manhattan's Chinatown, NYPD officers assisted federal agents in an ICE raid despite the city's sanctuary policies, arresting protesters who tried to block the operation. In New Orleans, Operation Catahoula Crunch not only targeted immigrants but also sent a message to a Democratic-led city about who controlled its streets. In Tucson, ICE agents used pepper spray on demonstrators and a newly elected congresswoman during a raid protest, raising questions about proportionality and respect for elected oversight. Public space felt more conditional.

Legal and administrative tools reinforced this squeeze on dissent. Texas's abortion-pill law turned private citizens into enforcers, inviting lawsuits against providers and helpers across state lines. In New York City, Mayor Eric Adams issued executive orders restricting city support for investment decisions aligned with the BDS movement and directed a review of protest rules near houses of worship, potentially narrowing where and how people could demonstrate. At the federal level, Bondi's antifa tax investigations and the FBI's probe of lawmakers added a layer of legal risk to certain forms of political speech and organizing. Protest became easier to frame as a threat.

Yet resistance adapted. The 50501 Movement organized a nationwide Cyber Monday boycott of major retailers seen as aligned with the administration, using consumer power as a nonviolent form of protest. Starbucks Workers United expanded a nationwide strike over stalled bargaining and alleged retaliation, mobilizing thousands of baristas across many cities. These actions did not rely solely on permits or public squares. They turned economic behavior into a field of contestation, harder to police yet still vulnerable to surveillance and retaliation. Dissent shifted to where it could.

Behind these conflicts lay a deeper fusion of public power and private interest. The administration used a golden-share arrangement to exert control over US Steel's decisions, blocking a plant closure and demonstrating the state steering a private firm's actions. At the same time, the Pentagon and Commerce Department awarded a $620 million loan package and equity warrants to Vulcan Elements, a startup backed by Donald Trump Jr. This intertwined industrial policy with family-linked finance, raising clear conflict-of-interest concerns in military supply decisions. Governance and gain overlapped.

The Trump family's broader business ties reinforced this pattern. Reports indicated they leveraged government positions to advance cryptocurrency and real estate ventures. World Liberty Financial, a Trump-family crypto firm, faced potential Nasdaq delisting due to regulatory noncompliance and money laundering, highlighting the risks posed by politically connected firms operating in lightly regulated sectors. The administration launched

"Trump accounts," government-funded investment programs for children that directed public funds into private financial products, further blurring the line between public policy and private finance. Public funds flowed through private channels.

Foreign-linked capital and diplomacy were integrated into this framework. Steve Witkoff, serving as a peace envoy, maintained a real estate partnership with sanctioned billionaire Len Blavatnik, raising questions about whose interests influenced his work. Jared Kushner's firm, Affinity Partners, continued to receive large fees from Saudi and other foreign sovereign investors even while he advised on foreign policy. Together, Kushner and Witkoff helped craft Ukraine peace proposals that aligned with Russian territorial demands and Saudi commercial logistics, embedding private foreign investors' interests into U.S.-backed diplomatic efforts. Kushner participated in Moscow negotiations without a formal government appointment, while still maintaining these foreign financial ties, testing the limits of the Logan and Emoluments Clauses. The line between envoy and investor became blurred.

Policy decisions related to energy and trade followed the same pattern. The administration issued export permits for four new LNG terminals, reversing an earlier pause and prioritizing producer interests and foreign sales over domestic price stability, with regulators predicting higher gas prices for U.S. consumers. Tariffs that increased federal tariff revenue by 281 percent served as a broad consumption tax, raising costs for households without a direct legislative tax increase. China's increased research spending and advanced manufacturing capacity during this period set the backdrop for these policy choices, yet the response favored politically connected firms over wide-based investment. Strategic policy leaned toward patrons.

Information control and narrative management linked these strands together. The White House launched a "media offenders" website, naming and shaming outlets for supposed bias and creating a searchable database of claimed malpractice. This used government platforms to discredit critical journalism and redirect public distrust toward independent media. At the same time, the administration stopped publishing key federal economic indicators, forcing reliance on private data during rising job cuts. With official figures withheld, the public's ability to assess economic performance and connect it to policy decisions weakened. Darkness spread where data should be.

The information environment within the government also deteriorated. The chaotic cabinet meeting celebrating contested strikes and repeating false claims about wars and drug prices showed how disinformation could be normalized at the highest levels. The FBI's internal turmoil under Kash Patel, along with its shift away from right-wing extremism, changed which threats were documented and pursued. The National Security Strategy released that week endorsed European far-right ideas on migration, warning of "civilisational erasure" and urging U.S. support for nationalist parties, exporting domestic identity politics into allied democracies. Official doctrine echoed fringe rhetoric.

Science and culture weren't spared. Vaccine advisory panels reshaped under RFK Jr. considered and then voted to limit universal hepatitis B vaccination for newborns, moving away from long-standing evidence-based recommendations. This signaled politicization of scientific guidance and risked eroding trust in immunization programs. Defense Secretary Hegseth shared a fake book cover of a beloved children's character shooting traffickers, and the White House used pop star Sabrina Carpenter's song in an ICE arrest video without permission. Both acts co-opted cultural symbols to normalize militarized enforcement, prompting artist backlash but also reaching millions with state-crafted imagery. Entertainment became a vessel for policy.

Amid this backdrop of managed opacity, some pockets of forced transparency emerged. House Democrats and the House Oversight Committee released new photos, videos, and estate documents from Jeffrey Epstein's private island, exposing ties to political and economic elites. Bipartisan members of Congress pressed Attorney General Bondi to release Epstein files on schedule under the new

Epstein Files Transparency Act. U.S. District Judge Rodney Smith ordered the release of Epstein grand jury transcripts, applying the statute to unseal materials traditionally kept secret. These actions did not resolve questions about elite impunity, but they broadened the documentary record in ways that future investigators and the public could access. The archive expanded even as other records receded.

Accountability for political violence made some progress. The FBI arrested and later obtained a confession from Brian Cole Jr., the suspected January 6 pipe bomber who had placed devices near party headquarters. The Department of Justice tried to re-incarcerate Taylor Taranto, a pardoned January 6 defendant, after concerning behavior near lawmakers' homes. In Utah, prosecutors charged Matthew Scott Alder with manslaughter for a fatal shooting at a protest, highlighting legal limits on armed "security" at demonstrations. These cases showed that some forms of extremist violence still received serious legal responses, even as other parts of the system were being manipulated to protect insiders. The rule against political violence was not yet abandoned.

Courts and Congress, overall, offered uneven resistance. Judge Beryl Howell's injunction against broad, warrantless immigration arrests in Washington, D.C., reaffirmed constitutional standards for seizures and added documentation requirements for agents. A federal court in Alabama chose a student-drawn state senate map to fix Voting Rights Act violations, actively correcting racial vote dilution. Costco sued the administration over emergency tariff powers, testing judicial limits on executive trade authority. The Federal Trade Commission and state attorneys general filed an antitrust lawsuit against Amazon over algorithmic pricing, aiming to reduce platform power. In these cases, institutions still acted in a clearly constitutional manner.

But higher courts often moved in the opposite direction. The U.S. Supreme Court approved Texas's new congressional map, adding GOP-leaning districts and allowing a plan previously labeled racially gerrymandered to stand during primaries. The

Court also agreed to hear a challenge to Trump's order restricting birthright citizenship, putting core Fourteenth Amendment protections under review. The appellate stay that kept the troubled Florida immigration facility open, along with Judge Charles Breyer's doubts about prolonged federal control of the California National Guard, showed how much now depended on the makeup and instincts of specific panels. Judicial independence appeared more uncertain.

In Congress, oversight itself became a contested area. Armed Services Committees examined the boat strikes. Judiciary Committees scheduled hearings on FBI Director Kash Patel's leadership after the leaked "rudderless" report. Meanwhile, House Judiciary Chair Jim Jordan subpoenaed former special counsel Jack Smith for closed-door testimony, raising concerns that oversight could be used to threaten prosecutors or leak selectively about sensitive investigations. House Democrats filed a discharge petition to force a vote on extending health insurance tax credits, using procedural tools to address affordability even as leadership resisted. The Taiwan Assurance Implementation Act showed bipartisan support for a contentious foreign policy stance, limiting executive flexibility toward China. The same tools served very different purposes.

Economic stress permeated all of this. Tariffs acted as a regressive tax. Deportations hindered job growth and local spending. Health insurance costs increased without a replacement plan. The Transportation Security Administration introduced a $45 fee for travelers needing temporary identity verification, adding another barrier to mobility. State and local actors tried to mitigate some of these pressures: attorneys general in several states secured settlements and filed suits against dollar stores for deceptive pricing; the FCC capped prison phone rates; New York City and San Francisco streamlined permits and reduced fines for small businesses; Utah and other states advanced balcony-solar laws; Texas and Oklahoma secured regional haze plans for air quality. These measures provided relief at the margins, but they did not alter the federal macro-environment. The headwinds remained formidable.

Throughout this period, the moral baseline sagged. Character, ethics, and restraint were tested by the president's use of pardons for corrupt officials and foreign traffickers, threats against immigrants, and casual talk of denaturalization. Truthfulness eroded as disinformation about immigrants, wars, and the economy spread from the highest offices. Good faith declined when autopen acts were invalidated and when emergency powers and private enforcement schemes were used to bypass normal processes. Stewardship weakened as protections for LGBTQ+ prisoners were removed and economic data were suppressed. Courts and civil society responded in some areas, but their efforts were mainly reactive—they were on defense.

The small weekly change on the Democracy Clock masked the true extent of these shifts. What changed was not the presence of rights or institutions, but the cost of exercising them and their resilience under pressure. Laws remained on the books. Courts still functioned. Elections loomed. Yet clemency shielded the powerful, citizenship became more conditional, security forces aligned more with regime priorities, and information about the economy and public health became easier to manipulate from above. The erosion didn't occur suddenly but steadily, with a practiced hand wielding familiar tools to make extraordinary changes seem routine.

CHAPTER 57
WEEK 47: CITIZENSHIP AND POWER FOR SALE

A week of hardened borders, leader-centric security, and AI-era crony capitalism, where resistance held the clock still but not the moral floor.

The forty-seventh week of Trump's second term did not hinge on a single order or shock. It unfolded as a dense layering of moves that treated power as something to be extended wherever it encountered only friction, not firm resistance. Immigration, national security, regulation, media, and even the physical shape of the White House were all affected. The pattern was not improvisation. It was consolidation: existing tools used more boldly, limits tested more openly, and the costs of pushing back raised for those who tried.

At the close of the previous period, the Democracy Clock stood at 8:11 p.m. By the end of this week, it remained at 8:11 p.m., a net change of zero minutes. The stillness in the measure did not mean stasis in the system. It reflected a balance between heavy authoritarian pressure and a patchwork of institutional and civic resistance that managed only to hold the line. Executive power pushed outward—over immigration, war, and regulation—while courts, some legislatures, and civil society forced partial retreats or imposed conditions.

The week's movement lay not in the hands of the clock, but in the deepening strain on the moral and institutional foundation beneath it. The clearest arena where that strain showed was immigration. The administration stopped Afghan asylum decisions and paused immigration from nineteen non-European countries, redefining nationality and origin as security risks. At the same time, it rescinded an ICE directive that had protected non-citizen veterans from deportation and asked the Department of Veterans Affairs to compile internal reports on non-citizen staff, many of whom are veterans, for potential enforcement use. These choices did not just tighten rules; they redrew the boundary of belonging, signaling that even military service or government employment offered no stable shield if one's passport or birthplace fell on the wrong side of the new line. The message was blunt.

Alongside these exclusions, the administration proposed a "Trump Gold Card" that would sell U.S. citizenship for one million dollars. In a week already marked by nationality-based bans and the stripping of veteran protections, the idea of a purchasable path to full membership in the polity made the hierarchy explicit. Wealth would not just buy access or speech; it would buy status itself. Citizenship, once seen as a civic bond and legal minimum, was now treated as a commodity, available to those who could pay and revocable for those who could not. The terms of belonging were being priced.

Policy design was complemented by physical build-out. The government signed a $140 million contract for Boeing 737s dedicated to deportation flights, turning removal into an industrial operation with its own fleet. It created a militarized National Defense Area along the California border by transferring public land to the Navy, empowering military personnel to apprehend migrants in a zone where civilian oversight is limited. Reports from Fort Bliss described beatings, sexual abuse, and illegal deportations inside a large detention camp. In North Carolina, an ICE dog was set on Wilmer Toledo-Martinez during an arrest, causing severe injuries and delayed medical care. These were not isolated abuses; they reflected the operating conditions of a system built to move large numbers of people with minimal rights and limited visibility.

Enforcement agencies began targeting specific communities more deeply. ICE activity increased in Somali neighborhoods in Minnesota. Afghan asylum seekers who had attended check-ins and court dates were still arrested, sending a message that good-faith compliance offered no safety. At the border, agents detained commentator Hasan Piker, a U.S. citizen, and questioned him about his views on Trump and Gaza. ICE revoked DACA and imprisoned Muslim photojournalist Ya'akub Vijandre over social media posts, blurring the line between immigration enforcement and punishing speech and religious identity. In another case, immigration authorities sought to deport Yana Leonova, a defendant extradited to the U.S. for trial, threatening to end a long-standing criminal case for a swift removal. The line between law enforcement and threats grew thinner.

The cumulative effect was a two-tier system where some people —often based on origin, faith, or politics—lived under a rights-reduced regime. Yet, this expansion also sparked resistance. Illinois passed HB 1312, banning civil immigration arrests at courthouses, hospitals, campuses, and daycares, and giving people the right to sue officers who violated those protections. Grassroots groups like Siembra trained businesses and local governments on how to demand warrants and uphold Fourth Amendment rights during raids. Churches across the country staged nativity scenes depicting detention and gas masks, turning religious imagery into a critique of immigration policy. These efforts did not dismantle the deportation system, but they showed communities learning how to navigate and challenge it. Resistance evolved as the system hardened.

Beyond the border, the administration expanded its claims over war and security. A new National Security Strategy redefined U.S. interests around sovereignty, anti-immigration priorities, and alignment with Russia, and explicitly called for ending NATO as a permanent organization. In public remarks, Defense Secretary Pete Hegseth said President Trump could order military strikes without Congress, defending unilateral actions off Venezuela. Trump himself refused to rule out ground invasions in Venezuela, Mexico, and Colombia, suggesting large-scale interventions with little debate or consultation. The document and rhetoric marked a move away from a rules-based order toward a leader-centered view of force.

On the water, this approach had deadly results. In the Caribbean, a U.S. strike on a suspected drug boat left survivors in the water; reports indicated a follow-up attack killed them, raising serious war crimes concerns. Pentagon lawyers later suggested sending any captured survivors to El Salvador's CECOT prison, known for torture. At home, the administration deployed Guard troops from West Virginia into Washington, D.C., under a declared crime emergency despite low crime rates, and federalized the city's police, leading to the police chief's resignation. It also attempted to federally deploy California's National Guard during immigration protests, but a federal court ordered the troops back to state control. The boundary between domestic policing and military force blurred.

Oversight followed these moves, arriving late and only partially effective. Congressional Democrats urged the Pentagon to release unedited footage of the Caribbean strike, with Senator Mark Kelly considering a subpoena. Lawmakers moved to withhold part of Hegseth's travel budget until the footage was produced, using appropriations as leverage for transparency. The House approved a $900 billion defense authorization bill that funded the military while tying some funding to troop levels abroad, Ukraine aid, and the release of the strike video. Simultaneously, the Pentagon opened an investigation into Kelly and colleagues over a video urging service members not to follow illegal orders, blurring the line between civilian oversight and military discipline. A Defense Department inspector general report found that Hegseth mishandled classified information on Signal, but he faced no significant consequences. Security measures were used first; accountability, when it occurred, was partial and contested.

Law and justice followed a similar pattern of imbalance. President Trump pardoned Representative Henry Cuellar and his wife on federal bribery charges, nullifying a corruption case involving alleged foreign money. The move signaled that clemency would be used to protect political allies rather than uphold standards. At the same time, the administration accused rivals of mortgage fraud while excusing similar conduct by Trump, and federal prosecutors in Brooklyn moved to drop a high-profile FIFA bribery case "in the interest of justice." Over two hundred former DOJ Civil Rights Division staff issued a public letter warning that purges, mission changes, and case dismissals had hollowed out the division responsible for enforcing voting and anti-discrimination laws. The law was being bent, not shared.

Control over independent agencies became another battleground. Trump dismissed FTC Commissioner Rebecca Slaughter, the last Democrat on the commission, challenging long-standing limits on presidential power over independent regulators. The Supreme Court heard arguments on whether presidents can remove such officials at will, a case with implications for the autonomy of agencies that oversee competition and consumer protection. In New Jersey, courts permanently barred former Senator Bob Menendez from holding state or local office following his corruption conviction, demonstrating that some judicial actors still imposed lasting consequences. In another case, federal courts ruled that Alina Habba's appointment as U.S. Attorney was unlawful because it bypassed Senate confirmation, forcing her resignation from that role while she took on a senior advisory position. The message was mixed: formal rules about appointments still mattered, but loyalty could be rewarded elsewhere.

Electoral rules and civil rights were pulled in different directions. The Supreme Court permitted Texas's redrawn congressional map to take effect despite strong evidence that it diluted minority voting power, indicating tolerance for partisan and racial gerrymanders. Meanwhile, in Indiana, the state Senate rejected a Trump-backed mid-decade gerrymander despite explicit threats that federal funding would be cut if lawmakers did not comply. In Missouri, the People Not Politicians coalition submitted far more signatures than required to force a referendum on a congressional map that eliminated a Democratic district. A federal judge temporarily blocked prosecutors from accessing key evidence in the James Comey case on Fourth Amendment grounds, and a Maryland court ordered the release of Kilmar Ábrego García from ICE custody, later barring his re-detention without a final removal order. A federal grand jury declined twice to indict New York Attorney General Letitia James on contested mortgage-fraud charges. These rulings showed that parts of the judiciary still resisted overt politicization, even as other decisions favored entrenched power.

Economic policy and regulation increasingly reflected elite lobbying and were intertwined with personal and foreign interests. The administration promoted a national AI framework intended to override stricter state rules, echoing language from venture-capital firms like Andreessen Horowitz. OpenAI and allied companies lobbied Congress to prevent state-level AI laws in favor of a unified, more permissive federal standard. At the same time, AI industry donors established a $100 million "Leading the Future" group to influence the 2026 elections, backing candidates sympathetic to their regulatory goals with undisclosed funds. In this environment, policies on a transformative technology were being shaped in close consultation with those who stood to profit most from light oversight.

Strategic technology exports became bargaining chips. Trump agreed to permit the sale of advanced Nvidia H200 AI chips to China in exchange for a revenue-sharing arrangement, leveraging national-security assets for short-term gain. The House's China competition committee opposed this move, warning that such chips could bolster China's military and surveillance capabilities. In parallel, the Justice Department unsealed a guilty plea in "Operation Gatekeeper," a case involving illegal AI chip exports to China, highlighting how enforcement struggled to keep pace with illicit trafficking and high-level policy deals. The line between protecting critical technology and monetizing it blurred.

Media and capital entered the same sphere. Jared Kushner's Affinity Partners helped organize a foreign-funded hostile takeover bid for Warner Bros. Discovery, using $24 billion from Middle Eastern sovereign wealth funds. The deal raised concerns about foreign influence over a major U.S. media company, while the administration could influence regulatory approvals. Trump announced $12 billion in tariff-funded aid for farmers harmed by his trade policies, redistributing resources to a key political base without structural reform. He said he would appoint a Federal Reserve chair committed to immediate interest-rate cuts regardless of economic conditions, linking monetary policy to partisan goals and investor preferences. The Environmental Protection Agency rolled back toxic chemical regulations and PFAS drinking-water standards, while a new executive order targeted proxy advisors that promote ESG and DEI criteria, aligning regulatory posture with corporate and investor interests.

Healthcare and social policy shifted through a combination of executive actions and congressional gridlock. The administration announced a settlement to end Biden's SAVE student loan repayment program, using litigation instead of legislation to dismantle a major debt-relief program. Trump supported allowing Affordable Care Act premium subsidies to expire, positioning the White House to reshape coverage by letting premiums increase and encouraging people to choose less-regulated products. In the Senate, competing bills—one to extend subsidies, another to redirect funds into health savings accounts and catastrophic plans—failed to advance. Analysis by Popular Info projected steep premium increases and coverage losses for up to twenty-two million people if subsidies lapsed. Risks and costs were being shifted from public pooling to individual markets, not through open debate but through inaction and procedural tactics.

Meanwhile, House leadership removed IVF coverage for service members from the defense authorization bill, using control over a must-pass measure to impose an ideological stance on military family health. An advisory committee revised long-standing newborn hepatitis B vaccination recommendations under pressure from anti-vaccine arguments, and the administration announced upcoming changes to vaccine regulations based on unverified death claims. These actions signaled an anti-expert shift in health policy, where anecdote and ideology could outweigh established evidence. Yet within the same state, technocratic efforts persisted: the FDA sought public input on testosterone therapy, agencies renewed advisory committees and data collection efforts, and the FCC adopted multilingual Wireless Emergency Alert templates to improve access to emergency information. The result was a dual-track state, with one lane for ideological capture and another still functioning as a conventional bureaucracy.

Information systems and media were transformed in ways that encouraged speculation, propaganda, and leader-centered branding. CNN and CNBC partnered with Kalshi to integrate prediction markets into news coverage, embedding betting odds into political and economic reporting. The CFTC's limited insider-trading rules for these markets, exposed by watchdogs, created opportunities for those with nonpublic information to profit and influence perceived probabilities. Paramount and CBS News leaders aligned hiring and editorial policies with Trump's ideological agenda, while foreign-backed capital sought to acquire Warner Bros. Discovery, raising the possibility of a major news ecosystem tilted toward regime interests.

The White House launched a portal inviting citizens to submit examples of media bias, creating a government-managed grievance channel that could be exploited to target disfavored outlets. Trump described the economy as "A-plus-plus-plus-plus-plus" despite conflicting indicators, insisting on personal success while blaming predecessors for problems. The administration planned to replace national park imagery on entrance passes with Trump's face, politicizing a neutral public symbol and prompting legal challenges over the use of federal programs for personal glorification. In response, the 50501 Movement released an archive of Trump's 2025 Truth Social posts, documenting his directives, conspiracies, and harassment attempts to preserve a record that might otherwise be deleted or altered. House Democrats on the Oversight Committee published thousands of Jeffrey Epstein photos featuring prominent figures, while survivors' lawyers and Senator Ruben Gallego pressed DOJ to release more files, highlighting both the power and limits of selective transparency.

Surveillance and intimidation against dissenters and marginalized communities increased. At the border, Hasan Piker's questioning about his political views and Ya'akub Vijandre's detention over social media posts demonstrated how border and immigration authorities could be used to suppress speech. Trump called Somali Americans "garbage" and attacked female reporters, normalizing demeaning rhetoric from the presidency toward minorities and critics. After he labeled Representative Marjorie Taylor Greene a traitor, she reported hundreds of threats from both the left and the right, showing how incendiary language from the top could lead to personal danger. In North Carolina, a House select committee accused the Chapel Hill School Board of "grooming" children over DEI initiatives, using legislative hearings to intimidate educators and suppress inclusive curricula. Words were paired with real risk.

The chilling effect spread into schools and communities. A UCLA report found that ICE crackdowns had created fear and bullying among immigrant students, reducing attendance and increasing harassment. Former DOJ Civil Rights Division staff warned that the division's cuts had weakened voting rights and anti-discrimination protections. The administration threatened sanctions on the International Criminal Court to block investigations of U.S. and Israeli officials, framing international accountability as hostile. Online, researchers documented artificial engagement boosting for extremist Nick Fuentes by anonymous and foreign accounts, demonstrating how algorithmic manipulation can widen the reach of far-right figures. Surveillance expanded downward; impunity remained concentrated at the top.

Yet the week also showcased a mosaic of resistance. Courts blocked the federalization of California's Guard deployment in Los Angeles and struck down Habba's unlawful U.S. Attorney appointment. A Maryland judge ordered Ábrego released from ICE custody and later prohibited his re-detention without a final removal order. The Indiana Senate's rejection of a Trump-backed gerrymander, despite explicit threats of lost federal funds, showed some Republican legislators would still defy the president on electoral rules. Illinois's HB 1312 created legal protections around courthouses and hospitals. Missouri organizers gathered signatures to force a referendum on a gerrymandered map. Miami voters elected their first Democratic mayor in nearly thirty years on a pro-immigrant platform, flipping a city in a county Trump had carried. The pushback was real.

Congress also showed flashes of restraint. It funded the House Ethics Committee and the China competition committee, preserving internal accountability and strategic oversight. Lawmakers tied parts of Hegseth's travel budget to the release of strike footage and conditioned defense spending on transparency and European commitments. Representative Brian Fitzpatrick and allies initiated a discharge petition to compel a vote on extending ACA premium credits, using procedural tools to challenge leadership's agenda. Civil society organized boycotts against corporations seen as aiding ICE or retreating from democracy commitments, trained communities to resist raids, and used religious symbolism to protest detention. These actions did not reverse the overall trend but demonstrated that the system still had actors willing to spend political and social capital to slow it.

The battle over symbols and memory continued through the week's end. The National Trust for Historic Preservation sued to stop a $300 million demolition of the East Wing for a new White House ballroom, alleging that the project was proceeding without the necessary planning, environmental, or constitutional reviews.

The case framed the ballroom not just as construction but as an effort to reshape the presidency around personal glorification. The plan to put Trump's face on national park passes carried the same logic into everyday civic life, turning a shared emblem of public land into a leader's calling card. Meanwhile, churches' nativity scenes depicting detention and gas masks, school districts' responses to antisemitic incidents with education and discipline, and independent archives of Trump's posts and Epstein's materials all worked to present alternative narratives about who counts and what the country remembers.

Taken together, Week 47 signaled a deepening of authoritarian practices without a corresponding leap in the clock. Executive power over war, immigration, and regulation was asserted more boldly. Laws were openly bent to favor allies and oppose critics. Economic and media structures grew more aligned with regime-friendly capital and foreign patrons. At the same time, courts, legislatures, states, and civic groups exerted increasing effort just to prevent further erosion. The moral baseline—character, ethics, restraint, truthfulness, good faith, stewardship—continued to decline, even as isolated rulings and protests indicated it had not yet collapsed. The clock's stillness reflected that tension: a democracy not yet visibly collapsing, but held in place only by resistance that now had to work just as hard to preserve the present as it once did to build a better future.

CHAPTER 58
WEEK 48: MEMORY AS INSTRUMENT

Law, force, and narrative tightened around the presidency, turning immigration, archives, and media into coordinated tools of control rather than constraint.

The forty-eighth week of Trump's second term did not depend on a single order or spectacle. Its shape arose from the way law, force, and story were pulled into closer orbit around the presidency. Immigration, protest, healthcare, science, media, and archives all shifted slightly, mostly in the same direction. The pattern was not improvisation; it was consolidation: a state more willing to categorize people into tiers, to call ordinary conflict "terrorism," to bend institutions toward loyalty, and to treat memory as another tool of control.

At the start of Week 48, the Democracy Clock showed 8:11 p.m. It ended the week at the same public time, with a small inward shift of 0.3 minutes. The face remained the same; the hands moved closer to midnight. This shift reflected the week's character: no new coup against the constitutional order, but a steady tightening of tools that make future ruptures easier. Courts added new permissions to doctrine. Agencies revised rules and websites. The Justice Department treated a transparency law as optional. Each step was limited in form but radical in effect, deepening the sense that power now anticipated acting without real restraint.

The clearest line ran through immigration. Midweek, the Supreme Court issued a ruling that, in practice, legalized racial profiling in immigration enforcement. The decision allowed aggressive, race-based raids and sweeps, giving immigration agents broad latitude to target communities based on appearance and origin. Constitutional protections that once limited such discretion were narrowed. On paper, the Court spoke in the language of enforcement and deference; on the ground, it opened the door to mass operations that treat entire neighborhoods as suspicious.

These operations followed swiftly. Immigration and Customs Enforcement detained U.S. citizens and demanded they carry immigration documents, blurring the line between citizen and noncitizen in daily practice. In North Carolina, ICE and allied forces doubled arrests and conducted heavily armed raids in Latino neighborhoods, moving through residential streets in tactical gear. The message was clear: presence itself became a risk factor. Families who had lived for years amid a mix of fear and routine now faced a more overt, quasi-military posture.

Children were not spared. At the border, Customs and Border Protection used a coercive advisal document on unaccompanied minors, threatening lengthy detention and prosecution of sponsors to induce "voluntary" return. The form turned legal rights into bargaining chips, exploiting children's vulnerability to secure outcomes that would be harder to justify in open court. In this environment, the administration's earlier decision to freeze asylum decisions and halt many immigration applications for Afghans and nationals of travel-ban countries gained a sharper edge. Combined with an expanded travel ban that included additional African and Middle Eastern states and Palestinian document holders, the policy architecture and street-level tactics reinforced each other.

Yet resistance persisted. In Durham, North Carolina, the city council declared municipal workplaces "Fourth Amendment workplaces," requiring judicial warrants for ICE to enter private spaces at work. Voters in Bucks County, Pennsylvania, elected a sheriff who campaigned on ending a 287(g) partnership with ICE, using local authority to pull law enforcement back from federal involvement. Lawsuits challenged violent, warrantless ICE detentions of lawful residents and their citizen children, and civil rights groups sued over abuses during raids and protests. Federal courts, in a series of rulings, continued to strike down blanket policies denying bond hearings to detained immigrants and ordered the return of a deported man, Kilmar Ábrego Garcia, emphasizing that some judges still insisted on individualized review. Even within the Catholic Church, the appointment of an archbishop outspoken against harsh immigration policies signaled moral opposition from a major religious institution.

While immigration enforcement intensified, the language of war seeped further into domestic and foreign policy. The president signed an executive order designating illicit fentanyl and its precursors as weapons of mass destruction. This did not create new chemicals but changed the tools available to confront them. By recasting fentanyl as a WMD, the administration could leverage Pentagon and intelligence authorities designed for national defense, not domestic crime. The line between policing and war powers blurred, with emergency-style frameworks creeping into everyday governance.

Abroad, the White House ordered a naval blockade of sanctioned oil tankers entering and leaving Venezuela and labeled its government a foreign terrorist organization. This was not a declared war but involved military force and terrorism designations against a sovereign state with limited congressional oversight. The blockade sat uneasily within existing legal frameworks, raising questions about the legal basis for such an escalation. At home, terrorism language extended inward. Texas prosecutors and the Justice Department charged eighteen alleged "North Texas antifa" members with terrorism-related offenses after a protest at an immigration detention center turned violent. The FBI opened domestic terrorism investigations into anti-ICE activity in at least twenty-three regions, treating threats to immigration enforcement as security threats.

Congress attempted to investigate the use of force at sea. Lawmakers demanded unedited footage and legal justifications for U.S. military boat strikes in the eastern Pacific, amid reports that the war secretary had ordered a Caribbean strike to "kill them all." Navy leaders publicly denied that phrasing, but conflicting accounts about the orders and strikes clouded public understanding. The Senate's annual defense authorization bill responded by requiring the war secretary to provide strike videos to Congress—a modest oversight measure in a field where information was being carefully managed. Meanwhile, activism persisted—environmentalists in North Carolina mobilized calls to block a gas pipeline expansion, and advocates organized vigils to honor those who died from poverty—but such actions now faced a growing threat of being labeled disorder or even terrorism.

Civil rights became more limited for two groups: transgender youth and immigrant children. The House passed a bill making gender-affirming care for minors a federal felony, with long prison terms for providers. The measure claimed to be about child protection, but its real aim was to criminalize a type of medical care that many families and doctors see as essential. At the same time, the Defense Department's TRICARE program finalized a policy excluding hormone therapy for minors with gender dysphoria from coverage, denying military families' children access to that care through federal benefits. Together, law and policy indicated that trans youth would be treated as outside the circle of protected autonomy.

Immigrant children faced a different but related challenge. The coercive advisal document used on unaccompanied minors turned their legal process into a pressured choice. Lawsuits argued that threatening children with prolonged detention and sponsor prosecution to induce "voluntary" return violated due process and statutory protections. Elsewhere, civil liberties were strained. In Tennessee, a man was jailed for thirty-seven days over a meme about the killing of a prominent conservative figure, leading to a civil-rights lawsuit that raised serious First and Fourth Amendment concerns. In Texas, terrorism charges against detention-center protesters blurred the line between political activism and terrorism.

Despite this, some institutions pushed back. Local and federal election authorities oversaw Democratic victories in Miami and other traditionally Republican areas, showing that competitive elections and peaceful transfers of local power continued. In Indiana, a Republican-controlled legislature rejected the president's gerrymandering plan despite threats to cut infrastructure funding, demonstrating that state-level actors could still oppose overt electoral manipulation. California banned legacy admissions at public universities, prompting some private schools to forego state funds rather than change their practices, thereby using funding as leverage to promote more merit-based access. In Washington, the House passed a measure to restore union rights at federal agencies, and a federal court blocked the administration from withholding funding and imposing fines on the University of California over campus policies, limiting the use of civil-rights investigations as a pretext for ideological coercion. Yet even here, pressure grew: a Georgia Senate committee investigated District Attorney Fani Willis over her prosecution of Trump, signaling that those seeking accountability might themselves become targets.

The story that justified much of this enforcement was built as carefully as the legal tools. The Department of Homeland Security launched an "ARRESTED: WORST OF THE WORST" website highlighting alleged crimes by "criminal illegal aliens." The site selectively showcased extreme cases, even though ICE's own statistics showed that most detainees lacked criminal records. Official channels thus curated a picture of immigrants as dangerous outliers, using data presentation to stoke fear. On the streets, ICE's racialized operations—such as stopping Representative Ilhan Omar's son during a surge targeting Somali communities, and heavily armed raids in Latino neighborhoods—made that narrative visible. The FBI's terrorism framing of anti-ICE activity completed the loop: propaganda primed the public, and policing practices reinforced the story.

Activists and local governments responded with their own tools. Cities and advocacy groups coordinated know-your-rights trainings and alert systems to help residents withstand raids. Durham's warrant requirement for workplace entries created a local legal barrier. Within the Democratic Party, groups like Indivisible encouraged primary challenges to incumbents seen as too corporate or soft on Trump, trying to strengthen opposition. Environmental and anti-poverty organizers used vigils and call-in campaigns to keep other issues in view. Yet the president's own rhetoric worked against this. When filmmaker Rob Reiner was murdered, Trump used social media to link his death to "Trump Derangement Syndrome" and to disparage him posthumously. Critics were not just wrong; they were portrayed as deranged enemies whose suffering could be folded into partisan messaging.

Beneath these conflicts, the social safety net and worker security were being restructured. The administration and its allies in Congress advanced a "big, beautiful" healthcare bill that projected roughly $911 billion in Medicaid cuts and imposed new work requirements. The bill promised innovation and efficiency, including incentives for artificial intelligence in rural hospitals, but its main effect was to reduce long-term support for low-income patients. In Alaska, a proposed 35 percent cut to High Intensity Drug Trafficking Area funding threatened local capacity to address fentanyl and overdose deaths. House leadership blocked and delayed votes on extending enhanced Affordable Care Act premium subsidies, even after a discharge petition signed by enough members to force a future vote. Procedural control allowed a small group to block the majority's will on a policy that affects insurance costs for millions.

Veterans' care moved toward privatization. The Department of Veterans Affairs announced plans to cut up to 35,000 healthcare jobs and shift more veterans to private providers. Public health services shrank; private contractors gained. At the same time, the president announced a one-time $1,776 "warrior dividend" payment to most service members, framed as a personal gift tied to tariff revenues. To fund it, the administration redirected housing allowance money meant for ongoing support into short-term checks. The gesture made headlines and created goodwill, but it replaced structural benefits with a symbolic payout. A new drug pricing program, branded "Trump RX.gov" and introduced with pharmaceutical executives, promised lower prices without clear mechanisms, blending policy with personal branding in a sector already influenced heavily by lobbying. All this occurred amid reports of net job losses—41,000 positions over two months—pointing to economic weakness that would make cuts to safety nets even more painful.

The knowledge infrastructure supporting public policy faced increased pressure. At the Environmental Protection Agency, officials proposed nearly doubling the safe level of formaldehyde exposure after lobbying from industry, shifting regulatory standards in favor of chemical producers potentially at the expense of public health. The General Services Administration aligned the Federal Management Regulation with deregulatory goals, simplifying management rules and changing how federal property and contracts are managed. Oversight mechanisms were not eliminated but were loosened, making it easier for contractors and reducing strict control.

More significant was the move against climate science. The administration announced plans to dismantle the National Center for Atmospheric Research and cancel its federal funding, including $109 million allocated for operations in Colorado. NCAR had long provided data and models for weather, climate, and disaster readiness. Cutting its funding weakened an essential public good institution and indicated a move away from investing in shared scientific infrastructure. Simultaneously, billions in federal research funds for universities were frozen as part of an ideological push in higher education, threatening campus finances and research capacity. The funding freeze used federal dollars to pressure universities into political conformity, reinforcing the message that dissenting institutions could lose vital support.

Disputes over institutional memory also intensified. Preservation groups and courts challenged Trump's plans to demolish or modify historic federal buildings, including proposals for a White House expansion, seeking legal review and public input. The National Archives and Records Administration requested public comments on proposed federal records disposition schedules and convened an advisory meeting on classified information for non-federal entities, aiming to uphold norms around preservation and access. Other agencies continued routine regulatory activities—pesticide risk assessments, contract audit data collection, drug and device guidelines, and survey updates—highlighting normal government functions. Yet the contrast was clear: while many technical processes persisted, the key levers of science and education were being manipulated to serve ideological agendas.

Public health governance became increasingly politicized. As Health and Human Services Secretary, Robert F. Kennedy Jr. spread misinformation about the measles vaccine, contributing to a major outbreak. He also institutionalized this misinformation by removing statements on the CDC website asserting that vaccines do not cause autism. The deletion silenced a settled scientific consensus. At the same time, he replaced all voting members of the CDC's vaccine advisory committee with anti-vaccine advocates and appointed a non-scientist as acting CDC director. Advisory bodies that previously grounded immunization policies in evidence were now serving as platforms for skepticism.

The ideological influence extended beyond the government. The Heritage Foundation appointed Scott Yenor, known for opposing aspects of civil rights laws and equality for women and LGBTQ+ people, to lead a major center, signaling an effort to promote revisionist narratives about rights. These developments occurred even as other parts of the health system continued legitimate work: the CDC sought OMB approval for data collection on health programs and overdoses, and awarded a grant to study neonatal hepatitis B vaccination in Guinea-Bissau; the Food and Drug Administration issued guidelines and approvals affecting drugs, devices, cosmetics, and tobacco warnings. The result was a divided system: some areas followed evidence-based practices under leadership that increasingly viewed science as optional.

Economic power and personal gain became more openly linked. Stephen Miller sold stock in MP Materials shortly after a favorable deal by the administration boosted its stock price, highlighting the risk that policy decisions could directly benefit officials' investments. Trump Media & Technology Group announced a multibillion-dollar merger with a speculative fusion energy company while Trump was president, a deal dependent on Department of Energy decisions. This merger intensified conflicts of interest between presidential regulatory power and the financial interests of the president's own firm. Abroad, the Albanian legislature changed laws to permit development on protected Sazan Island for a Jared Kushner resort project, granting "strategic investor" status and easing environmental protections. In Serbia, a Trump Tower Belgrade redevelopment collapsed amid a document-forgery scandal, underscoring how politically connected deals often depended on flexible local regulation.

In the U.S., the Justice Department filed a brief claiming it would be legal to distribute federal grants only to Republican-led states. The filing didn't allocate funds itself but openly defended partisan discrimination in federal spending, challenging long-standing norms of equal treatment among states. The president urged the Federal Reserve to cut interest rates further to boost asset values, a move that would benefit wealth holders, including himself, even as tariffs increased costs for small manufacturers. One such firm, a guitar pedal maker, reported that tariff-driven input costs were limiting hiring and investment. The administration manipulated inflation data that used shutdown-related placeholders to claim housing costs were flat, and the president cited those figures as proof of economic success. Official statistics were not just interpreted; they were manipulated to fit a narrative.

Other actors navigated this landscape. A Michigan utility petitioned regulators for expedited, ex parte approval of a large data center project, seeking limited review of its impact on electricity prices and climate goals. The FCC launched a new computer matching program to verify eligibility for communications subsidies by cross-checking SNAP and Medicaid data, expanding data-sharing across programs. Members of Congress requested internal documents from dollar-store chains over pricing discrepancies and arbitration clauses, using oversight to investigate practices that burden low-income consumers. Abroad, Japan and India advanced their own investment and reform agendas, reshaping labor and financial rules to attract capital. These actions demonstrated that not all economic governance was captured, but they unfolded in a shadow system where presidential business interests and partisan gains increasingly influenced key decisions.

The struggle over narrative and memory was likely the most obvious thread. Inside the White House, staff put up biased plaques under presidential portraits, rewriting descriptions of recent presidents in partisan terms, and removed Joe Biden's image in favor of an autopen graphic. An official historical display turned into a curated story of legitimacy and grievance. At the Kennedy Center, a board mostly made up of Trump appointees voted to rename the venue after Trump, even though they lacked congressional authority to do so. The attempt used control over a national cultural monument to boost the sitting president's image. Meanwhile, Trump publicly pushed for building a triumphal arch in Washington as a top domestic priority, placing a personal monument above more urgent public needs.

Media outlets felt the pressure. Trump filed a multibillion-dollar defamation suit against the BBC over its January 6 coverage, using civil courts to challenge critical reporting on his role in the Capitol attack. ABC News settled a separate defamation case by paying his legal fees and contributing to his presidential library, despite a weak case. CBS and Paramount/Skydance also settled another Trump lawsuit and appointed a pro-Trump ombudsman and an "anti-woke" editor-in-chief at CBS News. Major broadcast networks aired a prime-time Trump speech with clearly partisan content, even though they had previously refused similar requests from Democratic presidents. Each of these decisions could be justified as business judgments, but taken together they showed how legal risks and regulatory pressures nudged outlets toward showing deference.

Regulators also signaled alignment. FCC Chair Brendan Carr told senators that the commission was not independent and aligned itself with the administration, and the FCC changed its mission language accordingly. At the same time, the commission refined data collection and rule schedules for Wireless Emergency Alerts, shaping how emergency messages reach the public. The president ordered the federal government to close on December 24 and 26 and issued an executive order setting new pay rates for federal employees and uniformed services, emphasizing his control over the routines and rewards of public service. A new National Security Strategy framed immigration and alliances as threats to civilization, and an executive order on space dominance focused strategic planning in the White House. A White House spokesperson went further, suggesting that the country would be "lucky" to have Trump serve a third term, normalizing talk of bypassing the Twenty-Second Amendment.

Beneath these symbolic steps was a quieter but important fight over archives. The Epstein Files Transparency Act required the Justice Department to release records by a clear legal deadline. Instead, DOJ delayed and heavily redacted the files. When the deadline arrived, the department announced only partial releases, with extensive blackouts in documents that included detailed FBI notes about procuring underage girls. The content that was released was disturbing, but the way it was done fueled suspicion that powerful figures were still being shielded. In response, Senators Jeff Merkley and Ben Ray Luján vowed to block civilian nominations until they were briefed on DOJ's plans, using their advice-and-consent powers to press for compliance. House Oversight Committee Democrats released more photos from Epstein's estate ahead of the deadline, trying to keep the pressure on and the issue in the public eye. Yet by the end of the week, the main fact remained: a transparency law had been treated as negotiable by the executive branch.

Across these areas, the moral baseline lowered. Character and restraint were strained by the promotion of personal monuments, casual talk of a third term, and willingness to label opponents as deranged or criminal. Ethics became less clear as presidential business ventures merged with regulatory decisions and federal grants were openly discussed as partisan spoils. Truthfulness declined with misrepresented economic data, manipulated crime statistics, and the removal of accurate vaccine information from official sites. Good faith eroded when transparency laws were ignored and civil rights rhetoric was used to justify exclusion and punishment. Stewardship faltered in dismantling climate research centers and freezing university funds.

Yet, the week also revealed that not all institutional authority had weakened. Courts blocked some overreaches, from unlawful immigration detention to politicized university funding threats. Congress added oversight language to defense bills and used tools like discharge petitions to force future votes. Local governments and civil society organized to defend rights and highlight other crises—poverty, climate, corporate abuse. Religious leaders and state actors sometimes prioritized principles over pressure. These responses did not reverse the week's trend but set boundaries that had not yet been crossed.

Over the course of the term, Week 48 feels less like a turning point than a deepening of existing patterns. Law was used more assertively as a weapon rather than a limit. Emergency frameworks seeped further into everyday policy. The civil service and knowledge institutions were pushed harder to align with ideological and personal agendas. Memory—through plaques, archives, and media deals—was curated more openly by those in power. The Democracy Clock's slight inward shift signified a quiet consolidation: rights and procedures remained, but invoking them now required more effort and carried greater risk, while those in power found it easier to act first and justify later, if at all.

CHAPTER 59
WEEK 49: FILES AS INSTRUMENTS OF POWER

A week when transparency laws, courts, and agencies kept their formal shape while their inner workings bent toward secrecy, loyalty, and selective punishment.

The forty-ninth week of Trump's second term didn't depend on a single order or speech. Instead, it showed how a government can keep its formal appearance while its inner workings are turned toward secrecy, loyalty, and fear. The surface looked familiar: agencies issued press releases, courts issued opinions, Congress held hearings. Beneath, the levers connecting law to power were being shifted, gradually, away from public oversight. The forms remained, but the function changed.

At the end of the previous period, the Democracy Clock showed 8:11 p.m. By the end of this week, it stayed at 8:11 p.m., with a tiny change of 0.1 minutes. The public time didn't shift, but the machinery behind it did. This small numerical change reflected a pattern of steady consolidation rather than sudden rupture: transparency rules were weakened, executive defiance of courts became normal, and tools of law and information were more openly used to protect allies and punish critics. The clock's stability was due to slow, incremental damage, not an explosion. The general direction was clear.

The clearest window into that shift was the Epstein files. Congress had passed a law—the Epstein Files Transparency Act—requiring the Justice Department to release records on a set schedule. Instead, the department missed deadlines, released groups of documents with illegal redactions, and quietly moved or misfiled sensitive materials. A photo of Trump with Epstein disappeared from the public database, then reappeared after public outcry, while misleading images of political opponents remained. Officials announced they had suddenly "discovered" 1.2 million unreviewed records, as if the large volume excused the failure to comply. On paper, the law still existed. In practice, it was treated as optional.

This wasn't just a clerical mistake. It was a pattern. Files were downloaded, re-uploaded, and rearranged multiple times. Some letters were later found to be fakes, yet the department's public statements obscured that, letting doubt linger over genuine complaints as well. Each action could be explained by caution or confusion. Taken together, they represented a nationwide breach of transparency rules. The winners were the power networks mentioned in the files, whose exposure was slowed or softened. The losers were Congress, whose law was ignored, and the public, which learned that even clear legal commands could be bypassed when they challenged elite interests.

The same actions fueled a second shift: using law as a weapon instead of a limit. The Epstein case was not just about secrecy. It was about who controls the story. Selective releases spotlighted some names and kept others hidden. Redactions favored allies in office while leaving past or rival figures more exposed. At the same time, officials were accused of judge-shopping in a high-profile case and ending crypto investigations involving top figures' personal stakes. The department's social media, once just a channel for official messages, was used to target critics and boost the president's complaints. Instead of constraining the executive, legal tools were bent to serve it.

This weaponization followed a clear power logic. Those close to the president gained a buffer against scrutiny, while those out of favor faced a more aggressive, unpredictable state. The line between prosecution and politics blurred. Courts still issued rulings, and some judges resisted, but daily decisions about which cases to pursue, which documents to release, and which narratives to endorse moved further into partisan territory. The law's outer shell remained, but its core weight shifted.

Executive defiance of checks extended beyond the Justice Department. On immigration, the White House pushed ahead with National Guard deployments across multiple cities to provide enforcement support, even after the Supreme Court blocked earlier efforts to deploy state troops in that role. New orders tried to limit Guard activity to federal property or "support" functions, but the effect on the ground was the same: uniformed soldiers near courthouses, detention centers, and protest sites. A federal judge blocked an effort to cut homeland security grants to states that refused to cooperate with mass deportations, calling it unlawful retaliation. Yet the administration indicated it would seek alternative ways to punish those jurisdictions, viewing court setbacks as obstacles to be circumvented, not boundaries to be respected.

In these conflicts, the president and his inner circle were clear winners. They showed supporters that they would push past legal limits in the name of security and control. Governors, mayors, and state legislators who resisted faced funding threats and public attacks. The judiciary upheld some boundaries, but each time, the executive pushed from a new angle. Oversight existed but no longer reliably influenced behavior; it merely increased the costs of certain tactics, which the White House appeared willing to pay. Federal power was also wielded more openly to reward friendly regions and punish adversaries. The administration moved to block California's planned phase-out of gas-powered cars, framing a state climate policy as a threat to national interests.

Meanwhile, it sought to cut or condition homeland security grants to "sanctuary" jurisdictions that refused to assist federal immigration sweeps until a court intervened. National Guard deployments for immigration enforcement focused on Democratic-led cities, even when the official rationale was neutral. The message was clear: align with the president's agenda or face federal pressure on your budget, policies, and streets. This selective punishment went beyond bruising local pride; it shifted the balance of federalism. States and cities attempting to chart their own course on climate, immigration, or public safety found that the federal government could reach into their finances and security. The winners were those whose leaders embraced the president's line, gaining quicker access to funds and favorable treatment. The losers were those who didn't, along with residents who saw national policy as a tool against their local choices.

Inside the administrative state, agencies were repurposed to serve private and ideological interests. Interior and environmental regulators canceled or suspended major renewable energy projects, including offshore wind, on pretextual grounds. In one case, officials invoked a defunct "Department of War" in a national security rationale that read more like a fig leaf than a legal analysis. A low-income solar program was terminated, even as fossil fuel projects moved ahead. At the Veterans Affairs department, health policy was subordinated to abortion politics, with orders to end certain forms of care regardless of medical judgment. Crypto enforcement was quietly pulled back in cases where senior officials had personal holdings, raising clear conflict-of-interest concerns.

The winners were political appointees and outside contractors who could step into the gaps left by departing career staff. The losers were the institutions that depend on long-term expertise and nonpartisan judgment: the foreign service, regulatory agencies, and enforcement arms that require continuity to function. As capacity drained away, the cost of saying no to political pressure rose. Those who stayed faced a choice between quiet compliance and marginalization.

Civil liberties and dissent came under pressure through both overt and subtle means. Immigration enforcement was scaled up into a semi-permanent infrastructure of control: record numbers of people held in ICE detention, plans for 80,000-bed warehouse-style facilities, harsh deportation practices, and official messaging that mocked migrants as "self-deporting" if conditions were made unbearable. National Guard deployments to cities, even when limited on paper to federal property, cast a shadow over protests near courthouses and detention centers. The FBI deprioritized a far-right neo-Nazi group with insurgent aims, sending a signal about which threats the state chose to confront and which it could tolerate.

In this environment, citizenship itself became more stratified. Non-citizens, and often citizens of certain backgrounds, faced a harsher, more militarized state. Their movements were tracked, their protests chilled, their legal protections thinner. At the same time, elite crimes—especially those tied to sexual abuse, financial fraud, or political corruption—remained obscured behind redactions and procedural fog. Surveillance and coercion flowed downward. Impunity flowed up.

The press, which might have tied these strands together for the public, faced its own squeeze. Violence against journalists covering immigration protests rose sharply, with reporters assaulted or detained as they tried to document enforcement actions. Trump labeled the New York Times a national security threat, moving beyond the familiar "enemy of the people" rhetoric into language that implied legal consequences. The Justice Department and the White House used official channels to collectively insult reporters, turning institutional accounts into instruments of ridicule. In this climate, CBS pulled a fully vetted 60 Minutes segment on deportations at the last minute, reportedly for political reasons, even as the same piece aired abroad.

These developments did not shut down the press. They changed its risk calculus. Investigative reporters who probed elite wrongdoing or harsh enforcement practices now faced not only online harassment but physical danger and the possibility of being cast as threats to the nation. Editors had to weigh the cost of angering a government that controlled access, regulation, and public funding. State-aligned outlets, by contrast, thrived on access and amplification. Independent media was not banned; rather, it was starved of safety, certainty, and reach.

Information itself became a tool of control. The president's economy speech blended false claims with conspiracy content about COVID and the 2020 election, reinforcing a disinformation ecosystem that had never been dismantled. Official social media accounts mocked migrants, attacked the press, and spread narratives that blurred the line between policy and propaganda. The chaotic handling of the Epstein files—staggered releases, contradictory explanations, sudden document "discoveries"—added to a sense that no single account could be trusted. Oversight bodies and the public alike struggled to keep up.

This chaos was not random; it had a structure. By flooding the space with partial disclosures, inflammatory rhetoric, and shifting explanations, the administration made it harder to focus on any one abuse long enough to force change. The winners were those in power, who could move from one controversy to the next while the previous one remained unresolved. The losers were citizens, lawmakers, and judges trying to piece together a coherent picture from fragments.

Even memory was curated. The removal and later quiet restoration of the Trump-Epstein photograph, the selective inclusion of misleading Clinton imagery, and the Justice Department's control over the narrative around fake letters all pointed to an emerging practice: archives as instruments of politics. What could be controlled was highlighted or framed. What could not be controlled was erased, at least for a time. Government records, once regarded as a neutral base for future inquiry, became another field of contest.

Courts and parts of Congress did not stand idle. The Supreme Court blocked certain National Guard deployments for immigration enforcement. A federal judge halted funding retaliation against sanctuary states and constrained an attempt to rename the

Kennedy Center after Trump, treating it as an improper use of public institutions for personal glorification. Other judges pushed back on ICE abuses. On Capitol Hill, bipartisan anger over the Epstein noncompliance prompted members to consider legal action to enforce the transparency statute. A House bill sought to restore federal workers' bargaining rights, even as the executive branch celebrated job cuts.

These acts of resistance mattered. They showed that institutional muscle remained and that not every test of power would succeed. But they also revealed limits. House leadership avoided tough votes and suppressed testimony from special counsel Jack Smith, wary of direct confrontation. Court rulings were narrow and often came after the fact, trimming the edges of policies rather than reshaping their core. The executive learned where the lines were and how far they could be bent without breaking.

No major hearings or rulings were scheduled within the week that promised immediate reversal. Instead, the period ended with ongoing investigations, lawsuits filed, and oversight letters sent. The real deadlines lay in the slow process of litigation and the next rounds of document production, where the same patterns of delay and partial compliance were likely to recur. The system moved, but at a pace that favored those already in power.

In the course of the term, Week 49 signaled a deepening of existing habits rather than a new shift. Transparency laws were treated as suggestions. Executive power challenged judicial and legislative checks, retreating only when forced and then seeking new routes. Agencies that once served broad public missions were steered toward the interests of donors and ideological allies. Journalists and dissenters faced higher costs for doing their work. The formal structures of democracy remained intact, but the ease with which they could be used by ordinary people, and the reliability of their ability to constrain those at the top, continued to decline. The clock's face did not move, yet the gears behind it slipped another tooth.

CHAPTER 60
WEEK 50: CONSOLIDATION AS GOVERNANCE

With the clock frozen, the administration deepened its use of law, security, and narrative to personalize power and stratify rights without new formal shocks.

The last week of the year brought no surprises. Instead, it revealed a clear pattern. In areas like immigration, security, public spending, and information, the same approach was used: law, force, and narrative. Each action could be justified as policy, management, or a necessary response. Together, they showed a government more willing to treat institutions as extensions of individual will and faction interests. That was the point.

At the end of Week 49, the Democracy Clock read 8:11 p.m., and it stayed at that time after Week 50—a zero-minute change. This stillness didn't mean nothing happened; it meant that the actions of the week reinforced existing patterns rather than creating new ones. Executive power was exercised more confidently without new formal authorities. Laws were more openly bent to favor friends and oppose enemies. Security forces and information systems were moved further toward regime priorities. Courts and civil society pushed back in some areas but not enough to shift the overall balance.

The most notable change was in immigration. Within the bureaucracy, the Justice Department and USCIS issued guidance to handle between one hundred and two hundred denaturalization cases each month. What was once rare—revoking citizenship—became a routine objective. Meanwhile, USCIS stopped naturalization ceremonies and green-card interviews for nationals of nineteen countries linked to earlier travel bans. The official reason was security. The result was a freeze on legal pathways for people based on their country of origin, not their actions.

On a personal level, these changes affected individual lives. Immigration officers deported Moises Sotelo, a vineyard manager in Oregon, tearing him from his family and job. Other officers pulled individuals out of cars and courthouse hallways, turning everyday spaces into zones of fear. The FBI sent additional agents to Minnesota to investigate fraud involving Somali communities, including denaturalization referrals. While many financial crimes were genuine, focusing on one immigrant group blurred the line between targeted enforcement and group stigmatization. That boundary is important.

Behind these cases, the coercive infrastructure expanded. ICE increased detention capacity with warehouse-style facilities near logistics hubs, supported by long-term funding. The agency launched a $100 million recruitment campaign for new agents, marketed in "wartime" language and aimed at specific ideological groups. Immigration enforcement was no longer just a series of cases; it had become an industrial system, scaled up and branded as a cause.

At the top, the president claimed personal control over that system. In public statements, he asserted that immigration enforcement, criminal law, and even forcible removals were under his direct command. This was not just a technical description of the chain of command; it was a claim that the coercive powers of the state came directly from him. The Department of Homeland Security echoed this message in a softer tone, using a Japanese artist's work without permission in a social media post that depicted a peaceful America after deportations. The image transformed mass removal into an idyllic vision by appropriating art as state propaganda.

Law followed a similar pattern in the realm of reproductive rights and criminal punishment. A federal appeals court allowed the administration to end Medicaid funding for Planned Parenthood in twenty-two states and the District of Columbia. The decision did not ban care outright but cut off reimbursements supporting clinics serving low-income women. In Kentucky, state police and prosecutors charged Melinda S Spencer with fetal homicide after a self-managed abortion, even though state law did not explicitly criminalize such acts. Prosecutors stretched existing statutes to reach conduct that lawmakers had not clearly forbidden. These actions occurred amidst broader health-policy retrenchment. The administration let enhanced Affordable Care Act tax credits expire after a forty-three-day shutdown, raising insurance costs for millions. Simultaneously, the Drug Enforcement Administration and Health and Human Services extended pandemic-era telemedicine flexibilities for prescribing controlled substances, the fourth such temporary extension. Emergency tools once justified by crisis now became part of the regular regulatory landscape. Emergency had become routine.

Courts did not speak with a single voice. A federal judge issued a temporary restraining order to protect Imran Ahmed, an anti-disinformation advocate, from detention while his lawsuit proceeded. Another judge dismissed with prejudice an indictment against TikTok streamer Carlitos Ricardo Parias after finding violations of due process in an alleged assault on federal agents. Judge Amy Berman Jackson ordered the administration to continue funding the Consumer Financial Protection Bureau despite executive resistance, defending Congress's intent to create an independent consumer watchdog. Meanwhile, violent crime and murder rates continued to decline from their 2021–2022 peaks. The shift toward punitive measures in reproductive and immigration law cannot be explained as a response to rising crime; it was driven by ideological choice.

The president's use of formal powers against disliked regions and communities made this choice visible. He vetoed a bipartisan bill that had unanimous support to improve drinking water in Colorado, a measure focused on public health rather than partisan politics. He also vetoed a bill that would have funded an Everglades project benefiting the Miccosukee Tribe, citing ideological objections. In both cases, the veto was used not to check overreach but to punish and send a message. The targets were clearly identified.

Cultural and public spaces were merged into the same sphere. The Kennedy Center Board of Trustees amended its bylaws so that only Trump-appointed trustees could vote, and approved a renaming that included the president's name. The center is a congressionally chartered arts venue, designed to stay independent from daily politics. Concentrating control among one president's appointees and rebranding the building around him blurred that line. Artists responded by canceling shows in protest, using their absence as a form of speech.

In Washington, the administration ended the National Links Trust's lease to manage public golf courses without a plan for a replacement. Workers and residents were left uncertain as renovations stopped. The decision disrupted public recreation and raised questions about whether new, politically connected operators would step in. Meanwhile, Social Security backlogs exceeded six million cases after budget cuts, delaying benefits for vulnerable individuals. These were different areas—golf courses and disability claims—but both showed how public goods were destabilized in ways that could favor private or insider interests.

Not all uses of public power trended this way. New York and Vermont enacted climate superfund laws requiring major polluters to fund resilience projects and emissions reductions. These state measures shifted costs onto large emitters instead of taxpayers at large. They contrasted with federal vetoes and rollbacks, illustrating how subnational governments could still use law to protect shared resources. The difference was clear.

Security forces, both domestically and abroad, were increasingly portrayed as tools of political and religious narratives. In major U.S. cities, federal agents appeared in military fatigues, armed with assault rifles, to control protests. The administration pushed to deploy National Guard troops in Democratic-led cities but then withdrew them after court rulings and political pushback. These episodes showed how the threat of military force could be raised and then partially pulled back, establishing a new norm where such deployments were considered possible responses to domestic dissent.

Overseas, the pattern continued. U.S. forces launched strikes in Nigeria and Syria against Islamic State-linked militants, described by officials as a "Christmas present" for the group and linked to protecting Christians. The CIA reportedly carried out a drone strike on a Venezuelan port facility as part of regime-change efforts. The U.S. military tried to seize the oil tanker Bella 1 en route to Venezuela but was blocked when Russian forces moved to protect the vessel. Meanwhile, the president threatened military action against Iran over its repression of protests, speaking personally rather than through official channels.

Real security threats did exist. A federal court held a detention hearing for Brian Cole Jr., a suspect in the January 5 pipe bomb case, considering his mental health and risk factors before ruling to keep him detained pending trial. Law enforcement in North Carolina arrested a radicalized teenager who planned New Year's Eve attacks on Jews, Christians, and LGBTQ+ people. These cases showed the state acting to protect targeted minorities and public safety. But they also provided a backdrop for broader crackdowns on protest and immigration, justified by the language of security.

Information and memory became battlegrounds. CBS and 60 Minutes withdrew an investigative report on CICOT from broadcast and official archives, even as illegal copies circulated online. The removal showed how a major media outlet could suppress reporting on sensitive political issues. The administration imposed visa bans on European anti-disinformation figures, calling their work censorship. The message was clear: those enforcing platform rules or exposing propaganda could be seen as enemies rather than allies.

Meanwhile, the Justice Department's handling of Jeffrey Epstein's records grew more opaque. Advocates accused the DOJ of unlawfully restricting the release of files through redactions and delays. The department admitted it was reviewing over five million documents, far more than initial estimates, and only revealed millions of additional undisclosed records after congressional pressure. Changing timelines and figures fueled distrust, raising concerns that powerful associates might be being protected. The suspicion was justified.

The president and his allies filled the resulting space with their own narratives. Fundraising emails disguised as surveys warned supporters that they would lose tariff rebate checks, steering them into donation funnels built on false premises. The White House shared misleading images of a dead bald eagle beneath wind turbines, using old foreign photos to falsely claim domestic harm from renewable energy. Trump amplified Kremlin narratives by falsely accusing Ukraine of attacking Vladimir Putin's residence, aligning U.S. discourse with an authoritarian adversary's propaganda. On trade, the administration celebrated tariffs as a national triumph while quietly implementing carve-outs and delays after exporter lobbying, which reduced effective rates on semiconductors, furniture, cabinets, and Italian pasta.

The same logic of selective pressure and protection influenced the justice system's treatment of elites and ordinary people. Reports surfaced that young spa workers from Mar-a-Lago had been sent to Epstein's home for sexual exploitation, raising questions about potential complicity and protection of vulnerable women and minors. Yet, the release of Epstein-related documents remained slow and partial. By contrast, the state moved quickly and aggressively against immigrants facing denaturalization quotas and women like Melinda Spencer facing new homicide charges for self-managed abortion. TROs and dismissals in some high-profile cases showed that some judges still enforced rights, but the overall pattern pointed toward a two-tier system.

Legislatures and quasi-public bodies have become arenas for displays of punishment. The U.S. House of Representatives censured Al Green for interrupting the president during a joint session, punishing his floor speech without stripping his formal voting rights. It also passed a resolution condemning Representative Chuy Garcia's retirement timing as an effort to influence his successor's election. In Tennessee, the state House expelled Justin Pearson and Justin Jones for leading a gun policy protest from the floor, using the harshest punishment against members who challenged the majority on procedural and substantive grounds.

The governance change at the Kennedy Center followed the same pattern. By limiting voting to Trump-appointed trustees and renaming the institution to include his name, the board transformed a national arts venue into a symbol of personal loyalty. In North Carolina, a Select Committee on Oversight and Reform criticized the Chapel Hill School District under the guise of accountability. Republican leaders portrayed their efforts as necessary reform, even as grassroots groups like Public School Strong organized to defend public education. Oversight was used as a tool to pressure schools rather than support them.

The president urged Republican senators to eliminate the filibuster, pressing for a Senate where a simple majority could pass sweeping laws without minority-party leverage. In this context, legislatures functioned less as forums for discussion and more as stages where power was displayed and dissent was disciplined. Civil society responded where it could. Activists organized public comments opposing policies targeting trans youth. Artists boycotted the renamed Kennedy Center. Yet, the formal rules of representation were being bent towards control.

Economic policy added another layer to the week's story. The administration made significant budget cuts to healthcare, science, and anti-hunger programs, weakening public services that help cushion the impact of hardship. It allowed expanded Affordable Care Act subsidies to lapse, raising premiums for many. The Social Security Administration, strained by funding cuts, faced severe caseload backlogs, leaving more than 6 million claims pending. In North Carolina, lawmakers planned new tax cuts for the wealthy and corporations despite budget delays that threatened childcare centers and healthcare providers. At the same time, organized interests secured relief.

After warnings from exporters and foreign governments, the administration delayed higher tariffs on furniture and cabinets and reduced antidumping duties on Italian pasta. Earlier carve-outs had already lowered effective rates on semiconductors and other goods. China responded with a fifty-five percent tariff on U.S. beef and reduced soybean purchases, squeezing American farmers caught in the crossfire. Rising corporate bankruptcies and household financial stress signaled a fragile economy where risk was pushed downward, while those with access to power could negotiate softer landings.

Regulatory agencies often acted in ways that favored industry. The EPA revoked a 2024 rule on reclassifying major pollution sources under the Clean Air Act, restoring a more flexible 2020 standard that industry preferred. It granted a no-migration variance for hazardous waste disposal at a Clean Harbors facility, allowing an exception to land disposal restrictions based on technical findings. Other EPA actions—approving South Carolina's regional haze plan, revising the Taconite Federal Implementation Plan, and updating information collections—demonstrated that the machinery of environmental governance was still moving forward. However, the overall trend of high-profile decisions leaned toward deregulation.

Against this backdrop, civil society and subnational actors mounted targeted resistance. In North Carolina, Indivisible and allied activists organized a Long March against racial gerrymandering, a multi-day protest to highlight Black voter disenfranchisement under the state's maps. The same network urged support for the Block the Bombs Act, aiming to end U.S. funding for Israeli military actions in Gaza, and mobilized public pressure on the Senate to block unauthorized attacks on Venezuela, invoking Congress's war powers. These efforts sought to reestablish legislative control over war and foreign policy.

Grassroots groups worked to defend public schools from legislative attacks and oppose policies targeting trans youth. In New York City, a democratic transfer of local executive power occurred as Zohran Mamdani was sworn in as mayor, opening the door to new urban policies. Federal advisory and statistical processes—such as the EPA's Local Government Advisory Committee renewal and the Census Bureau's request to continue questionnaire pretesting—continued to function, preserving channels for expertise and public input. The exposure of a large Medicaid fraud scheme in Minnesota by federal investigators showed that oversight of public funds still operated effectively in some areas.

These threads—centralized executive control, weaponized law, militarized security, curated information, economic stratification, and scattered resistance—came together during a week in which the formal clock did not advance. The lack of numerical change did not mean safety. Instead, it marked a period in which earlier shifts were reinforced rather than newly created. Executive authority was exercised with less restraint and more personalization. Institutions that might have checked that authority were pressured, repurposed, or bypassed, even as some judges and state governments held firm.

The moral baseline continued to decline under the weight of these choices. Character, in the sense of aligning words with duty, gave way to personal grievance in vetoes and threats. Ethics became blurred as public assets and programs were steered toward allies or left to decay. Restraint was scarce in the use of immigration powers, military signals, and punitive legislative measures. Truthfulness eroded amid waves of disinformation and selective disclosure. Good faith and stewardship were strained as transparency laws were tested and long-term capacities—such as social insurance, public health, and civic education—were weakened.

Week 50 is recorded as a period of consolidation rather than upheaval. The tools of state power stayed the same, but their application changed. Rights and procedures remained official, yet using them became more difficult and costly. Civil society and subnational actors demonstrated that democratic vitality has not vanished. They also revealed how much of the responsibility for defense had shifted away from the federal government. The Democracy Clock maintained its pace, not because the threat diminished, but because the country had already entered this phase and was learning how easily it could become the new normal.

CHAPTER 61
WEEK 51: WAR, OIL, AND ENFORCEMENT AS RULE

> *A near-static clock masks a week when war powers, immigration raids, and economic policy were fused into a single project of personalized executive rule.*

The week demonstrated concentrated power. War, immigration enforcement, economic policy, and public narratives all worked toward a single goal. What may have once been separate areas—foreign intervention, domestic policing, budget decisions, and information—became tools in a unified effort. This pattern did not depend on new laws. Instead, it relied on willpower, speed, and the ability to decide which rules to follow and which to ignore.

At the end of the previous period, the Democracy Clock read 8:11 p.m. By the end of Week 51, it stayed at 8:11 p.m., with a net change of just 0.2 minutes. The clock's face did not jump forward, but its internal mechanism shifted. Executive power was asserted over war and oil without prior approval. Security forces acted as if their main client was the regime, not the public. Law and transparency bent around elite interests. Courts, Congress, and civil society registered resistance—war-powers votes, impeachment articles, protests, and investigative reporting—but mostly after the fact, and rarely with enough power to reverse existing actions. The balance tilted further toward rule by decree.

The clearest example of this was seen in Venezuela. Early in the week, President Trump ordered a military operation to seize Nicolás Maduro, viewing capturing a sitting foreign leader as a presidential discretion. The operation was presented as a law enforcement action against narco-terrorism, but it involved lethal maritime strikes that killed thirteen people and a covert incursion to remove a leader from his own territory. Congress was not consulted beforehand. Intelligence briefings required by law for such actions did not reach key members. The presidency acted first and explained later, if at all.

Beyond that military action, a broader plan took shape. The administration announced plans for the U.S. to seize and control tens of millions of barrels of Venezuelan oil. Sanctions were eased not to restore Venezuelan sovereignty but to route crude through U.S.-controlled channels. Energy Secretary Chris Wright and the president described a future where American taxpayers would finance the rebuilding of Venezuela's oil infrastructure, with companies later reimbursing costs and earning profits. At the same time, billionaire Paul Singer bought Citgo at a steep discount, a windfall made possible by the very instability U.S. actions had helped create. Oil and force moved together.

Trump did not hide his reasoning. He claimed he had the authority to use military force to seize other countries' oil and mentioned Greenland as a potential target for coercive takeover, even suggesting payments to residents. He dismissed international law as a meaningful limit, arguing that his morality, not treaties, defined his boundaries of power. In this narrative, Venezuela was portrayed as a collapsed state needing rebuilding, and U.S. control of its resources was viewed as mutually beneficial. The language of humanitarian rescue and reconstruction disguised a simple truth: war powers and sanctions were being used to secure assets for a select group of allies and corporations.

Institutions responded, but slowly. Members of Congress

reported receiving no briefings on the Venezuela strikes despite legal requirements to notify. Representative Ted Lieu publicly declared the attack illegal without congressional approval. The Senate passed a bipartisan War Powers Resolution aimed at limiting further military intervention in Venezuela, reaffirming that the power to declare war lies with the legislature. Meanwhile, the Supreme Court, in a separate case, rejected Trump's claim of authority to deploy federalized National Guard troops in Chicago, indicating judicial limits on domestic force still existed. Yet Maduro was already in a New York courtroom, charged with narco-terrorism and related crimes, while Venezuelan authorities, in the chaos after the coup, detained journalists and quashed protests. Courts and international civil space were pulled into an operation they had not authorized.

If Venezuela showed how military and economic influence could be projected abroad, Minnesota demonstrated how security forces could be directed against citizens internally. The Department of Homeland Security and ICE sent about two thousand federal agents to the state in a large surge, justified by accusations of Somali-linked fraud. This operation overwhelmed detention centers, most holding people without criminal records. Communities saw the surge not as targeted law enforcement but as an occupation, with agents patrolling streets, neighborhoods, and outside hospitals. The scale resembled a domestic military deployment rather than routine policing.

In Minneapolis, this surge resulted in the death of Renee Nicole Good, a U.S. citizen and legal observer, during an ICE raid. Federal agents claimed she used her car as a weapon and posed an immediate threat. However, video footage later confirmed by independent outlets showed her driving away from agents, not toward them. On scene, medics and a doctor were prevented from reaching her after she was shot. She died without prompt medical help, in a scene under the full control of federal officers. The message to observers of state authority was clear: proximity to enforcement could be deadly, and even basic duties of care could be ignored.

The Minnesota operation was not isolated. During the same week, DHS detained Dulce Consuelo Díaz Morales, a U.S. citizen, for twenty-five days despite evidence of her citizenship, and Border Patrol agents shot two people outside a Portland hospital during an immigration-related stop. ICE and Border Patrol activities nationwide led to at least nine shootings and multiple deaths in custody. Detention numbers rose, including individuals with no criminal background. Enforcement extended beyond borders and high-risk targets to cities, hospitals, and homes, treating mere presence as grounds for suspicion.

The public responded quickly and broadly. Local leaders in Minneapolis demanded that ICE leave the city. Protests and vigils for Renee Good spread nationwide, organized by groups like Indivisible and broader coalitions under banners such as "ICE OUT FOR GOOD." Demonstrators gathered at federal buildings to protest immigrant detentions at Guantanamo Bay and to challenge senators' votes on social programs and immigrant treatment. Calls to abolish ICE moved from the margins to the center of the debate. Communities organized ICE Watch trainings, teaching volunteers how to verify and document enforcement actions in real-time. Even as this civic infrastructure grew, DHS sent more agents into Minnesota, and detention facilities remained overcrowded.

Control over the story of what had happened became its own battleground. DHS and the Trump administration labeled Renee Good a domestic terrorist, claiming she had weaponized her vehicle and was connected to a broader left-wing threat. Vice President JD Vance criticized media coverage, accusing reporters of misrepresenting the incident and hinting at links to a terror network. The administration released selective bodycam and cellphone footage to support its story while withholding other evidence and blocking state investigators from accessing the full record. The FBI took exclusive control of the shooting investigation, excluding Minnesota's Bureau of Criminal Apprehension. Independent journalists and outlets pushed back. Reuters and others verified video showing Good driving away, not charging agents. Their work highlighted the importance of investigative reporting in challenging official claims about state violence. However, the cost of that work increased. Reporters who challenged the DHS account were smeared as biased or dangerous. The administration's approach—curated evidence, broad labels, and attacks on the press—implied that those documenting abuses would themselves be treated as enemies.

The same pattern appeared in how the administration handled January 6. On the anniversary, Trump issued broad pardons and commutations for participants in the Capitol attack. He described them as peaceful patriotic protesters and called Democrats who certified the election villains. Official channels portrayed the insurrection as a serious injustice against its supporters rather than an attack on constitutional order. The White House narrative, echoed by aligned media, recast an attempt to block the transfer of power as an act of loyalty and bravery. Here, too, there was institutional resistance. The Senate unanimously approved a resolution to install a plaque honoring Capitol Police officers who defended the building on January 6. The plaque served as a physical symbol that the attack was real and that those who resisted it were justified. Yet the administration's mass pardons and revisionist rhetoric had already changed the landscape. Paramilitary-style violence aligned with regime interests now carried a presumption of impunity, while those opposing it risked being labeled unpatriotic or corrupt.

Beyond these headline events, the law was increasingly used as a weapon rather than a limit. Reports emerged of federal agents kidnapping individuals off the streets as perceived enemies of the state, blurring the line between lawful arrest and political abduction. In Kentucky, prosecutors charged Melinda S. Spencer with fetal homicide after a self-managed abortion, stretching a statute that did not apply to the pregnant person herself. At Stanford, university prosecutors pursued felony conspiracy and vandalism charges against students over a pro-Palestinian protest, showing a willingness to treat campus dissent as a criminal matter rather than a disciplinary issue. The scope of criminal law expanded as its neutrality diminished.

Inside the state, those who questioned or challenged this trend faced retaliation. Defense Secretary Pete Hegseth issued a formal reprimand of Senator Mark Kelly and began proceedings to strip his retired rank and pension after Kelly urged service members to refuse unlawful orders. The move used military disciplinary tools against a sitting senator, chilling lawful dissent and blurring civilian–military boundaries. At the Justice Department, Trump fired senior ethics attorney Joseph Tirrell without a stated reason, removing a career official tasked with enforcing internal legal norms. These actions sent a clear message: internal critics of illegality or overreach would face personal consequences.

The story of unlawfully appointed U.S. attorneys demonstrates both the reach of politicized appointments and the remaining power of judicial checks. Trump-appointed lawyer Lindsey Halligan continued to serve as a U.S. attorney even after her appointment was declared unlawful, leading federal courts to require her to justify her use of the title. In New York, Judge Lorna Schofield ruled that acting U.S. attorney John Sarcone did not legally hold his position. Meanwhile, the Justice Department appealed dismissals of charges against political figures made by these invalid appointees, extending uncertainty over prosecutions that had already been compromised from the start. Courts were willing to enforce appointment rules, but the executive's desire to bypass them had already influenced who was charged and how.

Economic policy aligned with these displays of power. The Venezuela operation was not only about regime change; it was also about money. Singer's favorable purchase of Citgo, the easing of the oil embargo, and the administration's plan to oversee Venezuelan crude exports placed key assets under the control of politically connected investors. Trump met with oil company leaders at the White House and assured them of "total safety and security" for their investments in Venezuela, promising state backing to safeguard private ventures abroad. He suggested that U.S. taxpayers fund the recovery of Venezuela's oil industry, with companies later covering costs—shifting political and financial risks onto the public while maintaining potential gains for firms.

At home, the administration proposed increasing the U.S. military budget from $1 trillion to $1.5 trillion for 2027, with Republican lawmakers and Treasury Secretary Scott Bessent suggesting that speculative fraud cuts would cover the difference. Meanwhile, Trump revoked billions of dollars in childcare funding and planned significant workforce reductions at FEMA, threatening the federal government's disaster response capacity. An executive order tightened rules on defense contractors' stock buybacks and dividends, ostensibly to ensure performance but also to increase executive control over a sector already linked to state power. A Trump family cryptocurrency venture, World Liberty Financial, applied for a national banking license, raising concerns that businesses tied to the president's family might receive favorable regulatory treatment.

Corporate money flowed back into politics in ways that reinforced this alignment. Some firms, like Airbnb, kept pledges to withhold donations from lawmakers who opposed certifying the 2020 election, signaling ongoing concern for democratic norms. Others, including major insurers and media companies, resumed funding election deniers, normalizing their role in politics. In contrast, New York City and State announced a universal childcare plan offering two years of free care for two-year-olds, and California advocates proposed a one-time 5 percent tax on billionaires to fund education, food, and health services. These local initiatives presented a different model—one that directed public resources toward broad social infrastructure rather than militarization and foreign extraction.

Transparency, a fundamental component of democratic oversight, was directly challenged. Under the Epstein Files Transparency Act, Congress required the Justice Department to release documents related to Jeffrey Epstein and to justify any redactions or withholding. DOJ, led by Attorney General Pam Bondi, released less than 1 percent of the documents and missed statutory deadlines. It failed to provide the necessary justifications or reports to Congress. Names of politically exposed individuals remained concealed. In response, Representatives Ro Khanna and Thomas Massie, from opposite parties, moved toward using inherent contempt against Bondi and asked a federal judge to appoint a special master to oversee the releases. The fight was not about a single case but about whether the executive could ignore transparency laws with impunity.

A similar pattern played out in Minneapolis. The FBI took exclusive control of the investigation into Renee Good's killing, shutting out Minnesota's Bureau of Criminal Apprehension and blocking state investigators from accessing evidence. DHS was accused of lying about the circumstances of the shooting and misrepresenting key facts in public statements. Selective release of video footage allowed the administration to shape the narrative while keeping the full record out of independent hands. Here, too, Congress responded: House Democrats filed articles of impeachment against DHS Secretary Kristi Noem, alleging obstruction and abuse in handling the case, and lawmakers threatened to withhold DHS funding unless ICE reformed its practices. Yet the underlying investigations remained under federal control.

Not all transparency mechanisms failed. The Equal Employment Opportunity Commission announced a public Sunshine Act meeting on voting procedures and organizational changes, following open-meeting norms. The Environmental Protection Agency issued notices on environmental impact statements, hazardous waste permit information collection, and Superfund settlements, inviting public comment and scrutiny. These routine disclosures demonstrated that the machinery of open government still operated in many areas. However, they also underscored the selectivity of opacity: when elite crimes, politically sensitive archives, or controversial uses of force were involved, the same government that published technical rules on chemicals and air quality often chose to seal, delay, or sanitize information.

Federal power was also wielded unevenly across different regions. The Justice Department sued twenty-two states for refusing to provide complete voter lists, including sensitive data, advancing a national voter file project that could enable aggressive roll purges. The administration sued California cities over local natural gas restrictions in new construction, challenging their climate policies. In Minnesota, DHS framed its extraordinary enforcement operation as a response to Somali-linked fraud, targeting a specific ethnic community and pushing detention facilities beyond capacity. These actions employed legal and security tools to pressure disfavored jurisdictions and populations, often those opposing the administration politically.

Legislators and local leaders sought ways to push back. House Democrats, led by Representative Robin Kelly, filed impeachment articles against Secretary Noem over the Minneapolis shooting. Members of Congress threatened to withhold DHS funding unless ICE altered its course. The Senate's War Powers Resolution on Venezuela, though subject to veto, reaffirmed a constitutional boundary. In New York City, Mayor Zohran Mamdani was sworn in and immediately revoked all executive orders issued by his indicted predecessor after the indictment date, signaling a break with perceived corruption and a new vision of executive power. Protest networks, from antiwar organizers in Grand Rapids to nationwide ICE vigils, advocated for alternative models of security and care. These efforts demonstrated that federalism and civil society still provided tools of resistance, even as the costs of using them increased.

Information control extended beyond security and scandal into health, economics, and climate. The administration eliminated federal guidance on childhood vaccines and promoted a new food pyramid that encouraged alcohol use as a social lubricant, sidelining evidence-based public health advice in favor of ideological and economic narratives. Allegations emerged that Trump had leaked confidential jobs data before its official release, giving insiders an advantage and undermining trust in the neutrality of economic statistics. The December jobs report itself was weak, and advisors downplayed its significance by attributing it to data issues rather than policy failure. In the same week, the administration withdrew the United States from the UN Framework Convention on Climate Change and dozens of other international organizations via presidential memorandum, reducing U.S. engagement in cooperative rule-making and undermining global frameworks for shared problems.

Against this high-profile retreat, agencies like EPA continued their technocratic work: reviewing industrial chemicals, updating state air quality plans, and seeking nominations for scientific advisory committees. These actions indicated a divided state. On one side, headline policies and presidential memoranda shifted the country away from multilateral commitments and evidence-based guidance. On the other, career staff and regulatory processes persisted, maintaining a baseline of environmental and procedural governance. The tension between these layers defined much of the week's tone.

Several scheduled and pending actions loomed over the period. The Senate's War Powers Resolution on Venezuela awaited final decision and possible veto. The House Judiciary Committee planned upcoming testimony from former Special Counsel Jack Smith, providing another avenue to examine past executive conduct. In the Epstein case, the request for a special master and discussions of inherent contempt set the stage for a confrontation between Congress, the courts, and DOJ over compliance with the transparency statute. Impeachment articles against Secretary Noem and threats to DHS funding indicated that immigration enforcement practices would remain under close scrutiny.

During Trump's second term, Week 51 did not introduce new strategies but rather applied familiar ones with greater confidence and scope. Security forces were deployed to protect power rather than people, both abroad and on American streets. Laws were stretched and used selectively to punish enemies and protect allies. Economic decisions regarding oil, defense, and social spending further fused governance with a narrow business network. Transparency laws and investigative norms bent under pressure, especially where elite exposure was at stake. Meanwhile, courts, legislators, journalists, and protesters continued to act, maintaining lines of accountability that had not yet been broken. The small progress made during the week on the clock reflected this uneasy balance: a deepening erosion of guardrails, offset but not reversed by institutions still willing to challenge how power is wielded.

CHAPTER 62
WEEK 52: OCCUPATION AS GOVERNANCE

A federal immigration surge turns Minnesota into a test site for domestic force, legal impunity, and curated memory, even as states and courts push back.

The fifty-second week of Trump's second term did not depend on a single order or speech. Instead, it unfolded as a convergence: immigration enforcement on a war footing, economic power wielded as personal leverage, and the information system bent to protect both. The core focus was Minnesota, where a federal operation turned a metropolitan area into something close to occupied territory. Around that core, law, money, and narrative were adjusted to make such operations easier to launch, harder to question, and safer for those carrying them out.

At the end of the previous period, the Democracy Clock stood at 8:11 p.m. By the end of this week, it had moved to 8:12 p.m., a net shift of 0.2 minutes. The change was small, but it reflected a series of significant actions: federal agents using lethal force and mass detention in a disfavored state, the Justice Department recasting civil rights issues as assaults on federal officers, and the executive branch tightening control over oil revenues, tariffs, and health coverage. The clock advanced because these actions expanded the presidency's ability to operate without effective oversight, and because the institutions meant to check that power were pushed into reactive, fragmented resistance.

The story in Minnesota began with scale. Operation Metro Surge sent thousands of ICE and Homeland Security agents into Minneapolis–St. Paul, conducting door-to-door raids at homes and businesses, stopping people on the street, and demanding papers. Within days, more than 2,400 people had been detained, deported, or transferred, including visa holders and refugees. The impact on daily life was immediate. Immigrant neighborhoods emptied. Families stayed indoors. The presence of federal agents, armored vehicles, and chemical munitions made the operation feel more like a domestic deployment than routine law enforcement.

The killing of Renee Nicole Good, a U.S. citizen, transformed that sense into a concrete case. Good was shot by ICE agent Jonathan Ross during an enforcement action, in circumstances that quickly became contested. Federal officials described a dangerous encounter. Community witnesses and early video suggested a different story. What was not in dispute was the outcome: a woman dead in her own city, killed by a federal officer operating under a mandate that had never been debated as war.

The surge didn't end with Good's death. ICE detained four members of the Oglala Lakota Nation in Minnesota, deported a gravely ill detainee in a vegetative state who soon died, and recorded four migrant deaths in custody in the first ten days of the year. In Texas, a medical examiner ruled that another detainee, Geraldo Lunas Campos, had died of asphyxia at an ICE facility, raising the possibility of homicide. Taken together, these events revealed an enforcement system where loss of life was no longer an exception but a recurring feature.

Minnesota's response to the situation was notably extensive. The state attorney general and Hennepin County attorney launched their own investigations into Good's killing, directly challenging federal claims of "absolute immunity" for ICE agents. The state, along with Minneapolis and St. Paul, sued to stop Operation Metro Surge, citing unconstitutional stops, detentions, and racial profiling. The ACLU of Minnesota filed a class-action lawsuit describing agents stopping Somali and Latino residents based on race, demanding papers, and making arrests without probable cause. In their filings and public statements, state officials called the operation a "federal invasion."

Other states acted similarly. Illinois sued over a separate DHS operation, Operation Midway Blitz, accusing federal agents of warrantless detentions and using chemical weapons. California passed laws allowing state authorities to arrest federal agents for specific abuses on state soil. Illinois established an accountability commission to receive complaints about federal immigration officers. New York's attorney general launched a portal for residents to submit evidence of misconduct by federal agents. These measures didn't stop the Minnesota surge, but they signaled a shift. States were creating their own oversight systems to monitor and, where possible, limit federal enforcement. Congressional and public reactions added further pressure. Representative Shri Thanedar announced plans for an Abolish ICE Act, pointing to deaths in custody and the Good shooting as evidence that the agency's current form was unsustainable.

Democratic lawmakers held a field hearing in St. Paul called "Kidnapped and Disappeared," hearing testimony from families and advocates about the raids' effects and warning DHS to keep records. Polls showed that 46 percent of Americans now supported abolishing ICE, an astonishing figure for an agency formed less than 25 years earlier. Latino focus groups expressed regret over supporting Trump, citing immigration tactics and economic issues. Even as this backlash grew, federal officials moved to limit oversight. ICE and facility operators near Minneapolis blocked members of Congress from visiting a detention center, despite a judge's ruling that they had the right to access it. Homeland Security Secretary Kristi Noem issued a policy that more broadly restricts congressional oversight visits to ICE facilities.

These actions, along with the scale and tactics of the raids, made Operation Metro Surge seem less like regular law enforcement and more like a federal occupation shielded from outside scrutiny. If Minnesota's surge demonstrated federal power on the ground, the handling of Renee Good's case showed how the law could be used to protect that power. The Justice Department decided to frame the shooting mainly as an assault on a federal officer, rather than as a possible civil rights violation. This framing guided all subsequent actions. The FBI took over the investigation, sidelining Minnesota's Bureau of Criminal Apprehension and limiting local prosecutors' access to evidence. Reports indicated that agents had left and possibly tampered with the crime scene and were withholding body-camera footage. The federal inquiry focused on whether Good had attacked Ross, not on whether Ross had unlawfully used deadly force.

Inside the Justice Department, this approach sparked open resistance. Senior officials in the Civil Rights Division resigned after being prevented from investigating the Good killing as a civil-rights issue. Federal prosecutors in Minnesota also stepped down rather than continue a case they believed had been politically redirected. Their departures reduced the department's ability to enforce civil rights laws and indicated that internal checks were being overridden when they conflicted with protecting federal agents. The department's official decisions reinforced that message. DOJ declined to open a civil-rights investigation into the Good shooting, stating there was "no basis" for such a probe, even as protests and resignations grew. It later refused to treat another ICE shooting in Minneapolis as a civil-rights case, again prioritizing the protection of agents over scrutinizing their conduct.

In both instances, the Justice Department's choices signaled to federal officers that lethal force against civilians, in the context of immigration enforcement, would not be examined through a rights lens. State-level investigations in Minnesota and Oregon provided a contrast. Oregon's attorney general launched an inquiry into border agents' shooting of two undocumented immigrants in Portland, asserting state interest in policing federal use of force. Minnesota's own investigation into Good's death continued despite federal obstruction. These efforts demonstrated that some jurisdictions were willing to challenge the Justice Department's narrative, but only with limited evidence and constrained jurisdiction.

The overall pattern was clear. Federal law enforcement power was being used to shield ICE and DHS from accountability, while those within the system advocating for civil rights enforcement were marginalized or removed. The justice system's formal structures remained, but their practical role shifted: from neutral mediator between the state and citizens to defender of the state's agents against the citizens. Alongside these legal strategies, the administration worked to shape public understanding of Good's death and the Minnesota operation.

Within days of the shooting, President Trump endorsed a baseless claim that Good was part of a paid left-wing agitator network. Vice President J.D. Vance and DHS released a short, tightly framed video of the incident, first leaked to a partisan outlet, that portrayed Ross as a victim and hid key context. The 47-second clip became the main piece of official accounts, even as longer footage and witness statements suggested a more complex scene. The smear campaign intensified. Trump and Vance labeled Good and her wife as "domestic terrorists," claiming she had tried to run over an agent with her car, despite video evidence contradicting that claim. These statements were not mistakes. They were repeated, amplified through sympathetic media, and used to justify both the shooting and the broader operation. In this narrative, Good was not a citizen killed by the state; she was an enemy whose death justified harsh measures.

Information control extended beyond this case. ICE resisted releasing updated use-of-force policies and heavily redacted documents under the Freedom of Information Act. The Pentagon imposed new restrictions on defense reporters, leading mainstream journalists to leave the Pentagon press corps and creating room for pro-administration voices. The Department of Defense also moved to take editorial control of Stars and Stripes, the long-standing independent newspaper for service members, removing protections that maintained its independence.

Government messaging also targeted a narrower audience. The Labor Department and White House used rhetoric and imagery in official social-media posts that unions and observers said resembled Nazi slogans and white supremacist literature, including a cartoon asking, "Which way, Greenland man?" These cues did not alter policy by themselves but helped define who belonged inside the national "we" and who was an outsider, linking this identity politics to the administration's enforcement agenda.

Journalists questioning these narratives faced direct pressure. The FBI raided the home of Washington Post reporter Hannah Natanson as part of a leak investigation, seizing her devices. Officials claimed she was not a target, but the search sent a clear message to her sources and other reporters with federal connections. At the White House podium, Press Secretary Karoline Leavitt criticized a reporter who called ICE's defense of the "Good shooting" a "left-wing activist," framing critical questioning as partisan hostility. CBS News staff raised concerns that a report on Ross's condition relied too heavily on politicized leaks, illustrating the difficulty of covering a story when the government controls both evidence and narrative.

Despite this pressure, the information battle was not entirely one-sided. Over a thousand "ICE Out For Good" protests and vigils took place nationwide, highlighting deaths in custody and the Minnesota raids. Portland saw demonstrations against border patrol shootings, with arrests that underscored protest risks. Polls and focus groups indicated public support for the administration's immigration tactics was waning, even among some who supported Trump in 2024. The narrative space narrowed but remained open.

While law and information were being manipulated around the Minnesota operation, the Justice Department and allied agencies also targeted other critics and independent institutions. The raid on Natanson's home was one example. Investigations into lawmakers were another. DOJ opened probes into Representative Elissa Slotkin and three other House Democrats for a video where they reminded troops of their duty to refuse illegal orders. Military leadership launched inquiries into Senator Mark Kelly's public comments on the same topic, and Defense Secretary Pete Hegseth formally censured Kelly and ordered a review of his retirement grade.

These actions blurred the line between genuine concern about civil-military relations and the use of investigative authority to suppress oversight. The lawmakers' statements focused on the law of armed conflict and the duty to disobey unlawful orders, a fundamental principle of military ethics. Treating those statements as potential misconduct or criminal incitement inverted the usual hierarchy. Instead of civilian leaders scrutinizing the executive's use of force, the executive and its appointees were scrutinizing legislators for raising questions. The Federal Reserve also became a target. President Trump publicly threatened criminal charges against Fed Chair Jerome Powell over interest rates and building renovations. The Justice Department subpoenaed the Fed and launched a criminal investigation into Powell's testimony about renovation spending. Prosecutors in Washington, D.C., even threatened indictment, widely seen as a way to pressure rate cuts. Global central banks issued a joint statement backing Powell and warning against political interference—an extraordinary move highlighting how far the confrontation had gone.

Meanwhile, the Justice Department relaxed guidance that discouraged federal prosecutions for simple cannabis possession, reopening an enforcement channel that had disproportionately affected marginalized communities. It also sued 23 states and the District of Columbia to obtain sensitive voter information, including birth dates and partial Social Security numbers, claiming to be cleaning voter rolls. A federal judge in California blocked that effort, ruling DOJ was not entitled to that data, but the move itself showed a willingness to centralize voter info at the federal level. Amid this aggressive, selective enforcement, some courts and states still imposed limits. Judge Amir Ali ordered the reinstatement of whistleblower attorney Mark Zaid's security clearance, finding its revocation was politically motivated. Judge William Young prepared a protective order for noncitizen academics targeted over pro-Palestinian speech, checking the use of immigration powers to silence political expression. The Supreme Court, in an earlier decision now in effect, rejected Trump's claim of authority to deploy federalized National Guard troops in Illinois, reinforcing boundaries on domestic military use.

Other judicial decisions went the opposite way. The Third Circuit reversed a ruling that had released Palestinian activist Mahmoud Khalil from ICE detention, ruling that lower courts lacked jurisdiction over his claims and deferring to restrictive immigration laws. The Supreme Court agreed to hear cases challenging Trump's global trade tariffs imposed under emergency economic powers and revived a Republican lawsuit over Illinois's mail-in ballot deadline, expanding candidate standing to challenge election rules. These cases aren't decided yet, but their acceptance signals a Court willing to revisit presidential economic powers and open new paths for voting litigation.

Legislative efforts to check war powers and alliance policies had mixed outcomes. The Senate advanced, then narrowly rejected, a resolution requiring congressional approval for future military actions in Venezuela, maintaining broad presidential discretion. Lawmakers also debated a Save NATO Act to limit the president's ability to unilaterally attack NATO allies, reflecting concerns that war powers could be used to weaken key alliances. House Republicans moved to hold Bill and Hillary Clinton in contempt for ignoring Epstein-related subpoenas, intersecting with another dispute over transparency in that case.

The most visible aspect of executive power in foreign policy was economic. The administration took control of Venezuelan oil and its revenues without full congressional approval, declaring a national emergency that blocked repayments and placed assets under U.S. control. Trump then announced a 25 percent tariff on any country trading with Iran, using access to the American market as leverage against third parties. These moves extended emergency economic powers into long-term foreign asset management and trade policy, with little legislative oversight.

The handling of Venezuelan oil revenues linked foreign policy to domestic political motives. The first U.S. sale of seized Venezuelan crude went to Vitol, a company whose executive heavily funded Trump-aligned political committees. Executive orders protected the proceeds from courts and creditors, making it hard to trace how the money might be used. Simultaneously, the Trump Organization entered multi-billion-dollar development deals with Saudi-backed Dar Global in Diriyah and Jeddah, strengthening financial ties between the president's business and a foreign government involved in major security interests.

At home, economic tools were used in ways that blended policy with pressure. The administration refused to extend Affordable Care Act premium subsidies, risking coverage losses and reshaping healthcare access without new laws. New federal dietary guidelines emphasized red meat and full-fat dairy, raising questions about industry influence on public health advice. A Labor Department rule change lowered wages for foreign farmworkers, and the Trump Organization hired foreign workers at those reduced wages, showing how regulatory shifts could directly benefit connected employers.

Tariff policies created their own feedback loop. Reports indicated manufacturing jobs declined despite high tariffs, challenging claims that protectionism was reviving industry. Polls showed widespread public disapproval of Trump's economic policies. Meanwhile, China and Canada finalized a $1 trillion strategic trade agreement, including tariff cuts on electric vehicles and agriculture, indicating a shift in global trade alliances that could reduce U.S. influence. While these developments did not change the administration's direction, they highlighted the costs associated with its approach.

The fight over transparency and archives extended through

several of these sectors. Congress passed the Epstein Files Transparency Act, requiring the Justice Department to release investigative records. DOJ ignored the law's deadlines, leading Representatives Ro Khanna and Thomas Massie to ask a federal judge to appoint a special master and monitor to enforce compliance. Judge Paul Engelmayer ordered DOJ to explain its noncompliance. When the department finally acted, it released less than one percent of the files, contradicting the statute's clear purpose.

ICE's secrecy around its use-of-force policies followed the same pattern. Even under FOIA, the agency heavily redacted documents, leaving the public and oversight bodies with little understanding of when agents were authorized to use lethal force. Simultaneously, DOJ sought detailed voter data from states, and the General Services Administration proposed adding fraud indicators to the Federal Audit Clearinghouse. The National Archives invited public comment on records disposition schedules—a routine step that gained importance in a climate where politically sensitive records could be sealed, sanitized, or destroyed.

The Epstein case intersected with partisan maneuvering. House Oversight Chair James Comer moved to hold the Clintons in contempt for defying subpoenas related to Epstein, even as DOJ itself failed to release the broader set of files mandated by law. The release of former special counsel Jack Smith's testimony, where he asserted proof beyond a reasonable doubt of Trump's criminal schemes, added another layer of unresolved accountability to the public record. These developments showed a government that demanded transparency from some actors while fiercely resisting it when elite networks and donors were involved.

Amid these pressures, some institutional safeguards still operated. Judges restored a whistleblower lawyer's clearance, protected noncitizen academics' speech, and rejected federal demands for intrusive voter data. States sued to stop abusive enforcement operations, created commissions to monitor federal agents, and passed laws affirming their own authority to hold those agents accountable. Congress recognized Capitol Police for defending the legislature on January 6 and considered measures to limit presidential war powers and alliance policies, even when those measures failed.

Upcoming cases are already scheduled. The Supreme Court has agreed to hear cases on Trump's emergency tariffs and on state bans of transgender girls in sports, and has revived litigation over Illinois's mail-in ballot deadline. The Epstein transparency lawsuits will return to court as the DOJ's minimal release is challenged under the statute. Minnesota's and Illinois's suits against DHS, along with the ACLU's class actions, will proceed in federal court, forcing judges to determine how far federal immigration operations can extend into states.

This week's movement on the Democracy Clock was modest in minutes but heavy in content. Federal agents acted as a domestic security force in a disfavored state, backed by a Justice Department that reframed civil-rights questions as threats to federal officers. The executive branch seized foreign assets, threatened global tariffs, and withheld health subsidies, using economic tools in ways that blurred policy with personal and political gain. Information about these actions was curated, leaked, and withheld to favor the state's narrative, while journalists and lawmakers who challenged that narrative faced raids and investigations. Courts and states did not stay aside, but their responses were uneven and often reactive. The result was not a dramatic rupture but a deepening of patterns: law as weapon, security forces aligned with power, and memory shaped by those who hold both.

EPILOGUE

This book concludes where it must: with the measurement complete, the frame closed, and the period in view. What follows is not an argument, a warning, or a prediction. It is a consequence.

To measure something is to change its status. What was once an impression becomes evidence. What was once episodic becomes cumulative. What could be dismissed as temporary gain or loss becomes durable. The work of this book has been to make democratic erosion visible while it was still unfolding—not to dramatize it, but to hold it in view long enough to evaluate.

That act does not require agreement. Readers may differ in the importance they assign to particular weeks or in their interpretation of specific events. Disagreement is not a flaw of the measure. It is evidence that the record exists as more than assertion. What matters is that the changes documented here are no longer scattered or vague. They have been organized sequentially, assessed against consistent standards, and fixed in time.

Visibility has its own implications. Once patterns are seen, they cannot be unseen. Once cumulative effects are traced, they cannot be reduced to isolated events without deliberate effort. This remains true regardless of whether institutions respond, remedies are pursued, or future volumes extend the work. Measurement does not resolve democratic strain; it confirms that the strain is real, persistent, and observable.

The weeks covered in this book do not determine the outcome of this period. They define its condition. They show how power was exercised, how constraints worked or failed, and how democratic time moved under pressure. That is sufficient for judgment, even where it is not sufficient for closure.

History often turns not on what was foretold, but on what was recorded clearly enough to be remembered. This book claims no more than that. It offers neither reassurance nor despair. It offers a line of sight. What was visible here will remain visible, whether it is acted upon or not. That is the difference between erosion that can be named and erosion that is allowed to fade into noise.

The measure stands.

ABOUT THE AUTHOR

Jim Vincent is a U.S. citizen, born and raised in the United States, where he lived for five decades. He now resides in Australia, with children and grandchildren still living in the country he considers home. His work reflects both a sustained engagement with American democratic institutions and a concern for their durability over time.

Living outside the United States has shaped his perspective in two ways: by creating distance from the country's internal political polarization, and by providing daily exposure to another functioning democratic system. From that vantage point, he approaches American governance not as an abstraction, but as a lived structure —one that can be examined, compared, measured, and evaluated.

Vincent is the founder of *Jim Vincent US*, an independent publication focused on democratic accountability, institutional resilience, and the practical conditions required for self-government to endure. He is the author of the *American Renewal* trilogy—*American Renewal*, *American Restoration*, and *American Redemption*—which examines the historical foundations, structural failures, and civic obligations of modern democracy.

His writing emphasizes clarity over rhetoric and documentation over assertion. He writes with the conviction that democratic systems are not sustained by sentiment alone, but by attention, record, and accountability.

He can be reached at https://jimvincentus.substack.com

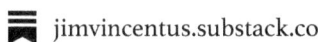
jimvincentus.substack.com

amazon.com/stores/Jim-Vincent/author/B0F87XPWCL

ALSO BY JIM VINCENT

The American Renewal Trilogy

American Renewal

American Restoration

American Redemption

Other Works

Essays on Tyranny: Resisting Trump's Attack on Democracy

Every Day: Turning Betrayal into Recovery

The Quiet Habit of Giving

www.ingramcontent.com/pod-product-compliance
Lightning Source LLC
Chambersburg PA
CBHW071327080526
44587CB00017B/2750